KW-407-819

A Jurisprudence of Power

*Victorian Empire and
the Rule of Law*

R. W. KOSTAL

OXFORD
UNIVERSITY PRESS

OXFORD
UNIVERSITY PRESS

Great Clarendon Street, Oxford, OX2 6DP,
United Kingdom

Oxford University Press is a department of the University of Oxford.
It furthers the University's objective of excellence in research, scholarship,
and education by publishing worldwide. Oxford is a registered trade mark of
Oxford University Press in the UK and in certain other countries

© R.W. Kostal, 2005

The moral rights of the authors have been asserted

First Edition published in 2005; reprinted 2006
First published in paperback 2008

All rights reserved. No part of this publication may be reproduced, stored in
a retrieval system, or transmitted, in any form or by any means, without the
prior permission in writing of Oxford University Press, or as expressly permitted
by law, by licence or under terms agreed with the appropriate reprographics
rights organization. Enquiries concerning reproduction outside the scope of the
above should be sent to the Rights Department, Oxford University Press, at the
address above

You must not circulate this work in any other form
and you must impose this same condition on any acquirer

Crown copyright material is reproduced under Class Licence
Number C01P0000148 with the permission of OPSI
and the Queen's Printer for Scotland

Published in the United States of America by Oxford University Press
198 Madison Avenue, New York, NY 10016, United States of America

British Library Cataloguing in Publication Data
Data available

Library of Congress Cataloging in Publication Data
Data available

ISBN 978–0–19–955194–1

Links to third party websites are provided by Oxford in good faith and
for information only. Oxford disclaims any responsibility for the materials
contained in any third party website referenced in this work.

PLYMOUTH UNIVERSITY
9 009730182

For Leslie

General Editor's Preface

One of the standard justifications for British imperialism was that it brought colonial territories and their inhabitants within the rule of law. Until the British Empire was dismantled in the second half of the twentieth century this justification continued to be regularly offered as a counter to the anti-colonial movement. And even today, when the Empire is no more, legality and respect for the rule of law continue to feature in attempts by historians to produce balance sheets of the merits and demerits of British imperialism. It was in the Victorian period, at the height of British imperialism, that the role of legality in colonial administration became a subject of a particularly impassioned public controversy. The occasion was the violent suppression, in 1865, under martial law – whatever that meant – of a supposed insurrection in the Morant Bay area of Jamaica, the Governor at the time being Edward Eyre. Underlying this controversy was the uncomfortable realization that there exists a symbiosis between law and the violence employed to maintain its authority when that authority is thought to be threatened. Both before and after the Governor Eyre controversy there have been other occasions when the suppression of colonial insurrections has given rise to public debate, and there is currently such a historical debate over the suppression of the 'Mau Mau' rising in Kenya in the 1950s. But somehow the intellectual heavyweights of Victorian Britain conducted such debates with a touch of class which is no longer available.

There have been a number of studies of the Jamaica affair, but when Professor Kostal approached me some time ago to discuss the possibility of producing a new study I encouraged him to do so; the end product seems to me to have shown that I was right. He has made a major contribution to the understanding of Victorian thought and Victorian attitudes to colonialism, and in particular to the place of legalism in those attitudes, a subject which historians of colonialism have rather neglected. And the issues which so excited the Victorian intelligentsia – the role of respect for legality in countering feared challenges to government under law – have a timeless quality, as is particularly obvious as I write this. It is a pleasure to welcome Professor Kostal's book to this Modern Legal History Series.

A. W. Brian Simpson

Preface to the Hardback Edition

How is a constitutional nation to contend with the nakedly brutal realities of empire? Can such a country rule over alien lands and peoples without corrupting its defining ideals? In the late 1860s the English governing class was frequently absorbed and deeply perplexed by these questions. When I first came upon this fact, while reading contemporary newspapers and journals for another book several years ago, I had never heard of the Morant Bay rebellion or of Governor Edward Eyre. But after only a little reading it was evident that in early November 1865 news had reached England that the colonial authorities in Jamaica had ruthlessly suppressed an uprising among the island's black peasantry, and that they had done so under a proclamation of martial law. It was also apparent that these reports quickly had become the subject of controversy, and that the controversy involved an explosive convergence of politics (the formal exertion of power) and law (the formal restraint of power). A casual glance at published sources indicated that the Jamaica suppression, patently an official campaign of terror and punitive violence, had brought about some very interesting effects in England. From the outset, leading English politicians and thinkers began to discuss the episode in terms of legal principles and procedures. In time, moreover, the politicians and thinkers seemed largely to have surrendered the dispute to lawyers and judges. The combatants also appeared broadly to agree that the Jamaica controversy was not only about politics, but the basic legal rules governing politics. For an historian of Victorian law and society, this seemed a story worthy of more systematic investigation.

I have been at work on this project for many – too many – years and in that time have accumulated a great many academic debts. The project was financed principally by a generous Program of Research Grant from the Social Sciences and Humanities Research Council of Canada. While undertaking the majority of the archival research for the book, I was a Visiting Scholar to the School of Advanced Study at the University of London. I am extremely grateful for the kindness and hospitality shown me there by Dr. Terry O'Brien and his staff at Senate House. I also benefited from use of the facilities at the Institute of Historical Research, and from the seminar in imperial history conducted by Dr. Andrew Porter. In this time-frame, I profited immensely from conversation and correspondence with Gad Heuman, Stefan Collini, Josh Getzler, Miles Taylor, Bernard Semmel, Michael Taggart, David Sugarman, and Richard Cosgrove. During a research trip to Jamaica I was hosted by my friend Las Neuman, and with him as my expert guide made an unforgettable trip to Morant Bay. At the National Library of Jamaica nothing would have been accomplished but for the skilful assistance of Mrs. Eppie D. Edwards.

At my home institution at the Faculty of Law, the University of Western Ontario, I have enjoyed the unflagging support and patience of Dean Ian Holloway, and that of my colleagues. I am also grateful to the Law Foundation of Ontario, and to the Work Study Program of the Province of Ontario for underwriting the cost of student research assistance. In 1997, the law student (and now Crown Attorney) David King prepared an archival research brief of simply astonishing comprehensiveness and accuracy. I subsequently benefited from the diligent work of law students Risa Kirshblum, Kelly Gonsalves, Michael DeVries, Phillip Casey, and Martin Painter. I want to extend special thanks to law students Darryl Keen, John Nicholson, and Roslynn Kogan, all of whom made crucial contributions to the project in its final phase. Frances Lethbridge, Veronica D'Souza, and Tigger Jourard provided invaluable service in the preparation of the text. Leslie Lauinger helped shape up the bibliography. I would be remiss if I failed to acknowledge the unrivalled expertise and efficiency of University of Western Ontario's Legal Research Librarian, Marianne Welch. Finally, I want to acknowledge the personal and intellectual debt owed to my friend and mentor, Professor Craig Simpson. Craig has been my *confrère* from the beginning to the end of this work.

Turning to the staff, past and present, of Oxford University (Clarendon) Press, I do not like to think where my writing career would be were it not for the support of Richard Hart. Richard commissioned my first work for the Clarendon Press, and encouraged me in the proposal of this book. The book was proposed under Richard's auspices, but was warmly endorsed and carried to fruition under the direction of the Senior Commissioning Editor, John Louth. I am also grateful to Gwen Booth and Fiona Stables for their skill and diplomacy in shepherding me through the arduous process of making a manuscript into a book. The book's prose and scholarship were greatly enhanced by the meticulous reading and judicious advice of Anna Hodson, the copy-editor. My largest debt at the Oxford Press is owed to Brian Simpson, the General Editor of *Oxford Studies in Modern Legal History*. Brian took great pains with a rather raw first draft of the present script. My work has benefited enormously from his knowledge and suggestions, and from his unfailing professional courtesy and respect. Of course, for the errors and misjudgements that have gone uncorrected, I alone am responsible.

Preface to the Paperback Edition

A number of people have made vital contributions to the preparation of the paperbound edition of *A Jurisprudence of Power*. I am grateful to John Louth, Senior Law Editor at Oxford University Press, in affording me the opportunity of publishing a long book in a more exact but less expensive imprint. Dr. Gwen Booth, Development Editor at Oxford Press, also has been instrumental in the publication process. Elmandi du Toit rendered invaluable aid in getting the book through the final stages of production. Anna Dekker read the first edition of the book with a precise eye and marvelous skill, and suggested many pertinent amendments. Dr. Christopher Ricks, Co-Director at Boston University both of the Editorial Institute and its impressive James Fitzjames Stephen project, read the book with great care, and offered a number of helpful suggestions. Frances Whistler, the other Co-Director of the Stephen project, leant her formidable learning in recommending alterations to my depiction of Stephen's career as a lawyer and journalist to 1865. Frances also suggested some useful improvements to the entries for Stephen in the index to the first edition. I am especially grateful to her for these beneficial amendments.

As always, I have received invaluable institutional support from the Faculty of Law at The University of Western Ontario, and from administrative assistant, Emilia Hugel. Emilia, with all of the other persons I have inadequately thanked, worked very hard in helping me produce a cleaner edition of the book. However, I fear that some mistakes of text, fact, and interpretation will have persisted into the paperbound edition of *A Jurisprudence of Power*. Of course for these remaining errors I alone am responsible.

Contents

Abbreviations

Adm	Admiralty Records, National Archives of England
BFASS	British and Foreign Anti-Slavery Society, Rhodes House, Oxford
BL	British Library
CUL	Cambridge University Library
CD	Diary of Frederick Chesson, John Rylands Library, Manchester
CL	Cornell Library
CO	Colonial Office, National Archives of England
DNB	Dictionary of National Biography
FHP	Frederic Harrison Papers, London School of Economics
GSP	Goldwin Smith Papers, Cornell University
JC Minutes	Minutes of the Jamaica Committee, Rhodes House, Oxford
JRC	Jamaica Royal Commission, British Parliamentary Papers
JRO	Jamaica Record Office, Spanish Town, Jamaica
NLS	National Library of Scotland
PP	British Parliamentary Papers
SLSA	State Library of South Australia
WO	War Office, National Archives of England
UCL	University College London

Introduction

> History is made up of episodes, and if we cannot get inside these, we cannot get inside history at all.
>
> Edward Thompson, *The Poverty of Theory*

This book is about the centrality of law in the world-view of the English political class of the 1860s. Its more specific subject-matter is the prolonged conflict that arose in England over the suppression of the Morant Bay uprising in Jamaica. On 11 October 1865, a crowd of black men and women attacked and burned the court-house at the southeastern vestry town of Morant Bay. The chief magistrate and seventeen other persons, most of them white men, were beset and killed as they fled. When apprised of these events, the Governor of Jamaica, Edward John Eyre, proclaimed martial law in the afflicted district, and despatched regular soldiers and militia to put down the insurrection. This the soldiers did with vigour, killing and torturing hundreds of black Jamaicans – that is to say, British subjects – in the process. When reports of these events reached England during the first week of November 1865, they became the focus of what *The Times* later called 'one of the most acute public controversies of the later half of the nineteenth century.'[1]

Although the 'Jamaica affair' (as contemporary writers often called it) has not been the subject of a general historical treatment for more than forty years,[2] the incident has generated an extensive, rich, and varied historiography.[3] We have detailed accounts of the causes and contours of the Morant Bay uprising and suppression.[4] There are compelling histories of the subsequent controversy in England from the standpoints of imperial policy, social psychology, and race relations.[5] Historians also have commented extensively on the role in the affair of

[1] 'Death of Ex-Governor Eyre', *The Times* (3 Dec. 1901), 8.

[2] See Bernard Semmel, *The Governor Eyre Controversy* (London, 1962).

[3] These works are more closely examined in the Appendix.

[4] See generally, Thomas C. Holt, *The Problem of Freedom: Race, Labor and Politics in Jamaica and Britain, 1832–1938* (Baltimore, Md., 1992); Gad Heuman, *'The Killing Time': The Morant Bay Rebellion in Jamaica* (Knoxville, Tenn., 1994); Mimi Sheller, *Democracy after Slavery: Black Publics and Peasant Radicalism in Haiti and Jamaica* (Gainesville, Fla., 2000), 203–46; Catherine Hall, *Civilizing Subjects: Colony and Metropole in the English Imagination, 1830–1867* (Chicago, Ill., 2002).

[5] These works are more closely examined in the Appendix.

prominent intellectuals such as Thomas Carlyle[6] and John Stuart Mill.[7] However, a premiss of the present study is that these works, while worthy enough on their own terms, have failed to apprehend that the Jamaica affair was understood, described, and contested largely in terms of legal language and procedures. Historians of the Jamaica affair, put off perhaps by the 'maze of technicalities' associated with legal matters,[8] have overlooked an exceptional opportunity to identify and analyse the legal components of English political language and behaviour in the mid-Victorian era. Similarly, in their broad indifference to the history of the mid-Victorian legal system, scholars have barely considered how political ideas and concerns might have affected the legal writing, pleading, and decision-making spawned by the episode. This book, therefore, describes the Jamaica controversy as an important episode in the legal history of English politics, and the political history of English law.

Before elaborating more fully on the main historical sources, questions, and theses of this study, it will be useful to survey the main contours of Jamaican constitutional and socio-political history in the years immediately preceding the Morant Bay uprising. What was the structure of colonial government in Jamaica? How were legal powers divided between colonial and imperial authorities? What circumstances led to the uprising and suppression in Jamaica during October 1865? What laws governed public emergency?

Jamaica formally became a British territory in 1670, fifteen years after Cromwell's naval forces defeated the Spanish garrison on the island.[9] The ensuing evacuation of Spanish people and institutions in Jamaica later created uncertainty about the laws governing British immigrants to the island,[10] uncertainty arising from a peculiar distinction in British imperial law between 'conquered' and 'settled' colonies.[11] In conquered territories, any 'civilized' laws in place at the moment of conquest continued in force until expressly discontinued by Parliament or the Crown. In settled colonies, on the other hand, British

---

[6] For Carlyle and the Jamaica affair, see particularly, Gillian Workman, 'Thomas Carlyle and the Governor Eyre Controversy: An Account with Some New Material', 18 *Victorian Studies* (1974), 77–102; Holt, *The Problem of Freedom*, 284–6; Catherine Hall, 'The Economy of Intellectual Prestige: Thomas Carlyle, John Stuart Mill, and the Case of Governor Eyre', 22 *Labour/Le Travail* (1989), 167–96; Catherine Hall 'Competing Masculinities: Thomas Carlyle, John Stuart Mill and the Case of Governor Eyre', In C. Hall (ed.), *White, Male and Middle-Class: Explorations in Feminism and History* (London, 1992), 255–93, 268–76.

[7] For Mill and the Jamaica affair, see Stefan Collini, *Public Moralists: Political Thought and Intellectual Life in Britain, 1850–1910* (Oxford, 1991); Bruce L. Kinzer, Ann P. Robson, and John M. Robson, *A Moralist In and Out of Parliament: John Stuart Mill at Westminster, 1865–1868* (Toronto, 1992), 184–217.

[8] George Ford, 'The Governor Eyre Case in England', 17 *University of Toronto Quarterly* (1947–8), 219–33, 233.

[9] For a narrative overview of the political history of British Jamaica in the seventeenth century, see Clinton V. Black, *The Story of Jamaica: From Prehistory to the Present* (London, 1965), 42–51.

[10] This uncertainty is reflected in a memorandum written in the wake of the Morant Bay suppression by the law officers of the Crown to the Colonial Secretary, Edward Cardwell. See 'Disturbances in Jamaica', 24 Jan. 1866, CO 885/2.

[11] Kenneth Roberts-Wray, *Commonwealth and Colonial Law* (London, 1966), 540–2.

immigrants were entitled to all of the legal privileges and immunities of British subjects in their homeland.[12] By this reckoning, British Jamaica was a legal hybrid. It was a conquered colony which only briefly contained a conquered population with 'civilized' laws. In 1662, although Jamaica's final status had not yet been determined, Lord Windsor was given leave to govern the island as a 'settled' colony under its own constitution.[13] This became the operative premiss of Jamaican government for the next two hundred years. However, in the aftermath of the martial law of 1865, a number of basic questions about the legal status of Jamaica and its population were revisited and contested. According to the letter of imperial law, was Jamaica a 'conquered' or 'settled' colony? Were its British settlers entitled to the same protections (as against, for instance, the introduction of martial law) enjoyed by citizens in Britain? Did the legal rights and immunities of white British settlers in Jamaica extend to the black men and women whose ancestors had been brought to the colony in chains?

In the late seventeenth and eighteenth centuries, British Jamaica was developed as a slave colony dominated by local and absentee planters of sugar cane. It was the site of almost ceaseless conflict between the planter oligarchy and the colony's governors, and between the white minority and the enslaved majority. These struggles unfolded within a 'representative' constitution,[14] the central feature of which was a Legislative Assembly elected by a tiny elite of enfranchised white planters. Insofar as the Jamaica constitution had a fixed purpose, it was to provide the planter class with the legal powers needed to foster the production and export of sugar while it safeguarded the scattered white population from the perils of slave insurrection. The guiding principle of Colonial Office policy in this era was that the planters were to be left to pursue these goals with a minimum of interference from the imperial government and its agents.[15] However, this policy did not ensure that relations between legislative and executive branches of colonial government would be free of friction. In fact, such friction was an endemic feature of Jamaican politics.

The first principle of Jamaica's constitution was that the Legislative Assembly, elected by the colony's wealthiest landowners, would be the principal source of public law and revenue in the colony.[16] Its second principle was that these functions were to be subject to the influence and oversight of the colony's chief executive officer, the Governor. Appointed by the Colonial Office, holding the commission of the Sovereign, the Governor had powers enough to obstruct but

---

[12] Ibid. See also D. B. Swinfen, *Imperial Control of Colonial Legislation, 1813–1865: A Study of British Policy towards Colonial Legislative Powers* (Oxford, 1970), 6.

[13] Ibid. Lord Windsor also introduced a Royal Proclamation which purported to bestow the legal rights of British citizenship on the offspring of British settlers in Jamaica. Black, *Story of Jamaica*, 50–1.

[14] W. P. Morrell, *British Colonial Policy in the Mid-Victorian Age* (Oxford, 1969), 378–9; C. V. Gocking, 'Early Constitutional History of Jamaica (with Special Reference to the Period 1836–1866)', 6 *Caribbean Quarterly* (1960), 114–33.

[15] Michael Craton, *Empire, Enslavement and Freedom in the Caribbean* (Kingston, Jamaica, 1997), 1–25.   [16] Gocking, 'Early Constitutional History', 116.

not to control the business of the Assembly.[17] In Jamaica, however, by law and convention, the will of the Assembly prevailed over the will of the Governor, especially in fiscal matters.[18] The Governor might delay, but could not override legislation. And while the Colonial Office had the power to disallow colonial legislation,[19] in practice disallowance was regarded as an 'extreme remedy', one to be used sparingly.[20] In 1865, Parliament passed the Colonial Laws Validity Act, which provided that a colonial statute was to be regarded as legally valid unless it was clearly repugnant to an Act of the imperial Parliament.[21] This development had at least one important consequence for the history of the Jamaica controversy. The statutes passed by the Jamaica Assembly governing the use of martial law, and later governing indemnification for the use of martial law, were good laws until such time as the Government in London took active steps to invalidate them.

In the mid-nineteenth century Jamaica's political and constitutional history was shaped by two pivotal events: the complete emancipation of the slaves by Parliament (after five years of transitional 'apprenticeship') in 1838,[22] and the collapse of sugar prices after the repeal of imperial protective tariffs in 1846.[23] The prevailing view in the Colonial Office in this period was that Jamaica's planter oligarchy was too racist and dissipated to govern justly in the post-emancipation era. So long as the black freedmen were unenfranchised (and the Colonial Office thought them unready for the vote), there was no way of curbing the dogmatic race and class politics of the old white elite. In 1839, Lord Melbourne's government fell on a bill that would have placed Jamaica under the direct government of the Crown.[24] For the next fifteen years economic and political conditions in the colony continued to decline. By 1854 Jamaica's public finances were a shambles. Facing fiscal disaster, the colony's Legislative Assembly agreed to relinquish some of its powers in exchange for new imperial loans.[25] Henceforth, political authority was to be shared between the Assembly (forty-seven members elected by 2000 enfranchised persons), a Legislative Council (seventeen Crown appointees), the Governor, and an Executive Committee (the Governor and three Assemblymen). However, these changes quickly led to political gridlock,[26] and Jamaica's formal politics became even more deeply divided by class and racial enmities. Relations between governors and legislators went from bad to worse. The constitutional

---

[17] The Governor possessed a 'vaguely defined delegation of the royal prerogative to him as agent of the King'. Ibid., 115.   [18] Ibid., 116.
[19] Swinfen, *Imperial Control of Legislation*, 4.   [20] Ibid.   [21] Ibid., 172–3.
[22] Among white Jamaican planters, the emancipation of the slaves was an unwelcome imposition, one which was fiercely resisted. See Holt, *Problem of Freedom*, 1–35; Hall, *Civilizing Subjects*, 174–208.
[23] The price of sugar began to decline in 1816. Imperial preferences on sugar were not completely removed until 1854. Morrell, *British Colonial Policy*, 377.
[24] Gocking, 'Early Constitutional History', 119–23. Ten years later, the Jamaica Assembly declined responsible government on the theory that it would decrease its power over fiscal policy. Morrell, *British Colonial Policy*, 382–9; 399–403.
[25] Swinfen, *Imperial Control of Legislation*, 4.
[26] In general, the remnants of the old planter elite lined up against a shifting coalition of urban merchants, professionals, 'coloured' persons, and Jews. Morrell, *British Colonial Policy*, 402–3.

'reforms' of 1854 had only aggravated the colony's crushing social and political problems.

In the winter of 1862, Edward John Eyre, who had held appointments in the colonial service intermittently since 1845, was appointed Acting Governor of Jamaica. In May 1864 (before it was obvious to the Colonial Office that he was in over his head) Eyre was given the office outright. It was Eyre's enduring misfortune to have assumed full executive authority in a colony wracked by economic depression, racial hatred, and political paralysis.[27] In confronting the crisis, the new Governor faced two significant disadvantages. First, Eyre was ill-equipped both by temperament and intellect to navigate in a financial, political, and racial maelstrom. Second, he would have the advantage of almost no useful assistance from the colonial elite. In the early 1860s, Jamaica was notoriously short of wise statesmen.[28]

The colony was short of statesmen but not population. In 1864 Jamaica contained some 440,000 citizens, more than 350,000 of whom were former slaves or the progeny of former slaves.[29] Approximately 80,000 colonists were regarded as persons of 'coloured' or mixed race. Fewer than 14,000 were viewed as 'white' persons. With few exceptions, black and coloured Jamaicans were desperately poor. There was little cash employment. In droves they had abandoned (irregular and irregularly paid) employment on the sugar estates to squat on vacant land in the rugged hills. In the early 1860s the inevitable hardships of back-country farming were exacerbated by prolonged drought. The general distress of the peasantry intensified when the exigencies of the American Civil War began to chase up the price of food and other essential goods.[30] And then there was the colony's antiquated system of local justice. In Jamaica, mundane legal disputes over land, labour, and petty crime invariably were tried before lay magistrates recruited from among the planters and their close associates. Local justice, the most important surface of contact between the black poor and the colonial state, was meted out mainly by habitually racist white men who had class (sometimes directly personal) interests in the outcome of prosecutions and trials. It was not wholly by chance, therefore, that the Morant Bay uprising began at a parish courthouse.

For two years preceding the Morant Bay rebellion, black and coloured community leaders, supported by a handful of white missionaries and assorted malcontents, pressed the colonial government for social, economic, and political reforms.[31] George William Gordon, a prominent coloured landowner, legislator, and Native Baptist convert, was the most conspicuous and tenacious advocate of these claims.[32] In this period Gordon was in constant collision with Governor

---

[27] See generally, Ronald V. Sires, 'Governmental Crisis in Jamaica, 1860–1866', 2 *Jamaican Historical Review* (1953), 1–26, 15; Heuman, *'The Killing Time'*, 44–5.

[28] Sires, 'Governmental Crisis', 16.

[29] These statistics cited by *The Times* (15 Mar. 1866), 8.

[30] Sires, 'Governmental Crisis', 19; Heuman, *'The Killing Time'*, 44–5.

[31] Ibid., 63–77; Sheller, *Black Publics*, 212–18.

[32] Gordon was born in 1820, the son of a wealthy planter and a slave woman. He inherited a number of large landholdings, some of which were located in the parish of St. Thomas-in-the-East,

Eyre and the white planter elite. Gordon was not alone in this role. In St.Thomas-in-the-East, the southeastern parish of the colony, Paul Bogle, a black Native Baptist preacher (and associate of Gordon), led a populist movement for political and land reform. However, the agitation spearheaded by Gordon, Bogle, and other reformers failed to produce tangible results. As the suffering of Jamaica's black communities increased in 1864, and as one after another reformist initiatives were rejected or ignored by the authorities, the political tension became palpable. Protest meetings were more frequent, political rhetoric more heated. By the end of 1864, rumours of impending violence abounded. Then, in January 1865, Edward Underhill, an official of the Baptist Missionary Society in England, sent a letter to the Colonial Office documenting the plight of the Jamaican peasantry, and the potential for violence.[33] If the island was to avert open rebellion, Underhill warned, the Government needed to take urgent steps to address the grievances of black Jamaicans. During the first months of 1865, Underhill's letter received wide publicity in England, and was the focal point of a series of angry public meetings in Jamaica. But the Colonial Office did not take any remedial action. As for Governor Eyre, he did not budge from his long-held belief that the principal cause of distress among Jamaica's blacks was their stubborn unwillingness to work.[34]

The bitter political conflicts of the early 1860s were the direct by-products of Jamaica's convulsive past. The most important fact about Jamaica in this era, indeed, in the entire arc of its history as a British colony, was slavery. Jamaica's legal and political culture was forged within a brutally coercive but endemically insecure system of unfree plantation labour.[35] The survival of the slave system had depended on the ability of scattered pockets of white men to maintain control over large and recalcitrant concentrations of black men. This had not been a simple task. In 1673, fewer than twenty years after the British conquest of Jamaica, the island experienced the first of a long succession of bloody slave revolts and suppressions.[36] From these experiences white Jamaicans learned a visceral fear of the island's black population. In 1865, nearly twenty years after emancipation, Jamaica's whites remained haunted by the spectre of black violence. The catastrophic slave revolt in nearby Saint Domingue (Haiti) in 1791 had never been forgotten. The Jamaican slave revolt of Christmas 1831 was part of the active memory of elderly white colonists.[37] There was also the fresh recollection of the Indian Mutiny. The massacre of white soldiers and civilians by Indian army mutineers in 1857–8 only intensified the dread among white Jamaicans that one

the site of the uprising of 1865. By the early 1860s, profligacy and careless investments had left Gordon deeply in debt. Heuman, *Oxford DNB*, online 74415.

[33] Heuman, 'The Killing Time', 55–60.

[34] Morrell, *British Colonial Policy*, 406–7; Heuman, 'The Killing Time', 48.

[35] For a stark and comprehensive account of the brutal character of Jamaican slavery, see generally, Trevor Burnard, *Mastery, Tyranny and Desire: Thomas Thistlewood and his Slaves in The Anglo-Jamaican World* (Chapel Hill, NC, 2004).

[36] For a concise survey of slave revolts in Jamaica, see Heuman, 'The Killing Time', 33–42.

[37] Mary Reckord, 'The Jamaica Slave Rebellion of 1831', 40 *Past and Present* (1968), 108–25, 120.

day they might be overwhelmed and exterminated by the black majority. The civil unrest associated with the Jamaican tax riots of 1859 further heightened this anxiety.[38]

The insecurity of whites had always been the central premiss of public law and planning in the colony. In 1681 the Legislative Assembly passed the first of an unbroken chain of statutes permitting the Governor and his privy councillors, on any credible news of slave conspiracy or rebellion, to proclaim martial law and apply maximum military force against rebels. In 1866, Alexander Heslop, Jamaica's English-educated Attorney General, summarized this point: '[F]rom the time of the actual settlement of [Jamaica] as a British possession,' he stated, 'there never has been a day during which martial law, or the power of declaring martial law, has not been a normal provision of the statute book.'[39] The imperative of the colony's emergency law was to provide the military with the legal powers necessary to crush insurrectionary activity before it could become dangerously widespread. Given that everywhere on the island whites were vastly outnumbered by blacks, and that regular army and militia forces were small and ill-equipped, the main tenet of colonial security doctrine was to institute a reign of state-backed terror against black rebels and their communities. Terror – the ruthless and sometimes indiscriminate use of torture, burnings, and summary execution – was seen as having two salutary effects: it broke the morale of active rebels while it deterred potential rebels. The quick and unhindered application of terror, it was further reckoned, would tend to undermine the plausibility of insurrection as a practical political option.

It is unremarkable that Jamaica's colonial officials were often preoccupied with public security. More intriguing is that the same officials, in the face of dire public emergency, were also preoccupied with legality. Even during the period of slavery in Jamaica, the operative assumption among executive decision-makers was that their actions had to conform with the strictures of law. In ordinary times, this meant conformity with statutory and common law. In extraordinary times, in the context for instance of slave insurrection, it meant conformity with the requirements of 'martial law'. When in December 1831 the western parishes of Jamaica were the scene of widespread slave insurrection,[40] the authorities did not simply lash out. On receiving word of the uprising, the Governor (the Earl of Belmore) took pains to abide by the statute governing the proclamation and enforcement of martial law. When the military quickly suppressed the rebellion and captured scores of suspected rebels, most prisoners were tried (either before military tribunals or civilian slave courts) before they were punished. While clearly many of these trials were *pro forma* (and they led to the conviction and execution of no fewer than 344 enslaved men[41]), remarkably, some accused slaves were acquitted.[42]

---

[38] Heuman, '*The Killing Time*', 38–42.   [39] *JRC Minutes*, Q. 16,245–16,247.
[40] Reckord, 'Jamaica Slave Rebellion', 121.   [41] Holt, *Problem of Freedom*, 14.
[42] For records pertaining to these trials, see *CO* 137/185. See generally, Reckord, 'Jamaica Slave Rebellion', 121–2.

That in the aftermath of a slave rebellion the authorities had observed even cursory legal constraints suggests a deeply ingrained deference to the forms of law.

The same fastidiousness about legal proprieties was displayed by Edward Eyre during the Morant Bay rebellion. Before he would move to proclaim martial law, Eyre was cautious to consult the senior law officers of the Crown, and to heed their advice regarding proper procedures.[43] And when some members of the Privy Council urged him to proclaim martial law over the whole of the colony, Eyre, troubled by the legal and economic ramifications of this move, limited its purchase to a single parish. This was only prudent. As the Governor of a British colony, Eyre did not possess an arbitrary discretion to spill blood, even that of dark-skinned rebels. Eyre knew this, just as he knew that one day his superiors at the Colonial Office would invite him to prove that in putting down the rebellion he had acted in accord with local and imperial law. In the result, Eyre struggled with this proof.

Edward Eyre was not the first British colonial governor to become embroiled in controversy over the proclamation or implementation of martial law. Before 1865, there had been at least five such cases. In 1824, Governor John Murray of Demerara was castigated in Parliament for the profligate use of military tribunals in the aftermath of a slave revolt.[44] In 1848, the use of martial law by Governor Ward to crush an insurrection in Cephalonia[45] led to controversy at home, if one quickly overtaken by the fierce and sustained conflict sparked by the martial law of the Governor (Lord Torrington) of Ceylon in 1848.[46] Torrington's conduct became the subject of a parliamentary select committee investigation in 1849 and a motion of censure in 1851. The process ultimately led to Torrington's dismissal and disgrace. Seven years later, in 1858, martial law was once again the subject of controversy in England, this time with regard to the suppression of the Indian Mutiny. During the insurrection, Indian rebels had occasion to massacre English civilians, including (in the notorious incident at Cawnpore) women and children. The English political class broadly supported the savage suppression which followed, a suppression facilitated by martial law. In this case, the Governor-General of British India, Lord Canning ('Clemency Canning', as he was branded by critics), was bitterly assailed in England for having taken steps to *limit* the punitive discretion of the army under martial law.[47]

---

[43] These decisions will be more carefully documented and examined below, Ch. 2.

[44] Particularly controversial was the court martial of the English missionary John Smith. Charles M. Clode, *The Military Forces of the Crown: Their Administration and Government* vol. ii (London, 1869), 482–3. This and the other controversies involving British governors and martial law are discussed at greater length below, Ch. 4.   [45] Ibid., 502–03.

[46] The implementation of martial law in Ceylon touched off the most prolonged and intense controversy over the subject before the Jamaica affair. See my article, 'A Jurisprudence of Power: Martial Law and the Ceylon Controversy of 1848–51', 28 *Journal of Imperial and Commonwealth History* (2000), 1–34.

[47] See generally, Michael Maclagan, *'Clemency' Canning: Charles John, 1st Earl of Canning* (London, 1962), 114, 135–43; S. Gopal, *British Policy in India, 1858–1905* (Cambridge, 1965), 1–2; Saul David, *The Indian Mutiny, 1857* (London, 2002), 237–8.

Although these clashes produced a body of professional and lay commentary on the law of martial law, they did not give rise to an authoritative treatise or high court precedent. As a consequence, when Edward Eyre began to weigh his response to news of the Morant Bay uprising in October 1865, the law in this field was perilously uncertain. The fact of the matter was that Eyre's legal advisers – although they acted on the contrary assumption – could not provide dependable answers to some very basic questions. What *was* martial law? What did it mean to proclaim it over a territory? What new powers and immunities, if any, did it call into being? Did the power to proclaim martial law flow from statute or Royal Prerogative? These questions raised still others: did martial law apply exclusively to armed insurrectionists in the field, or did its powers extend to detainees? In other words, was the ambit of martial law limited to the immediate and local restoration of the peace, or did it go further to license exemplary and deterrent punishments?[48] If martial law extended to detainees, were they entitled to a military trial prior to punishment? In either event, were officials accountable to the common law for actions taken under martial law? Was it conceivable that in a British territory some uses of military power stood outside the ambit of law? The Jamaica controversy can plausibly be described as an attempt by an alliance of English intellectuals, politicians, and social activists to settle these questions decisively.

As matters stood in October 1865, English lawyers did not agree even on the definition of the term 'martial law'. The relevant literature contained at least three distinct meanings.[49] According to the famous statement of Lord Wellington during the Ceylon debate of 1851, the term was a misnomer; martial law was not law at all, but the 'will of the General who commands the Army'.[50] Under a proclamation of martial law, Wellington contended, the General's will was constrained only by his practical judgement. In another account, one later endorsed by the Lord Chief Justice of England,[51] martial law was the temporary displacement of civilian rule by 'military law' (the body of laws passed by Parliament governing the military forces of the Crown)[52] while the army defeated armed invasion or insurrection. These definitions were similar in describing martial law as standing apart from the common law. But according to yet another and radically different account of the term, martial law was nothing more than an exotic instance of the common law defence of public necessity.[53] It was a defence

---

[48] For a discussion of this line of debate, see A. W. Brian Simpson, *Human Rights and the End of Empire* (Oxford, 2001), 58–62.

[49] The competing definitions of martial law were summarized in the *Solicitors' Journal* (16 Dec. 1865), 140–1.   [50] *Hansard*, cxv (1 Apr. 1851), 880.

[51] See Frederick Cockburn (ed.), *Charge of the Lord Chief Justice of England to the Grand Jury at the Central Criminal Court, in the Case of The Queen against Nelson and Brand* (London, 1867), 82–91.

[52] Taken together this law was known as the 'Military Code', consisting of the Mutiny Act and the Articles of War. Judge-Advocate General, Sir David Dundas M.P., *Second Report of the Select Committee on Ceylon, PP* (1850), xii, Q. 5431.

[53] As we will see in Ch. 5 below, this theory of martial law was advanced by the great jurist and barrister James Fitzjames Stephen. For a summary of the theory, see *Law Times* (20 Jan. 1866), 163. The theory was later defended by Dicey. See Simpson, *End of Empire*, 60–2.

pleaded by public officials when called into court to justify an intentional interference with the person or property of another. Martial law was a legal privilege or excuse for any conduct undertaken (reasonably and honestly) in order to subdue the armed enemies of the Crown. The privilege of martial law was a means of legitimating an action, usually an extreme and violent action, otherwise culpable. By this account, importantly, martial law did not provide public officials with an unfettered discretion. Nor did it sanction an arbitrary or wanton use of force. Martial law was not the absence of common law, but a continuation of a subset of common law principles during the temporary abatement of the common law courts.

The definition of martial law was one vexed question, the nature of the legal authority to proclaim martial law another. While it was broadly accepted that the sovereign Parliament was entitled to introduce any law, including a law proclaiming martial law in a British territory, at this point agreement ended.[54] In 1865, the character of martial law, indeed, whether such a thing continued to exist as a 'prerogative' (or 'exclusive')[55] authority of the Crown and its agents, was a tangle of conflicting propositions. According to one school of thought, the Petition of Right (approved by Parliament in 1628) had terminated the royal prerogative to proclaim martial law in Britain or her colonies, full stop. Other legal commentators agreed that the Petition of Right had terminated martial law in Britain, but claimed that it did not apply in the colonies. Still others asserted that the Petition of Right applied in the colonies, but could be overridden by a valid colonial statute. If this were not perplexing enough, still other lawyers contended that the only effect of the Petition of Right was to extinguish the royal prerogative to proclaim martial law in *peacetime*. It had nothing at all to do with the legal rights and immunities of the Crown during a public emergency. In this view, executive officials, in Britain and the empire, possessed an unassailable common law prerogative to proclaim martial law in the face of armed invasion or insurrection.

In October 1865, the law of martial law was dauntingly complex, perhaps utterly incoherent. But these difficulties did not make it any less pertinent. The academic fact that the law of martial law was unsettled did not alter the practical fact that it was an essential part of the security apparatus of many colonies in the empire. To officials like Governor Eyre, officials charged with the awesome responsibility of preserving white British lives and property in the empire, martial law was not a debating point. In the advent of an emergency such men had to act with (in the often-repeated phrase) 'promptitude and vigour' even if, as agents of the British Crown, they also had to act within a framework of law. Remote in time

---

[54] These points are discussed and documented in detail below, Ch. 4.

[55] In this technical sense the term 'prerogative' denoted the exclusive legal powers of the Crown and its agents as established by common law. Here the state (the 'Crown') was comprehended as an entity distinct from Parliament. A prerogative power, then, was one that might be exercised by an agent of the Crown (a colonial Governor, for instance) without the sanction of Parliament or a subordinate legislature created by Parliament. See generally, O. Hood Phillips and Paul Jackson, *O. Hood Phillips' Constitutional and Administrative Law*, 6th edn (London, 1978), 266–71.

and space from London, there was nothing for an executive official to do but make decisions, if on the best available legal advice. As for Governor Eyre, when he received word that the black peasantry in the southeastern parish of Jamaica were in open rebellion, he followed the well-established protocol. His first move was to consult with the colony's senior military officer, Major-General L. S. O'Connor, about the deployment of armed forces. But his second move, not incidentally, was to consult with his senior legal officer, Attorney General Heslop, about the use of these forces in accordance with the emergency laws of the colony. O'Connor advised the Governor to deploy troops. Heslop advised the Governor to convene a Council of War with a view to proclaiming martial law.

Eyre accepted this advice without apparent hesitation, and in so doing committed himself to his Attorney General's very sure (if not unproblematic) views on what this signified.[56] The central thrust of these views was that for 200 years the imperial government in London had permitted the Jamaica Assembly to promulgate a body of security law that suited local conditions. As Heslop summarized in 1866, '[T]he sun never rose and set on Jamaica as a country in which the English law prevailed with regard to martial law.'[57] Statutes governing the proclamation and use of martial law had been on the books in Jamaica since the 1670s. None of these statutes, including those passed and amended after emancipation, had ever been disallowed by the Colonial Office.[58] It had been clearly understood by both parties that where British colonists were vastly outnumbered by black men and women, martial law was a wholly indispensable and legitimate facet of a colony's legal arsenal.

During the suppression of the Morant Bay rebellion and afterward, Heslop was steadfast in his opinion that Governor Eyre, if he followed the procedures laid down in the colony's martial law statute, was legally entitled to proclaim martial law over all or any part of the colony. Heslop was equally confident that the proclamation of martial law meant that civilian law was suspended in favour of the unhindered discretion of military commanders in the field and that this discretion applied both to active combatants and to men captured in the field. But the Attorney General was less certain that martial law entailed comprehensive legal immunity for the exercise of this discretion. While it was possible that martial law provided this immunity,[59] it was also possible that it did not. On this point, Heslop hedged his bet. When the rebellion was suppressed, he advised Jamaica's Executive Council to introduce a bill to the Assembly which, when passed, would permit the Governor to issue certificates of legal indemnity (or immunity) covering any person who had taken any action in an honest effort

[56] Heslop testified on these points before the Jamaica Royal Commission. See, for instance, *JRC Minutes*, Q. 16,200. Heslop's views on martial law are discussed at length below, Ch. 2.

[57] Ibid.

[58] Moreover, on three occasions after emancipation, but prior to the Morant Bay uprising, the Colonial Office had consented to amendments to the martial law statutes. Ibid., Q. 16,200–16,240.

[59] This position was later defended by the leading scholar on martial law. See W. F. Finlason, *Commentaries upon Martial Law* (London, 1867), 267.

to suppress the rebellion. If immunity was not provided by the common law of martial law, surely it would be provided by the Governor exercising a statutory power. This otherwise sound course had one potential flaw: a colonial indemnity act, while valid *per se*, could be disallowed by the Government in London.[60]

This brings us back to our narrative overview of the Jamaica uprising and its subsequent suppression under martial law.[61] In October 1865 the black peasantry of the eastern parish of St. Thomas-in-the-East (in the county of Surrey) were especially hard-hit by the effects of drought. The essentials of life were scarce, the suffering great. The simmering anger of this community had been given sharp political focus by George Gordon, a landowner in the parish, and by the preacher firebrand, Paul Bogle. In a succession of public meetings during the previous year Gordon and Bogle had made provocative (Governor Eyre later called them 'openly treasonous') remarks about the obstinacy and venality of the colonial regime.[62] By the summer of 1865 Bogle began openly to discuss the possibility of armed resistance. There is evidence that his followers began to drill.[63] By October 1865, mounting political tension in the parish was exacerbated by a series of angry clashes at the petty sessions of the peace held in Morant Bay. For Bogle and his followers, the courthouse at Morant Bay had become a symbol of their oppression.

On 9 October, Baron von Ketelholdt, an expatriate German and planter–magistrate in St. Thomas parish, issued a warrant for the arrest of Bogle and a score of others. The next day an attempt was made to effect their arrest in their upland villages. This ended in the rough ejection of the police, accompanied by threats against von Ketelholdt's life. In response, the Baron mustered the local white militia and sent an urgent plea to the Governor for help. These precautions in place, von Ketelholdt decided to convene a vestry meeting at the Morant Bay courthouse on 11 October. Late in the afternoon of that day, a large and variously armed group of black Jamaican men and women followed Bogle into the main square. Von Ketelholdt came into the square with a squad of militiamen and ordered the people to disperse. When they did not, von Ketelholdt read the Riot Act. When the crowd still did not disperse, and after a hail of stones was directed at the Magistrate, the militia was ordered to fire on the crowd. The crowd temporarily fell back and then surged forward. Von Ketelholdt and his retainers fled inside the courthouse. After a further exchange of gunfire, the building was put to the torch. When the occupants attempted to flee, eighteen of their number (including von Ketelholdt, an Anglican clergyman named Herschell, and some

---

[60] In May 1866, the Colonial Office asked the Attorney and Solicitor General of England for their advice regarding the legal consequences of their disallowing Jamaica's Indemnity Act. For inquiries and answers, see Law Officers to Edward Cardwell, 8 June 1866, *CO* 885/11. The point is discussed below, Ch. 2.

[61] This account has been assembled from contemporary and subsequent magazine articles, and from the accounts provided in Holt, *Problem of Freedom*, 263–309; Heuman, 'The Killing Time', 1–130; Hall, *Civilizing Subjects*, 243–65.   [62] Heuman, 'The Killing Time', 59.

[63] Heuman argues that the Morant Bay uprising was deliberately planned and organized, and Bogle was at the centre of these activities. Ibid., 80–3.

coloured vestrymen) were mobbed and killed. Some thirty-five others escaped. Although there were other unprotected white and coloured persons present in the town, Bogle and his followers did not seek them out. Instead, they melted away into the hills. In the course of the next two days two bands of armed blacks – neither party led by Bogle – killed two more white planters on their remote sugar estates.

When Eyre was apprised of these events, there was reason for nervousness. The Governor had fewer than 1,200 uniformed soldiers (500 of whom were black West Indians), two field guns, and two small naval vessels at his disposal.[64] When he proclaimed martial law and moved to suppress the uprising, Eyre was able to spare only 500 regular troops and a few companies of lightly armed militia. This gave rise to a contention repeated many times by Eyre and his apologists in subsequent months: in order to forestall a more general and potentially catastrophic rebellion in Jamaica, it had been imperative to break rebel morale by recourse to a reign of terror under martial law.

When pressed with credible evidence of widespread revolt, Eyre's response was swift, fierce, and, as he endeavoured to make certain, fully sanctioned by Jamaican law. In a series of actions which will bear closer scrutiny in the second chapter of this study, Eyre consulted with his legal officers and called for the Council of War to convene the next morning. On 13 October, after a heated debate concerning the geographic scope of the proclamation, the Council unanimously agreed that martial law would be proclaimed in the 'county of Surrey, except in the city and parish of Kingston'. In the next handful of days, the colonial government's makeshift military, facing no organized resistance and without the loss of a single man, quickly restored order in the eastern districts of the colony. It was what happened *next* which became the source of nearly four years of rancorous debate and litigation in England.

Although the period of martial law lasted thirty days, the resistance was crushed in the first seven. For the remainder of the period, and often with the direct knowledge and approval of Governor Eyre, the military engaged in what one commentator later called a 'hell-like saturnalia' of retaliatory violence.[65] Under the proclamation of martial law, no fewer than 439 black Jamaicans, as an English magazine story later recounted, 'were either shot down or executed, sometimes with, sometimes without the formality of a trial, and over 600, amongst whom were included a number of women, were flogged, in some cases with revolting cruelty'.[66] The black population of St. Thomas parish, in short, was subjected to a protracted and calculated reign of terror. Its most celebrated victim was the coloured landowner–politician, George Gordon. When the Morant Bay court-house was attacked on 11 October, Gordon was at his house near Kingston. While

[64] Colonel North, quoted in *Hansard*, ccxii (8 July 1872), 819.
[65] Charles Roundell, as quoted in John Gorrie, *Illustrations of Martial Law in Jamaica, Jamaica Papers No. VI* (London, 1867), 3.
[66] 'The Case of Governor Eyre', *Cornhill Magazine*, n.s. xii (1902), 209.

his role in the uprising remains murky, it was not alleged, then or later, that Gordon had been directly involved in acts of violence. Nor did he try to take flight. On 14 October, Gordon, still at his home in Kingston, learned that a warrant had been issued for his arrest. On 17 October, he surrendered to the authorities.

Before the uprising, Gordon had been Eyre's most persistent and influential critic. With Bogle he had also been one of the two main lightning rods of black discontent in the eastern section of the colony. After consulting with the Attorney General, the Governor personally oversaw Gordon's arrest on charges of high treason and sedition. Then, with Gordon in custody, Eyre made a stunning move. He ordered the prisoner removed from the civilian jurisdiction of Kingston for trial by a military tribunal at Morant Bay. Gordon was put ashore there on 21 October. Denied access to a lawyer, and most other vestiges of civilian criminal justice, he was tried, convicted, and sentenced to execution. On 23 October, after the proceedings and verdict had been reviewed and approved of by Eyre, Gordon was hanged 'from the centre arch of the ruined courthouse'.[67] Eyre later explained to the Colonial office that he had taken these steps both because Gordon had conspired to foment armed rebellion and because he was a potential rallying point for further rebellion. Eyre emphasized that the senior law officers of the Crown had wholly endorsed his decision and its reasoning.

News of the massacre of whites at Morant Bay reached England on 3 November. During the next two weeks it became clear, to general relief, that the uprising had been short-lived. But, on 17 November, the Jamaica story took a strikingly different turn. English readers learned that in the aftermath of the rising the people of the eastern parish of the island had been subjected to a prolonged and ruthless regime of martial law. Sensational stories began to circulate that as many as 2,000 persons had been massacred by the military, and that 'eight miles of dead bodies' had been left to rot along a Jamaican road.[68] It was also learned that the coloured politician George Gordon (and scores of other prisoners) had been executed by military courts. Immediately a clamour was raised. As the journalist Justin McCarthy recalled of December 1865, 'For some weeks there was hardly anything talked of, we might say hardly anything thought of, in England, but the story of the rebellion in Jamaica, and the manner in which it has been suppressed.'[69] In its initial phase, the loudest and most persistent critics of the suppression were members of Christian missionary and philanthropic groups with links to Jamaica. Their principal allegation was that Governor Eyre had personally sanctioned and supervised a campaign of brutal (and *illegal*) retaliatory

---

[67] 'The Case of Governor Eyre', *Cornhill Magazine*, n.s. xii (1902), 209.

[68] In the immediate aftermath of the suppression, the Jamaican authorities themselves believed the correct figure to be in the range of 2,000 dead. 'Jamaica', *Dublin Review* vii (1866), 406–7. However, *The Times* (7 Apr. 1866), 8, was vindicated in its refusal to lend any credence to the early casualty figures.

[69] Justin McCarthy, *A History of Our Own Times*, vol. iii (New York, 1895), 356.

violence against the black people of St. Thomas-in-the East. The arrest, trial, and execution of Gordon was cited as only the most shocking example of this official lawlessness. By mid-December, some prominent Liberal and Radical parliamentarians (John Bright, Thomas Hughes, Peter Taylor, and, from his retreat in France, John Stuart Mill) also had spoken out against the Jamaica suppression. Behind the scenes Bright began to urge that a 'powerful committee' be formed to coordinate the protest. If Bright was to have his way (and, in the end, he did), the newly formed 'Jamaica Committee' would raise funds for a very specific purpose. He wanted the Committee to engage 'able lawyers' and to prosecute Governor Eyre for the murder of Gordon.[70]

English conservatives were quick to respond to these developments. In late December 1865, both Thomas Carlyle and John Ruskin published letters defending Eyre and denouncing his critics. It was agreed that, should the need arise, the two men would organize a committee devoted to the vindication of the beleaguered Governor. With regard to the Jamaica question, the *Daily Telegraph* glumly observed in 1867, 'our greatest men are most remarkably divided. We have eminent philosophers divided into hostile camps; distinguished scientific men take opposite sides; professed philanthropists act apart; and the names of Liberal politicians, popular writers, famous travellers, and leading divines might be taken from the list of supporters on both sides.'[71]

The Jamaica Committee, this grand coalition of Christian activists and secular liberals, was formed at a London hotel on 19 December 1865. During the next three years the Committee instigated most of the main developments of the Jamaica affair. The Committee espoused two aims, one short and one longer term. First, to persuade the Government to institute a thorough investigation of events in Jamaica. Second, to persuade the Government to prosecute criminal wrongdoers in the English courts of law. The second aim, temporarily shelved until the final report of the Jamaica Royal Commission was released in June 1866, was the primary objective of most of the Committee's leadership cadre. Their mission was to cause leading members of the Government and judiciary to state unequivocally that a proclamation of martial law did not license officials to kill and torture with impunity. The Committee wanted official acknowledgements that serious crimes – even murders – had been committed during the Jamaica suppression, and that the culprits would be prosecuted in England for these crimes. Put more sweepingly, the Committee wanted senior officials of state to admit that civilian and military agents of the Crown were always and everywhere legally accountable for their official acts, even when those acts took place under a proclamation of 'martial law'. At the end of the Parliament of 1866, however, the senior ministers of Lord Derby's Conservative government not only refused to admit these things but endorsed the contrary view. In suppressing the uprising,

---

[70] Bright to McCarthy, 6 Dec. 1865, as quoted in Justin McCarthy, *Reminiscences*, vol. i (New York and London, 1899), 80–1.   [71] *Daily Telegraph* (8 Feb. 1867).

Disraeli stated, the former Governor Eyre and his regular military officers had acted both rightly and legally. Neither Eyre nor his officers would be prosecuted on the initiative of the Government or its law officers.

On this news, the Jamaica Committee quite literally took the law into their own hands. In the course of the next thirty months, they instituted no fewer than three private criminal prosecutions in the English courts (two for murder) against Edward Eyre, and another murder prosecution against two regular military officers, Colonel Abercrombie Nelson and Lieutenant Herbert Brand. These cases, the *Newcastle Chronicle* commented in 1866, 'raised issues of the deepest and gravest importance'.[72] When after many months of litigation these prosecutions ended indecisively, the Committee threw its support behind a private civil lawsuit against Eyre. Although none of these cases delivered a positive verdict, the Committee's legal programme generated a vast body of commentaries, opinions, legal treatises, and judicial pronouncements on the English law of emergency and political violence. In the result, in fact, the Jamaica Committee succeeded in provoking the most protracted and significant public discussion of the idea of the rule of law during the Victorian era.

If the advent of the Jamaica controversy proved one thing, it was that in November 1865 little about the law of martial law was certain. It was obvious only that martial law existed as a feature of colonial law and that, when activated, it almost invariably generated protest and recrimination. It was not obvious, however, whether martial law had a legitimate existence within imperial law and, if it did, whether it existed within or outside the common law. Much of the confusion stemmed from the fact that the subject of martial law raised fundamental questions about British politics and jurisprudence. Martial law was proclaimed only when the very existence of the state was in doubt, only when the civilian legal system was under siege. Inevitably, then, martial law was about taking extreme and extra-legal measures in order to rescue the basis of all law, the state. Could these measures be subject to law? Was 'martial law' law, or was martial law a state of non-law, a state of official and pragmatic *lawlessness*? This order of inquiry, at bottom philosophical in nature, was beyond the ken of most lawyers, certainly of most politicians and imperial administrators.

The Jamaica affair, of course, did not unfold in an historical vacuum. On the contrary, the reason why the suppression became (and then remained) controversial was that it was so closely linked in the public mind to other contentious social and political issues. Anti-slavery activists were attracted to the Jamaica affair, not only because of fellow-feeling for black Jamaicans, but because the actions of the Governor and the military (and the approval those actions had received in some quarters in England) were seen to reflect a rising tide of anti-black racism among the English governing classes. Liberals and Radicals were attracted to the Jamaica case because they saw the suppression, and more particularly the unwillingness of conservatives

---

[72] *Newcastle Chronicle* (14 July 1866).

to condemn the suppression, as evidence of a resurgent authoritarianism in English politics. In these circles, the agitation surrounding the Second Reform Bill (introduced to Parliament by the Liberals in 1866) and the Jamaica affair were of a piece: both were attempts to introduce or reinforce the accountability of political actors to law and law-makers; both were sites for contesting the fundamental questions of English political jurisprudence. How, and by whom, was political power to be assigned or withdrawn? What were the boundaries of legitimate political dissent? Did some public officials possess a prerogative to suspend the operation of the common law? What was martial law, and did it exempt officials from subsequent legal accountability? If it did provide this exemption, where did that leave the central precept of English jurisprudence that laws always were to prevail over men?

Such questions, when treated as historical inquiries, can have substance only in the context of relevant and accessible source materials. Like previous scholarly works on the Jamaica affair, this book makes substantial use of newspaper and journal literature, as well as published essays, letters, and pamphlets. A private diary and some unpublished letters also figure here, as do the transcribed speeches of politicians and other public orators. The enormous body of relevant government documents is another rich source of primary materials. As has been stated, however, the present study is founded on the observation that a complete history of the Jamaica affair must also be a history of legal ideas and courtroom conflicts. Political and intellectual luminaries such as Carlyle, Mill, Ruskin, and Bright propelled the affair, but they did not do so alone. The interventions of English lawyers and judges – James Fitzjames Stephen, Hardinge Giffard (Lord Halsbury), W. F. Finlason, Lords Cockburn and Blackburn, to preview only the most well-known figures – had as much, sometimes far more bearing on the shape and outcome of the Jamaica controversy. Accordingly, the book delves into a set of sources which have *not* been examined systematically by previous scholars: the plethora of published legal literature – articles, essays, treatises, memoranda, commentaries, oral submissions, jury charges, pleadings, and reported judgements – on the Jamaica conflict.

Taken together, this material provides ample documentation of the perceptions and actions of members of what I will call, somewhat inexactly, the English 'political class' of the late 1860s. Here I am referring to that aggregate of persons – thinkers, journalists, social activists, officeholders, and politicians – who by their documented writings, speeches, and actions, created the amalgam of thoughts and deeds that came to be known as 'the Jamaica controversy'. The political class were the persons who actively instigated, resisted, described, and sustained the Jamaica affair, the persons who gave it pith and substance. The body of *A Jurisprudence of Power* should be read as a long answer to an integrated set of historical questions about their habits of thought and action. Some of these questions are specific to the empirical content of individual chapters, and are set forth and answered in those chapters. Some of these questions, however, resonate throughout all seven chapters of the book.

Why, for instance, only a handful of years after the traumatic Indian Mutiny, did the suppression of a rebellious community of black men and women become the subject of prolonged conflict in England? What patterns are discernible in the way in which English journalists and political activists described and comprehended the Jamaica affair? How and why did law, lawyers, and litigation become so central to the controversy? Why did the Jamaica affair generate such a large and divisive literature on 'martial law'? How did writers comprehend the legal nature of martial law, and its place in the English constitution? How did the Jamaica episode fare in the courts of law? Is it correct, as one important historian of the Jamaica affair has suggested, [73] that the legal initiatives of the Jamaica Committee 'had absolutely no effect'? Is it correct, then, that the repeated attempts by lawyers and judges to make sense of the law of martial law were of little historical moment or consequence? If this suggestion is incorrect, what might be the basis of the contrary hypothesis? What contribution did the Jamaica litigation make to the unfolding English jurisprudence concerning the use and abuse of political and military power? How did the English governing class answer a question posed repeatedly in the context of the Jamaica affair: 'How is a country committed to the rule of law to administer a vast and sometimes dangerously recalcitrant empire?' Finally, what does the Jamaica affair reveal of the broader political psyche of the English governing class in the late 1860s?

A Jurisprudence of Power advances two sets of ten theses. The first concerns the Jamaica affair itself, its language and its internal dynamics. The second set concerns the larger significance of the episode for our understanding of English political consciousness in the mid-Victorian era. By their nature the first set of theses are directly accountable to the empirical content of the book's seven chapters. Borrowing Edward Thompson's words, they are about 'getting inside' an episode of English history. The second set of ten theses, by *their* nature, are necessarily more speculative and conjectural. In fact, these theses are offered to readers not so much as arguments but as plausible inferences. They are a self-conscious attempt to get 'outside' the episode.

The first ten theses are as follows:

(1) That the language used by the English governing class to describe and evaluate news of the Jamaica suppression reflected the deep penetration into public discourse of legal terms, criteria, and concepts. From its inception, the 'Jamaica affair' was understood and transacted largely in terms of law and legality.

(2) That the legal-minded discourse of the Jamaica affair was rhetorically powerful and widely embraced. It tended to accentuate matters which the governing class cared about a great deal (the legal regulation of political and

---

[73] Catherine Hall, 'Rethinking Imperial Histories: The Reform Act of 1867', 208 *New Left Review*, (1994), 3–29, 13. For a similar view, see Collini, *Public Moralists*, 146.

military power) and marginalize matters which it cared about a great deal *less* (the status of dark-skinned persons in the empire).

(3) That by the end of December 1865, it was broadly agreed that the Jamaica suppression had exposed some stark and alarming ambiguities in the English jurisprudence pertaining to martial law, and the use of political and military power during public emergencies.

(4) That in keeping with the legal-mindedness of the Jamaica debate, the Russell government instituted an official inquiry dominated by lawyers and legal conventions. One of the central purposes of the inquiry was to discover the degree to which the suppression had conformed to the law of martial law.

(5) That the enduring purpose of the Jamaica Committee was to cause the English courts of law to pronounce definitively on martial law, and on the principle of the universal legal accountability of political and military actors and conduct. In pursuit of this goal the Jamaica Committee evinced an unflagging faith in the acuity and integrity of English high court judges.

(6) That the Jamaica affair spurred English lawyers to create a new but highly disputatious technical literature on the law of martial law. This material was written to influence public debate, and did so appreciably. However, the legal propositions advanced in these texts were strongly influenced by *a priori* political tenets and preoccupations. The legal literature of martial law became a site of political and ideological conflict.

(7) That when the leaders of the Jamaica Committee decided to pursue the Jamaica controversy in the courts of law, they relinquished control over their project to the professional judgment, language, and procedures of lawyers. The process of litigation inevitably involved the inexact translation of the aspirations of the Committee into legal pleadings and submissions.

(8) That English law lacked an effective mechanism for the resolutions of constitutional conflict. The private criminal prosecution, while it afforded access to the courts, was a maladroit means of pursuing abstract legal and political goals. The constitutional aims of the Committee were consistently derailed by the practical concerns and sympathies of English grand juries.

(9) That while English high court judges enjoyed great prestige, and were seen as having a crucial role in resolving the Jamaica controversy, the judges ultimately proved unable to distil a coherent body of principles concerning the law of martial law. Judicial pronouncements on martial law were confounded by personal ambivalence and political confusion.

(10) That the Jamaica Committee failed to achieve a decisive legal precedent about the law of martial law, but succeeded in causing the English governing class to confront the contradiction between the love of power and the love of law.

The second set of theses arises from a single question, one which will be discussed at some length in the concluding essay of the book: through the keyhole of the Jamaica affair, what can be seen of the general moral and political consciousness of the English political class of the late 1860s? What can be detected of their most fundamental assumptions and habits of thought?

The second set of ten theses is as follows:

(1) That the English political class of the late 1860s were Hobbesian pessimists about human nature. In this view, human beings, when left to their own devices, were naturally inclined to egotism, aggression, and violence.

(2) That the political class increasingly embraced the idea that secular law and legality – not Christian religion – were the essential bulwark of a society against the natural licentiousness of men. The moral imagination of the English, even among the most pious Christians, fundamentally was a legal imagination.

(3) That the Jamaica suppression became controversial because it called into question the moral – hence legal – integrity of the English people. There was general unease, skilfully exploited by the Jamaica Committee, not only that English officials had engaged in a vicious and prolonged reign of terror in Jamaica, but that they should later claim that what they had done was completely *lawful* under the doctrine of martial law.

(4) That the Jamaica affair mainly concerned the moral and legal framework governing white Englishmen at home, not black subjects abroad. The suppression became controversial in England because it exposed the tectonic stresses created by the nation's embrace both of the will to power and the rule of law.

(5) That the Jamaica suppression was sustainable as a subject of controversy because it aroused the nation's Burkean qualms about the potentially corrosive effects of empire on the English national character. Even the rising tide of 'scientific' racism could not fully eliminate the intuition – reinforced by the Indian Mutiny – that the non-white empire depended on coercion not consent, and that coercion would corrupt the coercer.

(6) That by broad consent the Jamaica affair was channelled into the English legal system. Because of its growing commitment to secular modernity, the English governing class not only tolerated but institutionalized the legal investigation and evaluation of the suppression. The final reconstruction and assessment of the Jamaica affair were assigned to judges, not clerics. Public sin was rightly expunged in courtrooms, not churches.

(7) That for most members of the English governing classes, conservatives and liberals, the principle of political and military accountability to law was sacrosanct. The radicalism of the Jamaica Committee was in insisting on

the legal accountability even of imperial officials who crushed insurrection among the dark-skinned peoples of the empire. The conservatism of their opponents was in insisting on an imperial exception to the rule of law in the governance of alien peoples.

(8) That the Jamaica litigation stimulated a fierce, prolific, if ultimately indecisive exchange among English lawyers, jurists, and judges over whether there could be a doctrinal accommodation between imperialism and constitutionalism, between mastery and legality. This exchange focused on the history, legal pedigree, and political implications of the law of martial law.

(9) That English constitutional law operated less as a body of substantive principles than as a reservoir of legal narratives about state power and its proper limits and constraint. When the judges pronounced on the law of martial law they drew on these narratives according to their sense both of legal propriety and political expedience.

(10) That although the moral, political, and legal issues raised by the Jamaica affair were not resolved by debate or litigation, the English governing class, more candidly and openly than the elites of other European states, were willing (at this historical moment) to confront the contradictions generated by their political choices in the world. More than the elites of other states they were willing to engage in a vigorous if ultimately indecisive reassessment of their jurisprudence of power.

The ensuing study consists respectively of seven analytical narrative chapters, an epilogue, a final thematic essay and an historiographical appendix. The seven empirical chapters trace the historical development of the Jamaica affair in rough chronological order. Chapter 1 examines the way in which the English governing class described and conceptualized news of the Jamaica suppression. The second chapter considers the investigation and litigation of the Jamaica affair in Jamaica during the first half of 1866. Chapter 3 examines how, in the second half of 1866, the Jamaica affair was revitalized as an English political and legal controversy. This chapter focuses on how English ideologues and intellectuals formed alliances to define and litigate the issues arising from the suppression in Jamaica. The fourth chapter delves into the voluminous technical legal literature which was generated in response to the Jamaica affair and litigation. This section considers the doctrinal content and also the political mainsprings of this writing, and how it affected the larger public debate on the affair. Chapter 5 examines the first attempts by the Jamaica Committee to bring the controversy to a decisive conclusion in the English criminal courts, and the motives, strategies, and decisions of the lawyers and magistrates who litigated the Jamaica cases. The sixth and seventh chapters focus on the content of and public reaction to the grand jury charges, first of Lord Chief Justice Cockburn in the case of *The Queen v. Nelson and Brand*, and then of Justice Blackburn in *The Queen v. Eyre*. These chapters closely examine the legal and political underpinnings of the charges, the public reaction they engendered, and the unprecedented dispute that arose between the judges. The Epilogue provides an account of the civil litigation in *Phillips v. Eyre*, and the final winding down of the Jamaica affair in 1870. It also provides a postscript to the law and politics of martial law in the later British empire. The book is then brought to a close with an interpretative essay, 'A Jurisprudence of Power', which attempts to elaborate on the principal themes of the book.

1

'The Country of Law': Reconstructing the Morant Bay Uprising in England

Of all the Martial Laws I have heard of, this is the most dreadful. The Queen is a good and kind lady, but her soldiers are being fierce men of war; they are let slip now, like bloodhounds in the hunt and nobody can pull them in . . . I have no doubt that Gordon is hanged by this time . . .

Letter of Louis MacKinnon, Kingston, October 1865 [1]

Judging by his own despatches, we can only conclude that Gov. Eyre is flagrantly ignorant of the constitutional law which, as the agent of the Queen, he is bound to administer.

Law Magazine, Jan.–Mar. 1866.

The first reports of the violence at Morant Bay – a *mélange* of Jamaican newspaper clippings and private letters – reached England by packet ship in the first week of November 1865.[2] This material had been written more than three weeks earlier, and by persons unaware of the full extent of the rebellion, or the efficacy of measures taken to suppress it. The common theme of these reports was that white men in Jamaica already had been killed and mutilated by black men, and that the fate of the entire white population of the island still was in doubt.

With the arrival of further packet ships in the following ten days, however, it became apparent that the safety of Jamaica's small and scattered white communities had been secured, if only because of the decision, pluck, and manly resolve of Governor Edward Eyre and his tiny complement of regular troops and militiamen. The rebellion had been snuffed out in its infancy, and for this 'great relief' was widely expressed.[3] If there was to be any ensuing controversy about the Jamaica violence, or so it seemed early in November 1865, the controversy would be confined to the causes of the revolt.[4]

---

[1] MacKinnon to Sheldon, 20 Oct. 1865, Cardwell Papers, CO 30/48/42.

[2] The first news arrived by transatlantic telegraph from Halifax. See Douglas Lorimer, *Colour, Class, and the Victorians: English Attitudes to the Negro in the Mid-Nineteenth Century* (Leicester, 1978), 182. [3] *The Times* (17 Nov. 1865), 9.

[4] See summary of newspaper editorials on this subject in the *Pall Mall Gazette* (14 Nov. 1865), 2.

When the English political class received the startling news from Jamaica it was fully acquainted with the potentially lethal perils of rebellion in the non-white empire. In November 1865, after all, the white men and women of Cawnpore had been dead for fewer than eight years. Within the space of just twenty years, moreover, British troops had suppressed violent uprisings in Ceylon and the Cape Colony.[5] And now, just as the country came to grips with the October rising in Jamaica, Fenian insurrectionists were taking up arms in Ireland and Canada. It is hardly surprising, then, that Edward Eyre, when he composed his first official despatch to the Colonial Office in the wake of the bloodshed, was unembarrassed by the extraordinary measures he had taken to restore public safety and order. In fact, Eyre appears to have expected ample praise, even reward, for his conduct.

As it turned out, he got neither. In England the period of general thanksgiving about Jamaica was short-lived. By the end of the second week of November criticisms of the moral (and legal) character of the suppression were in wide circulation. By the end of the third week the Jamaica affair had become a matter of national controversy, and the defenders of Governor Eyre were very much on the defensive. In the first week of December, only a month after news of the Jamaica rising had reached England, the cabinet already had resolved (privately) to suspend Eyre from his duties while a Royal Commission undertook a thorough investigation both of the rebellion and suppression. In the second week of December, these decisions were announced publicly. How had this reversal come about? Why had the suppression of some rebellious blacks, men with white blood on their hands, become the subject of bitter controversy? What was it about the news from Jamaica that had caused so many prominent men, men inured to the bloody exigencies of imperial rule, to censure Governor Eyre and his soldiers? How, and under what banners, did they coalesce into a coordinated association? What was the nature of their criticisms, and how were they translated into action?

In addressing these questions, this chapter examines the period from early November 1865 to the point, just before Christmas, when the Jamaica controversy was temporarily becalmed by the Liberal government's decision to send a Royal Commission of Inquiry to the island. The chapter is broken down into three short studies: the first describing the evolution of opinion on the Jamaica affair; the second examining the organized response of some private persons and organizations; and the third addressing the response of the Liberal government. Looked on as a whole, the chapter documents the crystallization of a political language about the Jamaica controversy, and how it came to be comprehended not only as a moral and political issue, but even more fundamentally as an issue of constitutional law.

---

[5] For an overview, see Clode, *Military Forces of the Crown*, vol. ii, 481–511.

I. The Jamaica Affair as a Problem of Law

From late November until mid-December 1865 England's legion of journalists and political pundits generated a veritable storm surge of reportage and polemic on the Jamaica rising and suppression, one which all but swamped what *John Bull* called 'our newspaper-ridden generation'.[6] These accounts were so numerous, and yet so contradictory, that even the most discerning reader could not have known what had gone on there. 'Distance and difference of colour,' the *Spectator* observed, 'interpose so greatly as to slow the [English] imagination in realizing what has happened'.[7] Every new item reaching England was founded on second-, third-, and fourth-hand information, liberally embellished by supposition, opinion, or both. In its first account of the uprising on 3 November, *The Times* cautiously reported the 'most unpleasant piece of intelligence' that a 'rebellion is *said* to have commenced among the negroes in the eastern portion of the island of Jamaica' (emphasis added).[8] But for more detailed and reliable information English readers would have to wait for another two full weeks.[9] 'The English Press,' an editor at *The Times* later lamented, 'has no correspondents in the island, and for anything like trustworthy intelligence must be dependent on official documents or the chance letters of respectable private persons'.[10]

But the uncertain reliability of the Jamaica news did not deter the formation of strong opinions about its implications for politics at home. This was only natural. After all, most English commentators were as one with readers and listeners in their sturdy indifference to the fate of Jamaicans, living or dead, black or white. The defining truth of rebellion journalism and discourse, of the Jamaica controversy as a whole, is that nearly from the outset it was appropriated and reconstructed as a means of contesting political positions and propositions in *England*.

During the first days of the week of 13 November, the accounts of the Jamaica uprising published in England's principal newspapers continued to emphasize the ruthless violence of the black insurrectionists. *The Times*, to select a representative example,[11] published military bulletins (written in mid-October) which documented alleged 'barbarities committed by the negroes' which, as Major-General O'Connor cautiously termed it, '*appear* to have been of a fiendish character' (emphasis added).[12] Somewhat less cautiously, O'Connor's bulletin also reported

---

[6] *John Bull* (13 June 1868), 404.　　[7] *Spectator* (27 Jan. 1866), 89–90.

[8] *The Times* (3 Nov. 1865), 7. The admirable caution of *The Times* had limits. In the same piece the editor expressed doubt that the black peasantry of Jamaica, fully endowed with the privileges of British citizenship, could have rebelled on their own accord. On this premiss the newspaper stated that 'it was by no means improbable that some of the negroes [of Haiti] may have been practising upon the population of our dependency'.

[9] Governor Eyre's first post-uprising despatch (written on 20 Oct.) was made available to English reporters on 19 Nov.　　[10] *The Times* (2 Dec. 1865), 8.

[11] See also *Manchester Guardian* (14 Nov. 1865), 6–7.

[12] Official Bulletin of Major-General O'Connor, 14 Oct. 1865 as reprinted in *The Times* (13 Nov. 1865), 9.

that the 'plan of the rebels is to murder all of the white and coloured men first, then the children, and to keep the women as servants and for their own pleasure'. Articles reprinted from Jamaica's newspapers described 'lawless bands spreading murder and devastation in the parish of St. Thomas-in-the-East'.[13] *The Times* published a private letter written by an (unnamed) white Jamaican who claimed that the 'whites who have fallen in the hands of these savages have been doomed to slaughter without distinction of age or sex. They tear out the tongues of their victims, cut off the breasts of women, and strangle and mutilate little children, and practice all the enormities that render the insurrection in Santa Domingo the darkest page of history.'[14] The violence being visited on defenceless whites was nothing short of horrific, and the country had yet to receive reliable information that it had been stopped.

In the same week, 13 November, *The Times* ran an editorial which decried the 'horrible outrages' of the Jamaican rebels, and insinuated that they had been the direct and predictable consequence of an overly indulgent stance toward negroes since their emancipation.[15] It was also insinuated that the insurrection had been fomented, at least in some important measure, by the irresponsible meddling of Baptist missionaries. The 'best policy for any people who have to deal with the black race,' the editorial concluded, 'is to keep a strong hand over them'. Other newspapers, conservative[16] and liberal,[17] suggested that unrest among Jamaica's black population had been manifest for many months, but that Lord Russell's government had negligently failed to take necessary steps to avert violence. In the initial judgement of most English political pundits, blame for the Jamaica debacle was properly assigned to officials in London, not Spanish Town.

The editorial tone of the reporting on Jamaica began to change with the arrival, on 16 and 17 November, of more detailed and dependable information about what had happened in the colony. The change became even more pronounced when, on 19 November, the government quickly published the first post-rebellion despatch of Governor Eyre (written to Edward Cardwell, the Secretary of State for the Colonial Office, on 20 October).[18] When the despatch and news reports were read together, the *Pall Mall Gazette* summarized, it was obvious that 'the rising of the negroes has been at once and effectually trampled out'.[19] It was also plain that the rebels had been suppressed with 'unsparing severity'. Still, even a liberal-minded paper such as the *Pall Mall Gazette* was not ready to contend that

[13] As reprinted from the *Colonial Standard*, ibid.
[14] As reprinted from the *New York Daily News*, ibid.   [15] *The Times* (13 Nov. 1865), 8.
[16] Report of the *Evening Standard* as summarized in the *Pall Mall Gazette* (15 Nov. 1865), 2.
[17] The *Daily News* reported that the Jamaican authorities had been forewarned that an insurrection was imminent, and suggested that prompt action might have prevented the loss of life. But the *Daily News* also suggested that 'the chief cause of political discontent of the Negroes . . . is the fact that the island is governed by the old slave-holding class'. As reprinted in the *Pall Mall Gazette* (14 Nov. 1865), 2.
[18] Eyre's despatch was published in the Government *Gazette* only two days after it arrived from Jamaica. *The Times* (8 Jan. 1866), 8.   [19] *Pall Mall Gazette* (17 Nov. 1865), 1.

Governor Eyre had been guilty of wrongdoing or even misjudgement. Although 'two hundred rebels shot or hanged sounds a large number of victims to the vengeance of the law in a few days', the *Gazette* remained of the opinion that the uprising in Jamaica had been of a dangerous 'half-sepoy character', one which 'requires and deserves to be treated with far severer and more exemplary punishment'.[20] The decision made by Governor Eyre first to proclaim martial law and then to crush the rebels with all available force, the *Gazette* still contended, would be exonerated as one of the 'strictest justice and the truest mercy'.

Such votes of support became much rarer after English commentators had a chance to submit Eyre's long despatch to more deliberate scrutiny. His report provided a remarkably detailed and candid record of the ruthless character of the suppression. The commencement of the Jamaica controversy can be traced to the publication of this official document.

Eyre's report began by making two very telling preliminary points.[21] The first was to inform Cardwell that among the first persons whom he consulted upon learning of the violence at Morant Bay was his Attorney General, Alexander Heslop.[22] No important determination about the suppression had been made without advice from the senior law officer of the Crown. It is obvious that Eyre thought it terribly important to assure his superiors that he had been alert to the legal implications of his decisions, and had complied with the law. Secondly, Eyre took pains to establish a historical context for his official conduct. Every one of his key decisions, the Governor emphasized, had been influenced by the receipt of apparently credible descriptions of the 'most frightful atrocities'. On this information – the only information in his possession – it had seemed to Eyre that the 'whole outrage could only be paralleled by the atrocities of the Indian mutiny'.[23]

Eyre's first despatch on the uprising and suppression was written in an appropriately detached tone, but one which betrayed a measure of defensiveness. As an experienced official of the British Empire, Eyre knew that his decision to apply violence under martial law had to be justified militarily and legally. He also knew that this rule applied even when the objects of the violence were black men and women who had spilled the blood of whites. Eyre's despatch described how the 'extreme urgency of the case, and the magnitude of the interests at stake' had rendered it absolutely necessary to apply severe levels of violence against the rebels under a proclamation of martial law. It described how in a moment of great peril the Governor had moved quickly to use a small military force to avert the second catastrophic insurrection in the empire in eight years. The despatch repeatedly underlined that the decision to proclaim martial law in St. Thomas-in-the-East,

---

[20] Ibid.

[21] Eyre to Cardwell, 20 Oct. 1865, in 'Papers Relating to the Insurrection in Jamaica', *Annual Register*, 1865, 277–86.

[22] 'I immediately sent for the Executive Committee, and after a hurried consultation with them, and with the Attorney General ...' Ibid., 279. (Eyre's consultations with his Attorney General are explored in greater depth below, Ch. 2.)   [23] Ibid.

and to send troops there to quell revolt, had been endorsed by all of the colony's leading legal and military men. Thus, as much as Eyre's first despatch imparted basic information about the suppression, it was meant to anticipate and answer legal questions about what had been done in the name of the Crown.

Eyre's description of what had been done to quell the uprising was interestingly guileless and unguarded. It volunteered, for instance, that the rebellion had been effectively contained and crushed within a week of its first outbreak, and that 'No stand has ever been made against the troops'.[24] The despatch further reported that the supposed leaders of the insurrection had been quickly rounded up. ('We have been singularly fortunate in capturing or shooting a large number of the principal ringleaders in the rebellion.'[25]) Strangely, however, Eyre also contended that the colony continued to be in 'the greatest jeopardy', so much so that the summary trial and punishment – including execution – of alleged rebels continued at the time of writing. And then Eyre offered another startling piece of information. George Gordon, the coloured politician and Native Baptist agitator, had been arrested in Kingston (a place not under martial law) and, on the Governor's personal order, transported to Morant Bay for trial by a military court. The report almost casually added that Gordon had been executed just before Eyre had completed the present despatch to the Colonial Office. Finally, with this despatch Eyre enclosed a sheaf of reports written by various military men in the field. The reports graphically (and even proudly) described a series of brutal acts of retribution against suspected rebels. Clearly Eyre was confident that his superiors in London would view this material as evidence of a job well done. In this he soon was sorely disappointed.

In his official reply to Eyre dated 17 November, Cardwell offered some perfunctory congratulations to the Governor for the 'spirit, energy and judgment' in suppressing the rebellion. But just two paragraphs later Cardwell registered his great consternation over the various 'measures of severity' that Eyre had either ordered or approved. In a line which must have startled the Governor, Cardwell hoped that it be 'evident' to Eyre that his despatch contained 'many passages which will require to be explained'.[26] In the meantime, Cardwell relied on Eyre's assurance that the measures he had taken to suppress the rebellion indeed were a 'merciful substitute' for the even more vigorous suppression that would have been required by a full-scale revolt. Cardwell also indicated that he expected to read in the next despatch that Eyre had 'arrested the course of punishment' so soon as he was able to do so.

Eyre's despatch also did not win many admirers in the English political press. While The Times held fast to its view that a potent dose of martial law had been the only prudent course in Jamaica,[27] England's liberal-minded papers began to entertain grave doubts. As the Pall Mall Gazette observed on 20 November, 'The

[24] Annual Register, 1865, 285.   [25] Ibid.   [26] Ibid., 287.
[27] The Times (20 Nov. 1865), 8.

despatch of Governor Eyre is the first cool and collected account that has been received of the course of events in Jamaica, and certainly one of the most remarkable documents that ever was printed in English newspapers.' The editor guessed that many English readers would be stunned by its unselfconscious descriptions of brutal retaliatory violence against black Jamaicans. 'The despatch,' the *Gazette* wrote with macabre understatement, 'is full of hanging.'[28] And the newspaper thought that while 'it *may* be true that the measures taken were necessary to stamp out the first sparks of servile war' (emphasis added), the Governor's own admissions 'raised the far less agreeable possibility' that he had committed 'a terrible wrong to the black population of Jamaica by magnifying the massacre at Morant Bay into the first symptom of a general explosion'.[29] The *Gazette* called for a 'clear and impartial inquiry' into the uprising and its suppression. On 22 November the *Manchester Guardian* took a similar position: 'Every candid man must feel that the more the Jamaica business is investigated, the worse it looks for the colonial authorities.'[30] The circumstances surrounding the arrest, court martial, and execution of Gordon seemed particularly to require a full explanation and justification.

Eyre's despatch was little short of a public-relations disaster for Eyre and for the Government. Its main achievement was to foster the perception that in the wake of a minor uprising Eyre's military forces had gone on a bloody rampage against the black peasantry of Jamaica. The subsequent publication in England of the private letters of some militia and regular officers who had implemented martial law (some of these letters had previously been published in the Jamaican papers) put the matter beyond serious doubt. The letter of Captain Ford, a cavalry officer, proudly drew a 'picture of martial law' in which he and his men had taken sport in shooting black men and women in the back as they fled for their lives.[31] A militia colonel, Francis Hobbs, openly boasted of how he had terrorized then executed the servant of one of the leaders of the uprising.[32] Another officer, the soon notorious Provost-Marshal Ramsay, blithely reported that he had hanged (without trial) one black prisoner merely for having made an angry face after a severe flogging. This and a host of other letters recounted in minute detail how government troops had hunted, burned out, shot, and whipped scores of men and women, sometimes without benefit even of a drumhead court martial. A litany of appallingly cruel and purely vindictive actions, actions committed by officials of the Crown, now were self-admitted matters of public record.

But the lasting significance of these letters, as the *Dublin Review* later pointed out, was not so much their gruesome content but the insight they gave into 'the public feeling in Jamaica, and the degree to which it was shared by Mr. Eyre and

---

[28] *Pall Mall Gazette* (20 Nov. 1865), 1.   [29] Ibid.

[30] *Manchester Guardian* (22 Nov. 1865), 2.

[31] This and other notorious letters of similar type were quoted at length in an article in the *Spectator* (2 Dec. 1865), 1330–1.

[32] Hobbs had tethered the man to his horse while threatening him with his revolver. Hobbs's letter was published in a number of leading papers, including *The Times* (17 Nov. 1865), 9.

the other authorities'.[33] Far from being concerned that their actions would incur official disapprobation or sanction, the writers had related their most grisly deeds with unhidden pride. One journalist recalled that 'Every writer seemed anxious to accredit to himself with the most monstrous deeds of cruelty.'[34] As the *Glasgow Sentinel* pointed out on 25 November, 'the negro revolt in Jamaica has been suppressed and public attention has been attracted from the outbreak to its suppression'. The *Sentinel* agreed that there was 'something disgusting in the way the military officers speak of the execution of the negroes'. But more alarming was the fact that British subjects had been subjected to 'high-handed justice'. In these pages Governor Eyre was compared unfavourably to Lord Canning who during the closing stages of the suppression of the Indian Mutiny (so it was claimed) had averted an even more bloody revenge. In Jamaica, however, Governor Eyre had lost his nerve and, in so doing, had tolerated a wholly 'illegal mode of punishing the insurgents'.

And while the *Dublin Review* and other political journals[35] expressed incredulity and shock over the military letters, from a historical point of view the attitude of the soldiers was entirely understandable. First, there was a local explanation. The militia officers were recruited from a class of white colonist who seethed with racial hatred and fear of blacks.[36] When white lives were taken at Morant Bay, they felt entitled to exact a terrible revenge. There was also an imperial explanation. When they wrote their letters and reports the regular officers might be forgiven for thinking that they had done no more than what had been necessary to ensure that the scattered white population of Jamaica did not experience the horrors of the Indian Mutiny. Having achieved this result, the idea that the officers, whatever violence they might have perpetrated, 'could merit anything except reward and honour does not seem to have crossed their minds'.[37] At the local level, too, this assumption was borne out. Not even the most gross and seemingly excessive use of force generated as much as a reprimand. Neither the commanding officer of the military, General O'Connor, nor the highest civilian official, Governor Eyre, had indicated anything but approval of all actions taken against suspected rebels during the month-long period of martial law.

The publication of Eyre's despatch and the assorted military letters in England caused the rapid fragmentation of published opinion on the issue. While many prominent commentators remained convinced that it had been necessary to crush the rebels by any possible means, the opposite view now also was being forcefully expressed. But even as the discussion became more fractious and emotionally

---

[33] *Dublin Review*, vii (1866), 408.

[34] McCarthy, *A History of Our Own Times*, vol. iii (London, 1895), 357.

[35] The editors of the *Quarterly Review* (120 (1866), 221) were of a similar mind: 'To us nothing in the whole affair is so painful and revolting as the tone in which some British officers thought fit to write regarding shooting or punishing negroes'. But the *Review* thought that the most 'unaccountable thing' was that senior military and civilian officials could have received such letters without delivering the 'sternest reproof' to their authors.   [36] Heuman, '*The Killing Time*', 97–110.

[37] *Dublin Review*, viii (1866), 409.

charged, it is also possible to discern the emergence of broad agreement on one key point: that the crucial implications of the Jamaica affair related to the inviolability of English laws not of Jamaican blacks.

On 25 November the radical historian and labour activist Edward Beesly[38] made this first of many interventions into the Jamaica affair. In a long letter to the labour paper the *Bee-Hive*, he endeavoured to make his goals and allegiances clear. 'I protest,' Beesly assured readers, 'I am no negro-worshipper…Some negroes may be men of ability and elevated character, but there can be no doubt that they belong to a lower type of human race than we do, and I should not like to live in a country where they formed a considerable part of the population.'[39] The real issue presented by the suppression in Jamaica was not that scores of black labourers had been massacred under cover of law, but that scores of white labourers might now meet the same fate in England. Beesly's letter warned that the apologias (those 'horrible articles') that had been written about military actions in Jamaica 'prove something more than the wickedness of the writers; they show what sort of views are found to be acceptable to the well-to-do part of the community'.[40] To Beesly's reckoning, if the powerful would countenance the suspension of all legal niceties and protections in St. Thomas-in-the-East, they would also do so in London east.

The Jamaica controversy did not consist only of polemical newspaper editorials and letters. Historians have often recorded that in the last days of November and the first of December 1865 a series of public 'Jamaica Meetings' were held in most of the larger cities and boroughs of England. It is equally well known that these meetings were organized (or provoked) mainly by Christian evangelicals and anti-slavery activists (known collectively by the name of their London meeting place in the Strand, Exeter Hall).[41] Although a great many speeches were made at these meetings, by Exeter Hall men and otherwise, historians have paid surprisingly little attention to their rhetorical content.

One of the first and most widely reported of the Jamaica Meetings was convened by the mayor of Manchester (at the behest of a petition signed by 600 citizens) on 27 November. The meeting had been instigated by its main speakers (the anti-slavery activist and radical M.P. for Rochdale, T. B. Potter, and Jacob Bright, the younger brother of the great radical reformer and M.P., John Bright), as a means of pressuring the Liberal government to institute an inquiry. The meeting

---

[38] Edward Spenser Beesly (1831–1915) was a Comtian, and had been Professor of Modern History at University College London since 1860. See Joseph A. Baylen and Norbert L. Gossman (eds.), *Biographical Dictionary of Modern British Radicals*, vol. ii (New York, 1977) 53–8; Vogeler, *Oxford DNB*, online 38832.

[39] *Bee-Hive* (25 Nov. 1865) Beesly also spoke of the equal entitlement of blacks to fair treatment and wages.

[40] Ibid. The *Bee-Hive* had not been a friend of anti-slavery during the American Civil War. Under the editorship of George Troup, the paper railed against 'anti-slavery fanatics'. See generally, Howard Temperley, *British Antislavery, 1833–1870* (Columbia, SC, 1972), 250; R. J. M. Blackett, *Divided Hearts: Britain and the American Civil War* (Baton Rouge, La., 2001), 150.

[41] Temperley, *British Antislavery*, 39, 66–7.

also should be seen as the start of the process by which some political radicals (led by John Bright), while they vented outrage against the brutalities of the suppression, began to co-opt the Jamaica controversy as a means of consolidating support for the cause of constitutional reform. Without exception these meetings emphasized the secular and legal implications for *Englishmen* of the use of martial law in Jamaica.

At the outset of the Manchester meeting, Potter moved and then defended a resolution that there should be a 'strict and impartial investigation on the part of the Government . . . into the origin and causes of the outbreak, and especially into the legality and necessity of the severe measures adopted for its suppression'.[42] While this was predictable enough, Potter's defence of the resolution touched on themes that would continue to define the main contours of the Eyre controversy.

Potter's speech was woven together by repeated appeals to the legal sensibilities of his English audience. Governor Eyre, Potter asserted, had clearly 'lost his head' in the face of a mere spasm of unrest. The horrific retaliatory violence he had set in motion was a 'disgrace and dishonour to the English name'. More adamantly than many commentators, Potter acknowledged that terrible atrocities had been committed against subjects of the realm ('for though coloured men, these were Englishmen.')[43] But this, decidedly, was *not* the crucial point of his address. In the body of his speech, Potter reviewed how Eyre and his officials had acted in contempt of the most sacred constitutional rights of Englishmen, of how von Ketelholdt had ordered soldiers to discharge their muskets into a political assembly of British subjects. Invoking the memory of Peterloo, he reminded Mancunians of 'how dangerous it was to fire on the people'. Potter also referred to how George Gordon, the leader of the political opposition in Jamaica, had been torn from the protection of the civilian courts only to be handed over to the 'tender mercies of a court-martial'. Potter was among the first publicly to suggest that for the subsequent execution of Gordon, Eyre and his officers had been 'guilty of murder'. This assertion was reinforced by Jacob Bright's speech, who warned that the British government was apt 'to screen high class offenders', however guilty.[44] 'It was but truth,' Bright added in closing the speeches, 'to say that the killing of Gordon – No, Murder! – had stirred the profoundest patriotic feeling in the British heart'.[45]

---

[42] *The Times* (28 Nov. 1865), 5.

[43] Potter went on to allege that he had 'heard men speak with deep regret of the atrocities they had themselves witnessed during the Indian Mutiny . . . when [innocents] were massacred with the greatest cruelty because the authorities and the soldiery had been worked up to a feeling almost of barbarity'. Ibid.   [44] Reported in *Reynolds' Weekly* (3 Dec. 1865).

[45] John Bright used almost the identical rhetoric at a political banquet held at Blackburn on 1 December. At the conclusion of a long and widely reported speech in support of electoral reform, Bright expressed hope that 'the Governor of Jamaica and his accomplices will have to stand at the bar of justice for the murder of Mr. Gordon'. In Bright's opinion, 'there was no murder more foul than that which is done under the pretence of law'. Reported in *Manchester Guardian* (1 Dec. 1865), 3.

The Manchester meeting ended with a resolution that the Prime Minister be presented with a 'memorial' which would recount the misdeeds of Governor Eyre, and their grim significance for a nation governed by laws. 'The Englishman loved his country,' the memorial read, 'because it was the country of law, and because in it he was never subject to the caprices of a despotic will.' The memorial sounded a note that would have made a staunch American republican proud: England was a country in which the subject, 'no matter what his colour, his extraction, his position in society…had inalienable rights, the first of which was that he could never be punished for any crime for which he had not been legally tried and convicted'. Moreover, the memorialists steadfastly rejected the notion that the proclamation of something called 'martial law' might provide a blanket legal immunity for those who had acted 'without justice, with cruelty and an utter abandonment of reason'. The memorial ended on a prophetic note. Were it to prove that 'a British Governor had in one single case annihilated all law…the country would never be appeased until that Governor be put on his trial'. The memorial was presented to Lord Russell the next day.

The general agitation concerning the Jamaica affair intensified with the publication in the English newspapers on 1 December of the poignant last letter of George Gordon. The letter, addressed to his (it was inevitably reported, British-born and caucasian) wife, was composed in the hour before his execution. It was a minor masterpiece of gallows valediction. After a courtly thank you to Colonel Nelson (the commanding officer) for having been 'kind enough' to inform him that he would be hanged within the hour, Gordon turned to the injustice of his court martial and conviction. 'I do not deserve this sentence;' he wrote, 'for I never advised or took part in any insurrection.'[46] Gordon professed to have done no more than to 'seek redress in a legitimate way'. Finding himself condemned for his most deeply felt beliefs, he likened himself to the Christian saviour who had suffered to 'relieve the poor and the needy, and to protect…the oppressed'. Gordon then returned to the more prosaic subject of his trial: 'The judges seemed against me and from the rigid manner of the Court I could not get in all the explanation I intended.' The prosecution's witnesses had perjured themselves. Gordon's final request was that his wife should write to prominent Englishmen (among others, to the famed reformist politician and lawyer Lord Henry Brougham[47] and the anti-slavery activist Louis Chamerovzow)[48] in order that they should know that, innocent of any civil crime, he had been sent to the gallows by a military

---

[46] Ibid., 8.

[47] Brougham's name was not mentioned accidentally. Gordon had corresponded with him over the years. Forty years earlier, in 1824, Brougham had been a leading figure in the campaign to exonerate the Baptist missionary John Smith, who had been sentenced to death by a military tribunal for fomenting a slave rebellion in the slave colony of Demerara. See *Manchester Guardian* (8 Dec. 1865), 2.

[48] Chamerovzow was an evangelical social activist who was connected to Baptist missionary groups in Jamaica. In 1865 he was the General Secretary of the British and Foreign Anti-Slavery Society. Temperley, *British Antislavery*, 79.

tribunal. 'I did not expect,' Gordon again lamented, 'that not being a rebel, I should have been tried and disposed of in this way. I thought his Excellency the Governor would have allowed me a fair trial.'

As the soldiers came for him, Gordon closed with some heartbreaking sentences which wavered between last farewells to his wife and final lamentations about the injustice of his treatment. 'You must do the best you can,' he told his wife, 'and do not be ashamed of the death your poor husband will have suffered.' He then offered a blessing to the men who had come to lead him to the gallows. But even at the very end, the legal injustice of his predicament was close to Gordon's mind. In the postscript to his letter Gordon informed his wife that he had 'asked leave' to see his solicitor, 'but the General said that I could not'. Minutes later, Governor Eyre created a martyr, and the means of his own undoing.

It is perhaps understandable that Gordon should have devoted so many of his last words to matters of law. His life had been built on twin pillars of faith: faith in the grace of the Christian God, and in the justice of the British imperial state. In the shadow of the gallows the former was affirmed, the latter shaken to its core. Gordon had fervently believed that like any other British subject he possessed the right to express political dissent. The final letter reflected his genuine bewilderment (he 'little expected' and 'did not expect') that this right had been taken away by a military tribunal, just as now, so his life would be. His final hope was that some eminent men (like Brougham and Chamerovzow) would be roused, if not by the plight of one coloured man, then by the blatant illegality of his execution. This hope was not misplaced.

Gordon's letter was like a godsend to a small but growing body of Englishmen already inclined to assail Governor Eyre and his officials. The letter served a number of useful purposes at once. It particularized and humanized a protest which might otherwise be accused of political and legal abstractness. Gordon's letter also made it more difficult for the Jamaica affair to be dismissed as an unnecessary fuss about some dead black men. As the *Fortnightly Review* stressed, Gordon was 'nearly white'.[49] Further to the point, he had been 'educated' (at an English boarding school), was 'prosperous' (he had owned estates in Jamaica), and had married a white English woman.[50] It seemed pertinent to add that Gordon had been 'known personally to many gentlemen in England'. In short, Gordon's life was white, English, and respectable enough to have been of real value. All the more reason to resent that he had been 'slain in violation of the law'. By mid-December 1865, Gordon's execution, more precisely, its alleged *illegality*, had become the dominant theme of the Jamaica controversy. As the *Fortnightly* put the matter, Gordon's executioners had committed a 'judicial murder'.[51] The *Freeman*, the clarion of anti-slavers and Baptist missionaries, called for Lord Russell to

---

[49] *Fortnightly Review* (1 Dec. 1865), 240–7.
[50] In fact, Gordon was all but officially bankrupt when he died, and his wife was Irish born.
[51] *Fortnightly Review* (1 Dec. 1865), 244.

prosecute Governor Eyre for 'his murderous and illegal trial' of Gordon.[52] The less emotive *Spectator* agreed that 'the presumptive evidence grows stronger each mail that the judicial murder of Mr. Gordon was the murder of a morally innocent man, as well as a pure illegality'.[53] Even the conservative sheet, *John Bull*, had come to think it incumbent on Governor Eyre to show 'that he has not exceeded his legal powers' in the proclamation of martial law generally, the execution of Gordon specifically.[54]

The arrival of Gordon's last letter coincided with the publication in England of Governor Eyre's post-suppression speech to the Jamaica legislature.[55] The speech was an unstinting defence of everything that had been done by the colonial authorities to crush the revolt. Shrewdly, Eyre likened the uprising at Morant Bay to the sepoy mutiny, and claimed that the government's forces had repelled a 'diabolical conspiracy to murder the white and coloured inhabitants of the island'. The Governor railed against the 'pseudo philanthropists', 'political demagogues', and the 'scurrilous press' who (he claimed) had incited the 'ignorant, excitable and uncivilized [black] population' of the island to revolt. For the proclamation, duration, and implementation of martial law, for the military execution of Gordon, or for any other act of suppression, Eyre expressed no apology or regret.

The political fires emanating from Jamaica were stoked by a number of factors, the Governor's official utterances prominent among them. The gruesomely boastful letters of militia officers, and the heart-rending final letter of Gordon also figured in the rapid change of public temper. All of this lent credence to reports that the repression had been on a massive scale. Rumours circulated and placards alleged that there had been 'Three Thousand Executions' in St. Thomas-in-the-East and that a road eight miles long was so 'strewn with dead bodies as to render [it] impassable'.[56] The slaughter was 'wholesale and indiscriminate', the *Glasgow Sentinel* informed readers on 2 December.[57] The Maroon allies of the authorities, it was said, had perpetrated a series of 'shocking barbarities' against alleged rebels and their families.[58] Another Scottish paper thought both that 'there was some exaggeration in all this, but enough remains true to render this counter-massacre in Jamaica one of the greatest scandals which has fallen on the country for a long period'.[59] While no one was in a position to know whether 100, 1,000, or 5,000 British subjects had perished under the martial law, there was a ready market for

---

[52] *Freeman* (6 Dec. 1865), 784.　　[53] *Spectator* (2 Dec. 1865), 1330–1.
[54] *John Bull* (9 Dec. 1865).
[55] *The Times* (29 Nov. 1865), 9; *Manchester Guardian* (30 Nov. 1865), 3.
[56] *Weekly Times* (3 Dec. 1865). Many critics operated on the assumption that the repression had claimed more than a thousand black lives. In its final report, the Jamaica Royal Commission calculated that 439 black Jamaicans had been executed or killed by the forces of the Crown. This figure probably does not account enough for the number of blacks slain in the back country. For the most authoritative discussion of the repression, see generally, Heuman, '*The Killing Time*', 113–30.
[57] *Glasgow Sentinel* (2 Dec. 1865). For a sceptical assessment of these reports, see *The Times* (13 Dec. 1865), 8.　　　　　　　　　　　　　　[58] *Morning Star* (9 Dec. 1865).
[59] *Glasgow Morning Journal* (30 Nov. 1865).

salacious and macabre speculation. Grub Street publishers rushed into print with illustrated penny pamphlets promising readers 'SPECIAL AND AUTHENTIC DETAILS' on the 'INHUMAN BUTCHERIES & RUTHLESS ATROCITIES'. At the same time, the *Spectator*, one of the most respectable liberal journals, chastised *The Times* for having failed to report that 2,000 men and women had been executed in Jamaica during the four weeks of martial law.[60]

With all this new grist to be milled, additional Jamaica Meetings were held in Lambeth, Brighton, Liverpool, and Bristol[61] during the first ten days of December. The Lambeth meeting, which drew over 1,000 people, was advertised as a public discussion of a memorial which proposed to condemn the conduct of Governor Eyre as 'cruel, tyrannical and subversive of the rights of British subjects'.[62] The meeting was chaired by the Revd. Newman Hall (of Exeter Hall) who, after providing an account of the suppression, declared his hope that 'Governor Eyre and his allies had done nothing unconstitutional'. The memorial under consideration deplored the 'barbarous measures' adopted by the government in Jamaica against the negroes of Jamaica, and a number of speakers, to be fair, alluded to specific atrocities. But the thrust of their initiative did not concern the plight of Jamaican blacks. What the proposers wanted was for the Prime Minster to 'uphold constitutional law and punish violators of it'. What most troubled them was the evidence that suggested at Morant Bay the people had been fired upon 'in order to discourage constitutional and lawful agitation for the redress of wrongs and grievances'. The memorial credited Lord Russell for having long identified with 'struggles for liberty and human rights', and he was called upon to vindicate the 'true value and blessing of constitutional law'. The resolution to send the memorial passed easily on a voice vote.

In Brighton, the speakers followed an almost identical script.[63] The chair, William Coningham M.P. (a political radical and associate of Exeter Hall), opened the meeting by stating of the Jamaica suppression that a 'more atrocious violation of every divine and human law had never been heard of, or a more open flagrant violation of the principles of the British constitutionalism... Were the Magna Carta, the Bill of Rights, and the Habeas Corpus mere fictions that they were violated with impunity in one of the dependencies in which the same laws were maintained that existed in this country?' In the wake of the transgressions perpetrated by British officials against British subjects it was vitally important that the Government undertake a 'full, searching, impartial investigation', so that the 'honour of the British nation might be purified, and the rights of the subject protected'. An M.P. named White alleged that Governor Eyre had orchestrated a 'panic-terror' in Jamaica, and that terrible crimes had been committed in the name of the Crown. White reminded the audience that in 1802 Governor Wall

---

60 *Spectator* (2 Dec. 1865), 1330.
61 The Bristol meeting generated a brief report in *The Times* (15 Dec. 1865), 5.
62 *Daily News* (2 Dec. 1865), 2.   63 Ibid. (6 Dec. 1865), 2.

had been 'tried, condemned and executed at the Old Bailey on a charge of wilful murder' (for having wrongfully caused the death of a soldier). White wanted the wrongdoers in Jamaica also to be made accountable for their crimes, and in so doing to 'wipe away the stain from our country's honour, and to vindicate the majesty of British law, so atrociously violated'.

In Liverpool, the centre of the West Indies trade, just as in Manchester, Lambeth, and Brighton, Jamaica Meeting speakers equated British honour with British law.[64] While the Mayor acknowledged that opinion was divided on the causes of the Jamaica affair,[65] on one point there was a wide consensus: it was vital to discover 'whether the means by which it had been suppressed have or have not been in violation of the constitution'. This theme was central to the longest speech of the evening, that given by a Canon McNeile.[66] McNeile told the assembly that prior to taking holy orders he had been a lawyer, and that his legal training had taught him the virtues of withholding judgement until all of the evidence was in. What was needed to resolve the Jamaica affair was not political partisanship, but a 'grave judicial inquiry'.[67] England was likened to a 'practiced jury', one that would bring in the correct verdict when the time was right. This sentiment was cheered.

It is striking about the speeches of the Jamaica Meetings that in rhetorical content they so closely resembled Edward Beesly's letter to the *Bee-Hive*. With regard to martial law in Jamaica, Exeter Hall Christians and the Comtian atheists were in broad agreement that what had happened in Jamaica posed a palpable threat to the civil and political rights at home. If the Exeter Hall men indulged in a measure of solemn hand-wringing about the plight of black men in the colonies (while Beesly candidly admitted that he did not care about any black men living anywhere), both camps were of one mind on the proper point of emphasis: if Gordon could be hanged by martial law in Jamaica, John Bright could be hanged by martial law in England.

In the space of just more than two weeks the Jamaica affair had been transformed from a narrative about the salvation of Jamaican colonists into a narrative about the destruction of the English constitution. The commentators who had supported the suppression now were badly wrong-footed. A leading colonial politician had been executed after a ramshackle trial. The Governor of the colony admitted that brutal punishments had been inflicted for many days, even weeks, after the rebels had dispersed. Senior military officers had boasted openly about acts of appalling cruelty. The *London Review*, once a vigorous defender of the suppression, now conceded 'that the negroes have been treated with a merciless and undiscriminating severity that is wholly unjustifiable'.[68] The white population of Jamaica, including its Governor, had been 'seized by a wild and unreasoning panic', one which had led inexorably to a period of 'blind, passionate

---

[64] For an approving editorial comment on the meeting, see *The Times* (13 Dec. 1865), 8.
[65] *Manchester Guardian* (12 Dec. 1865), 5.   [66] *The Times* (12 Dec. 1865), 5.
[67] Ibid.   [68] *London Review* (2 Dec. 1865), 580–1.

vengeance'. The Liberal government was left with no choice but to undertake an official investigation. And while *The Times* had resisted this conclusion, on 2 December its editors admitted that the tide had turned in the Jamaica affair and 'it was not now black insurgents who are on trial, it is Mr. Eyre . . . and the other officers, military and naval, who were engaged against the negroes, or who sat on the Courts-martial'.[69] No longer was the Jamaica affair about the heroic salvation of a colony but whether the Governor and his soldiers 'honestly did their duty, and did not exceed it'. On 7 December *The Times* admitted that the available evidence, although incomplete, was damning enough for the authorities in Jamaica that an official investigation of their conduct was required.[70]

By the beginning of December 1865, then, the editors at *The Times* were committed (implicitly) to two important propositions: (1) that in the face of civil unrest there were legal limits to what could be done by the authorities; and (2) that it was at least *possible* that in Jamaica those limits had been exceeded. These propositions already had become the subject of discussion and opinion in the newspaper press. They also were quite naturally the province of England's extensive legal press. In December 1865, the two leading legal weeklies, the *Solicitors' Journal* and the *Law Times*, suddenly bristled with Jamaica-related leaders, technical comments, and letters. Two other legal periodicals, the *Jurist* and *Law Magazine*, began to publish longer essays on the constitutional status of martial law, the legality (or otherwise) of the arrest, trial, and execution of Gordon, and on the potential criminal culpability of Governor Eyre and his soldiers. Here was a political wrangle to which lawyers and legal journalists could make a vital contribution.

'The summary execution of Mr. Gordon in Jamaica without legal trial,' the editor of the *Law Times* boldly opined on 2 December 1865, 'appears, on the face of the dispatches, to be wholly illegal'.[71] Then, like any good lawyer, the writer spelt out the grounds of this submission. At English law, the taker of life, whether a private person or government official, bore the onus to justify his action. The men who had executed Gordon had thus far offered none. Gordon had not been 'taken red-handed in any overt act of rebellion, or even sedition, which alone can legalise a drum-head court martial and a summary execution'. 'No lawyer,' the *Law Times* flatly declared, 'would hesitate for a moment to pronounce [Gordon's] trial to be illegal and his execution murder – *in point of law.*' Gordon's executioners were murderers *prima facie*. Their only recourse was to demonstrate that they acted 'at a time when necessity overrules all law'. 'If Governor Eyre can show this,' the leader sombrely concluded, 'he will be enabled amply to justify the execution of Gordon; if not he will have been guilty of a grave crime. It is for *him* to show that he *was* justified.'

The *Solicitors' Journal* was equally adamant on the same points. The Jamaica affair had given rise to 'one of the gravest constitutional questions which could

---

⁶⁹ *The Times* (2 Dec. 1865), 8–9.   ⁷⁰ *The Times* (7 Dec. 1865), 8.
⁷¹ *Law Times* (2 Dec. 1865), 59.

arise in the present day, viz: The limit of military authority in times of civil disturbance.'[72] As early as 25 November, the editors of the paper advanced the unreserved opinions that the transfer of Gordon to Morant Bay had been illegal, that the court martial which tried him had lacked authority to do so, and that Gordon's execution had been murder (as much as if 'Brigadier Nelson were to be seized in the streets of London, tried by a jury of Baptist ministers at Exeter Hall, and hung from a belfry on the order of Sir Morton Peto').[73] In mid-December the *Journal* published a long essay on the 'all-important and indeed, vital, question' of the nature and legal status of martial law.[74] (The essay argued for a narrow legal definition of martial law, and suggested that a heavy onus would fall on Governor Eyre and his soldiers to establish that they had the legal authority to flog, shoot, and hang scores of British subjects.)

Although these were highly contentious and politically charged issues, and although the *Solicitors' Journal* coverage of them attracted the criticism of some subscribers, the editors refused either to scale back or apologize.[75] While the *Solicitors' Journal* avoided comment on the personal culpability of Governor Eyre, it continued to endorse a very controversial position on the issues posed by the Jamaica affair: 'We have said, and we repeat it, that the execution of a man *guilty* of high treason, by virtue of the sentence of a military tribunal, is *murder* by the law of England unless that man was actually taken in arms.'[76] Not only was this position not retracted under criticism, but was reinforced by even bolder language: 'the judicial murder of a British subject, however justly he may have merited his fate, is of graver import than the horrors of the India mutiny itself'. The one was merely the spasm of the mob, the other 'the inroad of executive power upon the province of law'.

Of the legal periodicals that took a position on the legal implications of the Jamaica affair, only the *Jurist* entertained serious doubts about the legal culpability, *prima facie*, of Governor Eyre for the arrest and execution of George Gordon. In early January 1866, the *Jurist* published the first of a number of lengthy studies of martial law and the English constitution, studies that merit close attention later in this study.[77] After a long review of the relevant law, the article concluded that the treatment of Gordon *might* have been 'perfectly legal'. The matter was said to turn on 'whether there was any reasonable ground for proclaiming martial law in the district where he was tried, and holding him to be connected with, and privy to, the murders there committed'. By the same token, the *Jurist* agreed that for the execution to be privileged, Governor Eyre would have to demonstrate both that martial law was 'proclaimed honestly, and in the belief of its necessity', and that Gordon's trial had conformed at least to the rules of 'natural justice'. The simple

---

[72] Response to letter of E. J. Barron, *Solicitors' Journal* (16 Dec. 1865), 146.
[73] *Solicitors' Journal* (25 Nov. 1865).
[74] 'Martial Law', *Solicitors' Journal* (16 Dec. 1865), 140–2.
[75] See letter of E. J. Barron, *Solicitors' Journal* (16 Dec. 1865), 146.   [76] Ibid.
[77] See *Jurist* (6 Jan.1866), 507–10. These essays are analysed at greater length below, Ch. 4.

proclamation of martial law did not provide a blanket immunity. For the time being, the journal was content to let the subject rest.

II. The Jamaica Committee and their Lawyers

The Governor Eyre controversy, as we have seen, was not entirely a product of journalistic reaction to news from Jamaica. In fact it was actively cultivated as a public issue by the leading lights of the three main constituents of Exeter Hall: the Baptist Missionary Society, the British and Foreign Anti-Slavery Society, and the Freedmen's Aid Society. The members of Exeter Hall were united by their commitments to nonconformist Christianity and to the spiritual and temporal improvement of non-white persons within the empire, commitments that had been reinvigorated in the early 1860s by the American Civil War.[78] The role of Exeter Hall in the early phases of the Jamaica controversy and particularly in the formation (by the leaders of Exeter Hall and some radical politicians and activists) of a 'Jamaica Committee' has been exceedingly well documented.[79] Still, the subject merits revisiting. The various historians of the Committee have overlooked or underplayed at least two important matters. The first is the process by which the Christian evangelical and secular elements within the Jamaica Committee came to be united by a common political language rooted in legal notions and goals. The second is the process by which the Committee began to surrender control over their cause to the concepts, procedures, and prerogatives of lawyers.

One of the key players in the foundation of the Jamaica Committee was John Bright M.P.[80] Like many of the leading figures in English radicalism in this period, Bright was not monolithically opposed to the British empire.[81] But in keeping with his rearing as a Quaker and a northern manufacturer, Bright was an inveterate critic of certain tendencies within British imperial policy, specifically, of its mercantilist and militaristic bent.[82] Bright was also an ardent abolitionist and, more pertinently to the Jamaica affair, a dedicated adversary of what he called 'irresponsible power' at home and in the colonies. In 1858, after some initial hedging, Bright had been one of the few eminent English politicians to have

---

[78] Temperley, *British Antislavery*, 248–9; Heuman, '*The Killing Time*', 56–9.

[79] Hall, *Civilizing Subjects*, 407–24; Temperley, *British Antislavery*, 258; Blackett, *Divided Hearts*, 76–7, 168–9.

[80] For the best brief overview of John Bright's life and career, see Taylor, *Oxford DNB*, online 3421.

[81] Bright tended to support imperial policies that suited northern cotton and other manufacturing interests. His criticisms of empire were rooted in a combination of anti-mercantilism and the Burkean position that the exercise of absolute power over foreign peoples and cultures would inevitably lead to the corrosion of political integrity at home. Miles Taylor, *The Decline of British Radicalism, 1847–1860* (Oxford, 1995), 51, 292–3.

[82] For an examination of Bright's fierce opposition to the Crimean war, see G. R. Searle, *Entrepreneurial Politics in Mid-Victorian Britain* (Oxford, 1993), 97–101.

spoken out against the atrocities committed by the British army during the suppression of the Indian Mutiny.[83] Bright was severely criticized for these speeches,[84] and for his tendency to view the British empire, in the word of *The Times*, as 'one monstrous and uniform inequity'.[85] But it was a primary characteristic of Bright's personal and political character to thrive on the repulsion he inspired in England's conservative elites. In the news of the Jamaica suppression, Bright saw an unmistakable sign of the deep rot in England's domestic politics. And while Bright was a 'friend of the negro', and no doubt genuinely deplored the suffering of black Jamaicans under martial law, he immediately seized on the Jamaica suppression principally as a means of galvanizing popular support for political reform in the home countries. Bright wanted to use Jamaica as a lever in the general democratization of political power. Toward this goal Bright was willing to commit sizeable sums of his own fortune, but he also committed his sway over other evangelical philanthropists, and over friendly publications such as the radical newspaper the *Morning Star*.[86]

Another vital figure in the inception (and documentation) of the Jamaica Committee was the Mancunian anti-slavery activist Frederick W. Chesson. Chesson was the son-in-law and protégé of the former radical M.P. and zealous anti-slaver George Thompson.[87] Chesson was a sometime journalist who published articles in the *Morning Star*. In 1859, Chesson had founded the London Emancipation Society, an organization which attempted to rally British support for the North during the American Civil War.[88] Cobden, Bright, and Stuart Mill were also members of this association. In the early 1860s, Chesson also worked closely with Louis Chamerovzow, the president of the British and Foreign Anti-Slavery Society (BFASS),[89] and leader at Exeter Hall. When the Jamaica affair began to unfold in November 1865, Chesson, with the strong encouragement of Bright,[90]

---

[83] When reports reached England in 1858 of the extreme severity of the suppression in India, Bright denounced these violent excesses. On this point, Bright was chastised in *The Times* (21 May 1858), 9. For Bright's earlier reluctance to oppose the suppression, see Taylor, *British Radicalism*, 294–5.   [84] For example, in *The Times* (21 May 1858), 9.

[85] Ibid.

[86] The *Morning Star* was operated by Bright's brother-in-law and, for all intents and purposes, was the voice of Bright's vision of free-trade radicalism and its associated causes. Until he became a cabinet minister in 1868, Bright made regular visits to the *Star* in order to converse with its writers and editors. In some instances Bright all but dictated stories. When the Jamaica story began to unfold in December 1865, for instance, Bright advised the paper to prepare an article, and '*in a grave and forcible style befitting the case*'. See Bright to Justin McCarthy (a journalist with the *Morning Star*) in McCarthy, *Reminiscences* vol. i, 80–1. For this reference the author is indebted to Bridget Brereton, *Law, Justice and Empire: The Colonial Career of John Gorrie, 1829–1892* (Kingston, Jamaica, 1997), 36–7.

[87] Swaisland, *Oxford DNB*, online 38853; Temperley, *British Antislavery*, 237, 240–3.

[88] Temperley, *British Antislavery*, 254–5.   [89] For background, see ibid., 66–8.

[90] Chesson and Bright were well known to each other, and on 13 November 1865, only a week after the Jamaica story broke, Bright urged journalists at the *Morning Star* to contact Chesson for background information. In the first week of December Bright was already urging the formation of a 'powerful committee' on Jamaica to cause the Government to commence an official investigation. McCarthy, *Reminiscences*, 80.

worked assiduously to persuade the same network of philanthropists, politicians, and freethinking ideologues to form common cause. Importantly to the historical record, Chesson kept a detailed diary of his efforts. As one of the few windows to the inner workings of the Jamaica Committee, this diary is cited extensively in this study.

Chesson's diary records that in mid-November 1865 he acted as a liaison between his network of contacts and the Baptist Missionary and Freedmen's Aid societies. His aim was to forge a united front in the effort to cause the Liberal government to prevent further retaliatory violence in Jamaica and to institute a full inquiry into the causes of the revolt and circumstances of the suppression.[91] In fact, Chamerovzow's group, BFASS, already had taken action on Jamaica. At a special meeting held on 20 November, the executive resolved to implore Edward Cardwell not to sanction the actions of Governor Eyre until 'further intelligence' had been received from Jamaica. Meanwhile, in the typical English fashion the BFASS also moved to bolster the legal credibility of its criticisms and concerns. Before the meeting of 20 November, Chamerovzow had written to two lawyers, Vernon Lushington[92] and the venerable Henry Brougham, 'for advice on the legal points of the issues raised' by the suppression of the Morant Bay disturbances.[93] Chamerovzow wanted to know whether they supported the idea of a public inquiry into the Jamaica affair, and whether the BFASS were on solid ground legally when they asserted that 'the authorities of the island have been committing murder under cover of martial law'.

Both lawyers responded before the next general meeting of the BFASS. Chamerovzow informed the assembly that Lord Brougham advised them to make an 'immediate application to Mr. Cardwell for a full inquiry'. As for Lushington, he thought 'a full investigation indispensable'. Both lawyers, Chamerovzow continued, 'consider there is a strong prima facie evidence of excessive severity and actual illegality'. The executive of BFASS resolved that Lushington (Brougham was too elderly) be consulted for a fuller briefing 'on the law of the case'. While the consultation was being arranged, BFASS continued to rally 'friends of the cause' while it primed the newspaper press with information about the situation in Jamaica. The next week Lushington advised BFASS both

---

[91] *CD*, 17 Nov. 1865. Chesson's diary described a meeting with leaders of the Baptist Missionary Society. The main subject of discussion was how to counteract the accusation (made in several conservative newspapers) that the insurrection in Jamaica had been incited by irresponsible missionaries. It was agreed that the Liberal government was to be lobbied to appoint a commission of inquiry. On 30 November, Chesson attended a meeting of the Freedmen's Aid Society (chaired by Fowell Buxton) in which it was resolved that he would join forces with the BFASS in pressuring the Prime Minister for an inquiry.

[92] Lushington was then a young and ambitious barrister and social activist who was known to be interested in radical causes. Vogeler, *Oxford DNB*, online 53968.

[93] The choice of Brougham and Lushington was not accidental. Both men had been instrumental in the legal controversy surrounding the missionary William Smith, prosecuted for his alleged role in the Demerara slave uprising of 1823. This episode is discussed below, Ch. 4.

to pressure the Liberal government to commence an official inquiry and to make plans to send its own 'private commission' to Jamaica.[94] This advice was immediately accepted.

On 30 November the executive of the BFASS met with its counterparts in the Freedmen's Aid Society. Among those present was Edmund Beales, the radical lawyer and champion of political reform, along with the Christian Socialist and trade union activist J. M. Ludlow. The meeting was attended by the ubiquitous lawyer for progressive associations and causes, William Shaen.[95] In effect, this was an emergency summit of the elite of England's anti-slavery activists. The anti-slavery activist, evangelical, and wealthy brewer Thomas Fowell Buxton[96] was in the chair. Chesson took notes in the role of provisional secretary. His diary records that the attendees were 'red hot' on the Jamaica affair, and agreed readily that their concerns about it needed to be expressed in some more systematic manner. It was decided that the various English anti-slavery societies and their allies should coordinate their efforts by forming a new committee devoted only to the Jamaica issue.[97] By 4 December the provisional committee had persuaded Peter Taylor, the radical M.P. for Leicester and fellow-traveller of the anti-slavery movement,[98] to put his name to a circular advertising a foundational meeting of the 'Jamaica Committee'. From that point forward Taylor remained at the leading edge of the agitation over the abuse of martial law in Jamaica.

Before this meeting could take place, a deputation of some 250 men from all corners of the country (including all of the leaders of Exeter Hall and more than a dozen sympathetic M.P.s) met with Cardwell (the Prime Minister did not attend due to illness) at Downing Street on 9 December.[99] The delegates had come to discuss the Jamaica affair, and they arrived in a foul mood. Chamerovzow was the first to address the Colonial Secretary, and in a prepared statement set forth two key demands: that Governor Eyre be recalled, and that there be a 'searching investigation' of what had happened in Jamaica. Chamerovzow made a third demand about the future legal culpability of those who had orchestrated the suppression in Jamaica. He asked that the Government withhold its consent from any 'Bill of Indemnity presented to the Legislature of Jamaica'. Shorter statements were read to Cardwell by Fowell Buxton, by Peter Taylor, and by one of the most tireless

---

[94] *JC Minutes*, 24 Nov. 1865.

[95] Born in 1821, by 1865, Shaen was the pre-eminent London solicitor for radical social and political causes. He was a Unitarian in religion, a Chartist-cum-Radical in his politics. Shaen was closely connected politically and socially with Peter Taylor M.P. M. J. Shaen (ed.), *William Shaen: A Brief Sketch* (London, 1912); Baylen and Gossman, *Modern British Radicals*, vol. ii, 450–1; Slinn, *Oxford DNB*, online 50082.

[96] Fowell Buxton (1837–1915) was a deeply devout Quaker who had long been dedicated to the anti-slavery cause. Baigent, *Oxford DNB*, online 32225.

[97] *CD*, 30 Nov. 1865. In early December, John Bright also was lending his support to this idea. See Bright to McCarthy, 6 Dec. 1865, as reprinted in McCarthy, *Reminiscences*, 80–1.

[98] Taylor was also from a family of prosperous northern merchants and manufacturers who were dissenters in religion. In the 1860s Taylor was at the forefront of the push for manhood suffrage. Ruston, *Oxford DNB*, online 27070. [99] *The Times* (11 Dec. 1865), 12.

advocates of the Jamaica cause, writer Tom Hughes M.P.[100] When he was given a chance to reply over the catcalls, Cardwell announced that the Government had already decided that there would be a 'full, impartial and independent inquiry' of the Jamaica matter, and that Eyre would be suspended from his duties pending the outcome of the inquiry. Cardwell then urged the delegation not to prejudge the matter, and to make some allowance for the fact that the Governor had acted in the context of a serious public emergency. Many delegates took great exception to this suggestion, and began to press forward, shouting questions and angry remarks at the minister.[101] When the din quieted, Cardwell offered further assurances that the inquiry would be fair and impartial, accepted the thanks of one or two of the leading delegates, and then took his leave.

On 12 December the Russell government formally announced the creation of a Royal Commission to investigate the causes of the Jamaica rebellion and the circumstances of its suppression. The Government also announced that Edward Eyre was to be suspended (until the Commission rendered its final report) in favour of Sir Henry Storks, a career colonial official. Storks would also act as the chairman of the Jamaica Royal Commission. As for Eyre, he would remain in Jamaica until the Commission finished its work.

While there was some carping in the Tory press,[102] the weight of published opinion was that, as the *Athenaeum* put it, 'Lord Russell has done something to calm the conscience of England.'[103] In keeping with the use of legal metaphors in describing the controversy, the *Athenaeum* concluded that 'Mr. Eyre is arraigned on his own statement of the facts, and some of his subordinate agents are absolutely condemned out of their own mouths.'[104] In a similar vein, the *Saturday Review* commented that 'if the early allegations of Mr. Eyre's apologists had been supported by evidence, his resort to martial law would have been approved even by the steadiest supporters of constitutional freedom'.[105] But the plain fact was that Eyre and his many sympathizers back in England had lost the first round of the Jamaica controversy. The best that the Eyre forces now could hope for, in the pointed words of *Punch*, was that the English public would 'retain its judicial attitude' when it evaluated the findings of the Royal Commission.

---

[100] By 1865, Hughes (1822–96) was a committed Christian socialist devoted to trade unionism and the improvement of the condition of the working classes. In the course of the next three years Hughes frequently used his fame as a popular writer to advance the policies of the Jamaica Committee. Mitchell, *Oxford DNB*, online 14091.

[101] It was reported in some of the newspapers that when Cardwell stated that Eyre was to be suspended, that one of the delegates shouted, 'Yes, by the neck!!!' See *The Times* (13 Dec. 1865), 12; *Daily Telegraph* (11 Dec. 1865), 4. Leaders of the delegation later denied that the remark had been made.

[102] On 22 Dec., for example, the *Morning Herald* asserted that a 'fatuous clique' had intimidated Russell into these decisions when there was 'not even a *prima facie* case against Governor Eyre'.

[103] *Athenaeum* (16 Dec. 1865), 83–4. The political implications of the decision to institute an inquiry is discussed at greater length below, Ch. 2.

[104] *Athenaeum* (16 Dec. 1865), 83–4.   [105] *Saturday Review* (16 Dec. 1865), 746.

The same day that the Government announced its decision on Jamaica, 12 December, BFASS held a large evening meeting at Exeter Hall. The members discussed a number of possible policies on Jamaica. But in the final two hours the main subject on the floor was whether the BFASS should support a resolution that, upon his recall to England, Edward Eyre be put on trial for the murder of Gordon.[106] Just as in the Jamaica Meetings, the rhetoric employed at this event was perceptibly free of religious verbiage. Not one orator, not even the Wesleyan and Baptist ministers, thought it pertinent to state that Eyre and his soldiers had violated the laws of God, i.e. that they had *sinned*. On the other hand, virtually every speaker contended that they had violated the secular laws of the 'transmarine empire', i.e. that they had committed *crimes*. The first speaker, William Coningham M.P., urged the audience to view the official inquiry as preliminary to the 'ulterior object' of subjecting Eyre to a 'trial by jury' for the murder of Gordon. The Quaker anti-slavery activist G. W. Alexander[107] contended that 'Christian men' could not stand by when under 'the proclamation of martial law . . . men, women and children were hunted like wild beasts, and flogged and destroyed without any evidence of their guilt'. Minutes later, the Revd. W. Arthur, a Wesleyan minister, stood to move a resolution that the assembly 'record its indignant protest against violations of law and justice'. The way to restore the 'honour of England', Arthur contended, was 'to seek when wrong was done to have it fairly judged and justly punished'. Toward this end he thought the Crown should be advised 'to refuse its sanction to any Indemnity Bill' that might foreclose the chance of a proper legal accounting.

The remainder of the speakers did not deviate from these (conspicuously temporal) themes. Henry Richards 'dwelt upon the illegal and unconstitutional character of martial law'. The Revd. Newman Hall introduced a note of caution, but not with regard to the secular and legal preoccupations of the meeting. He suggested only that the call for the criminal prosecution of Eyre was premature, and that the country 'must wait patiently for a fair trial of the authorities accused, whose case ought not to be hurried through as judicial matters had been hurried in Jamaica'. This suggestion garnered little support. Overwhelmingly, the sentiment of the assembly was that grave crimes had been committed by colonial officials in Jamaica, and these crimes needed to be vigorously prosecuted and punished in the English courts of law. Even when addressing an audience consisting (it may fairly be presumed) mainly of decidedly religious men, the Exeter Hall speakers chose to define their perceptions and aims in terms of secular law.

With the Jamaica Royal Commission now in the offing, Chesson felt even greater urgency to establish the organizational and financial basis for the Jamaica Committee. The first general meeting of the Jamaica Committee was to be held in London at Radley's Hotel on 19 December. In the ten days prior to this meeting

---

[106] Ibid.   [107] Temperley, *British Antislavery*, 69–70.

Chesson, along with Bright, Chamerovzow, and Charles Buxton M.P.[108] (philan-thropist and cousin of Fowell Buxton), acted as a provisional executive. Due mainly to the intercession of Bright, initial donations of £500 were secured.[109] The provisional executives also decided on another step: Shaen was instructed to 'obtain the opinion of [the eminent barristers] Edward James Q.C. and Fitzjames Stephen on the legal questions involved in recent transactions in Jamaica'.[110] This opinion was so urgently required that it was requested before the Jamaica Committee could hold its first general meeting.[111]

The first meeting of the Jamaica Committee brought together London's leading anti-slavery activists – Chesson, Charles Buxton, Chamerovzow, and the like-minded politicians Bright, Taylor, and Hughes.[112] The radical lawyer and labour activist Frederic Harrison, along with his friend E. S. Beesley, were also present. Buxton, who had previous experience with protest of the kind contemplated,[113] was elected to chair the Committee, and Taylor and Chesson to the positions of treasurer and secretary respectively. The first topic of discussion was the urgent matter of the Royal Commission. The Commissioners were soon to embark for Jamaica to begin their investigation. It was quickly agreed that it was imperative that the Commission's work be closely monitored by an agent of the Jamaica Committee. It was also agreed that in order to be effective, the Committee's agent in Jamaica should be a lawyer. The Scottish barrister and anti-slavery activist John Gorrie was proposed for (and soon agreed to undertake) this task.[114] It was announced that the Committee had already collected £500 to pay for the legal mission to Jamaica.[115]

The Jamaica Committee met again two days later.[116] Legal matters remained at the top of the agenda. It was resolved that the Committee would 'assume responsi-bility' for the opinion being prepared by Stephen and James. It was further

---

[108] Charles Buxton was a highly erudite and extremely wealthy philanthropist and Liberal politi-cian. In the early 1860s he was instrumental in mustering British support for abolitionism in the Americas. Smith, *Oxford DNB*, online 4244.   [109] *JC Minutes*, 16 Dec. 1865.

[110] Ibid., 21 Dec. 1865.

[111] Bright shared the view that it was imperative for any new committee on the Jamaica question to retain legal counsel. In a letter written to Justin McCarthy on 6 Dec. 1865, he advised that 'able lawyers should be engaged'. Bright also wanted the legal implications of the affair 'discussed by some good lawyer in your columns'. He recommended J. M. Ludlow for the task. McCarthy, *Reminiscences*, 80–1.

[112] *CD*, 19 Dec. 1865.

[113] In 1858, Buxton (with John Bright) had been one of the few M.P.s to raise probing questions about the conduct of British military forces during the final stages of the suppression of the Indian Mutiny. For Buxton's interventions in this regard, see *Hansard*, cxlix (18 Mar. 1858), 360–7 (20 July 1858), 1786.

[114] Gorrie was in his mid-thirties when the Jamaica affair began, and already well known as a professional man who was committed to radical social and political causes, including anti-slavery. Although he later recalled having been taken completely by surprise when he was asked (by Shaen) to travel to Jamaica for the Jamaica Committee, he was an obvious choice for the job. See Brereton, *Law, Justice and Empire*, xi–xiii, 36–7.

[115] According to Chesson, the money was raised when Bright met with a number of wealthy bene-factors of the BFASS. *CD*, 16 Dec. 1865.   [116] *JC Minutes*, 21 Dec. 1865.

resolved that Shaen should be officially retained as the Committee's solicitor. Shaen was immediately instructed to set to work on yet another legal matter. It had come to the attention of the Committee that the colonial legislature in Jamaica intended to pass an indemnity bill which might immunize public officials from civil and criminal prosecutions for actions taken during the period of martial law. Shaen was asked to draw up a petition 'requesting Her Majesty to withhold her consent to any bill of indemnity which may be sent from Jamaica'. Then the legal mission to Jamaica was discussed. It was agreed that there would be work enough there for two barristers, and that a junior should be found to go out with Gorrie. In the result, the Committee had trouble finding a willing candidate. As the *Morning Advertiser* reported on 22 December, 'lawyers of high rank cannot afford to undertake the task. No man can be expected to give up his practice of £3,000 a year for such an occupation as this.' The *Advertiser* hoped that 'fit men' could be found. On 29 December, after some wrangling about fees, Chesson was able to secure the services of a young English barrister called J. Horne Payne.[117] Gorrie and Horne Payne were to sail to Jamaica at their earliest convenience.

Meanwhile, the executive leadership of BFASS met separately from the Jamaica Committee in order to discuss the Royal Commission. The conclusion was reached that a great deal of investigatory and support work needed to be done among the victims of the suppression, and that it would not be practicable for the work to be undertaken by the two barristers sent out by the Committee.[118] It was resolved that the BFASS should retain an English solicitor who might travel to Jamaica to coordinate these efforts, and to share their fruits with the barristers of the Committee. In late December, William Morgan, a solicitor closely tied to the BFASS in Birmingham, was retained and sent to Jamaica as 'special correspondent' of the Society.[119] His instructions were to compile an exhaustive list of Jamaican men and women who had been killed or injured at the hands of Eyre's forces, and to assess the degree to which popular grievances with the colony's local courts and property law had contributed to the outbreak of violence. In Morgan's retainer, BFASS underlined their expectation that with 'the Government Commission on the one hand, and the exertions of the legal gentlemen who represent the Committee on the other, the vindication of the principles of the British Constitution and of British law will now be amply secured'.[120] While this was an ambitious goal, in time Morgan proved useful enough to Gorrie and Horne Payne that the Committee executive in London decided to assume complete responsibility for his £100 fee.[121] In this way another lawyer had been added to the

---

[117] *CD*, 30 Dec. 1865.   [118] As reported in *JC Minutes*, 5 Jan. 1866.
[119] Morgan and two Quakers, Thomas Harvey and William Brewin, sailed for Jamaica in the third week of January 1866. *Law Times* (20 Jan. 1866), 167. See also Hall, *Civilizing Subjects*, 412–13.   [120] *Law Times* (20 Jan. 1866).
[121] *CD*, 15 Jan. 1865.

Committee's burgeoning legal payroll. Barely a month after its inception, the association already had come to employ no fewer than five lawyers, four barristers and a solicitor.

After Gorrie and Horne Payne sailed for Jamaica, the executive of the Jamaica Committee concluded that it would be useful to publish the terms of their retainer in the newspapers.[122] The retainer was drafted in terms of a public manifesto, and it is very revealing of the Committee's central preoccupations. The letter began with the assertion that, on any fair reading of the former Governor's own official despatches, Eyre had been 'guilty of acts of illegality and cruelty'.[123] (We might query whether the placement of the word 'illegality' before 'cruelty' was purposeful.) In sending lawyers to Jamaica, readers were assured, the object of the Committee was not to 'secure the victory of one party to the contest over the other'. The aim of the Jamaica Committee was 'solely to vindicate the supremacy of the English law'. For this reason, Gorrie had been specifically instructed *not* to advocate for any individuals in the colony, but to act rather as a 'commissioner on the part of the Committee, to assist in ascertaining and placing in the clearest and most distinct light the facts that have recently transpired'. To facilitate this goal, Gorrie was asked to cooperate closely with the lawyers on the Royal Commission, and with any Jamaican lawyer acting on behalf of victims of the suppression.

But as the Jamaica Committee's letter made clear, there was another and overriding reason why two barristers, at great expense, were to be sent to Jamaica. At the conclusion of the investigation, and after the Royal Commission had issued its final report, it was acknowledged that 'Governor Eyre and his subordinate officers may have to be put on their trial for acts of illegality and cruelty, in all probability amounting to murder'. Gorrie was to collect evidence that might support such prosecutions. Crucially, moreover, Gorrie also was to do everything in his power to prevent the Royal Commissioners from doing anything that might prejudice or preclude a successful criminal prosecution.[124]

From its inception, the founding members of the Jamaica Committee were emphatic that the central issue arising from the Jamaica affair was the accountability of political and military men to law. They were equally adamant that the opinion of educated men about the affair would hinge on the perceived legality – or otherwise – of the proclamation and use of martial law by government officials in the colony. So fervently was this view held by the leaders that they moved to secure professional legal advice on these matters some days before the organization had even been formally constituted.[125] The barristers Stephen and James had been instructed to prepare a memorandum which answered a list of pressing legal

---

[122] *JC Minutes*, 30 Dec. 865.

[123] *Facts and Documents relating to the Alleged Rebellion in Jamaica, Jamaica Papers No. 5:* (London, 1866), 80.

[124] Ibid. 81. The Royal Commissioners were later instructed to caution all witnesses.

[125] The earlier decision to secure a formal legal opinion on martial law was endorsed by the Jamaica Committee's executive body at its second meeting on 21 Dec. *JC Minutes*, 21 Nov. 1865.

questions. What was the precise compass of the term 'martial law'? Had Eyre acted 'illegally and criminally' in the arrest, removal, and execution of Gordon? Were military officers immune from punishment when they carried out orders during martial law? If crimes had been committed, how might they be prosecuted and tried? Would a colonial indemnity act exonerate officials from prosecution and punishment in England?

What was wanted from lawyers was not objective legal scholarship, but some credible technical backing for a cause. Stephen and James were paid to provide it. Fitzjames Stephen was an obvious choice for the Jamaica Committee's commission. In December 1865 Stephen was an experienced (if not especially dedicated or successful) circuit barrister[126] and promising scholar of criminal law.[127] In his parallel career as an intellectual journalist, Stephen had written against American slavery.[128] That he was the son of the distinguished Clapham Sect abolitionist, lawyer, and imperial civil servant James Stephen[129] could only have counted in his favour.[130] Although it is not known who suggested that Stephen should be offered the Jamaica Committee's research work,[131] it is not hard to guess why. It is also easy to comprehend why, for all Stephen's credentials, the Committee also retained the services of Edward James Q.C.

With his thirty years at the bar (twice those of Stephen), a Queen's Counsel for twelve years, the 'undisputed leader' of the Northern circuit,[132] James possessed what Stephen did not: great stature as a practising barrister. He was the quintessential 'lawyer's lawyer', renowned mainly for his minute knowledge of commercial law. His signature was certain to give credibility, even *gravitas*, to any legal opinion. This was especially useful to the Committee given the politically charged nature of the issue at hand. In selecting James it also did not hurt that he was a Liberal M.P. (for Manchester), and connected politically both to the governing party in Parliament and to some of the leading members and natural supporters of

---

[126] Radzinowicz generalized that Stephen's 'vocation at the bar was a very, very hard struggle and that he never became an eminent, or even a successful, barrister'. See L. Radzinowicz, *Sir James Fitzjames Stephen 1829–1894 and his Contribution to the Development of Criminal Law* (London, 1957), 7.

[127] See K. J. M. Smith, *James Fitzjames Stephen: Portrait of a Victorian Rationalist* (Cambridge, 1988), 44–72; Smith, *Oxford DNB*, online 26375.　　[128] Smith, *Victorian Rationalist*, 42.

[129] In his memoirs Henry Taylor recalled that in the decade after 1836 Stephen the elder 'virtually ruled the Colonial Empire'. Quoted in Smith, *Victorian Rationalist*, 1. See also 'Editor's Introduction' (R. J. White), J. F. Stephen, *Liberty, Equality, Fraternity* (Cambridge, 1967), 6.

[130] Throughout this period Stephen regarded himself both as a practising lawyer and as a gentleman thinker and writer who earned by his pen. He laboured to develop his legal scholarship (specializing in criminal law) but even more tirelessly to establish himself as an intellectual journalist who wrote on a wide variety of subjects including theology, literature, law, and politics. While Stephen published widely, he established especially strong ties with the *Saturday Review* and after 1865, the *Pall Mall Gazette*. In the general election of October 1865, he had stood unsuccessfully as a Liberal candidate. See James A. Colaiaco, *James Fitzjames Stephen and the Crisis of Victorian Thought* (London, 1983), 1–25.

[131] In *Portrait of a Victorian Rationalist*, Stephen's leading biographer, K. J. M. Smith, stated (without specific documentation) that Mill made the approach in January 1866. With respect, this must be mistaken. The approach to Stephen was made while Mill was in France, and had yet to attend his first Jamaica Committee meeting.

[132] *Law Times* (9 Nov. 1867), 20–1. James died suddenly of an infection in November 1867.

the Jamaica Committee.[133] By retaining Stephen and James as a tandem, the Jamaica Committee looked to have the best of both worlds. Stephen the scholar would research and draft the opinion.[134] James the lawyer would review and endorse it. Stephen's scholarship would be used to inform the internal decision-making of the Jamaica Committee; James's signature would be used to convince the public of the accuracy and disinterestedness of the opinion.

Whoever did the work, whether Stephen alone or Stephen with James's input, it was done speedily. A nearly complete draft of the opinion was made available to Shaen, and then to Chesson, before the end of December. In Chesson's opinion the barristers had produced 'a most lucid and able document'.[135] The final version was delivered to Shaen on 13 January 1866, and was reviewed by the whole executive two days later. The minutes do not record discussion on the subject, but it is plain that the Committee had got what it had wanted. Chesson noted in his diary that the Committee decided that the 'admirable opinion' of Stephen and James should be released to the press in the form of a case comment.[136] By 19 January 'CASE: *Ex parte* Jamaica Committee' had been published in most of the country's leading newspapers and legal periodicals. The first great legal salvo in the Governor Eyre controversy had been fired.

The Jamaica Committee's press release consisted of three parts: a prologue explicating the Committee's motives for commissioning a legal opinion on the Jamaica affair; the list of seven legal questions and sub-questions for which the committee desired answers; Stephen and James's answers, and the legal basis for their answers.[137] The prologue informed the public that one of the 'first acts' of the Committee 'was to cause the following case to be submitted on its behalf' to two eminent lawyers. The committee had solicited the opinion in order to discover, first, 'what steps are open to them to assist their fellow subjects in Jamaica to obtain the protection of the law; and if the law had been broken, to bring the guilty parties to justice'. In the second place the Committee wanted to know what 'steps [were] open to them as Englishmen to vindicate constitutional law and order, if constitutional law and order have been illegally set aside by the government in Jamaica'.

Toward these ends, the Jamaica Committee had sought clarification of a number of points of law in the form of answers to seven discrete questions. The lawyers were asked to base their answers only on the information found in the official documents that thus far had been given to the public. The seven questions of the Committee, we have seen, focused on the legal meaning and import of the term

---

[133] *Law Times* (9 Nov. 1867). Although it is noteworthy that James was a moderate Liberal who, in the general election of 1865, had defeated Jacob Bright, the Radical candidate.

[134] Stephen's first biographer, his brother Leslie, claimed that Stephen 'drew the opinion which was signed by Mr. James and himself'. The opinion was later published, little altered, as Stephen's own work in his *History of Criminal Law*. See Leslie Stephen, *The Life of Sir James Fitzjames Stephen* (London, 1895), 228.   [135] *CD*, 30 Dec 1865.

[136] *CD*, 15 Jan. 1866.

[137] As reprinted in the *Law Times* (27 Jan. 1866), 179–80; (3 Feb. 1866), 201–2.

'martial law', and on the legality of the arrest, removal, court martial, and execution of George Gordon. The Committee also wanted to know about the potential liability of subordinate officers for their actions under martial law, and particularly for the violence visited on men and women 'in the absence of any appearance of organized resistance'. Finally, the Committee wanted to understand its options in the event that the Governor and his subordinates *had* broken the law. What were 'the proper modes of bringing them to trial', and what if any 'indemnity' would the perpetrators enjoy as a result of immunities granted by the colonial legislature? The answers submitted by Stephen and James were lengthy and technical. (They were long enough that the editors of the *Law Times* published them in two separate parts. The Committee's private publication of the opinion ran to some twelve pages.) But what is more remarkable is that its leadership thought that the publication of a legal opinion, replete with case and statutory references, was indispensable to the advancement of their aims.

The first task of the Jamaica Committee lawyers had been to determine the 'meaning of the term martial law, and . . . the legal effect of a proclamation of martial law'.[138] Their historical research revealed that in 'very early times' officials of the Crown sometimes exerted a law martial (a kind of summary justice) 'over troops in actual service'. With the passage of time, some English monarchs deigned to employ the law martial 'in time of peace or emergencies, and especially for the punishment of breaches of the peace'. According to Stephen and James, the first usage had been rendered obsolete by the creation of a standing army regulated under the Mutiny Acts, and the second was outlawed by Parliament when it passed the Petition of Right in 1628. All this seemed clear enough. But problems had cropped up when these archaic meanings of martial law had become conflated with 'the common law right of the Crown to repel force by force in the case of invasion or insurrection'. On this key point, Stephen and James concluded that 'the suppression of revolts by military force was undoubtedly legal' (in the sense that particular acts of suppression might be privileged by the defence of public necessity). On the other hand, 'the subsequent punishment of offenders by illegal tribunals' was barred by the provisions of the Petition of Right, and thus was undoubtedly illegal.

The opinion then considered whether Jamaica's colonial assembly could 'confer upon Governor Eyre any other power than he already possessed at common law'.[139] Stephen and James concluded that it could not. The jurisdiction of the Jamaica assembly was derived, not from Parliament, but from a Royal Commission, and because 'the Crown cannot authorise legislation inconsistent with the law of England, it could not authorise the Jamaica Legislature to confer

---

[138] Ibid. (27 Jan. 1866), 179.
[139] Ibid. (3 Feb. 1866), 202. The opinion also concluded that the legislation did not confer any special martial powers. Instead, the Act only provided regulations for mustering and disciplining the colonial militia.

upon the Governor or anyone else powers inconsistent with the Petition of Right'. The Jamaican legislation which Eyre had used to proclaim martial law was 'repugnant' to an Act of Parliament and was therefore a nullity. It was the further opinion of Stephen and James that upon careful scrutiny the Jamaica legislation invoked by the Governor did not purport to provide any new or special powers. The statute promulgated rules by which 'martial law' was to be used and, in so doing, actually *limited* the common law power to confront an armed invasion or insurgency.

Having established these general propositions of law, Stephen and James returned to the remaining six questions which had been posed by the Jamaica Committee. As for the actions taken against Gordon, their legality would pivot on whether, as a matter of fact, the actions 'had been necessary for the suppression of open force, and the restoration of legal authority, to put him to death'. Based on their reading of the official despatches, the lawyers did not think that 'such could have been the case'. The fact that Gordon had been arrested in Kingston, and the authorities had not judged Kingston to be enough threatened to be subject to martial law, 'shows conclusively' that 'no necessity for the assumption of arbitrary power existed then and there'. The same reasoning held for the court martial which tried and convicted Gordon. In the absence of evidence that the trial had been 'immediately and unavoidably necessary', the soldiers at Morant Bay had no jurisdiction over him. 'Their province,' it was clear, 'was to suppress force by force, not to punish crime.'

Their final conclusion was that the violent actions of suppression ordered by Governor Eyre, or ordered or carried out by soldiers in the field, were all crimes *prima facie* which could be prosecuted in England, by any person in England. The mere fact that these actions had been undertaken under a proclamation of martial law did nothing to widen the (undoubted) common law right of any officials of the Crown to implement 'measures of excessive severity' if they were 'absolutely essential to the restoration of the power of the law'. It was of course open to any person accused of having committed a crime during the suppression to plead, and then prove, that their actions were privileged by necessity. As to the legal effect of an Act of Indemnity passed by the Jamaica Legislature, Stephen and James professed more doubt. Still, on the principle that it was not 'competent' of a colonial assembly to 'pardon crimes committed against the laws of England', the lawyers 'were inclined to think that such an Act would be no answer to an indictment in England'. This was a matter of sufficient legal difficulty, however, that Stephen and James thought that, in the event that the Legislature passed such an Act, some person should cause its legality to be reviewed by the Judicial Committee of the Privy Council.

The reaction of the newspaper press to the publication of the Stephen–James opinion was predictably partisan. The liberal press praised it for its impartiality and lucidity on a crucial point of constitutional law. The *Daily News*, by way of example, called the opinion a 'calm judicial statement of English law', and claimed that the 'eminence of the gentlemen who have given it is undeniable'.[140] When the opinion had been absorbed it was bound to 'satisfy the public that there is still such a thing as the supremacy of law'. Conversely, the tendency of the conservative press was to dismiss the opinion as a shabby political manoeuvre. According to the *Morning Herald*, the opinion was secured by a 'tyrannous cabal' joined together on behalf of 'that teeming and festering population of idle negroes'. A legal opinion had been secured and paid for in order to 'justify the [Jamaica Committee] in the violent and extravagant course which they seem to contemplate', in particular to try Governor Eyre in an English court of law.[141] Interestingly, however, while it condemned the aims of the Jamaica Committee, the *Herald* did not impugn the accuracy of the Stephen–James opinion. The newspaper even expressed gratitude to the Committee for having 'put difficult questions on a tangible footing'. After all, the story noted, the Committee's own lawyers had conceded that indemnity legislation passed in Jamaica might act as a 'bar' to the indictment of the Governor and his officers. In this way the Jamaica Committee had given its lawyers 'rich presents to curse its enemies, instead of which, like a pair of Balaams, they had blessed them altogether'.

The Jamaica Committee was more sanguine about the results of its legal research. On 24 January the Committee's executive decided that both Stephen and James were to be retained as its 'standing counsel'.[142] It was assumed that their skills would be needed again when the Royal Commission, and the Committee's other two barristers, Gorrie and Horne Payne, reported findings from Jamaica. In the aftermath of the legal opinion of Stephen and James, it was now widely assumed that in the wake of official investigations in Jamaica, there would be unofficial, that is, private, prosecutions in England. (The *Law Times* seemed almost giddy at the prospect of the spring bringing forth 'the rare spectacle of a grand State trial'.[143]) But for the remainder of the winter of 1866, the Committee was preoccupied with fund-raising, and with the serious problem created by fraudulent canvassers.[144] Thus far the Committee had taken in some £565 (most of which had been secured by Bright). A great deal more would be needed if the Committee hoped to mount a major legal offensive in the spring.

To this point we have described the activities mainly of those who, on hearing of events in Jamaica, had quickly concluded that serious and criminal wrongdoing had been committed during the suppression. Little has been said about those who opposed them. The first point to underline in this regard is that Governor Eyre and his officers did not enjoy any *organized* support in England until the summer of 1866. Until that time the pro-Eyre position was championed mainly by letters

---

[140] *Daily News* (17 Jan. 1866).   [141] *Morning Herald* (18 Jan. 1866), 4.
[142] *JC Minutes*, 24 Jan. 1866.   [143] *Law Times* (20 Jan. 1866), 163–4.
[144] It had come to the attention of the Jamaica Committee that a man named Edmundson had passed himself off as an agent of the Committee, and had absconded with a sizeable sum of money. *CD*, 16 Jan. 1866, 17 Jan. 1866.

and editorials in *The Times*[145] and other conservative newspapers. In December 1865 an obscure Scottish journalist named Hamilton Hume began to circulate admiring biographical sketches of Eyre (which he published as a long piece in January 1866).[146] A few distinguished men, Sir Roderick Murchison, Lord Elcho, and John Ruskin most notably, also published letters of praise for Eyre.[147]

Eyre's proponents of course took great exception to the allegation that he was a murderer. But in so doing they did not put forward contrary positions on the relevant law. In a speech which garnered wide publicity in the Tory papers, Elcho preferred to emphasize Eyre's heroic personal qualities, how his cool-headedness and decision had saved the Jamaica colony and 'the lives of every white man in it'.[148] Ruskin's approach was only slightly different. In an open letter on the Jamaica affair he slammed the 'Radical movement against the Governor' whose telescopic philanthropy intervened on behalf of former slaves of Jamaica while it ignored the wage slaves of England.[149] In the same letter Ruskin famously declared fealty to conservatism ('they are for liberty, and I am for lordship; they are the mob's men, and I am a king's man . . .'). The men of the Jamaica Committee were entreated to 'reserve their impeachments, or turn them from those among us who have saved colonies to those who have destroyed nations'.

But at the close of December 1865, and for some months afterward, personal interventions of this sort on behalf of Eyre became increasingly rare. Even among the most conservative writers of *The Times, Standard*, and *Herald* there was at least a grudging acceptance that the Jamaica suppression had given rise to a 'painful crisis', one which called for thorough investigation.[150] As the credibility of Eyre's explanations eroded, the legal and racial dimensions continued to divide public opinion. The Jamaica Committee had succeeded in demonstrating, at the very least, that Eyre and his soldiers might have committed serious crimes, including (technical) murders, in putting down the Jamaica uprising. At the same time, those crimes, *if* they were crimes, had been perpetrated by whites who appeared honestly to believe that they faced extermination at the hands of a vast black majority. The racial dimensions of the case were salient enough that it quickly became conventional even in the radical writing on the Jamaica affair to criticize Eyre and his senior officers without sympathizing with their black victims. As the

---

[145] See, for instance, the letter of Rear-Admiral J. Lort Stokes, *The Times* (7 Dec. 1865), 5.

[146] 'Edward John Eyre, Governor of Jamaica, with an account of his early life', *British Army and Navy Review*, iv (Jan. 1866), 1–15, 100–211.

[147] As will be seen in subsequent chapters, with Thomas Carlyle these men would ultimately move to organize a committee to defend Eyre against attempted criminal prosecutions. For a more thorough description of the material published in support of Eyre in December 1865, see Geoffrey Dutton, *The Hero as Murderer: The Life of Edward John Eyre, Australian Explorer and Governor of Jamaica, 1815–1901* (London, 1967), 310–11.   [148] *The Times* (7 Dec. 1865), 5.

[149] On 20 December, Ruskin published an open letter in which he chastised erstwhile friends (Thomas Hughes and Mill were named) for having contributed to what Ruskin called 'this fatuous outcry against Governor Eyre'. See, e.g., *Manchester Guardian* (21 Dec. 1865), 3.   [150] Ibid.

Royal Commission began its work in Jamaica in January 1866, England's political class had time to ponder two large questions. Was it the fact of the matter that some or all of the actions perpetrated in Jamaica under martial law were crimes? If the Governor and his officers had committed crimes, was it prudent for an imperial nation to prosecute them?

III. The Liberal Government Responds to the Jamaica Affair

The response of Lord John Russell's government to the Jamaica rebellion and suppression is one of the more minutely researched aspects of the early phases of the Eyre controversy. When read together, the careful work of Arvell Erickson[151] and B. A. Knox[152] offers a detailed picture of the Government's decision-making. But as valuable as these studies are as meticulous narrative reconstructions, they do not display great analytical ambition or reach. More specifically this work does not explain *why* a British government, only a handful of years after the sepoy mutiny in India, responded so sternly to the conduct of Governor Eyre and his officers. Eyre had taken very deliberate and successful steps to quell a rebellion among a turbulent majority of black men, a rebellion that had taken white lives, and had imperilled many more. What was it about these steps that Russell's Government did not like? Further to the point, what explains the striking dissonance between the perceptions and expectations of the Governor in Jamaica and those of his masters in England? Bearing these questions in mind, it is worthwhile to revisit the key figures and the relevant documentary record.

When news of the Jamaica insurrection and suppression reached England in early November 1865, Lord Russell's premiership, only weeks old, was in a tenuous position. The death of Palmerston in early October had left the Liberals without sure leadership or definite policies.[153] The news came when Parliament was in recess, and just as Russell (with Gladstone, Chancellor of the Exchequer and Liberal leader in the House of Commons) had begun to forge a legislative agenda, one committed to an inevitably divisive bill on general electoral reform.

The Jamaica affair looked to present a dilemma for the leaders of the Liberal Party in Parliament. On one hand, their legislative agenda, especially the proposed Reform Bill, would depend on the goodwill of reform-minded Liberals and parliamentary Radicals. Members of these groupings would want the Government to deal harshly with Governor Eyre. On the other hand, moderate and conservative

---

[151] Arvel B. Erickson, 'Edward T. Cardwell: Peelite', 49 *Transactions of the American Philosophical Society* (1959), 5–67; 'Empire or Anarchy: The Jamaica Rebellion of 1865', 44 *Journal of Negro History* (1959), 99–122.

[152] Bruce A. Knox, 'The British Government and the Governer Eyre Controversy, 1865–75', 19 *Historical Journal* (1976), 877–90.

[153] K. Theodore Hoppen, *The Mid-Victorian Generation, 1846–1886* (Oxford, 1998), 245.

Liberals would expect a more Palmerstonian response to the Jamaica affair. As was often remarked in the press[154] (and at least once by Edward Eyre privately)[155] in his long tenure as premier Palmerston was always steadfast in his support of colonial officials who had got into trouble, even when they had committed blatant errors.[156] If Russell acted with un-Palmerstonian reproachfulness toward Eyre, he would be likely to alienate large numbers of Liberal M.P.s and voters.

In the end, however, these more political calculations were not the mainsprings of the Government's early decisions about the Jamaica affair. Evidence strongly suggests that all three of the main decision makers – Cardwell, Russell, and Gladstone – were quickly of one mind that in the suppression of the Jamaica uprising Governor Eyre had made serious and even unforgivable mistakes, i.e. that he had superintended over an unnecessary, and unnecessarily brutal, slaughter of fellow subjects. To be sure, that these things had happened under the watch of a Liberal government was politically embarrassing. But the main reason why the Cabinet moved so quickly in deciding to suspend Eyre and institute a thorough investigation (by three Conservatives, no less) was that the Jamaica affair was embarrassing morally. Under a cloak of legality, the Governor and his senior soldiers had delivered (what many senior Liberals thought was) a grievous blow to England's international reputation as a humane nation governed by law.

As supremo at the Colonial Office, Edward Cardwell was the Government's 'point man' with regard to the Jamaica affair. With the assistance of senior civil servants, and occasionally on the advice of Cabinet, he received reports and issued instructions from colonial Governors. In 1865 Cardwell was a highly experienced politician who had held a number of cabinet posts.[157] Cardwell was also a lawyer by training, a man with a deeply ingrained respect for the 'majesty' of English law and justice.[158] While he was not a proponent of further democratic reform of the colonial governments, most especially of those populated mainly by non-whites, Cardwell thought the colonies, like the mother country, should be governed by

154 The *Daily Telegraph* (11 Dec. 1865), 4, remembered the 'steadfast courage which was ever displayed by Lord Palmerston in defending his subordinates against unfair attack'. The *Law Times* (30 Dec. 1865), 113, recalled the 'proud boast of Lord Palmerston that he always stood by his men, and never deserted them until guilt was proven...Had he been living, he would have quitted office rather than have abandoned Governor Eyre to his enemies, or accepted any complaints against him until proof of guilt was given.'

155 In a letter to Henry Taylor written in January 1866, Eyre complained that Palmerston would not have taken the course taken by Russell. In his reply, Taylor reminded Eyre that 'it was also Palmerston's way to take the measure of his power, and to yield reasonably to a pressure which he knew he could not resist'. Taylor to Eyre, 31 January 1866, Cardwell Papers, *CO* 30/22/16a.

156 See, e.g., *Law Times* (30 Dec. 1865), 113.

157 Erickson, 'Cardwell: Peelite', 7–9. In his youth, Cardwell passed up a career in the law to become a politician. He became a loyal Peelite, noted for his 'somewhat austere devotion to public service'. Before his appointment as Minister in the Colonial Office, Cardwell had held a number of cabinet positions in Peelite and then Liberal governments. Throughout his long career Cardwell was a dogged and skilful advocate of governmental reform. Bond, *Oxford DNB*, online 4620.

158 Erickson, 'Cardwell: Peelite', 6.

recourse to established and civilized laws.[159] This legalistic view of the Jamaica affair clearly influenced his perspective both on Governor Eyre and Eyre's critics.

As previously noted, in his first post-rebellion despatch Eyre provided a frank, even recklessly frank, picture of the ruthless methods by which the insurrection had been suppressed. The despatch reflected Eyre's untroubled conviction that what had been done had been both necessary and just. The historian B. A. Knox thought that Cardwell felt 'uneasy' about the tone and content of Eyre's report.[160] Arvell Erickson, on the other hand, thought that Cardwell had found the report 'shocking'.[161] Judging by the content of the first three responses written by Cardwell to Eyre, it would seem that Erickson was much closer to the mark. In roughly equal degrees, Cardwell's replies transmitted their author's pervasive doubt, distaste, and despair. They communicated an oblique yet unmistakable warning to Eyre that his explanations and justifications were unconvincing, and if they (and the evidence supporting them) were not rendered more convincing, there would be a reckoning.

While it is true that in the opening passages of Cardwell's first post-suppression despatch,[162] he offered some praise and congratulations to Eyre, in light of what followed, these expressions must be seen as *pro forma*. On any sensible reading of the document, Cardwell meant to deliver a rebuke.[163] Finished on 17 November 1865, and before he had met with the Cabinet, Cardwell's despatch made two points abundantly clear. The first was that the norms of civilian law and justice in a colony could not be disturbed or superseded except in the case of overwhelming public necessity. The second point concerned Eyre's first post-rebellion despatch; Cardwell believed that it had signally failed to make out a strong case for the 'measures of severity to which [Eyre] felt it necessary to have recourse'.[164] So much was Cardwell anxious on this point that he set forth the test on which Eyre's decisions would be judged. The Governor would be obliged to demonstrate that his measures amounted to a 'merciful substitute for much larger measures of punishment

---

[159] Ibid., 42.   [160] Knox, 'British Government', 879.

[161] Erickson, 'Cardwell: Peelite', 45.

[162] In all probability, Cardwell drafted his first two replies to Eyre, those written on 17 and 23 Nov., without consultation with Cabinet colleagues or even the senior bureaucrats at the Colonial Office (Frederic Rogers, the Permanent Under-Secretary, and Henry Taylor, his chief lieutenant). There is no evidence that Cardwell met or communicated with Cabinet colleagues on the Jamaica affair until the last week of November. Knox, 'British Government', 880. Both Rogers (himself a lawyer) and Taylor were inclined to take a far more lenient stance towards Eyre's conduct. In a private note to Rogers written on 16 June 1866, Taylor reiterated his previously stated view that the vigorous use of martial law had been necessary, and that 'the execution of Gordon was the one decisive blow which silenced the agitators in the west and secured the colony'. See Cardwell Papers, *CO* 30/48/43. See also Morrell, *British Colonial Policy*, 420.

[163] Here the present writer is obliged flatly to disagree with Erickson ('Cardwell: Peelite', 46) that Cardwell's letter was a 'model of kindness, suspended judgment and lucidity'. While the letter was lucid enough, it also made plain that the plausibility of the Governor's account was in doubt, and that it was incumbent upon him to justify what (to that point) appeared wholly unjustified. It seems unlikely that Eyre thought the letter either kind or non-judgemental.

[164] Cardwell to Eyre, *Annual Register* (1865), 287.

which would have had to be executed had the rebellion been allowed to gather head and extend itself'. And in its general tone and phrasing the despatch strongly insinuated yet another point: that Cardwell harboured very grave doubts that the measures deployed by Eyre, once they were thoroughly explicated, would pass this test.

Cardwell's legal training figured in the way in which he put particular queries and comments to the Governor, and in how he situated them within a general account of a colonial governor's legal obligations in a time of emergency. Eyre had rightly viewed it as his duty to take energetic steps to crush a violent challenge to public order and authority. However, Cardwell informed the Governor, it equally had been his duty to 'arrest the course of punishment as soon as [he] was able to do so, and had exerted [himself] to confine it to ascertained offenders and to cases of aggravated guilt'.[165] Here, and in other passages, Cardwell adverted to the *limits* of martial law. Even if circumstances warranted a proclamation of martial law, civilian justice ought to have been restored at the earliest possible moment. Even when martial law had been justly proclaimed, moreover, the authorities were obliged to respect the principles of natural justice with respect to the identification and punishment of offenders. Cardwell also expressed the expectation that it was the responsibility of a governor to grant a 'general amnesty except to actual murderers' after a rebellion had been quelled. At all times and in all places, Cardwell insinuated, the bywords of an English governor were justice and mercy. This was the standard by which Eyre's conduct was to be measured.

Having had an opportunity to review Eyre's first report in more depth, including the reports from military officers which Eyre had enclosed, on 23 November Cardwell was moved to write a second official note to Eyre, one that underscored Cardwell's earlier concerns. If the Governor had not already done so, he was to terminate martial law and its military tribunals, and order the restoration of the 'ordinary course of legal inquiry, and of the judicial trial and punishment of offenders'.[166] Cardwell wanted to be sent copies of the proceedings of the courts martial, and 'of the evidence taken in the various cases'. With respect to the graphic descriptions of retaliatory violence, he expressed his 'earnest hope that they may be capable of full explanation'. But, so that there would be no mistake on the matter, Cardwell also warned Eyre that in many instances 'the severity inflicted would not appear to have been justifiable'. He also took this opportunity to request more information concerning the arrest, trial, and execution of Gordon. Specifically, he wanted a more complete explanation of why it was that Gordon 'was arrested at Kingston, to which martial law did not extend, and taken to Morant Bay for trial, under martial law'.[167]

Once again, Cardwell had informed Eyre that his judgement would be measured against a legal standard. He expected to 'see it clearly established that [Gordon] was not executed until crimes had been proved in evidence against him;

---

[165] Cardwell to Eyre, *Annual Register* (1865), 287.   [166] Ibid.   [167] Ibid.

and that the prompt infliction of capital punishment was necessary to rescue the colony from imminent danger, and from the horrors of a general or wide spread insurrection'. It was unmistakable that Cardwell already entertained grave doubts about the legality and propriety of Eyre's decisions, especially with regard to Gordon. 'Her Majesty's Government,' Cardwell stated in his penultimate paragraph, 'await with much anxiety your explanation on this subject'. Near the end of his despatch he told Eyre that he was 'satisfied to wait patiently for the justification which you will send of the points which now appear to require justification'.[168] It is also worth repeating that Cardwell sent these despatches on 23 November, or inside of a week of having received Eyre's first post-rebellion report. In other words, Cardwell communicated serious misgivings about the morality and legal character of the suppression *before* it was made into a national *cause célèbre* by an assortment of evangelicals, anti-slavery activists, radical politicians, and campaigning newspaper writers.[169] By the time he drafted his second despatch Cardwell already had decided that his official correspondence with Eyre would be published in the parliamentary *Gazette*. (Cardwell's parallel *private* correspondence with Eyre in this period was not released to the public.) The publication of official despatches, Cardwell privately informed Eyre, 'will probably be the best antidote to the disposition to condemn your proceedings . . . which a part of the press seems to exhibit'.[170] In light of the foregoing, however, it is difficult to credit Cardwell's assurance that he had published Eyre's despatches in order to help the Governor.

Behind the scenes, Cardwell was being advised on the political implications both of Eyre's actions in Jamaica and his own responses at home. On 18 November, Cardwell received a note from Sir Charles Phipps, the Queen's private secretary.[171] Phipps had been present in Jamaica in the bloody aftermath of the slave revolt of 1831–2, and the early reports from Morant Bay were a chilling reminder of them. Because colonial Governors represented the sovereign personally, the Queen and her secretary took a keen interest in the Jamaica affair. Phipps was alarmed especially by the news that Gordon had been arrested in a civilian jurisdiction and transferred to the summary justice of the courts martial. This was an illegal act for which, Phipps was certain, 'many will be severely blamed'. By the same token, he also alerted Cardwell to the dangerous precedent that would be set were Eyre and his senior officers to face punishment. In the event of a similar

---

[168] Ibid.

[169] It was with a clear conscience, therefore, that on 24 November Cardwell was able to provide Henry Brougham with his personal assurance that the Government already had asked Eyre for 'full information' and 'much explanation' about the period of martial law in Jamaica. Cardwell hoped that 'these explanations will remove much of the anxious feeling which is entertained about the measures of authority, by proving that a scene of extreme public danger' justified the use of force. See Cardwell to Brougham, 24 Nov. 1865, Brougham Papers, *UCL* Add. MS.

[170] Cardwell to Eyre, 17 Nov. 1865, Cardwell Papers, *CO* 30/48/42

[171] Phipps to Cardwell, 18 Nov. 1865, Cardwell Papers, *CO* 30/48/42.

emergency in another part of the empire, 'the authorities and officers will be disheartened and intimidated by the experience of the censure from home, and will be afraid to incur any responsibility'. In weighing his response to the Jamaica affair, Cardwell was urged to bear in mind that the strict limitation of force in the colonies might make them even more difficult to govern.

Before the end of November the entire Cabinet met to discuss the Jamaica case.[172] At that meeting it was agreed that Cardwell should continue to press Eyre to justify the prolongation of martial law and of the removal of Gordon to Morant Bay. On 1 December Cardwell sent a third post-rebellion despatch to the Governor, one which (more openly than before) declared his dissatisfaction with Eyre's previous reports. The despatch instructed Eyre to answer a long list of specific questions about what had been done under the proclamation of martial law.[173] More interestingly, however, the despatch also included an even more explicit statement of Cardwell's view on the *law* of martial law. Cardwell wrote that 'all martial law supposes an overwhelming public necessity, which makes it absolutely necessary to dispense with the securities and forms of ordinary law. It is therefore only justifiable so long as that necessity exists: and martial law should cease the moment the public safety will permit.' On the question of martial law and the treatment of Gordon, Cardwell candidly admitted that he found it 'difficult to understand how it can be right to carry a person away from a district which it has not been thought necessary to proclaim, and try him in a proclaimed district'. Such a course, Cardwell wrote, *might* be justified by the existence of a 'systematic conspiracy, headed by Gordon' to massacre Jamaica's white minority. However, he stressed, the existence of such a conspiracy had only been alleged, not proved. 'These considerations,' Eyre was informed, 'press very much upon the Cabinet'.[174] Cardwell put the Governor on notice that 'a full investigation of such circumstances as thus stated . . . must take place either here, or in Jamaica'.

If he had not known it before, it was now plain to Eyre that he was in serious trouble. He had overseen the summary execution of hundreds of British subjects on the assumption, an incorrect one, that the political and military necessity of this course would be readily comprehended and accepted in London. This was perhaps an understandable error given the nearness in time of the massacres at Cawnpore. As we have seen, Eyre himself had been quick to invoke this point.[175] Although (as we will see in the following chapter) Eyre had not been unmindful of the legal implications of martial law, he had thought that these would be eclipsed by the political and military exigencies faced by him in the colony. On having read Eyre's October despatches, Charles Phipps perceptively remarked that they were written by a man who hadn't 'the slightest appearance of an expectation that anything that had been done would be questioned in England. On the contrary,

---

172 For a full account of this meeting, see Knox, 'British Government', 880.
173 Cardwell to Eyre, 1 Dec. 1865, *CO* 137/394.   174 Ibid.
175 Eyre to Cardwell, 20 Oct. 1865, *Annual Register*, 279.

his only anxiety appeared to claim the largest share in the acts which one here supposed to entail so heavy a responsibility.'[176]

The reports which Eyre wrote after receiving Cardwell's despatches of November 1865 were understandably nervous, even dejected, in tone. In one of his replies, Eyre made this plaintive remark: 'I could not imagine that I should have been called upon to defend myself against attacks made by my fellow-countrymen at home for acts done in good faith.'[177] But now there was no question that in fact Eyre *was* being called upon to defend himself, and even by his master at the Colonial Office. In response, Eyre's later despatches featured a number of exculpatory strategies.[178] First, he tried to shift responsibility. In his capacity as civilian Governor, Eyre explained, he had attended only to the 'general arrangements for the suppression and punishment of the rebellion'.[179] The trial and punishment of specific prisoners had been supervised by military officers in the field, who reported only to their commanding officer, General O'Connor. While it was possible that some things were done that could not be justified, these things necessarily had been left to the discretion of 'subordinate authorities, differing greatly in character, ability, temper, experience and judgment'. Eyre's second strategy was to claim that overwork and fatigue (the 'thought, work, and anxiety' associated with saving the western districts of the colony, the 'pressure which has seriously affected my health') had prevented him from being more vigilant of the conduct of subordinates.[180] During the key moments of the suppression, the Governor had been able to take no more than a 'hurried glance' at reports from the field. In short, it had been all but 'impossible' for him to have prevented or curbed excesses.

As time progressed, and as London continued to press for further explanation and justification, Eyre prefaced his report with a self-pitying description of his physical decline. In his despatch of 24 December Eyre related how his 'powers have been sadly overtaxed lately; there has been more work to get thru' than any man however strong could accomplish. I have had to work under the disadvantage of failing health [Eyre lived until 1901!] – and the work has been of a horrifying and anxious kind.'[181] But the Governor was able to summon enough strength to lecture Cardwell on the legal dimensions of his conduct. 'Martial law,' he stated, 'implies a state of war during which even in the best regulated armies many evils necessarily arise.' By its nature martial law was 'an arbitrary exercise of power authorized by any law (though since covered by the Indemnity Act) and only justifiable as a measure of public safety'.

---

[176] Phipps to Cardwell, 24 Dec. 1865, *CO* 30/48/42,
[177] Eyre to Cardwell, Jan. 1866, *JRC Eyre Papers, PP* (1866), xxx, 19.
[178] When these despatches were published by the Government in February 1866, *The Times* (7 Feb. 1866), 10, remarked that Eyre clearly had been alarmed by Cardwell's first post-rebellion communication, and that his tone now was 'apologetic throughout'.
[179] Eyre to Cardwell, 8 Dec.1865, *Annual Register*, 290–1.   [180] Ibid.
[181] Eyre to Cardwell, 24 Dec. 1865, Cardwell Papers, *CO* 30/48/42.

In January 1866 Eyre completed his long awaited final report to Cardwell on the uprising, and on the methods used to suppress it.[182] This document is important both because it was Eyre's most comprehensive justification for his actions, and because it figured so prominently in subsequent debates in England about the meaning and significance of the Jamaica affair. The final report decidedly was not a *mea culpa*. On the contrary, Eyre maintained more fervently that everything he had done to suppress the Morant Bay rebellion had been both necessary and legal. His despatch, then, was composed as an argument for his complete vindication.

The argument, as Eyre made clear, was grounded in six premisses about race and security in the tropical empire. The major premiss was that 'the negroes, from a low state of civilization and being under the influence of superstitious feelings could not properly be dealt with in the same manner as might the peasantry of a European country'.[183] The danger presented by the racial character of negroes was compounded in Jamaica by the fact that they greatly outnumber the whites. The central problem for the Governor of the island, then, was how to make 'an adequate effect upon such a population, numbering as they do some 350,000 against 13,000 whites who are scattered amongst them in isolated and unprotected positions'? Eyre argued that it had been imperative, if new trouble was to be averted, to continue the period of martial law until all of the leaders of the insurrection had been captured and tried summarily. To have moved sooner would have 'done away with the impression which it was so necessary at the time to make upon the minds of the negroes throughout the island'. In other words, it had been necessary to round up and punish the leaders in order to terrorize the black majority still at large.

Eyre's remaining five arguments amplified why it had been incumbent upon him as Governor to act swiftly and unrelentingly to crush the rebellion. As a race the negroes 'are most excitable and impulsive', and if Jamaica's blacks had been afforded any reason to believe that the rebellion might succeed, it would have instantly spread to the central and western sections of the colony. The negro was also 'most reticent', and it is 'almost impossible to arrive at anything like correct details of their plans and intentions'.[184] The leaders among the negro population had exercised a 'reign of terror' over their black brothers in order to maintain discipline in the ranks of the rebels. Although the opening spasm of violence occurred in just one parish, Eyre 'had good reason to believe that disloyalty, disaffection, sedition and rebellious intentions existed in almost every other parish of the Island'. And as for a possible race war on whites, the black men of the island had only to look to the history of the neighbouring island of Haiti for a model. To meet this potentially lethal threat the Governor had had only 1,000 troops in the entire colony. For all of these reasons, then, Eyre considered that he was 'fully justified in continuing

---

[182] Eyre to Cardwell, Jan. 1866, *JRC Eyre Papers, PP* (1866), xxx, 19.   [183] Ibid., 1.
[184] Ibid., 2.

martial law...until...the rebellion itself was so crushed out as to deter any similar outbreak elsewhere'.[185]

In the balance of his despatch Eyre offered up evidence in the form of a series of fragmentary testimonials (given by white officials and civilians) as to the gravity of the threat, and the necessity of martial law. He then attempted to dispel reports in England that the suppression had claimed thousands of black lives. Eyre believed that no more than 500 had been killed in the field or executed by the forces of the Crown.[186] But for the 'prompt suppression of the rebellion and the severe punishment which followed', Eyre ventured to say, the number of lives lost, white and black, would have been far higher.

But, in terms of saving his position and career, these arguments were in vain, and not only in the eyes of Cardwell. Before Eyre could send his December despatches to England, the cabinet had already decided that the Governor would be suspended pending an official inquiry.[187] Gladstone had been the strongest voice in Cabinet on this point.[188] He had a long-standing interest in martial law and its use in the colonies (he had once made a long speech in Parliament on the subject during the Ceylon controversy of 1851),[189] and when the Jamaica affair began to unfold fourteen years later, he immediately began to keep a file of newspaper reports.[190] In salon conversation, too, Gladstone had made no secret of his 'deep emotion' about the Jamaica affair, nor of his view that the good name of the country had been sullied by the violent excesses of Eyre's martial law.[191] In notes made for his own reference on 1 December 1865, Gladstone recorded his alarm at the large number of 'violent deaths' in Jamaica, and that persons ('like Gordon') had been 'deported *into* districts under martial law'. He also noted that while the Government had been 'told of the signs and threats of strife throughout the island, no evidence is supplied'. While the decision to suspend the Governor and institute a public inquiry would placate the Radical wing of the Liberal party as it approached a potentially bruising battle over electoral reform, there can be but little doubt that Gladstone acted out of personal conviction that Eyre had committed errors of act or omission for which, regardless of political consequences, he deserved the sack.

When Lord Russell met a delegation of Jamaica activists in Downing Street on 12 December, he expressed similar sentiments. What had occurred in Jamaica, he stated, 'has affected the government with very great pain'.[192] The 'whole matter,'

---

[185] Ibid., 3.   [186] Ibid., 17.

[187] On 7 December, just before the cabinet's decision was announced, Milner Gibson, the Radical M.P. and President of the Board of Trade, confided in Bright that even the most vocal critics of Eyre's actions in Jamaica soon would agree that the government had 'taken the proper course'. Bright was assured that the cabinet was taking 'a most serious view of the Jamaica horrors' and that there would be a 'full and impartial enquiry, a *real* one, and a commission will carry out that purpose'. Bright Papers, BL Add MS. 43,388, f.110.   [188] Knox, 'British Government', 880.

[189] See my 'A Jurisprudence of Power', 19–20.

[190] Gladstone's notes, 1 Dec. 1865, Gladstone Papers, BL Add. MS. 44,754.

[191] *CD*, 24 Jan. 1866.   [192] See account in *The Times* (14 Dec. 1865), 12.

he later repeated, but particularly the 'unbecoming levity' with which some soldiers had described atrocities and violent actions, 'is one exceedingly painful'. While the Prime Minister reiterated how important it was that the Governor not be 'prejudged', he informed the assembly that Eyre would be suspended from his duties pending the completion of a full inquiry. According to *The Times*, the sincerity of Russell's remarks had not been doubted by those who heard his address.[193] For all intents and purposes the protesters had got what they wanted, at least for the moment. Many protest meetings were postponed or cancelled.[194] Attention was turned from public inquiry to the public inquirers, and from England back to Jamaica itself.

IV. The Country of Law: The End of the First Phase of the Jamaica Affair

In November and December 1865 the English political class struggled mightily to make sense of the Jamaica bloodshed. The frenetic reporting, editorializing, and speech-making about Jamaica did not make matters any easier. If the reading and thinking public agreed on one point it was that the episode merited further investigation and consideration. As the Government moved to assemble a Jamaica Royal Commission, observers were left to contend with a set of four contradictory propositions:

(1) That the Jamaica crisis began when a multitude of black men reverted to their natural state of resentment, aggression, and savagery, *or* that the crisis was exacerbated when white men, *British* white men, reacted with an excessive and lawless ferocity.

(2) That only the firmness and decision of Governor Eyre had prevented the slaughter of Jamaica's scattered white community, *or* that Governor Eyre and his soldiers had confused martial law with the licence to eliminate political opposition, and to kill, maim, and destroy with impunity.

(3) Martial law was an essential tool of imperial statecraft in the tropics, *or* martial law in the tropics was a threat to law and liberty at home.

(4) Jamaica was saved! *or* the honour of England was irrevocably stained!

By the end of November 1865, the advocates of the four critical propositions – this diverse coalition of dissenting Christians, secular Radicals, and hybrids of

---

[193] See account in *The Times* (14 Dec. 1865), 12.
[194] *Manchester Guardian* (16 Dec. 1865), 4. Not all new meetings were cancelled, however. On 22 December, the mayor of Ashton convened a Jamaica Meeting in the town hall. A resolution was passed condemning the execution of Gordon, but it was agreed by a majority that debate on a resolution urging the criminal prosecution of Eyre should await the outcome of the government's inquiry. *Manchester Guardian* (22 Dec. 1865), 3.

both – had forged a common and potent rhetoric about the affair. The unifying theme of their rhetoric was secular. The suppression was depicted as an egregious, even dangerous betrayal of England's basic secular law, its constitution. This betrayal was properly viewed as a source of great shame. After all, Englishmen loved their country (as T. B. Potter M.P. had put it) 'because it was the country of law'. Under Edward Eyre's malign direction, however, Jamaica had been reduced to a country of lawlessness. Such a thing could not be tolerated.

Eyre's critics coalesced around a number of (still only vaguely formed) theories of his criminal culpability. To some minds, Eyre's crime was the product of erroneous racial assumptions. Black men and women had been deprived of their legal rights as British subjects solely because of the dark complexion of their skin. ('[T]his meeting,' the Revd. John P. Hopps moved before an assembly in the city of Ashton, 'desires to assert emphatically the principle that all races under Her Majesty's government are entitled to the rights of freemen.'[195]) But to more minds, the essence of Eyre's crime was not that he had whipped and executed some black persons in Jamaica, but he had gone about it in a way that threatened the civil liberties in England. Most of Eyre's critics focused on the fact that the suppression generally, and Gordon's execution particularly, had been carried out under martial law. In this view, the Governor and his soldiers had committed a grave political crime. They had used an inconsequential riot as a pretext for the elimination of political opponents. If this precedent were to be left unchallenged, executive officials in England might be tempted to adopt the same tactic.

In mid-December 1865, the leading critics of Governor Eyre coalesced as the Jamaica Committee, an association made up of a strange blend of mid-Victorian England's most and least religious men. The leaders of the Committee rallied around a purely secular dogma. The central twine of their alliance was the mutual conviction that Eyre and his soldiers had broken the *temporal* law of Britain. Their central strategy was to use legal principles as a means of generating broad-based support for its cause. Their central aim was to cause the government to hold the offenders accountable to the law, and thereby to vindicate the legal rights and privileges of the British people at large. The leadership of the Jamaica Committee was so strongly committed to this agenda that their first collective action, agreed upon before the association was formally constituted, was to retain a solicitor in order that he might retain eminent barristers so that they might create an authoritative legal opinion. Once created, that opinion was to serve both as a manifesto and as a blueprint for future actions including, if necessary, the criminal prosecution of officials.

Although by December 1865 there was broad agreement among the English political class that the Jamaica affair raised important legal and constitutional issues, there was much less agreement about what these issues were, and how they were to be resolved. In fact, a great many serious and important figures were

---

[195] Resolution of some petitioners of Ashton, *Manchester Guardian* (22 Dec. 1865), 3.

concerned about the fact that Governor Eyre and his soldiers might have made some serious errors in suppressing the Jamaica rising.

Certainly this ambivalence was felt by Edward Cardwell. Cardwell read Eyre's first post-uprising despatch with a lawyer's detached and sceptical eye. (And when he might have 'buried' this document for some weeks or months, he chose to publish it in the parliamentary *Gazette*.)[196] Cardwell quickly concluded that the Governor's conduct called for further explanation and justification. But while Cardwell adopted an unyielding line in his despatches, and then agreed with the Cabinet's decision to suspend Eyre pending a full inquiry, he also hesitated to draw firm conclusions about the legal and political ramifications of his conduct. When he met the delegation of Eyre's critics on 9 December, for instance, he persisted (over catcalls and howls of derision) in urging that due allowance be given for the fact that the menace posed by the Jamaican uprising had been real, and that the Governor had been under enormous pressure to act decisively. In a speech made at Oxford on 1 January 1866, Cardwell revisited this point, venturing that 'one thing has never been disputed, and that is by great promptitude on the part of the authorities, and by the skilful disposition of the troops, comparative safety was speedily restored to all persons of whatever race or colour'.[197] While Cardwell was worried about the legal implications of the martial law in Jamaica, he still was not wholly convinced either that Eyre had been wrong to proclaim it, or that he had committed crimes during its implementation. (In January 1866, Cardwell instructed his senior civil servant, Sir Frederic Rogers, to ask the law officers of the Crown to prepare thorough legal opinions on these questions.)[198] At least one of the liberal journals thought that Cardwell's flexible stance on Eyre was the result of a politician's 'amiable desire to displease nobody'.[199] But it was more than that. Like many of his contemporaries, Cardwell was repelled by what had been done in Jamaica. He struggled to form a coherent policy on the suppression, and on the larger question of how to have an empire, and an empire based on laws.

For there to be controversy there must be activism and *resistance*. When one reads the modern-sounding polemics of the Jamaica Committee and its fellow-travellers, it is easy to forget that in December 1865, and afterward, there were good and compelling reasons for English persons to support (or at least not to condemn) what had been done to suppress the Jamaica uprising. These reasons stemmed from the inescapable fact that the empire, most especially the burgeoning empire in the tropics, was a dangerous place. No one who had read the many lurid accounts of the murder and defilement of white men (and white women!) by Indian sepoys could doubt this. By these lights, so *The Economist* remarked, the dispersed white population of Jamaica might be forgiven for having felt and

[196] This politically brave action was much applauded in an editorial of *The Times* published on 8 Jan. 1866, 8.   [197] *Manchester Guardian* (3 Jan. 1866), 4.
[198] The opinion was requested on 18 January 1866, and is to be found at *CO* 885/2. The opinion is discussed at greater length below, Ch. 4.   [199] *Spectator* (10 Feb. 1866), 150–1.

reacted like a 'menaced class'.[200] When the blacks took up arms and used them, it was understandable that 'the whites felt like men in the presence of an almost irresistible yet somehow *insulting* danger'. Jamaica's whites not only had had to confront the prospect of being wiped out, but by masses of their racial inferiors. In such circumstances it was understandable that the white minority looked to '[a]ny means, no matter what, the use of thunderbolts had thunderbolts been available... if only to prevent the storm'. In the judgement of *The Economist*, these facts explained what had happened in Jamaica, even if did not excuse everything the authorities had done to restore public security and order.[201]

To many English commentators it was a matter of simple common sense that in the tropical empire the colonial authorities needed less law and more ready recourse to military coercion and terror. For this reason Governor Eyre's supporters, as much as his critics, could claim a legitimate interest in the legal implications of the Jamaica violence. The *Morning Herald* recognized that there 'was something in the very nature of martial law which is repugnant to the English temper... Yet that in extreme cases it is necessary no one can deny.'[202] There were British colonies and possessions, the newspaper explained, where 'the power of government is so weak and so ineffectually supported by armed force' that the authorities faced a stark choice: invoke martial law or be 'overwhelmed'. Jamaica was just such a colony, and Governor Eyre 'most emphatically' had faced just such a case. For these reasons, the Jamaica case had grave implications, and not only for Eyre and his officers. On 14 December 1865, the *Daily Telegraph* summarized the point in this way: '[I]t must be remembered that the case of Mr. Eyre today, may, at any future time, be the case of some other colonial Governor. In her dependencies all over the world England stands confronting hostile races. In many of the distant settlements the British are looked upon as intruders, and are constantly exposed to extreme peril. It is therefore necessary that... its subjects in those place have large powers... and should feel confidence in the resolution of the Home government to sustain them in the legitimate exercise of those powers.'[203]

That England ought to be a country in which the powerful were beholden to law was no longer, in 1865, a very widely contested proposition. But what the crisis in Jamaica brought into question was whether the same political shibboleth could be safely invoked in the nation's far-flung and racially diverse empire. It could not have been entirely accidental that on 2 December 1865 the *Lancet* published an article titled

---

[200] *The Economist* (2 Dec. 1865), 1455.

[201] In fact, *The Economist* thought that the known facts suggested that unjustifiable excesses had been committed, and that 'black persons being subjects of Great Britain, deserve and require strict investigation'. In Jamaica, *The Economist* observed, the key actors, white and black, had behaved as if 'Jamaica was the world'. It was essential now for the government to demonstrate the supremacy of English law, 'to show to both that a power distant from local prepossessions, calm, fearless, and for political purposes, omnipotent, will at last resort control, and judge, and if necessary punish their acts'. Ibid.   [202] *Morning Herald* (26 Jan. 1866), 4.

[203] *Daily Telegraph* (14 Dec. 1865).

'The War of Race'.[204] The piece consisted both of an admiring retrospective of the racial theories of the Scottish anatomist Dr. Robert Knox, and a pointed commentary on order and security in the tropical empire. Knox was credited for having 'discovered' that 'human character, individual and national, is traceable solely to the nature of race to which the individual or nation belongs'. Knox also championed the idea that racial groups had distinct, unequal, and unreconcilable differences, differences which led inexorably to ceaseless conflict, even war, between them. According to the *Lancet*, the Jamaican insurrection already had been 'foretold on scientific principles'. It had been inevitable in that colony, just as inevitably it would happen again, that the men of coloured races would seek to exterminate their white masters. In this inexorable struggle between the races 'only one can be master, the dark races or the white'. If it is to be the white race, the *Lancet* warned, the blacks 'must be constantly kept down with a rod of iron'. If the English were to increase and maintain their empire, it would not be by the gentle ministrations of lawyers, but 'as military masters lording it over a sort of serf population'.

By mid-December 1865, as the members of the Royal Commission prepared to embark for Kingston, the lines of conflict over the Jamaica affair had become clear. On one side were those who contended that England was defined by its ancient jurisprudence of power, that it was bound by honour and tradition to undertake a thorough and impartial investigation of the Jamaica uprising and suppression. Within these ranks some men called for the eventual criminal prosecution of any persons, civilian officials and military men, who had committed crimes while acting in the service of the Crown. On the other side, a side which for now was less well organized and vocal, were those who thought that Governor Eyre and his soldiers could not be justly criticized, still less prosecuted, for having done their duty in harrowing circumstances. By all indications the colonial officials in Jamaica had moved decisively and effectively to prevent a general insurrection, one that would have claimed scores of white lives. Within these ranks some men called upon their countrymen to admit some hard facts. A sprawling empire of non-white, non-Christian peoples could not be safely governed within a scrupulous constitutional framework. In such places, where the white colonists and administrators would be perpetually outnumbered by teeming masses of hostile peoples, there could be no substitute for the prompt invocation of martial law, and all of the means of coercion and terror implied by that term.

---

[204] *Lancet* (2 Dec. 1865), 626–7.

2

'The Blood that Testifies': The Jamaica Controversy in Jamaica

He complained of the indignity offered him in the hearing room by having to sit between two 'niggers'; he described with great glee his own conduct in leveling a revolver at a big black fellow on a grey horse; he gloried in . . . browbeating the Commissioners, calling Mr. Gurney a mere 'drawing room man'; and during one violent gesticulation dropped a revolver out of his pocket.

Major-General Forbes Jackson, February 1866

Servile insurrections and proconsular delinquencies not infrequently reminded the Roman that he was a citizen of a vast empire.

North British Review, June 1866

'That this country has been profoundly affected by the executions in Jamaica,' the *London Review* observed on 16 December 1865, 'no one who takes even the most cursory glance at the newspaper reports can doubt.' With the arrival of every packet ship from Kingston it was more abundantly clear that British soldiers and civilians, many of high rank, had committed atrocities in Jamaica. It was also clear that the perpetrators were strongly inclined not to downplay or disavow but to boast about even the most vicious things done in the name of the Crown. It now was broadly agreed among English politicians and political writers that these revelations raised fundamentally important moral and, inevitably, legal questions. In the shadow of the Indian Mutiny, that most dangerous and dispiriting of mid-Victorian colonial rebellions, imperial Britain still was capable of bad conscience. This chapter concerns the peculiarly English way in which that conscience was evinced.

When in late December 1865 a bevy of English officials embarked for Kingston to institute the Jamaica Royal Commission (hereinafter, the JRC), the Jamaica affair, in a manner of speaking, was re-exported to its point of origin. For interested parties back in the mother country, there was little to do but watch for the next newspaper report from the island. 'Here, as at home,' the correspondent of *The Times* wrote from Kingston in January 1866, 'the appointment of the Royal Commission has occasioned a lull in politics, and people are waiting for the evidence which is now being prepared on both sides of the question.'[1] For the first five months of 1866, the Jamaica controversy, as an English phenomenon, was in suspended animation.

We have seen that in the final weeks of 1865 the Jamaica affair had been reconstructed in England as a story about law or, more precisely, as a story about the legal boundaries of legitimate state violence. The Jamaica policy of the Russell Government bore this stamp. The centrepiece of that policy was the JRC, a body made up of the Acting Governor and, not incidentally, two highly experienced criminal court judges. These men were selected because they were thought to know how to ferret out the truth in situations where lies would be ubiquitous. Lawyers, criminal lawyers especially, knew how to ask questions and evaluate contradictory evidence. They also knew something else of interest to the government: how to render an informed opinion about the legal ramifications of evidence. In the words of *The Times*, the JRC was constituted as a 'solemn judicial inquisition'.[2]

The JRC left a detailed public record of its work, and this record has attracted a considerable amount of historical research.[3] A good deal is known about the witnesses, what they were asked, and what the Commissioners thought about the answers given. For the most part, the scholars who have read this material have come to admire the Commissioners for their energy, tenacity, and integrity. Still (and due largely to the fact that historians have not focussed enough on the quasi-judicial character of the process) a number of apposite questions about the JRC have gone unasked. How did the Commissioners comprehend the nature of their task? What choices were made about how best to complete the inquiry, and why? Was it significant to the inquiry that two of its three principals were lawyers? How did the Commissioners deal with attempts by outsiders, lawyers particularly, to participate in the process? How was the final report of the JRC perceived in England, and what if any lasting significance did it have for the Jamaica controversy? Is it historically significant that the Government instigated such an inquiry?

The Russell Government was not content merely to investigate what had happened in Jamaica. Early in 1866, before the JRC filed its report, the Colonial Office already was preparing to start criminal proceedings both against black rebels suspected of sedition and treason and white officials suspected of illegal floggings and executions. These prosecutions have not received close attention

---

[1] *The Times* (9 Feb. 1866), 7.   [2] *The Times* (10 Feb. 1866), 9.
[3] Morrell, *British Colonial Policy*, 418–22; Ronald Hyam, *Britain's Imperial Century, 1815–1914: A Study of Empire and Expansion*, 2nd edn (London, 1993) 152; Susan H. Farnsworth, *The Evolution of British Imperial Policy during the Mid-Nineteenth Century: A Study of the Peelite Contribution, 1846–1874* (New York, 1992), 242–250; Heuman, '*The Killing Time*', 164–74. In these accounts, when the work of the JRC is evaluated, it is uniformly praised. Hyam called the final report of the JRC a 'masterly and notably impartial document'. Farnsworth thought the final report 'complete [and] balanced'.

from scholars.[4] In this regard, a number of additional questions require answers. What motivated the Colonial Office (with the support of the acting Governor) to commence criminal prosecutions? Who was selected for prosecution, and why? What role did the Jamaica Committee play in these matters? Were the accused permitted to rely on the Jamaica Indemnity Act? What was the attitude of Jamaican judges and juries to these cases? To what extent did the racial politics of the colony affect the outcome of prosecutions? Is it historically significant that the Government instigated these prosecutions?

In the opinion of Sir Henry Storks (the official who replaced Edward Eyre), the 'chief evil' in Jamaica, the factor which more than any other explained the violence there, was the 'absence of a general principle to abide by the laws'.[5] Storks' view was widely shared among the leaders of the Liberal Government. The idea of legality, more particularly of legal action and reform, predominated the Government's response to the Jamaica quandary. A quasi-judicial inquiry was begun; criminal prosecutions were started; the Jamaican constitution was over-hauled.[6] To the modern observer, to many contemporaries, the Government's obsession with things legal was more than passing strange. After all, in the 1860s Jamaica faced profound economic and social crises.[7] The sugar economy had collapsed, and nothing viable had taken its place. The colony was densely populated but desperately poor. Race relations were hopelessly poisoned. But the leaders of the imperial state in London either did not want – or did not know how – to respond to the Jamaican crisis at the level of political economy. What it thought to do, what it could do, was to consult lawyers and mount a series of legal initiatives.

I. The Jamaica Royal Commission

On 12 December the Government announced that the Queen would commission a general inquiry in Jamaica, that it would assemble there with all urgency, and that it would investigate both the causes of the rebellion and the circumstances of the suppression (including the execution of Gordon). The English press greeted this announcement with almost universal praise.[8] 'Reasonable Englishmen of all parties,' the *Daily Telegraph* maintained, 'must have received with satisfaction the news . . . that the Government had decided on appointing a Royal Commission to inquire into the recent proceedings in Jamaica.'[9] The *Fortnightly Review* observed that 'the action of the Government with regard to Jamaica has met with general

---

[4] For the best treatment, see Heuman, '*The Killing Time*', 174–7.

[5] *The Times* (29 Aug. 1866), 6.   [6] See Morrell, *British Colonial Policy*, 421, 427–32.

[7] For a contemporary survey of economic and social conditions in Jamaica in 1865, see *Westminster Review* 88 (July, 1868), 189–225.

[8] A few journals thought that the inquiry was both premature and founded on the regrettably *un*-Palmerstonian assumption that any beleaguered colonial governor was guilty until proved innocent. *Law Times* (30 Dec. 1865), 113.   [9] *Daily Telegraph* (3 Dec. 1865), 6.

approval . . . there is every desire that justice shall be done to all parties.'[10] In the opinion of the *Spectator,* the Government had moved 'with more promptitude than was expected, and with equal justice and caution'.[11] Although *The Times* was not entirely convinced of the need for an inquiry, it accepted that legally trained civilians should review the proclamation and implementation of martial law in Jamaica.[12] The recurrent theme of these editorials was that the Jamaican uprising had stained the honour of the country, and that a forthright investigation was an indispensable first step in removing the stain.[13] 'Lord Russell,' the *Athenaeum* stated on 16 December, 'has done something to calm the conscience of England.'

The JRC had been advertised as a 'full and impartial' investigation, and the Russell Government took pains to appoint to it men who would command respect across party and ideological lines. There were a number of reasons to take such pains. The first was that the Cabinet genuinely wanted to know what had happened in the colony. The second was that any (even subtle) attempts to rig the inquiry were certain to be detected, and with unhappy consequences for Russell's fragile governing coalition just when it hoped to rally support for a Reform Bill.[14] The third reason brings us back to the law. When it instituted the inquiry, the Government knew that it might uncover evidence of official wrongdoing. In fact, the instrument creating the JRC specifically mandated investigation of allegations that 'excessive and unlawful severity was used in such suppression'.[15] With these serious legal implications looming so large, the Government wanted to be sure that the JRC's work would be done methodically and fairly. It also wanted the final report to be seen in this light.

The position of President of the JRC, the Government decided, was to be filled by an interim governor. Little time was wasted in selecting Sir Henry

---

[10] 'Less we could not have expected from a ministry whose head is Earl Russell and one of whose members is William Ewart Gladstone.' *Fortnightly Review* (1 Jan. 1866), 363.

[11] *Spectator* (16 Dec. 1865), 1394.

[12] *The Times* (4 Jan. 1866), 8. Only the most fanatically Tory newspapers took issue with the inquiry, accusing the Liberals of having answered the 'dictation of the Radical school'. The *Morning Herald* (22 Dec. 1865) contended that Exeter Hall 'have intimidated Lord Russell into sending out a Royal Commission for the purpose of putting on his trial the Governor who has suppressed a formidable revolt in Jamaica . . .That inquiry, they are determined, shall result in the ruin of the governor, and in the complete exculpation of the innocent blacks. . .They have sent out counsel to take part against the governor, and talk of sending others to aid him and espouse the cause of convicted felons against the lawful authorities, whose prompt and energetic action saved Jamaica.'

[13] This decidedly was the opinion of George Lewes at the *Fortnightly Review* (15 Dec. 1865), 362: 'By this time all the world rings with the stories, supplied by the actors therein, of the "massacres" in Jamaica; and whatever the upshot may be, it will take years to efface the stain upon our reputation.'

[14] 'Reform, as our readers know, is not the only rock ahead of Ministers. There is Jamaica, which involves the fate of Mr. Cardwell as well as Mr. Eyre, and, if Mr. Cardwell, surely of the Cabinet.' *Fortnightly Review* (1 Jan. 1866), 760.

[15] As reprinted in W. F. Finlason, *A History of the Jamaica Case* (London, 1869), 57–8. The criminal prosecution of officials was so real a possibility that the Government sought legal advice on this eventuality two months before the JRC issued its Final Report. See replies of Crown Law Officers to Frederic Rogers, 24 Jan. 1866, *CO* 885/11. These replies and other legal correspondence between the Colonial Office and the Crown's lawyers is discussed below, Ch. 4.

Knight Storks – a former soldier and career imperial administrator – for the post.[16] Storks had impeccable credentials as an imperial troubleshooter.[17] In the previous twenty-five years he had served both in military and civilian capacities in the Cape Colony, Ionia, Turkey, and the Crimea. Storks was promoted to the rank of Major-General in 1862, and was appointed the Governor of Malta in 1864. He was widely regarded as a man of intelligence and tact. His appointment was praised across the political spectrum of the press. Here was a civil servant, as *The Times* put it on 13 December, who had precisely the skills needed to 'pacify Jamaica and to reconcile the demands of equity with the interests of public order'. Storks brought to the JRC, the *Quarterly Review* later observed, 'not only a familiarity with the routine of civil administration, but also an unaffected courtesy of manner and a singular tact in treating delicate and difficult questions'.[18]

The appointment of Storks got the JRC off to a promising start. However, by the time Storks sailed for Jamaica on 18 December, it was obvious that the Cabinet intended for the heaviest lifting to be done by two lawyers recruited from the senior ranks of the profession (on the recommendation of some senior judges).[19] But there was a catch point. It would not be easy to find qualified legal men willing to say farewell to family, friends, and fees while they spent three weeks at sea before toiling for untold months on an arduous, even harrowing assignment. The two legal positions on the JRC remained unfilled at the end of December 1865. 'There has been a good deal of difficulty in choosing Commissioners,' the *Pall Mall Gazette* reported on 2 January, 'in as much as a more delicate and difficult task has seldom been committed to such a body.' Finally, Cardwell's office succeeded in persuading two eminent barrister-magistrates, Russell Gurney M.P. and John Blossett Maule Q.C., to accept appointments to the JRC.

When he was approached for the JRC, Russell Gurney was the sitting Conservative member for Southampton. He was a barrister and, due to his appointment as Recorder for London, a seasoned criminal law judge. He was also, at £3,000 a year, the senior legal adviser of the City of London. When they learned of the Government's plans for Gurney, the City's mayor and aldermen were reluctant to grant him leave.[20] (If we can take him on his word, Gurney was equally reluctant to ask for it.) When Gurney accepted the appointment, he assured his constituents that the position 'was not sought for by me, and had I consulted my

---

[16] Storks previously had been High Commissioner of the Ionian Islands and Governor of Malta. See *DNB*, xviii, 1312–13; Lloyd, *Oxford DNB*, online 26595.

[17] 'Again and again, Sir Henry Storks has been called in to solve some difficulty which was not of his own making.' *The Times*, as reprinted in the *Manchester Guardian* (14 Dec. 1865), 4. Storks was seen to have done a particularly good job of coping with an independence movement on the Ionian islands. *The Times* (4 Jan. 1866), 8. For a less admiring assessment of Storks' career, see *Saturday Review* (16 Dec. 1865), 141.   [18] *Quarterly Review*, 120 (1866), 232.

[19] *Law Times* (6 Jan. 1866), 132–3.

[20] The Mayor and Aldermen of the City of London were very perturbed both to lose the services of Gurney for some months, and that the Government had made an agreement with Gurney without their knowledge or consent. *Daily Telegraph* (28 Dec. 1865), 2. *Law Times* (30 Dec. 1865), 113.

own ease or my own wishes, I should have persisted in declining it'.[21] There was
only one reason why he had changed his mind: 'the inquiry is one the importance
of which it would be difficult to overestimate. Feeling this, I thought that I was
not the person to decide upon my fitness to conduct it.'[22]

In many respects Gurney was ideally suited for the JRC, especially from the
perspective of the Cabinet. His Conservative credentials would deflect any suggestion that he was the Government's compliant servant. By the same token, Gurney
was also a cousin of the Quaker banker and Jamaica Committee member, Samuel
Gurney.[23] As the *Morning Herald* later commented, Russell Gurney was 'connected by family ties to the denomination most interested in proving [Eyre] in the
wrong'.[24] Thus, when his appointment was announced in early January 1866, it
was universally applauded. '[P]robably,' the *Pall Mall Gazette* opined, 'there is not
a man in the legal profession whose personal character has conciliated a greater
amount of respect.'[25] He would at once detect 'any inhumanity which might be
found in the conduct of the stronger race' while he resisted 'any maudlin sympathy with crime'. Here was a man, crucially, whose predilections about the Jamaica
affair – if indeed he had any – were not easily surmised.

A few days later the Government announced that John Blossett Maule, senior
barrister of the Midland Circuit and for the previous six years Recorder of Leeds,
had been selected as the third member of the JRC. In background, personality,
and training Maule strongly resembled Gurney, and his appointment was greeted
with similar enthusiasm. The *Law Times* noted that Maule had garnered the
'highest recommendation from the judges on the [Midland] circuit'.[26] Although
he had not cut his judicial teeth in London, the *Pall Mall Gazette* informed readers
that Maule had held a 'leading position as a criminal lawyer [in Yorkshire], which
gives as much and as varied experience of evidence and of crimes as London
herself'.[27] Maule's legal peers respected him, especially for his 'experience, his
strong common sense, and his remarkable vigour in whatever he undertakes'. Like
Gurney, he had defended, prosecuted, or adjudicated hundreds of criminal cases,
and in one of the country's largest cities. It also stood in Maule's favour that he was
not closely aligned with any political party.[28]

When Gurney and Maule sailed for Jamaica in the first week of January,
the consensus, even among those who (like the editor of the *Law Times*) objected
in principle to the inquiry, was that the JRC could not have been 'better
constituted'.[29] The three Commissioners, the *Daily Telegraph* contended, were

---

[21] *Law Times* (6 Jan. 1866), 132–3.   [22] Ibid.
[23] Although it was not a matter of comment, Gurney was connected by blood to Fitzjames
Stephen and the Clapham sect. Curthoys, *Oxford DNB*, online 11774.
[24] *Morning Herald* (20 June 1866), 4.   [25] *Pall Mall Gazette* (2 Jan. 1866), 1–2.
[26] *Law Times* (6 Jan. 1866), 125.   [27] *Pall Mall Gazette* (2 Jan. 1866), 1–2.
[28] One historian described Maule's politics as 'moderate Liberal'. See Knox, 'British Government', 881.
[29] *Law Times* (6 Jan. 1866), 125.

men 'in whose ability and character the public can put the fullest trust'.[30] The editor of the *Law Times* thought that in Gurney particularly, 'a better choice could not have been made. Mr. Russell Gurney is the best criminal Judge now upon the bench, *and the investigation is substantially into a criminal charge*' (italics added).[31] Even the rather jaded white commentators of Jamaica found little to complain about in the choice of Commissioners.[32]

In England and Jamaica there was a remarkably broad consensus that the JRC's mission was essentially forensic, and being so it was best completed by seasoned barristers, preferably judges. As the *Quarterly Review* later summarized the point: 'Mr. Gurney and Mr. Maule are lawyers, who bring to any investigation of facts the acuteness and precision which long practice at the Bar, and no small experience on the bench, make normal habits of mind.'[33] The leader in the *Saturday Review* agreed that the task of the Commissioners will 'be not only to collect evidence, but to sift it and to weigh it with patient impartiality which belongs exclusively to professional lawyers'.[34] As the *Saturday Review* conceded, the 'opinion of a layman, especially of a soldier, on the legality of Gordon's trial would be absolutely worthless'.[35] It was not lost on these observers that the JRC had not only an investigative but a judicial function. Questions of the legality of actions (the removal and court martial of Gordon was only the most frequently cited), and of potential culpability for actions, would inevitably be raised. Gurney and Maule, the *Pall Mall Gazette* contended, were 'excellently selected' because their credentials 'were rather those of the judge than the advocate'.[36] If it was inescapable that the conduct of English soldiers and officials was to be judged, then it was seen as vital that it be done by men schooled in that business. As the *Daily News* commented, the two lawyers were ideally suited to 'collect the information that shall enable the central administration to judge whether its subordinates should be supported or removed, or punished by further proceedings'.[37]

Interestingly, *The Times* endorsed an even stronger line. As 'barristers and criminal judges', it explained, Gurney and Maule harboured 'a natural bias in favour of the time-honoured system they administer, and a jealousy of that hateful thing almost unknown in English annals, called martial law'.[38] It was also observed that the JRC's senior secretary, Charles S. Roundell, was 'also a barrister, and the evidence to be brought before it will probably be in a great measure prepared by lawyers'. By *The Times*, by virtually all observers in the press, the

[30] *Daily Telegraph* (1 Jan. 1866), 4–5. [31] *Law Times* (30 Dec. 1865), 113.
[32] *Falmouth Post* (26 Jan. 1866), 2. A tireless defender of the white elite in Jamaica, the *Falmouth Post* assured readers that the Commissioners were certain to be 'strictly impartial and satisfactory'.
[33] *Quarterly Review* 120 (1866), 232.
[34] *Saturday Review* (16 Dec. 1865), 141. In the opinion of the *Daily Telegraph* (3 Dec. 1865), 6, lawyers should be represented on the JRC 'not because lawyers are naturally wiser than any other class...but because their intellects are trained by habitual practice to weigh the relative value of conflicting testimony'. [35] *Saturday Review* (16 Dec. 1865), 141.
[36] *Pall Mall Gazette* (2 Jan. 1866), 1–2. [37] *Daily News* (23 Dec. 1865), 3–4.
[38] *The Times* (4 Jan. 1866), 8.

thoroughly lawyered character of the inquiry was seen as right and proper. It would ensure that the 'constitutional principles' impugned by the Jamaica rising and suppression would be carefully reviewed, not by soldiers or politicians, but by 'minds eminently civilian in their training and modes of thought'.

The official mandate of the Queen for her Royal Commission was published on 30 December 1865. It recounted how 'grievous disturbances' had broken out in Jamaica, and how the disturbances had been suppressed 'with great loss of life, and it is alleged that excessive and unlawful severity has been used in the course of such suppression'. Consequently, a 'full and impartial inquiry' would be made into the 'origin, nature, and circumstances of the said disturbances, and with respect to the measures adopted in the course of their suppression'.[39] The inquiry would be conducted by 'persons not having borne a part in the government of our island during the existence of the said disturbances nor in the suppression thereof'. The two main tasks of the JRC were to 'gather evidence' and report 'any opinions which you think fit to express thereon'.

But what was meant by this? Were the Commissioners to offer 'opinions' on the moral, political, or criminal culpability of the individuals mentioned? *The Times* thought that the Government had selected lawyers in order to receive opinions on potential legal culpability.[40] 'For their own sake,' the paper stated, 'Governor Eyre and his subordinates must be virtually placed on their trial; they cannot be examined here, for all the evidence against them is in the West Indies'.[41] The *Law Times* agreed that the main task of the JRC was to determine whether criminal charges ought to be laid, and against whom.[42] The more liberal journals also endorsed this view, if with more righteous vigour.

II. The JRC in Jamaica: Getting Down to Business

The key figures of the JRC, including the Jamaica Committee's legal watchdogs, began to assemble in Kingston in mid-January. They were accompanied by some half-dozen 'special correspondents' from England's leading newspapers.[43] The correspondent for *The Times*, Frederic Clifford, devoted his first report to the (unexpectedly prompt) arrival on the island of Storks, and to the state of feeling in the colony toward the JRC.[44] His report made the plausible claim that the colony's populace was deeply polarized along racial lines.[45] Among the white community (a smattering of Baptist missionaries and activists excepted), 'No one of them entertains the least doubt that Mr. Eyre will be triumphantly "acquitted"'. Even

---

[39] As reprinted in Finlason, *History of the Jamaica Case*, 57–8.
[40] *The Times* (4 Jan. 1866), 8.   [41] Ibid. (13 Dec. 1865), 8.
[42] *Law Times* (30 Dec. 1865), 113.
[43] The *Daily Telegraph, Daily News, Morning Herald*, and *The Times* were among the newspapers who sent correspondents.   [44] *The Times* (30 Jan. 1866), 9.
[45] For a similar view, see *London Review* (3 Feb. 1866), 136–7.

those whites who had criticized Eyre before the rebellion 'now support him warmly'. In fact, Jamaican whites 'complained loudly that in England too little allowance has been made for the...danger to which the white population were hourly placed'. In this view, it was self-evidently the case that Eyre had saved the island from becoming another Haiti.

Clifford also reported that Kingston's black community was expressing equal (if more naive) confidence that the JRC would identify and punish those officials who had broken the law during the suppression. When Storks' ship arrived in port, the black men on the dockside 'shook hands and looked triumphant'.[46] Clifford, a man who entertained all of the conventionally bigoted assumptions about 'the negro's character',[47] was struck both by the unexpected 'intelligence' of many of the black men he met, and that these same men were 'saying loudly that Governor Eyre was to be hanged, and that the chief authorities here would be sent to the Penitentiary'. Both the black and the white populace of the colony, then, had invested considerable trust in the idea that the JRC would further justice.

For their part, the Jamaica Committee barristers Gorrie and Horne Payne were leaving nothing to chance. As neither man had any previous connection to the island or its people, they soon cultivated an alliance with William Morgan, the Baptist solicitor sent out to Jamaica by the Birmingham chapter of the BFASS.[48] Morgan provided an essential link to Jamaica's Baptist missionaries and black communities.[49] Within days of their arrival Gorrie and Horne Payne were besieged by black Jamaicans wanting legal advice and representation.[50] There was so much work of this kind that they retained (as Storks reported to Cardwell) 'two of the best attorneys in Kingston',[51] a coloured and Jewish lawyer, D. P. Nathan, and a white lawyer, S. C. Burke. (Ironically, both men had been members of the Council of War which in October 1865 had voted unanimously for the proclamation of martial law.)[52] They forged an alliance with William Phillippo,

---

[46] Ibid.

[47] Clifford was a veritable repository of racial stereotypes and cliches. He had not been in Jamaica ten days when he confidently reported that the blacks of Jamaica were, among other things, 'an excitable race' 'easily – too easily – wrought upon and led' 'liable to sudden and almost unaccountable excesses of rage' 'with many good qualities, crossed by much which requires humouring, management and firm control'. *The Times* (9 Feb. 1866), 7. It is understandable, then, that Clifford was so much admired by the editors of Jamaica's *Falmouth Post* (6 Mar. 1866), 2. But the correspondent of the *Daily Telegraph* (17 Mar. 1866), 7–8, also did not hide his contempt for 'negroes' and the self-appointed 'champions of sable humanity'. He assured his readers (7 Mar. 1866, 7) that 'the question, already closed among ethnologists, as to the inferiority of the negro, needs no reopening...he is capable of being trained...but he rarely if ever excels as a chief in command'.

[48] Hall, *Civilizing Subjects*, 410–11.

[49] His work was seen as so important to them that the JC's executive in London decided to assume responsibility for his expenses and fees. *JC Minutes*, 31 Jan. 1866.

[50] It was reported by the correspondent of the *Daily Telegraph* (13 Feb. 1865), 5–6, that Gorrie gave 'audience to large numbers of negroes every day' before the JRC's hearings commenced. See also Brereton, *Law, Justice and Empire*, 42.

[51] Storks to Cardwell, 6 Jan. 1866, Cardwell Papers, *CO* 30/48/43.

[52] Burke was himself called before the JRC to explain why he had urged Governor Eyre to proclaim martial law. *The Times* (12 Apr. 1866), 10. See also *JRC Report*, *PP* (1866), xxxi, Eyre,

an English-trained barrister (son of James Phillippo, a leading Baptist missionary) who had been retained by the white Baptist community.[53]

In despatching lawyers to Jamaica one of the main goals of the Jamaica Committee was to gather evidence for the future criminal prosecution of Governor Eyre (and his most culpable subordinates) for the murder of Gordon. 'Mr. Gordon's case', the Committee reminded Gorrie and Horne Payne soon after their arrival, 'has attracted the greatest attention in this country from his position and his name being known here, and we should be glad for the minutest information on the steps that were taken in his case.'[54] As we have seen, in England, the Committee's fund-raising drive was beset with problems;[55] more money would be raised if the Gordon case remained in the spotlight. Reversing earlier instructions, Gorrie now was advised that 'it may be important as soon as possible to institute criminal proceedings against some one or more of the military officers'.[56] The Committee's lawyers were to consult with local attorneys and advisers in order to proceed with charges as soon as they 'could be instituted with a reasonable hope of success'.

On 23 January, only a few days after the arrival of Gurney and Maule, the JRC commenced its official work in the 'cool, comfortable' executive council chamber of the government buildings in Spanish Town. According to the correspondent of *The Times*, the proceedings opened quietly, attracting 'no crowd, and little excitement'.[57] Storks began by reading aloud the Queen's Commission, and then attended to rules governing the press. (Newspapers could publish any evidence presented to the JRC except when that evidence was likely to prejudice a person who had not yet testified.) When Storks completed his opening remarks, Gorrie introduced himself and Horne Payne, informing the Commission that the two lawyers 'attended on behalf of Mrs. George W. Gordon and numerous other parties, who alleged they had suffered from those measures taken in suppressing the disturbances'. Phillippo made a similar introduction on behalf of his Baptist clients. With this Storks adjourned the hearings until the following day. But the reporter from *The Times* noted that after the first session of the JRC 'the *status* of the Bar before the Commissioners does not appear to have been quite settled'.[58] The crucial question of the *locus standi* of the unofficial barristers and attorneys had not yet been resolved. At the commencement of the second session, however, and before any important witnesses could be called, Gorrie applied for the right to cross-examine any evidence that bore directly on the legal interests of his clients.[59] A great deal turned on this application. If granted, the work of the JRC would be

---

Q. 46,578. Ironically, the two lawyers later complained of the miserly fees paid them by the Jamaica Committee. *Falmouth Post* (19 June 1866), 2; *JC Minutes*, 9 May 1866.

[53] See Hall, *Civilizing Subjects*, 194. Special correspondent of *The Times* (13 Feb. 1866), 9.
[54] *JC Minutes*, 31 Jan. 1866.
[55] See *CD*, 13 Jan. 1866, 16 Jan. 1866; *JC Minutes*, 15 Jan. 1866.   [56] Ibid.
[57] Correspondent of *The Times* (13 Feb. 1866), 9.   [58] Ibid.
[59] *Falmouth Post* (2 Feb. 1866), 2–3. See also *The Times* (3 Mar. 1866), 9.

slowed dramatically; witnesses were likely to be far more guarded in their testimony. On the other hand, if Gorrie's request was denied, the integrity and legitimacy of the commission would be called into question. Critics would plausibly claim that the Government was not serious about getting at the truth.

The Commissioners adjourned to deliberate. Upon their return, Storks informed the assembly that the JRC was 'not to be looked upon as acting for the Crown, but for all parties interested'.[60] In general, questions would be put to witnesses only by or through the Commission. However, in circumstances where testimony tended to incriminate a third party, that party would be 'allowed to test the accuracy of such evidence and to submit counter evidence in reply'.[61] Further, counsel would be welcome to *suggest* questions to the Commission. Although this ruling initially disappointed Gorrie, the Commission ultimately permitted the Jamaica Committee lawyers to put (or cause to be put) more than a thousand questions to witnesses.[62]

Acting Governor Storks kept a close eye on Gorrie and Horne Payne. He commented on this in a despatch to Cardwell of 6 February 1866.[63] Before the hearings began, he recalled, he had had some qualms about the fact that the two British barristers were being so zealous 'in preparing what may be called their "case"'.[64] When the hearings actually began, Storks admitted that he and his fellow Commissioners had also had 'some difficulty in defining the "status" of these gentlemen'. But soon thereafter Storks became confident that the lawyers 'now understand our mission and their position, and . . . we have had no more trouble with them'. For his part, Gorrie, only two weeks later, reported to London that he 'was on the best of terms with Sir Henry Storks and often dined at Government House'; in fact, he was also now so much at ease with Gurney and Maule that he felt he could 'make suggestions privately when he thought that things were going at all wrong'.[65] Whatever tension or misgivings that had existed at the beginning of the inquiry, it soon had given way to the fraternal customs of the bar.

Having established a working relationship with the lawyers from the Jamaica Committee, Storks tackled another thorny problem. When the Government drafted the Commission for the Jamaica inquiry, it neglected to invest it with the power to subpoena witnesses. (In England, a number of commentators observed that the Commission had created an interrogative body which had no compulsory interrogative power.)[66] This was a serious problem. Before Gurney and Maule left for Jamaica, rumours were already afoot that persons unknown had secured a legal opinion which advised that the 'civil and military officers' involved in the suppression of the Morant Bay rebellion could freely 'decline to appear before the JRC'.[67] If free to decline, many would doubtless do so.

---

[60] Ibid.   [61] Ibid.
[62] By rough count, in the first ten days of JRC hearings, Gorrie asked or prompted about 5 per cent (380) of the more than 9,000 questions put to witnesses. In the second ten days of hearings, Gorrie and Horne Payne asked 791 of 14,382 questions. In the final ten days of the hearings the Committee's lawyers asked no fewer than 1,500 of some 6,800 questions.
[63] Storks to Cardwell, 6 Feb. 1866, Cardwell Papers, *CO* 30/48/43.   [64] Ibid.
[65] *CD*, 2 Mar. 1866.   [66] See leader in *Daily News* (12 Feb. 1866), 4.   [67] Ibid.

After all, it was reasoned, the persons most likely to be asked awkward questions would have 'heard all sorts of unpleasant suggestions about the law of murder, the illegality of proclaiming martial law, and the fate of Gov. Wall'.[68] Those called to the hearing room clearly would not be keen to 'say anything whatever that may be used against [them] at a future time'. In its haste to start the Jamaica inquiry, the Cabinet appears not to have considered these procedural issues. The *Law Times* summed up the situation in this way: 'The truth, we believe, is that the Government have suddenly discovered that they have no power to issue a summons to examine on oath in the colony. It is doubtful that such a power exists in England; certainly it cannot exist in the colony without the concurrence of the colonial Legislature.'[69] The JRC, the *Pall Mall Gazette* reminded readers, was not invested with the power of a real court of law. The Commissioners, by the same token, 'are not committing magistrates [and] cannot examine witnesses on oath'.[70] The only way to cure this disability was for the Jamaica legislature – a body notoriously protective of the white elite – to pass a law. In the result, however, the Jamaican legislature, demoralized and facing extinction, lacked either the political will or coherence to rebuff Storks' official request for an enabling statute. Storks had arrived in Jamaica on 6 January.[71] The JRC got subpoena powers on 18 January.

But the mere fact that the JRC had been given subpoena powers did not mandate their use. 'It is extremely difficult to say,' the *Pall Mall Gazette* reflected on 2 January 1866, 'what they [the JRC] are to do when they get to Jamaica, and what exact form their investigations will take.' There were no established ground rules for such inquiries, and no means to account for local contingencies had rules existed. The Government had given Storks and his co-Commissioners a job to do, and then left them to do it. Had the Commissioners been of a mind either to skew or truncate the inquiry in some fashion – to refuse to hold hearings outside of Kingston or Spanish Town, for instance – there was nothing to stop them. But this is not what happened.

From the outset the JRC was determined to discover the pertinent facts of the rebellion and suppression, as perceived both by whites and blacks. In order to attain this goal, the Commission adopted a remarkably flexible approach. Its original plan, to gather evidence in chronological order, was quickly abandoned as impracticable.[72] Owing to the 'strangeness of the circumstances in which they were placed', the Commission decided to elicit evidence from such witnesses 'as were at hand'. In order that more witnesses (particularly among the black peasantry) might be heard, hearings were held at Morant Bay and other villages in the eastern parishes.[73] When one of the Committee's lawyers informed the

---

[68] *Pall Mall Gazette* (2 Jan. 1866), 1–2.   [69] *Law Times* (6 Jan. 1866), 125.
[70] *Pall Mall Gazette* (2 Jan. 1866), 1–2.   [71] Morrell, *British Colonial Policy*, 421.
[72] *JRC Report, PP* (1866), xxx, 505.
[73] According to the white press in Jamaica, however, 'Baptist Missionaries and radical Agitators' had been busy 'collecting money from an ignorant and easily deluded Peasantry' in order to subsidize travel to the JRC hearings. *Falmouth Post* (26 Jan. 1865), 2.

Commission that he had a list of 500 persons who wanted to testify to the 'excesses committed by magistrates, officers, soldiers, or Volunteers',[74] a compromise was hammered out. It being impractical for so many individual persons to be deposed, the Commission agreed that they would allot extra time to 'a selection of typical cases'.[75] In this way, the Commission ensured that it had garnered evidence on all of the major kinds of transgressions in all of the localities that had been under martial law. When it finished its work in March 1866 the JRC asserted, with credibility, that 'no material witness, of whatever colour or party, has been denied a patient hearing; no material evidence has been excluded by a too rigid circumspection'.[76] Under pressure of time, having to contend with uncomprehending, incomprehensible,[77] obstinate, or, in one notable case, even menacing[78] witnesses, the JRC questioned 730 people in the course of 60 hearings. Their testimony filled 1,100 large folio pages.[79] The documents and appendices of the final report filled another 600 pages. It took another 41 pages for the JRC to summarize its findings. And although some of these findings later attracted critics, its methods and tenacity in fact-gathering did not. Even the lawyer–scrutineers retained by the Jamaica Committee, the men in the best position to know, did not dispute the fundamental integrity of the investigative process. They did not complain because they had little to complain of.

While Gorrie and Horne Payne were not able freely to cross-examine witnesses, for the most part they were content with the interrogations undertaken by Gurney and Maule. In most instances, too, the Committee's lawyers were able either to suggest questions or put some questions directly to witnesses. Occasionally, when for instance Gorrie and Horne Payne were not given free rein to cross-question Governor Eyre, there was friction in the hearing room. But even in that case Gorrie was permitted to put a limited number of questions to Eyre, and later to undertake more uninhibited questioning of the military officers who tried and executed Gordon. Gorrie was also allowed to put a series of probing questions both to Colonel Thomas Hobbs and Gordon Duberry Ramsay, two of the most ruthless field officers during the martial law.[80] When it is remembered that the JRC was not a criminal trial of accused persons, the latitude given to the Jamaica

---

[74] See account of the correspondent of *The Times* (17 Mar. 1866), 9.   [75] Ibid.

[76] *JRC Report, PP* (1866), xxx, 506.

[77] So that the black Jamaican dialect could be better understood, the JRC employed black policemen as translators.

[78] The most menacing undoubtedly was Major-General Forbes Jackson, a Jamaican magistrate who had been a British officer in India during the Mutiny. It is obvious that Jackson did not disguise his utter contempt for the JRC, its Commissioners, and proceedings. Before he gave testimony, he complained bitterly of having been seated between 'two niggers' (policemen). He gesticulated so angrily during one answer that a revolver was flung out of his clothes on to the floor. When pressed to answer a question he threatened to leave the hearing room. At another point he referred to Russell Gurney as a 'mere drawing room man', and proudly offered that if any militia officers were called butchers, that he was a 'double butcher': *Daily News* (3 Mar. 1866), 7–9; *John Bull* (10 Mar. 1866).

[79] *Quarterly Review* 120 (1866), 233; *Dublin Review* 7 (Oct. 1866), 362.

[80] By rough count, Gorrie put some 175 questions to Hobbs (see especially, *JRC Minutes, PP* (1866), xxxi, Q. 37,267–326), and Payne put at least 11 questions to Ramsay (ibid., Q. 31,274–643).

Committee lawyers was generous. Although Gorrie and Horne Payne could not fully deploy the techniques (leading questions, the laying of verbal traps, etc.) of the trial cross-examination, they were able to pin witnesses down to specific accounts of what they had and had not done.[81] In the final result, moreover, the hearings generated evidence enough to support criminal indictments of over a dozen military and civilian officials, including Edward Eyre.

III. 'Little Facts': Investigating the Jamaica Terror

Of the hundreds of witnesses heard by the JRC, two deponents, Eyre and his Attorney General, Alexander Heslop, are of special importance to the jurisprudence of political and military power in the mid-Victorian period. Between them the two officials had made most of the critical decisions regarding the proclamation and implementation of martial law in Jamaica. For its part, the JRC comprehended that they had a mandate to explore these decisions, and their basis in law. The record of their interviews with Eyre and Heslop, when supplemented by official despatches (which were also closely examined and published by the JRC), underscores the prominence of legal ideas and concerns at a moment of colonial crisis.

This is a propitious moment briefly to discuss the background and personality of the man who, from November 1865 until July 1868, was never far from the vortex of bitter political and legal conflict. Edward John Eyre has been the subject of admiring biographies,[82] hagiographies,[83] unyielding attacks,[84] character sketches,[85] and cultural analyses.[86] The basic facts of his life are well known. Eyre was born into the family of an unprosperous Yorkshire clergyman in 1815. After an indifferent career at a number of nondescript public schools, he emigrated to Australia while still in his teens. After some success in sheep-ranching, Eyre devoted time and money to a number of daring expeditions into the outback of southwestern Australia. While these journeys did not accomplish anything of great importance, their sheer audacity brought Eyre to the attention of colonial officials. In time Eyre was appointed to the post of 'Protector of the Aborigine' in

---

[81] As mentioned, Gorrie reported that he had forged a very constructive working relationship with the JRC's English barristers, Gurney and Maule. On one occasion Gorrie complained that the brother-in-law of Ramsay had been employed as one of the solicitors to the JRC. This complaint, Gorrie reported to the Jamaica Committee, resulted in the 'dismissal of that obnoxious individual'. On another occasion, Gorrie suggested to Gurney that he had tended in his examinations 'to lean toward the white witnesses while pressing the blacks as if he believed that they alone were speaking falsely'. This suggestion, it was noted, had led to 'an evident improvement'. *CD*, 2 March 1866.

[82] For the most intelligent and comprehensive work, see Dutton, *Hero as Murderer*.

[83] Hamilton Hume, *The Life of Edward John Eyre* (London, 1867).

[84] Lord Olivier, *The Myth of Governor Eyre* (London, 1933).

[85] Jan Morris, 'Eyre: A Portrait', 35 *Encounter* (1970), 3–13.

[86] Catherine Hall, 'Imperial Man: Edward Eyre in Australasia and the West Indies 1833–66', in Bill Schwarz (ed.), *The Expansion of England: Race, Ethnicity and Cultural History* (London, 1996), 130–70.

South Australia, a job which (by some accounts) he undertook with considerable sympathy for native people.[87] His perceived success in this post led to a series of colonial appointments spanning the next twenty years. By 1864, the year he was sent to Jamaica as Acting Governor, Eyre was a seasoned imperial functionary.

As an administrator Eyre was undoubtedly conscientious and disciplined, but also anxious and brittle. More damagingly, Eyre lacked the depth of intelligence, education, and innate self-confidence to overcome a sorely felt sense of social inferiority when among high-born gentlemen.[88] Eyre's manner and bearing generally inspired respect but not admiration. Like many self-made men, he was never at ease with authority or power. Eyre was easily offended and, as was frequently the case in the period of the post-rebellion controversy, prone to bouts of self-pity.[89]

In the twenty years prior to the Morant Bay rebellion, Eyre had striven to make himself useful to the empire. In some ways, as historian Catherine Hall has observed, Eyre had become 'imperial man', the personification of the empire's administrative ideology.[90] The idea of racial hierarchy – that the white-skinned peoples were preordained by nature and God to dominate the black-skinned – was the central pillar of this ideology. By 1865, the comparatively benign racial paternalism of Eyre's young manhood had been displaced by a far less benign set of racial dogmas. When he was Governor of Jamaica Eyre believed that black people were incorrigibly idle and barbarous, and that they could be ruled only by coercion or the threat of coercion. This racialist dogma was so thoroughly embraced by Eyre that in official despatches he cited it as the first justification of martial law: 'First. That the negroes from a low state of civilization and being under the influence of superstitious feelings could not properly be dealt with in the same manner as might the peasantry of a European country.'[91]

This digression will be brought to a close with a final comment. If Edward Eyre might usefully be understood as 'imperial man',[92] he was a member of the subspecies *Homo angliensis*. Although he agreed that the white man needed to rule the black with sternness, Eyre never forgot that he was an *English* colonial governor whose power was limited by law. Even when Eyre received word that seventeen white people, a magistrate included, had been killed by an organized force of black rebels, he did not presume that he could use force with impunity. In fact, the evidence is clear that Eyre had been mindful of the legal implications of his decisions – even that he himself might be held to account for them – at all pivotal moments of the suppression. In January 1866, suspended from his duties, facing a formal interrogation, Eyre had reason to be apprehensive.

---

[87] For this view, see Dutton, *Hero as Murderer*, 153–4.

[88] In 1866, Acting Governor Storks noted of Eyre that among the reasons that it was inadvisable that Eyre should be reinstated as Governor was that he was 'perhaps not high bred enough for the planters, people who are not gentlemen, a group of "snobs" in other words'. Storks to Cardwell, 6 Feb. 1866, Cardwell Papers, *CO* 30/48/43.   [89] Morris, 'Eyre: A Portrait', 6.

[90] Hall, 'Imperial Man', *passim*.   [91] Eyre to Cardwell, *JRC Eyre Papers, PP* (1866), xxx, 15.

[92] Hall, 'Imperial Man', *passim*.

Eyre was called before the JRC on 31 January, precisely one week after hearings had commenced. Storks found Eyre to be cooperative if wary.[93] On first meeting Eyre, Storks was favourably impressed, commenting that he was 'a Gentleman, and I should say a very energetic and conscientious man'.[94] While Eyre appeared 'very unwell' physically and mentally, any fears that he would attempt to obstruct the work of the JRC were quickly allayed. As for his wariness, this was both understandable and prudent. After news of the suppression reached England, for Eyre things had gone from bad to worse. Cardwell's despatches were sceptical, even aggressive. He was suspended from his office. With regard to the JRC, it was obvious that it had not been sent to Jamaica simply to exonerate the Governor. And then there were the Jamaica Committee barristers. What was their purpose if not to assemble a criminal case against the former Governor? Would Eyre's testimony before the JRC contribute to this result? These questions must have crossed Eyre's mind when, like all of the other witnesses, he was cautioned by the Commission that 'no witness was obliged to answer any question likely to incriminate himself, and that if he did answer . . . it might be used against him'.[95] Eyre chose to answer every question, if sometimes only evasively.[96]

Until the day of Eyre's testimony, the proceedings of the JRC had been only lightly attended by spectators. Eyre's appearance drew a far larger audience, some sixty people, mostly coloured or black.[97] Eyre arrived with the Bishop of Kingston and some assorted 'friends', but without a lawyer.[98] Out of respect for his position, the Commissioners stood when he entered the hearing room, and when he left ninety minutes later.[99] After the caution was read, Eyre was questioned about two general issues. The first was purely factual. What had the Governor done to suppress the insurrection? The second concerned lawful authority. What justification, that is, what *legal* justification could the Governor offer for his decisions, in particular, for the proclamation and duration of martial law, and for the arrest and execution of Gordon?

The Commission began with Eyre's decisions on the first news of violence at Morant Bay. Here Eyre was asked to do little more than verify the authenticity of the JRC's copies of the despatches that Eyre had received and sent.[100] As Eyre gave his answers, one of the recurring themes was that all key decisions had been made upon consultation with his legal and political advisers. Eyre explained how von Ketelholdt's call for military aid had reached him on the morning of 11 October and how, in response, he summoned his Executive Committee and Heslop, the

---

93 Storks to Cardwell, 6 Feb. 1866, Cardwell Papers, *CO* 30/48/43.
94 Storks to Cardwell, 7 Jan. 1866, Cardwell Papers, *CO* 30/48/42.
95 As quoted in the *Manchester Guardian* (3 Mar. 1866), 5.
96 It is possible that Eyre felt safe in answering the questions because he believed that he would be shielded from legal culpability by the indemnity statute passed by the Jamaica Assembly after martial law ended. Eyre made inquiries about the legal effects of the disallowance of the indemnity statute by the Colonial Office. See Storks to Cardwell, 7 Apr. 1866, *CO* 137/405.
97 *The Times* (3 Mar. 1866), 9.   98 *Daily News* (3 Mar. 1866), 7–9.
99 *The Times* (3 Mar. 1866), 5.
100 As reported by the correspondent of *The Times* (3 Mar. 1866), 9.

Attorney General. Only 'with their concurrence', had Eyre despatched orders to his senior military officers.[101] The flow of reports that Eyre received in these hours all signalled that a 'very serious rebellion had broken out'.[102] Eyre met with his advisers again that night. The result, Eyre testified, 'was that *we* considered it expedient that martial law should be declared' (emphasis added).[103] At this point, Eyre was advised by Heslop that a proclamation of martial law could only be issued with the approval of a 'Council of War' consisting of the Governor, privy councillors, Assemblymen, and the senior law and military officers of the colony. In an effort to bolster the legitimacy of this body, Eyre (and later, Heslop) asserted that it comprised 'nearly equal numbers from all three leading classes, white, coloured, and Jews, and representing fairly all shades of politics'.[104] Martial law was not proclaimed until the Council met and debated the question on the morning of 12 October, and only after the Attorney General and the Chief Justice (Bryant Edwards) agreed that it was urgently necessary.[105] The only point that had been much debated was the scope of the proclamation, more particularly, whether civilian jurisdiction was to be superseded in Kingston. In the end, Eyre decided that he 'did not think it absolutely necessary'.[106] This decision later had serious repercussions in the case of George Gordon.

The JRC was keenly interested in the question of the chain of command on the island during martial law. What were the standing orders of the officers in executing martial law? Who had given what orders, and to whom? When questioned on these points, Eyre distanced himself from the specific actions of the colony's senior military officers. After he signed the martial law proclamation, Eyre testified, he did not presume to interfere with how the professional military men did their jobs in the field. Eyre's belief, one backed by his law officers, was that 'during martial law the supreme power was vested in the military authorities'.[107] Eyre described how he had 'directed all the movements of the troops while [he] was with them; but [how] with the subsequent details I have nothing to do'.[108] This was a stance which contradicted Eyre's private attestation to Cardwell of his complete moral and legal responsibility for what was done in the suppression.

Gurney also questioned Eyre on the subject of the duration of martial law. Implicit in this questioning was that the *undue* prolongation of martial law was unwise if not illegal. Gurney asked Eyre to 'state [his] reasons' for keeping martial law in place for 'nearly a fortnight' after (many reports indicated) the rebellion had

---

[101] In fact, however, General O'Connor learned of the outbreak before and independently of the the Governor, and issued the order for troops to sail for Morant Bay while Eyre was still in transit. *JRC Minutes*, Q. 3873. See Eyre's testimony, ibid., Q. 3860-2.

[102] Ibid., Q. 46,578. The seriousness of the violence at Morant Bay was confirmed to Eyre by a naval officer on the evening of 12 October. See ibid., Q. 3902.   [103] Ibid., Q. 3881.

[104] Eyre made this point in his second session before the JRC. Ibid., 46,578.

[105] Ibid., Q. 3894–6. (There is no record that D. P. Nathan, the coloured Jewish lawyer later arrested as a conspirator, objected to the proclamation.)

[106] Ibid., Q. 3955–7. (See also discussion of Q. 46,578, below.)   [107] Ibid., Q. 3972.

[108] Ibid.

been crushed. In his response Eyre described how in the days at issue 'there were still large numbers of rebels in custody who had not been dealt with, and because there were apprehensions of serious disturbances in other districts'.[109] When asked for the evidence that corroborated these 'apprehensions', Eyre referred rather vaguely to communications from 'various persons'. Gurney pressed Eyre to reveal whether he had had 'any official report' warning of renewed rebel activity. We detect discomfort when Eyre invoked a faulty memory and then referred obscurely to the accumulation of numerous 'little facts' all of them 'indicatory that the country was very unsettled'.[110] Still unsatisfied, the JRC asked for the 'large number of reports' that Eyre alleged to have collected on this point. He offered none.[111]

Eyre's travails were not over. The next subject of inquiry was the 'case of Mr. Gordon'. Gurney quickly established that Gordon had been arrested on Eyre's personal order, and in a place – Kingston – still under the jurisdiction of the civilian courts. When asked to justify this arrest, Eyre again referred to 'little facts' that he 'had heard from every quarter' that Gordon, beyond question an intimate of Bogle's, 'had been the prime instigator of the outbreak' in St. Thomas-in-the-East.[112] Eyre thought it important to note that the 'same opinion was universally entertained in Kingston'. Warming to the subject, he also reported how a number of men, themselves facing the gallows for treason, had identified Gordon as their leader. When asked for the names of these men, Eyre, again, could not provide a single one. After a few more perfunctory inquiries, Eyre was invited to retire. The entire session did not last two hours.

On some vital points, especially with respect to the continuation of martial law, his testimony had been damagingly vague. Eyre appears to have realized this. Seven weeks later, and on his insistence, Eyre made a second appearance before the JRC. In his opening address he stated that as 'the labours of the Commissioners [were] drawing near to a close...I am desirous of giving further evidence'.[113] During his first visit before the panel, Eyre explained, he had 'had to refer to a great many documents, dates, names and circumstances, and it is very important I think that my statement should now be made in connected form, uninterrupted by cross-questions'. Eyre then told the Commission that he desired to read a sworn statement into the record, along with a large sheaf of supporting documents, and then to be 'cross-questioned upon any part of it'. The JRC acceded to this request, but transparently the Governor was attempting to effect damage control. It is obvious that Eyre thought that the JRC mattered, and that if he did not make a strong case for himself, that it would continue to matter. Eyre thought this strongly enough that he had sought assistance in assembling the documentary materials for the second hearing.[114] He wanted them to prove a

---

[109] *JRC Minutes*, Q. 3986.   [110] Ibid., Q. 3986–9.
[111] Some were, as Eyre admitted, only 'verbal communications'. Ibid., Q. 3990–2.
[112] Ibid., Q. 4004.   [113] Ibid., Q. 981.
[114] By this time the colonial government had retained the services of the Jamaican barrister R. J. Walcott to defend the interests of 'Eyre and the Executive Committee'. *The Times*

critical point: that prior to the outbreak at Morant Bay, more emphatically after the first white blood was shed, 'all respect for constituted authority had been undermined, rights of property and law were set at defiance, and it was clear that only the most stringent measures could save the colony from impending anarchy and ruin.'[115] These 'actual circumstances' which Eyre had faced in Jamaica, he asserted, were 'greatly misunderstood in England, and the steps taken by the local Government were grossly misrepresented'.[116]

This was especially true concerning the subject of martial law. In revisiting this point, Eyre strove to demonstrate that on learning of the rebellion it was 'at once his duty to proclaim martial law', and that this decision had been unanimously supported by the Council of War which was comprised in 'nearly equal numbers from all the leading classes, white, coloured, and Jews'.[117] Eyre was equally adamant that given his 'great anxiety' for the safety and security of the island as a whole, it had also been 'a matter of essential policy' to continue martial law for a month ending 13 November. These claims were substantiated by a large sheaf of letters from sundry parish officials. When these were admitted to the record, Eyre requested to file the statements of 'parties of position and influence' (statements written *after* the suppression) to justify why it had been necessary to retain martial law for a month.[118] To that point, the Commissioners had been indulgent of Eyre. On this matter, they dug in their heels: letters written after the period of martial law would not be received in evidence, 'as they would only be expressions of opinion upon the subject as to which they (the Commissioners) had to decide'.[119] These exertions took up all the JRC's time on 20 March. The cross-examination of Eyre and his evidence was adjourned to the next day.

On the second day the Commissioners finally began to lose patience with the ex-Governor. Once again Eyre tried to introduce hearsay evidence – the testimonials of various Jamaican whites – that he had faced a widespread conspiracy to overthrow the colonial government. When the panel would not admit these documents, Eyre tried to read them into the record. Exasperated, Storks finally admonished Eyre to 'endeavour, in the course of [his] remarks, to distinguish between what is argument and what is evidence'.[120] But when Eyre persisted, the Commissioners recessed to confer privately. When they reconvened, Eyre was told that he might allude to documents 'upon which [his] judgment was founded', but he was not to offer his opinion as to why these documents were reliable. The Governor also was to desist from making 'speeches'. In response Eyre protested that he was 'in the position of an accused person' and that he ought to be given 'an opportunity of stating in his own words the ground of his action and the justification of it'.[121] Eyre was not persuaded by the Commission's assurances

(3 Mar. 1866), 9. It is not known whether Eyre consulted with Walcott about his second appearance before the JRC.

[115] *JRC Minutes*, 989.   [116] Ibid.   [117] Ibid. Q. 46,578.
[118] Ibid., Q. 46,588–9.   [119] Ibid., Q. 46,590.   [120] Ibid., Q. 46,608.
[121] Ibid., Q. 46,623.

to the contrary: 'I think the tenor of the Jamaica Royal Commission,' he stated, 'certainly the voice of public opinion in this country and in England, indicates that I am virtually upon my trial, although not in so many words.'[122]

The remainder of the session was devoted to the arrest, trial, and execution of Gordon. On this sensitive subject Eyre was questioned, rather briefly and gingerly, by Gurney. The tenor of Eyre's evidence was that Gordon had been arrested on good information that he had committed high treason in St. Thomas parish, a place that was put under martial law. It was therefore correct that his fate had been decided by a military tribunal in that parish. At this juncture, Gorrie stood up to insist that he be given the opportunity to 'examine His Excellency further with reference to Gordon's case'.[123] Gurney replied that Gorrie could submit a list of questions so that the Commissioners might consider 'how those questions bore upon the inquiry', and whether they should be put to the witness. Gurney reiterated that the Commission was not 'testing the guilt of anybody', and that it was unwilling therefore to sanction a thoroughgoing cross-examination. On hearing this answer Gorrie petulantly remarked that 'if he could not cross-examine Mr. Eyre directly upon the Gordon case, he should put no further questions at all respecting it'. An examination that had been scheduled to last the entire day was thus completed inside of an hour. Eyre did not return for further questioning. Having put in his evidence, Eyre declined any further participation in the inquiry.[124]

When it is looked at as a whole, Eyre's experience before the JRC was neither particularly alarming nor reassuring. The Commissioners had not questioned him aggressively, and had not permitted Gorrie to do so.[125] By the same token, Eyre had been questioned enough, and was awkward enough in his own defence, to reveal his vulnerability. Now it was a matter of record that the Governor had stood by passively when he knew that atrocities were being committed in the name of the Crown. It was also clear that Eyre had personally overseen the arrest and transportation (to courts martial) of a number of British subjects who later were beaten, executed, or both, without benefit of trial. The execution of Gordon, more pointedly, had not been convincingly explained or justified. Eyre had left this vital task to his former Attorney General.

Alexander Heslop is a fascinating, if nebulous, Jamaica character. In some striking ways, he was the alter ego of George Gordon. Like Gordon, Heslop was a 'coloured' man, born of a white planter father and a slave (or ex-slave) mother in 1818.[126] Unlike Gordon, however, Heslop never deviated from his alignment

---

[122] *JRC Minutes*.   [123] *The Times* (3 Mar. 1866), 10.

[124] Storks to Cardwell, 6 Feb. 1866, Cardwell Papers, *CO* 30/48/43.

[125] Interestingly, Gorrie did not complain about the decision of the JRC to his retainers in England. He later suggested questions concerning the arrest of Dr. Bruce. *JRC Minutes*, Q. 4037–43.

[126] For Heslop's biography, see his obituary in the Jamaica *Daily Gleaner* (1 May 1879). The *Falmouth Post* (23 Feb. 1866), 2, emphasized that a number of educated coloured men like Heslop held high office in Jamaica. This was offered as proof that racial hatred, at least toward educated persons of colour, was not much in evidence in the colony.

with Jamaica's ruling elite. In the 1830s Heslop was expensively educated in England. After graduating from Oxford in 1840, he married the daughter of an English army officer and became a student member of the Inner Temple. When he was called to the Bar in 1844, Heslop returned to Jamaica to practice law. From 1849 to 1859, Heslop held a seat in the Colonial Assembly (ironically enough, for St. Thomas-in-the-East). From 1855 to 1871 – that is, for the ten years before and six years after the Morant Bay rising – he held the office of Attorney General.[127] In October 1865 Heslop was a seasoned lawyer and colonial official. It would seem fair to venture of Heslop that in regard to Jamaican law and government he knew as much as any man then alive. For this reason Heslop had been one of the first Jamaican officials to be called before the JRC.

When read the caution on 14 February 1866, Heslop declared, with detectable defensiveness, that 'having nothing to conceal, I shall feel no difficulty in answering any question which is at all pertinent to this inquiry'.[128] The JRC questioned Heslop on two subjects: on the law of martial law in Jamaica generally, and on Heslop's role in the suppression specifically. With respect to the general question, Heslop began with an overview of Jamaica's historical preoccupation with questions of race, demography, and internal security. He described how martial law, while an extraordinary and outmoded device in England, was a 'normal provision' of Jamaica legislation and had been so from the beginning of British dominion there in the late seventeenth century.[129] After all, he explained, Jamaica had been settled by small numbers of white men who imported large numbers of black slaves. There was never a time, even more acutely after the black revolution in nearby Haiti, when Jamaica's scattered whites did not fear extermination by its enslaved blacks. According to Heslop, one of the unchanging objects of Jamaican law had been 'to put strong powers in the hands of the Government because the free population was a very small fraction compared with the mass of the population'.[130] The emancipation of the slaves, he further offered, had only exacerbated the sense of vulnerability felt by the small white community.[131] Jamaica's robust security law had been born of these hard political facts.

The JRC asked Heslop to describe the legal framework within which Governor Eyre and his officers suppressed the Morant Bay rebels. As senior law officer in the colony at a moment of crisis, Heslop's opinion was of obvious importance. But when the Commission pressed him for detailed technical information on martial law, Heslop grew irritated and impatient.[132] The Commissioners decided to hold the line of questions in abeyance, and to ask Heslop about the legal advice he had given to Eyre before and during the suppression. The Attorney General explained how on 11 October 1865, only hours after von Ketelholdt's last message was

---

[127] Gad J. Heuman, *Between Black and White: Race, Politics, and the Free Coloreds in Jamaica, 1792–1865* (Westport, Conn., 1981), 61.   [128] *JRC Minutes*, 321.

[129] Ibid., Q. 16,200.   [130] Ibid., Q. 16,245.   [131] Ibid., 321.

[132] When pressed for more detail on the subject of martial law, Heslop finally tersely remarked that 'I have now stated all that I am prepared to say upon the question.' Ibid., Q.16,247.

received at Spanish Town, he had been summoned to a meeting of Eyre and General O'Connor.[133] The main topic of discussion was martial law, and the law and procedures governing its proclamation. As a result of this meeting, Eyre issued an order for the Council of War to convene the next morning. Heslop remained fully convinced of the legitimacy of this body, and its recommendations. He described the Council as a 'perfect mixture of all political parties, men of all shades of colour and all shades of local politics'.[134] He remembered that it was agreed unanimously that the situation was grave enough to justify a proclamation of martial law in the six parishes of the County of Surrey.[135] The single point of debate was whether the proclamation should include the city and parish of Kingston. According to Heslop, he (with Chief Justice Edwards[136]) strongly urged that Kingston be *excluded* from the proclamation.[137] Had it been otherwise, Heslop recalled stating, it would have 'paralysed the commerce of the whole country'. Eyre concurred, and it was then resolved that martial law would last for one month commencing 12 October, and would apply in all of Surrey except Kingston. Heslop himself proceeded to draft the proclamation.

The JRC eventually came to the more contentious subject of the courts martial, and especially the court martial and execution of Gordon. According to Heslop's evidence, on 13 October he had been invited by the Governor to travel with him by steamer to Morant Bay.[138] Martial law was proclaimed immediately upon the Governor's arrival. Prisoners already had been taken and collected, and the courts martial were convened on 14 October. Heslop then revealed that in his capacity as a militia captain he himself had been a member of the court martial on the first day. He had been so ill during the proceeding, in fact, that he heard evidence while lying prone on a mat. In all, Heslop participated in the trials of ten black persons, nine men and a woman, every one charged with treason and murder in the attack on the Morant Bay courthouse. Seven of the accused, Heslop recalled, were tried 'all at once'.[139] Four men were sent to the gallows. The woman's life was spared on the pragmatic grounds that her execution might incite rebels still at large.[140] Heslop assured the JRC that the charges against suspected rebels had been proved as conclusively as 'in any ordinary court of justice'.[141] All of the accused, the woman included, had been proven to be 'guilty participators and actual actors in the murderous atrocities'.

After some digression on other issues, the Attorney General was asked some more searching questions, some by Gorrie, about the legal character of martial law, and of the charges that had been levied against prisoners. Had they been tried as prisoners of war or as criminals who had broken civilian law? Heslop answered

---

[133] *JRC Minutes*, Q.16,174.   [134] Ibid., Q. 16,199.   [135] Ibid., Q. 16,175.
[136] Ibid., Q. 16,189.
[137] Ibid., Q. 16, 193. In response to Q.16,308 Heslop responded that 'Martial law … is one of the worst political evils; and I did not think it ought to be extended over an area larger than that where the actual outbreak had taken place.'   [138] Ibid., Q. 16,248.
[139] Ibid., Q. 16,266.   [140] Ibid., Q. 16,268.   [141] Ibid., Q. 16,267.

that he 'tried them under what is called martial law, which I take is the law of self-defence'.[142] He then stated that martial law was no more or less than 'the law of resisting force by force'.[143] For reasons that are not clear, neither the Commissioners nor Gorrie interrogated Heslop on the point. The subject of martial law, as well as the matter of Heslop's personal involvement in the first courts martial, were left behind without further inquiry. The JRC did not ask Heslop to comment on such matters as the admissibility and weight of the evidence he had heard, or whether the various accused had been afforded help in making out defences. The question of the procedural fairness of these trials was not revisited even when Heslop revealed that Baron von Ketelholdt (and a number of other persons who had been killed by the mob at Morant Bay) had been Heslop's 'personal friends'.[144] When he was asked about the arrest, court martial, and execution of Gordon, Heslop had a convenient answer: he simply had not been consulted on the legality (or otherwise) of any of these steps.[145] But, again, the JRC did not probe. It is not easy to say why this was the case. In fact, the despatches that Eyre wrote to Cardwell during and after the JRC hearings point to Heslop's much deeper, if indirect, involvement in a number of controversial events, the execution of Gordon included.[146] In this regard, Heslop was treated even more delicately than the former governor.

The Commission was rather harder on soldiers. Brigadier-General Abercrombie Nelson, commander of the Queen's forces at Morant Bay, and his subaltern, Lieutenant Herbert Brand, were both summoned to testify. Nelson was surprisingly forthcoming, especially in light of the fact that one Jamaica militia officer, Duberry Ramsay, already had been charged with the murder of a prisoner held during the period of martial law. Nelson was the ranking military officer at Morant Bay during the period of martial law. Brand was one of his subalterns. On Nelson's orders, Brand presided over the court martial, conviction, and condemnation of Gordon. We have seen that, in the eyes of the English political class Gordon's arrest and execution was the single most visible and fractious episode of the Jamaica affair. It was the episode which most cried out for legal justification and, in the absence of justification, would most cry out for punishment. For these reasons the examination by the JRC of Nelson and Brand was always likely to be among the pivotal moments of the inquiry.

Nelson had returned to England in December 1865, only to be ordered back to Jamaica two weeks later. If the army attempted to shield him from the prying questions of the JRC, it did not succeed. He was interrogated by the JRC over a series of days in early March 1866. The main subject of inquiry was his role in the court martial and execution of Gordon. Nelson recounted how as the commanding officer at Morant Bay, he had received Gordon as a prisoner to be tried by

---

[142] Ibid., Q. 16,388 and *passim*.
[143] The *Falmouth Post* (23 Feb. 1866), 2, noted with 'much pleasure' that Heslop's testimony corroborated the 'views we have often expressed'. [144] *JRC Minutes*, Q. 16,318.
[145] Ibid. Q. 16281–82. [146] These issues will be explored at length in Ch. 3 of this book.

court martial for treason. He then described how he had afforded Gordon very little scope to mount a defence, and had personally intervened to reject the attempt by a Jamaican solicitor (Wemyss Anderson) to assist Gordon in his defence.[147] The JRC then moved on to the circumstances of Gordon's execution. Gordon had been tried and condemned on 21 October 1865, a Saturday, but was not executed until the following Monday. The JRC (rather charitably) suggested to Nelson that the reason for the delay might have been 'to give Gordon the opportunity of being reprieved'.[148] Nelson did not hesitate to reject this suggestion. He had delayed Gordon's execution for the simple reason that he did not like to execute men on Sunday. As Nelson had informed General O'Connor, there being 'no *military* reason why the sentence should not be deferred', he simply decided to postpone Gordon's execution until Monday.[149] Both the sentence and the short delay in carrying it out had been endorsed by O'Connor and Eyre.[150] When the JRC persisted in suggesting that the possibility of a late reprieve had *also* influenced Nelson's decision to delay the execution, Nelson finally if half-heartedly conceded that the idea had 'floated through [his] mind'.[151]

Nelson was unembarrassed about his role in the suppression. He was a military officer whose task it had been to vanquish 'rebels' by any means at his disposal. In his view, the proclamation of martial law had authorized him to pursue this task without giving the slightest quarter. When asked whether by his definition a 'rebel' was 'a man in arms', Nelson unhesitatingly replied that he had given the term an even more 'general acceptation'.[152] He had acted on the premiss that the entire population of Surrey 'were all rebels'. The entire area, in his mind, was 'an enemy country, in full possession of the enemy'.[153] Martial law had authorized him to make war on a civilian population. 'Martial law was proclaimed by the Council,' Nelson stated, 'and I was sent to carry it out; and as a soldier I went and did my best.'[154]

Lieutenant Brand, a young but quite experienced naval officer,[155] had been ordered to preside over the court martial of Gordon. In this task Brand was assisted by two other even more junior officers. In Brand's two appearances before the JRC, the most testing questions were asked by Gorrie. Brand was asked to describe and explain the trial procedures he had adopted in trying Gordon on capital charges. In the early going, Brand proved a surprisingly compliant

---

[147] Nelson was on board a naval vessel when he received the lawyer's note. Nelson threw the letter over the side. *JRC Minutes*, Q. 33,862. See also criticism of Nelson in the *Daily News* (16 Apr. 1866), 4.
    [148] *JRC Minutes*, Q. 31,129.   [149] Ibid., Q. 31,097.
    [150] Nelson received a private letter from Eyre. Ibid. Q. 31,102–7. Nelson had read the proceedings of the trial to O'Connor who in turn read them to two members of the Executive Council who sent them to Eyre (and as Eyre reported to Cardwell) 'without any expression of dissent'. Eyre to Cardwell, 6 Apr. 1866, *CO* 137/405.   [151] *JRC Minutes*, Q. 31,134.
    [152] Ibid., Q. 33,839.   [153] Ibid., Q. 33,843.   [154] Ibid.
    [155] Dutton reported that Brand, although he was only twenty-six in 1865, had seen action in the Crimea and China prior to his duty in Jamaica. Dutton, *Hero as Murderer*, 284.

(perhaps naive) witness. With little apparent hesitation he conceded that he had little knowledge either of court martial procedure or the source of the authority under which he had acted.[156] He had not been much concerned that the charges against Gordon were not carefully specified.[157] Nor had he been worried that Gordon was convicted on the evidence of witnesses who had been given reason to hope that their lives might be spared in exchange for damning testimony.[158] Brand made plain he had viewed the courts martial as the annoying formality which preceded conviction and punishment.

But if he did not know it when he began giving testimony, Brand's subsequent interrogation at the hands of Gorrie alerted him to potential trouble. When he was questioned on how the court martial had evaluated the evidence against Gordon, Brand's responses became increasingly terse and defensive.[159] He fell back on the evasion that in courts martial it was enough to acquit or condemn on two of three votes. The presiding officers were sworn 'not to divulge' how they voted on guilt or innocence.[160] When confronted by the suggestion that Gordon's conviction had not been supported by credible evidence, Brand could deny that he himself had voted to convict the accused.[161] But even this strategem quickly wore thin. By the end of his examination on 3 March 1866, Brand began to fall back on a faulty memory. He also flatly refused to answer awkward questions.[162]

Brand plainly had a rough time in the JRC's hearing room. Circumstances dictated a smoother passage for Duberry Ramsay. Ramsay was a Crimean War veteran who, one historian claims, had been decorated for his part in the charge of the Light Brigade.[163] When the rebellion began, Ramsay was, in the local nomenclature, a 'Provost-Marshal' (or Sheriff) based in St. Thomas-in-the-East parish.[164] When it was quickly suppressed, Brigadier-General Nelson appointed Ramsay as commandant of a makeshift prison camp set up at Morant Bay. For nearly a month Ramsay ran the camp with a raging and sadistic mania. On his direct orders dozens of prisoners were mercilessly flogged before being subjected to summary trial and execution.[165] These punishments were meted out randomly

---

[156] *JRC Minutes*, Q. 32,482–9.   [157] Ibid., Q. 33,344–52.

[158] Many of Gorrie's questions fixed on the court martial of Gordon, and the court's reliance on the evidence of a condemned black prisoner named James McLaren. It was suggested to Brand that he had insinuated to McLaren that his own life might be spared in return for testimony against Gordon. Ibid., Q. 32,445.

[159] Ibid., Q. 33,345. When Brand testified that he had tried and executed a man on a charge of 'mutiny', he was pointedly asked, 'mutiny against whom and against what?' Brand's reply: 'against the Queen, I suppose'.   [160] Ibid., Q. 32,481.

[161] For example, in a case where a man had been convicted of treason on flimsy evidence, Brand denied that he himself had thought the evidence amounted to treason. Ibid., Q. 33,393.

[162] When asked to define 'treason' or to recall what evidence had been taken to amount to treason in specific cases, Brand refused to answer. Ibid., Q. 33,413–18. When asked about his operative definition of a 'capital' crime, Brand similarly refrained. Ibid., Q. 33,410–12.

[163] Ramsay gained a reputation for harshness during his tenure as Provost-Marshal. *Daily News* (30 Mar. 1866), 5.   [164] Dutton, *Hero as Murderer*, 284.

[165] For the most detailed account of Ramsay's conduct, see Heuman, '*The Killing Time*', 137–43.

against some, with calculation against others. In one instance, Ramsay had a
man beaten until he agreed to implicate his son in the uprising. When the man
finally muttered some incriminating words, both he and his son were immediately hanged. Another incident got Ramsay into serious trouble. In late October
a man named George Marshall was brought to Morant Bay for being a black
person on the move without a military pass.[166] When Marshall was brought
into the camp ('very thin and rather sick,' a witness stated[167]), Ramsay sensed
resistance in the man. Dispensing with a court martial, he had Marshall tied to a
field gun and fifty lashes applied to his back. After the forty-seventh lash,
Marshall, shrieking and writhing in pain,[168] his back now 'like a bit of raw beef,
bleeding very profusely', turned toward Ramsay and made an angry grimace
with his teeth.[169] With this Ramsay ordered Marshall taken down and hanged.
Marshall was 'thrown on his back, his hands and feet tied, a rope put round his
neck and thrown over a rail'. He was then dragged to the steps of the courthouse
and 'hoisted up as you would a barrel of flour'. Minutes later, as he was
still showing signs of life, 'a huge white stone was taken and put between his
arms tied behind him'. When word of this kind of conduct finally reached
Nelson, he reproached Ramsay and ordered the arbitrary beatings and
executions to stop.[170]

The JRC certainly had a great many reasons to be interested in Ramsay's
testimony. His conduct had come to symbolize the abuse of power under martial
law.[171] In February 1866 he became the first white Jamaican to be charged with a
criminal offence (the murder of George Marshall) as a result of actions taken
during martial law. It was also of interest that Ramsay had acted as prosecutor in
the court martial of Gordon.

Ramsay was questioned by the JRC on 1 March 1866. Before the proceeding,
the panel already had determined not to ask him anything which 'might prejudice
him' in his forthcoming trial.[172] Questions were confined mainly to Ramsay's
contribution to Gordon's court martial. As prosecutor, Ramsay had been responsible for the disposition of evidence against the accused. It quickly became obvious that Ramsay, while he knew something of rules of due process in British
criminal justice, had been utterly oblivious to them in the case of Gordon. Neither
Ramsay nor anyone else had spent much time preparing a credible case against
Gordon. To make up for this, Ramsay put into evidence a series of unauthenti-
cated documents written by men who might have been called as actual
witnesses.[173] Ramsay's witnesses, moreover, had been recruited from the ranks
of prisoners in his camp,[174] from persons, in other words, with the most obvious

---

[166] Ramsay had himself instituted rules that no man or woman was to be on the open roads without numbered passes issued by him. See *JRC Minutes*, evidence of Augustus Lake, Q. 14,210–12. See
also *Colonial Standard* (22 Oct. 1866).   [167] *JRC Minutes*, Q. 14,281.
   [168] Summary of Marshallech's evidence, *The Times* (3 Mar. 1866), 7–9.   [169] Ibid.
   [170] Nelson finally forbade Ramsay from inflicting 'any summary punishment'. See *JRC Report*, 525.
   [171] *Daily News* (3 Mar. 1866), 5.   [172] *JRC Report*, 525.
   [173] *JRC Minutes*, Q. 31,442.   [174] Ibid., Q. 31,319.

incentive to trade damning testimony against Gordon for clemency in their own cases.[175]

Having got these points on the record, the JRC's examination of Ramsay came to an abrupt end. He was not interrogated about the many other prosecutions, whippings, and executions he had supervised. The Jamaica Committee's lawyers respected this embargo, even though in early February they had been instructed by the executive in London 'as soon as possible to institute criminal proceedings against some one or more of the military officers'.[176] It was enough perhaps that the JRC had amassed a substantial amount of evidence that might be used against Ramsay in future proceedings.

IV. Local Justice: Magistrates' Courts and the Prosecution of Rebels

To a not insignificant degree the Morant Bay uprising was born in Jamaica's local courts of law. One of the most frequently cited and sorely felt grievances of black Jamaicans in the early 1860s was the poor standard of justice meted out by the local or 'petty' courts. Conversely, many of the colony's whites regarded the petty courts as bastions of impartial justice.[177] These courts – the leading edge of the colonial state in many black communities – were operated mainly by white planter magistrates.[178] When the paid or stipendiary magistrates who once presided over Jamaica's local courts had either died or retired, they were replaced by planters.[179] (In 1865, out of the several hundred Jamaican magistrates only seven were stipendiary.)[180] This meant that disputes between blacks and whites over vitally important matters such as title to land or entitlement to wages were decided by men who, for reasons of class and race, were not disinterested in the outcome. And while the petty courts were seen as inimical to blacks, whites routinely used them to advantage. By 1865, particularly in parishes (like St. Thomas-in-the-East) where squatting was a widespread practice, scores of black men had been embittered by encounters with local magistrates.[181] It was not by chance, then, that the Morant Bay rising was precipitated by an especially rancorous sitting of the petty sessions of

---

[175] Some witnesses later attested that Ramsay had told prisoners that anyone who could give evidence against Gordon 'will save his life and be rewarded'. As reported by the special correspondent to *The Times* (17 Mar. 1866), 9–10.   [176] *JC Minutes*, 15 Jan. 1866.

[177] '[I]n no part of the British Empire,' the *Falmouth Post* (26 Jan. 1866), 2, asserted, 'is Justice more mercifully administered than on this island'.

[178] 'As creole employment on estates declined and planters and peasants came increasingly to occupy two different worlds, their main points of contact were the courts of petty sessions.' Holt, *The Problem of Freedom*, 288–9.

[179] One of the few remaining stipendiaries on the island in 1865, a man named Jackson, gained a reputation among local whites for being too lenient with black litigants (he was called the 'nigger magistrate'), and was removed from his position by the authorities. See 'The Case of Mr. Gordon', *Law Magazine* 22 (1866–67), 31.   [180] Letter to the *Daily News* (7 Feb. 1867), 5–6.

[181] Holt, *The Problem of Freedom*, 288–9; Heuman, '*The Killing Time*', 69–72.

the peace.[182] Nor was it accidental that Bogle's 'army' razed the Morant Bay court-house as it massacred magistrate von Ketelholdt and his retainers.

The JRC was aware of these facts, and accordingly asked relevant witnesses a great many questions about the character of local justice in Jamaica. One of its chief witnesses in this regard was Justice Alan Ker. Ker was a colonial judge of great experience.[183] Born in Scotland in 1818, called to the Bar at the Middle Temple in 1842, Ker practised law as an 'equity draftsman and conveyancer' until 1851, when he accepted the perhaps more intriguing office of Attorney General in Antigua. After stints as Chief Justice of two minor island colonies in the British Caribbean he was appointed to the High Court of Jamaica in 1860. Ker remained a puisne judge of that court until his death in 1885. Estimated by his testimony before the JRC, Ker was a candid, perhaps even a recklessly candid, man. (This trait may explain why he was never promoted to Chief Justice of Jamaica.) Before the JRC began investigating local justice in the colony, Ker had already got himself into hot water when he claimed publicly that the magistracy of the parish of St. Ann routinely heard cases in which they had a personal interest.[184] Ker's willingness to criticize members of the white elite in Jamaica was enhanced by the fact that, as he himself stated, he was 'not connected by birth, marriage or ownership of land with Jamaica'.[185] His sensibilities were those of an independent and highly intelligent outsider who happened also to be a markedly idealistic barrister and judge.

Ker needed only little prompting from the JRC to deliver a caustic indictment of local justice in Jamaica. The local courts were expensive, cumbersome, and physically inaccessible; so much so, Ker explained, that most black peasants were 'absolutely shut out' of them as plaintiffs.[186] These failings, bad as they were, paled by comparison to the problems presented by the island's 'volunteer' Justices of the Peace. 'I think it right to state,' Ker stated, 'that I have for years past come to the conclusion that the present system of the unpaid magistracy in Jamaica is the most unsatisfactory that could well be conceived.'[187] Warming to his subject, Ker went on to even more bold assertions: 'Of 270 magistrates that hold the JRC of the peace, from personal observation and knowledge of a good many, I should say that more than half were utterly unfit to hold that trust, unfit by want of education, capacity, social position, and pecuniary independence.' The chronic inadequacy of the petty court bench, Ker believed, stemmed from a

---

[182] For description of these incidents, see *JRC Report*, 508–9.

[183] See obituaries in *The Times* (1 Apr. 1885), 10; *Law Times* (4 Apr. 1885), 416.

[184] On 21 November 1865, Ker sent a letter to Governor Eyre's secretary which stated that the people of St. Ann had 'real grievance' with the magistrates in the parish because the judges and clerks often had a direct financial interest in the outcome. When seventeen magistrates sent a letter of protest Ker was forced (by Governor Storks) to apologize. In his apology of May 1866, however, Ker admitted only that his letter had been 'faultily worded': 'I was discussing not what the Justices *do*, but what the people *think*. And they think (and constituting 19/20ths of the population, their prejudice must surely count for something) that they cannot get impartial justice from a tribunal *presided over by persons whose interests they believe to be antagonistic to their own*.' Ker to Edward Jordan, Misc. Correspondence, May 1866, *CO* 137/406.   [185] Ibid.

[186] *JRC Minutes*, Q.14,541.   [187] Ibid., Q.14,586.

dearth of men of the 'highest grade' in Jamaica. It was Ker's view that in 'several parishes here there is no person occupying the rank of what is commonly called "a gentleman" or anything approaching to it'.[188] There was no room to doubt, moreover, that the failure of local justice had contributed substantially to the 'disaffection' felt by the black peasantry toward the colonial government. Given his record as a vocal critic of local justice in Jamaica, Ker's testimony was not unexpected. Still, it was deeply resented by the local white establishment.[189]

While Justice Ker was by far the most blunt critic of local justice in Jamaica, he clearly was not alone in his view. Heslop also had affirmed that in general the colony's magistrates were 'not sufficiently educated men', and that there was 'a cloud of suspicion thrown over their decisions from the fact that in many instances they are connected with estates as owners or otherwise'.[190] Heslop agreed with Ker that at the root of the problem was the relative financial and intellectual poverty of the island's white elite. It was simply too hard to find local men with sufficient character, erudition, and inclination to serve as unpaid justices of the peace. This was why 'as a general rule the magistrates are not technically and legally up to their art'.[191] This low opinion of the state of the local courts had been shared even by the former Governor Eyre himself. The 'great evil in this country,' Eyre once generalized to Cardwell, 'is . . . the want of good and independent magistrates'.[192]

The issue of local justice figured prominently in the Report of the JRC which was published in April 1866. The criticisms lodged by Ker and other officials had found their mark. In its final assessment of the principal causes of the rebellion, the JRC recited the frustrated desire of black squatters to gain freehold title to patches of abandoned or undeveloped land.[193] The JRC also noted how this frustration was magnified by the fact that conflicts over land were litigated in local courts and before magistrates who were 'principally planters and persons connected with the management of estates'.[194] The most imperative legal assertions of the black peasantry had thus been 'adjudicated upon by those whose interests and feelings are supposed to be hostile to the labourer and the occupier'. In the eyes of black peasants, the petty sessions of the peace had become so corrupt that in some counties they had set up parallel tribunals complete with judges, summonses, and fines.[195] The JRC concluded that 'the want of confidence generally felt by the labouring class in the tribunals' had provided 'an additional incentive to the violation of the law'. Although the JRC did not recommend specific reforms, its findings lent momentum to a proposal, then under consideration by the Colonial Office, that the island's local magistracy be replaced by a

---

[188] Ibid., Q.14,587.
[189] Ibid., Q.14,541. The *Falmouth Post* (20 Feb. 1866), 2, accused Ker of having 'sneered at the class from whom the magistracy are chosen' without having facts to buttress his claims.
[190] Ibid., Q. 16,416.   [191] Ibid., Q.16,488.
[192] Eyre to Cardwell, 24 Nov. 1865, Cardwell Papers, *CO* 30/48/42.   [193] *JRC Report*, 515.
[194] Ibid.   [195] *Westminster Review* 88 (1867), 207.

complement of professional or stipendiary magistrates recruited in Britain. In the meantime, on the basis of other findings of the JRC, Acting Governor Storks sacked a number of magistrates implicated in 'acts of great barbarity' during the suppression.[196]

In the summer of 1866 the Colonial Office began to plan the systematic reform of local justice in Jamaica. But this was a longer-term project, one which took a back seat to the second track of the Government's response to the rebellion and suppression of October 1865: the criminal prosecution of persons, black and white, who had committed serious crimes when they fomented or suppressed the rebellion. While these prosecutions were always likely to exacerbate political tensions on the island, the determination to prosecute always trumped political considerations.

When the rebellion and suppression were over, three categories of men and women were vulnerable to prosecution in the criminal courts: (i) black Jamaicans who might have committed crimes during the uprising, but who had not yet faced trial; (ii) white Jamaicans suspected of political crimes (such as sedition or conspiracy) with regard to the events leading to the uprising; (iii) white military personnel who had allegedly committed crimes against blacks during the suppression. With the strong backing of the Colonial Office, Storks quickly instituted prosecutions in all three categories.

But first there was the question of what do with the 111 persons languishing in the colony's jails as a result of convictions by courts martial during the period of martial law. In November 1865, Governor Eyre had decided to detain these prisoners until they could be tried by a special court created by Crown Warrant in late January 1866. Toward this end, the Jamaica legislature passed a law giving the Governor the unfettered right to hold prisoners arrested under martial law as long as needed before trial.[197] When Storks arrived on the island, however, he was strongly inclined to release all of the martial law prisoners (pending selective rearrest and prosecution in the civilian courts). It is revealing of his mindset that Storks did not give the order until he had been advised by his Attorney General that it was permissible. 'As I had considerable doubts of the legality of such sentences by courts martial,' Storks confessed to Cardwell in Februrary 1866, 'and still greater hesitation about the legal power I possessed to keep these parties in confinement after martial law had ceased, I consulted the Attorney General on the subject'.[198] When Heslop informed the Governor that he believed that the continued detentions were illegal, Storks hesitated again, this time on the grounds that their release would exacerbate the 'excitement and ill-feeling' in the colony,

---

[196] One of the first to be dismissed was William Pitt Kirkland, a magistrate who had ordered black men and women flogged with wire cats at Bath. Storks to Cardwell, 20 Apr. 1866, *CO* 137/404. See also Storks to Kirkland, 14 Apr. 1866, *JRO* 1B/5/81. The dismissal of Kirkland was prompted by his testimony before the JRC.

[197] This statute is discussed in a memorandum written to Cardwell by the Law Officers of the Crown, 6 Jan. 1866, *CO* 885/11.   [198] Storks to Cardwell, 12 Feb. 1866, *CO* 30/48/44.

especially among the white population. Storks did not let these political considerations delay him for long. For this essentially legal problem he found a legal
solution. On the further advice of Heslop he instructed the Attorney General to
introduce a writ of *habeas corpus* into the High Court on behalf of one prisoner, a
white journalist called Sydney Leviens.[199] Chief Justice Edwards granted the writ,
and in so doing effectively nobbled the detention statute.[200] With this decision in
hand, Storks released all of the prisoners, and then ordered the rearrest of the
worst offenders on new charges. Sydney Leviens, for instance, was returned to
detention on charges of sedition and conspiracy.

As a whole this policy was not as draconian as it might first have appeared.
Much to the chagrin of former Governor Eyre,[201] only a handful of the 111 original prisoners (and only those directly implicated in the killings at Morant Bay)
were prosecuted for the capital offences of murder or treason. On the instructions
of Heslop, the Crown routinely proceeded against the prisoners on the lesser charge
of sedition or felonious riot.

None of this sat well with Eyre. When in February 1866 Eyre learned that the
Crown would not pursue convictions for treason, he wrote Heslop to register his
protest.[202] Heslop's reply was remarkably frank. He had reviewed the files and
sought the opinion of one of Jamaica's most eminent barristers as to the likelihood
of securing convictions for treason.[203] Although the opinion indicated that such
convictions were obtainable, Heslop admitted to Eyre that he had rejected this
advice because of 'merely political' concerns; in particular, Heslop had been moved
by 'consideration of the effect which a verdict of "Guilty of Treason" would have
had in the mother country'. In Heslop's view, 'Nobody [Eyre did not count?]
wanted to see 84 people even sentenced to be hung'. If politics had not been a
factor in the prosecutorial policy of the Colonial Office, it now clearly had affected
the policy of Jamaica's formidable Attorney General.

But while the colonial government would not seek to hang any of the black
political agitators, it was not so forgiving that it did not seek to put them behind

---

[199] Ibid.

[200] 'Mr. Cardwell, who was a lawyer before he was a Minister,' the *Saturday Review* mused on
20 January 1866, 'would be startled by the discovery that any law can be set aside by an English court
as unconstitutional.' This was seen as the effect of Chief Justice Bryan's ruling that under the statute
the Governor might only arrest and detain for the purpose of imminent trial, not general detention.

[201] It is easy to comprehend why Eyre was deeply frustrated by this. In previous months he
had defended martial law and actions taken under it on grounds that the government had been
confronted by a vast and highly coordinated conspiracy to overthrow the state. Eyre had hoped that a
series of successful and highly visible treason prosecutions would strongly corroborate this claim.

[202] Eyre's letter does not survive. The substance of the exchange is found in Heslop's response. See
Heslop to Eyre, 2 Apr. 1866, *CO* 137/405.

[203] The barrister J.S. Williams prepared the opinion. In a letter to Eyre, Williams informed the
former Governor that the lesser charges of riot were proceeded with 'not from any fear of an unsuccessful verdict on the higher charge of treason, but solely on account of the severity of the punishment, and
in consideration of the fact that most of the principal offenders had already met with the doom of
traitors'. Williams reminded Eyre that he was 'wholly relieved of any responsibility for the higher
charge of treason not having been proceeded with'. Williams to Eyre, 6 Apr. 1866, *CO* 137/405.

bars. The trials of the men who were alleged to have fomented the rebellion, these 'political prisoners' as even Storks called them,[204] took place before the Special Commission of the Court of Oyer and Terminer in Kingston and Spanish Town commencing in late January 1866. The Commission consisted of the three justices of the High Court, Chief Justice Edwards and Justices Ker and Cargill, sitting along side four lay judges.

These arrangements immediately attracted criticism.[205] That members of the local white elite would be permitted to preside in politically sensitive cases raised the spectre of class and racial bias. Unfavourable comment of a similar kind arose about the fact that the single grand jury consisted of fifteen 'principally white' planters, merchants, and clerks from Surrey, the parish of the uprising.[206] Some Jamaicans doubted that men accused of rebellion, men who before the rebellion had opposed a regime dominated by the same lay judges and jurors, could receive fair hearings. Then there was the fact that the trials were to be held in two towns simultaneously. The Jamaica bar was not numerous. Would there be enough barristers to defend those who could pay for professional representation? In response to these criticisms, the colonial government offered assurance that the appointment of lay judges was 'merely in compliance with custom, and will have no voice in administering the justice which, as all admit, flows impartially from the Jamaica Bench'.[207] As for the racial and social composition of grand juries, and the problems associated with the trials, nothing could be done.

The first cases began with the grand jury's evaluation of charges against three black and two white persons (a black policeman, two black preachers, a white physician, and the white newspaper publisher, Sydney Leviens) for conspiracy to commit sedition and, in Leviens' case, seditious libel. A big audience, mainly of black and coloured persons, filled the benches of Kingston's largest courtroom.[208] Heslop appeared for the Crown, William Phillippo for some of the accused. Chief Justice Edwards charged the grand jury. The issue, the jurymen were told, was whether specific utterances or writings had 'had a tendency to produce mischief by perverting the minds of Her Majesty's subjects in this colony, and by creating dissatisfaction with the Government'.[209] The charge made no reference to the political contexts of the impugned words, although in fact most had been uttered at 'Underhill meetings' organized by Baptist missionaries in the spring of 1865.[210] In the result, the grand jury found 'true bills' against (indicted) all of the accused.

The indictment of Leviens generated the most comment in England. A journalist based in Montego Bay, Leviens had been a thorn in the side of the

---

[204] When Gordon was arrested, his personal papers were seized. They revealed an extensive political correspondence with men like Sydney Leviens of Montego Bay and Dr. Bruce of Vere. These men were arrested by Eyre on the strength of these documents. See *JRC Report*, 536.
[205] *The Times* (13 Feb. 1866), 9.   [206] *Falmouth Post* (2 Feb. 1866), 1.   [207] Ibid.
[208] Ibid.   [209] *The Times* (13 Feb. 1866), 9.   [210] Heuman, '*The Killing Time*,' 44–62.

Governor[211] and colonial establishment in Jamaica for years prior to the uprising at Morant Bay.[212] In 1865, Leviens published a series of truculent personal attacks against Eyre in his *County Union* newspaper ('the most decidedly agitating articles', Eyre called them).[213] Leviens had been equally abusive of Jamaica's white oligarchy. The final straw fell in the aftermath of the rebellion. Before the fires had cooled Leviens published editorials claiming that the bloodshed was entirely due to the disastrous failings of Eyre and his government. It is obvious from his official despatches that by the time of the uprising Eyre had developed an intense loathing of Leviens.[214] Then, in the wake of Morant Bay, Eyre learned that Leviens and Gordon had been regular correspondents. Armed with this material, Eyre issued 'express orders' that Leviens be arrested in Montego Bay (a place outside the jurisdiction of martial law) and taken to Morant Bay for court martial.[215] Leviens' solicitor attempted unsuccessfully to gain his release by writ of *habeas corpus*. Fortunately for the prisoner, however, by the time he reached Morant Bay, Brigadier-General Nelson already had supervised the court martial and execution of Gordon. Nelson was perhaps understandably nervous about executing more persons, some of them *white* men, who had come from outside the jurisdiction of martial law, and whose crimes predated the period of martial law. Nelson informed O'Connor that he would not court martial Leviens, or other similarly situated prisoners, unless expressly ordered to do so.[216] This perhaps explains why Leviens stayed alive long enough to be tried by the Special Commission.

When Gorrie learned of Leviens' case in mid-January 1866, he began to press Storks for his immediate release.[217] Gorrie also alerted his masters in London that Leviens had been a determined political opponent of Eyre, but now was languishing in jail awaiting trial for sedition and conspiracy to commit sedition. Upon receipt of this despatch, the Jamaica Committee immediately decided to take up Leviens' cause, and to publicize his plight in the English press.[218] But, as matters unfolded, Gorrie was unable to persuade Storks to stop the prosecution, and Leviens faced trial in mid-February 1866. The indictment charged Leviens with having published two seditious libels in the *County Union* before and after the uprising (on 12 May and 17 October 1865). The first piece was a screed against

---

[211] Leviens published an article critical of the fact that the Governor had spent £150 of public funds for the purchase of a piano. He later claimed that he had been arrested 'simply to gratify the revenge of Mr. Eyre for the personal attack I had made on him relative to the piano'. Leviens to Colonial Secretary, 7 Oct. 1867, *CO* 137/427.

[212] Heuman, '*The Killing Time*,' 59–60, 151–3.   [213] *JRC Minutes*, Q. 4026.

[214] In a post-rebellion despatch to Cardwell, Eyre defended the Leviens arrest, calling Leviens the 'Jew editor of the *County Union* newspaper' and 'one of the greatest scoundrels working'. Eyre to Cardwell, 23 Oct. 1865, Cardwell Papers, *CO* 30/48/42.

[215] The letter in question was written to Dr. Bruce of Vere, and it indicated that Leviens would write editorials to 'screen' Bruce and others from 'the charge of anarchy and tumult' that would certainly follow from their political work. *JRC Minutes*, Q. 4016–20.

[216] Nelson to O'Connor, 5 Nov. 1865, *JRC Appendix, PP* (1866), xxx, 1159.

[217] *CD*, 31 Jan. 1866.   [218] They are discussed under this heading, ibid.

colonial misgovernment in Jamaica. The second asserted that the main cause of the recent uprising was that the Governor and his circle had taken it upon themselves 'to make their will the law of the land, and that law is cruelly obnoxious to the people'.[219] The editorial challenged Eyre to offer some explanation for his failed policies. 'What will [Eyre] write to the Colonial Secretary,' Leviens asked, 'as to the blood that testifies against his fatal misrule?' Importantly, however, Leviens' editorial also included an important disclaimer: that while the government's failures were many and serious, 'they are not justification of the rebellion that has taken place, nor are they brought forward as such.'

Heslop called witnesses to prove that the impugned articles put into evidence came from Leviens' newspaper.[220] However, the official account of the trial does not record what arguments were made as to why the articles were seditious.[221] The charge to the jury also was not recorded. What is more certain, however, is that in the 1860s sedition still was a very broadly defined crime, and that for any judge or jury so inclined, there was ample scope for conviction whenever the charge was laid.[222] In the result, the jury brought in a verdict of guilty, but recommended that the Special Commission exercise 'mercy' in sentencing on grounds that Leviens had disavowed rebel violence. Leviens was sentenced to one year in gaol.

On 22 February 1866, Leviens stood trial again (this time with ten others) on charges of conspiracy to engage in sedition, riot, and rebellion.[223] This prosecution had an unusual importance for Edward Eyre. In his official despatches to the Colonial Office, Eyre had repeatedly claimed that Gordon was arrested, tried, and executed as the linchpin of a wide conspiracy to overthrow the government and massacre Jamaica's white population. Leviens and his co-accused were said to be Gordon's main (surviving) co-conspirators. Their conviction would tend to bolster the Governor's position. Knowing this, the lawyers for the Jamaica Committee volunteered to defend Leviens and three other alleged co-conspirators.[224] After a short trial, the accused men, Leviens included, were acquitted. Most of the accused walked free from the courtroom. Leviens continued to serve his sentence for sedition in a Kingston gaol.

Leviens remained in gaol through the spring and into the summer of 1866. In June, the Jamaica Committee instructed Shaen to intercede on his behalf with the

---

[219] Jamaica needed something more from its Governor 'than the mere rearing of chickens in Flamstead' (the Governor's mountain retreat). For copies of the editorials, see *JRC Appendix*, 1161.

[220] *Falmouth Post* (16 Feb. 1866).

[221] *Papers Laid before the Jamaica Royal Commission, PP* (1866), xxx, 330–3.

[222] According to one treatise on English constitutional law published in 1866, a person could be convicted of seditious libel for making any writing which made 'contemptuous, indecent or malicious observations on the person of the king or his government'. The treatise writer emphasized that the definition was 'susceptible of an elastic meaning, and accordingly the Crown, when strong enough has been in the habit of punishing almost every obnoxious criticism on the acts of government'. Herbert Broom, *Constitutional Law: Viewed in Relation to Common Law, and Exemplified by Cases* (London, 1866), 520.

[223] *Papers Laid before the Jamaica Royal Commission, PP* (1866), xxx, 337–42.

[224] Special correspondent to *The Times* (17 Mar. 1866), 9–10.

Colonial Office. A letter was sent to Lord Carnarvon contending that Leviens had been too harshly sentenced for a libel 'of a very moderate character', and that he would have served his entire sentence before lawyers could perfect an appeal before the Judicial Committee of the Privy Council.[225] For this reason Carnarvon was asked to remit the remainder of Leviens' gaol term. His aides at the Colonial Office considered the matter, advising that some of Leviens' editorial writing had in fact been dangerously seditious. While the first of the two impugned pieces (written in May 1865) 'might have been supposed to be mere railing without contemplating practical results', the editorial Leviens wrote in the wake of the rebellion was a work of 'menace and fierce triumph'. When one took into account the timing of this piece, an aide wrote, 'the article of 17 October appears to me to have been a most wicked and malignant libel and not to be too severely visited with a sentence of twelve months imprisonment'. With this advice in hand, Carnarvon decided to defer to the judgement of Jamaica's new Governor, Sir John Grant. In late August, Grant reviewed Leviens' case with the Chief Justice of Jamaica and released Leviens on time served. A number of the other 'political prisoners' received pardons at the same time.[226]

The remission did not cause Leviens to forgive and forget. With the aid of the Jamaica Committee he continued his appeal against his conviction for seditious libel in the Judicial Committee of the Privy Council. In Leviens' view, one evidently shared by his allies, his arrest, detention, and prosecution were illegal acts perpetrated to suppress legitimate political dissent. 'I was arrested,' Leviens asserted in a letter to the Colonial Office in October 1867, 'in violation of all law, and in outrage of my rights as a British subject.'[227] He had been prosecuted and gaoled by the colonial regime for no other reason than that he published the opinion – an opinion not since changed – that the 'cause of the outbreak was the misrule of the Colony'. Leviens' appeal, although it no longer mattered to his personal liberty, was pursued in order to vindicate the principle of the 'inviolability of English law'. In addition to his appeal, Leviens petitioned the Colonial Office for monetary compensation for his wrongful imprisonment.

In the result, Leviens got neither. The Judicial Committee dismissed his appeal without a hearing, on the grounds that Grant's pardon made the appeal moot. This meant that there would not be a pronouncement of a high court on the issues raised by the charge of seditious libel specifically, or on the legitimacy of the proceedings at the Special Commission generally.[228] As for his claim to

---

[225] Shaen and Roscoe to Cardwell, 26 June 1866, *CO* 137/409.

[226] When Storks left he recommended that Leviens' sentence be remitted by Grant. Grant did not want to make a decision while Leviens' petition to the home government still was unanswered. Grant to Carnarvon, 24 Aug. 1866, Cardwell Papers, *CO* 30/6/134.

[227] Leviens to Colonial Secretary, 7 Oct. 1867, *CO* 137/427.

[228] When the Colonial Office was determining whether it would oppose Leviens' appeal, it was reminded by the Clerk to the Privy Council that, given that the applicant already had been pardoned, the sole motivation of the Jamaica Committee was 'to upset, if they can, the proceedings of the Special JRC in Jamaica'. Henry Reeve to Carnarvon, 24 Jan. 1867, *CO* 137/428.

compensation, an unnamed senior civil servant eventually advised Lord Buckingham, Carnarvon's successor as Colonial Secretary, that Leviens had been one 'of the more wicked and malignant of those whose conduct endangered Jamaica in 1865'. According to this memorandum, although in the Leviens case a long incarceration had not befallen 'a rebel, a murderer and an outlaw, it may be debated whether it fell upon a man who was much better'. Leviens received no compensation from the government.

V. The Criminal Prosecution of Jamaican Militia Officers and Volunteers

Some of the most savage acts of repression under the martial law were ordered or committed by white Jamaican militia officers. The prosecution of these men in Jamaican criminal courts raises some points of contrast. On one hand, British imperial officials had proved illiberal enough to prosecute journalists for publishing intemperate criticism of a colonial government. On the other hand, the same officials were also prepared to prosecute white Jamaicans, some of considerable social station, who used excessive force against black men and women during martial law. Jamaica's criminal justice system was capable of rendering convictions in cases involving seditious activity prior to the uprising. What remained unclear in the first months of 1866 was whether the same system would render convictions in cases involving abuses of power and office. As Cardwell knew well, these cases were certain to test the political will and integrity of the imperial authorities. They also underlined the fact the Colonial Office still had not arrived at answers to a number of important legal and political questions. What was the legal import of the Indemnity Act passed by the Jamaica Assembly in November 1865? Who might invoke this statute? Could its provisions be invoked in Jamaica before the statute had gained the formal assent of the imperial government in London? Would the Colonial Office exercise its prerogative to disallow the Indemnity Act?[229]

In December 1865, Cardwell directed his staff to commence an official correspondence with the law officers of the Crown, Attorney General Roundell Palmer and Solicitor General Robert P. Collier.[230] The first order of business was for the lawyers to undertake a review of the legal ramifications of the seven statutes passed by the Legislature of Jamaica in the immediate aftermath of the suppression. In this regard, Cardwell was well aware of one starting point, the Colonial Laws Validity Act (which had been passed by his own government in June 1865).[231] Under this law, the provisions of a colonial statute were to be regarded as

---

[229] The disallowance prerogative is described by Swinfen, *Imperial Control of Legislation*, 2–3.
[230] Law Officers to Colonial Office, 6 Jan. 1866, *CO* 885/11.
[231] See generally, Swinfen, *Imperial Control of Legislation*, 167–83.

valid unless they were either 'repugnant to the provisions of any Act of Parliament extending to the colony',[232] or when expressly disallowed by the imperial government. The default position, then, was that colonial legislation operated by Order in Council unless the government took positive steps to negate it.[233] Before he would take such steps, Cardwell needed more information both about possible repugnancy and the legal effect of the Indemnity Act and the other legislation passed by the Jamaica Assembly in the aftermath of the suppression.

Two of these statutes were of particular and urgent relevance to the prosecution of persons for crimes committed during the suppression. One created the Special Commission that would try all persons charged with crimes committed prior to the October uprising (Palmer and Collier did not think this problematic).[234] The other, the indemnity statute, raised more complex legal issues. There had been speculation in the newspapers that this statute would 'protect Governor Eyre and his subordinates from a criminal prosecution, unless it is expressly disallowed by the Imperial Government'.[235] It was obviously of the greatest importance for Cardwell to know whether this would be the effect of the law. If this was the effect of the law, moreover, Cardwell needed to know what would be the effects of its disallowance.

Cardwell's inquiries necessitate a brief digression on the subjects of martial law and legal indemnity as they were understood by Alexander Heslop, the leading authority on the subject in Jamaica. As Heslop stated before the JRC, he comprehended martial law as the temporary displacement of civilian law by unbridled military authority. Martial law was proclaimed in order to provide military officers with the latitude needed to restore or defend public order. In Jamaica, as elsewhere in the empire, a tradition (born largely of revolts of slaves or native peoples) dictated that any person who was obliged to break civilian law in order to put down rebellion would later be protected by a statutory indemnification. Certainly that had been the operative assumption of Eyre and his officers when martial law was proclaimed and implemented in October 1865.[236] In Heslop's opinion, if martial law was to have any useful effect, it was absolutely essential that those charged with its operation did not fear criminal or civil liability.

The Jamaica Indemnity Act of 1865 included a preamble and only three discrete provisions, all drafted to provide the widest indemnity to as many persons (who had acted on the side of the authorities) as possible. The preamble asserted that martial law had been proclaimed in order to suppress persons threatening 'the general massacre of all loyal and well disposed subjects'.[237] The first section indemnified 'civil and military authorities' for 'all acts ordered or done during the

---

[232] 28 & 29 Vict. C. 63, s 11.   [233] Swinfen, *Imperial Control of Legislation*, 12–14, 172–3.

[234] Law Officers to Colonial Office, 6 Jan. 1866, *CO* 885/11.

[235] Letter to the *Daily News* (16 Dec. 1865), 4.

[236] As Eyre later explained to Cardwell, he had assumed 'the sole responsibility of arresting Gordon without establishing martial law ... and trusting to an act of indemnity being afterward enacted to cover any derivation from a strictly legal course'. Eyre to Cardwell, Jan. 1866, *CO* 137/402.   [237] Ibid.

continuance of martial law' in order 'to suppress the said insurrection' either 'within or beyond the proclaimed districts'.[238] The second section indemnified 'the Governor' or 'persons acting under his authority' for actions taken to 'put an end to the said rebellion'. This provision also indemnified any other person who had acted '*bona fide*' to put down the revolt. The final section of the statute stated that the Governor might issue a 'certificate' that was to amount to 'conclusive evidence that any act was done under the authority of the Governor, or was done *bona fide* in order to suppress the rebellion'. In other words, the Governor was empowered to dispense a presumptive immunity from any civil or criminal liability to anyone he thought deserving of it.

In their joint reply of 6 January, Palmer and Collier were indecisive about the effect of these provisions.[239] They advised Cardwell, rather unhelpfully, that 'an enactment of this description *may* turn out to be proper' (emphasis added). The letter then expressed concern that the Indemnity Act was promulgated on the assumption, recited in the Preamble, that martial law had been proclaimed in order to avert a 'general massacre' of loyal subjects. In other words, the Act was founded on a factual premiss which now was fiercely contested. On this basis alone, Palmer and Collier recommended that the 'Royal sanction to this Act should be withheld until the [Royal] JRC had reported, or, in all events, more information had been received'. Not surprisingly, this decidedly vague advice did not satisfy the Colonial Office. Another inquiry about the potential indemnity of Eyre and his military officers was made by the law officers again near the end of January.[240] Palmer and Collier were asked to answer three additional questions. Could a Governor of Jamaica be 'proceeded against at law' if he had proclaimed martial law in the absence of a demonstrable necessity? Were military officers who had acted under a valid proclamation of martial law liable to any legal process, on the alleged ground that they exceeded the necessity of the case, or on the ground that the proclamation itself was unnecessary? Finally, were *civilians* who had acted under orders within a proclaimed district liable to any legal process?

To these questions Palmer and Collier made prompt and concise replies. If in good faith and in accordance with local law a Jamaican Governor and his war councillors proclaimed martial law over a district, they could not later be 'proceeded against at law, on the alleged ground that there was no sufficient necessity'. Similarly, military officers who had given orders under a proclamation of martial law were 'not liable to any legal process on the alleged ground that they have exceeded the necessity of the case'. On these two points, Palmer and Collier could be definite. With regard to liability of civilians, the lawyers thought that the question would turn on the particular facts of a case. Their inclination was that

---

238 Statutes of Jamaica, 29 Vict. C. 1. For annotations, see W. F. Finlason, *A Treatise on Martial Law as Allowed by the Law of England in Time of Rebellion* (London, 1866), 228–30.
239 Law Officers to Colonial Office, 6 Jan. 1866, *CO* 885/11.
240 Law Officers to Colonial Office, 1 Feb. 1866, ibid.

persons who acted in good faith and under the orders of an officer charged with the task of implementing martial law 'would not be liable to any legal proceedings'. If the lawyers were correct in these conclusions, there would be very little room for the successful prosecution of anyone who had taken part in the Jamaican suppression.

But the opinion of Palmer and Collier was just that, an opinion, one written only for the internal consideration of the Colonial Office. Cardwell was not bound to accept or publicize it. In fact, he did neither. Nor did he take any immediate action on the disallowance of the indemnity statute. What Cardwell did do, however, was to instruct the colonial authorities in Jamaica to move ahead with the criminal prosecution of some of the more notorious white militiamen, starting with Duberry Ramsay.

We have seen that during his time as prison camp commandant at Morant Bay, Ramsay had presided over a large number of sadistic floggings and executions. The incident involving Marshall was the most publicized case. When Eyre was suspended, no action had yet been taken on the matter. Soon after Henry Storks arrived in Jamaica, a letter was sent to Ramsay asking for further written explanation of his role in the Marshall execution. Ramsay did not bother to deny that he had ordered the man hanged without trial. In his reply to Storks, Ramsay recalled that 'one man [Marshall] was particularly violent, and stated to be one of the worst of the rebels . . . On looking at him he threatened my own life.'[241] He explained that when Marshall 'shook his fist and growled', Ramsay executed him for instigating mutiny. This explanation did not impress Heslop (who, ironically, had watched Ramsay operate in the role of court martial prosecutor). Heslop ordered Ramsay's 'immediate arrest for murder'.[242] But, being the cautious lawyer that he was, Heslop advised Storks that Ramsay could not be arrested on a statement 'made in the course of public duty'. Storks decided to dismiss Ramsay from his post as police inspector and place him under surveillance until 'information can be obtained to found the ordinary proceedings'.[243]

On 20 February 1866 Ramsay was arrested for the murder of Marshall, and because of what the magistrate called the 'peculiar circumstances of the case', released on heavy bail.[244] Ramsay was the first white Jamaican to face criminal prosecution for his role in the suppression. His prosecution became, *de facto*, a test case in the legal accountability of British officials for criminal acts committed within the jurisdiction of the martial law. The naked injustice and arrogance of Marshall's treatment (he had not been involved in the rebellion, and was executed in front of a coloured newspaper reporter and at least three white

[241] Ramsay to Jordan, 6 Jan. 1866, *CO* 137/407.
[242] Ramsay explained that he had had Marshall flogged without trial because he was 'particularly violent' and to 'keep the others quiet'. Marshall had been executed, Ramsay stated, when 'he threatened my own life'. Ibid.   [243] See ibid., notations of Heslop, 15 Jan. 1866.
[244] Bail was set at £400 plus £400 in sureties. It was highly unusual, and controversial, for bail to be granted in a capital case. Special correspondent of the *Daily News* (30 Mar. 1866), 5.

witnesses)[245] shocked and infuriated a number of colonial officials, including Storks. As Storks put the matter in a private letter to Cardwell, 'There can be no excuse for such acts as Mr. Ramsay admits he has committed.'[246]

Ramsay was brought before a panel of eight examining magistrates, all white and coloured men, none of them lawyers, in Spanish Town on 23 February. At this first 'committal hearing' stage of criminal proceedings, the magistrates were only to decide whether there was *prima facie* evidence enough to justify remanding Ramsay to a grand jury at Morant Bay. Against custom, the hearing was held *in camera*.[247] The Jamaica Committee's junior barrister in Jamaica, Horne Payne, made an appearance in court to enter the signed depositions of witnesses against Ramsay. Ramsay was defended by J. S. Williams (the same Jamaican barrister who had been retained by a number of the white witnesses before the JRC).

According to sketchy accounts of what transpired in the hearing room,[248] the proceedings began with the preliminary objection by Williams. He submitted that 'as the offence complained of was committed in the proclaimed district during martial law…civil courts had no jurisdiction'. In such a case, Williams argued, Ramsay was responsible only to 'the general commanding, or to a military court by that officer convened'. Horne Payne replied that a Jamaica statute of 1848 gave the magistrates jurisdiction to perform their tasks 'during the existence of martial law'.[249] Without making an explicit ruling on this important point, the magistrates permitted Horne Payne to call evidence. Four witnesses (three of whom, including Lake, had appeared before the JRC) testified that Ramsay had hanged Marshall without benefit of trial. None of the witnesses heard or saw Marshall threaten Ramsay, although undoubtedly he had clenched his teeth in pain and anger. When these witnesses were finished, Horne Payne informed the court that he had more witnesses to call, but they were at Morant Bay. Horne Payne asked for the court either to commit Ramsay to trial on evidence heard, or to remand him to a court at Morant Bay.

In reply Williams asked the magistrates to dismiss the warrant because 'there was not now, nor was there hereafter likely to be, any evidence that the act charged against his client had been done maliciously, or was beyond the functions of the Provost-Marshal, or was not covered by the Act of Indemnity'.[250] Horne Payne rebutted by submitting that such points of law 'were questions for the judge or the jury in the High Court'. After hearing these submissions, the panel of magistrates

---

[245] The reporter was Augustus Lake of the *Colonial Standard. JRC Minutes*, Q.14,284–6. The incident was also witnessed by Captain Ford of the Volunteers and the captain of a trading schooner. See also the special correspondent of *The Times* (17, 19 Mar. 1866).

[246] Storks to Cardwell, 18 Jan. 1866, Cardwell Papers, *CO* 30/48/43.

[247] Given that almost all of the key evidence against Ramsay already had been publicized during the JRC, it was odd that the hearings were closed to the public. The *Daily News* (30 Mar. 1866), 5, speculated that the magistrates either were afraid of there being a riot among the blacks or they wanted to avoid the scrutiny of the press while they perpetrated a 'mere burlesque of justice'.

[248] See *Pall Mall Gazette* (31 Mar. 1866), 7; *The Times* (30 Mar. 1866), 5.

[249] *The Times* (30 Mar. 1866), 5.   [250] Ibid.

conferred for a few minutes and then discharged Ramsay on a vote of five to three. While the majority did not offer reasons, the three dissenting judges 'recorded their dissent, and their opinion that Ramsay ought to have been committed for trial'. Ramsay went free, although it was later reported in an English newspaper that 'he found it necessary to draw a revolver in order to keep off an excited and angry crowd'.[251]

This was only the first skirmish in a protracted legal conflict. The day after Ramsay was discharged, the Attorney General had him rearrested. (To the dismay of some observers, Ramsay was then released on bail by a magistrate who was a blood relative.)[252] Aware now that a typical panel of Jamaica magistrates was unlikely to commit Ramsay to the grand jury, Heslop arranged to proceed on a 'preferred indictment' directly to the grand jury of the East Circuit Court at Morant Bay. Ramsay's position was made even more uncomfortable when, in April 1866, the JRC submitted its Report. The report noted that 'a great deal of evidence was laid before us with a view of proving undue severity during the existence of martial law in reference to the conduct of Mr. Gordon Ramsay, the Provost-Marshal'.[253] In order to reassure Cardwell that every effort would be made to secure a conviction in the Ramsay case, Storks assigned Heslop to the prosecution. 'Since nice and difficult points of law will be involved in this trial,' Storks wrote in a despatch of March 1866, 'the Attorney General will conduct the case on the part of the Crown.'[254]

While at the end of spring 1866 the prosecution of Ramsay still had not got before the grand jury, the move had a number of other important effects. First, it signalled to all interested communities – to white and black Jamaicans, the British public, and the Jamaica Committee – that the Russell Government was prepared to proceed against a prominent white official of the colonial state for actions taken during the period of martial law. The rearrest of Ramsay underlined the Government's resolve. The prosecution also stimulated further debate within the Colonial Office concerning the law of martial law and indemnity legislation. There were two very big questions which could no longer be deferred or evaded. Did the proclamation of martial law in Jamaica bestow on men like Ramsay the legal authority to torture and kill with impunity? If it did not, did the indemnity legislation provide legal immunity to those who committed acts of torture or summary execution?

If the prosecution of Ramsay can be taken as a guide, the Colonial Office, the legal opinion of its law officers notwithstanding, proceeded on the premiss that the answer to both of these questions was negative. This policy was seen as alarming enough to Eyre that on 7 April 1866, two days before the JRC rendered its Report, he wrote from Jamaica explicitly to urge Cardwell not to disallow the

---

[251] Ibid. (3 Mar. 1866), 10; *Pall Mall Gazette* (13 Nov. 1866), 9.
[252] Chesson remarked in his diary that the Ramsay prosecution had been a 'fiasco thus far, owing to his liberation on bail by the Magistrate . . . and who is a relative of his family'. *CD*, 23 Mar. 1866.
[253] *JRC Report*, 525.   [254] Storks to Cardwell, 10 Mar. 1866, *CO* 137/401.

Indemnity Act.[255] In his letter Eyre contended that the statute had the 'same practical legality' as the recent legislation of Parliament which had suspended *habeas corpus* in Ireland. The letter then made another and, to Cardwell, more worrying assertion: '[E]ven if the local laws referred to were now disallowed yet as they have been in valid operation for some time subsequent to the transactions to be covered by them, and as they are essentially retrospective, the indemnity provided would still remain complete.' This contention, in combination with other doubts about the effect of the indemnity law, caused Heslop to conclude that the Ramsay case could 'not proceed to trial until the recent act of Indemnity shall have been disposed of by Her Majesty's government'.[256] Storks' despatch informing the Colonial Office of this development prompted Cardwell to write this personal notation on 5 May: 'This makes a decision with regard to the Act of Indemnity urgent.'

Of particular concern to Cardwell and his senior secretaries was the notion that the Indemnity Act might shield men like Ramsay from the law, even if it were disallowed by the home government. On this point, Sir Henry Taylor and Sir Frederic Rogers, the senior civil servants at the Colonial Office, contended that a Jamaica statute could not 'have the force of law after it ceased to be law'.[257] Still, neither man was confident that they understood all of the legal ramifications of this legislation, or of the effect of the Colonial Laws Validity Act. In the result, they recommended to Cardwell that yet another elaborate set of questions and sub-questions – more than a dozen in all – be put to the law officers of the Crown. This time Palmer and Collier would be asked even more precise questions, and more precise answers were expected in return. Some of the questions related specifically to the potential liability of Eyre for the execution of Gordon (a subject to be examined in depth later in this study). Other questions pertained to men like Ramsay, and whether a certificate of indemnity issued by the Governor would provide a defence for an act 'so barbarous or unjust as to merit punishment', and whether the Governor could withhold a certificate for the perpetrator of such an act. It was also specifically asked whether the Indemnity Act would cover the person 'who from malice, or passion, or otherwise' exceeded orders by putting a prisoner to death without trial.

The reply of Palmer and Collier, dated 8 June 1866, was typically concise (one folio page shorter than the two-page recital of assumptions and questions).[258] In their view, the legislature of Jamaica had had the legislative authority to create an indemnity for those who had implemented martial law. But the two lawyers were not certain whether 'the Act would supply a defence to such a charge as that of murder which is *malum in se*, and an offence against Imperial law'. In other words, it was not clear to them whether the indemnity could be extended to an act which, by definition, involved the guilty or wicked intent of the perpetrator.

---

[255] Eyre to Cardwell, 7 Apr. 1866, *CO* 137/405.   [256] Eyre to Cardwell, 21 Apr. 1866, ibid.
[257] See notations of Taylor on letters of Storks and Eyre, 1 May 1866, ibid.
[258] Law Officers to Colonial Office, 8 June 1866, *CO* 885/11.

What Palmer and Collier could more confidently aver was that the Governor was obliged to grant certificates of indemnity to persons who had acted in good faith and within the ambit of their authority. Any actions by their nature 'barbarous and unjust', conversely, would not satisfy these criteria. The lawyers were of the opinion, moreover, that the Indemnity Act could be pleaded as a defence at trial, but that it would not 'cover an excess of orders, from malice or passion, or the putting to death of a person without trial, unless in self-defence or in circumstances of imminent danger'. With regard to the potential liability of Eyre personally for the arrest of Gordon, and for his removal from the jurisdiction of the civil courts for summary trial and execution in a court martial, the lawyers made this pointed remark: 'After giving this subject very careful consideration, we are apprehensive that the Governor may be liable to an indictment for murder.' The officers concerned in the trial and execution of Gordon were similarly vulnerable.

It was obvious that the legal issues thrown up by the suppression were complex. It was obvious, too, that the Crown's lawyers were out of their depth in attempting to resolve them. (In fact, the Government's legal intelligence on the law of martial law and indemnity was in such an uncertain state that Cardwell's successor at the Colonial Office felt obliged to seek new advice on the same questions.)[259] In the late spring of 1866, however, Cardwell had no alternative but to make a decision on further criminal prosecutions based on information at hand. On 18 June, in a despatch written after the publication of the JRC's final report, Cardwell instructed Storks not to attempt 'any very minute endeavour to punish every act which may now be the subject of regret'.[260] On the other hand, Cardwell was emphatic that 'great offences ought to be punished', and that the Colonial Office would rely on Storks 'to accomplish this necessary object, and shall expect a full report on the measures which have been taken with that view'. With regard to the Indemnity Act, the Government's decision was that it would not be disallowed, but that indemnification would be extended only to those actions which the perpetrator 'reasonably and in good faith considered to be proper for the purpose of putting an end to the Insurrection'. Storks was expressly instructed 'not to give certificates under the Indemnity Act in cases in which there is reasonable ground to question the propriety of them'.[261] On Storks' order, Heslop prepared a protocol for the prosecution of the most serious cases.[262] The road was clear, in other words, to

[259] Remarkably enough, however, under Carnarvon the Colonial Office revisited these questions with the Crown lawyers yet again, in 1867. See Law Officers to Colonial Office, 2 Feb. 1866, ibid.

[260] The despatch was published in the *Daily News* (21 June 1866), 2.

[261] In the end, Storks gave out only one certificate of indemnity, to an official who had been sued for false imprisonment by a man he had arrested and detained under the direct order of Eyre. Storks to Carnarvon, as quoted in Finlason, *History of the Jamaica Case*, 347.

[262] In a memo prepared in July 1866 under the title, 'In Re Martial Law, Jamaica 1865', Heslop recommended that the most serious offenders should be summoned for committal hearings, and that the Crown proceed wherever a 'just conviction' might be obtained'. Heslop thought that Ramsay should be prosecuted at the next sessions. Ibid., 347–8.

move forward with the prosecution of Ramsay, and any other white Jamaicans who had committed heinous acts during martial law.

When in July 1866 the Conservatives formed a government led by Lord Derby, Cardwell was replaced by Carnarvon as Colonial Secretary. On 5 August Sir John Grant, the career Indian civil servant,[263] relieved Storks as Governor of Jamaica. These major political and personnel changes, however, did not signal a change in policy about the Jamaica prosecutions. In one of his first communications with Grant, Carnarvon ordered the Governor to continue the vigorous investigation of possible crimes committed by white against black Jamaicans, and on the principle that 'every case of hardship deserves enquiry'. 'I have repeated that direction in very pointed language,' Carnarvon wrote.[264]

On top of the Government's list of prospective accused was Duberry Ramsay.[265] Ramsay's case, along with those of three other white accused (charged with the lesser offences of unlawful flogging),[266] came before another grand jury of the East Circuit Court at Morant Bay on 18 October 1866.[267] The proceedings were held in a temporary courthouse, the permanent one having been burned down by Bogle's rebels the year before. The presiding judge was Alan Ker. In light of what Henry Storks called 'the nice and difficult points of law' raised by the charge, Heslop was assigned to put in the case for the Crown.[268] Once again, J. S. Williams acted as defence counsel for Ramsay (and the other accused). Due to rumours beforehand that feelings about the cases were running high among local blacks, and that there might be a 'disturbance' during the session, the witnesses were conveyed to Morant Bay by naval vessel. The Governor also sent a detachment of armed police and some regular troops.[269]

The grand jury was made up of only fifteen (instead of the customary twenty-three) men.[270] One newspaper reported that the jury 'consisted of persons taken from all classes', including seven coloured men and one black.[271] The purpose of the grand jury was to decide whether there was sufficient evidence to justify a trial. Ker delivered a long and carefully rendered charge in the case, both on the evidence and on the law of martial law.

Ker began by asking the jury to put themselves in Ramsay's place in the moments immediately after Marshall was cut down from the field gun, his back a

---

[263] Grant's previous post was Lieutenant-Governor of Bengal, where he had been sent to defuse a serious conflict between the planters and indigenous cultivators of indigo. 'The problem to be solved in Jamaica is so Indian in its character that I can conceive of no one so likely as an Indian to grapple with it.' Cardwell to Storks, 16 June 1866, Cardwell Papers, CO 30/48/43. See also DNB, xviii, 766–8.   [264] Carnarvon to Grant, 15 Aug. 1866, Cardwell Papers, CO 30/6/43.

[265] Ramsay's prosecution had been delayed for several months for lack of a decision from the Colonial Office on the indemnity statute. See Storks to Cardwell, 21 Apr. 1866, CO 137/405.

[266] John Woodward and James and Christopher Codrington were also charged on preferred indictments for the illegal flogging of women. See Colonial Standard (22 Oct. 1866), 2.   [267] Ibid.

[268] This had been decided before Storks was succeeded by Grant. Storks to Cardwell, 10 Mar. 1866, CO 137/401.   [269] Colonial Standard (24 Oct. 1866), 2.

[270] The Attorney General had great difficulty finding even fifteen eligible men who were willing to serve. Grant to Carnarvon, quoted in Finlason, History of the Jamaica Case, 356.

[271] For this account and quotes, see Colonial Standard (22 Oct. 1866), 2.

bloodied mess. Would they, as Ramsay had done, have seen him to 'savour of mutiny, and requiring therefore an exceptional display of vigour'? Or was the decision to hang Marshall 'mere wantonness of power'? Ker explained to the grand jury that in the absence of lawful justification all homicide is murder. To this he added that if at the time of the hanging 'the ordinary law of the land had been supreme...this would have been murder, and murder of the first type'. That raised the question of whether 'the prevalence of martial law' might affect culpability for such an act. Ker thought that 'unquestionably' it did. The rationale for martial law was the urgent suppression of armed invasion or insurrection. It enabled military men to take extraordinary measures – measures otherwise illegal – to restore the authority of the Crown. But having made this statement, Ker qualified it. Martial law did not 'by any means authorise or sanction every deed assumed to be done in its name. It stops far short of that.' There were legal boundaries on the use of martial powers during an emergency. Martial law, in other words, was delimited by a body of *law*. 'No greater error exists,' Ker told the jury, 'than to suppose that the subjecting of a district to the military power authorises excess on the part of those who administer that power...Reason and common sense must approve the particular act.' By definition, for instance, acts of bare revenge were unreasonable and illegal. 'The vindictive passions,' Ker elaborated, 'are prohibited their exercise as...peremptorily during military rule as in the tranquil and orderly state. Excess and wantonness, cruelty and unscrupulous contempt for human life meet with the same sanction from martial, nay more than from ordinary law.' Such a rule, Ker concluded, was essential to prevent a regime of martial law from 'degenerating into an instrument of mere private malice and revenge'.

Ker then turned to the subject of the Jamaica indemnity statute of November 1865. On this point his charge was terse: 'Indemnity Acts can only be pleaded in a Court of Justice by those who have fulfilled the conditions to which I have made reference in the earlier part of this address.' Specifically, in order for Ramsay to enjoy the protection of the Indemnity Act, his decision to hang Marshall without trial, in the eyes of a reasonable man, had to have been necessary for the purposes of suppressing the rebellion. This was an issue of fact for the petty jury at trial. It was for the grand jury to decide only whether the Crown had made out a *prima facie* case that Ramsay's conduct toward Marshall had been unnecessary.[272] 'Upon this subject,' Ker pointedly told the jury, 'I owe it to the administration of justice to remark that you ought not to have doubt.' Although he did not think it appropriate to say so explicitly, Ker clearly intimated that the jury should find a 'true bill' and send the case to trial.[273] On the procedural rules, at least twelve grand jurors had to agree on that course. Less than half an hour later, the jury returned with

---

[272] A finding of a 'true bill' would mean only that Ramsay would face an indictment and trial before a petty jury.

[273] According to the reading of the *Manchester Guardian* (15 Nov. 1866), 2, Ker's charge was 'very heavily and distinctly in favour finding a true bill against Ramsay'.

their verdict: 'In the Queen against Ramsay, no bill.'[274] As Governor Grant summarized in a despatch to Carnarvon, the grand jury had acted 'in direct opposition to the charge of the presiding judge'.[275]

On the basis of his standing instructions from the Colonial Office, Grant instructed Heslop to gather more evidence against him.[276] But the Governor now entertained serious misgivings about the efficacy of further prosecutions. In his despatches after the 'deplorable' verdict in Ramsay's case, Grant informed Carnarvon that it was unlikely that any Jamaican grand jury (as they would consist always of substantial white and coloured men) would ever find a true bill against a white man for actions taken during the suppression. A very strong criminal case had thrice been derailed, the third time after the jury had heard the 'full, exhaustive and remarkably lucid' charge of a high court judge. It was hard to imagine what more could be done. 'The personal grievance and the public evil are great,' Grant wrote, '[b]ut the fault is not with the Government.' The Crown had pursued the criminal cases 'thoroughly and judicially, in all its legal and moral bearings'. The best course for the future, Grant believed, was to dismiss Ramsay from his government post[277] and to carry on with thoroughgoing reforms to the colony's petty courts and, perhaps, its grand jury system.[278]

In the course of the next few months Carnarvon reluctantly concluded that Grant was correct, that Jamaica's 'class system' would prove an insuperable barrier to criminal convictions of white men. On 16 November 1866, Carnarvon informed his aides that the Ramsay case underscored that 'there will be a failure of justice in all similar cases tried in Jamaica'.[279] After further communication with Grant and the civil servants in London, Carnarvon reluctantly confirmed that the 'political prepossessions' of the class of Jamaicans who sat on grand juries precluded

[274] In five cases where white militia officers were accused of having committed violent crimes against black prisoners, the result was the same. In every case (the new cases centred mainly on some arbitrary floggings during the martial law) the Attorney General preferred a charge to the grand jury, the Crown presented uncontradicted evidence of guilt, the presiding judge urged the grand jury to indict, and the grand jury declined to do so. *Pall Mall Gazette* (13 Nov. 1866), 9.

[275] As quoted in Finlason, *History of the Jamaica Case*, 356.

[276] Grant to Carnarvon, 8 Nov. 1866, 24 Dec. 1864, *CO* 137/408. D. P. Nathan (the coloured and Jewish solicitor who had been retained by the Jamaica Committee) was approached by the Attorney General's office to assist in assembling a stronger criminal case against Ramsay, and new cases against other white militia officers. In the last months of 1866, Nathan investigated some thirteen cases of alleged violent abuse and murder during martial law. In the result, criminal charges were laid against five other white men.

[277] It appears that Grant's intervention here was to make permanent the dismissal of Ramsay first ordered by Storks in January 1866. At that time, Storks wrote to Cardwell to inform him that Ramsay had been sacked: 'There can be no excuse for such acts as Mr. Ramsay admits he has committed.' Storks to Cardwell, 18 Jan. 1866, Cardwell Papers, *CO* 30/48/43. Although Ramsay had not been convicted of a criminal offence, and continued to 'claim justification for his actions', Grant insisted that 'he still must be dismissed'. Grant to Carnarvon, 8 Nov. 1866, *CO* 137/408.

[278] Grant was so discouraged by the verdicts of the grand jury that he recommended 'the abolition of the grand jury system [in Jamaica], as at best useless for any of the true ends of justice'. Grant to Carnarvon, 24 Oct. 1866, *CO* 137/407.

[279] Notation to despatch of Grant to Carnarvon, 24 Oct. 1866, ibid.

'the adequate punishment of persons chargeable with signal inhumanity'.[280] Unless circumstances changed, the Government would not initiate any further prosecutions for crimes committed by whites during the martial law.[281] Carnarvon further decided that it would not be practicable to prosecute Jamaicans in the English courts. Instead, Carnarvon instructed Grant to go forward with the creation of a new local court system complete with stipendiary magistrates. (Action on the colony's grand jury system awaited a full report.[282]) Carnarvon also issued instructions which will be considered at length later in this study: that the Colonial Office draft a set of rules governing the use of martial law in the colonies.[283]

VI. The Case of Ensign Cullen and Dr. Morris

Legal jeopardy was also felt by some of the regular soldiers who participated in the suppression. During the first week of martial law, Ensign Francis Cullen was put in command of a detachment of some fifty black soldiers from the 1st West Indian regiment. His orders were to march inland from Morant Bay and to pacify the northeastern sector of Surrey.[284] What happened on this mission is revealing both of the attitudes of some regular military officers toward alleged rebels, and of the willingness of the JRC to ferret out information that was not flattering either to the officers or to the Crown. This story also usefully brings our attention back to the kind and quality of investigative work done by the Commission, the stance of the British authorities toward this information, and to the question of legal accountability in the Jamaica affair.

According to Cullen's sworn testimony before the Commission, his assignment had not been very eventful. The regiment had received no fire from rebels, and itself fired only one shot.[285] There were perhaps ten (Cullen was unable to recall accurately) courts martial and executions. Another twenty or so men, and one woman, were flogged.[286] To be sure, the regiment had passed some unburied corpses on the road, but Cullen did not know who they were or who had killed them. Cullen provided this evidence on 5 March 1866. But by then the JRC had heard a number of black witnesses testify that Cullen was a sadistic killer who

---

[280] Notations on despatch of Grant to Carnarvon, 24 Dec. 1866, *CO* 137/408.

[281] Ibid. The subject of further prosecutions for crimes committed during the suppression was raised in Parliament by Charles Buxton in March 1867. Charles Adderley, Under Secretary for the Colonies, answered that after having failed multiple times to persuade grand juries in Jamaica to indict white militia officers, the Government had decided that it would be fruitless to persist. *Hansard*, clxxxvi (21 Mar. 1866), 275–80. [282] Ibid.

[283] This idea was first suggested in a despatch from Storks to Cardwell, 16 Mar. 1866, *CO* 885/3. See also Carnarvon to Lord Derby, 5 Dec. 1866, *CO* 30/6/138. These rules are discussed at length, below, Epilogue. [284] Heuman, '*The Killing Time*', 116–17.

[285] *JRC Minutes*, Q. 34,634.

[286] The JRC asked Cullen whether any men had been 'pelted' or 'obliged to kneel down and thank the officers for having flogged them'. Ibid., Q. 34,687–90.

had been party to a number of murders during the martial law.[287] The story had been repeated that Cullen and Morris had taken custody of four prisoners near a post-office close to the (plundered) sugar estate of Duckinfield. When one of the four slipped his restraints and escaped into a cane field, the three others were shot to death by Cullen while Morris looked on.[288]

The JRC interviewed Morris for the first time on 10 March 1866. Morris had been the first surgeon on the scene in the aftermath of the violence at Morant Bay. On him fell the grisly job of collecting and examining the bodies of the twenty-two persons who had been killed by the rebels. On his own evidence, however, Morris was very far from a squeamish or timorous man. He told the JRC (with no evident hesitation) of the occasion when he fired his revolver into a man struggling in his death throes after a hanging.[289] On another occasion he took his sword and 'ran through' a man who had been executed moments before.[290] Morris was less forthcoming, however, when the JRC asked him to verify that he had killed a total of eleven black prisoners during the martial law. Morris denied having done so. Morris also denied that he had written a letter to his father claiming to have slain nine people with his sword and revolver, a letter later published in a Jamaican newspaper.[291] According to Morris, he had not even pointed his revolver at a person the entire time of his 'expedition' with Cullen's regiment.

In time the JRC had enough reason to doubt the veracity of Cullen's original statements that he was recalled for re-examination. In this second session Cullen was confronted with specific allegations (made in one instance by a coloured schoolteacher[292]) that he had watched Morris shoot to death without provocation 'a boy sitting on some steps' and a man named Billy Gray.[293] Cullen testified that the allegations were 'positively untrue'. Later the same day, the JRC pressed Cullen about the three men shot near the post-office. Had Morris whispered to him that the men should be 'put on the road and then shot'? Cullen stated that at the relevant times Morris had been too ill with fever to have committed these crimes.[294] In still a third session that day Cullen was recalled and again swore, after some hedging about 'great confusion of circumstances at that time', that the shootings had not occurred.[295]

The JRC persisted. On 3 April it insisted again on the re-examination both of Cullen and Morris. In an extraordinary move, the JRC arranged a police-style line-up of military officers including Cullen and Morris. Three witnesses were asked to identify the two officers from the line of men, and then to recount their allegations against them. Although they had never met Cullen or Morris before or after the day of the alleged shootings, all three witnesses identified them from the

---

[287] The 'apparently credible witnesses' against Cullen and Morris included a postmaster, the schoolmaster, and the keeper of the local lighthouse. *Daily News* (1 May 1866), 5.

[288] *JRC Minutes*, evidence of Abraham Donaldson, Q. 48,038, *passim*.

[289] Ibid., Q. 39783.   [290] Ibid., Q. 39,952–4   [291] Ibid., Q. 39,960–8.

[292] Ibid., evidence of John Anderson, Q. 45,289.   [293] Ibid., Q. 47,569–87.

[294] Ibid., Q. 47,636–68.   [295] Ibid., Q. 47,790–860.

line-up.[296] The recollections of these witnesses were also strikingly similar and specific. Cullen's detachment had come to rest at a back country post-office in the Plantain Garden District. Morris had taken sick from fever and took himself into the building to lie down. Soon thereafter four prisoners had been brought in. The commotion caused by the escaped prisoner roused Morris from the post-office.[297] Outside he found Cullen preparing to flog the three remaining prisoners. Morris approached Cullen and whispered into his ear. With this the men were cut down from their whipping post. One of the witnesses was Cyphus Hills, a black rural police constable assigned to Cullen's regiment at the time of the incident. Hills testified that he saw Morris and some black soldiers take the prisoners over to the side of the road and shoot them as Cullen looked on.[298] Another witness, John Duany, was more specific. The prisoners had been tied to the fence and shot one by one.[299] The dead men then were buried near where they had fallen.

The JRC tried to be even-handed in the matter. On the same day, 3 April, four enlisted men (all but one identified as 'black' or 'brown') of the 1st West Indian regiment were brought in to testify. In turn each man steadfastly denied that any prisoners had been shot by Morris or any other person with the detachment. One witness claimed that he had been with Morris in the post-office during the entire length of his illness with fever, and that the surgeon had not left the building.[300] Another witness, a young Irish corporal named O'Connor, told the JRC that he had not heard a single firearm discharged, or even a man flogged, during the entire expedition.[301] It should be noted here that one of the black soldiers, Corporal Hunter, had been identified by Duany as one of the men who had participated in the shootings.[302]

When all of the witnesses had been interviewed, Cullen and Morris were recalled a final time. Morris was asked to comment on the testimony that he had just heard. He admitted that he had been taken ill at the post-office and carried inside. He denied that any prisoners had been brought to the post-office or shot. Cullen was also asked whether he had heard the evidence presented that day, and upon thinking it over, if he wanted to correct his previous accounts. Cullen did not. Like Morris he flatly denied that while at the post-office he had been brought prisoners or that they had been shot.

When Cullen and Morris were called and then recalled to give evidence before the Commission, Duberry Ramsay already had been brought before magistrates on a charge of murder. There no longer could be any doubt but that the colonial authorities were prepared to bring white men, even well-connected white men, to book for crimes committed during the suppression. Clearly Cullen did not think himself safe from criminal prosecution because he was a soldier. Men so secure do not need to lie.

---

[296] See, for example, evidence of the schoolteacher Anderson, Q. 48,371–5.
[297] Ibid., Q.48,038–71.   [298] Ibid., 48,444–85.   [299] Ibid., Q. 48,914–16.
[300] Ibid., Maddocks, Q. 48,785.   [301] Ibid., O'Connor, Q. 48,750–64.
[302] Ibid., Q. 48,898.

It is all but certain, moreover, that Cullen, Morris, and the soldiers of the 1st West Indian regiment blatantly lied to the JRC. The prosecution of Ramsay and the presence of the JRC gave them good reason to do so. Their careers, even their necks, were on the line. The men who testified that they witnessed shootings, on the other hand, had not themselves been ill-treated by Cullen's detachment. They had no obvious reason to lie about the actions of white and black men who had not harmed them personally. It is hard to imagine, moreover, that so many witnesses, witnesses not part of a military unit and not in peril of prosecution, could have colluded in telling the same blatant untruth.[303] But there is another, more material, reason to conclude that Cullen and Morris were liars. Their evidence was that *no prisoners had been taken or shot*, full stop. In the summer of 1866, the alleged murders of the three men at the Plantain Garden post-office were investigated by the authorities. The bodies of the three missing men were found, their gunshot wounds located precisely where witnesses had stated they would be.

The Report of the JRC, while it did not explicitly conclude that Cullen and Morris had perjured themselves, clearly implied it. On the extant evidence, Carnarvon requested of the Commander-in-Chief that he institute a court martial.[304] 'The more I consider the affair,' Governor Grant wrote of the Cullen and Morris case to Carnarvon in October 1866, 'the more I am impressed by its serious character.'[305] 'My own belief was that so horrible a story could not be true,' Grant confessed, 'but the finding and identification of the bodies leaves too little room now for doubt.' To the Governor's reckoning, the case against Cullen and Morris was 'morally the worst case of all, worse than Ramsay's'. Ramsay had executed Marshall in a 'frenzy of excitement', while the execution of the prisoners struck Grant as 'inconceivably cold-blooded'. Grant predicted that there would be a scandal in England if Cullen and Morris faced only court martial and dismissal for such crimes. He recommended that they be tried for murder in the civil courts irrespective of the finding of a court martial. However, Grant was also of the view that it would be better for Jamaica if the trials took place in England. The whole matter, Grant added, 'makes ones blood run cold'. But before his despatch could reach Carnarvon, Grant learned that the grand jury at Morant Bay refused to indict Ramsay. Proceedings against Cullen and Morris in the civilian courts no longer looked viable.

In the Colonial Office in London, Sir Frederic Rogers drafted a despatch to Grant stating that 'if you should see no rational prospect of true bills being found [against Cullen or Morris], even on the amplest evidence, by a Jamaican grand jury, the only course to be taken . . . will be to abandon the prosecutions'.[306] This

---

[303] As Grant later commented to Carnarvon: 'If the case of the prosecution is false, it is the result of one of the most remarkable conspiracies and the most consistent fabrications ever contrived.' Grant to Carnarvon, 24 Nov. 1866, Carnarvon Papers, *CO* 30/6/143.

[304] *Hansard*, clxxxiv (2 Aug. 1866), 1890–1.

[305] Grant to Carnarvon, 8 Oct. 1866, Carnarvon Papers, *CO* 30/6/143.

[306] Draft despatch to Grant, 31 Oct. 1866, *CO* 137/408.

despatch was never sent; the Colonial Office had already decided to discontinue the prosecution policy. A final despatch from Grant suggested that his Government should prosecute Cullen and Morris on the principle of the matter, that the authorities 'should not omit to do what is right so far as their powers extend'.[307] But before civilian officials acted, in October 1866, Cullen and Morris were tried in Jamaica by an army court martial, charged with various military offences (*not* including murder) under the Mutiny Act.[308] In London Carnarvon remained convinced that Cullen and Morris, if they were convicted of military offences, should be prosecuted in the civilian courts for murder.[309] After thirty-six days of hearings, both men were acquitted. One contemporary lawyer concluded of the verdict that the members of the court martial had either ignored the evidence, or had concluded that the evidence had been a 'complete fabrication'.[310] There was no other way to explain the outcome of their trial. These were the first and last legal proceedings brought against the two men.

VII. The Final Report of the Jamaica Royal Commission

In the wake of the Jamaica uprising and suppression the legal preoccupations and initiatives of the Colonial Office and local government were many and varied. In order to achieve some sense of their nature and content, our attention moved away from the quasi-judicial investigations of the JRC. It is time now that the work of the JRC is brought back into focus.

The JRC finished hearing evidence on 3 April 1866. In fifty-one days of hearings more than 700 witnesses had answered more than 70,000 questions. The Commissioners had heard from those who had perpetrated, observed, and received violence. They heard from black, white, and coloured witnesses from every stratum of Jamaican society, and of the colonial state. The enormous body of oral and documentary evidence collected by the JRC was then assembled for publication in 2,000 folio pages. The *Dublin Review* likened the collection to a 'mighty ocean of print'.[311] The *Report*, forty-one folio pages long, was finished inside of one week after the completion of hearings. It was a staggering – if unavoidably contentious – feat of fact-gathering, synthesis, and analysis.[312]

The *Report of the Jamaica Royal Commission* was divided into four parts. The first part consisted of a ten-page introduction to (and defence of) the methodologies and procedures of the investigation. The second consisted of the Commissioners' findings with regard to the origins and outbreak of the Jamaica

---

[307] Grant to Carnarvon, 14 Nov. 1866, *CO* 30/6/143.
[308] Finlason, *History of the Jamaica Case*, 339–41.   [309] Quoted ibid., 341.
[310] W. F. Finlason, the prolific scholar of all of the legal dimensions of the Jamaica affair, thought that Cullen and Morris were 'clearly guilty of murder'. Ibid.
[311] *Dublin Review* 7 (Oct. 1866), 362.
[312] The JRC cost Parliament almost £9,000. *Falmouth Post* (28 Aug. 1866), 1.

'disturbances'. The third part addressed the suppression under two subsections, 'Measures Adopted' and 'Conduct of Persons engaged in the Suppression'. The first subsection of part three addressed the proclamation of martial law, and military operations, and provided a numerical summary of punishments inflicted. The second included further details about punishments, the courts martial, the George Gordon case, the treatment of political prisoners, and remarks on the duration of martial law. The Commissioners set forth their final conclusions in the final, and most brief, section of the report. As a whole package, the report was calculated both to inform and persuade.

In the first ten pages of the report the Commissioners described and vigorously defended their *modus operandi*. There is an unmistakable tone of self-justification in this section, and understandably enough. The Commissioners knew that in some quarters their findings, whatever they were, would be castigated. They thus began by listing the numerous serious impediments to the inquiry. There had been too little time. It had been difficult to interview witnesses in a sensible order. Then there was the 'still more serious complexion in the nature of the evidence itself'.[313] The Commission had persevered with scores of ill-educated black witnesses who spoke in an unintelligible dialect, could not comprehend questions, and misunderstood the nature of the Commission's work. Still other witnesses, 'even of the educated class, could scarcely be restrained from giving opinions...as equivalent to facts.'[314]

The final report emphasized that these problems, as formidable as they were, had not stopped the Commissioners from fulfilling their mandate. If the Commissioners had erred in any direction, they had erred by affording 'too great a facility in giving audience to all persons of whatever class'. Readers of the report were urged to accept 'that any incidental formal defects will be thought of minor consequence, in comparison with the object which throughout we have regarded as paramount – that of fullness, thoroughness and impartiality'. The Commissioners then made another important point. The JRC had not been just any sort of investigation. From the outset the Commissioners had endeavoured for their inquiry to be of a 'judicial character'.[315] Witnesses had testified under oath. They had been properly cautioned about self-incrimination. So that the appropriate arm's length could be maintained between witnesses and Commissioners, all depositions, summons, and related documentation had been handled by a team of subordinate lawyers and clerks. Further, witnesses had been permitted to bring lawyers, and their lawyers to suggest and, on some occasions, to put questions to other witnesses. In making these arrangements, the Commission asserted, it had been guided by only one aim: 'the ascertainment of the truth'.

Some of the 'truth' ascertained by the Commission supported a crucial contention of the former Governor Eyre. The Commission found that what

---

[313] *JRC Report*, 506.   [314] Ibid.   [315] Ibid., 507.

happened at Morant Bay in mid-October 1865 was not a mere riot, but the first phase of what might have become a catastrophic armed rebellion. The Governor was credited for having correctly surmised that the violence had unfolded according to a 'preconcerted plan, and that murder was distinctly contemplated'.[316] It was also noted that Eyre had not been alone in holding this view. In fact, almost every important political and legal official in the colony, including the Chief Justice, the Attorney General, and some of the Governor's erstwhile political opponents, agreed that the circumstances justified the proclamation of martial law. The Council of War, the Commissioners further concluded, had 'good reason for the advice which they gave, and the Governor was well-justified in acting upon that advice'.[317] Had 'more than a momentary success been obtained by the insurgents,' the report further concluded, 'their ultimate overthrow would have been attended with a still more fearful loss of life and property'.[318] For these reasons the Council of War 'would have incurred a serious responsibility if, with this information before them, they had thrown away the advantage of the terror which the very name of martial law is calculated to create in a population such as that which exists in this island'.[319] On this issue the Commissioners went so far as to state that '*praise* is due to Governor Eyre for the skill, promptitude, and vigour which he manifested during the earliest stages of the insurrection' (emphasis added).[320]

It is worth noting that the Commissioners did not, however, attempt to define the term 'martial law,' or comment on its place in the British constitution. Instead they operated from the unquestioned premiss that the proclamation of martial law was valid under a Jamaica statute. Their problem was not with martial law *per se*, but the way in which it was implemented. In this regard the Commission found that there had been a series of grievous mistakes and abuses. First, some military officers had inflicted unnecessary and, in some instances, even 'positively barbarous' punishments.[321] Second, many of the courts martial had been slipshod in their rules, procedures, and decision-making. While it was acknowledged that courts martial could not have 'maintained the same perfect regularity and adherence to technical rules' as civilian courts, the Commissioners insisted that there were 'certain great principles which ought under no circumstances to be violated'.[322] Third, the Governor had kept martial law in place for too long, and his soldiers under too little oversight.

The Commission focused on the Gordon case as a particularly egregious example of these failings. Although Gordon's conduct had not been without fault before the rebellion (the record showed that on several occasions he had recklessly inflamed his 'ignorant and fanatical followers'), there was no doubt that Gordon's court martial had been profoundly flawed: 'the evidence, oral and documentary, appears to us to be wholly insufficient to establish the charge upon which

[316] Ibid., 512. [317] Ibid., 517. [318] Ibid., 538. [319] Ibid. [320] Ibid.
[321] Ibid., 539. [322] Ibid.

[Gordon] took his trial.'[323] The Commission was less plain-spoken on a number of other important issues relating to Gordon's case. It did not comment, for instance, on the problematic legality of his arrest, transportation, and trial. Nor did it venture an opinion on whether Gordon's executioners had committed culpable murder.

The ambivalent treatment of the Gordon case reflected a deeper ambivalence about the use of terror as an instrument of government in the empire. On one hand, the JRC accepted that it would sometimes be the case – especially when rulers were greatly outnumbered by the ruled – that a colonial government needed recourse to unfettered military coercion. In other words, martial law was an indispensable weapon of imperial rule. The incipient rebellion at Morant Bay was seen as presenting a case in point. On the other hand, however, the final report of the Commission also reflected some liberal instincts. The JRC referred to martial law as a necessary but palpable *evil*. The preamble of the proclamation document, the JRC stated, 'did not in any sense exaggerate the magnitude of the evils attending martial law'.[324] The Commission viewed the history of martial law as a history of 'mischief and calamities'; its implementation 'must ever be considered as amongst the greatest evils'.[325] No matter how the authorities attempted to control it, the JRC repeated, 'the evils of martial law must be very great.'[326]

The Commission attempted to address these tensions by distinguishing between three aspects of the Jamaican martial law: the initial necessity of its proclamation, its actual implementation, and its duration. The Governor merited praise on the first but not the second or third counts. He had neglected to give military officers precise instructions on the use of violence. The severe punishments inflicted, the JRC concluded, 'seem to us to have been far greater than the necessity required'.[327] Recourse to capital punishment was 'unnecessarily frequent'; the burning of houses was 'wanton and cruel'. The infliction of brutal floggings had been 'reckless' and, in one location, 'positively barbarous'. These problems had been compounded when martial law was continued 'in its full force' for an entire month, at least two weeks longer than warranted by necessity. The unjustified continuation of martial law caused many subjects in the colony to be 'deprived for longer than the necessary period of the great constitutional privileges by which the security of life and property is provided for'.[328] This was perhaps the Commission's single most damning criticism of Governor Eyre.

As the JRC finished its work in Jamaica, it was almost universally agreed among colonists that the three Commissioners had carried out their duties with skill, energy, and good faith. 'I am told,' Cardwell wrote to Henry Storks in April 1866, 'that the representatives of the anti-Eyre party express approval ... in high terms of the way in which the Commissioners have conducted the inquiry, and I trust that Mr. Eyre

---

[323] *JRC Report*, 535.   [324] Ibid., 517.   [325] Ibid., 516, 537.   [326] Ibid., 537.
[327] Ibid., 506.   [328] Ibid., 539.

and the white party in Jamaica show this feeling also'.[329] In April 1866, Frederick Chesson, the Secretary of the Jamaica Committee, recorded in his diary that Gorrie had spoken 'very highly of the Commissioners, especially of Sir Henry Storks, who is an honest and able man, and very favourably impressed with the negroes'.[330]

The final report of the JRC reached London at the end of April 1866. Cardwell and other leading members of the Government then took the next six weeks to 'mature their opinion as to the course they ought to follow'.[331] Among the many crucial issues which remained unresolved was the possible disallowance of the Jamaica indemnity statute. By this time the matter had been intensively but indecisively discussed between Cardwell and senior officials of the Colonial Office for more than three months. As we have seen, behind the scenes Eyre continued to lobby strenuously for the Government's assent.[332] Cardwell also was aware that the criminal prosecution of Ramsay could not proceed until the indemnity question was cleared up.[333] A decision on disallowance could not be postponed much longer. On 18 June, the Royal Commission's final report and evidence finally were laid before Parliament. Later that day the Government published its official response to the Jamaica affair in the form of a despatch from Cardwell to Storks. The document laid out the Government's final position on the Jamaica affair, and in so doing placed its stamp on a particular reading – if not an entirely forthright or decisive reading – of the legal nature and implications of martial law.

The central message of the despatch was that the Government 'generally concur' with the conclusions of the Jamaica Royal Commission.[334] Governor Eyre had faced 'planned resistance' to colonial authority and, with the information then available to him, had been correct to accept advice from his Council of War to proclaim martial law in the area of insurrection. Cardwell went so far as to state that the Governor and his councillors might have 'incurred a serious liability if, with the information before them, they had thrown away the advantage of the terror which the very name martial law was calculated to inspire.' But there were limits to Cardwell's 'commendation'. The Government also agreed with the JRC that martial law, and the punitive measures of martial law, remained in force too long. As a result, many of the executed persons were 'neither ringleaders of the horror nor actual participants in the actual murder or outrage'. While the Government did not 'impute to Mr. Eyre any personal cognisance at the time of those measures', at the same time when martial law is proclaimed, it was a Governor's 'bounden duty to restrain within the narrowest possible limits the severities incident to that law'. The Government was mindful that 'good government is not the object of martial law. Example and punishment are not its objects;

---

[329] Cardwell to Storks, 16 Apr. 1866, Cardwell Papers, *CO* 30/48/43.
[330] *CD*, 16 Apr. 1866.   [331] *London Review* (23 June 1866), 691–2.
[332] See the extensive notations on this subject of Henry Taylor, 1 May 1865, *CO* 137/405.
[333] Storks to Cardwell, 21 Apr. 1866, ibid.
[334] As reprinted in the *Daily News* (21 June 1866), 2.

its severities can only be justified, and as far as, they are absolutely necessary for the immediate establishment of the public safety.' With regard to Gordon the Government believed that while his arrest was justified, he ought to have been kept in detention until he could be tried in the civilian courts. Gordon's execution, therefore, was unjustified. With regard to the subject of indemnity, the Government's position was that it would not cover acts 'either by the governor or by subordinate officers, unless they (such as in the case of the governor) might reasonably and in good faith consider them to be proper for the purpose of putting an end to the insurrection'.[335] In this regard, the Government also was of the view that Jamaica's martial law statute of 1844 provided 'as complete indemnity as the Indemnity Act itself'. The Government nonetheless decided to leave the law in place while continuing with the criminal prosecution of any officials who had not acted reasonably or in good faith. As for Edward Eyre, the Government decided that he would not be restored to his previous office. Effectively, Eyre's career as a civil servant official was over. The despatch made no mention of a possible criminal prosecution.

These decisions ramified, if not altogether clearly, for the law of martial law. The Government had given its blessing to the view that a colonial governor was legally entitled to proclaim martial law whenever in possession of credible evidence of armed insurrection. (Whether this power was derived from statute or Crown prerogative, Cardwell did not say.) In such circumstances, in fact, the governor of a colony would face censure if he did not so act. The Government was also definite that martial law, while it permitted officers in the field to use extreme violence in crushing revolt, did not imply a boundless discretion to injure lives and property.

For a number of reasons Cardwell's despatch did not end the Jamaica controversy. First, the despatch was a political and not a legal document. While it indicated how and why a Government would exercise its executive discretion, it was not bolstered either by an act of Parliament or a court decision. Second, the week after the despatch was published, Lord Russell's Liberal government fell. There was nothing to prevent the new Conservative government from taking a different position on the Jamaica affair. Finally, while a large segment of the English political class appeared to agree with the Commission's findings, and with the thrust of Cardwell's despatch, a number of influential men did not.

By the time the Jamaica documents were published in the mother country, England, as the *Daily News* put it, had become 'powerfully engaged' by domestic (the Reform Bill) and foreign (the Prussian–Austrian conflict) events.[336] Still, the issues raised by the JRC's report generated a very extensive commentary. Three points were particularly contentious. The first concerned the JRC itself. Had the Commissioners done a good job of getting at the truth of what had happened in Jamaica? The second related to the specific conclusions of the JRC. Were they

---

335 As reprinted in the *Daily News* (21 June 1866), 2.
336 Ibid. For further discussion, see below, Ch. 3.

coherent and compelling? The third point concerned the Government's response to the Report. Had Russell and his cabinet made the right decisions about the future of the colony, about the use of martial law, about Governor Eyre, and about the question of legal culpability?

On the first point only was there a substantial consensus: the JRC had done everything in their power to complete a thorough, fair-minded, and conscientious inquiry. *The Times*, although it had been wary of the enterprise, thought that the basic findings of the Committee were 'decisive'.[337] The *Manchester Guardian* concluded that in 'the midst of this heated partisanship . . . the Commissioners held their impartial way'.[338] 'No one,' the *Guardian* contended, 'can question the impartiality of Sir H. Storks and his colleagues.' The staunchly conservative *Morning Herald* was equally impressed with the 'remarkable way' in which the Commissioners had accomplished a difficult mission. It thought that their final report should be 'accepted as a judicial determination of an earnest and angry controversy'.[339] In fact, as an exercise in the *pursuit* of empirical truths, a pursuit sponsored by a sitting government, the JRC was seen as an almost unqualified success. The basic facts of the Jamaica uprising and suppression had been found out; what mattered now was the interpretation of these facts.

In their assessment of the specific conclusions of the JRC, the conservative papers claimed that they vindicated Edward Eyre. The *Morning Post*, for instance, drew attention to the finding that there '*was* an insurrection, and that insurrection would probably have spread through the length and breadth of Jamaica if prompt and vigorous measures had not been taken for its suppression.'[340] Along the same lines, the *Evening Standard* ventured that the Report would 'bitterly disappoint those who would hunt Mr. Eyre to his ruin'.[341] For the *Standard*, the key conclusion of the JRC was that Eyre had been compelled by circumstance 'to demonstrate the superiority of the white race'. The *Morning Herald* endorsed the view that Eyre deserved to be commended for having invoked measures 'by which the horrors of a servile warfare were averted'.[342] 'Revolutions,' the paper reminded readers, 'are not made of rosewater, and rebellions are not put down with kid gloves.' By the same token, it could not be evaded that the Commission had reproached the former governor. The *Herald* thought that Eyre's sins were slight and excusable, and that he should not be 'even temporarily disgraced'. But this was very much the minority view, even among the conservative papers. *The Times* took the position that as Governor of the colony Eyre bore the responsibility both to proclaim martial law and to revoke the proclamation when it was no longer necessary. The Governor's explanation for why he had not done this, and why he

---

[337] *The Times* (20 June 1866), 9.   [338] *Manchester Guardian* (21 June 1866), 2.

[339] *Morning Herald* (20 June 1866), 4. The *Dublin Review* rejected the use of the word 'judicial' in describing the JRC because it could not decide the innocence or guilt of men as a matter of law. (Oct. 1866), 398.   [340] *Morning Post* (19 June 1866).

[341] *Evening Standard* (20 June 1866).   [342] *Morning Herald* (20 June 1866), 4.

had not kept his soldiers on a tighter leash, was 'clearly inadequate'.[343] Because of this 'grave error of judgment' it was 'impossible' that Eyre should 'resume the government of Jamaica'. On this point *The Economist* was in complete agreement: Eyre's misjudgement was properly understood as a 'political more than a personal offence, and Mr. Cardwell inflicted the highest political penalty now enforced; he broke the offender's career'.[344]

The liberal papers also generally endorsed the view that Eyre's main fault was not in the proclamation but regulation of martial law. The *London Review* believed that Eyre had failed miserably in this part of his duty: 'Herein lies the gist of the charge against [the] Governor ... the powers of law were strained – or, rather, law and justice were equally defied – in order that a spirit of the wildest revenge might have full swing.'[345] 'No one can doubt,' the *Manchester Guardian* concurred, 'that unless this wholesale destruction of life and property was absolutely necessary for the restoration of order, it was entirely indefensible.'[346] '[H]aving found it necessary for the safety of Jamaica to let the dominant caste loose,' *The Economist* summarized, 'the Governor could neither recall it to discipline, nor keep its fury within legitimate bounds.'[347] Eyre's great error was to have considered martial law 'as a mode of government, not merely an instrument intended only to subdue the resistance which makes government impossible'.

Among the more radical newspapers, comments on the findings of the Royal Commission were more blistering. The *Examiner* thought that the Commission had issued a 'whitewashing report'.[348] Its conclusions were seen as 'feeble and timid', and reflected 'a manifest anxiety to exculpate the authorities'.[349] Even as the Commissioners catalogued the 'foulest misdeeds', the *Daily News* lamented, 'from the beginning to the end of the Report they do not decisively condemn a single person'.[350] By these lights the Government was equally culpable for having failed to make up the shortcomings of the JRC. In his 'hesitating censure', the *Spectator* observed, Cardwell had missed the opportunity 'for marking powerfully the will of the country with regard to the treatment of a dependent and inferior race'.[351] When his colony was plunged into crisis, Governor Eyre had proved himself an 'energetic military administrator, and no more'. That Eyre had not acted from private malice (when he permitted the military to hang Gordon and scores of others) 'may absolve him of a *sin*, but not

---

[343] *The Times* (19 June 1866), 11.   [344] *The Economist* (30 June 1866), 765.
[345] *London Review* (23 June 1866), 691–2.   [346] *Manchester Guardian* (21 June 1866), 2.
[347] *The Economist* (30 June 1867), 764–5.
[348] *Examiner* as reprinted in the *Daily News* (26 June 1866), 5.
[349] Letter of Buxton to *The Times* (30 June 1866), 12. The Jamaica Committee held this view officially. See also John Gorrie, *Illustrations of Martial Law in Jamaica. Jamaica Papers no. VI* (London, 1867).
[350] *Daily News* (20 June 1866), 4. The opinion that the JRC report had not gone far enough in its 'adverse expressions' was shared by Gladstone. Gladstone to Cardwell, 13 June 1866, Gladstone Papers, BL Add. MS. 44536, f. 60.   [351] *Spectator* (23 June 1866), 683–4.

of a political crime'. What was crucial now, 'for the sake of the British Empire' was to 'mark with strongly expressed, graphic censure, if not some *act* of punishment . . . that British justice is no respecter of persons, and exists for the equal protection of all'.

VIII. Jamaica through the Prism of Law

In the summer of 1867 the *Westminster Review* published a long essay on how Jamaica had come to ruin.[352] The colony's downfall was traced to the introduction of slavery, and to the 'exhaustive system of agriculture which always accompanies slavery'.[353] In the nineteenth century the fragile sugar economy was further undermined by the removal of protective tariffs. By the 1860s Jamaica's tiny white community, now reduced by debt and dissipation, struggled to maintain mastery over a teeming population of free but impoverished and increasingly desperate black men and women. But the instruments of white domination – a discredited legislative body and a corrupt local judiciary – were antiquated and weak. At the same time the main sources of discord among blacks – the system of landholding, the importation of coolie labour, the persistence of drought – were intensifying. In these dire circumstances, a few incendiary black preachers were able to induce a spasm of violence on one side, grim retaliation on the other.

All of this was very well known to the politicians and imperial bureaucrats charged with the task of responding to the Jamaica crisis. They knew that the colony's social and economic structure was broken. What they did not know was what to do about it. The mid-Victorian imperial state did not possess the knowledge, resources, or will to rebuild an entire society. What they could do, however, what their training predisposed them to do, was to undertake a series of restorative legal initiatives. If the Colonial Office did not know how to repair a broken economy, it did have some notion of how to reform a constitution, reorganize a court system, and prosecute criminal wrongdoers. By these lights it made sense that two of three men sent out to investigate what had happened in Jamaica, the two who would shoulder most of its weight, were lawyers. Their job was to find who had done what to whom, and with what legal authority. In the meantime, the Colonial Office consulted other lawyers about a new constitution, about the nature and implications of martial law, and the operation of acts of indemnity. Jamaica's profound social and economic malaise was pushed into the background as the Government in England coordinated a multi-faceted legal assault on the island. In the 1860s English imperial statecraft was the preserve of the lawyer–bureaucrat, not the political economist.

---

[352] 'Jamaica', *Westminster Review* 88 (July 1867), 188–225.   [353] Ibid.

The British Government's legalistic response to the Jamaica affair was the product of deeply ingrained habits of mind. Cardwell, Rogers, and Henry Taylor – the principal architects of the Government's post-rebellion Jamaica policy – had all been educated as lawyers. They saw the world through the prism of law. It was therefore entirely the natural thing, and eminently the *practical* thing, to respond to the Jamaica crisis by holding some men accountable in the courts, while more far-reaching changes were wrought to the colony's legal institutions. The predisposition of the Government to act through law, moreover, was strongly encouraged from outside. After all, the most vocal critics of the Jamaica suppression were themselves intensely preoccupied with its legal and constitutional implications. The most persistent allegation about the conduct of Governor Eyre and his soldiers was that it had been illegal. In this way a broad consensus was formed between the Government and its antagonists that law should be at the forefront of investigation and intervention in Jamaica.

One of the most interesting things about the JRC, then, is what it was *not*: it was not a panel of assumed experts (insofar as such experts existed) primed to diagnose and redress the ailing political economy of the colony.[354] By the same token, what the JRC actually *was* is significant enough. From its inception the JRC was conceived of (and almost universally embraced) as a quasi-judicial body charged with the mission of discovering facts about some very troubling events. In perfect good faith the Government assumed – and almost no one disputed this assumption – that the important facts to discover about Jamaica were *legal* facts. Had it in fact been lawful for Governor Eyre to proclaim martial law? If so, was it kept in place for too long? What had been done to British subjects during the period of martial law? Was it possible that some officials might have broken the law of public emergency?

Gurney and Maule were thought superbly equipped to answer such questions, and in a manner that would be comprehensible and acceptable both to the Government and the English political class. They were also superbly equipped to do their job while remaining detached from specific political men and their agendas. The Royal Commissioners were given very ample latitude to gather, assemble, and analyse evidence free of outside interference. Some years after the JRC finished its work, Gurney recalled that he and his co-Commissioners had 'entered upon [their task] with no other feeling than eliciting the truth; and we were fully determined to declare the truth when elicited'.[355] Self-congratulatory though this statement was, its credibility was not seriously disputed by contemporaries. In virtually every respect, but

---

[354] It is worth noting that in 1866 England had enormous social and economic problems of its own, and yet the main item on the nation's political agenda was constitutional reform.

[355] Gurney was clearly proud of his work with the Commission, and in 1872 he found cause to remind the House of Commons that it had produced an objective report on what had happened in 1865. *Hansard*, ccxii (8 July 1872), 836–41.

especially in its dogged fact-gathering, the selection and operation of the JRC were justly hailed in England as a model of upright governmental practice. In the wake of an acutely embarrassing colonial episode, and in the context of an increasingly rancorous domestic politics, the Russell government had mounted a remarkably bipartisan and uninhibited investigation into the conduct of important figures of state. And when it is borne in mind that the key subjects of investigation were white, that they had successfully stemmed an armed uprising among blacks, the relative autonomy of the JRC is all the more noteworthy.

It was widely agreed that the JRC had got on with its work with 'an impartial hand'.[356] Recalcitrant white witnesses were given no quarter. Black witnesses were sometimes condescended to, but never silenced. Before the JRC hearings ended, the most pertinent questions had been put to the most pertinent witnesses, irrespective of race or social status. Almost invariably those who complained of their treatment at the hands of the Commission (Major Forbes Jackson, for instance) were white men. And, their dented sense of racial pride notwithstanding, these witnesses had good reason to resent the JRC. They were questioned closely and without undue regard for their station. Furthermore, witnesses were aware that their evidence, although it could not be used against them directly, might well trigger criminal investigations and prosecutions. Indeed, much to the chagrin of men like Duberry Ramsay, in 1866 the Colonial Office instigated such litigation. Edward Cardwell, and his Tory successor, Lord Carnarvon, were genuinely repulsed by what Ramsay (and a score of other white men) had done in Jamaica, and in the name of the Crown. As Englishmen, however, their moral sensibilities had a decidedly legal aspect. They did not hesitate to use all of the resources and procedures at their disposal to prosecute white Jamaican officials for murder and other felonies. Had the Ramsay prosecution been successful, moreover, many more such prosecutions would have followed.

But the legal response of the British Government to the Jamaica affair was not all of a kind. While the Colonial Office was prepared to prosecute officials who had committed atrocities in the name of the Crown, equally it prosecuted white, black, and coloured men for their supposed roles in fomenting the uprising. The imperial state was not so liberal-minded that it was prepared to forgive, for example, the post-rebellion philippics of Sydney Leviens.[357] Leviens was detained under martial law, kept in detention after martial law lapsed, released, rearrested, and then tried on two occasions for different serious offences. The decision to remit Leviens' sentence, when it came in

---

[356] *The Times* (13 Apr. 1866), 9.

[357] 'I was very anxious,' as Governor Grant once reported to Carnarvon, 'that it should not be understood that a seditious libel in such a place as Jamaica was a trifling offence.' Grant to Carnarvon, 24 Aug. 1866, Carnarvon Papers, *CO* 30/6/143.

August 1866 (half his sentence served), was made only grudgingly.[358] Colonial rebellion was not a trifling matter, and those who encouraged it, in deeds or words, felt London's wrath.

It also did not escape the attention of the Colonial Office that the Morant Bay uprising had started at a courthouse, and that the main object of the mob's rage was a local magistrate. After the endorsement of the dissolution of the Jamaican Assembly and the move to direct rule from London, the most important reform introduced to Jamaica after the uprising was the shake-up of the local courts. When boiled down to essentials, these policies reflected the Whiggish catechism that the central strut of all politics was legitimacy; that legitimacy was a product of consent; that consent was the natural residue of the comprehensive accountability of power to law. The main thrust of the Government's response to the Jamaica controversy, then, was to reaffirm – to Jamaican whites and blacks alike – the legitimacy of British power over the island and its inhabitants.

In its final report the JRC had wanted it both ways. On one hand, it implied that legal norms were an essential feature of a British government, even in the context of great public emergency. In this spirit the Commission decried the fact that so many British subjects had been subject to torture and execution without minimum due process of law. On the other hand, the JRC aligned itself with the view that martial law and martial practices were essential, if regrettable, features of imperial state practice. These powers could be compromised only at risk of white British lives in another colony. The JRC was unwilling to make any pronouncement or draw any conclusion that might impair the ability of colonial officials to do what was necessary to avoid another Cawnpore. As the *Law Times* warned, the too harsh punishment of the soldiers and officials who implemented martial law would 'paralyse the arms of all future Governors, and render the lives and properties of all Englishmen unsafe wherever they are dwelling amidst another race who form a majority'.[359]

In the late spring of 1866, most English political commentators were satisfied that the Jamaica affair was over. A thorough investigation had been made, a balanced report had been written. Beyond this, a senior colonial executive had been dismissed, and the most sadistic Jamaican officials prosecuted. For most this was enough, or too much. But for the radical politicians, intellectuals, and philanthropists of the Jamaica Committee, this was not nearly enough. The lingering problem was that the nature, character, and constitutional status of martial law still had not been clarified.[360] In fact, some

---

[358] And in large measure because during martial law Leviens had been subjected to an 'absurdly illegal' arrest, transportation, and period of imprisonment. Ibid.

[359] *Law Times* (6 Jan. 1866), 125.

[360] 'Another point which ought to be more distinctly cleared up by judicial proceedings is the real meaning and nature of the proclamation of martial law.' *Dublin Review* 7 (Oct. 1866), 403.

Government officials had endorsed a broad reading of the doctrine. The opinions of Alexander Heslop, the legal engineer of Jamaica's martial law, had not even been lightly challenged. And then there was the unsettled question of Eyre, and his potential criminal culpability for the arrest, trial, and execution of George Gordon. These unresolved issues were soon at the focal point of a renewed Jamaica controversy in England.

3

The Drawing-Room Men: The Jamaica Controversy in 1866

Men who know only of risings and civil war by books have been free in their condemnation of acts which, because they are not likely to be done in England, these critics hastily inferred, ought not to be done in Jamaica.

Quarterly Review, July 1866

As far as Mr. Kingsley and his associates have any intelligible purpose, they must desire to vindicate the principle that human life and positive law, however sacred, are less inviolable than the duty of repressing anarchy . . .

Saturday Review, October 1866

The truth is that the insurrection of the negroes, and the manner in which it was suppressed, raised a series of questions not merely local, casual, or personal, but entering very deeply into the science of politics and public morality.

Manchester Guardian, November 1866

When in December 1865 the Russell government announced that a Royal Commission would investigate the Morant Bay rebellion and suppression, the Jamaica controversy was temporarily quieted. But in the course of the winter and spring of 1866, Jamaica gradually re-emerged as a focal point of English political discussion. In part this was attributable to the steady flow of new information about what had actually happened in Jamaica, and especially about what had happened to Gordon. The Jamaica controversy also was given momentum by the rancorous debate over the second Reform Bill, and by heightened interest in the basic tenets of government, and over the boundaries of legitimate political dissent. In this time, Radicals pressed an intriguing if emotive question: if the law could countenance the summary execution of George Gordon in Jamaica, could it also countenance the summary execution of John Bright in England?[1]

The first chapter of this book discussed English politicians, political activists, and pundits and how they conceptualized, articulated, and wrote about the first

---

[1] Reform League speakers became fond of this suggestion during the summer of 1866. See, for example, account in *The Times* (31 July 1866), 3.

reports of the Jamaica rebellion and suppression. It was observed that legal vocabulary and understandings figured prominently in the reconstruction of these events. The second chapter concerned the re-exporting of the Jamaica crisis to Jamaica, and the means and character of the Government's response. It was observed that the formal investigation was undertaken mainly by lawyers, and that while they completed their work the Government implemented a series of legal initiatives (including criminal prosecutions both of black and white men). The chapter at hand focuses once again on members of the English political and intellectual elite – the 'drawing-room men' as Major Forbes-Jackson had so contemptuously labelled them – and their engagement with the Jamaica affair from the time in January 1866 when English readers began to receive new and significant information from Jamaica, until the following August when Parliament debated the Jamaica question.

A more or less complete transcript of Gordon's trial was published in the leading English newspapers during the last week of January 1866, or little more than one week before the Liberal government announced that a second Reform Bill would be introduced during the forthcoming session of Parliament. By the time the bill was introduced on 12 March (followed by a bill concerning the redistribution of seats on 7 May), the Gordon case, the law of martial law, and constitutional reform at home had all become inextricably linked. Many of the men – John Bright, Goldwin Smith, John Stuart Mill – who called for the greater legal accountability of Governor Eyre, now were leading the fight for the greater legal accountability of Parliament to male voters. By the same token, those who had risen to the defence of Governor Eyre, Carlyle and Ruskin most notably, also loudly opposed a more democratic suffrage. While it was not a point that was carefully articulated by participants in these debates, at bottom, reform of the franchise and the Jamaica affair raised the same question: what was the nature of legal accountability in a constitutional state?

This chapter has a number of integrated aims. The first is to pose a set of questions about Gordon's arrest and trial. Why was the Gordon case seen as so signally important? Why was the legality of his arrest and trial so fiercely contended? What were the political ramifications of the clash over Gordon? The second aim of the chapter is to undertake a careful examination of the terms by which parliamentarians, during the tense and choleric London summer of 1866, debated the Jamaica affair. How did leading politicians and political writers comprehend the Jamaica rebellion and suppression? How did they come to grips with the legal dimensions of the arrest, trial, and execution of Gordon, and with the larger questions relating to the legality and constitutional status of martial law? Were there 'Liberal', 'Tory', and 'Radical' conceptions of martial law? Did the politicians carve a distinction between the domestic and imperial law of state emergency? Did English intellectuals present a coherent account of these issues? What were the terms of debate with regard to the parliamentary clash over Jamaica, and how was it evaluated (in turn) by political commentators?

The chapter has one additional aim: to examine the internal dynamics of the Jamaica Committee and the process by which its leaders decided to dedicate most of its resources to criminal prosecutions in the English courts of law. We have seen how in its infancy the Committee was organized and funded principally by an alliance of Christian activists and missionary leaders. In the earliest stages of the controversy these men had been concerned mainly about the need to obtain justice for the scores of black Jamaicans who had suffered at the hands of the military. But we have also noticed the inclination of even these deeply religious men to favour a legal over a scriptural understanding of the Jamaica affair. (One of their first initiatives was to secure legal advice on martial law generally, on the execution of Gordon specifically.) In fact, by the end of the summer of 1866 it was exceedingly rare for a leading member of the Jamaica Committee to talk about the implications of the suppression in terms of those who actually endured it. By then Charles Buxton (the Christian philanthropist) had been replaced by John Stuart Mill (the secular humanist) as the chairman of the Committee. Under Mill's leadership, the focus of the Committee was fixed squarely on the implications of the Jamaica episode for England, and on the idea of using the English courts to shore up some basic principles of English constitutional law.

I. January to May 1866: Reconstructing the Arrest and Trial of George Gordon

'It is one of the compensations of the evils of this terrible Jamaica tragedy', the *Daily News* observed on 30 January 1866, 'that it is finding out some of the least expected weak points of our character at home.' The occasion for this remark was the publication (on 24 and 25 January) in a number of important daily newspapers of the first complete and seemingly reliable account of the trial by court martial of George Gordon. The upshot of the new information was plain: Gordon had been sent to the gallows on shabby evidence mustered during a sham trial. To many English observers, this news was disquieting enough. But for the country's radicals and malcontents, the really worrying aspect of the Jamaica episode, the best reason to take notice, was that a number of prominent Englishmen were attempting to validate (what the *Daily News* called) this 'utter subversion of the law'.[2] It was this combination of revelation and justification, then, which spurred further action on the Jamaica affair.

In some sense, as the *Spectator* pointed out, the Gordon case had taken on an almost 'accidental importance'.[3] After all, during the suppression a great many other British subjects had been apprehended and executed by the authorities, some even more arbitrarily and brutally than Gordon. But these men and women

---

[2] *Daily News* (30 Jan. 1866), 4.   [3] *Spectator* (27 Jan. 1866), 89.

and *their* deaths had not become *causes célèbres*. As the writers at the *Spectator* knew very well, there were cogent reasons for the discrepancy. Of the scores of Jamaicans who had been killed in the bush or in military camps only Gordon had been a 'man of influence and station, a member of the Jamaica Assembly, and one who surrendered himself unhesitatingly to the demand of the Government'.[4] When Eyre killed Gordon, he eliminated the colony's most important opposition politician and, as was well known in England, a painful source of vexation and embarrassment to the Governor. For these reasons Gordon's execution presented the spectre not only of murder, but in a country of laws one of the most heinous of all crimes, *political* murder.

But there were still other reasons – racial, social, emotional, and promotional – why the Gordon case became the focal point of the Jamaica affair. As the *Manchester Guardian* summarized, Gordon was regarded by the English as 'being a man chiefly of white colour, and connected by the closest possible ties with white people [his wife was Irish, and he was known personally by many English Baptists], by his possession of large property, and by private letters [the poignant last letter to his wife, particularly] written by him after the massacre'.[5] For anyone interested in making political hay of the Gordon case, these were invaluable (if posthumous) attributes. Their potential as munitions in a propaganda war was not lost, least of all by the leaders of the Jamaica Committee. In January 1866 the Committee was in something of a bind. It now was publicly committed to the rather extreme (and as yet unsubstantiated) contention that Gordon had been arrested and tried unlawfully, and that his execution amounted to culpable homicide. Already it had buttressed this view with a legal opinion, and had published it in the newspapers.[6] The Committee also had devoted itself to the very expensive business of sending lawyers to Jamaica, and in paying local lawyers and clerks to assist them over a period of several months. This was an ambitious agenda, made more so by the fact that the Committee's first fund-raising efforts had not generated the sums hoped for, and then were seriously damaged by an impostor.[7] For all of these reasons by mid January the leaders of the Committee were in desperate need of a potent symbol for its cause, of something or someone to keep the Jamaica story on the front pages of newspapers and in the pocketbooks of benefactors.

The story of the demise of George Gordon was always the presumptive favourite in this regard. Much had been made of Gordon's case in December 1865. All that was needed to revitalize the issue was proof that Gordon had been the victim of an unlawful arrest, court martial, and execution. Fortuitously for the Jamaica Committee, that proof was soon forthcoming. At some point in early

---

[4] Ibid.   [5] *Manchester Guardian* (26 Jan. 1866), 2.

[6] This opinion is discussed at length below, Ch. 4.

[7] It only recently had been learned that a man named Edmundson had solicited unauthorized donations and had made off with the money. *CD*, 13, 15 Jan. 1866.

January 1866, one of the Committee's executive officers, Louis Chamerovzow (in his capacity as chairman of the BFASS) learned that a coloured Jamaican reporter named Augustus Lake had witnessed Gordon's court martial, and that he was prepared to give over his notes. On this news, the Committee immediately sent instructions to Gorrie that he was to contact Lake and obtain the papers.[8] (The Committee was so anxious in this regard that they authorized Gorrie to offer Lake employment with the *Illustrated London News* in London 'should he lose his situation in consequence of furnishing you with [the documents]'.) Gorrie was also instructed to continue his investigations into 'cases of even more indisputable murder', but, as the Committee's despatch underlined, 'Mr. Gordon's case has attracted the greatest attention in this country from his position and his name being known here, and we should be glad of the minutest information on the steps that had been taken in his case'.[9] But before Gorrie could receive these instructions, Lake communicated directly with Chamerovzow and arranged to give over a copy of his trial notes.[10] The subsequent release of the notes was then carefully stage-managed by Chamerovzow (probably with the approval of the other members of the Jamaica Committee executive), commencing with some proactive public relations work on Lake's background and character.

Augustus Lake, Chamerovzow undoubtedly knew, was not a man of unassailable credibility. In October 1865 Lake had been a reporter for the *Colonial Standard* newspaper, a paper aligned with Jamaica's white elite before the uprising, and strongly approving of the use of martial law in putting it down. More to the point, Lake had been assigned to cover the implementation of martial law at Morant Bay. The first stories he returned brimmed with praise for Duberry Ramsay (he was called 'the right man in the right place'),[11] and the methods Ramsay had employed to punish alleged rebels. Lake was the only reporter to witness the court martial of Gordon. He took copious notes on the evidence and procedure, and sent them to his editor in Kingston. At first the editor held the story back,[12] fearing that it would inflame the black community in the colony. In its place the *Standard* ran a general report that Gordon had been convicted after a trial that in every relevant respect was 'very impartial'.[13]

Some weeks after martial law ended, however, Lake suddenly and dramatically reversed course. He quit writing for the *Colonial Standard* and publicly recanted the despatches he had filed for that newspaper from Morant Bay. In a letter published in Kingston on 24 December 1865, and then reprinted in England's *Daily*

---

[8] *JC Minutes*, 15 Jan. 1866.   [9] Ibid.
[10] That this transaction had taken place was intimated in a letter published by Chamerovzow in the *Daily News* (19 Jan. 1866), 2.
[11] Letter of Augustus Lake, republished in the *Daily News* (19 Jan. 1866), 2.
[12] As late as 30 January 1866, the Jamaica press still had not published any specific information about Gordon's trial. See report of the special correspondent to *The Times* (30 Jan. 1866), 9.
[13] See *Falmouth Post* (9 Mar. 1866), 1.

News (under a letter written by Chamerovzow) on 19 January 1866, Lake explained that he had been repulsed by what he had witnessed at Morant Bay, but that he was so frightened of reprisal that he 'dared not have given [the facts] in their true character'.[14] As a coloured man working in dangerous proximity to Ramsay, Lake 'thought that the only safe course was to endorse, for a time, the many acts lawlessly perpetrated at Morant Bay'. But now that the period of retribution was over, and a new Governor had taken Eyre's place, Lake felt that it was safe to reveal what he knew of 'evil doings' during martial law. His letter related eyewitness accounts of a number of floggings and hangings, including a harrowing account of the torture and execution of George Marshall. Lake also disclosed that he had taken verbatim notes of the court martial of Gordon, that these notes were 'in the present mail to the Anti-Slavery Society', and that they would demonstrate conclusively that Gordon had been 'cruelly slain by the authorities'.

With a cover letter written by Chamerovzow, Lake's transcription of the Gordon trial was sent to all the leading English newspapers during the final week of January 1866. While his personal character and reliability remained a matter of contention,[15] the essential accuracy of Lake's report was widely (if not unanimously)[16] conceded. 'It appears probable,' the *Pall Mall Gazette* concluded, 'that the report is both correct and as complete as any report is likely to be.'[17] A close friend of the Jamaica Committee, the *Daily News* perhaps had a vested interest in the hyperbole that Lake's transcript had been 'publicly certified by the ruling powers themselves'.[18] Most newspapers (*The Times* being a good example)[19] said nothing at all about the accuracy of Lake's report while they offered extensive commentary on the court martial and its political implications. Their unstated assumption was that English readers were in possession of the same information available to Governor Eyre when he authorized Gordon's execution.

Lake's transcript was treated as an authentic artifact of the suppression in Jamaica, one of very substantial significance. Its publication caused a number of leading commentators to offer their first definitive judgement about the Jamaica affair. The *Manchester Guardian*, for instance had repeatedly warned against the 'blind precipitancy' of strong or final conclusions about the affair.[20] As late as 12 January it had cautioned readers against prejudging either the justice, or otherwise, of Gordon's execution, or of the propriety, or otherwise, of punitive actions

---

[14] *Daily News* (19 Jan. 1866), 2.

[15] Ibid. When Lake commenced his testimony before the Royal Commission, the *Falmouth Post* (16 Mar. 1866), 1, published a withering attack on his character and motives.

[16] One detractor was the *Daily Telegraph* (25 Jan. 1866), 4, which tried to dismiss Lake's report as a 'mere *ex parte* statement', one made by a man who had 'given inconsistent versions of the same events'. In the same editorial, however, the *Telegraph* admitted that the transcript underscored the need for a 'careful investigation' of Gordon's court martial.   [17] *Pall Mall Gazette* (25 Jan. 1866), 1.

[18] *Daily News* (25 Jan. 1866), 4.

[19] *The Times* (25 Jan. 1866), 8. The even more doggedly conservative *Morning Herald* also commented only on the implications of Lake's report. *Morning Herald* (29 Jan. 1866), 4.

[20] *Manchester Guardian* (30 Nov. 1866), 2.

against his executioners.[21] 'Throughout the discussions of the Jamaica question,' the *Pall Mall Gazette* declared, 'we have done our best to maintain a position of impartiality, and to impress... the importance of suspending judgments.'[22] Upon the publication of Lake's notes, however, both the *Gazette* and the *Guardian* abandoned their previous caution. 'The publication of the evidence in the Gordon case,' the *Guardian's* leader stated on 26 January, 'confirms the worst that has been said by the complainants.' On the assumption that Lake's notes were correct, the *Gazette* stated, 'we ought no longer to hesitate to speak decisively'. The case for the prosecution, the *Guardian* sombrely declared, was 'almost incredibly weak' and 'wretchedly insufficient'.[23] 'It is impossible,' *The Times* stated on 25 January, 'not to come to the conclusion that, if there be nothing more forthcoming than has been reported, there was no sufficient proof of Gordon's guilt'.[24]

The *Manchester Guardian* was only one of many newspapers to compile a long list of the trial's conspicuous defects. The bill of indictment had been insensibly vague. The officers who presided over the court martial had been comparatively young, and wholly inexperienced in the matters of courts martial.[25] The principal witnesses for the prosecution were themselves black prisoners of the martial law, men facing cruel punishments, men who had hoped, vainly, that they might secure pardon by implicating Gordon in the Morant Bay violence. In all but one case the evidence offered against Gordon was hearsay,[26] and none of the witnesses had been able to testify to an overt act of rebellion. To make matters worse, Gordon had been denied access to counsel and the opportunity to call defence witnesses. In short, Gordon's trial had been a charade.

As English journalists and political commentators groped for understanding of the Gordon case, almost invariably they compared his court martial to an archetypal *civilian* criminal trial, and on this benchmark found it wanting. The main goal of an ordinary civilian trial was to provide a forum for the presentation and examination of material evidence. 'The first thing that must strike any reader of [Lake's] minutes,' the *Guardian* observed, 'is that by far the greater part of the evidence... is of inadmissible quality.'[27] Gordon had been condemned mainly on the basis of the worst sort of hearsay. 'It would be a very great mistake,' the *Guardian* added, 'to suppose that this is merely a technical rule of lawyers.' In fact the rule was rooted in the 'obvious dictates of common sense and honour'. On this point *The Times* concurred: 'Depositions and hearsay evidence are such untrustworthy things that even martial law ought not to be administered in reliance on them.'

---

[21] *Manchester Guardian* (12 Jan. 1866), 2.   [22] *Pall Mall Gazette* (25 Jan. 1866), 1.
[23] *Manchester Guardian* (26 Jan. 1866), 2.   [24] *The Times* (25 Jan. 1866), 8.
[25] The senior officer, twenty-six year old Lieutenant Herbert Brand, had been in the navy for six years, the two junior officers four years and one year respectively. *Pall Mall Gazette* (25 Jan. 1866), 1.
[26] 'Only one of the witnesses,' the *Daily News* (25 Jan. 1866), 4, asserted, 'gave evidence to which an English magistrate would listen.' This was evidence of an alleged conversation between Gordon and Paul Bogle. The *Daily Telegraph* (25 Jan. 1866), 4, concurred on this point.
[27] *Manchester Guardian* (26 Jan. 1866), 2.

This last observation was made by a number of other papers. It was insisted that the evidentiary defects of Gordon's court martial were so many, substantial, and egregious that they were not excusable even in the context of a state emergency.[28] There was 'not a point in the proceedings,' the *Gazette* concluded, 'which is not an outrage not only to the rules of law, but on the plainest dictates of natural justice and common good sense'. Invoking English norms of justice, the *Gazette* concluded that Gordon was hanged on evidence 'upon which no magistrate in England would have committed a man for trial for larceny'. In a similar vein, the *Spectator* reckoned that the evidence 'was probably barely enough to have induced an English, or for that matter an Irish magistrate *to grant a remand*'.[29] To the *Spectator*, Gordon's trial was a 'parody of justice'. The *Pall Mall Gazette* saw a 'mockery of the forms of law'.[30] For the *Daily News* Gordon's case was likened to 'some insane burlesque of the forms of a court'.[31] Even *The Times* acknowledged that the case was a grievous insult to England's 'singular idea of administering criminal justice'.[32]

Most prominent English political commentators either condemned Gordon's trial and execution or simply did not defend them. But there were notable exceptions to this trend, and their diatribes reinvigorated the Jamaica controversy. Among the boldest contrarians were the editors at the *Morning Herald*. In an editorial on Gordon's case the *Herald* contended that pervasive 'negro partisanship'[33] had obscured the political essence of the matter. The fact of the matter was that Gordon had been a 'political agitator, who, by secret appeals and intemperate harangues…incited to violence a mass of ignorant men'. Whatever his intentions, Gordon's demagoguery had the effect of fomenting an armed rebellion and it was 'imperative that he should be arrested and put on his trial'. As for the proceedings at his court martial, they 'were no more open to objection than those of courts martial in general'. The worst that might be said against the officers of the court was that they were 'careful [more] of the spirit than the letter of the law'. As for the evidence presented against Gordon, the *Herald* saw it as various and compelling: 'culprits in England, even in our own time, have been sentenced to death on far weaker evidence than that which led to the hanging of the Morant Bay agitator.'

This kind of unblushing defence of the court martial and execution of Gordon infuriated the liberal press and, in the result, helped crystallize the Jamaica affair as a constitutional conflict in England. 'Last summer,' the *Daily News* remarked, 'nobody would have believed that there were people…presenting at all points the appearance of Englishmen who deliberately approve of hanging persons without trial.' The *News* thought that this posture, the 'justification of the utter subversion of law in the name of conservatism' was in fact symptomatic of a major shift in the temper of conservative political philosophy, one which tended to conflate opposition

[28] For a rare dissent on this point, see the *Morning Herald* (29 Jan. 1866), 4.
[29] *Spectator* (27 Jan. 1866), 89.   [30] *Pall Mall Gazette* (25 Jan. 1866), 1.
[31] *Daily News* (25 Jan. 1866), 2.   [32] *The Times* (25 Jan. 1866), 8.
[33] *Morning Herald* (29 Jan. 1866), 4.

to treason. It was a conservative politics which was forgetful that the 'securities of British law' were evolved to ensure that peaceful opponents of a government could not be hanged as traitors. As the *London Review* summarized, 'a man is not to be hanged, even though he has negro blood in his veins, because he is disagreeable.'[34] Gordon was a demagogue, the *Spectator* conceded, but 'demagogues are *permitted* under English law.'[35] John Bright, the editor continued, 'has said ten exciting sentences for every one that can be quoted from Mr. Gordon's speeches'. Would Bright face a summary court martial and execution after he gave an impassioned speech in favour of the extension of the franchise?

The public ruminations about the court martial and execution of Gordon opened up discussion also of the circumstances and implications of his arrest at Kingston and subsequent transportation to the military courts at Morant Bay. At this juncture, the personal hand of Eyre in Gordon's death began to come back into focus. In January 1866, Louis Bowerbank, a physician and *custos* of Kingston, arrived in England. Bowerbank had been a close adviser to Eyre before and during the suppression. He also had been a long-time antagonist of Gordon. The purpose of his visit to London is unclear. We know only that he spent a good deal of time justifying the actions of Eyre, and decrying those of Gordon.[36] On 27 January, Bowerbank published a letter in *The Times* recounting the events leading up to Gordon's arrest and execution. He picked up the thread of the story on 14 October, one day after martial law had been proclaimed in the County of Surrey. On that day the magistrates of Kingston met in a special session and voted to urge the Governor to declare martial law also in the city's precincts. A resolution was committed to paper and sent to Eyre at Morant Bay. When he received the request, Eyre immediately returned to Kingston. Told that Gordon was still at large, Eyre issued a warrant for Gordon's arrest before attending a meeting of magistrates. Eyre informed them that the rebellion at Morant Bay was 'crushed', and that his chief concern now was to prevent outbreaks in other parts of the island. Eyre also reiterated his strong opposition to the proclamation of martial law in Kingston. Such proclamation, Eyre remained convinced, would 'cripple and damage commerce' in the colony's most important town.

In the afternoon of the same day, before he sailed again for Morant Bay, Eyre returned with Bowerbank to the residence of General O'Connor. A policeman informed them that Gordon was present in the General's drawing-room with his physician, Dr. Alexander Fiddes. Gordon was surprised by Eyre's sudden entry into the room. He said, 'Oh, your Excellency.' Eyre replied that he could have no communication with a man who was to be made a prisoner. Bowerbank then approached Gordon and, by a symbolic laying on of hands, placed him under

---

[34] *London Review* (27 Jan. 1866), 117.   [35] *Spectator* (27 Jan. 1866), 89.
[36] According to Charles Buxton, Bowerbank had come to England to propagandize for Governor Eyre and the white ruling class of Jamaica, and with the 'express purpose of blackening [Gordon's] memory'. *Hansard*, clxxxiv (31 July 1866), 1772.

arrest on a charge of treason. Gordon was then taken away in Bowerbank's carriage. There Gordon professed his innocence of any treason, and explained that he had been ill in recent weeks. When told that he was to be taken directly aboard a naval ship destined for the courts martial at Morant Bay, Gordon said aloud that he was sure that he 'would die there'. Permitted a brief visit from his wife, Gordon twice repeated a request that he be allowed to consult with his Kingston solicitor, Mr. Airey. Bowerbank denied these requests. A few hours later, Gordon was put on board the *Wolverine* and transported to Morant Bay.

At the close of his narrative, Bowerbank expressed a number of opinions on its legal ramifications. It did not matter legally, Bowerbank contended, that Gordon had been transferred to the military courts in Morant Bay both because they were the only courts then in operation, and because it was correct in law that an accused person should be tried 'in the theatre of his designs'. As for the haste of the court martial, Bowerbank explained that 'the urgency of the case, the necessity of striking a prompt and decisive blow to crush the rebellion and save the rest of the island', had rendered it imperative that Gordon 'should be dealt with summarily'.

A short time after the Bowerbank letter was published, the *Daily News* printed an intriguing letter written by Dr. Fiddes, the Kingston physician. For twenty years Gordon had been one of Fiddes' patients and friends. The letter addressed two subjects: Gordon's suspicious absence from the vestry meeting at Morant Bay on 11 October 1865, and the events surrounding Gordon's arrest in Kingston on 17 October. With regard to the absence, Fiddes stated that immediately prior to the uprising Gordon had been to his surgery complaining of ill health. The doctor diagnosed bronchitis and ordered Gordon home to rest. According to Fiddes, then, it was an accident of fate, not political or military calculation, that caused Gordon not to be present at the meeting.

Fiddes' letter also went on to recount how, in the first days after the uprising, he had tried to alert Gordon that he was being sought by the colonial authorities. After some trouble, Fiddes located Gordon at the Kingston house of a relative. When Fiddes met up with him, Gordon already had decided that his best course was to surrender himself to General O'Connor without delay. (Unknown to Fiddes, Gordon had been urged by his wife and mother-in-law to take flight, but refused both because he believed himself innocent of wrongdoing, and because his solicitor had advised him that he could not be 'legally removed to a proclaimed district'.)[37] Fiddes recalled how, in the best tradition of Victorian civility, 'cards were sent to General O'Connor, who received us with the utmost civility and politeness.' In the meantime, Fiddes sent a carriage for Gordon's solicitor, Airey, who, in Fiddes's account, arrived in time to witness Gordon's arrest.[38] Soon

---

[37] *CD*, 31 Jan. 1866.
[38] Oddly enough, Fiddes' account put Airey in the General's house at the time of the arrest. He makes no mention, however, of Airey having intervened in any way. By contrast, Bowerbank does not mention that Airey was present at the moment of arrest. He recalled only the (potentially embarrassing) fact he had refused Gordon's request to consult his lawyer on his way to the Ordnance Wharf.

thereafter the Governor and Bowerbank suddenly entered the General's drawing-room and approached Gordon. The two men took Gordon's arm and 'in some-what hurried language, made him understand that he was their prisoner' and that he was to be transported to Morant Bay to be tried for treason by court martial. This turn of events caught Fiddes by surprise: 'martial law did not exist in Kingston,' the doctor recalled, 'and I entertained no idea that Mr. Gordon would be immediately transferred to a parish where it was in active operation.' From the hasty manner of the arrest, moreover, Fiddes instantly concluded that Gordon's fate 'was sealed'.

If Bowerbank's letter was an explicit *apologia* for Governor Eyre's actions with regard to Gordon, Fiddes's piece was a cleverly constructed indictment of them. The author took pains not to alienate English readers by warming too much to Gordon or his politics. Fiddes made clear that he been Gordon's friend and doctor, but decidedly *not* his political acolyte. In fact, he had thought Gordon 'eccentric in his views and notions of the people's rights, and somewhat peculiar in his religious observances'. Fiddes also admitted that, as an 'undeniable Anglo-Saxon', he had not forgotten that Gordon was 'a man of colour', a member of a group 'greatly inferior to ourselves'. But for all of this, Fiddes remained con-vinced that Gordon's arrest and court martial were motivated less by security concerns than personal and political enmities. In his letter Fiddes recalled how Eyre had dealt with Gordon in a 'fussy and excited' manner, displaying none of the 'dignified firmness' of General O'Connor. In sum, Fiddes depicted Eyre as a man who lacked conviction in his actions, as someone whose judgement had been corrupted by fear and loathing.

The letters of Bowerbank and Fiddes were not the only sources of public informa-tion to emerge concerning the circumstances of Gordon's arrest and trans-portation to Morant Bay. In April 1866, English newspaper readers learned that before he had decided what to do with Gordon, Eyre had conferred with the colony's Executive Council.[39] While the Council unanimously concurred with the Governor that Gordon should be detained under house arrest, a number of Councillors urged that Gordon not be handed over to the military. In their view, Gordon's detention did not pose an imminent threat to public security on the island. They recommended a 'patient' civilian trial when order had been restored. To his eventual detriment, Eyre chose not to follow this advice.[40]

This brings us to another interesting aspect of the Gordon case. We know that Eyre did not move to proclaim martial law until he had consulted fully with his Council of War, and with his Attorney General.[41] But as Heslop made clear to the Royal Commission, there were no further consultations between himself and the

---

[39] This information was imparted to the Jamaica Royal Commission by Henry Westmoreland, then a member of the Executive Council. Special correspondent to the *Daily News* (7 Apr. 1866), 2.

[40] One of the reasons Edward Cardwell offered to justify the dismissal of Eyre was that he had not adopted the advice of executive councillors to try Gordon before a 'regular tribunal'. Cardwell to Storks, reprinted in the *Daily News* (21 June 1866), 2.   [41] *JRC Minutes*, Q. 3894.

Governor during the duration, or even *concerning* the duration of martial law.[42] When he was questioned about the Gordon case, Heslop was very sure on this point (and Eyre did not challenge his recollection)[43]: 'I have not been consulted in the case of any one single arrest since the declaration of martial law.'[44] On further questioning, Heslop also maintained that he had known 'nothing at all about [Gordon's] arrest, personally',[45] nor was he consulted about Gordon's execution.[46] In Heslop's opinion, it simply had not been necessary to discuss these subjects with the Governor. The actual operation of martial law he regarded as the business of military men, not lawyers.[47]

This is a crucial point both about the Gordon case and the active assumptions of colonial administrators about martial law. Both Governor Eyre and his senior legal adviser acted from the premiss that the proclamation of martial law represented an extreme departure from the norms and procedures of civilian law. Because of the colony's history of slavery and slave insurrection, 'strong powers', stronger than those possessed by English officials, were available to the authorities in case of emergency.[48] One such power was the right to subject suspected rebels to trial by summary or 'drumhead' court martial and, upon conviction, execution. (Heslop had been so much convinced of the legality of this that he himself had sat on a court martial which condemned 'four or five' men to be hanged.)[49] As Heslop made clear, it was the nature of martial law that it had 'its own operation', one that was not limited by formal legal strictures or constraints, but alone by 'policy and common sense'.[50] Thus, when Eyre 'proclaimed martial law, and gave orders to a General to go to a proclaimed district,' Heslop explained, 'the Governor was absolved from personal responsibility'.[51] By these lights, Eyre had been fully justified in arresting Gordon, and in sending him for trial before a military tribunal in the jurisdiction of his alleged crime. And, once the military decided that it was necessary that Gordon be executed, the Governor equally had been entitled not to intervene with this *military* decision. Even as criticism of this decision mounted in 1866, Eyre maintained that he had been right not to interfere, and that the execution of Gordon 'had the most powerful influence in putting down sedition and deterring others from revolt'.[52]

When he moved against Gordon, Eyre knew that some of his actions contravened the strictures of civilian law. As he later explained to Cardwell, 'I preferred to take upon myself the responsibility of doing an illegal act by seizing G. W. Gordon and carrying him back to Morant Bay for trial.'[53] As he himself stated, Eyre was fully aware that these steps amounted to an 'arbitrary exercise of power not by any law (tho' since covered by the Indemnity Act) and only justifiable as a measure of

---

[42] Ibid., Q. 16,281.   [43] Ibid. Q. 3997–4004.   [44] Ibid., Q. 16,272, 16,273.
[45] Ibid., Q. 16,281.   [46] Ibid., Q. 16,282.   [47] Ibid., Q. 16,283.
[48] Ibid., Q. 16,245.   [49] Ibid., Q. 16,260–70.   [50] Ibid., Q. 16,281.
[51] Ibid.   [52] Eyre to Cardwell, 6 Apr. 1866, *CO* 137/405.
[53] Eyre to Cardwell, 24 Dec. 1866, Cardwell Papers, *CO* 30/48/42.

public safety'.[54] By the term 'responsibility', however, Eyre meant to denote political or *administrative* responsibility. He accepted that his action would have to be justified to his superiors at the Colonial Office. In the event that they did not accept these justifications, the result would be some form of internal discipline. Answering to Cardwell was one thing, answering to the courts quite another. With regard to any potential legal liability, Eyre informed Cardwell, he had been 'trusting to an act of indemnity (which has been passed) being afterwards enacted to cover any deviation from a strictly legal course if there was such a deviation'.[55] The question of whether Eyre had actually committed such a deviation, whether for instance he was guilty of Gordon's murder, would preoccupy the political and legal establishments in England in the months to come.

'We cannot pretend to think', the *Manchester Guardian* stated on 30 January, 'that any further information is required to convince fair-minded people that George Gordon was wrongfully convicted...but everything which helps elucidate the circumstances under which that lamentable error was committed is a matter of absorbing interest.' 'To us here sitting at home,' *The Times* observed, 'it seems impossible that any person of ordinary intelligence should glance over that meagre testimony...and not come to the conclusion that they were insufficient to hang a man upon.'[56] It was now only too apparent that the debate over the Gordon case could no longer be sensibly confined to the issue of whether Gordon had received a fair trial. By the end of January 1866, almost every respectable English commentator, even those who had doubted it before, accepted that Gordon's trial had been a macabre farce. Further to the point, the notion that Gordon's execution amounted to criminal murder now was even more widely entertained than before. '[T]here is not an unprejudiced lawyer in this kingdom,' so sober a voice as the *Solicitors' Journal* declared on 27 January, 'who will not be ready to admit that Gordon's execution was a *moral* as well as a *legal* murder.'

During the first weeks of 1866 English commentators debated the merits and demerits of Gordon's court martial without giving much consideration to a number of more fundamental issues. What, precisely, was a 'court martial'? Could such a court exert lawful jurisdiction over a British *civilian*? More specifically, when George Gordon was brought within the scope of martial authority in Jamaica, was he entitled to the procedural protections set down in the Mutiny Acts?[57] About such questions, there were arguments to be made, and made they were in forthcoming months, that the quality of Gordon's military trial was a moot point. The more material issue was whether the military had exerted a lawful jurisdiction over his case. In one account, it was never tolerable, even in

---

[54] Ibid.   [55] Eyre to Cardwell, undated, *CO* 137/402.

[56] That those involved *did* think themselves entitled to hang Eyre was offered as proof of their fear. *The Times* (30 Jan. 1866), 8.

[57] See generally, Finlason, *Commentaries upon Martial Law*, 207–8; Clode, *Military Forces of the Crown*, vol. i, 146–7.

the context of a proclamation of martial law, for a British military court to try a civilian prisoner. The ambit of authority under martial law did not extend to persons who had been captured and disarmed. By these lights, Gordon's trial by court martial and execution would have been wholly illegal even if military law and procedure had been followed to the letter.[58] Conversely, other lawyers contended that the court martial of Gordon had been perfectly legal both in theory and practice.[59] In this account, it was an intrinsic feature of martial law that commanders might use the drumhead court martial law as a means of restoring order in a place that had been disarranged by armed invasion or insurrection. Pursuant to this power, the drumhead tribunal could try any person who was honestly and reasonably suspected of having fomented or engaged in armed rebellion. Such tribunals, moreover, were not obliged to conform strictly with military law or rules of evidence. Given the practical difficulties involved, it was enough that the tribunal respected the rules of 'natural justice'. According to the most extreme version of this argument, there might be times during emergency when captured rebels might be lawfully executed without the slightest pretence of any trial.

In the winter of 1866, the pervasiveness of the view that Gordon had been legally executed presented a dilemma to the leaders of the Jamaica Committee. What actually was to be *done* about the apparently illegal and unjust execution of Gordon and others? Was it enough that Eyre had been suspended, his reputation in tatters? If the law against murder, against *political* murder no less, had been abrogated, were Eyre and other officials to be prosecuted like common criminals? Was it a good excuse, as a matter either of law or politics, that Eyre and his military men had acted in the good faith belief that the execution of Gordon and scores of other alleged rebels had been indispensably important to the salvation of the white population of the colony?

II. June–July 1866: The Jamaica Committee Finds its Voice

The progenitors of the Jamaica Committee were devoutly Christian men who came together to express a shared sense of outrage that civilian and military officials of an ostensibly Christian nation could have committed so many terrible sins against other subjects of the Crown. The agitators were also animated by the fact that so many English commentators had spoken in favour of the suppression. Their alarm was heightened by the fact that racial attitudes in Britain had hardened during the debate over the American Civil War.[60] It has gone largely

---

[58] This line of argument, crystallized in 1867 in the Grand Jury charge of the Lord Chief Justice, is analysed at length below, Ch. 6. See Cockburn (ed.), *Charge of the Lord Chief Justice*, 124–9.

[59] This line of argument, analysed at length below, Ch. 4, is set forth in Finlason, *Treatise on Martial Law*, 89–92.   [60] See generally, Blackett, *Divided Hearts*.

unnoticed, however, that the evangelicals and secular philanthropists who came together to promote public action on Jamaica did not talk about their mission in the language of religion, but of secular law. They were more likely to invoke the words 'illegality', 'murder', and 'prosecution' than 'immorality', 'sinfulness', or 'divine retribution'.

There were at least two reasons why the rhetoric of the Jamaica Committee was infused with legal and constitutional language. The first was pragmatic. Men like Chesson, Buxton, and Bright were only too aware that the mere fact that some black men had been ill-used in Jamaica was never likely to be the basis of sustained outrage in England. If their cause was to be advanced, its champions would need to make a more resonant appeal. The second reason concerned widely shared habits of thought. Assertions about legality were a ubiquitous feature of English political calculus and language. The tendency to reconstruct political events in legal and constitutional terms simply was a mark of being English. From the outset of the Jamaica affair, the leaders of the Jamaica Committee conceptualized and spoke of the Jamaica affair mainly in terms of legal criteria, and aims. But the preoccupation with law was even more pervasive. The first formal decision of the Committee was to seek expert advice about legal implications of the suppression.[61] The second was to retain Fitzjames Stephen and Edward James to work up a thorough and authoritative legal opinion on the Jamaica episode.

It is also important to note here that the leaders of Exeter Hall were nothing if not expert in the advancement of causes. Experience had taught that the proponents of a project were far more likely to enjoy success when their aims were advanced by a broadly based coalition. So it was that on 19 December 1865 – at a London public house – the Christian philanthropists of Exeter Hall reached out to a motley assortment of religious and secular parliamentary Radicals (Bright, Taylor, Henry Fawcett), radicals-at-large (Edmond Beales), Christian socialists (J. M. Ludlow, Thomas Hughes), labour activists (Frederic Harrison and Edward Beesly) and at-large political intellectuals (Goldwin Smith and, by correspondence from France, John Stuart Mill M.P.), to hammer out the organizational framework and agenda of a new political action committee. After some preliminary discussion it was unanimously agreed to form a new association, and that Charles Buxton M.P. should be its chairman. Chesson was elected secretary, and Peter Taylor, treasurer. Buxton was an astute choice as chairman. He was a polished, articulate, and well-schooled proponent of social causes.[62] It could not have hurt that he was also the wealthy heir to a vast brewing fortune, and had already given seed money to the Jamaica cause. It was appropriate, too, that the first chairman of the Jamaica Committee should so comfortably straddle the gap between the freethinkers and the leaders of Exeter Hall.

---

[61] In the first instance, opinions were solicited from Lord Brougham and Dr. Vernon Lushington. *BFASS Minutes*, 20 Nov. 1865.   [62] *DNB*, ii, 557–8.

According to the best historical sources relating to its internal politics – the private diary of Chesson, the official minutes of the Committee, newspaper reports of its public meetings – from its inception in December 1865 until the publication of the final report of the Royal Commission in June 1866, the executive body of the Committee operated without serious internal dissension. At its first meeting the Committee established (and then promoted[63]) three main objectives: to demand a 'searching Parliamentary inquiry' into the political economy of Jamaica (with a view to its Reform); to invigilate the work of the Royal Commission with a view to 'take such further action (both legal and otherwise) as may be deemed necessary'; and finally, to 'provide Mrs. Gordon and others … with competent legal assistance' as they engaged with the Royal Commission. These last two objectives were thought so important that the public was assured that 'the Committee were represented in Jamaica by five members of the bar'. However, no definite course was set with regard to future action. Wisely enough, that debate was postponed.

By January 1866 the Jamaica Committee was firmly committed to a twin-track programme of action. The first track concerned using lawyers to monitor events in Jamaica. The second track concerned England, and the struggle for public opinion. It is telling that in its efforts to gain the upper hand in this contest, the executive of the Committee did not rely on their own names and literary assets. Given the nature of the Jamaica controversy, and the perceived inclinations of the English political class, the leaders of the Committee quickly moved to augment their position with a publishable legal statement from the barristers Stephen and James on the law of martial law. The tacit assumption here was that in the war for English hearts and minds perceptions about legality would prove decisive. By these means the Committee hoped to put itself in a position to contend, with greater credibility, that Edward Eyre was a murderer.

The publication of the opinion of Stephen and James, now the Committee's official 'standing counsel',[64] was its most important public action during the winter of 1865–6. But the Committee remained active behind the scenes. One of their concerns was to keep track of the movements of persons suspected of having committed atrocities in Jamaica. For instance, when Abercrombie Nelson (Chesson described him as a 'tall, grizzly bearded, care-worn individual') arrived in England in mid-January, he was kept under surveillance.[65] Some executive members of the Committee, Goldwin Smith was one,[66] thought that preparations should be started for the criminal prosecution of Eyre himself. Smith thought this option

---

[63] The Committee's objectives were set forth in *Statement of the Jamaica Committee, Jamaica Papers No. III* (London, 1866), 3–7.   [64] *JC Minutes*, 24 Jan. 1866.

[65] *CD*, 17 Jan. 1866.

[66] 'The case of Mr. Gordon,' Smith informed a correspondent, 'which is an outrageous breach of the Petition of Right, will probably be carried before a court of law by the prosecution of Governor Eyre for the murder.' Smith to Waring, 4 Jan. 1866, *GSP*.

more pressing because, even in the face of revelations about Gordon's trial, so many English conservatives continued to defend the 'tyranny and cruelty' of the Jamaica suppression.[67]

But if the Jamaica Committee was to continue to wage legal war in Jamaica, or open a second front in England, it would need more money. By 24 January 1866, its first appeal for donations had garnered just £565 in cash and subscriptions. ('[The] money does not come in as fast as we hoped,' it was admitted to Gorrie.)[68] The new material on Gordon's court martial had stirred writers to take up their pens, but not so many readers to take up their purses. Still, even in the absence of a major new initiative, by 23 February the Committee had received more than £1,750 in donations.[69] This was money enough to keep its lawyers at work in Jamaica.

In February 1866 the Jamaica Committee acquired a major asset in the shape of the famed philosopher and newly elected M.P. for Westminster, John Stuart Mill.[70] Until that time Mill had been a supporter of the Committee only from his retreat in Avignon. But there is no question of his immediate and profound commitment to this cause. In December Mill had sent a strong letter of support to the Committee 'as soon as he heard of it'.[71] Mill wanted to be counted among those Englishmen who thought that the Jamaica suppression, especially the legal justifications offered for it, raised questions of the greatest public importance. He returned to England, convinced that nothing on Parliament's agenda in the coming year, 'not even the Reform Bill', would be 'more important than dealing justly with the abominations committed in Jamaica'.[72] As he became more directly engaged with the issue, Mill's writings and speeches on Jamaica reflected an unusual (for him) emotional fervour, even zealotry. For him it was a 'battle' that had to be won at all costs.[73] According to Chesson, at his first meeting of the Committee, he took 'a leading part in the conversation, and spoke with sense and judgment'. On most issues, but particularly on the need to prosecute Eyre, Mill's views were in accord with John Bright.[74] Although Charles Buxton was still the chairman of the Committee, together Mill and Bright soon came to dominate its public persona and policies.

---

[67] Smith to C. E. Norton, 16 Dec. 1865, *GSP*. Soon after the Jamaica Committee was formed, Smith also confided in Frederick Chesson that he believed that 'the High Church party had a good deal to do with events in Jamaica, notably Sir Frederic Rogers and the Under-Secretary [Henry Taylor]'. See also *CD*, 21 Dec. 1865.   [68] *JC Minutes*, 24 Jan. 1866.
[69] It had disbursed over £785, and had paid its local solicitor, William Shaen, £375. *JC Minutes*, 23 Feb. 1866.
[70] For basic biographical information on Mill, see Harris, *Oxford DNB*, online 18711.
[71] John M. Robson and Jack Stillinger (eds.), *John Stuart Mill: Autobiography and Literary Essays* (Toronto, 1981), 281.
[72] Mill to William Rae, 14 Dec. 1865, in Dwight N. Lindley and Francis E. Mineka (eds.), *The Later Letters of John Stuart Mill, 1849–1873* (Toronto, 1972), 1126.
[73] Mill to Fawcett, 1 Jan. 1866, ibid., 1131.   [74] Ibid.

The substantial body of scholarship regarding Mill's role in the Jamaica affair has yielded a number of useful generalizations.[75] First, while Mill felt genuine anger and shame about the systematic mistreatment of Jamaican blacks during the suppression, for him the Jamaica issue was never mainly about 'standing up for negroes'.[76] Mill was always mainly preoccupied with the ramifications of the episode for England's domestic politics, specifically, for what he saw as the constitutional bedrock of that politics. As Mill himself put it, the Jamaica episode threatened 'the first necessity of human society, law'.[77] What alarmed Mill most was not that the blood of black men had been spilled under the banner of martial law, but that so many otherwise reputable English politicians and journalists either would not condemn these events, or had openly endorsed them. For Mill this was unmistakable evidence that the English governing classes were beginning to backslide on the transcendent principle of British political culture: the supremacy of law and the constitution over men, and most especially over men of state. As Mill later recalled in his autobiography, it was not a mere coincidence that the men who had executed Gordon now were 'defended and applauded by the same kind of people who had so long upheld negro slavery'.[78] It was time to make a stand, to use the English courts of law to reassert the country's ancient jurisprudence of political power.[79]

In March and April 1866 the Jamaica Committee began to lose focus. The seemingly interminable work of its lawyers in Jamaica dragged on. Many of the Committee's leading lights – Bright, Ludlow, Beales, Hughes, Taylor, and Mill – now were fully embroiled in the fight over the Second Reform Bill. When the first murder prosecution of Duberry Ramsay ended in a 'fiasco',[80] and as the Committee's legal bills began to mount, Gorrie was recalled to England for consultation. Upon arrival, Gorrie advised the Committee that Jamaica's grand jury system was likely to prove an insurmountable barrier to criminal convictions.[81] By the beginning of May 1866, the Committee's treasury was all but empty. The legal mission to Jamaica had cost the Committee in excess of £2,000. (By themselves the three Kingston solicitors hired by Gorrie submitted accounts totalling almost £1,450.)[82] 'The Jamaican lawyers,' Chesson lamented in his diary entry of 9 May, '[soon] will have eaten up all our resources.'[83] (The Committee's executive authorized Shaen to pay these bills subject to 'certain deductions' as he saw fit.)[84] The

---

[75] For a detailed account of Mill's involvement with the Jamaica Committee, see Kinzer *et al.*, *A Moralist In and Out of Parliament*, 184–217. The larger body of historiography concerning Mill's role in the affair is further discussed below, Appendix.

[76] Mill to David Urquhart, 4 Oct. 1866, *Later Letters*, 1205.

[77] Ibid.   [78] John Stuart Mill, *Autobiography* (London, 1873), 281.   [79] Ibid.

[80] Ibid.   [81] *JC Minutes*, 23 Mar. 1866.   [82] Ibid., 9 May 1866.   [83] Ibid.

[84] Shaen made a number of deductions from the bills as submitted. According to a story published in the Jamaican newspaper the *Falmouth Post* (19 June 1866), Burke was offered £500 on his account of nearly £634; Nathan was offered £400 on his bill of over £476; Andrews was asked to take only £200 on his account of over £333. The three lawyers refused to accept this offer. A deal settling the dispute finally was worked out in October 1866. *Manchester Guardian* (13 Oct. 1866), 4.

financial position of the association had become so desperate that Buxton had to pledge an additional £100 from his own purse in order to sustain its activities until the final report of the Royal Commission was made public in June.[85]

The publication of the Commission's report, and the Government's response to it, was a pivotal moment for the Jamaica Committee. It obliged the executive leadership of the association finally to define a *primary* mission. Was it investigatory? hortatory? prosecutory? At its inception, the leading members of the Committee had agreed readily enough on the importance of the first two aims, but (excepting the prosecution of Duberry Ramsay in Jamaica) they deferred making a final decision on the last one. It was still to be hoped, moreover, that the Liberal government might take upon itself to bring criminal charges against Eyre and other senior military figures. But although the leaders of the Committee did not immediately commit themselves to this course, they did continue to lay the groundwork for this option. Legal opinions had been commissioned. Potential witnesses had been identified and interviewed. The movements of potential targets for prosecution, Nelson and Brand for instance, were kept under close watch. All that was needed to move forward was sufficient agreement, and money.

In early June 1866, just before the final report of the Royal Commission was to be tabled in Parliament, the barrister Frederic Harrison, a member of the Jamaica Committee's executive body, asked that the question of the possible criminal indictment of Eyre be put on the agenda for the next meeting.[86] (Harrison urged his friend Beesly to write a similar letter.)[87] The question no longer could be kept on the back burner, however divisive. The Committee met on 20 June. The meeting began with a discussion of Gordon's widow (who had arrived in England from Jamaica in mid-May). It was decided unanimously that the Committee's parliamentarians would vigorously support a petition that Mrs. Gordon should receive an apology and some financial compensation for the wrongful death of her husband.[88] The Committee then moved to the far more contentious issue of whether they should petition the Government to commence criminal prosecutions against Eyre and other officials. If it did not, would the Committee start private prosecutions? As Chesson wrote in his diary, 'upon the question of prosecution there was, as was always to be apprehended, a serious difference of opinion.'[89]

Neither Chesson's diary nor the minutes of the Committee provide much information about the arguments that were made for and against the prosecution initiative. It is certain only that Bright moved a resolution that the Government be asked to prosecute Eyre for the murder of Gordon. Bright also moved a contingency plan: if the Government declined to act against Eyre, that the Committee would support Mrs. Gordon in the private prosecution of Eyre. It is also apparent

---

[85] *CD*, 9 May 1866.   [86] Harrison to Beesly, undated, letter no. 14, *FHP*.   [87] Ibid.
[88] *JC Minutes*, 20 June 1866. The petition read like a criminal indictment of Eyre, as it outlined why the arrest, trial, and execution of Gordon had been 'wholly illegal'. Petition reprinted in *Daily News* (10 July 1866), 3.   [89] *CD*, 20 June 1866.

that Buxton remained steadfast in his objection to both proposals, but that the tide of opinion at the meeting ran strongly against him. As Chesson recorded: 'Mr. Buxton is an admirable man, but he always stops short of the thing needful.' In the end, the decision was taken to support a private prosecution if one was not started by the Government after it tabled the final report of the Royal Commission.

As we have seen, the Commissioners did not make specific findings regarding the potential legal culpability of civilian and military officials. As *The Times* observed, the Commission had commented extensively on such matters as Gordon's arrest and trial only to 'forbear to draw the legitimate inferences from the materials'.[90] As the legal writer W. F. Finlason later observed, these findings were no more than '*general* conclusions, and they are so general as to afford no guide as to the responsibility of particular parties'. Not surprisingly, the leaders of the Jamaica Committee strongly concurred with this view. Buxton thought that the report was 'feeble and timid'.[91] Even the most blatant misdeeds, Mill complained, had been only 'mildly condemned'. Further to the point, the tangle of legal and constitutional issues engendered by the Jamaica affair had been left unresolved. As for the Government, it decided that the proper penalty for Edward Eyre was that he should be dismissed from the colonial service. It was silent on the subject of criminal proceedings.

The executive meeting of the Jamaica Committee of 26 June 1866 was, according to Chesson's diary entry, the 'most interesting and important that has yet been held'.[92] Ahead of the meeting Buxton wrote to Chesson indicating that he would 'probably be prevented from attending', but setting forth the reasons why he remained resolutely opposed to the idea of backing Mrs. Gordon in a private prosecution of Eyre for murder. Buxton offered two main objections to the prosecution option. The first was that it had little chance of success. In order to prove an allegation of murder against Eyre, the prosecution would need to convince an English jury that Gordon's death had been 'wilful' in the sense that it was brought about dishonestly. In other words, the prosecution would have to prove that Eyre knew that there was no general conspiracy to make armed rebellion, and that Gordon had not been 'the prime mover of this design'.[93] In Buxton's view, however, the facts were indisputable that Eyre honestly had 'shared in the belief, universal at the moment among all the whites and coloured men of the island that such a conspiracy had existed, and that Mr. Gordon was, to a great extent, guilty of promoting it'. The prosecution, then, manifestly could *not* prove that Eyre had had the requisite *mens rea* or 'guilty mind' for the offence of murder. Buxton would not lend his name to a policy that was bound to fail.

Buxton's second objection concerned the matter of sentencing. In the unlikely event that Eyre was indicted by a grand jury and convicted by a trial

---

[90] *The Times* (19 June 1866), 11.   [91] Buxton letter, *The Times* (30 June 1866), 12.
[92] *CD*, 26 June 1866.   [93] Ibid.

jury, he would be sentenced to hang. Not one member of the Jamaica Committee, Buxton ventured to suggest 'would not be filled with utter dismay if we supposed that any steps we might take would send Mr. Eyre to the gallows'. Given that the Committee would have initiated the prosecution, but could not live with its possible (if implausible) consequence, it would then have to rely on some 'third party to step in and save us'. In any event, the probable result of the prosecution would be that '[Eyre] would be regarded by public opinion as a martyr who had been vindictively and cruelly assailed'. As matters stood, the punishment that Eyre had already received, while it was not 'adequate', would act as a 'sufficient warning to others'. The proper course of the Committee was to press Parliament to cashier the other officials and military men who had committed serious wrongs in Jamaica, and to compensate their victims. Buxton's letter warned that if his colleagues would not relent on the prosecution option, he would be compelled to resign as chairman of the Jamaica Committee.[94]

In the event, Buxton was present on 26 June. When the meeting was called to order, Buxton stood up and reread his letter. As Chesson remembered, this gesture received 'no support from anyone but his nephew' (Fowell Buxton). Bright then moved a resolution that the Committee provide financial and legal support to Mrs. Gordon in the criminal prosecution of Eyre. Chesson recalled that Bright supported his motion with 'a few pithy sentences', while Mill 'sustained it by his trenchant logic'. Beales, Ludlow, Taylor, and Smith also spoke in favour of Bright's motions, as did Shaen and Gorrie. In a straw vote, the resolution was endorsed by a count of 11–3.[95] True to his word, Buxton resigned as chairman of the Committee.

But this was not the end of the matter. When Buxton read newspaper accounts of the meeting, he thought that they gave a false impression that the Committee had been unanimous in their support for a criminal prosecution. Buxton desired to set the record straight. He did so by writing to *The Times*.[96] His letter described his objections to the prosecution proposal, and publicly announced his resignation. The schism within the Jamaica Committee now was a matter of public record. Then came an even more damaging blow, one which some Committee members attributed to Buxton's letter.[97] On 2 July, Gordon's widow informed Chamerovzow that she would not consent to act as the complainant in the criminal prosecution of Eyre (or anyone else) for the death of her husband. ('I shrink

---

[94] As reprinted in *The Times* (30 June 1866), 12.

[95] Later there was some dispute between Buxton and Bright on whether there had been a formal 'division' on the resolution to prosecute. In the special Committee meeting of 9 July, Buxton alleged that there had been a definitive vote. Bright denied it. See *The Times* (10 July 1866), 5. In a letter to *The Times*, Mr. Alfred Churchill indicated that he would have voted against Bright's resolutions had he been present at the Committee meeting of 26 June. As reprinted in the *Colonial Standard* (21 July 1866), 2.   [96] *The Times* (30 June 1866), 12.

[97] See remarks of Peter Taylor, as quoted in *The Times* (10 July 1866), 5.

from the step suggested.')⁹⁸ Mrs. Gordon thought it was more consonant with Christian virtue to 'leave Mr. Eyre and those who have aided him in his cruel proceedings in the hands of [God]'.⁹⁹ The Committee now was in crisis. An emergency meeting was called for 9 July.

When the July meeting convened at Radley's Hotel, Buxton was in attendance.¹⁰⁰ Peter Taylor chaired the session, relating how the meeting had been necessitated by Buxton's public letter of resignation. He opened discussion with some quibbling about whether the Committee had actually committed itself to a prosecution or, as Taylor believed, their position was that 'the Government ought to initiate a prosecution, and that they would press upon them to do so; and that, in the event of the Government not doing so, they would give Mrs. Gordon every assistance if she prosecuted'.¹⁰¹ Taylor admonished Buxton for having 'damaged the prestige of the committee in greater degree than its united enemies could accomplish'. He thought that Buxton's letter had encouraged the view, now seemingly embraced by Mrs. Gordon, that the proposed prosecution of Eyre was motivated by the spirit of 'personal vengeance'. Inspiring loud cries of 'hear, hear', Taylor disavowed this perception. The former Governor Eyre, he pointedly stated, was nothing to the Jamaica Committee as an individual man. If he was to be the target of criminal litigation it was not because of any personal feelings, but because Eyre was 'the impersonation of wrong'. Buxton was given the opportunity to reply. He repeated that 'he did not consider Mr. Eyre as guilty of wilful murder, but...as a man who most shamefully, criminally and cruelly misgoverned the colony of Jamaica'. Buxton thought this argument 'irresistible'. Buxton continued that he would support the criminal prosecution of Eyre 'for misgoverning the colony'. He would also gladly endorse the prosecution of the military men who executed Gordon. But under no circumstances would he endorse the prosecution of Eyre on a charge of murder. For the record, Buxton also took pains to allay the rumour that he had been in contact with Mrs. Gordon, and that he had dissuaded her from the idea of a private prosecution. Buxton stated categorically that he had not communicated with Mrs. Gordon, and that the decision not to prosecute was entirely 'voluntary on her part'. Buxton expressed regret that his actions might inadvertently have caused harm to the Committee.

When Buxton was finished, Bright dressed him down for having published a 'hastily penned fulmination against the Committee'. Bright likened Buxton to the man who promised to go tiger hunting with a friend, only to abandon him at the

---

⁹⁸ The charitable view was that Mrs. Gordon declined to prosecute out of a 'misguided sense of Christian forgiveness'. The less charitable view was that she was afraid that the trial would jeopardize her chance of gaining some financial compensation from the Government. *Falmouth Post* (10 Aug. 1866), 2. There is evidence that Mrs. Gordon already had collected a substantial sum from an insurance policy on her husband's life. In the *Manchester Guardian* (4 Dec. 1866), 2, it was reported that an English insurance company already had resolved to make a payment of £2,500 on the assumption that 'Gordon's execution was a judicial murder'.   ⁹⁹ *Daily Telegraph* (18 July 1866), 3.
¹⁰⁰ A transcription of the meeting appeared in *The Times* (10 July 1866), 5.   ¹⁰¹ Ibid.

moment of danger. Just as the Jamaica Committee was coming to the crucial if perilous moment 'at which they could do any good', Buxton had 'backed out and left them in the lurch'. Bright blamed Buxton's actions for having put off Mrs. Gordon. There was nothing now to do but confront the question. If the Government would not prosecute Eyre, and if Mrs. Gordon would not prosecute privately, should the Committee fill the breach?

Bright answered his own question: 'The fact was, unless they prosecuted Eyre, it would be better for them to dissolve.' That left the matter of the appropriate charge. To Bright's mind, there was no doubting that Eyre had engineered Gordon's death, and that for his efforts he should face the charge of wilful homicide. Bright bolstered this contention with a quite extraordinary claim: '[A]t the meeting of Parliament,' Bright explained, 'he discussed this question with one of the oldest and most esteemed judges in England, who said – not in his [Bright's] presence alone – that in his whole life he had never seen or known a case more distinctly of murder than the putting of Mr. Gordon to death.' This being so, and no lawyer of reputation had yet doubted it, then the Jamaica Committee members 'would make fools of themselves if they proceeded on any other basis than that of trying Mr. Eyre for murder'. On the other hand, Bright was not unrealistic about the difference between theory and practice in the law. He admitted that it was 'very likely the Grand Jury would ignore the Bill', especially if Mrs. Gordon was not the complainant. Bright put the question forward for further debate.

What followed was a short restatement of collective faith. The few men who spoke were lawyers, and they focused on the constitutional implications of the Jamaica affair. Edmond Beales, the barrister and leading Reform Bill activist, argued that 'if the Committee did not prosecute, then English law was for all intents and purposes a mockery, and there would be a strong feeling throughout the country that there was one law for the rich and another for the poor'. In the wake of this comment, Harrison moved that the Committee take 'immediate action in the prosecution of Mr. Eyre'. Gorrie told the Committee that 'having heard the evidence before the Jamaica Commission, and the statements of Mr. Eyre, he had no doubt that the latter was guilty of putting Mr. Gordon to death without sufficient cause, and in opposition to law'. Harrison's resolution was carried, only Buxton voting against it.

Mill was present for the debate, but his voice had not been heard until Beales moved that Mill be elected to replace Buxton as Chairman. This was carried unanimously. Mill spoke briefly to underline his emphatic support for the legal and constitutional motivations of the proposed prosecution. Eyre was to be prosecuted for murder, Mill explained over the applause of his associates, 'to ascertain whether there exist in *this country* any means for making a British functionary responsible for blood unlawfully shed, and whether that be murder or not' (emphasis added). Under Mill's leadership the Committee would not rest until Eyre was in the dock facing a charge of murder, whether as a result of governmental or private action. The main goal now was for the parliamentary members of the Jamaica Committee to convince the new (Tory) government that it bore the responsibility to start the prosecution.

The following day, 10 July, in the course of the first executive meeting chaired by Mill, Gorrie was asked to assemble a list of the 'chief criminal acts committed by Governor Eyre and his subordinates in Jamaica'.[102] Shaen read a report from Stephen concerning the potential criminal culpability of Eyre and his officers, and it was decided that Gorrie's list would be sent to Stephen as soon as it could be completed. It was also decided that Chamerovzow would call on Mrs. Gordon and make a final appeal that she might act as the criminal complainant.[103] In the result, Mrs. Gordon, although she did not relent, published an open letter in which she regretted that her first letter caused embarrassment to the Committee, and pledged not to interfere with the 'vindication of the great principles so outraged by Mr. Eyre'.[104] With or without the widow's support, the prosecution of Eyre would be expensive. The Committee's deliberations turned to the subject of fund-raising.

The Committee permitted the press to cover its meeting of 10 July. By then it was well known that it had pledged to bring a criminal case against Eyre. Most of the press were strongly opposed to the idea. The most obdurately conservative papers summarily dismissed it as 'absurd fanaticism',[105] as a 'vindictive and cowardly prosecution for the sake of clap-trap popularity with the most ignorant classes'.[106] But more papers, *The Times* for example, felt compelled to enumerate their objections. While it now accepted that the execution of Gordon had been 'a most serious error' and a 'grievous abuse of authority' for which there needed to be some accountability,[107] the editors did not accept that Eyre bore 'moral and legal criminality' for the death of Gordon, or any other person. In this view, the man had been punished enough by loss of reputation and office. This was a widely shared opinion in the press. As the editors of the *Manchester Guardian* put it, Eyre's actions, rash and regrettable though they were, were also 'wholly lacking in the element of moral criminality'. To proceed with the plan would thus be 'vain, foolish, and uncalled for'.[108] Eyre's 'administrative blunder,' the *Saturday Review* agreed, 'approximates to a crime,' but the editors did not think that 'any sane person would impute to Mr. Eyre wantonly homicidal intentions'.[109]

For the *Spectator*, the fact that Mrs. Gordon would not be the complainant discredited the prosecution option.[110] In this view, a criminal prosecution was supposed to be personal; it was supposed to be about getting justice, not in the abstract, but for a real person 'deeply wronged by Mr. Eyre's contempt for law'. If Mrs. Gordon will not prosecute, asked the editors of *The Age We Live In*, why

---

[102] *JC Minutes*, 10 July 1866.   [103] Ibid., 17 July 1866.
[104] *Daily Telegraph* (18 July 1866), 3.
[105] *Morning Herald*, as quoted in the *Pall Mall Gazette* (11 July 1866), 2.
[106] *Morning Advertiser* (31 July 1866).   [107] *The Times* (30 June 1866), 8.
[108] *Manchester Guardian* (11 July 1866), 2.   [109] *Saturday Review* (7 July 1866), 15.
[110] *Spectator* (7 July 1866), 735.

should the Crown (or anyone else) 'adopt a system of persecution'?[111] But for other journals, the personalization of the case was exactly what was not to be desired. The key to the case, the *Saturday Review* maintained, was understanding that Eyre's mistakes were administrative in nature.[112] By these lights the idea of prosecution was worse than absurd. If Eyre were actually convicted of a criminal offence for having made honest mistakes in carrying out his official duties, surely it would impair the judgement of other Governors. The next time a colonial rebellion occurred, the *Review* suggested, the executive in charge would be wise to 'wait till he heard of the massacre of a thousand whites, then sit down and pen a despatch to the Secretary of State'. Empires were dangerous places; they could not be governed by men afraid that the next decision made in a civil emergency would land them in the dock.

The legal trade paper, the *Law Times*, was adamant that the prosecution option was the 'unwise proceeding' of Mill, 'who seems, like too many philosophers to have every sense but common sense'.[113] Like the newspapers and political journals, however, the *Law Times* editorial consisted of a seamless mixture of political and technical objections. When the leader writer claimed that 'the Governor's fault was only an excess of severity in putting down an undoubted rebellion which, if he had failed to suppress, would certainly have resulted in the massacre of all the whites', it offered the most common *political* justification for his actions. The writer did not cite law demonstrating why an *excess* of severity, even in the context of an emergency of state, was not a criminal act. On the other hand, when the editors doubted that Eyre could be liable criminally for the action of a court martial, or that he could be convicted of murder in the absence of *malice prepense*, it at least was referring to some legal grounds of objection to the prosecution. In the same way the *Law Times* also alluded to the question of the grand jury. '[I]s there the remotest chance,' it asked, 'of any twelve men chosen by ballot being found who would convict the Governor of a colony ... of a crime of murder for an excess of severity in putting down the rebellion of a semi-barbarous race whose numbers were ten to one, and whose success would have been the certain massacre of every white man?' In such circumstances, the colonial executive who 'stopped to measure the precise amount of force required would be faithless to his trust'.

In moderate liberal and conservative circles, the received wisdom was that the proposed prosecution was seriously misguided. The only point of disagreement was whether the Jamaica Committee was about to make a malicious or merely foolish mistake. But there was some dissent from this point of view, especially in the labour and radical papers. For the *Weekly Times* Gordon's death was not an administrative error but a 'political assassination'.[114] The editors of the *Weekly Times* thanked heaven for the 'calm, philosophical, law-loving John Mill' and his

111 *Age We Live In* (14 July 1866).   112 *Saturday Review* (7 July 1866), 15.
113 *Law Times* (21 July 1866), 650.   114 *Weekly Times* (22 July 1866).

determination to make Eyre and his protectors accountable to the people. In a similar vein, the *Newcastle Weekly Chronicle* saw in the Jamaica controversy 'issues so deeply affecting ourselves that we are quite sure no impotent conclusion will altogether satisfy the English people'.[115] The execution of Gordon presented issues of the 'deepest and gravest constitutional importance'. These the *Chronicle* summarized: 'What security is there for the person if a functionary is allowed to put to death a political opponent? If Eyre's proceedings in Jamaica should become a precedent, the Bill of Rights would be of no value whatever, and popular orators like Mr. Bright would be reduced to depend for their freedom and their lives on the will of the arbitrary minister.' In this reading of the controversy, it was a matter of 'the highest moment' for the Jamaica Committee to fulfil its pledge to compel Eyre to face an English judge and jury. 'It is not enough,' the *Birmingham Post*'s editorial read on 11 July, 'that Mr. Eyre has been deprived of his office and, as we suppose, dismissed of his employment; or that naval and military subordinates have been handed over to the Admiralty and the War Office, for correction. Measures of this kind will neither satisfy public feeling, nor meet the justice of the case.'

On 12 July a writer to the *Daily News* attempted to rescue the Jamaica Committee from the pillory. The fact that almost all of the leading newspapers of the country had vehemently attacked the prosecution proposal was seen as emblematic of the 'laxity of public opinion with regard to the cherished rights and safeguards of British subjects'.[116] The writer urged that the prosecution be viewed as a matter of 'public duty, in dealing with a dangerous precedent', not as a question of mere 'personal feeling'. If Englishmen were to have their rights, Eyre's conduct could not safely be dismissed as 'an error of judgment... in a moment of excitement'. What if an English person was to 'assist his neighbours to "lynch" an unpopular individual', is it possible that he might be excused from 'judicial investigation' only because he was caught up in the excitement of the mob? The writer believed that the Jamaica Committee was moved only by the 'highest constitutional considerations', and that it was essential to the well-being of the nation that their initiative be shielded from the 'unjust charge of fanaticism'.

Such friendly comments notwithstanding, as matters stood at the end of July 1866 Mill and his associates had not won the hearts and minds of the majority of the press or, probably, of readers of the press. By the same token, they cared enough about public opinion, to say nothing about the public purse, to publish a new statement of self-justification. Drafted by Goldwin Smith, the *Statement of the Jamaica Committee*, published on 27 July, was a calculated response to the harsh criticism directed toward the prosecution initiative.[117] Its striking characteristic was

[115] *Newcastle Weekly Chronicle* (14 July 1866).
[116] Letter of '*Droits de L'Homme*' (12 July 1866), 5.
[117] *Statement of the Jamaica Committee, Jamaica Papers No III*, 3–7.

the tendency to reduce the political, economic, and racial dynamics of the Jamaica uprising and suppression to a syllogism of legal abstractions:

(1) it was unlawful for British subjects to be molested by officials or agents of state except in accordance with due process of law;

(2) the salient fact about the Jamaica affair was that British subjects had been assaulted and even killed by officials of state without due process of law;

(3) because there was credible evidence of such crimes, it was the 'duty of the Government to inquire into the case' in order to 'vindicate the law by bringing the offenders to public justice';

(4) when the Government neglected this duty, it fell upon private citizens to vindicate the law 'by an appeal to judicial authority'.

The statement then specified the constitutional principles that had been put into jeopardy. Its first contention was that the 'illegal execution of a British subject by a person of authority' is not a forgivable error of judgement, but a 'crime which will certainly be punished by law'. 'Our lives and liberties,' the statement continued, 'have not been, nor can they be safely allowed to be, under the guardianship of Executive government alone; and it is essential that they should remain, under the guardianship of the law.' Clearly the appeal here was not to the personal security of Jamaicans but to '*Our*' (read: English) 'lives and liberties'. What was needed was an authoritative declaration from a 'Court of Justice' about 'the jurisdiction of the courts of martial law'. The Committee desired to learn whether martial law was 'really law at all, or sanguinary licence which the law will repress and punish'. This agenda, it was admitted, could not be attained except by the application of great legal expertise. On this point the public were reassured that 'the Committee have hitherto consulted and would continue to consult, professional advisers of the highest eminence and most unbiassed judgement'.

Without justifying the selection of this case, the Committee's statement turned to the subject of Eyre's role in the execution of Gordon. It was alleged that Eyre 'was not only constructively but personally guilty' of these transgressions. Gordon, 'to all intents and purposes', died at Eyre's hand. The statement then attempted to rebut the contention that Eyre could not be guilty of murder for lack of evidence of 'private malice'. Echoing the argument made by the *Weekly Times*, the Committee argued that, if accepted, this theory would effectively immunize 'the crime which is the most dangerous to all of the community – the crime of a public functionary who abuses the power entrusted to him'. If the plea of 'good intentions' was as a legal defence to criminal charges made against an official, it would 'hold out to impunity all political homicide'. The Committee's intention was to seek punishment for the 'great offences of the great offenders'. It would not pursue any official who 'appears to be fairly covered by the plea of necessity'. But the Committee also wanted to underline that it would have no truck with rebels, and had 'no desire to abet resistance to lawful authority or to weaken the arm of the magistrate in preserving public order'. The prosecution of Eyre was to be an exercise in buttressing, not destroying, constitutional tradition. The legal mission of the Jamaica Committee, then, was depicted as essentially *conservative* in thrust.

An abbreviated version of the July statement became a staple of the Jamaica Committee's fund-raising publicity in the autumn of 1866.[118] Its central message was that the prosecution of Governor Eyre would be undertaken for the benefit of Englishmen. The goal of the Committee was to 'defend public liberty' from the incursions of the state. For this reason, the Committee asserted, it could justly claim the 'sympathy and support of all to whom public liberty is dear'. What was wanted from the prosecution was law, not blood or vengeance. Should Eyre be convicted of murder, the Committee would support an application for pardon. The prosecution was portrayed mainly as a symbolic proceeding. Eyre was to be treated not as a wicked person, but, in the words of Peter Taylor, as the '*impersonation* of wrong' (emphasis added). The prosecution was quite self-consciously contemplated as a kind of political allegory, the courts as a grand political theatre.

Mill's election to the chairmanship accentuated another important fact about the Jamaica Committee. Although it had been instigated by Exeter Hall, it was no longer committed mainly to a philanthropic agenda.[119] If 'Justice for the Negro' was once the Committee's principal slogan and goal, that had changed. So fastidious about his words, Mill in his inaugural speech as chairman did not once mention Jamaica or its people. The main aim of his chairmanship, he informed colleagues, would be to bring Eyre to justice in the English courts. The main aim of this project was to vindicate the principle of legal accountability in 'this country'. It is not coincidental that during the pivotal Committee meetings of June and July 1866, the leaders of Exeter Hall had remained almost comprehensively silent. Even more interestingly, the Exeter Hall men who did speak, Buxton excepted, firmly *supported* the direction given the Committee by Mill and Bright. As matters stood in mid-July 1866, the twin *raisons d'être* of the Jamaica Committee were to prosecute Governor Eyre for murder, and in order to affirm a point of English constitutional law. While the jurisprudence of political power clearly had implications for non-white subjects of the realm, it was a very far cry from the business of getting justice for the black Jamaican victims of the suppression.

III. July–November 1866: The Jamaica Controversy in Parliament

Before July 1866 the Jamaica affair had been only fleetingly and superficially discussed in Parliament. There were reasons for the strange quiet on a matter of such

---

[118] See, for example, 'The Jamaica Committee', *Daily News* (12 Oct. 1866), 3.

[119] At the Jamaica Committee meeting of 10 July, Peter Taylor remarked that the association had 'constituted themselves the advocates of the blacks'. However, very little either of the Jamaica Committee's programme or the rhetoric adopted to promote it actually related to colonials, black or white. See *The Times* (10 July 1866), 5.

public importance. Many of the leading members of the Jamaica Committee – Taylor, Mill, Bright, Hughes, Buxton – were also parliamentary Radicals who (for many purposes) were allied with the governing Liberals. The alliance was strengthened on the death of Palmerston, and with his successor's (Lord Russell's) decision to revive the question of constitutional Reform in 1866.[120] However, the Radicals did not assume that it would be an easy matter to pass a Reform Bill. Even if Russell could be counted on to introduce the legislation, the position of the Liberal party in 1866 was not strong, and a Reform Bill was unlikely to strengthen it. For this reason alone the Radicals were disinclined to make trouble for the Government over Jamaica. But another factor was that there simply was little to complain of in the Government's handling of the Jamaica affair. After all, only a few weeks after the Jamaica story broke in England, the cabinet already had instituted a far-ranging inquiry, one which the Jamaica Committee's own lawyers acknowledged was being undertaken fairly and conscientiously.

There was another good reason for the Jamaica Committee's M.P.s to hold fire. After the publication of Augustus Lake's transcript of Gordon's court martial, it became a commonplace that Gordon had been either wrongfully convicted, or convicted after a defective trial. It was also widely accepted that Gladstone – the most important Cabinet member after the Prime Minister – was outraged by the excessive violence of the suppression.[121] Until the publication of Cardwell's despatch on the findings of the Royal Commission on 22 June, the Committee could still entertain some small hope that the Attorney General would prefer indictments against Eyre and his senior officers. But when the Liberal government lost the Reform Bill, and resigned on 28 June, there no longer was any reason to hold back.

The rainy summer of 1866 was a time of political, financial, and physical malaise in England, especially in London. The new Conservative government of Lord Derby was feeling the weight of its inheritance. While cattle plague was wasting stock in the countryside, cholera was wasting people in the slums of the capital. The whole country, the *Daily Telegraph* reflected at year's end, seemed to 'lie under heavy shadows...shadows of war, pestilence and murrain among the herds...great wrecks, great conflagrations, great floods, civil troubles, clouds of disaffection and political bitternesses'.[122] And while the Liberal Reform Bill was dead, the extra-parliamentary agitation for Reform had become more intense and impatient. In such a time, the Conservative potentates were in no mood to be browbeaten on Jamaica, even if it were true that the alleged sins of Governor Eyre and his soldiers had not taken place under their watch.

As a sitting M.P., a passionate proponent of the prosecution initiative, and not so much tethered to the previous Government as Bright, Mill was the natural

---

[120] See generally, Maurice Cowling, 'Disraeli, Derby and Fusion, October 1865 to July 1866', 8 *Historical Journal* (1965), 31–71, at 34–7.   [121] Knox, 'British Government', 880.

[122] *Daily Telegraph* (31 Dec. 1866), 4.

voice of the Jamaica Committee in the House of Commons. At the executive meeting of 10 July, it had been agreed that Mill would put a series of Jamaica questions to Disraeli, Chancellor of the Exchequer, and Tory leader in the Commons.[123] On 17 July, Mill read his questions into the parliamentary record, and expressed the expectation that they would be answered in the House two days later.[124] All but one concerned the alleged criminal misconduct of individual soldiers and officials during the suppression, and were selected from a list compiled by Gorrie. The thrust of Mill's questions was whether the Government had taken steps to indict certain colonial officials and soldiers (some thirteen were named, including Heslop, Nelson, Brand, and Eyre) for criminal offences (ranging from unlawful arrests to floggings and executions) committed during martial law? And, if no steps had been taken, had the Government been advised 'that these acts are not offences under the Criminal Law'?

According to Mill's most meticulous (and sympathetic) historians, the ensuing clash over his Jamaica questions was not the shining hour of his brief parliamentary career.[125] In this account, when the matter came to a head in the House of Commons on 19 July, Disraeli subjected the philosopher to nothing less than a 'Parliamentary drubbing'. The episode deserves another look.

Certainly the debate began awkwardly for Mill.[126] When he asked to 'spare the House the monotonously painful details contained in the Questions of which he had given notice', Disraeli adroitly insisted that the House *not* be spared the details. The honourable member was to read 'the whole'. Mill was left to look the earnest pedant as he plodded through ten monotonously worded questions. The reading also drew attention to a weakness of reasoning. Disraeli accused Mill of some very unphilosophical question-begging. Specifically, Mill was accused of having put questions to the House 'in which opinions are also expressed'. Mill's questions had *assumed* some of the very points that remained in dispute. They assumed, for instance, that the actions of some officials were 'illegal' or 'unlawful', and this before the House had heard the opinion of the 'Law Officers of the Crown'. Disraeli further ventured that Mill's questions omitted the key fact that 'the proceedings complained of took place during the existence of martial law'. This was not an inconsequential oversight, 'for in a state of martial law there can be no irregularity in the constitution of the courts. Martial law supersedes all law.' This being the case, it was not obvious that any of the persons mentioned had committed crimes. At the very least, the major premiss of Mill's inquiry was a matter of doubt. Disraeli referred to the former Governor Eyre as a case in point. A Royal Commission had already found that the decisions made by Eyre during the suppression were not motivated by *malice prepense*, and that the appropriate punishment for these mistakes was dismissal. The Government, Disraeli told the

---

[123] *JC Minutes*, 10 July 1866.   [124] *Hansard*, clxxxiv (19 July 1866), 1065.

[125] Kinzer *et al.*, *A Moralist In and Out of Parliament*, 195–6.

[126] *Hansard*, clxxxiv (19 July 1866), 1064–9.

House, saw no reason to disturb these decisions. But nor would the Government disturb ongoing investigations into possible criminal misconduct in Jamaica. That was all the Chancellor had to say about Mill's questions.

As a matter of political theatre, there is no doubt that Mill had been upstaged by Disraeli. He had given a wily politician the chance to make him look foolish, and the chance was not squandered. But it would be easy to make too much of the encounter. Mill did not ask his ten questions expecting definitive answers from the Government. It is doubtful that Mill entertained the slightest hope that the Tories would commence criminal proceedings against anyone on his list.[127] In fact, Mill's questions were less inquisitory than promotional. He asked them in order to draw lines in the sand. In his answers, Disraeli had made clear that the Derby government would not pursue criminal proceedings, not, at least, in England, against the men who had orchestrated a bloody suppression. Such proceedings would have to be started by private persons: enter the Jamaica Committee. Thus, when he ridiculed Mill's questions, Disraeli did something for him of considerable tactical value. Disraeli had endorsed a broad reading of the law of martial law. A senior member of the Tory Cabinet had gone on public record that a former colonial Governor was entirely innocent of murder (or any other serious crime) because 'martial law supersedes ordinary law'. This was a rich grist for Mill.

Developments in the agitation for political reform soon made the grist even richer. When the Liberals' Reform Bill was defeated at the end of June 1866, extra-parliamentary agitation for manhood suffrage intensified. As noted, the leadership of the Reform League overlapped substantially with the leadership of the Jamaica Committee.[128] Edmond Beales was the President of the League. Harrison and Beesly both were executive members. Bright, Mill, and Hughes spoke at a number of Reform League rallies, as did the Jamaica Committee's solicitor, William Shaen.[129] On 23 July, only four days after Mill's parliamentary clash with Disraeli, the London authorities deployed a force of nearly two thousand foot and mounted police to clear Hyde Park of Reform League demonstrators. Injuries were caused, arrests made. As an exercise in state repression, Hyde Park was pretty small beer. But the incident had a symbolic resonance not lost on the Jamaica Committee. Here was a timely reminder that the English authorities remained able and willing to use force to suppress political dissent. One of the challenges faced by the Jamaica Committee in the summer of 1866 was to persuade their countrymen of the connectedness between martial law in Jamaica and political

---

[127] According to the *Morning Post* (20 July 1866), 4, 'it was overstepping the bounds of Parliamentary usage when [Mill] called on the Government to declare what course they proposed to adopt toward certain individuals under the assumption they had committed serious crimes'.

[128] See generally, Royden Harrison, *Before the Socialists: Studies in Labour and Politics, 1861–1881* (London, 1965), 82–3; Hall, 'Rethinking Imperial Histories'.

[129] Harrison complimented Shaen's speech in a letter to Beesly, letter no. 18, *HP*.

repression in England. The Hyde Park riots made this task a little easier.[130] As Peter Taylor told a large Reform demonstration held in Islington on 31 July (a meeting also addressed by Mill and Hughes),[131] 'the Tories are the same now as they were thirty years ago, and as they were last year in the Jamaica business.'[132] Taylor continued over cheers: 'I will, with regard to Jamaica, give you a rule of three sum. As the latitude of Jamaica is to the latitude of Hyde Park, so is the late George William Gordon to that of John Bright.' The Jamaica Committee orators were not the only ones to make such references. The Government's methods at Hyde Park, a Scottish newspaper editor ventured, was a sobering example of the 'importation of West Indian maxims into England'.[133] These developments, he warned, 'must be met in the old English way, or we may see the atrocities of an Eyre, a Nelson, or a Hobbs repeated in Dublin, Hyde Park or in a Lincoln's Inn Fields'.

By the summer of 1866 the Jamaica Committee was ready to commence private criminal prosecutions in England against Eyre and other officials. However, neither Eyre nor any of the other principal targets was in England. In the meantime, the Committee exploited opportunities to promote its ideas and agenda in the present Parliament. At an executive meeting held on 24 July, it was unanimously agreed that Disraeli's reply to Mill's questions 'involved an evasion of the chief matters which those matters brought before the House and implied that the existence of martial law proved the legality of the executions . . . in strict violation of the principles embodied in the Great Charter and Petition of Right'.[134] The attendees also discussed Buxton's intention to move resolutions in the House of Commons condemning Eyre and the Jamaica martial law. On this initiative, the House also was to be asked to vote compensation to innocent victims of the suppression, and pardon persons still facing charges related to the uprising. Buxton would also call for the Government to discipline any soldiers or civilians who committed 'great offences' during martial law. In order to speak to these resolutions without prejudice to the Jamaica Committee, Buxton had resigned his membership.

After some discussion the Committee's new leaders decided that Buxton's resolutions fell short on two key points. Buxton had not asked the House to condemn the

[130] The Hyde Park riots provided the Jamaica Committee with a splendid opportunity to fuse the prosecution of Eyre with domestic political concerns. The fusion created a broader base of support (especially among working men), and it helped the Committee raise money. At Reform meetings, the hat was passed round to advance constitutional change (a new Reform Bill) and constitutional principle (the Jamaica prosecution). As Chesson recorded in his diary on 28 September 1866, 'much money was collected at [the Reform meeting] in Rochdale'.

[131] All five of the principal speakers advertised to address the Islington meeting – Bright, Mill, Hughes, Fawcett, and James White – were M.P.s and members of the Jamaica Committee. All but White were executive members. For reasons they did not make known, neither Bright nor Fawcett came to the meeting. Hughes was present but refused to speak. *The Times* (31 July 1866), 3.

[132] *Daily Telegraph* (31 July 1866), 4.   [133] *Glasgow Morning Journal* (2 Aug. 1866).

[134] *JC Minutes*, 24 July 1866.

illegality of the execution of Gordon and others, and did not call for the criminal prosecution of the worst offenders.[135] It was agreed that a member of the Committee would need to make these deficiencies known to the House. According to Chesson's diary, Bright was to be asked to undertake this task. In the result, however, Mill gave the principal speech (buttressed by Hughes) for the Committee. The Committee also resolved to ask other 'friendly' M.P.s 'to emphasize the illegality of the Jamaica authorities' conduct'.

Buxton moved his resolutions in a long speech to the House of Commons on the evening of 31 July. It was the occasion for the first expansive parliamentary debate on the Jamaica affair, the subject, as Cardwell put it, 'which more than any other in recent times has stirred the feelings of the community'.[136] While there were misgivings among M.P.s as to the prudence of Buxton's resolutions, the idea that there should be some extensive debate on Jamaica, more particularly, on the findings of the Royal Commission, was widely accepted. 'It was a natural consequence,' the *Saturday Review* observed on 4 August, 'that the House should express some opinion on the facts which the inquiry had elicited.'

Although Buxton now was speaking for himself only, his speech deserves attention. It is revealing of how a highly cultivated English mind tried to reconcile the contradictions generated by his country's constitutional and imperial commitments. Buxton knew that if he was to make any headway with the House, his rhetoric would have to be very carefully honed. He knew that he was addressing a legislative body of a vast empire, a body which knew something of colonial insurrection and suppression, and one which did not think that they were only of antique interest. This suggests why Buxton began with a reassuring clarification: 'No one need fear that in supporting these Resolutions he would run any risk of hampering or increasing the responsibility of any Governor or other official who might have to deal with any insurrection that might arise on future occasions.'[137] Buxton stressed that his resolutions did not pertain to 'anything that was done *during* the suppression of the disturbances' (emphasis added). He was concerned only with the 'excessive severity' of punishments meted out *after* the rebellion had been crushed. He then drew from the evidence of the Royal Commission to describe examples in detail and at length. Returning to his former point, Buxton asked aloud how 'anyone who had any regard for the honour of England, dared to maintain that all this hanging, shooting and flogging that went on for more than a month, was necessary'.[138]

Buxton continued to step gingerly around what must have been a widely held assumption among his peers in the House: that the use – or threatened use – of extreme violence was absolutely indispensable to the governance of an empire. The memory of Cawnpore was, after all, fresh in the minds of all his listeners. He could not be seen suggesting that British officials in the colonies, often isolated and

---

135 *CD*, 24 July 1866.   136 *Hansard*, clxxxiv (31 July 1866), 1819.
137 Ibid., 1763–4.   138 Ibid., 1770.

vulnerable, should have their hands tied in the face of trouble. 'For argument's sake,' Buxton stated, 'he would admit the truth of what had been so often said, that it was not right for us, sitting at home at ease, to criticise the acts done by men in a great emergency.'[139] He hammered on the fact that the worst violence perpetrated by government officials in Jamaica occurred days or even weeks after 'everything like peril or panic, or what might be called an emergency, was over'. What was done on these days, then, was done 'in deliberate cold blood'.[140] To make the point more palatable to the House, Buxton likened the position of the Jamaicans slain by courts martial after the uprising was long over to the victims of Judge Jeffreys after the Monmouth rebellion of 1685. Buxton ended with an emotional appeal to the House to put aside partisanship and condemn the 'wild rage and vengeance' which had been perpetrated in Jamaica in the name of the Crown.[141] Before he yielded the floor, Buxton moved that his first resolution be put to a vote, 'That this House deplores the excessive punishments which followed the suppression . . . and especially the unnecessary frequency with which the punishment of death was inflicted.'

The first reply from the Government benches was made by Charles Adderley, the recently appointed Under-Secretary for the Colonies. Adderley was a scion of the Tory gentry.[142] In 1866 he had been an M.P. twenty-five years, and regarded himself an expert on colonial affairs. This was not the first time, incidentally, that Adderley had become embroiled in a debate over the use of violence to suppress rebellion in the colonies. In 1852 he had spoken in defence of Lord Torrington, and the use of martial law in Ceylon.[143] Adderley's stance was unsubtle. He attacked Buxton's assertions and motives comprehensively, conceding nothing. He began by chiding Buxton for having spoken as if he 'was the exclusive champion of the oppressed', and that all those who opposed his resolutions were 'the enemies of mankind'.[144] Adderley then moved to seize the legal high ground by claiming (rather fatuously) that the unfortunate incidents described by Buxton already had been evaluated as 'matters of trial by a properly constituted tribunal', the Jamaica Royal Commission. In Adderley's view, the final report of the Royal Commission ought to be regarded as the last word on these matters. There was no proper basis upon which the House could 're-open the case' or 'try the case over again'. The House of Commons, Adderley asserted, simply did not have the 'means' or 'witnesses' to do so. After all, unlike the Royal Commission, the Commons was 'no judicial tribunal'.

Much like Disraeli had done with regard to Mill's questions, Adderley objected to the tacit assumptions of Buxton's resolutions. In the first instance, he did not think it right to characterize the armed uprising at Morant Bay as a 'very trifling

---

[139] Ibid., 1772.   [140] Ibid., 1773.   [141] Ibid., 1785.

[142] *DNB*, 2 supplement, i, 18.

[143] Sixteen years earlier, in 1850, Adderley had pressed the Liberal government for the further investigation of the use of martial law to suppress a rebellion in Ceylon. See Kostal, 'A Jurisprudence of Power', 10.   [144] *Hansard*, clxxxiv (31 July 1866), 1785.

affair'. Here Adderley appealed to race prejudice. He reminded the House that black men vastly outnumbered white men in Jamaica. In Adderley's view, it was too easy (from a safe distance of England) to dismiss what happened at Morant Bay as a mere riot. That mere riot had cost the lives of more than a dozen white men, including a magistrate. The former Governor had had every good reason to believe that Morant Bay portended a bloody general revolt in Jamaica. Many months removed from the original outbreak, Adderley had heard credible rumours that there might be 'renewed disturbances' in Jamaica.[145] It was crucial, then, that Parliament made no move that might tend to inhibit the ability of imperial officials to respond vigorously to an insurrection.

Adderley thought that when he proclaimed martial law in Jamaica, Edward Eyre had had compelling reasons to do so. Further to the point, Adderley also contended that the proclamation of martial law should have a substantial bearing on the potential criminal liability of the former Governor and his officers. This, he alleged, is where Buxton's resolutions were most seriously flawed. They failed to take into account that martial law provided a blanket immunity to all those who acted in good faith to put down a threat to public order. Nothing that Eyre had undertaken *bona fide* to suppress the Jamaica revolt could have been 'illegally done'.[146] Warming to his subject, Adderley then elaborated his most controversial point: 'With regard to the recall of Governor Eyre, I do not think the case against him is yet made out . . . The law of the case is by no means settled. The illegality of Gordon's trial is a question still undecided.'[147] Adderley went so far as to suggest that the 'justice of Gordon's death' was at least arguable, and that 'there was a case [against Gordon] on which no jury would have acquitted'. This last assertion incited loud shouts of disapproval. Sensing that he might have overstated his case, Adderley did 'not wish to press that point'. He remained adamant, however, that the treatment of Gordon was in accord with the strictures of 'practical justice'. As for Buxton's resolutions, the first one was perhaps minimally acceptable. The remaining three deserved to be rejected out of hand.

For reasons that remain unclear, Mill (not Bright,[148] as Chesson had stated) addressed the House on behalf of the Jamaica Committee. In his *Autobiography*, Mill recorded that he thought his speech on this occasion 'the best' of his parliamentary career,[149] and Mill's historians have tended to agree with this assessment.[150] When Mill spoke to the resolutions it was with one thought in mind: he wanted to use the occasion to validate the decision of his Committee to prosecute Eyre for murder. In this regard, Mill was encouraged by Adderley's speech. Once again, a senior Conservative M.P. had advanced the very thesis about the law of martial law that the Jamaica Committee was determined to

---

[145] *Hansard*, clxxxiv (31 July 1866), 1787.   [146] Ibid., 1789.   [147] Ibid., 1793.
[148] According to the *Manchester Guardian* (3 Aug. 1866), 2, the debate had had 'much less vivacity' due to the (unexplained) absence of Bright from the House.
[149] Mill, *Autobiography*, 281.   [150] Kinzer *et al.*, *A Moralist In and Out of Parliament*, 203–6.

overturn in the courts. As Mill stated in his opening remarks, he 'could have desired nothing better for their cause'.[151] His speech defended the proposition that the issues raised by the conduct of state officials in Jamaica were so profoundly important that they should be given over to 'the only authority that is competent to pass a binding judgment on such acts – the authority of a judicial tribunal'.[152] As for the Royal Commission, it had been mandated to uncover the facts of the riot and its suppression, not to characterize those facts in the 'eye of the law'.[153] At the same time, the evidence gathered by the Commission strongly indicated that many culpable homicides had been committed during the period of martial law. In Mill's view, it was absolutely essential to the integrity both of British government and British law that these actions should result in criminal prosecution. 'Hitherto in this country,' Mill observed, 'the agents of executive Government have had to answer for themselves in the same Courts of Law as the rest of Her Majesty's subjects.'[154] If officers of the state are permitted to protect such persons from prosecution, he now warned, 'we are giving up altogether the principle of government by law, and resigning ourselves to arbitrary power'.

Having set forth his organizing principles, Mill spoke to the legal objections that had been put forward against the proposed criminal prosecution of Edward Eyre. While making some acerbic references to Disraeli's previous statements in the House, Mill endeavoured to refute the notion that a man could not be found guilty of murder if he honestly believed that killing a man was deserved or necessary. Mill thought that history abounded with examples of why this view had to be mistaken. Were the perpetrators of the St. Bartholomew's Day massacres innocent of crimes because they thought their victims were guilty? Was Robespierre free of all legal culpability because he strongly believed that the men and women he ordered guillotined had conspired against the Revolution?[155] From these rhetorical posturings, Mill turned to the law of martial law. The doctrine had been confidently propounded by leading Conservatives that any and all actions of government officials under a proclamation of martial law were immune from criminal prosecution. 'If that is our condition,' Mill told the House, 'we have gained little by historical struggles, and the blood shed for English liberties has been shed to little purpose.' But, according to Mill, the Conservatives were wrong about the law of martial law. Martial law was rightly understood as 'another word for the law of necessity, and that the justification of acts done under that law consists in their necessity'.[156] Quoting from the legal opinion of Stephen and James, Mill contended that *law* also governed the use of martial law, that there were limits on the power of those exercising its authority.[157] When these limits were exceeded, the perpetrators were, in the lawyers' words, 'liable civilly or criminally for such excess'.

---

[151] *Hansard*, clxxxiv (31 July 1866), 1798.   [152] Ibid.   [153] Ibid., 1799.
[154] Ibid., 1799–800.   [155] Ibid., 1801–2.   [156] Ibid., 1803.   [157] Ibid.

At this juncture, Mill returned to the subject of political fundamentals. He drew for the House a picture of a nation in which men were 'let loose from all law, from all precedents, from all forms'.[158] In such a place there would be no security, either for rulers or the ruled. But this was the kind of nation imagined by those who maintained that martial law was not governed by law, but was 'arbitrary power – the rule of force subject to no legal limits'. It boiled down to this: if the courts did not have jurisdiction to review the proclamation and use of martial law by the executive, then the lives of Englishmen depended only on the caprice of their political masters. What the Jamaica Committee wanted to know, what it intended to find out, is 'who are to be our masters; the Queen's Judges and a jury of our countrymen, administering the laws of England, or three military or naval officers . . . administering no law at all'.[159] The Committee, Mill pledged, would work tirelessly to 'assert the great principle of the responsibility of all agents of the Executive to the laws, civil and criminal, for the taking of human life without justification'.[160]

Mill had used his speech to connect the policies of the Jamaica Committee to the fundamental tenets of British politics. The speeches which followed had more modest aims. W. E. Forster, the veteran Liberal M.P. (and formerly of the Colonial Office), stood to offer his support to those of Buxton's resolutions which asked the Commons to 'condemn the misuse of strength'.[161] The remainder of his speech was a warning against the rising tide of authoritarianism and racism in the empire. Forster described martial law as the 'devil let loose', a licensed tyranny impossible to 'regulate so as to prevent loss of life and cruelty'. He recommended that the Government move quickly to reform any colonial laws which made it easier (than in England) for officials to proclaim martial law.[162] Forster also reminded the House that the violence of white officials in Jamaica had been motivated by 'the feeling of contempt for what was regarded as an inferior race'.[163] He expressed concern that so many of his countrymen subscribed to the view that the English could not 'afford to deal with other races on the principle of morality'. Having registered these cautions, Forster took pains to reject the proposal that the former Governor Eyre and his senior advisers and officers face criminal prosecutions. At all times these men had acted in good faith. Even their most serious mistakes were not criminal in nature. Here Forster's remarks surely reflected the sentiments of a great many liberal-minded Englishmen, a position informed at once by bad conscience, earnest concern, and pragmatic acceptance. This alignment agreed with the aims but not the means of the Jamaica Committee. But they did not have the Jamaica debate all their own way. Like Adderley before him, the ultra-Tory Baillie Cochrane conceded nothing to Mill, or even Buxton or Forster. In Cochrane's view, the only matter of importance before the House was the security of the white minority

---

[158] *Hansard*, clxxxiv (31 July 1866), 1804.   [159] Ibid., 1805.   [160] Ibid., 1806.
[161] Ibid., 1813.   [162] Ibid., 1811.   [163] Ibid., 1812.

populations in the non-white possessions of the empire. Governor Eyre had only done what had been necessary to prevent '500,000 [*sic*] of blacks to get the upper hand on the 15,000 whites'.[164] That Eyre had been dismissed was wrong, that he was threatened with criminal prosecution, an outrage. In maintaining this thesis, we will see, Cochrane was far from an isolated crank.

The remaining debate on Buxton's resolutions was comparatively shapeless. The Government's Attorney General, Sir John Rolt, spoke but would not comment on the 'legal questions' asked by Mill.[165] He confined his speech to quibbles about the form of Buxton's resolutions. Edward Cardwell rose to defend the handling of the Jamaica affair by the previous government. With Forster, Cardwell was at once ashamed of the violence committed or sanctioned by British officials after the uprising had been quelled, but unwilling to say that Eyre and others had committed crimes. He 'was convinced that [Eyre] acted in the real belief that he was discharging his duty'. The former Governor had done so, Cardwell hastened to add, within a colonial legal framework which permitted martial law to continue for a month 'irrespectively of any continuing necessity'.[166] For these reasons Cardwell thought that dismissal had been the right punishment for his errors of judgement. Following Cardwell, Tom Hughes made a brief speech which alluded to a number of historical cases in which British officials had been brought to account in the courts for crimes committed while in office. The last noteworthy intervention was made by Russell Gurney, the barrister who had sat on the Jamaica Commission. Gurney rose to address remarks made by Adderley (to the effect that Gordon had been properly convicted of treason) and by Buxton (that the uprising was unpremeditated and feeble). Gurney reiterated the conclusion of the Commission that the evidence on which Gordon was convicted was 'wholly insufficient',[167] and endorsed the view that the law regulating the use of martial law in the empire needed to be thoroughly reformed.

As Conservative leader in the House of Commons, Disraeli was the last to address the substance of Buxton's resolutions. Like so many of the previous speakers, Disraeli was anxious about the legal implications of the Jamaica case, and particularly the legal implications of censuring former Governor Eyre for having tolerated the excessive punishment of alleged rebels. Disraeli contended that rather than a resolution of censure, impeachment was the proper means by which an official of state was 'brought to justice in Parliament'.[168] On this point he thought it important to assert that, if passed by the House, the censure for excessive punishments could not be 'the foundation of an impeachment, because it was based throughout on the assumption that everything that was done was legal'. Disraeli did not stop there. He explained that the 'term "punishment" is an acknowledgment that it was the result of a legal act'. While the Jamaica affair was a matter of 'great shame and calamity in this country', Disraeli thought that it was

---

[164] Ibid., 1814. [165] Ibid., 1816. [166] Ibid., 1823. [167] Ibid., 1834.
[168] Ibid., 1838.

a very different matter to suggest that what had been done there to suppress rebellion was illegal. It was his unchanged view, on the contrary, that 'the action of the authorities was perfectly legal'.[169] But in order to put an end to the Jamaica affair, Disraeli was prepared to support Buxton's first resolution, but on two conditions. His Government would not concede either that anything illegal had been done, nor would it give any credence 'for the assumption that [the Government] are necessarily called upon to act against individuals'.[170] Excessive punishments would be deplored, but they would not lead to government-instigated prosecutions of senior officials in the English courts. This having been made unmistakably clear, Disraeli endorsed the passage of the first resolution, and pass it did.

In the final minutes of the debate, Buxton was given some indefinite assurances from the Government (by Adderley) that it would continue to support the investigation of potential criminal wrongdoing by civilian and military officials in Jamaica. The Government further pledged that it would permit the present Governor of Jamaica to address the question of compensation (from the public coffers of that colony), and that it would also permit the authorities there to remit the sentences of persons convicted of crimes associated with the uprising. These (distinctly open-ended) undertakings in hand, Buxton withdrew the last three of his resolutions. In the House of Commons, the Jamaica debate was over.

The majority of newspaper commentators thought that in promulgating his Jamaica resolutions in Parliament Buxton had conducted himself with grace and eloquence. The *Illustrated London News* admired his speech for its 'earnestness and manly pathos'.[171] The *Morning Advertiser* was impressed by his 'thorough mastery of the subject'.[172] *The Times* thought that Buxton had somewhat underplayed the danger of the Jamaica uprising, but conceded that he 'fairly represented the opinions of the less fanatical assailants of the late authorities'.[173] Buxton's arguments, the *Spectator* opined, were set forth 'in the grave, restrained way of a man who felt that he was in reality, though not in form, managing an impeachment'. The case he made, for his first resolution especially, was 'irresistibly strong'.[174] Even some of the conservative papers were prepared to concede that Buxton had spoken well and, as the *Saturday Review* put it, 'without the downright savage temperament which distinguishes the genuine philanthropist'.[175] But for all his elegance of expression and mastery of detail, what had Buxton accomplished? Stepping back from the series of Jamaica debates in Parliament in the summer of 1866, what had they revealed about the attitude of England's political elite about the issues raised by the Jamaica affair? What effect did the debates have on the policies of the Jamaica Committee?

---

[169] *Hansard*, clxxxiv (31 July 1866), 1839.   [170] Ibid.

[171] *Illustrated London News* (4 Aug. 1866), 10. The *Morning Post* (1 Aug. 1866), 4, congratulated Buxton for having provoked a long-overdue debate relating to the 'powers of the Crown and the rights of the subject' during moments of emergency.   [172] *Morning Advertiser* (1 Aug. 1866).

[173] *The Times* (1 Aug. 1866), 9.   [174] *Spectator* (4 Aug. 1866).

[175] *Saturday Review* (4 Aug. 1866), 132.

In terms of concrete political action from the Government, Buxton's resolutions amounted to little or nothing. But in terms of the symbolic dimension of politics, they were of obvious significance. The passage of the first resolution satisfied a widely felt need for a gesture of national contrition for what had happened in Jamaica. With this vote, the *Manchester Guardian* proclaimed, 'the nation is free from the taint of vindictive and wanton cruelty'.[176] This would help explain why Adderley was so severely mauled in the liberal press in the aftermath of the Jamaica debate. 'A more damaging speech,' stated the *Illustrated London News*, 'it is impossible to conceive; and what it wanted in skill and tact was not counter-balanced by propriety of demeanour, for he was petulant, captious and altogether unpleasant'.[177] Mr. Adderley had made a grave mistake, stated the *Manchester Guardian*, when he thought it 'possible to treat the subject of the suppression of the insurrection in any other than a penitent and apologetic strain'.[178] 'There have been few occasions in our history of late years,' the *Pall Mall Gazette* observed, 'when English statesmen had greater reason to speak the language of humility and regret.'[179] But 'far from being humble or apologetic', Adderley had been 'almost defiant'. The *London Review* made a similar comment: 'Nothing more feeble, more partial, more undignified in tone and temper, has fallen in recent times from the organ of an Administration... a painful exhibition of official incapacity.'[180] Although he had taken to his feet to 'deplore' the excesses of the suppression, the *Spectator* noted, 'in five minutes, giving way to the instinct of a true Tory, was extenuating or justifying them'.[181]

Adderley's speech was resented by liberals because it had not respected the ritual obligation of a beleaguered minister to do penitence. It was also detested for its unbending and even reactionary posture on legal and constitutional questions. The Under-Secretary had asserted that the excessive violence of the suppression, while regrettable, was not illegal because it occurred under a proclamation of martial law. Then Adderley had gone farther: Gordon's execution was justifiable and Eyre's hand in it forgivable. As *The Economist* observed, Mr. Adderley's defence of martial law left the impression that 'nothing done under martial law could be illegal', and that 'the Government in proclaiming martial law, means to abrogate all law whatever, and thus to tempt all officers entrusted with this exceptional power to misuse it without fear of any future responsibility'.[182]

Adderley's comments on martial law, coming as they did from a high official of state (and on the heels of Disraeli's comments on martial law), were widely seen to have grim implications for the civil liberties of Englishmen *at home*. If the Minister was correct in his theory of martial law, the *Spectator* contended, 'it would enable the Government on the occurrence of any riot in London to hang

---

[176] *Manchester Guardian* (3 Aug. 1866), 2.
[178] *Manchester Guardian* (3 Aug. 1866), 2.
[180] *London Review* (4 Aug.1866),115–16.
[182] *The Economist* (4 Aug. 1866), 907.

[177] *Illustrated London News* (4 Aug. 1866), 110.
[179] *Pall Mall Gazette* (1 Aug. 1866), 1.
[181] *Spectator* (4 Aug. 1866).

Mr. Adderley for having provoked it by denouncing workmen as rowdies'.[183] The people of London, the *Glasgow Morning Journal* observed of the Minister's speech, should be 'grateful to Lord Derby for putting Adderley in the Colonial instead of the Home Office'.[184] In a similar vein, the *Glasgow Sentinel* concluded that the 'Tory party is still of the opinion that might makes right, and that they have no conception of any higher law'.[185] The *Globe* focused specifically on the 'strange doctrines' that Adderley had endorsed in the case of Gordon: 'First he maintained that the law applicable to Gordon's case is by no means settled. This is a very important admission . . . If Mr. Gordon can be justly seized in Kingston and tried and executed by court martial in Morant Bay, any one of us might be justly seized in London and tried and executed by court martial in York or Inverness.'[186] As the *Morning Post* summarized, 'the House of Commons is preeminently the guardian of the liberties of the people, and the debate of last evening is chiefly remarkable as showing that in the opinion of the House no violation either of statute law or the constitution took place in Jamaica.'[187] For the editors at the *Globe*, the politicians had muddied a critically important issue of constitutional law, one which 'ought to be cleared up'.

We have seen that the Jamaica affair generated tensions within the upper caste of the Liberal Party. The affair produced similar tensions among Conservatives. When Adderley spoke for the Government in the House, he spoke with the approval of Lord Carnarvon, the senior official in the Colonial Office. This was a ticklish business for Carnarvon. As a member of the House of Lords, he could not speak to the matter himself in the House of Commons. At the same time, however, Carnarvon had reason to doubt that he and Adderley were *ad idem* on Jamaica. For Adderley, the Jamaica affair was an unfortunate incident that was best forgotten. For Carnarvon, it was a national disgrace that could not be forgotten, not, at least, until the country's honour had been restored.

Carnarvon did not leave the matter to chance. Prior to the debate on Jamaica in the Commons, he directed Adderley to *support* Buxton's first resolution.[188] When on 1 August Carnarvon learned that this had not been done, that Adderley had in fact *attacked* Buxton's resolution whilst he defended the execution of Gordon, he was appalled and infuriated. Carnarvon immediately admonished Adderley for having reneged on explicit instructions 'without any communication with me'. The failure to support Buxton's first resolution, Carnarvon continued, 'certainly altered the character of our position and destroyed the pace of accepting so much responsibility'. The Earl then excoriated him for having given 'the speech of a partizan vindicating the conduct of Eyre . . . it implies, if it does not actually give a support, to officers whose conduct has been very questionable, and it states an opinion with regard to the justice and legality of Gordon's trial, which called forth

---

[183] *Spectator* (4 Aug. 1866).   [184] *Glasgow Morning Journal* (4 Aug. 1866).
[185] *Glasgow Sentinel* (4 Aug. 1866).   [186] *Globe* (1 Aug. 1866).
[187] *Morning Post* (1 Aug. 1866), 4.
[188] Carnarvon to Adderley, 1 Aug. 1866, Carnarvon Papers, *CO* 30/6/134.

a disclaimer even from Russell Gurney'. In short, the speech given by Adderley was 'in terrible variance with the views which I have held and which I frankly expressed before now'. The Earl finished with a stern warning: '[I]f things are to go well there must be a complete understanding and concert between us.'

In making his reply, Adderley was defiant. He explained that the change of direction had been orchestrated by Disraeli 'and other cabinet ministers present'.[189] (The Conservatives had been taken by surprise, seemingly unnerved, by the 'sudden appearance' in the House of Mill, the man who seemingly had been so easily bested by Disraeli only two weeks earlier.) Adderley insisted that before the debate he had agreed only to 'keep our course open', and that when the time came he had done no more 'than necessary to redress violent injustice to Eyre (who has been guilty of nothing beyond grievous errors of judgment in the most trying circumstances)'. Adderley was repentant only about the remarks he had made about Gordon's execution: 'I confess I regret having said anything of this in the Debate.' With regard to future dealings with Carnarvon in the Colonial Office, Adderley indicated his respect for the Earl's position as 'Head of the Department'.

Adderley's speech did not change Carnarvon's mind either about his subordinate's speech or the larger issues at stake. When he spoke on the subject of the Jamaica affair in the House of Lords on 2 August 1866, the Earl was determined to reformulate the Government's position. The Earl of Romney, as if on cue, stood and asked if the Government would give some statement 'on the course of policy that was likely to be pursued in this matter'.[190] In his reply, Carnarvon strove for balance. He agreed that strong measures had been needed to suppress the Morant Bay uprising. It was equally clear, however, that many acts of 'cruelty', 'oppression', and 'injustice' had been committed in the name of the Crown. Some of the boasts that had been published by the perpetrators of such acts the Earl called 'indecent and absolutely disgusting'.[191] In Carnarvon's view, the civilian and military men who committed such misdeeds were deserving of 'very great blame'. But how was blame and responsibility to be assigned?

The Earl began with the Royal Commission appointed by the previous government. Carnarvon thought that the Royal Commission was properly understood, not as a quasi-judicial tribunal, but as a 'grand jury called upon to find whether there were fair grounds against these persons for making further investigation'.[192] The Earl noted that the military would soon convene courts martial against Cullen and Morris. The Earl then turned to the question of potential criminal wrongdoing by civilians. Thus far, only Duberry Ramsay had been prosecuted. But Carnarvon gave his assurance that investigations were ongoing, and that the current Governor of Jamaica, Sir John Grant, had been instructed to continue 'the most searching inquiry' into these cases, and into cases in which remission of

---

[189] Ibid.   [190] *Hansard*, clxxxiv (2 Aug. 1866), 1888.   [191] Ibid., 1890.
[192] Ibid.

sentences might serve justice.[193] But with regard to the more disputatious question of the possible legal culpability of Edward Eyre, Carnarvon was more cautious. The former Governor had acted with considerable courage and decisiveness, but then had become 'absorbed in the one paramount idea of crushing out this insurrection and saving the colony'.[194] In the process Eyre had forgotten that as Governor of all the colonists, black and white, it had been his duty to maintain 'perfect impartiality, and the power of rising above the panic and apprehension of the moment'. In this regard, Eyre had failed in his duty. However, the Earl did not say more about the potential legal consequences of such a failure.

Carnarvon then turned to the subject of law and martial law. Although the Earl was reluctant to discuss 'the legal technicalities' relating to this subject, he nonetheless felt compelled, like so many politicians before him, to venture some propositions.[195] While Carnarvon acknowledged that in times of 'dire necessity' it could be 'absolutely imperative to proclaim martial law', he thought that 'in such cases there are several rules which ought to be observed'. The first rule was that martial law was not to be prolonged for 'one single day or hour' past the last moment of necessity. The second was that the officers in charge of implementing martial law were 'accountable for any excessive acts'. In this regard, the former Governor Eyre had made two 'great mistakes'. He permitted martial law to continue in force beyond the point of any sensible necessity. He had also signally failed to impose 'safeguards' on the use of military power. Gordon's experience at the hands of the court martial was cited specifically as a 'most terrible case, and one that is indefensible'. Carnarvon weighed his next words carefully. Although the evidence which convicted Gordon was 'insufficient', when he endorsed the guilty verdict Governor Eyre had 'acted with the most complete *bona fides*'.[196] There was no evidence that he had been moved by 'personal feelings' toward the accused. For this reason, the idea of charging Eyre with murder was 'preposterous' and 'utterly repugnant to the common sense of Englishmen'. Dismissal from the Queen's service, the Earl believed, was punishment enough.

Most of the commentators who had expressed serious qualms about Adderley's speech found a welcome corrective in Lord Carnarvon's subsequent address in the House of Lords. In the view of *The Economist*, the Earl had adopted an 'entirely different tone' from that of his Under-Secretary.[197] Here was the 'cool, serene judgment of a mind inclined towards authority, but utterly averse from injustice, oppressive rigour, or concessions to the feeling of caste'. With fitting candour Carnarvon had admitted unreservedly that Gordon had been wrongly convicted and executed, and that martial law had gone on too long and with too little regulation. He had also given his assurance 'to revise the entire system of martial law in the colonies'. *The Economist* concluded that the Earl had found the voice of that

---

[193] *Hansard*, clxxxiv (2 Aug. 1866), 1891.　　[194] Ibid., 1892.　　[195] Ibid., 1893.
[196] Ibid., 1894.　　[197] *The Economist* (4 Aug. 1866), 907.

'immense class of moderate men who, knowing that it is sometimes necessary for a Government to kill people, still abhor the killing of those who have ceased from resistance'. The *Pall Mall Gazette* agreed that Carnarvon's speech would 'go far to do away with the evil impression justly excited by the partisanship of Mr. Adderley in the Commons'.[198]

Carnarvon had been the last senior minister of the Government to speak to the Jamaica affair in Parliament, and his words had a sense of finality about them. 'Except for the possibility that the Jamaica Committee may make a further exhibition of their weakness by instituting a criminal prosecution against Mr. Eyre,' the *Manchester Guardian* stated rather hopefully on 3 August, 'the public discussion of the question is at an end.'

Carnarvon's principled intervention made it easier for moderates to dismiss Mill's speech, and the prosecutorial initiative that it had portended, as shrill and extravagant. But Mill's contentions had struck a chord with radical commentators. Rather predictably, the *Morning Star*, the unofficial organ of advanced liberalism, described Mill's oration as 'brilliant'. Similarly, *Reynolds' Weekly* stated that it redounded 'greatly to their credit' that Mill and the Jamaica Committee were to pursue the 'slayers of Gordon' in the English courts.[199] Until a stand was made against the new apologists of martial law, the editors warned, 'nothing hinders the Tories from doing to the working classes of London what Eyre did to the blacks of Jamaica'. But the stance adopted by the *Glasgow Sentinel* was far more typical. Mill was praised for his 'indignant eloquence', and it was conceded that 'many things were done that were not only illegal but criminal'. But the *Sentinel* still did not think that public opinion supported the prosecution of Eyre.[200] Similarly, *The Economist* believed that as effective as Mill's speech had been, the philosopher had gone 'much too far, asking for a state prosecution'. In the same vein, the *London Review* contended that 'ably as the grounds for such a proceeding were stated [by Mill], they entirely fail to convince us of their propriety'.[201] Even in the unlikely event that Eyre was found guilty of murder, 'the common sense and feeling of the country would cry out against such a decision'.

When they were looked on as a whole, the Jamaica debates were generally seen as a setback for the Jamaica Committee. Buxton's very mild set of resolutions, after all, had found only grudging and piecemeal support in the Commons. Carnarvon's encouraging statements about the limits of martial law had undone some of the damage inflicted by the opinions expressed on martial law by Disraeli and Adderley. Then there was Mill's bid to shame the Government into indicting Eyre for murder; this had been an abject failure. As the *Saturday Review* summarized, 'all then that the House has done is this – it places on record its regret that certain criminal acts were punished with excessive severity.'[202]

---

[198] *Pall Mall Gazette* (1 Aug. 1866), 1.   [199] *Reynolds' Weekly* (5 Aug. 1866).
[200] *Glasgow Sentinel* (4 Aug. 1866).   [201] *London Review* (4 Aug. 1866), 116.
[202] *Saturday Review* (4 Aug. 1866), 132.

By the lights of the Jamaica Committee, however, the outcome of the parliamentary debates was not unexpected or discouraging. The leaders of the Committee had persuaded themselves that it now was widely understood in England that the Jamaica suppression had raised some critically important legal and constitutional questions, questions which only the country's highest courts of law were qualified to resolve. The interjections of Mill and Hughes during the debate were meant as public justifications for an *extra*-Parliamentary course of action. But in case the public was not yet fully persuaded, on 6 August 1866 Goldwin Smith published an open letter on the subject in the *Daily Telegraph*. The letter explained why the parliamentary debates had actually *strengthened* the determination of the Committee to press on with the prosecution of Eyre.[203] When Gordon and others were put to death without proper charge, trial, or legal justification, Smith argued, '[i]t was the duty of the Government to set the law in motion'. Speaking for the Cabinet, Disraeli and Adderley not only had 'declined the duty, but declined . . . on grounds which give rise to the most sinister reflections'. In essence, the Cabinet had asserted a new and alarming doctrine about its own power, that 'the lives of British subjects should be placed at the mercy of an agent of the Executive Government and his soldiery'. The same officials had told the country that 'martial law is the suspension of all law; and that when it has been proclaimed, British subjects are exposed to irresponsible slaughter'. In Smith's view, this was a proposition, now that it had been endorsed by senior politicians, which could not be left unanswered. 'This was a case, if ever there was one, for judicial investigation before an independent court of justice.'

Until the late summer of 1866 the sympathizers with Governor Eyre had been able to dismiss the threats of the Jamaica Committee with breezy contempt. However, when the politicians washed their hands of Jamaica, and when the Committee began to turn words into legal actions, this luxury no longer could be indulged in. The friends of Edward Eyre suddenly began to talk among themselves about the ways and means of defending a political case.

IV. August–December 1866: Making and Defending a Political Case

At the end of June 1866 the leading members of the Jamaica Committee agreed that they would take whatever steps necessary to cause an English high court judge to pronounce on the legal questions brought forth by the Jamaica affair. It was further resolved that the best method of achieving this aim was by the criminal prosecution of Eyre for the murder of Gordon. Before the parliamentary debates of July, some faint hope still was entertained by the Committee that the government might be persuaded to undertake the Eyre prosecution on its own initiative, and pay for it

---

[203] *Daily Telegraph* (6 Aug. 1866), 3.

out of public funds. When that hope was dashed, the Committee prepared to exercise its right to commence a private prosecution. And when it began to advertise these intentions, the leaders of the Committee took pains to emphasize that they were not interested in Eyre the individual man. (As Goldwin Smith stated in an open letter, he was not 'animated by vindictive feelings against a man whose name I never heard till I heard it connected to these transactions'.)[204] The Eyre prosecution was not about retributive justice, but a larger and public purpose. By prosecuting Eyre the Jamaica Committee hoped to vindicate vital constitutional principles relating to the accountability of civilian and military officials to law. In this sense, this was to be an explicitly political litigation.

In some respects the Jamaica Committee was well placed to succeed, at least in getting the prosecution started. The Committee had determined leadership and access to experienced and able lawyers. It was also accommodating that the English criminal justice system of this era continued to rely on private citizens to initiate and sustain prosecutions.[205] The initiative did not require the endorsement of the state. But then there was the problematic issue of money. On 4 August 1866, the executive members met to discuss how much its initiative might cost, and how to raise the requisite funds.[206] While there is no surviving record of the discussion, it is obvious that the executive quit the meeting knowing that law was not bought cheaply.[207] There would be an office (65 Fleet Street, London was selected) to maintain. The Committee's solicitor, William Shaen, would have to be extensively employed and recompensed. There would be barristers to fee, both for legal research and courtroom appearances. Witnesses needed to be brought from Jamaica, and then supported for weeks or months in England. If the Committee's political message and financial appeal were to get wide publicity, there would be pamphlets and circulars to print and pay for. With these particulars in mind, the executive determined that it would not be safe to raise less than £10,000. As a demonstration of their personal commitment to the cause, Bright, Mill, and Goldwin Smith all pledged £100 to what soon was advertised as 'THE TEN THOUSAND POUNDS FUND'.

By late September the fund-raising campaign had made headway, some £3,300 having been subscribed. Some money had been raised at Reform League rallies.[208] Hughes and Smith had held a series of town hall meetings to promote the 'aims and objects' of the Jamaica Committee, and to solicit donations.[209] At the end of

---

[204] Ibid.
[205] A. H. Manchester, *A Modern Legal History of England and Wales, 1750–1980* (London, 1980), 201. [206] *JC Minutes*, 4 Aug. 1866; *CD*, 4 Aug. 1866.
[207] In a private letter written in October 1866, Mill recalled that the Committee had agreed that 'the expensiveness of the attempt to get justice done in the Jamaica matter' would arise mainly from the costs associated with Jamaican witnesses and English lawyers. 'We may possibly not require the whole £10,000, but we thought after consideration, that it would not be safe to ask for less.' Mill to Thomas Thompson, 10 Oct. 1866, *Later Letters*, 1206. [208] *JC Minutes*, 28 Sept. 1866.
[209] For example, see report (the *Daily Telegraph* (28 Dec. 1866), 2) of a meeting at the Birmingham Town Hall addressed by Hughes.

August, an 'Indignation Meeting' organized by the Reform League was held in Bartholomew Close, London.[210] A succession of speakers urged a large crowd drawn from the 'working classes' of the city to support the Jamaica Committee in the prosecution of Eyre. It was resolved on a show of hands that a 'Tory government had as much right to shoot down the people in Hyde Park as had Mr. Eyre to murder hundreds of innocent people in Jamaica'. In November, the Anti-Slavery Society published a ringing public endorsement of the Jamaica Committee's prosecution strategy and urged its sympathizers to donate money.[211] By December 1866 the Committee's fund-raising circular featured the names of over 200 notable subscribers, including (and I will say more about some of these men presently) more than a dozen M.P.s, and another dozen academics (including Smith, Beesly, and T. H. Green). Even a few Church of England clergymen and retired military men listed their names. The appeal emphasized that the legal course contemplated would be 'very expensive' and that it would encounter a 'powerful resistance, backed by all the resources of wealth'.

In October the Jamaica Committee issued a statement informing the public that it had collected money and pledges enough to take the first steps toward the prosecution of Eyre (and perhaps some of his senior subordinates).[212] The plan was to lay a first charge 'by the time the courts resumed their sittings' in the autumn. Behind the scenes, Shaen was asked to prepare a legal brief on the procedural niceties associated with a private criminal prosecution for murder.[213] Fitzjames Stephen was asked to do more research on Eyre's criminal liability for the death of Gordon. The Committee also agreed that Augustus Lake, the Jamaican newspaper reporter who had witnessed Gordon's court martial, would be brought to England as the chief witness for the prosecution. Then, in a move which (as we will see in Chapter 5) greatly alarmed the friends of Eyre, the Committee retained the services of the celebrated barrister John D. Coleridge to undertake the in-court prosecution of Eyre.

This brings us to the defenders, proponents, and apologists of Edward Eyre, a subject as yet little considered. In the early summer of 1866, Eyre's proponents in the mother country were numerous and well connected, but not nearly so well organized as his critics. This is understandable. After all, Eyre still had not returned from Jamaica. The threat against him still seemed remote and hypothetical. It was one thing for Mill and a handful of radicals to *say* they were going to prosecute a former Governor for murder, quite another to do it. The idea that the Jamaica

---

[210] *The Times* (31 Aug. 1866), 7.

[211] It is interesting that the Anti-Slavery Society thought a public statement necessary. It suggests that the prosecution initiative was so controversial, and so distant from the routine work of the Society, that its leadership had felt some internal resistance. The statement emphasized that the prosecution would vindicate the 'rights and liberties' of 'all the Queen's subjects alike, irrespective of colour or race'. *Daily News* (10 Nov. 1866), 2.

[212] Printed in the *Daily News* (12 Oct. 1866), 3. See also ibid. (15 Oct. 1866), 4.

[213] *JC Minutes*, 28 Sept. 1866.

Committee would actually take steps to put Eyre in the dock was so perverse and unlikely that it was not taken seriously; that is, until the Committee began to raise the money needed to pay for it.[214] Then, only two weeks after the Jamaica Committee began to advertise its £10,000 fund, on 23 August, Eyre and his family disembarked at Southampton.

By the time he returned to England, Eyre had few friends among English political writers. The final report of the Jamaica Royal Commission had badly damaged his personal reputation and standing, even among conservatives. It was generally accepted that in his response to the Morant Bay uprising, Eyre, however well meaning, had committed a series of 'lamentable mistakes'.[215] After the parliamentary debate on these matters, the *Sun* newspaper strained to find something redeeming in the former Governor's conduct: 'There is one thing to say on behalf of Mr. Eyre, that those who criticise his conduct, and compare it to Lord Canning in India, are apt to forget and that is that he speedily suppressed the outbreak, while the authorities in India, by their tameness and hesitation, allowed the natives to make great encroachments.'[216] These comments were suggestive of a new maxim, one that was frequently invoked by Eyre's defenders: that wherever a white colonial population was vastly outnumbered by a non-white local population, and whenever non-whites engaged in or threatened insurrection, British officials were entitled to the widest possible latitude in the use of coercion and terror. It was this kind of thinking about security in the empire, far more than anything that was known about Eyre the individual, that explains why he was so warmly embraced by so many important men.

Eyre was fifty-one years of age when he arrived in England. He had a wife and five children. From 1846 until the time of his sacking in June 1866, he had been a career civil servant, one wholly dependent on his salary. When Eyre was summarily dismissed from the colonial service it was a deeply damaging blow to his pride, purse, and pension.[217] He did not accept it with equanimity.

That Eyre was unrepentant, and that he was bitterly resentful for having been dismissed from his position, was public knowledge in England before he arrived in Southampton on 22 August. On 24 July, at the ceremony held in Kingston to mark his departure for England, Eyre made a brief speech[218] (published in England on 18 August)[219] in which he declared that he 'had the consolation of

---

[214] The effort to raise the monies necessary to commence a prosecution was redoubled in the late autumn of 1866. *The Times* (13 Oct. 1866), 6.   [215] *The Times* (23 Aug. 1866), 6.

[216] *Sun* (3 Aug. 1866).

[217] When he was dismissed, Eyre was ten weeks from eligibility for a first-class pension, and a year from eligibility for the maximum pension. As things stood in 1866, he was entitled to about £500 instead of £1000 at age 65. Only 51 years of age in 1866, he was entitled to no pension at all until 1875. See 'The Eyre Defence and Aid Fund', *Daily Telegraph* (8 Sept. 1866).

[218] Eyre's remarks were given in reply to an expression of gratitude made by the Bishop of Kingston. The speech was reported by the *Falmouth Post* (31 July 1866), 2.

[219] See *Examiner* (18 Aug. 1866), 513.

feeling that there has been nothing in his conduct to merit dismissal, nothing to occasion self-reproach, nothing to regret'.[220] The English newspapers also published a letter Eyre had written to the Bishop of Kingston in which he referred to Gordon as the 'proximate occasion' of the Morant Bay uprising, and then stated that Gordon had 'suffered justly'.[221] In the same letter Eyre repeated the claim, one made many times before, that the execution of Gordon had been the crucial factor in discouraging black Jamaicans from mounting a general insurrection in the colony. Eyre's steadfastness aroused his allies, and enemies.

Upon his arrival Eyre's allies staged a testimonial banquet in his honour at Southampton's Philharmonic Hall. The event was hosted by the Earl of Shrewsbury and Talbot (a retired Admiral and owner of land in Jamaica)[222], and was attended by some 200 guests, including a colourful assortment of titled men and luminaries. The after-dinner speakers included the ultra-conservative Earl of Cardigan (the erratic commander–hero of the celebrated Light Brigade and enthusiast of martial punishments)[223], the Earl of Hardwicke (a retired admiral and Conservative politician), and Charles Kingsley,[224] the famed writer and Christian socialist. Their speeches were widely reported and commented upon. Cardigan wistfully recollected the days when Prime Ministers 'stood by' Governors 'whatever might be the cruelties, if they were cruelties, which had been perpetrated'.[225] Hardwicke made a less strident speech, admitting that when colonial insurrections were 'attended by great losses of life' it was right that there should be inquiries 'on a strictly legal basis'. The Earl was firmly convinced, however, that but for the prompt and decisive action of former Governor Eyre, Jamaica's 'white population would have been murdered'. Then Kingsley spoke.[226] In an address that severely damaged his reputation as a discerning observer of English affairs,[227] he began by praising the English aristocracy as the living embodiment of Christian chivalry. He then suggested that Edward Eyre, this heroic public servant, should himself be ennobled. Warming to his subject, Kingsley advanced the position that Eyre was so pure

---

[220] Discussed in the *Spectator* (18 Aug. 1866), 902.

[221] As paraphrased in the *Examiner* (18 Aug. 1866), 513.

[222] Dutton, *Hero as Murderer*, 338.

[223] Ibid., 339; Sweetman, *Oxford DNB*, online 3765.

[224] As a result of their mutual enthusiasm for the Christian socialist agenda, Kingsley was a long-time intimate of Hughes and Ludlow of the Jamaica Committee. In the 1860s, however, Kingsley was dissociated from political radicalism. In the fashion of Carlyle, Kingsley became a proponent of the 'heroic man' school of history. Hence his attraction to Eyre's cause. Vance, *Oxford DNB*, online 15617.   [225] All quotes from account in the *Daily Telegraph* (23 Aug. 1866), 2.

[226] Prior to the Jamaica rebellion, unsure even that Eyre was still alive, Kingsley had written two long and admiring articles concerning Eyre's Australian explorations. William H. Scheuerle, 'Henry Kingsley and the Governor Eyre Controversy', 37 *Victorian Newsletter* (1970), 24–7.

[227] Kingsley's speech was widely denounced in the liberal papers. *Spectator* (25 Aug. 1866), 937, lacerated Kingsley's speech as an 'explosion of flunkeyism'. The *Newcastle Weekly Chronicle* (1 Sept. 1866) denounced Kingsley as a 'mincing courtier'. The *Manchester Guardian* (24 Aug. 1866), 2, commented that Kingsley was 'wilfully uninformed' about Jamaica and its implications.

and great a man that his account of what had happened in Jamaica should be accepted 'upon trust'.

Eyre was last to speak. When he rose, the attendees (and women confined to the gallery) gave him a prolonged standing ovation. He then alluded to the many 'evil reports' that had circulated concerning his actions in Jamaica and expressed his gratitude that 'the people of England will respect and uphold a public officer who has endeavoured to do his duty faithfully'. Eyre was glad that so many of his countrymen understood 'the character of the negro', and the extreme danger and difficulty of the situation that arose in Jamaica the previous October. He graciously thanked the military officers who with him had 'saved a noble colony from ruin'. With this last remark the Governor accepted another enthusiastic ovation. But the evening did not end on a exultant note. An 'opposition meeting' (and fund-raiser) organized by the Jamaica Committee had been convened at a location nearby.[228] When the meeting broke up, a large and hostile crowd had gathered to 'hoot and howl' at the guests leaving (what their placards called) the 'Banquet of Death'.

Many of the same newspaper writers who had criticized the alleged excesses of the Jamaica Committee now were equally critical of the organizers of the Southampton banquet. *The Times* thought the event was 'very much to be regretted'.[229] Even on the generous assumption that the former Governor had done no more than necessary, these were not 'things to boast of, to be recollected with pride or pleasure, to be toasted at public dinners, and recounted for the satisfaction of ladies'. The organizers of the event caused Eyre to be 'unwisely raised to the dignity of a hero–martyr'.[230] That a man such as Eyre should be placed on a 'conspicuous pedestal as an English worthy,' one writer observed, '... rudely jars against the moral instincts of the nation'.[231] The *Pall Mall Gazette* reckoned that Eyre 'ought not to have accepted the invitation, and if he had known the dignified course, he would not have accepted it'.[232] The writers at the *Manchester Guardian* thought that the occasion was staged in order to rehabilitate a man who had been 'authoritatively condemned'.[233] Only the most partisan newspapers, the *Morning Post* on Eyre's part, the *Morning Star* for the Jamaica Committee, were willing to praise their respective camps.[234]

The Southampton banquet, this 'ostentatious show of opinion', as the *Manchester Guardian* termed it, was a political event. Unqualified support had been given as much to a political maxim as to a man. That principle, the *Guardian* abstracted, was that 'whatever the Governor of a colony may have done with

---

[228] The announcement that Eyre was to be publicly honoured upon his return from Jamaica prompted the Jamaica Committee to send one of its executive members, the long-time anti-slavery activist Henry Slack, to organize a counter-meeting. A large number of anti-Eyre placards were erected over the central part of the town. After the meeting ended, a large group of men collected outside the Philharmonic Hall to jeer at the guests as they left. See *Daily Telegraph* (23 Aug. 1866), 2; *Manchester Guardian* (23 Aug. 1866), 4.

[229] *The Times* (23 Aug. 1866), 6.   [230] Ibid. (14 Sept. 1866), 6.

[231] Letter of Arthur Hallam, *The Times* (19 Sept. 1866), 9.   [232] Ibid.

[233] *Manchester Guardian* (24 Aug. 1866), 2.

[234] See the summary of the newspapers in the *Pall Mall Gazette* (23 Aug. 1866), 2.

zealous intentions, he has an indefeasible right to be upheld by his superiors'.[235] On a more personal level, the banquet also underlined that Eyre had returned to England without contrition, unreconciled to his punishment, and unashamed to say so publicly. Some knowledgeable observers thought this an extremely unwise posture. They feared that Eyre's defiance, when combined with the political tenets of his supporters, would only encourage the Jamaica Committee to make good on its threat to prosecute. As Henry Storks confided to his successor, the new Governor of Jamaica, with his attendance at the Southampton banquet Eyre 'threw away a great chance of extricating himself from a very dangerous position, but the obstinacy of his nature and the imprudent promptings of those about him have gone far to ruin him'.[236] In the same way, W. E. Forster, the former Liberal Under-Secretary at the Colonial Office, wrote to Cardwell that 'if he [Eyre] has any friends with sense, which is doubtful, they ought to keep him quiet, for if he defends himself once more he will certainly provoke a prosecution'.[237]

It would seem, however, that in the two weeks immediately before Eyre's return from Jamaica his English friends took it for granted that the Jamaica Committee would commence a privately initiated and funded criminal prosecution of their man. On this assumption, the former Australian explorer, Hamilton Hume (the author of a profile of Eyre for the *British Army and Navy Review*), already had begun to organize a defence committee and, so one newspaper reported, to collect large sums of money to sustain its work.[238] Among Hume's first initiatives was to invite Thomas Carlyle to act as the association's first chairman. Soon thereafter, Hume was obliged publicly to deny that Carlyle had accepted the chairmanship of the committee (for it was still 'in the course of formation'),[239] but at the same moment was able to publish the great writer's first statement on the Jamaica affair.[240] When he wrote this letter, Carlyle was seventy-one years old, in frail health, and recently widowed. But he was strongly moved by Eyre's troubles.[241] His letter praised the former Governor as a 'just, humane, and valiant man, faithful to his trusts everywhere'. His quandary during the Jamaica rebellion was likened to that of a sea captain forced to cope with fire 'in the ship's powder-room at mid-ocean'. Carlyle was appalled that the Governor's prompt and firm response to this dangerous crisis had generated so much 'penalty and clamour' when it actually deserved 'honour and thanks, and wise imitation'. Carlyle called on his countrymen to reassert their historical commitment to 'order and the prompt suppression of seditions'.[242]

[235] *Manchester Guardian* (24 Aug. 1866), 2.
[236] Forster to Cardwell, 19 Aug. 1866, Cardwell Papers, *CO* 30/48/43.   [237] Ibid.
[238] The *Spectator* (18 Aug. 1866), 902, reported that £6,000 already had been 'raised for Mr. Eyre' by unnamed persons and for a 'defence fund'. See also Dutton, *Hero as Murderer*, 17, 168.
[239] Letter undated, as reprinted in *The Times* (12 Sept. 1866), 6.
[240] Ibid. Carlyle to Hume, dated 23 Aug. 1866. The letter is reprinted in Workman, 'Carlyle and the Governor Eyre Controversy', 91–2.
[241] Fred Kaplan, *Thomas Carlyle: A Biography* (Ithaca, NY, 1983), 491.
[242] Carlyle's motives for intervening on behalf of Edward Eyre have been extensively canvassed by scholars. In an important article on the subject, Gillian Workman remarked that 'Carlyle's

In late-August 1866, and for the first time in several months, John Ruskin also publicly reasserted himself on behalf of Eyre. We have seen that during the previous December Ruskin had published an open letter on Jamaica in which he affirmed his loyalty to Toryism ('I am a King's man') and condemned the public reaction against Eyre (that 'fatuous outcry'). In August 1866, at Carlyle's urging, Ruskin re-entered the fray when he took a leading part in the inaugural meeting of the Eyre Defence Committee on 30 August. Although he was a political dilettante who was ordinarily disinclined to get involved in such conflicts, in the coming months Ruskin devoted substantial time and effort to Eyre's cause, far more than did Carlyle. (In fact, Ruskin once privately referred to himself as Carlyle's 'henchman' on the Jamaica issue.)[243]

The first organizational meeting of the Eyre committee was held in London on 30 August. Carlyle attended and chaired the session, while insisting that it would be better for the association if the chair were occupied by a 'nobleman of power and influence'.[244] The meeting began with a discussion of names for the permanent committee. Should it include the word 'testimonial' (indicating a fund to be given over to Eyre for his personal use) or should the name be limited to indicate a legal defence fund? The attendees agreed that the title 'The Eyre Defence and Aid Fund' would satisfy all purposes. The Committee would take all steps to defend Eyre from the legal machinations of the Jamaica Committee while it also went on

---

involvement in the Jamaica controversy, like all his expressions of interest in the West Indies, was a result, not of any racist views, but of a life-long preoccupation with the condition of England, and a desire to force his lessons home' (Workman, 'Carlyle and the Governor Eyre Controversy', 85). However, this seems to be a needlessly constricted view of the matter. While it is clear that Carlyle did seize upon the Eyre case to chastise the English political community for its (alleged) complacency and sentimentalism, other motives were at work. In August 1866 Carlyle viewed Eyre, in his own words, as a 'faithful, valiant, wise, manful representative of the English Government', and richly deserving of support and protection. It was also easy for Carlyle to support Eyre because his victims had been black-skinned. Carlyle subscribed to the view that blacks were ill-suited to freedom, and that any attempts by them to use force against their white superiors needed to be put down with all necessary force. For bibliographical references and further discussion, see Appendix, below.

[243] Ruskin's fervent support for Eyre has long perplexed his biographers, who have almost invariably admired Ruskin's persona and cultural sensibilities, if not his reactionary politics and racism. One major biographer almost entirely ignores Ruskin's role in the Jamaica affair. (See John Dixon Hunt, *The Wider Sea: A Life of John Ruskin* (Toronto, 1982), 304.) Another biographer claims that Ruskin acted on behalf of Eyre only because he was in thrall to Carlyle. ('Ruskin's loyalty was not to Eyre, about whom he knew next to nothing, but to Carlyle. The elder sage had the odd effect of making Ruskin oblivious to reality.' Tim Hinton, *John Ruskin: The Later Years* (New Haven, Conn., 2000), 105.) Yet another scholar has suggested that Ruskin simply was a political neophyte who stumbled into the Eyre controversy without giving much thought to the political or legal implications of the former Governor's conduct. ('Ruskin's political doctrines,' one scholar has plausibly suggested, 'insofar as they have the coherence to be called that, were rooted in his allegiance to the quiet and hierarchically ordered life that he recalled from his childhood in Herne Hill.') Dinah Birch, 'Review: *John Ruskin: The Later Years*', *London Review of Books* (10 Aug. 2000), 30.

[244] *Daily Telegraph* (31 Aug. 1866), 2.

the attack against, in Carlyle's words, 'the fallacy that these noisy denunciations of Mr. Eyre were the deliberate voice of the people of England'. On the strength also of the names of Ruskin and Kingsley, the Committee would make an immediate call for donations. (No indication was given that substantial sums already had been collected.) An office and meeting place for the fund would be maintained in Pall Mall.

Behind the scenes, Hume, now the permanent secretary of the Defence Committee, wrote to Carlyle for encouragement to complete a biography of Eyre, one which an editor felt sure would be 'damned' by critics.[245] Carlyle wrote to Kingsley explaining that, given the chance, he would have appointed Eyre as '*Dictator*' over Jamaica for the next 25 years'.[246] For so valiant a figure such as Eyre to have become the subject of so many 'lamentations, shriekeries, and insanities', Carlyle blamed the Liberal government which he believed 'should have permitted no questioning and answering'. There was much harm to repair. But Carlyle was comforted by the idea that Charles Kingsley ('full of holy zeal') and the historian and journalist J. A. Froude would join him in the fight. In the result, Froude did not join the Eyre Defence Committee.[247] If Kingsley ever joined, which is in dispute, he had been too stung by criticism of his Southampton speech to partake in its meetings or work.[248]

The next meeting of the Defence Committee was held in London on 8 September.[249] It was again chaired by Carlyle; its ostensible purpose was to assess progress in the collection of money and names. Reporters were present. The meeting took an interesting turn when Ruskin made a statement concerning his reasons for joining the Committee. Ruskin emphasized that his motives might not be identical to those of many other members. He 'had joined the committee . . . in the simple desire of obtaining justice, not for black men only, nor for white, but for men of every race or colour'. Ruskin continued by stating that he 'detested all cruelty and all injustice by whomsoever inflicted or suffered', and that he would 'sternly reprobate the crime which dragged a black family from their home to dig your fields'. Having set forth these rather surprising premises, he began a discourse on the legal dimensions of the Eyre case.

[245] Hume already had been advised that such was likely. Hume to Carlyle, 13 Nov. 1866, *NLS*, 1768.
[246] Carlyle to Kingsley, 3 Sept. 1866, as reprinted in Workman, 'Carlyle and the Governor Eyre Controversy', 93.
[247] Froude backed out on the basis that he was too closely associated with *Fraser's Magazine*. Kingsley did not explain his retreat from the Committee. (He had been advertised as a member after the meeting of 31 August.) Kaplan, *Carlyle*, 491.
[248] Tennyson, with some hesitation over the excess of violence, supported Eyre because he had been motivated to protect the lives of whites in Jamaica. Dickens supported Eyre mainly on the grounds that the Jamaica Committee were canting hypocrites who neglected poor whites in England while fawning over lazy black men in the empire. See Dutton, *Hero as Murderer*, 354.
[249] *Daily Telegraph* (8 Sept. 1866), 3.

In Ruskin's view, the chief mistake being made by Eyre's critics was that they confused 'the office of a Governor with that of a judge'. The duty of a judge was 'only to declare and enforce law'. The duty of a British Governor, however, was 'to do what law cannot do, and to deal with such immediate events, and necessities arising out of them, as may be beyond the scope of existing law'. For this reason, the Governor's burden was much heavier than that of a judge. In the face of the extreme peril presented by the insurrection at Morant Bay, it had fallen upon Eyre to 'take upon himself the powers of the higher office, and do . . . that which needed to be done'. The only question of importance was 'whether Mr. Eyre, under circumstances of instant public danger did, or did not, do to the best of his power and ability what he believed to be his duty'. To Ruskin it was plain that Eyre had 'done his duty to the uttermost, with no bye-fears or base motives', and that his removal from office had been 'an act of national imbecility'. In a rhetorical flourish worthy of Carlyle, Ruskin described the persecution of Eyre as the 'act of a nation blinded by its avarice to all true valour and virtue . . . It was a suicidal act of a people which, for the sake of filling its pockets, would pour mortal venom into all its air and all its streams.' Ruskin equated Eyre's critics to people 'who would howl in the frantic collapse of their decayed consciences, that they might be permitted righteously to reward with ruin the man who had dared strike down one seditious leader, and rescue the lives of a population'. He held out hope that the majority of Englishmen were not so irreparably debased and corrupted. That was why he was willing to join the Eyre Committee.

From Ruskin's lofty pronouncements the meeting turned to the more mundane matters of Eyre's personal finances (it appeared that his dismissal would cost him most, perhaps all of his government pension), and the need to establish sub-committees to raise money in all the principal cities of the country. Hume was able to announce that Sir Roderick Murchison, the renowned scientist, had joined the Committee, and that an approach had been made to Tennyson.[250]

Decisions were also made about the Committee's propaganda. It was agreed that fund-raising circulars would stress that the Jamaica Committee was a creature of the Reform League, and beholden to it for money.[251] When the final version of the circular was published on 5 September, it alleged that the leaders of the Reform League had vowed to 'use every effort to make the perpetrators of atrocious crimes [in Jamaica] answer for their conduct before the legal tribunals of the country'.[252] The circular was published in the major newspapers the day after Eyre had been burned in effigy on Clerkenwell Green during a Reform meeting. By end of September, the battle lines were clearly drawn. As we have seen, the Jamaica Committee *was* receiving support from the members and supporters of

[250] Semmel, *Governor Eyre Controversy*, 114–18.   [251] Ibid.
[252] Reprinted in *The Times* (5 Sept. 1866), 6.

the Reform League,[253] while the Eyre Committee exploited the fear and loathing of the League's many rich and influential enemies.[254] By mid-October 1866, the Eyre Defence Committee had raised £4,000 in new subscriptions.[255]

Meanwhile Ruskin and Carlyle began to worry that Eyre, the 'heroic man' at the centre of their efforts, might have feet of clay. Ruskin in particular was concerned by reports that Eyre had performed poorly, perhaps corruptly, in his capacity as Governor of Jamaica.[256] With the aid of a 'conclusive' letter of explanation written by Eyre himself, Carlyle managed to reassure Ruskin on this point. But there were other problems. Both men agreed that Hamilton Hume was an earnest but limited man who was not up to a first-class biography of Eyre. Carlyle was especially doubtful about Hume's capacity to cope with the legal subtleties of Eyre's case. What was needed in Eyre's biographer, Carlyle believed, was someone with a 'lawyer's precision' (a man of 'real logic and law') to help Hume with the job.[257] The biography (with or without a ghost-writer, it is not clear) was completed and published in 1867.

In October, Carlyle stepped down as President of the Eyre Defence Committee. Although he remained with the Committee as a 'Vice-President', from this point forward Carlyle was mainly a figurehead. He was succeeded by Lord Shrewsbury. Murchison agreed to become the Committee's second Vice-President.[258] In the absence of systematic or complete Eyre Defence Committee records, it appears that Murchison was the most active member of the three-person executive.[259] Ruskin continued to work closely with the Committee in 1866, while Hamilton Hume handled the routine administrative tasks. At the executive meeting of 3 October, Hume reported on fund-raising efforts and how sub-committees had been formed in many of the larger cities and towns of

---

[253] For example, the large outdoor meeting on 30 August at Bartholomew Close in London. The meeting followed an interesting agenda. First, the speakers at the Southampton banquet for Eyre were denounced as 'champions of oppression and murder'. Then the chair of the meeting 'urged the working men of London to do all in their power to support the Jamaica Committee'. *The Times* (31 Aug. 1866), 7.

[254] On 28 September 1866, Hume published a letter in the *Daily Telegraph* stating that he had received 'an official communication' from the Reform League which proclaimed the League's firm commitment to those who were working to bring Eyre to 'justice' for the murder of Gordon. It was of obvious importance to the Eyre Committee that it widely publicize that the Reform League was its sworn adversary.

[255] This was a considerable sum, but as Murchison informed the public, the Committee thought that £10,000 would be needed to defend Eyre. Letter of Murchison, *The Times* (20 Oct. 1866), 10.

[256] Ruskin and Carlyle had been in receipt of information from a Jamaican newspaperman concerning some gaffes and improprieties allegedly committed by Eyre when he was Governor. Ruskin was inclined to take the information seriously, Carlyle to dismiss it. See Carlyle to Ruskin, 27 Sept. 1866; Ruskin to Carlyle, 29 Sept. 1866 as reprinted in George Allan Cate (ed.), *The Correspondence of Thomas Carlyle and John Ruskin* (Stanford, Calif., 1982), 119–21.

[257] Carlyle to Ruskin, 11 Oct. 1866, ibid., 122–3.   [258] *Daily Telegraph* (6 Oct. 1866), 2.

[259] This judging by the number of letters exchanged by Eyre and Murchison concerning the business of the Defence Committee. See Murchison Papers, *BL*, letters from Eyre, 1867–70. This material is discussed below, Epilogue.

Britain.[260] Solicitations had been sent to the commanding officers of all the regiments and ships of the armed forces, and soon were to be made to 'every individual member of the Civil Service of India'. Hume also was able to report that the Defence Committee had received endorsements from various Working Men's Conservative Associations. By the end of October 1866, the Committee had collected a large amount of money.[261] At least four members (Ruskin was one) subscribed £100.[262] One man, John Morant, donated £500 to the fund. By 3 November 1866, the Committee had collected thousands of pounds. The Committee now also could boast of a number of new 'name' enlistments to the cause, including the physicist Sir John Tyndall.

Tyndall's enlistment was particularly important to the Eyre Defence Committee, and a brief digression is required to understand why. In the period from August 1866 to the end of the year, the Jamaica Committee had got (what the *London Review* called) two 'literary and scientific windfalls' when T. H. Huxley and Charles Lyell joined its ranks.[263] Soon thereafter, Charles Darwin sent money to the Jamaica Committee and agreed that his name should appear on the Committee's circulars.[264] Herbert Spencer, the great proponent of biologicial and social evolutionism, also signed in this period. Most of the most eminent British scientists placed themselves squarely behind the Jamaica Committee and its determination to prosecute Eyre.[265]

Huxley quickly became a particularly valuable asset to the Jamaica Committee. In the weeks that followed his enlistment he not only became a member of its executive council, but began to publish a series of letters which explained and justified the Committee's legal methods and aims.[266] The most important of these was a rejoinder to some flippant remarks by the *Pall Mall Gazette* about the apparent connection between evolutionism, 'negrophilism', and allegiance to the Jamaica Committee. In his terse reply, Huxley made clear that he had not joined the Jamaica Committee either because of any scientific theory (or, he added, 'by any particular love for, or admiration of the negro'), but because the Jamaica affair raised issues of the 'profoundest practical importance'.[267] Huxley thought the country had to confront a large question: 'Does the killing of

[260] As reported in the *Daily News* (6 Oct. 1866), 6.

[261] The Eyre Defence Fund eventually raised some £13,000. *Hansard*, ccxii (8 July 1872), 807.

[262] *Eyre Aid and Defence Fund* (London, 1867), 25.

[263] *London Review* (3 Nov. 1866), 490.

[264] For an excellent summary of the involvement of the scientific community in the Jamaica affair, see Semmel, *Governor Eyre Controversy*, 118–27.

[265] The biologists who sided with the Jamaica Committee were motivated both by the political and constitutional issues at stake, but also by their loathing for the vulgar biological determinism and pseudo-scientific racism propounded by the pro-Eyre camp. See Douglas Lorimer, 'Race, Science and Culture: Historical Continuities and Discontinuities, 1850–1914', in Shearer West (ed.), *Victorians and Race* (Aldershot, 1996), 12–33, 26.

[266] Adrian J. Desmond, *Huxley: From Devil's Disciple to Evolution's High Priest* (Reading, Mass., 1997), 352–3.　　　　　[267] *Pall Mall Gazette* (31 Oct. 1866), 3–4.

a man in the way Mr. Gordon was killed constitute murder in the eye of the law, or does it not?' He was appalled by the proposition, put forward by the Eyre Defence Committee and many newspapers, that Gordon's execution was justified because Governor Eyre honestly believed him to be a bad man and a threat to public security. In an often-quoted phrase, Huxley contended that 'English law does not permit good persons, as such, to strangle bad persons, as such'. On the contrary, when the 'most virtuous of Britons' caused the execution of the 'greatest scoundrel' they committed murder. The decision by Eyre to endorse Gordon's execution, Huxley believed, had to be 'stigmatised by the highest authority as a crime'. Huxley shared the view, with Mill and Smith,[268] that the prosecution of Eyre was about fundamental political and legal principle, not retribution. As he explained in a letter to Charles Kingsley, 'Mr. Eyre's personality in this matter is nothing to me.'[269] Had it been 'practicable', Huxley would have preferred that the Committee prosecute Eyre's 'official hat'. This would at the very least have the effect of eliminating the taint of personal enmity or vindictiveness from the process. The point was to cause the courts to say what Parliament would not or could not say: that Gordon's execution was a 'political murder', as bad as any 'since Jeffreys' time'. Eyre was the vital instrument of the murder, and it was the mission of the Jamaica Committee to use his case to vindicate 'inflexible justice as between man and man' against the theory that some men, some men called 'heroes' by other men, stand outside the law.

When Tyndall joined the Eyre Committee, Huxley's public intervention already had lent a scientific gloss to the opposition. The fact that the Committee now could claim an eminent scientist for its own cause, especially given the racialist character of the claims it was making about the Jamaica affair, was especially valuable propaganda. Neither did it hurt the Committee's claim to political neutrality that Tyndall was a self-professed *liberal* in politics, one who professed that if he had a hundred votes at the next Parliamentary election, 'I would give them all to John Mill'.[270]

Huxley tried to detach his science from his politics. Tyndall did not. He quite deliberately tried to use his scientific reputation to buttress some of the key assumptions – particularly the racial assumptions – of the Eyre Defence Committee. In November 1866 Tyndall, not yet publicly pledged to either side of the Jamaica controversy, received some literature describing the aims of the Jamaica Committee. Tyndall used this as an opportunity not only to announce his allegiance to the Eyre Committee, but also to justify his choice in a lengthy open letter.[271] The letter elaborated on the themes of race and necessity.

[268] Mill later stated in an open letter that he did not have the 'smallest feeling of any sort . . . towards Mr. Eyre as a private man.' As printed in the *Pall Mall Gazette* (6 June 1868).

[269] Huxley to Kingsley, 8 Nov. 1866, as reprinted in Leonard Huxley (ed.), *Life and Letters of Thomas Henry Huxley* (London, 1900), 281–2.

[270] 'Report of the Eyre Defence Committee Meeting', in Hume, *Edward John Eyre*, Appendix C, 279.

[271] See 'Tyndall's Reply to the Jamaica Committee', ibid., Appendix B, 268–76.

Tyndall shared the view that Edward Eyre was an exemplary public servant who deserved not his nation's opprobrium, but gratitude. This view was based on what was taken to be some hard facts about the black and white races. Like all negroes in the tropics, Tyndall believed, Jamaican blacks were lazy and profligate at the best of times, savage and ruthless at the worst. In October 1865, they revealed their true stripes, and being of the 'same race and temper' as the murderous blacks of Haiti, set about to exterminate Jamaica's small white population. Which brought Tyndall to the predicament of the former Governor. When news of the Morant Bay atrocities reached him, Eyre was obliged to consider one thing only: how best to 'preserve the lives of 7,000 British men, and the honour of 7,000 British women from the murder and lust of black savages'. His only practical recourse was to proclaim martial law and then use its extraordinary licence to crush the rebellious impulse in the black majority. Tyndall was 'not prepared to deny that the period of punishment was too long, or that its character was too severe'. What he was prepared to deny was that Eyre, with recourse to only a tiny armed force, had any real choice but to make 'the name, power, and determination of England terrible throughout the island'.[272] Terror had been the only sure way for the white minority to avoid annihilation.

Tyndall then moved to the subject of Gordon, the 'taproot from which the rebellion drew its main sustenance'. According to Tyndall's reading of the official record, Eyre had been fully 'justified' in his general perception that Gordon had fomented the rebellion. However, if the Governor had committed a 'legal blunder' when he permitted Gordon to be executed, Tyndall thought that he had more than paid for it with the 'ruin of his career'. In the end, the crucial factor in Eyre's favour was that he had acted quickly to stem a bloody rebellion among a black majority, and in so doing 'saved the whole white population of Jamaica'. With this pronouncement Tyndall called upon the Jamaica Committee, 'in the name of all that is wise and dignified in human nature', to desist from the criminal prosecution of Eyre.

As it became increasingly likely (in the final weeks of 1866, the first of 1867) that the Jamaica Committee would soon move to prosecute Eyre, both Huxley and Tyndall became leading and frequently quoted spokespersons for their respective sides. In November 1866, Huxley wrote Tyndall to express regret that they had 'fundamentally different political principles'.[273] He hoped that they could 'agree to differ' without damaging their close friendship. While he too wanted to avoid personal recriminations, Huxley bluntly rejected the contents of Tyndall's open letter. It did not contain 'any important fact or argument' which he had not already considered, and rejected. Huxley remained convinced that the Jamaica affair was 'at bottom one of the most important constitutional battles in which Englishmen have for many years been engaged'. He would continue to press the agenda of the Jamaica Committee, whatever the cost.

---

[272] Ibid., 274.   [273] Huxley to Tyndall, 9 Nov. 1866, in *Life and Letters of Huxley*, 283.

And thus as the year 1866 came to a close the battle lines were drawn. It was obvious now that the Jamaica Committee was in earnest about the criminal prosecution of Eyre. It was equally obvious that a formidable association of intellectuals and grandees was prepared to invest considerable amounts of prestige and money in Eyre's defence.[274] As the *Manchester Guardian* remarked in November 1866, 'the strength and sincerity of the feelings stirred up by the late occurrences in Jamaica are shown by the inability of the question to die.'[275]

V. Conclusion: The Drawing-Room Men Contest the Jamaica Affair

The paradox of the Jamaica affair is that it so quickly stopped being about Jamaica and Jamaicans.[276] By the end of 1866 the affair had metamorphosed into a dispute over English law and politics. This was the result both of agency and circumstance. Under the leadership of Mill, the Jamaica Committee deliberately redefined the controversy. The Jamaica affair was no longer mainly about the violence done to a hapless black peasantry. It was now mainly about the violence done to the basic laws of England. The Gordon case illustrated the point nicely.

In January 1866 the English newspapers published the first detailed and credible information about Gordon's arrest, transportation, and trial. But for all the hand-wringing in the liberal newspapers about Gordon's unhappy demise, neither the Jamaica Committee nor the political press dwelled for long on this merely individual fate. Nor was it much interested in the implications of Gordon's execution for Jamaica's politics or constitution, nor even for Gordon's widow. Instead the Gordon case was seized on as an opportunity to discuss the law governing political dissent and repression at home. The question of the day was not whether martial law in Jamaica justified the execution of Gordon, but whether martial law in England would justify the execution of John Bright.

The crystallization of the Jamaica affair into a dispute about the civil liberties of Englishmen at home was assisted by a number of circumstances.[277] The first was the Reform Bill agitation. In the wake of the Hyde Park incident, it was especially cogent to link the repression of political dissent in Jamaica with the prospect of

---

[274] This decision was not discussed at the open meetings of the Eyre Committee. According to a letter written by Eyre to Carlyle, the arrangements were made quietly by one of the Committee's Vice-Chairmen. See Eyre to Carlyle, 29 Oct. 1866, in Workman, 'Carlyle and the Governor Eyre Controversy', 96.   [275] *Manchester Guardian* (24 Nov. 1866), 4.

[276] As one scholar has observed of Mill's 'point of reference' in the Jamaica affair, 'the events in the West Indies were ultimately subjacent: they provided the facts that illustrated general codes about questions of governance and rule'. Simon Gikandi, *Maps of Englishness: Writing and Identity in the Culture of Colonialism* (New York, 1996), 53. See also Lorimer, *Colour, Class, and the Victorians*, 197.

[277] 'But much of the extraordinary passion that went into dramatizing the Eyre case had its origin not in the case itself but in the strong differences of opinion on the question of how England, not Jamaica, was to be governed.' Kaplan, *Carlyle*, 488.

the same treatment at home. If a colonial Governor could use martial law to eliminate political opponents at the first hint of trouble, what would prevent the Home Secretary from doing the same thing to the leaders of the Reform League? This anxiety was made all the more palpable, moreover, by the Jamaica debates in Parliament. At the end of July 1866, senior members of the Tory government informed the House of Commons that Edward Eyre would not be prosecuted for crimes arising out of the Jamaica suppression. The simple reason for this decision was that he had broken no laws. All of the impugned actions of the former Governor had taken place under a proclamation of martial law. Martial law, Disraeli himself explained to the nation, sanctioned even the most savage repression, providing that it was undertaken in a good faith effort to restore public order. When cabinet ministers made such assertions, it was comparatively easy for men like Mill to consolidate the Jamaica affair as a controversy about the *English* jurisprudence of power.

Which brings us to the internal history of the Jamaica Committee. The Committee was originally conceived of as a vehicle of 'Jamaica-centric' activism by Christian activists and missionaries who wanted to redress wrongs done to black Jamaicans. It was natural, then, that the first chairman of the Committee was a renowned anti-slavery philanthropist, Charles Buxton. But from the beginning there was a faction within the Committee that was not mainly interested in the plight of black Jamaicans. While they agreed that many blacks had been treated abominably under martial law, their suffering, and retribution for their suffering, was not the point. The point was that Eyre had purported to suspend the operation of all law, and that no Government or court had yet to say that this was not possible under the constitution. Buxton and his Jamaica-centrism were permanently replaced by Mill and his legal-centrism.[278] On Mill's ascendancy the Jamaica Committee became entirely dedicated to the complete transformation of the Jamaica affair (a story about atrocities in Jamaica) into the 'Governor Eyre controversy' (a story about the law of England).

It is remarkable the degree to which the leaders of the Jamaica Committee were fixated on the law, the courts, and their capacity to resolve the issues arising out of the Jamaica affair. So much were men like Mill committed to this idea that they were determined to reduce the Jamaica affair to a single legal case, and at whatever the cost. The vehicle that was settled on was the criminal prosecution of Eyre for the murder of Gordon. Such a prosecution, or so it was imagined, would oblige the high courts to affirm that a proclamation of martial law, whatever was its real effect, did not permit government officials to arrest unarmed British civilians and subject them to summary military justice. Such a prosecution, so it was also

---

[278] Some committee members continued to draw attention to the plight of non-white peoples in the empire. While he vigorously endorsed the constitutional agenda of the Jamaica Committee, in his speeches in support of the Eyre prosecution Tom Hughes reminded his audience that a 'still greater question . . .[was] the duty of England toward subject races'. *The Times* (20 Nov. 1866), 7.

imagined, was vital to the integrity of the British constitution, and should be pursued even in the face of bitter resentment and hostility.

From the time it was announced in June 1866, until it ended more than two years later, the Jamaica Committee's prosecution initiative was almost universally condemned by all but the most radical commentators. The general consensus was that Eyre had made some serious mistakes in Jamaica, but that he had been punished enough by the loss of his career and pension. England needed to move on, while being mindful that the threat of 'servile insurrection' in the non-white colonies was real and ongoing. It was important, in this view, the *majority* view, that colonial governors were not so worried about their legal culpability that they might hesitate to act decisively in the next case.

But the core leadership of the Jamaica Committee was unmoved by such arguments, even when they issued from liberal quarters of opinion. While they pushed forward with their legal preparations, the public was assured that the prosecution of Eyre had nothing to do with settling personal scores. (As Huxley put it, were it possible the Committee would have been content to prosecute Eyre's hat.) It was freely admitted that Eyre was being used as a kind of prop in political theatre. The principles at stake were seen to justify the discomfort of the man who, after all, had overseen a policy of bloody repression. Basic laws were not matters to be arbitrated by public opinion. Going to court was not an election campaign. Whether a popular goal or not, the Committee wanted a high court judge, an unelected official, to state categorically that some kinds of actions were unlawful and punishable even though they occurred during a period of martial law, and even though they were approved of by high officials of state. By prosecuting Edward Eyre for murder the Committee looked to vindicate the country's most important secular ideal: the accountability of political decision-makers to the law.

4

The Tenets of Terror: Reinventing the Law of Martial Law

> The great questions respecting the nature and extent of martial law itself are of a very different nature. They appertain to the highest and most difficult chapters of political science.
>
> Letter to the *Pall Mall Gazette*, 19 Dec. 1866

> It is to be hoped that whatever may be the result of the inquiry into the lamentable proceedings in Jamaica . . . advantage will be taken of the opportunity to put the law on the subject of martial law into shape.
>
> *Solicitors' Journal*, 31 Dec. 1866

> [N]o one can doubt that the terror of speedy military punishment has a tremendous effect in checking an insurrection.
>
> *The Jurist*, 7 Apr. 1866

The Jamaica controversy was only days old when English political journalists began to expostulate on its legal nuances and ramifications. Their reports bristled with terms such as 'martial law', 'courts martial', 'murder', and 'indemnity', and with speculation about their meaning and application (especially) to the case of George Gordon. From the outset journalists treated legal ideas and principles as an intrinsic feature of the story.

Naturally enough, perhaps, England's two leading legal weeklies were uniquely placed to comment on the technical aspects of the Jamaica affair, and they did not wait long to weigh in. On 25 November 1865, the *Solicitors' Journal* reviewed the (apparent) facts relating to Gordon's arrest, trial, and execution and lamented that 'every principle of British law should thus have been set at nought by a British governor and British officers'.[1] A few days later, the *Law Times* ran its first article on Jamaica, stating that 'The summary execution of Mr. Gordon in Jamaica, without legal trial, appears, upon the face of the despatches, to be wholly illegal'.[2] But unlike its rival journal, the *Law Times* saw the relevance of another issue. It queried whether an action that was illegal '*in point of law*' might still be

---

[1] *Solicitors' Journal* (25 Nov. 1865).　　[2] *Law Times* (2 Dec. 1865), 59.

'justifiable' as a matter of necessity. To this question, as much political as legal, the journal did not yet deign to offer a definitive answer.

In 1866 *technical* legal writing on the Jamaica affair (writing undertaken by lawyers and based on a more or less systematic discussion of formal legal sources) proliferated. What began as a skirmish of letters and comments evolved into a full-scale battle of essays and treatises. Some of this work was commissioned by newspapers or associations, the Jamaica Committee being only the leading example, which already had made public assertions about the illegality of official conduct in Jamaica. This writing, while legal in content and outward appearance, was also a manifestation of specific political alignments and aims. And although most of the technical legal writing on the Jamaica affair was done by lawyers not in the pay of parties to the conflict, almost invariably this work had equally discernible political overtones. In many instances, the authors expressed specific conclusions not only about the potential criminal liability of key actors, but on the political expediency (or not) of martial law. And even when the authors themselves were either non-committal or silent on these points, their work could be adapted to these purposes by interested third parties.

When viewed as a body of work, the technical writing on the Jamaica controversy shared three assumptions. The first was that the controversy, at its core, was about the law of martial law. The second was that lawyers and legal institutions had a key role to play in resolving the conflict. The third assumption was that martial law, all but moribund in England, had been resurrected in the crucible of empire, and thus was renewed as a significant subject of public debate. These assumptions had observable consequences for how the subject-matter was researched, written, and published. Because martial law was dormant as domestic jurisprudence (it had not been proclaimed in England, Wales, or Scotland since 1745, not in Ireland since 1798), and because it was a facet of Britain's famously untidy constitution, research on martial law had necessarily to be based on a diverse array of legal and historical sources, some of which were antiquated and largely forgotten. At the same time, because the new scholars of martial law believed that they had a vitally important contribution to make to the resolution of the Jamaica controversy, they were careful to prepare and publish their work in a manner that would be accessible to educated laymen. Their work took many forms, including editorial letters, journal articles, pamphlets, treatises, and critical reviews of treatises. In almost every instance legal writers worked from the premiss that their readers, even the lawyers among them, knew little or nothing about martial law. How many people actually read their often turgid explanations of case reports and statutes, no one can say. It is clear only that in 1866 (and later) the editors of political journals and the publishers of books believed that there was a strong market for reading material on the law of martial law generally, the legal ramifications of the Gordon case particularly. As we will see, one publisher printed five stout volumes on martial law (and on the Jamaica litigation) in the space of two years.

The extensive legal literature that was generated during the Jamaica controversy has been almost wholly ignored by its historians.[3] It would appear that scholars have been deterred by the abstruseness of the law of martial law, its 'maze of legal technicalities'.[4] As a consequence, few of the writings that are discussed in this chapter have been carefully excavated. By the same token, virtually all of the historical questions that are posed here have not been posed before. To what degree, if any, did legal writers agree on the meaning, ambit, and implications of the term 'martial law'? To what extent, if any, were these disagreements driven by pre-existing convictions about formally *non-legal* factors such as race and empire? In short, did the legal writing on martial law have a politics and if so, what were its mainsprings?

I. The Raw Materials of Martial Law

When English legal writers began to undertake work on the law of martial law as it pertained to the Jamaica affair, they faced a formidable research and analytical challenge. The subject lacked for even one scholarly treatise.[5] As for the conventional sources of law, none was conclusive. The statute books of Parliament (but for an enigmatic provision of the Petition of Right) provided little guidance. And while over the course of the previous two centuries, a number of high court judges had pronounced upon various aspects of martial law, the law reports did not contain a leading or dominant precedent. For the determined legal writer there was nothing to do but work up a picture of martial law from disparate sources. When it came to constructing answers to the core questions about martial law, there was ample room for creativity.

Most of the writing on martial law that emerged in 1866 was interested particularly in the legality of the arrest, court martial, and execution of Gordon, and in the potential culpability of the former governor Eyre and the senior military officers who had implemented martial law in Jamaica. But in order to answer these questions, legal writers needed to make compelling arguments about five more fundamental issues. What manner of British law, if any, was 'martial' law? If there was a law of martial law, from what legal sources was it derived? When and by whom could martial law be proclaimed, and what powers did it bestow? Did martial law apply to civilians and disarmed prisoners? Could officials incur

[3] For discussion, see below, Appendix.

[4] Ford, 'The Governor Eyre Case in England', 219, referring to the complex litigation that arose from the affair.

[5] While some useful material was available on 'military law' (the law governing active officers and soldiers of the Crown), the subject of martial law (the law that *might* fill the vacuum left by suspension of civilian courts) lacked for a treatise, or even an authoritative precedent of the common law courts. For contemporary accounts, see generally, Henry Lord Brougham, *The British Constitution: Its History, Structure and Working*, 3rd edn (London, 1860); Thomas Erskine May, *The Constitutional History of England* (2 vols., London, 1861–3); Broom, *Constitutional Law*.

liability for actions taken under martial law? What was the legal effect, if any, of an indemnity statute? When these questions were answered, the Gordon and Eyre cases boiled down to matters of fact.

Because the formal sources of law on martial law – statutes and case reports – were so scant and indecisive, scholars of the subject felt obliged to cast their nets more widely. Predictably, they mined what they could from the scattered and unsystematic writings of previous law scholars. Less predictably, they also made frequent use of legal opinions on martial law that had been prepared by various Attorneys General (and other law officers of the Crown) for various government officials. A good deal of use was made of *Hansard*, and the parliamentary utterances on martial law of statesmen such as Burke, Brougham, Macintosh, and Wellington. Some writers also delved into documents and published writing on British constitutional history, particularly into those instances in which martial law had been proclaimed, and then later became the source of political and legal tumult.

The new legal literature on the law of martial law, and on the Gordon and Eyre cases, were amalgams (perhaps 'highly selective arrangements' is better) of sources of law and sources of *information* about law. The writers chose from an assortment of statutes, and reported cases were on one hand, published comments, dictionaries, legal opinions, parliamentary assertions, and public records on the other. The materials dated from many different historical eras and circumstances. It would be hard to imagine a more open-ended field of legal inquiry. By themselves, none of the documents yielded definitive answers about the core questions in dispute. In every instance, therefore, the new published work on martial law necessarily was the end result of hundreds of contestable choices about sources and, more importantly, about their interpretation and applicability to the facts of the Jamaica affair. In order to undertake an instructive analysis of this work, that is, in order to achieve some insight into the nature of the choices that were being made by its authors, the source materials must first be briefly elaborated. It might also be helpful to allude to some of the thornier problems of interpretation associated with those materials.

Almost every legal writer on the law of martial law commenced his work by drawing a distinction that had important implications for the scope of his research. That distinction was that 'martial law' was not to be conflated with 'military law'. According to this distinction, martial law was that body of law that governed officials of the Crown when, by reason of an emergency of state caused by invasion or armed insurrection, the civilian courts could not operate. Military law, by contrast, was that body of law that governed members of the armed forces of the Crown. While martial law might apply to civilians, military law could only apply to soldiers, seamen, and their uniformed officers. This distinction had important consequences for legal research. Martial law, if indeed it existed as a category of law in England, was derived from an array of legal sources. Military law, by contrast, was found exclusively in the military codes set forth in the Mutiny Act.

A common starting place for legal writing on martial law was the Petition of Right.[6] The Petition was passed by Parliament in 1628 to curb perceived abuses of the Royal Prerogative by Charles I, including the issuance by him of commissions permitting the bearers to exert the 'justice of martial law', that is to say, the law 'used in armies in time of war'.[7] The Petition reasserted the principle of Magna Carta that no free person should be imprisoned, outlawed, exiled, or executed except by 'due process of law'. In its Article VII the Petition roundly condemned the assignment by the King of commissions 'with power and authority to proceed within the land, according to the justice of martial law'. Article X implored the King that 'hereafter no commissions of like nature may issue forth to any person or persons'. For the mid-Victorian writer on martial law, the Petition of Right raised a cluster of difficult problems. What was the legal import of the phrase 'used by armies in time of war'? Did Parliament mean to imply that martial law was justifiable during time of war? What was the legal definition of the phrase 'in time of war'? Did armed domestic insurrection meet this definition? And then there was the question of the Petition of Right. Did its provisions apply to colonies and other imperial jurisdictions?

We will see that the legal writers on martial law frequently divided on these questions, and on the significance of another statute, the law passed by the Jamaica legislature in 1845 (and never disallowed by the Colonial Office) that permitted the Governor ('with the advice and consent [of] a council of war') to proclaim martial law in any district of the colony 'in the event of a disturbance or emergency of any kind'. As Alexander Heslop explained to the Royal Commission, the martial law legislation of 1845 was the last of a line of laws that reached back to the reign of Charles II.[8] This policy had a clear if unstated implication: since the island's inception as a British colony, Jamaican law-makers had been so much convinced of the importance of martial law that they created and maintained a ready statutory mechanism for its proclamation. In other words, neither these gentlemen nor their successors were content to rely on the hypothesis that the Governor, the senior representative of the Crown in the colony, could proclaim martial law as a matter of prerogative. The legislative approach seemed more certain, and much more in accord with the security needs of a small white population dwelling among a much larger population of slaves and former slaves.[9] But, whatever Jamaican legislators thought they had accomplished with the martial law statute of 1845, their designs were not unproblematic. In the aftermath of the use of martial law in 1865, legal scholars posed searching questions both about the meaning of the statute's

---

[6] 3 Charles I, c. 3.

[7] See generally, Lindsay Boynton, 'Martial Law and the Petition of Right', 79 *English Historical Review* (1964), 255–84.

[8] For Heslop's explication of this legislative history, see *JRC Minutes*, Q.16,200–46.

[9] For this reason, Heslop explained, 'the sun never rose and set on Jamaica as a country in which the English law prevailed with regard to martial law.' Ibid, Q. 16,200.

specific provisions, and about its validity in the face of the Petition of Right, and other laws of the mother country.

In his treatise on the law of martial law published in 1866,[10] the legal writer W. F. Finlason referred to more than *ninety* different reported cases. This speaks loudly of the fragmented nature of the subject-matter, and the absence of definitive precedents on the law of martial law. Case reports were cited by Finlason, and by other legal writers on martial law, mainly in order to document very specific points of law regarding a multitude of issues including the applicability of English law to the colonies,[11] the jurisdiction of courts martial,[12] the legal meaning of the term 'insurrection',[13] the operation of martial law in time of war,[14] and the criminal and civil liability of magistrates.[15] Very few of these cases arose out of an incident that had arisen in the context of a proclamation of martial law, and their value as an authority is highly contestable.

A small number of reported cases, however, were of more obvious relevance to the legal issues generated by the Jamaica controversy, and they were discussed at length in almost all of the more comprehensive treatments of the law of the subject. Two of these cases arose out of the Irish rebellion of 1798. In *Wright v. Fitzgerald*,[16] the plaintiff had been flogged on the order of the sheriff of Tipperary, and without benefit of trial. Martial law had been in place at the time of the flogging, and a bill of indemnity was passed when the rebellion was quelled. The plaintiff succeeded against the defendant in tort, on the theory that the defendant was not entitled to indemnity because the flogging had been arbitrary and cruel.[17] In *Wolfe Tone's Case*,[18] the applicant was an Irish rebel who had been captured on board a French naval vessel. Although he was a civilian, Tone was tried for treason by a court martial and was sentenced to be executed. Tone then applied to the King's courts for a writ of *habeas corpus*. The theory of the application was that because he was not a soldier, and because the civilian courts were operating at the time of his trial, the court martial had lacked jurisdiction. The Court agreed, and granted the writ. Tone famously died by his own hand before the writ could be executed. Read together these cases suggested that there were legal limits on the authority of any official exercising the powers of martial law, but their meaning and extent were contested by legal writers.

Five other cases were frequently cited in the works on martial law. In the 1774 decision in *Mostyn v. Fabrigas*,[19] the plaintiff claimed that on the order of Governor Mostyn he had been beaten and imprisoned without trial for

---

[10] Finlason, *Treatise on Martial Law*.
[11] *Bentinck v. Willink* (1842) 2 Hare's Rep. 1; 67 E.R. 1.
[12] *Grant v. Gould* (1792) 2 Hen. & Blackstone's Rep. 68; 126 E.R. 434.
[13] *The Queen v. Frost* (1839) 9 Carr. & Payne Rep. 129; 173 E.R. 771.
[14] *Barwise v. Keppel* (1766) 2 Wilson's Rep.; 95 E.R. 831.
[15] *Linford v. Fitzroy* (1849) 13 Q.B.R. 230; 116 E.R. 628.   [16] (1798) 27 St. Tr. 765.
[17] For a complete analysis of the case, see Patrick O'Higgins, '*Wright v. Fitzgerald* Revisited', 25 *Modern Law Review* (1962), 413–22.   [18] (1798) 27 St. Tr. 614.
[19] (1774) 1 Cowp. 160; 98 E.R. 1021.

allegedly having been party to sedition and mutiny against the Crown. The defendant, Mostyn, pleaded that at all relevant times he had been the Crown's representative, and that it was therefore his prerogative to maintain order and security as he saw fit, and with legal immunity. On the defendant's appeal against a substantial jury verdict, Lord Mansfield brushed aside the Governor's claim to immunity and upheld the jury's verdict. In *Grant v. Gould*,[20] a case involving a writ of prohibition to prevent the execution of the sentence of a court martial, Lord Loughborough stated that martial law no longer existed in England except as a jurisdiction of the military over soldiers. In *Governor Wall's Case*,[21] the accused was the former Governor of the West African island of Gorree on whose order three men were flogged to death. When seventeen years later Wall was tried in London for their murder, his defence was that the dead men had been mutinous, and that as Governor he had exercised an unreviewable prerogative to maintain discipline. Without interference from the judges a jury sent Wall to the gallows. In *The King v. Pinney*[22] the accused had been the Lord Mayor of Bristol during the Reform Bill riots of 1832. As a result of his indecision, the riots had got out of control. In pressing a charge of criminal dereliction of duty, the Crown submitted that Pinney had been under a legal duty to perform reasonably in the circumstances. Pinney pleaded that he had acted honestly and on best available advice. Having done so, he submitted, he could not be found guilty of a crime. Pinney was convicted as charged, a precedent that resonated among those interested in the prosecution of Edward Eyre.

All of these cases appeared to indicate civilian legal limits on the authority of Crown agents, even in the context of a period of political insecurity, open insurrection, or under proclamation of martial law. The nature and extent of such limits, however, as well as their applicability to Governor Eyre and other officials, was a matter of contention.

The case law on martial law was thin gruel, and legal writers frequently supplemented their discussion of cases with the extra-judicial statements of eminent judges and jurists. One often quoted passage was found in the *Institutes* of Sir Edward Coke.[23] In his short discussion of martial law, Coke, one of the draftsmen of the Petition of Right, asked rhetorically whether the 'soldier and justice' could share one bench. Coke thought that they could not. As long as the civilian courts were able to function, the courts martial had no jurisdiction over civilians: 'where the Common Law can determine a thing,' Coke wrote, 'the Martial Law shall not.' While he conceded that as a matter of practical necessity martial law might be invoked during times of war or armed insurrection, nothing short of this would justify its continuation. As Coke once stated in the House of Commons, 'God send me never to live under the law of conveniency or discretion'. With

---

[20] (1792) 2 Hen. & Blackstone's Rep. 68; 126 E.R. 434.
[21] (1802) 28 St. Tr. 36.   [22] (1832) 3 Barn. & Adolphus Rep. 966; 110 E.R. 349.
[23] J. H. Thomas (ed.), *Coke's First Institutes*, vol. iii (Philadelphia, Penn., 1836), 430.

Coke, Blackstone was sometimes quoted on martial law,[24] but principally for his endorsement of statements made by Lord Chief Justice Hale in the *History of the Common Law* (1736). In his brief discussion of the subject of martial law, Hale set forth three concise points. Of martial law, he declared, 'in truth and reality it is not a law, but something indulged, rather than allowed, as a law'.[25] He further concluded that 'this indulged law, was only to extend to members of the army, or, those of the opposite army, and never was so much indulged as intended to be executed or exercised upon others'. Finally, Hale stressed that 'the exercise of martial law, whereby any person should lose his life, or member, or liberty, may not be permitted in time of peace, when the king's courts are open for all persons to receive justice according to the law of the land'. In a footnote to his text, Hale further observed that it was not accidental that 'so little has been written on the martial law of England'.[26] This omission, he thought, was due to the fact that martial law always had been regarded as a 'temporary excrescence, bred from the distemper of the state, and not as part of the permanent laws of the kingdom'.[27]

While before 1866 there was no comprehensive treatise on martial law, there were at least three publications devoted to the subject of courts martial[28] and two on military law generally.[29] These books contained only small amounts of relevant material, even when they were supplemented by texts on the 'pleas of the Crown',[30] or on criminal law and evidence[31] (including the recently published work of one of the participants in the Eyre controversy, Fitzjames Stephen).[32] But even if the researcher's net was cast widely, there were not many good fish to catch.

To make up for the dearth of statutes and leading cases, legal writers often relied on constitutional histories of England[33] and, when there was greater ambition, on

---

[24] *Blackstone's Commentaries on the Laws of England*, ed. H. Broom and E. A. Hadley, vol. i (London, 1869), 412–13.

[25] Matthew Hale, *The History of the Common Law of England*, 6th edn (London, 1820), 42.

[26] Ibid.

[27] Ibid. Upon making this statement, however, Hale was quick to acknowledge that martial law is 'indisputably authorized by the legislature'. Parliament could pass a law proclaiming martial law whenever and wherever it chose.

[28] A. F. Tytler, *An Essay on Military Law* (London, 1800); J. McArthur, *Principles and Practice of Naval and Military Courts Martial* (2 vols., London, 1813); T. F. Simmons, *Remarks on the Constitution and Practice of Courts Martial*, 2nd edn (London, 1835).

[29] Tytler, *Military Law*, W. Hough, *Precedents in Military Law: Including the Practice of Courts Martial, the Mode of Conducting Trials, the Duties of Officers at Military Courts of Inquest, Courts of Inquiry, Courts of Requests, etc.* (London, 1855).

[30] In *A Treatise on the Pleas of the Crown* (London, 1716), William Hawkins stated that 'if persons take upon themselves to put others to death, either by virtue of a commission wholly unknown to our laws, or by virtue of any known jurisdiction, . . . as if the court martial in time of peace put a man to death by court martial, both the officers and judges are guilty of murder.'

[31] The most commonly cited works were *Russell on Crimes* and *Phillips on Evidence*. See, e.g., a bibliography of 'Authorities Cited or Referred to', in Finlason, *Martial Law*, xlvii–lii.

[32] James Fitzjames Stephen, *A General View of the Criminal Law of England* (London, 1863).

[33] Particularly, on Henry Hallam's *Constitutional History of England from the Accession of Henry VII to the Death of George II*, 7th edn (London, 1854), and on the constitutional histories of David Hume and Sir James Mackintosh.

the documentary sources (especially *Hansard*) relating to previous instances in which agents of the Crown had suppressed colonial uprisings under a proclamation of martial law. In fact, one form or other of 'martial law' had been proclaimed numerous times (including in Barbados 1805, 1816; Ceylon 1817, 1848; Demerara 1823; Jamaica 1831–2; Cape Colony 1835, 1846, 1850–1; Canada 1837–8;[34] Cephalonia 1849; India 1857–8; St. Vincent 1862) in the sixty years prior to the Morant Bay uprising. As an instrument of imperial statecraft, then, martial law was far from obsolete. Its use, and alleged abuse, in the empire had been the subject of public controversy a number of times in nineteenth-century England. In at least two instances, with regard to suppressions in Demerara in 1823 and Ceylon in 1848, the use of martial law became the basis of protracted political conflicts much like the one that had sprung up about Jamaica in 1865. Their potential value as (political, if not legal) precedents was understood by some of the legal writers on martial law and, for this reason, they merit brief comment.

In 1823 Demerara (British Guiana) was a colony of sugar plantations operated with an especially brutal regime of slave labour.[35] When the living conditions and general treatment of slaves continued to deteriorate, and when rumours began to circulate that they had been emancipated by Parliament, the slaves rose in revolt. Martial law was proclaimed as regular troops and militiamen crushed the revolt in a series of skirmishes. Courts martial were set up to summarily try and execute captured rebels. The authorities also arrested a white missionary named the Revd. John Smith. Smith was accused of having conspired with the slaves to foment rebellion. After a long but procedurally shoddy trial by court martial, Smith was convicted and sentenced to be executed. Before the sentence could be carried out, however, Smith died in a Demeraran jail. In all about 250 slaves were killed or executed during the five-month period of martial law. Three whites were killed during the short period of open insurrection.

When news of the revolt and suppression in Demerara reached England in 1824, an alliance of abolitionists, missionary societies, and liberal and Radical political figures instigated a series of investigations and parliamentary clashes. In June 1824 Henry Brougham and the eminent constitutional historian Sir James Mackintosh seized the opportunity to make impassioned speeches in the House of Commons both against the savage treatment of the rebel slaves and the missionary Smith specifically, and against permissive interpretations of the law of martial law generally. Brougham defended the position that martial law had been outlawed in England and the empire by the Petition of Right.[36] While conceding that the 'pressure of a great emergency' of state might justify a proclamation of martial law, Brougham argued that martial law, and special powers or immunities that it might entail, could not endure a minute longer than the emergency that brought it into

---

[34] For scholarship on the use of martial law in the Canadas, see Murray Greenwood and Barry Wright (eds.), *Canadian State Trials* (2 vols., Toronto, 1996, 2002).

[35] See generally, Michael Craton, *Testing the Chains: Resistance to Slavery in the British West Indies* (Ithaca, NY, 1982), 267–89.   [36] *Hansard*, xi (1 June 1824), 969.

existence. ('Created by necessity, necessity must limit its continuance.'[37]) Later in the debate, Mackintosh, citing Hale as his main authority, also contended that any attempt to prolong martial law beyond the point of emergency was mere 'usurpation'.[38] On this principle the court martial that had tried John Smith was illegal. Had the sentence of death been carried out, Mackintosh added, 'it would not have been an execution, but a murder'.[39]

Brougham and Mackintosh made the longest and most often quoted speeches on the subject of martial law, but they did not make the only significant statements. Representing the Tory government in the Demerara debate was Wilmot Horton, the Under-Secretary for the Colonies.[40] Horton did not have a lot to say about the law of martial law, but what he did say to the House on 1 June 1824 was cogent enough that the same words were frequently repeated during the Jamaica affair more than forty years later. Martial law, Horton agreed, was not something that could be invoked on any pretext. In his judgement, however, the Governor of Demerara had proclaimed martial law, and then kept it in place for five months, for only good reasons:[41] 'the continuation of this state of martial law,' Horton stated, 'will not be a matter of surprise to any man who knows the circumstances; who is aware of the disproportion existing between the slaves and the white population; and who reflects on the dreadful consequences that might result from a single day passing among those slaves in a state of insurrection.'[42] The tiny and scattered white population of Demerara had been terrified by the prospect of revolt, and then renewed revolt, after the first intercession of the military. They had been terrified also of the destabilizing effect on slavery of the evangelical preaching of men like John Smith. It had been their unanimous judgement, one that issued from men who actually faced the prospect of massacre by the black slave majority, that it was necessary for martial law to continue for some months after the initial outbreak of violence.[43] Horton, for one, thought the English government was in no good position to second-guess this judgement. The same view was advanced during the Jamaica controversy forty years later.

The Ceylon affair of 1848–51 was the next major instance of conflict over the law of martial law, especially as it related to empire. The affair began when reports arrived in England that some of the indigenous people of Ceylon had rioted against new taxes and long-standing grievances about British policies toward their Buddhist religion.[44] Fearing that riots marked the beginning of a generalized revolt under the leadership of a charismatic Buddhist leader, the Governor, Viscount Torrington, had taken advice from his privy councillors and proclaimed martial law. Just as in Demerara, a small contingent of British regulars and militia

---

[37] *Hansard*, xi (1 June 1824), 976.   [38] Ibid., 1046.
[39] Ibid., 1052.
[40] See generally, Emilia V. Da Costa, *Crowns of Glory, Tears of Blood: The Demerara Slave Rebellion of 1823* (New York, 1994), 288–9.   [41] *Hansard*, xi (1 June 1824), 1002.
[42] Ibid.   [43] Ibid., 1032.
[44] For a general account of this debate, see Kostal, 'A Jurisprudence of Power'.

quickly crushed the uprising. Again, just as in Demerara, martial law was kept in place for months after open resistance had been quelled. Ceylonese prisoners were tried, some were executed, by courts martial operating even as the civilian courts were open and functioning. In 1849 a number of political radicals successfully pressed the Russell government (in 1865 Russell had cause to reflect on this earlier experience) for a parliamentary inquiry into (among other issues) the use of martial law in Ceylon. When the investigation was completed almost two years later, the same men provoked a debate in both Houses of Parliament.

In the House of Commons the most noteworthy speeches on the Ceylon incident[45] were made by William Gladstone and the Attorney General, Sir Alexander Cockburn. Gladstone maintained that the Ceylon affair was a dispute over the 'highest and most sacred principles on which the government of mankind can be carried on'.[46] While it was understandable that the Governor had proclaimed martial law, the prolongation of it, the trial and execution of men by court martial when the civil courts were open, was the ultimate abuse of power. In a speech that was later quoted to discredit him, Cockburn (in 1866, the Lord Chief Justice of the Queen's Bench), spoke as the Government's chief legal officer. Instead of making a speech against martial law, or condemning Torrington for having abused it, Cockburn attempted to justify what had happened on the grounds that the Governor had acted out of the honest motive that it was necessary in order to save the colony from insurrection.[47] Whether Cockburn uttered these words because it was his genuine conviction or his political duty, was a question asked many times in 1867.

The most enduring statement about martial law made in the context of the Ceylon controversy was uttered by the Duke of Wellington in the House of Lords. In the spring of 1851 Wellington was a very elderly man who seldom took part in debate. He was moved to make an exception when the Earl Grey, during his speech on Ceylon, offered the casual remark that during his illustrious career Wellington had carried on whole campaigns under martial law, and had himself adopted 'measures of great severity and of wholesome rigour'.[48] This attribution clearly agitated the old general, and he levered himself to his feet to set the record straight. Martial law, Wellington stated, 'was neither more nor less than the will of the general who commands the army. In fact, martial law meant no law at all.'[49] In subsequent writing on martial law this statement was frequently quoted in support of the proposition that martial law was unlimited military discretion. However, it is clear that this is not what the Duke had meant. In the first case, Wellington was not referring to the law pertaining to civil unrest or emergency, but to the position of a military commander *vis-à-vis* foreign nationals in a military zone during time of war. In the second case, the Duke had taken pains to qualify

---

[45] *Hansard*, cxvii (26, 27 May 1851).   [46] Ibid., 209.   [47] Ibid., 227.
[48] *Hansard*, cxv (1 Apr. 1851), 852–6.   [49] Ibid., 880–1.

his aphorism, adding that it was incumbent on the commander always to fill the vacuum created by martial law with 'the rules and regulations and limits according to which his will has to be carried out'. (When Wellington himself had administered martial law in a part of conquered France, for instance, he decreed that 'the ordinary civil authorities should administer the law of the country'.)[50] Whatever martial law was, the Duke plainly did not think that it was the profligate use of limitless power. It is therefore telling of the politics of martial law as a subject-matter that these qualifications were rarely mentioned by those who quoted from Wellington's speech.

The Ceylon affair gave rise to another useful source of material on martial law: the solicited opinion of a law officer of the Crown. These were solicited in one of two ways. In some instances they were produced by the Attorney and/or Solicitor General (or on occasion by the Judge-Advocate General) on the formal request of some member of the Cabinet. In other cases, the Ceylon episode being one, the law officer provided his opinion after having been called to testify before a parliamentary select committee. But whatever the circumstances, on at least a half dozen occasions before the Jamaica controversy of 1865 the senior lawyers of the Crown had set forth their considered opinions on various aspects of the law of martial law.

In 1757 the law officers advised the Government that a proclamation of martial law did not suspend or stop 'the ordinary course of law and justice . . . any further than is absolutely necessary'.[51] In 1799 the Attorney General advised the Government that Parliament was entitled to pass a statute which 'in effect appears to recognize that it is part of the royal prerogative during the time of rebellion to authorize the King's general and other commanding officers to punish rebels according to martial law, by death or otherwise'.[52] The Attorney General expressed grave doubts, however, that civilians could be tried by martial law 'without an express Act of Parliament'. Such a doctrine was seen as 'unconsonant with several recitals [Coke and Hale were cited] and one enactment in that grand Act of Parliament, the Petition of Right'.[53] In the aftermath of rebellions in Canada in 1837–8 the Attorney and Solicitor Generals informed the Government that a governor of a colony has the 'power of proclaiming, in any district in which large bodies of the inhabitants are in open rebellion, that the Executive government will proceed to enforce martial law'.[54] Martial law was seen as a 'right arising from and limited by the necessity of the case', and does not 'extend beyond the case of persons taken in open resistance'. When the regular courts were open, there was 'no right in the Crown to adopt any other course of proceeding'.[55]

---

[50] An observation made by the editor of the *Pall Mall Gazette* (3 July 1867), 1.
[51] Joint Opinion of the Attorney and Solicitor Generals, Henley and Yorke, 28 Jan. 1757, as reprinted in William Forsyth, *Cases and Opinions on Constitutional Law* (London, 1869), 188.
[52] Opinion of Attorney General Hargrave, ibid., 191.   [53] Ibid., 192.
[54] Opinion of John Campbell and R. M. Rolfe, 16 Jan. 1838, ibid., 198–9.   [55] Ibid.

Before Sir David Dundas, barrister and Judge-Advocate General, was called to testify (as an expert witness) before the parliamentary select committee on Ceylon in 1850, he had taken it upon himself to study all of the available sources on the law of martial law, including the opinions of previous law officers of the Crown. Dundas was queried extensively by the select committee,[56] and for subsequent lawyers his testimony was a rich source of information and interpretation. In Dundas' view, agents of the Crown had an 'inherent right' to proclaim martial law and exert extraordinary powers to restore public order.[57] Crucially, however, Dundas thought that the proclamation of martial law invoked a body of unwritten *law*. When martial law was proclaimed by the Crown it was to serve notice of a new regime, not of official lawlessness, but of 'another measure of law, and another mode of pursuing it'.[58] It was therefore incumbent upon the officer implementing martial law to do so 'firmly, faithfully, and with as much humanity as the occasion allows'.[59] When these standards were met, officials were eligible for indemnity from civil or criminal prosecution for acts that might have been illegal under ordinary law.[60] But when an official did not live up to these minimum standards of conduct, Dundas thought that 'he ought to be brought into very great trouble for it'.[61]

Like the Demerara flap twenty years earlier, the Ceylon controversy did not generate any formal law on martial law. No seminal judicial decisions were rendered or statutes passed as a result of the uprisings there, or as a result of the political turmoil in England. Still, the parliamentary investigations, debates, and legal opinions made not inconsiderable contributions to the larger jurisprudence on the subject. What great and important men had said about martial law in Parliament was not law, but it was taken as relevant information about what the law was, or ought to be.

The proclamation of martial law in Ireland, Demerara, and Ceylon all had generated material that was exploited by the most comprehensive and sophisticated works on martial law published in England after 1865. But there was a glaring absence of material, an absence worthy of comment, drawn from an even more recent and dramatic episode: the suppression of the Indian Mutiny of 1857–8.[62]

In early May 1857, a number of Indian (or 'sepoy') regiments of the Bengal army of the East India Company (the ruling authority in British India) rose in

[56] *British Parliamentary Papers*, xii (1851), Q. 5431–520.   [57] Ibid., Q. 5475.
[58] Ibid., Q. 5437.   [59] Ibid., Q. 5432.   [60] Ibid, Q. 5506–7.
[61] Ibid., Q. 5515. Finlason held a different view of the import of statutes of indemnity. He thought that indemnity was to be invoked by officials who, while acting in good faith, committed 'some excess or irregularity, which may be without *wilful* criminality – through error, excitement or mistake'. See W. F. Finlason, *A Review of the Authorities as to the Repression of Riot or Rebellion, with Special References to Criminal or Civil Liability* (London, 1868), 89.
[62] The most important work on martial law to be published in the wake of the Jamaica controversy, a work that presented a seemingly exhaustive chronological list of instances in which martial law had been used in the colonies, did not mention martial law in India. See Clode, *Military Forces of the Crown*, vol. ii, 481.

mutiny against their British officers.[63] In some locales mutiny quickly transmuted into general revolt. With the collaboration of some disaffected Indian princes, the mutineer–rebels gained control over large swathes of territory. During the first months of the rebellion, scores of British soldiers and administrators were killed by rebel action. Then, in one of the most resonant events of British imperial history in the nineteenth century, in June 1857 more than one hundred British women and children were massacred by rebels at the garrison town of Cawnpore.[64] In British India and later in Britain proper, the violent death (and alleged sexual molestation) of white women during the revolt became a rallying cry for untempered revenge. The retribution subsequently meted out by British military forces was horrific.[65] Insofar as they thought about law, many field officers regarded martial law as a licence to exact revenge without restraint. In a number of regiments, the torture and summary execution of Indian prisoners became routine, systematic, and deliberately sensational.[66] A series of atrocities also were perpetrated by British forces against the civilian populations of recaptured cities, towns, and villages. By July 1857 the retributive terror had become so racially charged, merciless, and indiscriminate that the Governor-General of India, Lord Canning, moved to intervene. After consulting with his Executive Council, Canning issued an order (it was styled a 'resolution') requiring British officers to respect military law in the trial and punishment of rebel prisoners.[67] When news of these events reached England, however, the tendency among politicians and press was to castigate 'Clemency' Canning for an excess of tenderness toward murderous rebels.[68]

While the ruthlessness of the Indian suppression attracted some critical attention in England,[69] in contrast to the Ceylon episode of 1848, critics were few in

---

[63] For the best general account of the mutiny, see David, *Indian Mutiny*.   [64] Ibid., 182–200.

[65] Ibid., 191. For graphic illustration, see Christopher Hibbert, *The Great Mutiny: India 1857* (London, 1978), 124–33; Bruce Watson, *The Great India Mutiny: Colin Campbell and the Campaign at Lucknow* (New York, 1991), 105–6.

[66] Some prisoners were blown to pieces after being lashed to the mouths of cannon. David, *Indian Mutiny*, 145–6.

[67] For a copy of the 'Clemency' Resolution, see Maclagan, *Canning*, Appendix II, 324–7.

[68] Ibid., 136–43; David, *Indian Mutiny*, 237–8.

[69] We have noted that the exception proving the rule was the protest registered by John Bright. In the course of the debate on India in the House of Commons in 1858, Bright not only denounced the excesses committed by the British army during the suppression, but urged Parliament to wash the country's hands 'of the whole of our Indian policy'. For criticisms of this speech, see *The Times* (21 May 1858), 9. The question of the treatment of sepoy prisoners under martial law was briefly broached in Parliament on two occasions during the winter session of 1858. In February, the Earl of Ellenborough made a polite inquiry in the House of Lords about whether the authorities in Bengal had been prudent in executing so many captured mutineers. *Hansard,* cxlix (15 Feb. 1858), 1359–60. In March, Charles Buxton was among a small group of Liberal M.P.s who supported a motion for the Government to supply information about the instructions given British military officers regarding the treatment of mutineers and deserters. *Hansard,* cxlix (18 Mar. 1858), 346–73. During the debate on the motion one Mr. Rich M.P. went so far as to accuse the army of having engaged in an 'indiscriminate slaughter'. *The Times* (18 Mar. 1858), 6. For a contemptuous response to these accusations, see *The Times* (20 Mar. 1858), 8.

number and restrained in their rhetoric. Many questions were raised about the administrative competence of the East India Company;[70] many fewer were asked about how its armed forces had punished mutineers and rebels.[71] Despite abundant evidence that many 'innocent' Indian men and women had been mistreated under the martial law, there was no official parliamentary inquiry,[72] or even an effusion of condemnatory speeches and writings. Almost without exception,[73] moreover, the military men responsible for the most violent acts of suppression, not only were not criticized or prosecuted for their deeds, but generally were subjects of public admiration and reward. In the wake of the Indian Mutiny, the broad feeling among the English political class was that Indian rebels had been too treacherous, had spilled too much blood, and had defiled too many white women to merit much moral or legal concern.

But this is not to say that the law of emergency had been utterly irrelevant to the Indian episode as it unfolded.[74] Even in the face of a pervasive and dangerous revolt, the authorities did not dispense with (at the very least) the pretence of law. In May 1857, as the revolt was gaining momentum, the British authorities in Calcutta troubled themselves to pass legislation providing local executive authorities with new legal powers to proclaim their regions to be in a state of rebellion, and to exercise a broader and more draconian summary jurisdiction over alleged rebels.[75] The active assumptions here were that native Indians in British territories possessed some legal rights, and these rights could only be displaced by legislation, or by some other formal mechanism of law. Although the evidence is uncertain on this point, it would appear that local British authorities proclaimed martial law in the stricken districts before the military was sent in.[76] It was imagined that the recapture of these areas would proceed under the umbrella at least of military law. Lord Canning's intervention is particularly instructive in this regard. By July 1857, and before British forces had fully regained control of Bengal, the Governor-General of British India pointedly reminded senior military officers of

[70] In August 1858 Parliament moved to terminate the Company's governmental authority over India. Maclagan, *Canning*, 222–3.

[71] The colonial authorities in London did not think it either right as policy or practical in effect to attempt to influence the manner in which the East India Company suppressed the rebellion, or how it dealt with prisoners. See speech of Earl of Granville, *Hansard*, cl (15 Feb. 1858), 1363.

[72] There was one exception. It was perhaps not entirely coincidental that in October 1859 the Defence Commissioners asked the Judge-Advocate General, Thomas Headlam, to write a memorandum on the legalities of a proclamation of martial law in *England*. For a reprint of Headlam's report, see *Law Times* (3 Feb. 1866), 203.

[73] In 1857 some private soldiers were court martialled (but then acquitted) for having shot prisoners without orders. *The Times* (2 Dec. 1857), 8. Captain William Hodson was criticized (posthumously) in some quarters for having executed two captured Mogul princes with his revolver at Delhi in 1858. *The Times* (22 Jan. 1858), 7; David, *Indian Mutiny*, 305–6.

[74] The widespread use of martial law in India is imprecisely discussed in *The Times* (6 Feb. 1868), 8.

[75] The legal basis of the suppression is discussed in Simpson, *End of Empire*, 77–8.

[76] Joseph Minattur, *Martial Law in India, Pakistan and Ceylon* (The Hague, 1962), 17. For copies of the actual proclamations of martial law, see Charles Ball, *The History of the Indian Mutiny* (New York, *c*.1860), 129–38.

their duty to respect the strictures of military law. Canning plainly rejected the proposition, no doubt widely held by the military in the field, that when putting down a native revolt British officers wielded absolute power over lives and property. As matters stood at the outset of the Jamaica affair eight years later, it remained an open question whether Canning, or his military officers, had got it right about martial law.

It is striking about the Jamaica affair of 1865 that the law of martial law was so quickly and decisively thrust to the centre of the controversy. This turn of events caught many prominent government and military officials unprepared. The behaviour of Cardwell, the Liberal government's frontline minister in the Jamaica affair, is instructive in this regard. As we have seen, by mid-December 1865 Cardwell knew that the Government had to take a position on the Jamaica suppression, but that there was no plausible way for this to be done without also taking a position on the legality of Jamaica's martial law. More concretely, he knew that the Government had to take a position on the fate of Edward Eyre, but could not do so without also taking a position on the legality of his decisions.

In 1866, Cardwell, a highly able and experienced British statesman, did not make any important decisions about the Jamaica affair until he had consulted the law officers of the Crown. We have seen in this context that law officers (the Attorney General Roundell Palmer with the Solicitor General Robert Collier) initially had trouble finding their stride on the law of martial law.[77] Ultimately, however, they took a sharply defined position on most of the key questions.

Palmer and Collier were of the opinion, for instance, that the Petition of Right did not expunge the Crown's prerogative to proclaim martial law over a British territory faced with armed invasion or insurrection.[78] They further opined that in these circumstances the term 'martial law' connoted 'arbitrary military power, in accordance with the methods and usages of armies in the field'. But on the question of whether the same martial powers extended to soldiers and civilians captured or detained by the military, the law officers were less sure of themselves. On one hand they thought that the officers who (while under orders) subjected detainees to trial and punishment 'would not be civilly or criminally responsible for doing so'. On the other hand, they also thought that this privilege must be subject to some legal limits. In the end, Palmer and Collier aligned themselves with those commentators who contended that martial law did not provide comprehensive legal immunity to those who proclaimed and implemented it, even when supported by a statute of indemnity. While the indemnity would apply to any person who had acted reasonably and in good faith,[79] it would not extend to actions taken from 'an excess of orders, from malice or passion, or the putting to death of a person without trial, unless in self defence or in circumstances of

[77] For discussion of their memos on the subject, see above, Ch. 2.
[78] Palmer and Collier to Colonial Office, 24 Jan. 1866, *CO* 885/11.
[79] Ibid. See also, Palmer and Collier to Colonial Office, 1 Feb. 1866, *CO* 885/11.

imminent danger'.[80] And, while a subaltern might be legally excused for the summary execution of a person while under direct orders, the liability for a civilian governor was a different matter. On this reasoning, in fact, Palmer and Collier informed Cardwell that they were 'apprehensive that the governor [specifically, Edward Eyre] may be liable for an indictment for murder'.[81]

II. Contesting the Law of Martial Law: November 1865–June 1866

In late November 1865, when the Jamaica controversy was barely two weeks old, almost nothing about what had happened in the colony was known accurately. It was apparent only that there had been an uprising at Morant Bay and in the surrounding hill country, that some score of white men had died at the hands of black men, and that during the subsequent suppression as many as two thousand black peasants had died at the hands of government forces operating under martial law. It was also apparent that George Gordon, the colony's leading opposition politician, had been arrested in a civilian jurisdiction before being tried and executed by a military court martial.

But the paucity of complete or reliable information about what had happened in Jamaica did not deter lawyers (and not a few laymen) from making pronouncements on the legal niceties of the Jamaica affair. The law of martial law – its nature, scope, and status under the English constitution – suddenly was in prominence in the *political* press. This is an important point: the intense discussion of the law of martial law stimulated by the Jamaica affair did not take place only among lawyers. The burgeoning literature on martial law was often commissioned by or reprinted in the general political press.[82] The active assumption among political writers, editors, and publishers was that the law of martial law was of central importance to the entire community of English readers. It was assumed that the educated lay public wanted to know about the technical legal dimensions of the Jamaica affair, and that this information was essential to a complete understanding of the story. In this way and for these reasons legal and political journalism began to interface and overlap in the Jamaica reports until they became virtually indistinguishable.

The proliferation of technical legal literature on martial law did not lead inexorably to clarification of its subject-matter. By January 1866 it was painfully obvious that lawyers, even those without ostensible connections to the Jamaica

---

[80] Palmer and Collier to Colonial Office, 8 June 1866, *CO* 885/11.   [81] Ibid.

[82] For example, the *Daily News* (16 Dec. 1865), 3, reprinted a long essay on martial law previously published in the *Solicitors' Journal* (16 Dec. 1865), 140–1, and a shorter piece from the same journal on 6 Jan. 1866, 6. See also the opinion of William Willis, barrister, reprinted in the *Daily News* (3 Jan. 1866), 3. A long piece on martial law printed in the *Jurist* in April 1866 was reprinted in Jamaica's *Colonial Standard* (10 May 1866), 2.

Committee or its detractors, did not agree about the nature and content of martial law. The law of martial law quickly descended into a deep morass of theses and counter-theses, each one supported by a reported case or eminent authority. The law of martial law was unclear, and the lawyers who described it began to look like opportunistic politicians.

The *Manchester Guardian* was among many English newspapers to publish extensive, highly technical, and contentious commentary on the law of martial law in December 1865. On 7 December the newspaper published a fragment of a letter (with the contents of which the editors evidently agreed) in which the author claimed that a proclamation of 'martial law' was a legal nullity in the sense that it did not convey any special legal powers or immunities, and by itself was 'no protection against illegal acts'.[83] What martial law boiled down to was this: a pledge by the Government that it would 'do its best to obtain from the Legislature, at a future time, an indemnity for the illegal acts so done'. On this principle, the *Guardian* maintained, it was not necessary to argue about the alleged irregularities of this arrest or that court martial. More particularly, it was of no moment whether Gordon was hanged 'in a district where martial law had not been proclaimed as in one where it had'. What mattered was whether the relevant legislators would be 'satisfied, on reasonable grounds, that such an act was absolutely essential to the suppression of rebellion and the safety of the colony'. If a majority agreed that they were, the actors would be indemnified by statute. If it did not, they would be vulnerable to criminal prosecution and conviction.

This was a brash and forceful statement about the relative unimportance of legality during public emergency, and it provoked two interesting responses from a man, in all likelihood a lawyer, signing his name as 'G.W.H.'[84] His letters are interesting from two points of view. First, they (his second letter especially) were based on extensive legal research. Second, they struggled mightily, if not altogether successfully, to rescue constitutionalism and the rule of law from the logic of the *Guardian*'s initial piece.

G.W.H.'s first letter began with the Whiggish bromide that martial law had been banished from English law in the seventeenth century.[85] The Petition of Right, and some cursory references (from the constitutional historian Hallam and from Fitzjames Stephen) were offered in order to prove the point. G.W.H. then solemnly observed that any official who committed illegal acts under martial law 'places himself under a very grave responsibility'. He was somewhat less clear, however, about the nature of this grave responsibility. Did he mean that the official who broke the law during a state emergency could (or *should*?) not be indemnified by a legislature? G.W.H. did *not* mean that. He agreed with the indemnification theory of martial law, and with the notion that a legislature could

---

[83] *Manchester Guardian* (7 Dec. 1865), 3.
[84] 'G.W.H.' most probably was George Wirgman Hemming (1821–1905), a barrister, Chancery law reporter, and sometime journalist. Bedwell, *Oxford DNB*, online 33805. I am grateful to Neil Duxbury for this identification.   [85] *Manchester Guardian* (12 Dec. 1865), 5.

indemnify an official even for what ordinarily would be regarded as murder. But G.W.H. took pains to distinguish his position on other grounds. If an official, the Governor of Jamaica, for example, were to hang a suspected rebel in a place where 'martial law had not been proclaimed', that 'would throw aside even the semblance of legality'. He repeated that 'the proclamation of martial law affords alone a shadow of legality to proceedings taken in pursuance of it'. Put more concretely, the transfer of a man from a civilian jurisdiction to another place for trial by court martial 'is a gross violation of the laws and liberties which our ancestors struggled for centuries to obtain and preserve'.

These were fine platitudes, but they did not amount to an argument that the perpetrators of such 'gross violations' could not be indemnified by statute. G.W.H. had not made himself clear on this and other important points. Perhaps G.W.H. subsequently received communications about his letters from men who wanted to know more. Perhaps that is why on 25 December 1865 he sent a second letter to the *Guardian*, this one setting out his case with more legal precision. In this correspondence, G.W.H. referred to three different reported cases, Tytler's legal dictionary, and to a number of provisions in the Mutiny Act. He cited these materials to inform readers of the important difference between 'military' and 'martial' law. Military law applied to uniformed soldiers and consisted mainly of the provisions of the Mutiny Act. Martial law was much less palpable. It was the name given to the law that was 'supposed to exist' when, in response to armed invasion or rebellion, civilian law is supplanted by 'military tyranny'. In G.W.H.'s opinion, but one that was not clearly pinned down by authority, the vacuum created by the suspension of civilian law was filled automatically by military law. It was the legal duty of commanders to ensure that the strictures of military law were 'as nearly followed and adhered to as possible'. If, as appeared to have been the case in Jamaica, some officers failed to follow military law, they were not entitled to the indemnity of the legislature.

The letters of G.W.H. were seen as interesting enough from a legal standpoint that they were soon noticed and discussed in the *Solicitors' Journal*.[86] Their author was credited for bringing some technical accuracy to the public discussion of martial law.[87] The editor of the *Journal*, as we have seen, had taken a strong interest in the Jamaica affair from the time the story broke in England in early November 1865. For reasons that will stand close investigation at the conclusion of this chapter, the editor of the *Solicitors' Journal*, like so many of his contemporaries, was adamant that the question of the legal status of martial law, long dormant, was once again of vital importance to English law and politics. '[W]e are sincerely desirous,' the editor wrote on 6 January 1866, 'that the question should not be permitted to slumber until we have it authoritatively and unmistakably pronounced that no military court whatever . . . has any jurisdiction

[86] *Solicitors' Journal* (6 Jan. 1866), 198.
[87] Although G.W.H. feared that his meaning had been misconstrued by the editor. See his letter to the *Solicitors' Journal* (13 Jan. 1866), 232–3.

to try a British subject . . . without an express Act of the Legislature.' This point of constitutional law, the editor continued, 'is of more importance . . . than all the other issues involved in this question put together'. Clearly, then, Mill and the Jamaica Committee were not alone in holding this opinion.

From the outset the *Solicitors' Journal* was extremely interested in the Jamaica affair, and for some months after the story broke in England it published a series of forthright opinions about its legal implications. We have already noted that the first intercession of the *Solicitors' Journal* in the affair was an editorial published on 25 November 1865. But it was not previously mentioned that the editorial was prompted by a disagreement of two London newspapers, the *Evening Standard* and the *Daily News*, on the legal implications of the suppression. The *Standard* had defended the position that the steps taken to suppress the Morant Bay rebellion, including the arrest, transfer, trial, and execution of Gordon, had been necessary to the restoration of public order, and *ipso facto*, were lawful. The *Daily News*, we have seen, was one of the early proponents of the view that Gordon's execution was 'wilful murder'.

It was the opinion of the *Solicitors' Journal* that the *Daily News* had got it right: 'the act of putting Mr. Gordon to death was as much a murder . . . as it would be if Brigadier Nelson were to be seized in the streets of London and tried by a jury of Baptist ministers at Exeter Hall'.[88] The legal reasons for this conclusion were plain. Gordon was a civilian who had surrendered himself to the authorities in a civilian jurisdiction. The only basis under which the military court might have established jurisdiction over Gordon was if he had been engaged in 'armed resistance to the authorities in a proclaimed district'. In absence of jurisdiction, the military tribunal that tried him was no more than a 'mere voluntary association of private individuals', and its verdict had no legal validity. If charged with Gordon's murder the officers of the court martial could plead the defence of necessity, but with not much hope of success. Gordon had not engaged in 'actual warfare' against the colonial government. These were speculations about the law and its possible application to the Gordon case. But the *Journal* offered another more conspicuously political observation: 'there is not, we hope and believe, any division of opinion, at least among lawyers, that the execution of political prisoners by military courts is an evil of a greater magnitude than the rebellion itself'.

This observation was reinforced on 9 December 1865, when the *Solicitors' Journal* printed an item on martial law previously published in the *Morning Star* (the newspaper so closely connected with John Bright and other leaders of the Jamaica Committee). In a brief preface to the article, the editors candidly admitted that they had decided to reprint the piece because it 'enters with such care and research into the authorities which establish the proposition of law laid down by this Journal lately in Mr. Gordon's case'.[89] Written under the pseudonym 'Juridicus', the article began by referring to the late legal proceedings in Jamaica as a 'hideous

---

[88] *Solicitors' Journal* (25 Nov. 1866).   [89] Ibid. (9 Dec. 1865), 109.

travestie' (*sic*). The author then attempted to demonstrate that martial law, if indeed it was law at all, was 'only admissible in time of actual war, and when all the ordinary courts are closed'. His thesis was substantiated by standard quotes from (in this order) Blackstone, Hawkins (a treatise writer), Coke, and Hale. On this authority he restated his opinion that it was flatly illegal to apply martial law against civilians when the civil courts were open.

The decision of the *Solicitors' Journal* to run the 'Juridicus' piece is noteworthy because it originated in one of the most polemical of the general newspapers, and because at least one 'old subscriber' complained loudly in a letter to the editor that the 'Juridicus' piece was 'of a partisan character', and that the *Solicitors' Journal* had altogether prejudged 'the Jamaica question'.[90] It is also significant, however, because of the stridently political response to the complaint by the editor of the *Journal*. The 'limit of civil authority in times of civil disturbance,' he insisted, was 'one of the gravest constitutional questions which could arise in the present day'. The Gordon case raised the issue 'in distinct form', and therefore deserved 'so prominent a place' in the columns of the paper. It was further explained that before the 'Juridicus' letter was published, all references to the Gordon case had been excised. The editor denied having prejudged whether the persons who orchestrated the execution of Gordon could justify their actions, but restated his view that 'the judicial murder of a British subject, however justly he may have merited his fate, is of graver import than the horrors of the Indian mutiny itself'. The latter was the feckless action of a mob; the former is the 'inroad of the executive power upon the province of the law'. The editor ventured even a step further: 'there is now, we believe, a party in England which holds the Crown to be above the law, but if there be, we are politically opposed to that party.'

These statements might have been quotes from the manifesto of the Jamaica Committee (still being formulated when the editor wrote them). Here was the same insistence that the Jamaica affair was important mainly because of its implications for domestic politics. Here was the same insistence that the abuse of martial law in Jamaica, and the stubborn unwillingness of some political men to admit that it was illegal, posed a grave threat to English constitutional tenets and traditions. Here also was the foundation of the idea that Governor Eyre had to be prosecuted for murder in order to cause a high court judge to vindicate these principles.

The kinship between the *Solicitors' Journal* and the Jamaica Committee was further evidenced when another long article on martial law, one created and published by the *Journal* on 16 December 1865, was published (under the heading, 'From the *Solicitors' Journal*') in the *Daily News* on the very same day.[91] The central objective of the article was to examine whether 'in a British colony where the common law of England prevails, it is competent for the representative of the Queen ... to abrogate the common law of England'. The answer to this

---

[90] Ibid. (16 Dec. 1865), 146.   [91] Ibid. (16 Dec. 1865), 140.

question was seen to turn on the definition of the term 'martial law'. When the term was being used to describe the code of military procedure governing soldiers, martial law could be sensibly understood as a formal body of positive law. When the term was applied to the actions of armies in aid of the civil power, it was also possible to speak of law. The officers and soldiers of the Crown were fully accountable for their actions 'to the regular tribunals of the country'. However, when the term was being used to describe the suppression of 'actual warfare or riot', martial law was, as Wellington had stated, 'no law at all, but the expression of the will of the military commander'. The pertinent question then was, were there any limits on the commander's will when actual warfare or riot had ceased? The article argued strenuously that there were. It was observed that even Wellington's dictum was misleading because the dictates of 'humanity' imposed limits on conduct 'even in the most savage warfare'. (Commanders could face prosecution under military or civilian law if they, for instance, murdered in cold blood prisoners who had been disarmed.) But the law of open warfare, while it afforded great leeway to officers in the field, was not relevant to the allegations that had been made against Eyre and some military officers in Jamaica. In the great majority of those instances, prisoners had been subjected to summary punishments by courts martial, and armed resistance either had ceased or, in Gordon's case, had never occurred. What manner of 'martial law' applied to these men, and was it complied with?

In the opinion of the author, neither the military codes nor the martial law of 'open warfare' had any bearing on what had happened in the military camps set up in Jamaica in the relevant weeks of October 1865. The only species of martial law that was relevant was that which governed an army of occupation, in this instance, the 'laws of England and the customs of war'.[92] In fixing the standard of conduct it was relevant to observe that the Jamaican prisoners were not enemy aliens, but 'a population of natural born British subjects, speaking our language and brought up under our laws'. In these circumstances the officers bore a heavy onus to demonstrate that they had conducted themselves humanely and out of necessity. While the author did not want to evaluate the 'merits of the case', he ended his essay with a discussion of the trial, in 1802, of the former military governor Joseph Wall on charges that he had had a soldier flogged to death in 1782. Wall maintained that the flogging was absolutely necessary in order to maintain discipline within a dangerous outpost of the empire. The defence was rejected, and soon thereafter Wall was hanged at Newgate.

As for the editor of the *Solicitors' Journal*, it was obvious that he was inclined to believe that there was a body of law, 'martial law,' governing civilian and military officials even when there was a great emergency of state. It was also clear that the editor was inclined to believe both that Governor Eyre and his officers had broken this law, and that their transgressions, if left uncorrected, indicated a

---

[92] *Solicitors' Journal*, 141.

significant threat to English laws and liberties. Nonetheless, the editor stopped far short of calling for the criminal prosecution of Eyre or the officer who oversaw the execution of Gordon. At the same time, the *Journal* contended that the 'integrity of the law will not have been vindicated so long as either of the one or the other continues to hold her Majesty's commission'. This note of caution notwithstanding, there was no mistaking the stance of the *Solicitors' Journal* as detached or neutral. The prestige and professional expertise of the paper, whatever they amounted to, had plainly been committed to a position on the legal aspects of the Jamaica affair not unlike the one that was being evolved by the Jamaica Committee.[93] The editor of the *Law Times*, the main rival of the *Solicitors' Journal* in the world of English legal newspapers, assumed a much different posture.

In its first editorial on Jamaica, published on 2 December 1865, the *Law Times* affirmed that the 'summary execution of Mr. Gordon without legal trial, appears, upon the face of the despatches, to be wholly illegal'. It agreed, moreover, that what appeared to have happened in Jamaica had profoundly important legal ramifications, and that some officials, Governor Eyre particularly, would need to offer legal justification for their acts. The *Law Times* also conceded that in orchestrating the death of Gordon, Eyre and other officials might have 'been guilty of a grave crime'. However, unlike his counterpart at the *Solicitors' Journal*, the editor was far more inclined to emphasize that there were circumstances 'when necessity overrules all law'. If, for instance, the Governor was able to demonstrate that when he acted against Gordon the safety of the colony faced 'not a merely dubious alarm but a real and imminent danger', then he 'will be enabled amply to justify the execution'. Everything would turn on the proved facts about what Eyre knew at the relevant time, and the honesty and reasonableness of his response to the information. Unlike the rival publication, the *Law Times* was determined to 'suspend even an opinion until his defence is fully heard, and we ask lawyers, who must acknowledge the illegality of the act *per se*, to do the like'. Because of the centrality of its assertion that otherwise illegal acts might be privileged by a common law defence, we might call this the 'defence of necessity' theory of martial law.

The *Law Times* did not press this theory, or any other one about martial law, very hard in its pages during the final weeks of 1865. Even as the debate about the Jamaica affair and its legal ramifications raged in the larger community, the *Law Times* all but ignored the story. On 30 December it made a point of congratulating the Government for its appointment of Russell Gurney as a Commissioner of the Jamaica Royal Commission.[94] The occasion was seized also to make some remarks in support of Eyre. It was suggested that were Palmerston still alive he would have done far more to protect a senior civil servant from unfair criticism and ridicule. Palmerston, it was suggested, would have assumed that his Governor had done no more than was necessary to suppress a revolt until it was

---

[93] I have not been able to discover who was the editor of the *Solicitors' Journal*, or whether he was directly connected to the Jamaica Committee.   [94] *Law Times* (30 Dec. 1865), 113.

unequivocally proved otherwise. In the meantime he would also have seen that a man like Eyre, who faced attack from the lawyers in a well-organized cabal, was supplied with his own lawyer at the Government's expense. This was the least that could be done for a man who, had he not acted with alacrity, firmness, and decision, might now be in the dock for having failed to do enough to prevent a massacre of the colony's white population.

The *Law Times* offered some solace to the pro-Eyre camp, but more timidly and sparingly than the *Solicitors' Journal*'s interventions on the other side. It is also interesting that the *Law Times*, while it offered some encouragement to Eyre, did not offer any technical explanation for why he had not committed crimes in Jamaica. This was in stark contrast with the *Solicitors' Journal*, and the omission implied much greater ambivalence, possibly unease, about the role of law in colonial suppressions. It also reflected the deepening divisions within the English legal community about the Jamaica affair.

In January 1866, as the Royal Commissioners commenced their investigation in Jamaica, the public discussion of the law of martial law became more multilateral, intricate, and intense. Now it was the turn for the organ of Exeter Hall, the *Freeman*, to weigh into the debate. In an article called 'Authority of the Executive to Proclaim Martial Law', a barrister called William Willis put forward his own views on the subject. (The article was immediately reprinted in the *Daily News*.)[95] Willis began by setting forth some first principles. The first was that the putting to death of any individual in the British Empire was presumptively illegal until it was 'justified by the principles of *English law*'. His second principle was that 'the burden of showing all the circumstances which justify or excuse the killing devolves upon him who has taken life'. Governor Eyre and his subordinates, therefore, had either to privilege their conduct by some defence of law 'or they stand guilty of wilful murder'. Willis acknowledged that those Jamaicans killed in the course of open resistance (he assumed that there were some) had been 'lawfully sacrificed'. He also thought it uncontroversial that those who (reports indicated) had been captured only to be executed without any trial were murdered. The more debatable issue was the legal status of the executions ordered after trials by courts martial. This was a question that would turn on an exacting look at the legal history of martial tribunals from medieval times to the slave revolt in Demerara in 1823–4.

According to Willis's reading of these sources, the jurisdiction of a military tribunal over civilians began and ended with 'exigency, and the moment that exigency has ceased'. Whenever circumstances permitted civilian courts to operate safely, military courts, these 'rude substitutes' and 'anomalous tribunals', ceased to have authority to try prisoners. For Willis, this was the crucial point, one he buttressed with a quotation from Mackintosh's parliamentary speech in the 1824 controversy over the fate of the missionary Smith: 'As soon as the laws can

---

[95] *Daily News* (3 Jan. 1866), 3.

act, every other mode of punishing supposed crime is itself an enormous crime.'
Looking at the facts of the Jamaica suppression, Willis concluded, 'Governor Eyre
and his subordinates were guilty of murder'. Their only hope of avoiding conviction, a slim one, was to prove either that their victims were killed by reason of
pressing public necessity or that the law of Jamaica gave them some extraordinary
authority superseding the law of England. Willis guessed that no such defences
would be forthcoming.

For most of his long article, Willis maintained the tone and posture of a man
professionally disinterested in the ramifications of his analysis. In the final passages, the pretence was dropped. Much like the editor of the *Solicitors' Journal* and
the leaders of the Jamaica Committee, Willis was alarmed by the grim implications of Jamaica for domestic political traditions. Readers were warned that if left
unpunished, the deeds of Governor Eyre would 'establish a precedent that the
executive might on its own allegation of public danger take the lives of subjects
at its will and pleasure'. They were urged (the essay was written for Christian
evangelicals, after all) to become 'supplicants for justice'. This was essential both
to the vindication of ancient liberties and as a means of honouring Gordon the
'martyr', whose last moments were 'an expression of a virtuous life'.

Until the end of December 1865, most commentators on the law of martial
law, even the stodgy *Law Times*, had doubted the legality of much that had
happened in Jamaica. Then the debate took a decidedly different turn. On
6 January 1866, England's third legal trade paper, the *Jurist*, published the first of
a series of long articles on the subject. The initial piece, 'Martial Law in Jamaica',[96]
was not only much longer and more deeply researched than anything previously
published in England on the subject, it broke ranks with the other legal journals in
its conclusions.

The writer for the *Jurist* tenaciously defended a very clearly defined position on
the law of martial law: that in times of civil insurrection or invasion, English law
always had recognized that 'the Crown has the authority to proclaim martial law
by virtue of its prerogative to declare a state of war, and that the ordinary law of the
realm is for a time suspended'. The truth of this proposition, the writer observed,
had been obscured by the fact that 'for ages' the British 'had not known any
instance of martial law'. The problem now cropped up principally in the context
of the new empire. The Jamaica affair, however, presented an opportunity for legal
scholars to correct the 'errors' about the law of martial law which were apparent 'in
our recent text-books'.

To make these corrections, the author scoured the legal authorities. His
research produced yet another lumpy amalgam of potted history, selective quotation, and case analysis. From Bracton he gleaned the proposition that there were
numerous instances in which 'common law procedure' did not apply. Martial law
was one such instance. For the first time in one of these essays Hale (and

---

[96] *Jurist* (6 Jan. 1866), 507–11.

Blackstone quoting Hale), instead of being cited for their condemnation of martial law, were cited to prove that it was 'an entire error' to state that Magna Carta and the Petition of Right had laid down complete prohibitions of martial law. The prohibition was that martial law 'ought not to be permitted *in time of peace*'.[97] But when war or rebellion caused, in the words of Hale, a 'distemper of the State', martial law was indulged in as a 'temporary excrescence', an expedient imposed on men by the force of circumstance. When the military commander acted within a state of war, the 'most stringent, stern, and summary measures of repression' might be justified. But the writer used the word *might* advisedly. He agreed that even when martial law was lawfully proclaimed in the face of emergency, the English common law did not tolerate a legal vacuum. The void was instantly filled by the 'rules of natural justice'. Martial law, then, was 'no more or less than the application of the rules of natural justice to a state of war lawfully proclaimed'. Any person who exercised power under martial law was 'responsible' to Parliament and the courts for any 'excess or error', if on a stern test of criminal culpability. In order to find a man guilty of having abused the powers of martial law, it would have to be demonstrated that no person put in the same circumstances could have 'reasonably or honestly supposed' that the impugned measures were necessary.

Having set forth his legal propositions, the author of the *Jurist* piece commenced to apply them to the (supposed) facts of the Jamaica affair. Here the analysis is oddly unsystematic. It is mainly concerned with the arrest and transportation of Gordon, but, in a piecemeal way, also addresses the legality of the proclamation of martial law, and the executions which followed it. Starting with Gordon's arrest, a subject not carefully analysed by previous commentators, the author contended that since it was a long-standing principle of criminal law that 'crime is local', that an alleged criminal act should be prosecuted in the place of its occurrence, it had been perfectly proper for Gordon to be removed from Kingston to St. Thomas-in-the-East, the parish in which he was alleged to have committed the crimes of treason and sedition. The question then was whether it had been reasonable to proclaim martial law in that parish. The author concluded that there was a strong *prima facie* case that it had been. The black peasants of the parish had murdered officials of state. The Governor's privy councillors had agreed unanimously that the white population of the colony was in grave danger of extermination. Eyre's decision to sign the proclamation was therefore an honest and reasonable one. This left the question of Gordon's execution. *If* (and the author hedged on this point) it were the case that a man accused of treason or sedition was convicted after a 'fair and honest trial', that man might be 'lawfully executed' by a court martial in the field.

His factual information being so imperfect, the author did not dwell on these questions. Nor did he venture to analyse the legality, or otherwise, of the scores of

---

[97] *Jurist* (6 Jan. 1866), 507–11.

other executions, floggings, and burnings that had allegedly taken place in the four weeks after martial law was declared. Instead the author was content to focus on the issues raised by Gordon's arrest and execution. This was the real subject of interest. The author cited a long list of cases that purported to establish that it had been altogether legal to transport Gordon to Morant Bay, just as it had been completely lawful for the court martial to convict him of complicity in the massacre 'although he was not actually present'.[98] This section led to the author's final conclusion. *If* it was reasonable to have proclaimed martial law in St. Thomas-in-the-East, and *if* Gordon's trial was fair, the execution by court martial also was 'perfectly legal'.

The implications of the essay on martial law published by the *Jurist* were read with a skeptical eye by one 'E.M.S.', a letter writer to the *Daily News*.[99] If the *Jurist* was correct, the proclamation of martial law even in a small district 'is virtually the establishment of martial law over the whole district'. The Crown would be entitled to exert the 'terrible powers' of martial law against any person in any section of a colony simply by alleging that they were complicit with rebellious activities in the section under martial law. Although E.M.S. admitted that he was 'no lawyer', he wondered how the 'most pedantic' of legal experts could countenance such a principle. The writer worried that the new and expansive doctrine of martial law in currency reflected an ominous trend. In order to preserve the power and prosperity of the empire, he believed, Englishmen had become 'more and more ready to wink at high-handed authority, even though it hangs, shoots and flogs those who would disturb our business'.

The same anxieties, of course, had been very sharp spurs to the formation of the Jamaica Committee. We have previously noted that its founding members had resolved to obtain an opinion on the legal aspects of the Jamaica affair before the Committee had been officially inaugurated. James and Stephen had been retained to undertake the work during the third week of December 1865.[100] Their finished memorandum was in the hands of the Committee's executive by month's end and, after it was read and discussed internally, it was given to all the major newspapers on 13 January 1866.[101] There is an unmistakable haste in all this, and the reason for it is obvious. The public discourse on the legal dimensions of the Jamaica affair had unfolded rapidly and unpredictably. The Committee did not want to waste a minute before placing its stamp on this pivotal aspect of the debate.

As we have seen, it was not by accident that James and Stephen were selected by the Jamaica Committee. In James the Committee had got one of England's most venerable legal practitioners. In Stephen they had got one of England's most knowledgeable criminal lawyers and legal minds.[102] Neither man, it is worth

[98] Ibid., 511.   [99] *Daily News* (16 Jan. 1866), 6.
[100] *JC Minutes*, 21 Dec. 1865.
[101] See, for instance, in *The Times* (16 Jan. 1866), 3. The opinion was published without editorial comment.
[102] Even Finlason, a critic of Stephen's opinion on martial law, said of Stephen that he was 'the fittest exponent of the views of the prosecutors ... [He possesses] a Johnsonian vigour of intellect, a mind well trained and cultivated by scholarship, enriched by extensive reading, and

noting, was an actual member of the Committee. James's personal and political connections to the leading members of the Committee were actually quite tenuous. If he accepted the Jamaica brief for any other reason save that it was interesting (and paid) work, nothing in his biography suggests it. With Stephen it is wholly a different matter. He was an intimate both of the religious and secular wings of the Committee. Stephen was a Christian intellectual who knew the personalities and ideas of philosophic radicalism. With his friend Mill and many of the other leaders of the Jamaica alliance, Stephen believed passionately that the accountability of the powerful to law was the main hallmark of a civilized community. For an intellectual lawyer like Stephen – a man steeped in the works of Hobbes, Bentham, and Austin – the Jamaica brief was a plum assignment. Here was that rare instance when professional opportunity and philosophical convictions beautifully coincided.

From beginning to end the business of acquiring a legal opinion on the Jamaica affair was a thinly camouflaged political project. To be sure, the Jamaica Committee needed legal information. But they needed information that met two particular specifications. First, the information had to support its widely advertised view of the Jamaica affair (that Eyre had committed murder, etc.). Second, the information had to be supplied by lawyers who were not hopelessly compromised as partisan hacks. Stephen and James were chosen because they could be relied upon to deliver the 'correct' view of the law that would also have a patina of objectivity. In other words, the two eminent barristers could be relied upon to deliver a document that might influence public opinion in favour of the Committee's agenda. For an association that from its inception had portrayed the Jamaica affair as essentially a legal and constitutional crisis, this was an ideal way of making and disseminating potent propaganda.

Even the set of instructions sent by the Committee to Stephen and James was contrived also as a political statement (later to be published with the opinion). The document was styled, 'Case Submitted by the Jamaica Committee', and it began with the following statement: 'the committee desires to be advised what steps are open to them to assist their fellow subjects in Jamaica to obtain the protection of the law; and if the law has been broken, to bring the guilty parties to justice; and also what steps are open to them as Englishmen to vindicate constitutional law and order.' The lawyers were sent a sheaf of official documents and despatches relating to the Jamaica affair, and then were asked a set of seven interlocking questions. As much as possible the Committee endeavoured to maintain the appearance of distance between themselves and the lawyers engaged to answer their queries. What was denoted by the term 'martial law'? Were there reasons to believe that Governor Eyre had 'acted illegally and criminally' in the way in which he implemented martial law, particularly with regard to Gordon?

exercised by literary labours, together with no ordinary forensic power'. Finlason, *History of the Jamaica Case*, 374.

Gordon had been punished for alleged actions taken prior to martial law, and for some acts committed outside the proclaimed district. Had this been legal? Are officers who acted under martial law immune from prosecution? If they are not, how are they to be brought to justice? Can a private person institute legal proceedings against them? What would be the effect on liability of a bill of indemnity passed by the Jamaica legislature?

As for the written opinion itself, widely published in the English press after 13 January 1866, it too was framed to suggest that its authors had been routinely engaged to supply objective advice on points of law. The conventions of legal memoranda were strictly obeyed. The opinion was rendered under a formalized heading: 'Case: *Ex parte* The Jamaica Committee'. It was thus made plain that the authors had not asked these questions of their own accord. (In fact, they had been approached in the customary manner by Shaen, the Committee's solicitor.)[103] In preparing the opinion, the two lawyers meant to suggest that they had merely fulfilled a professional obligation like any other.

The opinion addressed the Jamaica Committee's inquiries consecutively.[104] Several pages were devoted to the initial question concerning the legal definition of the term 'martial law'. The lawyers noted that the term had 'been used in different times in four different senses'.[105] The first three were quickly dispensed with. In the medieval period the term referred to the authority 'exercised by the Constable and Marshal over troops in actual service'. This type of martial law was obsolete. Until the seventeenth century, various monarchs purported to give men commissions to employ martial law against civilians during peacetime. These were made illegal by the Petition of Right. The term 'martial law' also was used to describe the military law governing men in the regular military. This task had been subsumed by the Mutiny Acts. In the context of the Jamaica affair, Stephen and James observed, some people had spoken of a fourth meaning of martial law, one which they had 'inaccurately and improperly' conflated with the 'common-law right of the Crown and its representatives to repel force by force in the case of invasion or insurrection'.[106] In this *mistaken* view, martial law 'was not merely the suppression of military revolts by force, which is undoubtedly legal, but the subsequent punishment of offenders by illegal tribunals, which is the practice forbidden by the Petition of Right'.[107]

Stephen and James agreed that the common law gave the Crown very wide discretion in the suppression of actual rebellion. They strenuously disagreed, however, that this discretion had no limits. Commanders in the field, for instance, were not justified 'in the use of excessive or cruel means, but are liable civilly or criminally

---

[103] The normal proprieties in these matters were fully respected. See *JC Minutes*, 21 Dec. 1865.

[104] For a copy of the complete opinion, see *Facts and Documents Relating to the Alleged Rebellion in Jamaica, Jamaica Papers No. I* (London, 1866), 68–80. [105] Ibid., 72–3.

[106] Ibid.

[107] Ibid., 72. Stephen and James substantiated their claim by reference to specific passages of the Petition of Right, and by citing (without quotation) Hale's *History of the Common Law*.

for such excess'.[108] Secondly, the authority to do what was necessary to suppress rebels did not extend to the punishment of rebel prisoners: 'as soon ... as the actual conflict was at an end it would be the duty of military authorities to hand over prisoners to the civil powers'.[109] As for courts martial set up under martial law, these were not courts at all, but 'mere committees, formed for the purpose of carrying into execution the discretionary power assumed by the Government'. While members of such tribunals might be justified in doing 'whatever is necessary to suppress insurrection and restore peace and the authority of the law. They are personally liable for any acts which they may commit in excess of that power.'[110]

Stephen and James then turned to the Jamaican legislation 'under which Governor Eyre appears to have acted'.[111] Had the local statute conferred on him some extraordinary legal power? Their opinion was that it had not: 'The powers of the Jamaica legislature are derived not from Parliament, but from Royal Commission. As the Crown cannot authorize legislation inconsistent with the law of England, it could not authorize the Jamaica Legislature ... powers inconsistent with the Petition of Right.' Indeed, Jamaica's martial legislation, far from creating any new power, 'only limits the existing [common law] power, and provides regulations under which it is to be exercised'.[112] A similarly narrow view was offered on the subject of a Jamaican indemnity statute: 'It is not competent to the Legislature of Jamaica', the barristers concluded, 'to pardon crimes committed against the laws of England.'[113]

These propositions were grounded in a number of implicit (and contestable) assumptions.[114] On this reading of the law, a colonial governor (or any other executive official of the Crown) laboured under a positive legal duty to protect the King's peace against armed insurrection or invasion. If such a contingency arose, as perhaps it had done in Jamaica, the executive had no choice but to answer force with force. But for Stephen and James, the matter did not end there. The mere fact that an executive official did his duty did not by definition mean that he had done it lawfully, or that he enjoyed an immunity having done it unlawfully. Any action taken to suppress insurrection, however violent, was lawful if a reasonable man in the same circumstances would have regarded it as 'immediately and unavoidably necessary for the preservation of peace and restoration of order'.[115] That was the test. Whether an action did or did not pass this test was, when the action was disputed, a question for a trial jury to decide. For Stephen and James, then, the Jamaica affair hinged on a few straightforward issues of fact. On this basis they proceeded to examine the available despatches concerning Gordon's execution.

---

[108] *Facts and Documents Relating to the Alleged Rebellion in Jamaica, Jamaica Papers No. I* (London, 1866), 76.   [109] Ibid., 74.

[110] Ibid., 77.   [111] Ibid.   [112] Ibid., 78.   [113] Ibid., 79.

[114] The opinion assumed that the Petition of Right applied to the colonies, and that it applied when civil order was threatened by armed insurrection. It further assumed that the 'Crown', manifested in the executive prerogative of the Colonial Office, could not validate colonial legislation on martial law, or on any other subject matter, by arranging for the Royal Assent.   [115] Ibid.

Had it been immediately and unavoidably necessary to put him to death? Here the lawyers did not mince words. 'We see nothing whatever in Governor Eyre's despatch which affords any grounds for thinking that such could have been the case.'[116] Gordon was arrested in Kingston, a place (the Governor himself had decided) where there was no need for martial law. While he was in custody, moreover, he was 'disabled from doing further mischief, however guilty he might previously have been'.[117] Given the absence of military necessity, the military officers who tried Gordon 'had no powers at all as a court martial'. When they tried Gordon for a treason committed before the uprising, the military had fatally overstepped their authority. 'Their province', the opinion stated, 'was to suppress force by force, not to punish crime.' The upshot of this was that Gordon's execution, to take but one example, was a homicide for which the Governor (and the military officers involved) might be prosecuted in an English court.

These were bold conclusions, and too little has been said about how Stephen and James arrived at them. The main theme of their opinion was that martial law was a permutation of the common law defence of necessity. The main source of law cited in support was the Petition of Right.[118] Stephen and James use a discussion of the political history of the Petition to substantiate their claim that the statute permitted the suppression of revolt by military force, but not 'the subsequent punishment of offenders by illegal tribunals'.[119] At the conclusion of these passages, the lawyers struck a nice rhetorical pose. They stated of the Petition of Right (bolstered with short quotes from Coke and Hale) that 'these authorities *appear* to show that it is illegal for the Crown to resort to martial law as a special mode of punishing rebellion' (emphasis added). Before they would make a more definitive statement, the authors wanted to 'consider the authorities which look in the other direction'. The opinion then discussed the statutory proclamation of martial law by the Irish parliament in 1799. On its face this legislation seemed to contradict the Petition of Right. In order to dispel this view, the opinion cited the two famous Irish cases that arose from the proclamation (*Wolfe Tone* and *Wright v. Fitzgerald*) together with the testimony of Sir David Dundas before the Ceylon select committee in 1849. On the basis of this rather cursory treatment of the sources, Stephen and James began to pronounce their conclusion that the law of martial law was very limited in its scope, and that Governor Eyre had almost certainly overestimated its powers and immunities.

Stephen and James were eminent lawyers, and their considered opinion on martial law could not be easily dismissed. But neither was it shown any excessive deference. Having published the opinion on 13 January without editorial comment, *The Times* responded obliquely with publication of a legal opinion on martial law that had been prepared in 1859 by the then Judge-Advocate General, Thomas Headlam.[120] In response to questions put to him by the Defence

---

[116] Ibid., 78.   [117] Ibid., 79.
[118] The opinion also makes some token references to Coke and Hale.   [119] Ibid., 72.
[120] *The Times* (17 Jan. 1866), 7.

Commissioners about the legality of martial law in England, Headlam contended that martial law was 'so arbitrary and uncertain that the term law cannot be properly applied to it'. It remained an undoubted prerogative of the Crown to proclaim martial law, and the proclamation served as a kind of notice to inhabitants that the military had been empowered to take whatever measures were necessary for 'the public safety'. Martial law entitled commanders to 'overrule and disregard all private interests and rights'. But Headlam's report did not comment on the possible limits of this power, and more specifically on whether there could be culpability for the molestation or execution of prisoners taken under martial law. If *The Times* published this as answer to Stephen and James, no informed reader could have thought it a satisfactory one.

Critical assessments of a more direct and searching kind did not begin to surface for some weeks after it was published, but then were plentiful. The *Jurist* suddenly became an important forum for such material. On 3 February, the *Jurist* published a long letter on martial law written by 'A Barrister'.[121] The writer professed his 'extreme surprise' that two distinguished lawyers could have ventured the hypothesis that 'the proclamation of martial law in no way extends the power which every man has at common law of resisting . . . felonious violence'. He then advanced the counter-hypothesis that 'when martial law is proclaimed the military commander has an arbitrary discretion in the exercise of force'. This power implied 'far more than the mere resistance of actual present violence'. The writer further claimed that 'Lord Hale and the petition of right distinctly recites that in time of war (and in law rebellion *is* war) men may lose their lives by martial law.' The same authorities that supported the opinion of Stephen and James now were being cited against it.

The crux of the disagreement here was over the applicability of martial justice to persons who, in the larger context of war or armed insurrection, were no longer in open resistance to the government. What actions against civilians or disarmed prisoners, if any, might be legally justified? Stephen and James thought the military was not entitled to inflict summary punishments on such persons. The 'Barrister' disagreed, arguing at length that the military 'might act without magisterial authority, and not merely in the military execution of offenders – in the very act – but of wholesale attack upon the people, and shooting or cutting them down by the hundreds'. His evidence on this point was drawn from the history of the Gordon riots of 1780. In that instance, the military, after much hesitation on the part of civilian authority, was called in to clear the streets of rioters. The Attorney General then authorized an attack on the people. In the subsequent action, scores were killed and 'numbers of innocent persons were destroyed'. This act of suppression, it was conceded, was a 'terrible remedy, and only justifiable by a terrible emergency; but it *was* so justified, and it was, in effect, martial law'. Lord Mansfield himself had stated that these measures were both right and lawful. None of the military officers was indicted. No bill of indemnity was thought necessary to protect them from what was seen as a wholly lawful use of force under *de facto* martial law.

The crucial point of the letter writer was that the 'true scope of martial law' was much wider than supposed by the lawyers for the Jamaica Committee. It included 'not merely the response to actual outrage, but the removal of imminent danger to it, and the restoration of peace and confidence in a season of extreme public peril'. This conclusion was supported by the historian Hallam, who wrote that while martial law was reserved for 'extreme occasions', once in effect, it had 'a distinct and separate force and power, as distinguished from, though recognised by, the common law'. The writer thought that the 'bloody insurrection of a large number of an overwhelming majority, and an apparent imminent peril of the rising of the *whole*, surely would be such an emergency. And the *danger* would last some days after the suppression or cessation of *actual* outrage.' These principles were clearly set forth by the authorities, and the writer expressed his dismay that 'popular appeals and partisan opinions should be published which tend to mislead and distort public feeling on the subject of this terrible remedy for a terrible emergency'. The writer finished his letter with some comments on culpability for acts taken to suppress the Morant Bay rebellion. In his view, Eyre and his subordinates could not be convicted of any criminal offence for the execution of Gordon or other prisoners. His further opinion, one that would ultimately be put to the test, was that 'there was no judge in this country who would not tell a grand jury, that before they found the bill they must have evidence that acts done . . . after a proclamation of martial law were done, not honestly, but maliciously and wickedly'. The upshot was that there was no evidence to support such a claim.

It is worth observing that the *Jurist* letter was written after the English press had published new and fuller accounts of Gordon's trial, and in the wake of widespread criticism of the evidence which sent him to the gallows.[122] But the doctrine of martial law set forth in the *Jurist* was so expansive that this information was of scant importance. If at the time of the execution it was Governor Eyre's honest belief that he faced a state of rebellion, or the imminent relapse into rebellion, and if he had honestly believed that the execution of Gordon was essential to the restoration of order, he was legally entitled to Gordon's life. In the opinion of the letter writer, there could be no liability *ex post facto* for the honest exercise of judgement in a state of war. The contrary assertions of the Jamaica Committee's barristers were based on the fundamental misapprehension that martial law was only another name for the common law right to repel force with force. In fact, martial law was a far more potent doctrine. It was the legal name given to the unlimited authority of officials to preserve the security of the state at any physical cost to rebels or invaders.

---

[122] For further legal criticism of the trial, see letter of G.W.H. in the *Manchester Guardian* (10 Feb. 1866), 2.

In the early spring of 1866, the debate concerning the law of martial law took a more practical turn. In March English readers learned that the Jamaican authorities, abetted by the lawyers of the Jamaica Committee, already had attempted to prosecute Duberry Ramsay for having flogged and hanged a man without trial. Although this first effort did not succeed, it was obvious that the Committee was not thwarted, and that it planned to use the hearings of the Royal Commission to build stronger criminal cases against a large number of military men and civilians. The legal opinion of Stephen and James now had become the basis of a plan of action. When the editor of the *Jurist* learned of these developments, particularly that the Jamaica Committee was using the Royal Commission to 'get up proofs against Governor Eyre and his subordinate officers, upon which the committee may ground criminal proceedings',[123] once again he reached for his pen. In a long article on the Royal Commission published in April 1866, the *Jurist* complained that the Commissioners had used their 'moral compulsion' to cause men to incriminate themselves. In the name of justice the Commission was undermining it.

But the Royal Commission was seen to be making an even more serious mistake. Its entire proceedings, the *Jurist* argued, were based on a mistaken view of martial law. The Commission had correctly understood that under martial law the commander might choose to try and punish prisoners by courts martial. But when the Commission also began to inquire after the 'fairness' of the courts martial, they betrayed a fundamental misunderstanding of the law.[124] When it was rightly proclaimed, the essence of martial law was that it conferred 'an entirely absolute discretion in the military authorities'.[125] Under martial law commanders in the field were not bound by ordinary legal norms of due process or evidence. In fact, they were not bound to hold any trials whatsoever. While the *Jurist* did not go so far as to claim that an officer acting under martial law could never incur civil or criminal liability, it argued for a low threshold of exoneration. To be free and clear, an officer had only to demonstrate that he had had an honest belief in the guilt of condemned prisoners, and in the public necessity of their punishments. If the battlefield decisions of officers were later to be 'subject to review and reversal by persons who require legal evidence,' the *Jurist* reasoned, 'it is obvious that no one would ever sit upon a court martial, and the proclamation of martial law would be nugatory'.

The *Jurist* piece obviously was born of frustration. Too few observers had grasped that martial law was about coping with the extreme cases of war.[126]

---

[123] *Jurist* (7 Apr.1866), 127–34.   [124] Ibid., 128.   [125] Ibid., 129.

[126] The offending view was defended in a pamphlet published in April 1866 by George Young, a barrister at Gray's Inn. Ahead of the final report of the Jamaica Royal Commission, Young was moved to comment on whether Governor Eyre, in proclaiming martial law 'did violate the constitutional law of England'. It was Young's contention that the mere fact that martial law was proclaimed was not illegal *ipso facto*. The reason for this was plain: the elaborate legal protections enjoyed by British subjects prevailed only when there was peace. 'In a time of war and violence...,' he wrote, 'all these charters of public liberty, all these constitutional powers are necessarily suspended.' The single duty of the Crown in such circumstances is to restore order 'by all hazards and by all means'. A proclamation

In such urgent circumstances, when the very existence of the state and its citizens was in doubt, it was essential that officers of the state might 'strik[e] terror by some terrible examples'. And, in the wake of such examples, only two questions were pertinent: Did the authorities have an honest and reasonable belief in the existence of war or rebellion? Did the officers implementing martial law have an honest and reasonable belief both in the guilt of prisoners, and in the temporal necessity of their punishment?

Towards the end of June 1866, the Liberal government released the final report of the Royal Commission. The report concluded that the decision to proclaim martial law in St. Thomas-in-the-East had been both legal and justifiable.[127] The *Jurist* responded with a long and self-congratulatory article on how it had espoused 'the right view of the law on the subject'. But while the editor undoubtedly was correct that the Commissioners had (at least implicitly) acknowledged the legality of martial law for some purposes, he then pressed a number of much bolder and more dubious claims. The Commissioners were said to have 'followed out the law in impliedly holding all the executions [including the execution of Gordon], either on summary execution or by court martial, also [were] perfectly legal'.[128] While the *Jurist* conceded that the Commissioners did not explicitly *state* that these executions were legal, this was the logical implication of their other findings. For instance, when it commenced to examine the quality of justice meted out by the courts martial, the Commission implicitly endorsed their legality. And while the Commission thought that some of the trials were defective, and the number of executions excessive, it did not 'intimate that any of them were illegal'.[129]

In the view of the *Jurist*, the Royal Commission had got the law of martial law right, but the application of the law wrong. The criticisms of the Commission, the *Jurist* contended, 'were conceived in a spirit too strict, narrow, and technical'.[130] In evaluating the trial of Gordon and others, they imposed the standards of 'regular criminal procedure' on proceedings which, by their very nature, were highly irregular and expedient. In the context of martial law, the sole obligation of officers presiding over courts martial was to do 'substantial justice' to the best of their abilities. It was not to be forgotten, moreover, that the purpose of the courts martial was not only to punish but to deter. If insurrection was to be prevented or quelled, it was critical that commanders in the field might implement 'measures of military severity'.[131] It was necessary in other words, that the methods of suppression, including the use of summary justice by court martial, inspire terror

---

of martial law amounts to the giving of public notice that the law of the civilian courts was to be replaced by the 'law of the Sword'. Young held that the key question for the Commission was not whether martial law was legal, but whether 'Governor Eyre did not introduce too much, or extend too far, or continue too long, the perilous remedy of martial law'. George A. Young, *Notes on the Recent Events in the Island of Jamaica, and on the Right of the Crown to Proclaim Martial Law* (London, 1866).

[127] *Jurist* (30 June 1866), 267–71.   [128] Ibid.   [129] Ibid.   [130] Ibid., 270.
[131] Ibid.

in the rebels. 'This terror,' the *Jurist* once again reminded its readers, was 'of the *essence* of martial law; without it, it is nothing'. When viewed from this point of view, the courts martial of Gordon and others were, if anything, too scrupulous of the rights of the prisoners.

By the end of spring 1866, the field of public discussion was strewn with hypotheses and counter-hypotheses about the legal implications of the Jamaica affair. But two general shapes could be discerned in the rubble. The commissioned opinion of Stephen and James lent technical credence to the view that when they flogged and executed suspected rebels or rebel prisoners, Governor Eyre and military officers had overstepped their legal authority and were liable to a number of serious criminal and civil charges. The opinions published in the *Jurist* had set forth a contrary view. On the assumption that the Governor and his officers had acted on an honest and reasonable belief that the colony faced bloody insurrection, they were legally privileged in having taken any measure thought necessary to the restoration of order, including the corporal punishment or execution of prisoners. The legal issues raised by the Jamaica affair had generated a sizeable if discordant technical literature. But that literature now was about to redouble in its size and complexity.

III. The Legal Treatise as Polemic: W. F. Finlason's *Martial Law*

In June 1866, little more than a week after the Liberal government released the final report of the Jamaica Royal Commission, William Francis Finlason, a barrister of the Inner Temple, treatise writer, and long-time legal reporter for *The Times*, published a monograph on the legal aspects of the Jamaica controversy called *A Treatise on Martial Law as Allowed by the Law of England in Time of Rebellion*.[132] This was an historically significant publication, but not because it was brilliantly written and reasoned. In fact Finlason's book, although it contained some sharp observations and analysis, was often convoluted, sloppily edited, and tediously repetitive.

Finlason's treatise is important historically for other, more extrinsic, factors. One is the very fact of its publication in 1866. From this it can be inferred that by early January 1866 a professional legal writer perceived that the demand for legal knowledge about martial law had become so robust that a writer might justify the investment in it of hundreds of toilsome hours. And Finlason clearly had vital support in the line of thought. In June 1866 a legal publisher, Stevens & Sons, printed his book, a book that with all of its accessories was almost five hundred dense pages long. In other words, *A Treatise on Martial Law* was a major milestone in public discourse on the legal dimensions of the Jamaica affair.

---

[132] Stevens & Sons (London, 1866).

But Finlason's book is important also for what it contained: the most comprehensive discussion of martial law that had ever been written in English. No one before him had done nearly so much work to gather and organize the multitude of disparate legal materials associated with the subject. No one before him had done nearly so much to characterize the legal issues generated by martial law, and to make arguments about them. And this point leads us to the final reason why Finlason's book is so important to historians. *A Treatise on Martial Law* blatantly is a political book, a book that was meant to influence public opinion and the formation of policy about the Jamaica affair. Although throughout the text Finlason attempted to maintain the posture and tone of a disinterested scholar, he did not succeed. In fact his treatise was an unrelenting polemic in favour of a robust doctrine of martial law, a Clausewitzian rumination on the harsh racial and political realities of the burgeoning empire. The shadow of Cawnpore darkened every page. With the publication of *A Treatise on Martial Law*, Finlason became the mid-Victorian era's foremost authority on the legal technology of terror.

Before launching into a discussion of the specific contents of the treatise, something more needs to be said about its author. W. F. Finlason was one of that odd breed of English barrister who throve at the margins of his profession. Born into the minor Surrey gentry in 1819, Finlason became a student in the Middle Temple in 1841, but did not receive a call to the Bar for another decade.[133] It is easy to imagine that in the absence of extensive social connections Finlason struggled to get briefs. Not long after his call, Finlason became involved in law reporting. By the 1850s reporting and treatise writing had overtaken his work as a barrister on the South-Eastern circuit. By 1860 Finlason was chief legal reporter for *The Times*, and the author of numerous books and pamphlets on legal subjects.[134] When he published his long treatise on martial law, Finlason was a respected if not eminent lawyer.[135] And if, when the Jamaica story broke in November 1865, Finlason was a man of strong political convictions, his obituaries do not record it. When he died in 1895, he was not remembered for having run for public office or for his connections to a political party. He was recalled as learned of English law, and as an amiable gentleman who had known all the great legal luminaries, and who had become a repository of legal anecdotes. Not even one obituary recalled that thirty years earlier this seemingly innocuous jurist had been an important figure in a bitter political wrangle. Nor was it remembered that Finlason had penned a series of elaborate legal justifications for the ready and ruthless use of terror in the empire.

[133] For biographical detail, see *DNB*, xxii 637; Lobban, *Oxford DNB*, online 9462. See obituaries in *The Times* (13 Mar. 1895), 10; *Law Times* (16 Mar. 1895), 481; *Solicitors' Journal* (16 Mar. 1895), 324.

[134] Most of these works were annotated collections of cases or notable trials. Finlason had taken a special interest in the law of charitable trusts. Before he published his *Treatise on Martial Law* in 1866, none of Finlason's many published writings had concerned constitutional law.

[135] Finlason's relative obscurity in 1866 is underlined by the fact that the *Law Times* (23 June 1866), 580, in announcing the imminent publication of *A Treatise on Martial Law*, referred to him as 'Mr. Fieldson'.

And if by general disposition Finlason was mild-mannered, the pugnacious tenacity he exhibited in his published work on the Jamaica controversy must be taken as evidence of very deep convictions about his subject-matter and its implications. These convictions Finlason made plain in a letter he wrote to William Gladstone in February 1868.[136] 'When, two years ago, I first looked into the subject,' Finlason explained, 'it was from a sense of the injustice which was being done by a powerful combination.' The Jamaica Committee (when it published the opinion of Stephen and James) had begun to propagate an 'erroneous' notion of martial law that it was limited only to the 'common law defence of self-defence, or putting down actual force by force, to the case of actual present and physical necessity'. It was bad enough that the Jamaica Committee had been willing to circulate falsehoods about an important point of law, but far worse that it did so 'as a way to prove a man a murderer'. This course of conduct, Finlason contended, was 'alike unprecedented, illegal, and morally criminal'. In the result, Finlason had been 'moved to publish a work embodying what I knew to be a view of the law laid down by old authority, viz. That martial law is the *law of war*.' According to this law, the commander in the field could take whatever actions he deemed necessary and for so long as he thought necessary in order to effect the permanent restoration of order. 'It would be a ridiculous error', Finlason assured Gladstone, 'to limit the existence of this law of war to actual insurrection.'

A Treatise on Martial Law outwardly conformed to all of the conventions of formal legal scholarship. Assertions were made about the content of relevant propositions of law in the text, and then they were supported by authorities cited in long and detailed footnotes. But the intricate scholarly apparatus of the work could not obscure the fact that it was a sustained argument both about the legal nature of martial law and its ramifications for the Jamaica controversy. Finlason's treatise aimed to convince readers of three central theses. The first was that martial law was the law of war, and that it was a living feature of English law. The second was that martial law, while it was almost wholly moribund as a feature of English domestic law, would continue to be an indispensable tool of imperial statecraft. The third thesis was that under the law of war it was clear that neither Governor Eyre nor his senior military officers had committed crimes during the suppression of the Jamaica rebellion.

In the long Preface to *Martial Law* Finlason described his scholarly intentions, but in so doing he also revealed the political aims of his book. Formal writing on martial law, Finlason observed, was antiquated, fragmentary, and forgotten. Martial law simply had not been a pertinent subject in a country lacking any

---

[136] Finlason to Gladstone, 3 Feb. 1868, Gladstone Papers, *BL*, Add. MS. 44414. The letter was written to accompany a presentation copy of one of his later books on Jamaica. In the letter Finlason predicted (correctly) that Gladstone would be the next Prime Minister, and then unabashedly stated that he wanted to influence Gladstone's views on martial law. Not only was the subject of martial law of 'considerable historical and constitutional interest,' Finlason explained, 'but always also of some possible practical interest with reference to Ireland, India and the Colonies'.

recent experience of foreign invasion or armed rebellion. Even in the case of Ireland it had been possible for most of the nineteenth century to cope with rebellious activity largely within civilian structures of law and public order.[137] As an emergency power in Britain, Finlason asserted, martial law had become all but 'obsolete'.[138] As an emergency power in Britain's sprawling empire, however, it was 'far otherwise'. In this insight, in the bitter remembrance of the Indian Mutiny, Finlason had found the ultimate justification for his hefty treatise. If martial law now was to be routinely invoked in the empire ('as it is certain constantly to do in one portion or another of our widespread dominions or dependencies'),[139] it was time that a jurist set forth 'all that can be laid down upon the subject as a matter of law'.

The Preface commenced with a preliminary account of the meaning and status of martial law. When defined as 'the law imposed by the military power', did it still exist as a feature of English law? On this issue Finlason quoted Blackstone (citing Hale and the Petition of Right) that martial law 'can have no place in our *institutions*'.[140] But Finlason's italics signalled a key qualification. What the authorities stated was that martial law had no institutional legitimacy during *peace*time. The authorities were equally clear, however, that martial law had complete legitimacy during *war*time. On the contrary, the law was clear that it was the positive duty of public officials to proclaim martial law whenever civil society was threatened by an armed force 'too formidable to be dealt with, even by the military, when merely acting in aid of civil authority'.[141]

Having settled these definitional matters, Finlason introduced his second thesis: that the law of martial law, obsolete in the British mainland, had been revived by the military, demographic, and racial exigencies of the expanding empire. In most of Britain's foreign territories and dominions, he stressed, 'the military force is comparatively small, and the English inhabitants are a weak community, surrounded by an overwhelming mass of a population'.[142] In these places the white British population often was hopelessly outnumbered by dark-skinned people only recently emancipated from slavery, by people who had 'inherit[ed] all the evil passions and feelings of that hateful condition'.[143] In scores of remote outposts small and scattered communities of English men and women were constantly menaced by 'the revolt of the servile classes, or of the peasantry – a species of revolt which has been deemed the worst and the most dangerous'.[144] In the event of actual revolt (Cawnpore was the telling example), moreover, there was little hope that a besieged population might be saved by troops despatched from outside. If they were to have any chance of surviving an insurrection or, more hopefully, of *deterring* it in the first instance, the leaders of a colony needed to be

---

[137] As noted above, there was an exception to this generalization. In 1833, Parliament passed legislation which permitted some suspected rebels to be tried by courts martial. See Clode, *Military Forces of the Crown*, vol. ii, 168–75.   [138] Finlason, *Treatise on Martial Law*, v.
[139] Ibid., xlii.   [140] Ibid., iv.   [141] Ibid. xxiii.   [142] Ibid., v.   [143] Ibid., xx.
[144] Ibid.

able to 'strik[e] the rebellious masses with a terror inspired by the stern and summary severities of martial law'.[145]

Finlason did not mince words on this point: the future safety of British communities in the empire depended on the ready availability of terror: 'terror is of the very nature of martial law, and deterrent measures – that is, measures deterrent by means of terror – are its very essence.'[146] Martial law facilitated the coercion of human bodies and, even more emphatically, the coercion of human minds, 'by striking the rebellious masses with a terror inspired by the stern and summary severities of military law'. The point of martial law was to 'inspire a terror into the larger numbers of the rebels, in which alone the safety of a small loyal community can, under such circumstances, be found'.[147] The certainty of violent retribution would dissuade many groups from taking up arms in the first instance. But when they were not so dissuaded, a swift and ruthless show of force would cause men to put their arms down. '[T]he key to the whole question', Finlason reflected, 'is... the necessity for the terror inspired by the military measures to subdue a *spirit* of insurrection which prevails among a preponderating class of the population' (emphasis added).[148] For 'the true scope of martial law,' Finlason contended, 'is not so much the resistance of actual insurrection, as its suppression and prevention by terror'.[149] The very 'salvation' of the empire, Finlason contended, would depend first on the quick implementation of martial law and then on 'the promptness and vigour of military action'.[150]

If the indispensability of martial law in the new empire was the overarching political theme of Finlason's treatise, it was supported by two closely argued and carefully documented legal propositions. The first was that martial law persisted as an incontrovertible prerogative both of Parliament and, more controversially, of the executive agents of the Crown. When the highest executive or legislative authorities of state believed that there was 'a state of rebellion or civil war', it was their legal right to proclaim martial law.[151] The second was that martial law denoted the 'suspension of common law, and the application to the population of absolute, arbitrary, military power'.[152]

Finlason quickly dispensed with the sovereign right of Parliament to proclaim martial law. This right had been conclusively demonstrated in statutes passed by the Irish Parliament in 1798, and by Parliament in 1803.[153] It was also manifest in the annual recital by Parliament of the Mutiny Act (giving the armed forces jurisdiction to try and punish soldiers outside the common law). And, just as Finlason was writing his book, Parliament had moved to suspend the writ of *habeas corpus* in Ireland.[154] These statutes proved yet again that no legal claims or

---

[145] Finlason, *Treatise on Martial Law*, xxxii.   [146] Ibid.   [147] Ibid.
[148] Ibid., xxxv.   [149] Ibid.   [150] Ibid., 10.   [151] Ibid., 17.   [152] Ibid., vi.
[153] These statutes authorized the Lord Lieutenant of Ireland to enforce martial law in any part of Ireland without making a general proclamation and whether or not the civilian courts were operating. Ibid., 43–4.
[154] Ibid., 32. These acts, passed in 1848, and between 1866 and 1869, permitted the Irish authorities to arrest and detain persons without charge or trial. See generally, Simpson, *End of Empire*, 57–8.

entitlements, not even those that might be traced to Magna Carta, were impervious to adjustment, suspension, or termination.

The more interesting and contentious question was the nature and extent of the executive prerogative to proclaim martial law. In Finlason's view, the 'common law has always recognised the right of the Crown in a state of war ... to lay down such orders and rules of discipline as may be fit to enforce in the army ... these rules, and the usages of war, form the basis of what is called martial law'.[155] The state of war was 'any rising in arms for a general object', and included armed invasion, civil war, and insurrection. In the state of war, the common law is suspended, and persons in arms against the Crown 'forfeited their common law rights'.[156] When they acted as soldiers, rebels became 'liable to be treated as soldiers, and subject to the laws and usages of war'. Martial law was, in effect, a 'declaration of war by the Crown against the subjects, in consequence of a prior declaration of war by them against the Sovereign'.[157]

In and of themselves these points were not controversial. Even Stephen and James had conceded that martial law was justifiable in the face of emergency, and that soldiers acting under its banner were legally entitled to do whatever was necessary to restore order. Where Finlason departed from the lawyers for the Jamaica Committee was on the *boundaries* of military and civilian authority under martial law. Stephen and James had opined that martial law was (according to Finlason's paraphrase), 'strictly limited by necessity, in the strict legal sense of present, actual, instant, physical necessity'.[158] According to this account, the jurisdiction of martial law was limited to combatants acting in open resistance to the Crown. Stephen and James denied that 'there can ever be a *necessity*, in that stricter sense, for the summary trial of a man', and that 'all such trials and sentences were utterly illegal'. On these last points, Finlason defended a radically different view, one that was driven by a radically different set of political preoccupations.

We have seen that the legal sources for the British law of martial law were unusually dated, disparate, and disorganized. The prospective writer about the subject was presented with a virtually limitless range of choices about sources and their interpretation. It would be fair to say that the choices of Stephen and James were guided by their Whiggish sensibilities, and by their shared conviction that terrible wrongs had been committed by the authorities in Jamaica. The choices of Finlason, on the other hand, were guided by his anxiety for the security of Britons in the empire, and by his conviction that the law of martial law was rooted in the brutal realities of war, more specifically, imperial war between white and non-white peoples.

A conception of imperial war and its attendant horrors informed everything that Finlason wrote about the law of martial law. His premiss – not an insensible one – was that the gravest man-made threats to any civil society were foreign

---

[155] Finlason, *Treatise on Martial Law*, 2. In documenting these propositions, Finlason relied especially on the standard quotations of Hale, but also on Hawkins's *Pleas of the Crown*.
[156] Ibid., 4.   [157] Ibid., 58.   [158] Ibid., viii–ix.

invasion or armed insurrection. A civil society could have no more profound and urgent interest than to terminate such threats with the greatest possible prejudice. But rarely was this a simple matter. War, whether it was born of invasion or insurrection,[159] created conditions of the most extreme difficulty and uncertainty. When the site of war was some distant soil where 'there is a small white population in the midst of an enormous native population',[160] the turbulent dangers of war were only intensified. In such a context martial law, the declaration of war against the insurgents, was not a luxury but a necessity. The entire point of its proclamation was to enable professional military men to act decisively, even ruthlessly, to rescue and restore civil society.

Finlason's main concern was with the law of martial law and its bearing on rebellion in the burgeoning non-white empire. 'There,' he wrote, 'it may be of terrible importance, for it may at any moment afford the only really effectual means of suppressing a formidable rebellion which, if once allowed to make head, will be fatal.'[161] It will often be the case that in some distant colony there will be a 'vast preponderance of force . . . on the side of insurrection'. There the safety of the colony will depend on the 'most decided measures, which can only be taken under martial law'. Finlason was prepared to be more specific. On some occasions, circumstances might dictate that there be an 'indiscriminate attack upon those apparently assembled as rebels'.[162] In such situations, the martial power would be of but little use if commanders in the field were 'constantly harassed and paralysed by the fear of using it against those who may be comparatively, if not entirely, innocent'. The underlying logic of martial law was the same as the underlying logic of race war: to prevail at all costs, including at the cost of ordinary laws and liberties.

The peculiar perils associated with insurrection in the empire were key to comprehending why Finlason thought Stephen and James were wrong about the jurisdiction of martial law, and about its equivalence with the common law defence of necessity. For Finlason martial law was, because of its rootedness in the exigencies of war, something much wider and distinct. 'The scope of martial law,' he argued, 'was not merely the suppression of an actual insurrection or resistance of outward acts of rebellion.' Unlike the common law of riot, for instance, the law of martial law pertained more 'to danger than actual outbreak; it is prevention rather than resistance'.[163] At common law magistrates could only act to suppress actual riot, and in doing so were responsible for 'making out a strictly legal justification for their acts'.[164] It was obvious that such niceties, so vital to civil society, were utterly unsuited to the grim business of putting down an armed insurrection. In this regard, the 'difficulty and deficiency of the common law is met by the prerogative of the Crown for the proclamation of martial law'. Martial law was the legal facility for making war on an enemy and war, Finlason observed, is 'not limited to

---

[159] 'There can be no doubt . . . that an actual rebellion or insurrection is a levying of war.' Ibid., 16.
[160] Ibid., 19.   [161] Ibid., 10.   [162] Ibid., 6–7.   [163] Ibid., 27.
[164] Ibid., 32.

actual engagements'.[165] During war 'it is everything to anticipate the enemy'.[166] And finally to crush the enemy, especially in the context of native rebellion, it 'may be necessary to keep up the terror of military force, which has caused their cessation, until the removal of any danger of their renewal'.

The proclamation of martial law was understood by Finlason to be no more or less than 'a declaration of war by the Crown, against the subjects, in consequence of a prior declaration by them against the Sovereign'. In the context of rebellion, the proclamation justified 'the treatment of all that part of the population that is fit for fighting...*prima facie* as rebels; that is under suspicion of rebellion, whether or not they are found actively employed in support of the rebellion'.[167] In Finlason's view, 'in rebellion, there can be no *neutrality*.' This principle had far-reaching consequences. Every person in the field not acting in direct aid of the forces of the Crown was 'rightly and necessarily regarded as the enemy', and was rightly subject to 'absolute and arbitrary military authority'. This was the essence of martial law, that in reality it 'was no law at all, in the sense which that phrase is usually understood'.[168] Before a magistrate might punish or kill a man, he needed to concentrate on 'strict legal proof of guilt'. When the commander under martial law decided the fate of a man, he needed only to consider the potential impact of the punishment on the outcome of the war. Individual intent was secondary to military result.[169] 'The great object under martial law,' Finlason contended, 'was the security of the State, and to that the security of the individual must give way.'[170] The decision either to shoot, detain, flog, or execute prisoners was to be determined by military judgement tempered only by 'the usages of the service'.[171] Whatever the commander genuinely believed 'an absolute practical necessity' in suppressing rebellion *ipso facto* was a lawful measure. Neither, Finlason asserted, was it 'material to their legality, that [any measure] turn out in the event to have been excessive'.[172] Terror, by its very definition, could only be created by some excess of force.

The discussion of these general principles brought Finlason to the subject of prisoners and courts martial. The determination of what to do with prisoners taken under martial law was one that was to be based solely on what the commander thought likely to abet the war on rebel forces. It was not necessary in every instance, for instance, for prisoners to be punished as a result of conviction by 'formal trial, or any strict legal proof'.[173] Martial law, Finlason repeated again and again, 'operates chiefly by the terror of summary military executions, and by the rigid restraints of military discipline'.[174] In most instances, these restraints would dictate that prisoners would be tried and convicted by courts martial before any punishment was meted out. However, in other instances the circumstances of war might render it essential altogether to dispense with trials. The summary execution of prisoners, even those who were legally innocent of wrong, could be

---

[165] Ibid., xxx. [166] Ibid., 53. [167] Ibid., 59. [168] Ibid., 60–1.
[169] Ibid., 62. [170] Ibid., 69. [171] Ibid., xv. [172] Ibid., xvi.
[173] Ibid., 67. [174] Ibid., 71.

justified by a utilitarian calculus. The operation of martial law, Finlason assured his readers, 'even when inflicting military executions, is really merciful, for it is certain to save life in the long run'.[175] When commanders in the field convened courts martial they were 'as fully and as truly lawful tribunals...as the Courts of Assize'.[176] However, courts martial under martial law were not even bound by the rules of 'ordinary military law'.[177] Rather, they were to be regarded as part of the 'terrible powers' associated with the making of war against an enemy in arms. For this reason the officers presiding over courts martial were not bound either by ordinary procedural rules or 'the strict rules of evidence'.[178] It would be permissible, then, for officers to try and convict prisoners on grounds of a reasonable belief, a reasonable well-grounded suspicion, in their potential to commit further rebellious acts, or to encourage others.[179]

Finlason was aware that this generous reading of the ambit of martial law raised obvious questions. When could martial law be proclaimed? Could the official who proclaimed it later be found liable for suspending civilian law? What legal principles, if any, *limited* the powers of the persons who implemented martial law? Could *they* be held legally accountable for their actions?

With regard to the proclamation of martial law, Finlason was very definite. Martial law, he wrote, 'can never be required or justified unless there is a rebellion (or invasion) too formidable to be dealt with, even by the military, when merely acting in aid of civil power'.[180] It was a measure which could only be introduced as 'a measure of military necessity'.[181] On the second issue, accountability for the decision to proclaim martial law, Finlason was less definite: 'Whether there is an armed rising, which is a rebellion, or a levying of war against the Crown is a question of fact.'[182] In assessing the nature of a threat, officials of state – whether they be Governors, Viceroys, ministers of state or military officers – were obliged only to act in good faith. The decision of an official to proclaim martial law was the expression of 'a high discretionary authority vested in him by the Crown'.[183] By virtue of the office of the decision-maker, Finlason maintained, the decision was 'necessarily valid'. If later it became clear that the decision to proclaim martial law was made in good faith, but was 'rash, erroneous or ill-judged', it, like other political decisions, was 'liable to censure of the Crown or of Parliament'. Nearer the end of his book, Finlason summarized the point in a way which had obvious ramifications for the Eyre controversy: 'for errors the offending Minister was liable to reprimand, even loss of office, but he cannot be criminally liable.'[184]

The military officer who had implemented martial law in good faith could not later be punished in the criminal or civil courts. After all, the entire point of martial law was to give the military an extraordinary and independent authority to

---

[175] Ibid.   [176] Ibid., 90.   [177] Ibid.,107.   [178] Ibid., 99.
[179] 'The scope of martial law is not guilt, but mischief and danger.' Ibid., 104.
[180] Ibid., xxiii.   [181] Ibid., 53.   [182] Ibid., xxi–xxii.
[183] Ibid., 53. See also ibid., 17.   [184] Ibid., 314.

use force, and the terrifying threat of still more force, to crush rebellion. 'The measures to be taken under martial law', Finlason reminded readers, 'were military measures, to be taken entirely under military authority.'[185] In effect, then, martial law was about permitting military men to *make war* and, in case of rebellion, to make war on fellow subjects. Nothing was more likely to impede the efficacy of martial law (to say nothing of the officers' willingness to implement it)[186] than the threat of subsequent civil or criminal prosecution. It was plain to Finlason that one of the hallmarks of martial law was the broad authority it bestowed on the officials who declared and implemented it. Were it otherwise, if the decision to proclaim martial law could be easily second-guessed or its powers retrospectively revoked, 'no one could even venture to declare, or act upon, martial law, and put into force its terrible powers for the salvation of a colony or dependency'.[187]

By the same token, even Finlason acknowledged that there were some limits on the discretion of officers in the field to use violence against rebels, especially with regard to prisoners who had not been 'taken "red-handed" ' in the act of making war on the Crown.[188] First, there had to have been an honest belief that a punishment was necessary to suppress rebellion. Second, the officer, even when he was acting in good faith, was constrained by the 'usages' of the battlefield, by the customary law of war.[189] Finally, Finlason conceded that 'there is the duty imposed by those dictates of natural justice, which the law of England considers of universal obligation'. In making an investigation that might lead to the punishment of a prisoner officers were bound to observe 'those rules of common justice and humanity, which are universally obligatory'.[190] Even the most 'inferior and irregular tribunals' were obliged, before they sentenced a prisoner, to make some investigation, hear evidence, and permit some means of defence. There was a duty, in sum, of conducting 'a fair trial'. If an officer disregarded these duties, Finlason admitted, he could face criminal prosecution and conviction. But what Finlason did not admit is that the upshot of his discussion of natural justice was that it contradicted his repeated claim that the effect of a proclamation of martial law was 'to establish an absolute arbitrary authority over the district'. The commander had an absolute power to do what he thought fit in order to restore order, but not an absolute immunity for exercising that power. For a writer determined to excuse the actions which had been taken to suppress the rebellion in Jamaica, and Finlason was such a writer, this was a noteworthy, even curious, qualification.

This is a suitable point at which to discuss Finlason's use of sources. The reader of *Martial Law* cannot but be awed by the breadth of legal research on display in the work (research, remarkably enough, that must have been assembled in only a

---

[185] Ibid., 317.

[186] 'But it would be idle', Finlason wrote on this point, 'to tell a General to do all that might be thought necessary, in the opinion of a Middlesex jury, some months afterwards.' Ibid., xi.

[187] Ibid., 55. [188] Ibid., 87. [189] Ibid., xxxvii.

[190] Ibid., 84. Finlason added that the non-observance of these universal principles of justice would be evidence of the 'bad motive' of the officer.

few months). In this regard the book is much the superior to any other work published on martial law during the Jamaica controversy. At some point in his text Finlason quotes from and discusses well-nigh every case report, treatise, statute, constitutional history, and legal opinion that had even touched upon the subject to that point in time. His book is a veritable encyclopaedia of martial law and its deployments in British history. But if the fullness of Finlason's research is beyond reproach, the soundness of his technique in utilizing sources is open to question.

Finlason's *modus operandi* in writing *Martial Law* was conventional enough. Propositions of law were stated and arranged in the text, and source materials were cited and discussed in footnotes. On a great many of its pages, however, the footnotes overtake and even overwhelm the textual material. Many of the footnotes are imprecise and tangled. It is not always obvious how assertions made in the text are validated by the citation or quotation in a footnote. The book's discussion of the term 'martial law' furnishes an instructive example.[191] In order to establish that the term denoted 'absolute and arbitrary military authority', Finlason referred to the Petition of Right, Lord Loughborough's statements in *Grant v. Gould*, Lord Hale, and Simmons's treatise on courts martial. The first three sources are not quoted directly. The last source is quoted to the effect that martial law 'renders every man liable to being treated as a soldier'. But neither this statement nor the simple invocation of the other sources establishes that martial law bestowed powers suggested by the words 'absolute and arbitrary'. And in his zeal to substantiate other key points, Finlason also employed the old writer's trick of pruning quotations to suit his purposes. For instance, while Finlason quotes Wellington that martial law is 'neither more nor less than the will of the General in command', he omitted the ensuing sentences in which Wellington qualified these remarks.[192] These machinations underline the political imperatives of *Martial Law*.

These imperatives were also indicated by the structure of the book. When the sixty-five-page introduction is included, Finlason devoted less than a *quarter* of his treatise to the explication of the law of martial law.[193] The remainder of the work, more than 350 pages, addressed the 'practical illustration' of the law in the context of the Jamaica rising and suppression of 1865. 'That case,' Finlason stated, 'illustrated all the questions that can possibly arise with reference to martial law.'[194] The decision to focus on the Jamaica controversy was consistent with his stated conviction that 'the whole subject of martial law is preeminently so *practical* a subject that, though it is based on certain principles . . . it is best elucidated by practical illustrations'. It was also consistent with the unstated purposes of the book: to demonstrate at once that Governor Eyre had not committed crimes in Jamaica, and that martial law was a vital instrument of statecraft in the empire.

---

[191] Ibid., 59–60.   [192] Ibid., vii.
[193] Finlason's treatment of the law of martial law *per se* was completed on page 109 of a book 411 pages in length.   [194] Ibid., xxii.

The last 300 pages of *Martial Law* were based on Finlason's reading of the materials collected by the Jamaica Royal Commission. The 'first and fundamental point' about this evidence was that it clearly demonstrated the 'necessity for the declaration of martial law'.[195] Here was the archetypal case of why martial law mattered to security in the empire. The key here was race and numbers. As in so many other British colonies, in Jamaica a 'small white community were surrounded by, or rather scattered among, an overwhelming mass of a coloured race'. The 'enormous black peasant population,' as Finlason already had noted, was 'in their character singularly credulous and excitable'.[196] To make matters even more perilous, the large black population had advantage of 'a large island with much mountain, and wood, and bush'. In the face of this potential threat, and on this unfavourable terrain, the colonial authorities could rely on 'only 1,000 soldiers and scarce any police'.

But there were even more tangible reasons why it had become necessary for Governor Eyre to proclaim martial law. By October 1865 the Governor had been only too aware of a 'deep-seated and widespread spirit of rebellion, ready to break forth'.[197] He also knew that among the credulous masses of black people there was 'a man of great influence' (George Gordon), who had made a series of 'seditious addresses, in one at least of which [so Finlason alleged[198]], he incited the negroes to rise and massacre the whites'.[199] When on 11 October Governor Eyre learned that a large contingent of armed blacks had risen up and shed white blood at Morant Bay, there was no prudent alternative to the conclusion that the 'insurrection, if not checked, would speedily develop into rebellion'.[200] When the Governor and his privy councillors met to discuss these matters, they had quickly agreed that the small contingent of soldiers available to the Government could not possibly avert a widespread rebellion without the special powers of martial law.[201]

According to Finlason's analysis, there was no room for doubt that Governor Eyre had made the right, indeed, the *only possible* decision when he signed the proclamation of martial law, a document prepared and urged on him by his Attorney General.[202] There equally was no doubt that the senior commanders had been correct to deal with blacks in the rebellious districts 'as a body and in the mass as having a general and pervading character of rebellion – raising a

---

[195] Ibid., 111. Stephen and James, Finlason believed, had written their opinion before the Jamaica Commission had uncovered so much evidence that the rebellion in Jamaica had in fact been very real and dangerous. Their underestimations on this point helped explain why they thought that Governor Eyre and his officers had overreacted. See, for example, ibid., iii–iv, x.   [196] Ibid., 54.
[197] Ibid., 113.
[198] It was indicative of Finlason's active bias in this analysis that he accepted, without qualification, that in a speech prior to the rebellion, Gordon had urged black Jamaicans to replicate the massacres of whites perpetrated by black Haitians in 1793. In fact, Gordon denied having made the statement and the evidence that he had done so was far from conclusive. See Heuman, '*The Killing Time*', 148–9.   [199] Finlason, *Treatise on Martial Law*, 115.
[200] Ibid., 118.   [201] Ibid., 125–6.
[202] That Eyre had resisted the idea of including Kingston was evidence even of an excess of caution in this regard. Ibid., 299.

presumption against them of complicity in the rebellion'.[203] This presumption was reinforced by reports from the field that the rebellion was 'more serious and organized than had been expected',[204] leaving the officers with little choice but to deal sternly with prisoners who were implicated in violence. In this regard, drumhead courts martial were an unavoidable necessity, and the 'terror inspired by these summary trials and executions were made the means of deterring others from similar atrocities'.[205] Finlason was also convinced that Governor Eyre had been right in his controversial decision to keep martial law in place even for some three weeks after he learned that 'the rebellion was checked, headed, or hemmed in, and was crushed in the district first disturbed'.[206] When he made this determination, the Governor was in possession of seemingly reliable intelligence that many rebels had only retreated to their 'inaccessible fastnesses' in the hills, and that from there they might 'renew the rebellion at pleasure'. Quite properly, then, the decision to continue martial law for some weeks had 'turn[ed] upon military considerations' strongly urged on the Governor by senior officers in the field.[207] For the entire four-week period, the terror instilled by the continuation of martial law had been the Government's best insurance against new and more widespread rebellion.

Towards the end of his treatise, Finlason addressed the arrest, court martial, and execution of Gordon. Recall that the final report (and minutes of evidence) of the Jamaica Royal Commission were released just before Finlason published his treatise. As previously discussed, the report was critical of the operation of the courts martial in general, and of Gordon's trial in particular. According to the Commissioners, Gordon had been tried and condemned without 'any sufficient proof' of his complicity in the rebellion. According to Finlason, however, this conclusion was based on a profound misunderstanding of martial law. Finlason defended the legality of the initial arrest for the simple reason that it had been based on credible information that Gordon had helped foment the uprising at Morant Bay. The arrest had been justifiable on military grounds, and Governor Eyre had not been alone in thinking this. A number of persons 'in the highest position and of the best means of information, firmly believed [Gordon] to be the author of the rebellion'.[208] More importantly, as long as he remained alive he was a potential rallying point for insurrectionists all over the island. For Finlason, the legality of the subsequent transportation of Gordon to Morant Bay was equally uncomplicated. The transfer was lawful because of the ancient principle that 'crime is local'.[209] Gordon had made a number of inflammatory speeches in St. Thomas-in-the-East

---

[203] Finlason, *Treatise on Martial Law*, 141.   [204] Ibid., 145.   [205] Ibid., 149–50.
[206] Ibid., 253.
[207] Ibid., 218. 'In the opinion of the persons of the highest position, there still existed, not only in the district in which the insurrection had arisen, but in other and distant districts, the utmost disaffection and disloyalty, and the most alarming symptoms of rebellious spirit.' Ibid., 227.
[208] Ibid., 395.   [209] Ibid., 179.

before the violence erupted.[210] It had been right and proper, then, that he should stand trial at the place of his alleged sedition. From the point of view of legality, moreover, it was irrelevant that the parish was under martial law, or that Gordon had not been present in the parish at the precise time of the rebellion.[211]

The next important question concerned Gordon's actual trial and execution under martial law. Who, if anyone, had incurred liability for that notorious action? Finlason's first contention in this regard was that it could not be Governor Eyre. Gordon had been hanged by military men acting under martial law. It was simply not possible that Eyre, a political official, could be liable for an 'act of supreme military authority'.[212] (Finlason's view was not altered by the fact that Eyre had confirmed the finding and sentence.) If anyone bore legal responsibility for Gordon's execution, it was the group of officers who tried, condemned, and hanged him.

In addressing the potential liability of the military officers, Finlason's treatise returned to first principles. Under martial law, the officers possessed a (nearly) absolute discretion to do whatever they honestly thought necessary to put down a rebellion. For this reason, the officer who organized Gordon's trial, Brigadier Nelson, had not been legally obligated to follow even 'the strict rules of ordinary military law', still less the rules that prevailed in courts of common law.[213] It was incumbent upon the officers only to have held a trial that was 'fair' in the limited sense that it conformed with the minimum requirements of 'substantial simple justice, which are of universal obligation'.[214] This, Finlason believed, they had done.

He had many reasons for thinking so, reasons that were rooted in the political and military climate on the island during the days of Gordon's detention. The trial had taken place in the aftermath of a massacre of whites by black rebels. Gordon was charged with having conspired to cause these deaths.[215] During the trial, witnesses for the prosecution had testified in open court, and had given relevant testimony that pointed to guilt.[216] The accused had been given an opportunity to cross-examine his accusers, and then to rebut their evidence with his own testimony. If he had not been granted wide latitude to call defence witnesses, this was attributable to the military exigencies of the moment. The authorities feared that the rebellion might be rejoined at any moment, and that Gordon's living presence in the colony only exacerbated the

[210] Finlason was so anxious to justify Gordon's court martial at Morant Bay that he offered a reason for it that had not been suggested even by Eyre: that justice would not have been 'impartially administered' in Kingston because of the (supposed) racial fellow-feeling of 'coloured' men on petty juries. Finlason did not substantiate his supposition (it was false) that petty juries, anywhere on the island, were dominated by non-white men. See ibid., 393.   [211] Ibid., 178.
[212] Ibid., 177.   [213] Ibid., 192.   [214] Ibid., 403.   [215] Ibid., 406–10.
[216] Contrary to assertions made in the newspapers, the military men who tried Gordon did not have to call evidence to link the prisoner with particular acts of rebellion. Ibid., 401. With regard to standard of proof, Finlason maintained that the tribunal was entitled to convict and execute a prisoner if 'there was any evidence that could lead them, in fact, whether rightly or wrongly, to the belief of the prisoner's guilt'. Ibid., 194.

threat. When the trial was viewed in the context of these arduous circumstances, Finlason believed, the military men had actually done an admirable job of protecting Gordon's interests. He had been given a 'a patient hearing, full opportunity for cross-examination, comment or observation'.[217] What was there to complain of? 'The great question, both moral and legal,' Finlason firmly concluded, 'was whether the prisoner had had a fair trial, and this, it was clear, he had.'[218]

Finlason then made an even more stark claim. Gordon had been tried under martial, not common law. Therefore, the legality of his trial under martial law would not 'be affected one way or the other by a number of mere irregularities or departures from mere rules of procedure, nor necessarily by some degree of error, rashness, or want of care'.[219] At common law, *all* the measures taken against him were wholly illegal'. Under the jurisdiction of martial law, however, all the measures were legal insofar as the officers who implemented them were acting reasonably and in good faith to crush the rebellion. What Finlason appeared to be intimating was that the courts martial, in the end, were instruments of war, not criminal justice. What the critics of Gordon's trial, what the Royal Commissioners themselves had failed to recognize, was that the military officers, had they honestly believed it necessary to restore order, might have lawfully executed Gordon *without any trial*. When this was considered, it was clear, morally and legally, that Gordon's interests had been shown great consideration and indulgence.[220]

For a long book on a seemingly complex subject, Finlason's treatise was strikingly free of ambiguity. He entertained no doubt as to the continued existence in British law of a robust and capacious doctrine of martial law. He had no doubt but that, in the context of armed rebellion, it entailed a near-absolute discretion to treat subjects as enemy soldiers, and to continue so to treat them until military men were satisfied that the rebellion was finally crushed. Nor did Finlason entertain any doubt about the legal ramifications of the Jamaica affair. Governor Eyre had been right to proclaim, and to maintain, martial law for a full month. Gordon had been lawfully arrested, tried, and executed. Even Duberry Ramsay, the man who had been accused (even by the Jamaican authorities) of having hanged a man for having made an angry face after a brutal whipping, was fully exonerated by Finlason.[221] *A Treatise on Martial Law*, while it displayed the apparatus and veneer of a scholarly book, was in fact an elaborate *apologia*.

---

[217] Finlason, *Treatise on Martial Law*, 410.   [218] Ibid., 409.   [219] Ibid., 410.

[220] Finlason noted that on Gordon's cross-questioning the prosecution witnesses 'were not shaken in the least'. It did not seem to affect this judgement that Gordon was not a lawyer, and had not had time to prepare questions. Ibid., 407.

[221] In Ramsay's case, as we have seen, several witnesses testified before the Royal Commission that Ramsay had hanged a prisoner (Marshall) for having shown a flash of anger. But while the evidence of wrongdoing had been seen by the Attorney General of Jamaica to be compelling enough to justify a prosecution for murder, Finlason preferred the evidence of some British seamen that Marshall had 'distinctly threatened the life' of Ramsay. In Finlason's opinion, the execution of Marshall 'was fully justifiable as a matter of law'. Ibid., 370–1.

Finlason's book was replete with highly partisan material; but that is not to say that its arguments were inconsequential. It went far to explain why Britain – or, at the very least, the British Empire – could not do without a doctrine of martial law. All over the globe small and vulnerable communities of British men and women were being asked to govern teeming numbers of semi-civilized, non-white people. Ignorant, credulous, and excitable, these new subjects posed a constant and potentially lethal threat to those sent to govern them.[222] When rebellion was in the air, the invocation of martial law was always likely to be a critical dimension of any effective response. If, moreover, martial law meant anything less than the suspension of civilian law in favour of the unfettered power of the military, it was, in Finlason's words, 'an empty and unmeaning form'.[223] In the end, martial law was 'not so much a law as a power'.[224] It was the power to treat rebels, not as 'honourable enemies, entitled to the rights of war, but criminals who offend against the first of the laws of war, by raising war against their sovereign'.[225]

It is a safe conjecture that in the 1860s long-winded legal treatises only rarely were noticed by the English newspaper and political press. Finlason's book on martial law was the exception proving the rule, as it garnered substantial and sustained interest from the moment of publication. (Finlason's publisher, incidentally, was so much encouraged by the reception of the book that it published another four Finlason books on law and the Jamaica controversy in the next three years.) But *Martial Law* received a mixed reception both in the legal and political press. Many reviewers disliked the book, some intensely so. Others lavished praise. But on one point almost all of Finlason's readers agreed, lawyers and laypersons alike: the law of martial law was a subject of the greatest possible importance. Finlason's book, for all its faults, was a welcome addition to the national debate on the law governing emergency measures.

According to the *Law Times*, the Jamaica affair had demonstrated to the English political class that martial law 'is not dead, but sleeps'.[226] While the leader-writers at the *Dublin Review* did not think it likely that martial law would soon be revived as an instrument of state in England (or even Ireland), the issue was relevant because of 'the immense extent of the colonial and Indian dominions'.[227] But while the subject of martial law now was extremely pertinent, the *Morning Post* stated in its notice of Finlason's treatise, the English people had been left to 'guess' at the law governing its use. For this reason alone, the book was a welcome foray into a subject that had received almost no systematic research.[228] Few readers, however, admired the book for grace of style. In fact, there was a near consensus that the book was flabby, vastly overwritten, and hastily edited. The *American Law Review* slammed the treatise for its 'tediousness and prolix repetition',[229] the *Saturday Review* for its 'redundant language'.[230] It was abundantly

---

[222] Ibid., 277.   [223] Ibid., 327.   [224] Ibid., 309.   [225] Ibid., 342.
[226] *Law Times* (1 Sept. 1866), 762–3.   [227] *Dublin Review*, vii (Oct. 1866), 404.
[228] *Morning Post* (30 July 1866), 3.   [229] *American Law Review*, i (1866–7), 558.
[230] *Saturday Review* (14 July 1866), 40–2.

clear that the book had been rushed into print, willy-nilly, in order to reach the book stalls only a few days after the publication of the Royal Commission's final report.

But these were quibbles compared to the more trenchant reasons to repudiate Finlason's book. Foremost among these was its thinly disguised partiality. The editors of two legal periodicals were particularly unforgiving on this score. Here, they asserted, was a vulgar political tract masquerading as a work of detached legal scholarship. 'The book,' the *American Law Review* wrote, 'though called "A Treatise on Martial Law", is really an argument in defence of Governor Eyre.'[231] Finlason was accused of having rummaged through the law books with the plain (though never plainly stated) purpose of vindicating martial law generally, and its use by Governor Eyre particularly. In the opinion of the *Law Magazine*, Finlason had written a 'most able and learned argument on one side of the question'.[232] But the author was also sternly rebuked for having 'prostituted' the prestige and authority that had traditionally been ascribed to barristers when they spoke publicly on legal subjects. As the *Law Magazine* summarized: 'a member of the bar is not justified in writing a law book in the spirit of partisanship.'

Of the leading legal periodicals the *Jurist*, predictably enough, was an unalloyed admirer of Finlason's work.[233] (As we have seen, in the previous months it had published a series of long articles which defended an expansive view of martial law.) The *Law Times*, for its part, maintained its inconsistent, even erratic, line on the same subject. In its notice of the treatise,[234] the journal welcomed a book on a subject so 'prominently under public notice'. The review then described Finlason's main lines of argument, refraining from strident praise or criticism. With regard to one important issue, however, the *Law Times* registered a clear dissent: it rejected outright Finlason's contention that 'the constitution has vested in the Sovereign the right to resort to [martial law] without legislative sanction'. By the same token, the *Law Times* was unwilling to reject outright Finlason's idea that martial law bestowed an 'absolute discretionary authority' on military officers in the field. It would say only that '*if* Mr. Finlason has rightly expounded this fearful law – and he adduces his authorities – Governor Eyre must have a triumphal acquittal' (emphasis added).

The editors of the more liberal-minded political papers did not hide their contempt for Finlason's scholarship. These men worried about what the book signified about the political climate in Britain. In the opinion of the *Saturday Review*, Finlason's defence of a broad doctrine of martial law was symptomatic of a profound and unwelcome change 'in the temper of the people of this country in regard to matters of law, and especially those parts of the law which relate more particularly to the liberty of the subject'.[235] The 'legal effect and character of a proclamation of martial law', the *Saturday Review* asserted, was an issue which

[231] *American Law Review* 1 (1866–7), 558.   [232] *Law Magazine*, 22 (1866–7), 40.
[233] *Jurist* (21 July 1866), 296–7.   [234] *Law Times* (1 Sept. 1866), 762–3.
[235] *Saturday Review* (14 July 1866), 40–1.

'vitally affects our interests'. And yet the historical moment had come to pass when a lawyer was prepared publicly to endorse the 'high prerogative view of the subject', one that 'would appear to authorise martial law in Kent on the strength of the Fenian raids in Canada'. For the *Pall Mall Gazette*, Finlason's treatise signalled the birth of a 'New Doctrine of Martial Law'.[236] The 'gist of the thick volume lately published by Mr. Finlason', the newspaper warned, was to 'supply a legal justification for all acts, however atrocious and despotic', whenever a local government thought that the public peace was threatened. This was worrying enough. But even more alarming was the fact that Finlason, and the writers who had endorsed his views, had 'put forward this monstrous doctrine with a calm and ease which proves that they suppose themselves to be putting forward nothing new or startling'. What they were doing, in fact, was 'rendering popular, propositions which if they were true would destroy every security which exists for our freedom'. The suppression of the Hyde Park riot was seen as a harbinger of things to come. In this view the Tory establishment in England was beginning to claw back hard-won liberties, and they now had their own legal ideologues to clear the way. It was now socially acceptable to praise the virtues of the martial state. That this could be the case, that such notions 'should not be universally scouted as the worst of all legal heresies, is melancholy proof of the general neglect into which the legal securities for our liberties have fallen'.

In the liberal papers, then, Finlason was viewed as a political writer with political aims, the chief one being to champion an altogether 'new' doctrine of martial law, one which understood the executive branch of government as having wide-ranging powers to suppress dissent in the empire, and more alarmingly, in the home countries. But if the liberals did not like his book, in the late autumn of 1866 Finlason could take comfort in the fact that it now dominated a topical field of discussion. The *Morning Post* thought that the work merited a 'place in the library of every educated man'.[237] The *Athenaeum* urged the book on 'those who desire to form an opinion on a matter which is likely to attract much attention'.[238] If nothing else, Finlason had proved that the law of martial law had become a critically important political subject-matter.

IV. Taming the English Tiger: Frederic Harrison's Six Letters to the *Daily News*

It is a safe conjecture that five-hundred-page law books rarely make an impression on a political controversy. Finlason's *Treatise on Martial Law* is the exception that proves the rule. In part it was a question of timing. When Finlason published his book the English political class was interested in the law of martial law, and its

---

[236] *Pall Mall Gazette* (23 July 1866), 1–2.   [237] *Morning Post* (30 July 1866), 3.
[238] *Athenaeum* (11 Aug. 1866).

implications for the Jamaica controversy. That would help explain why such a
hefty work got published, and why it received notices in so many leading newspapers and journals. But it was also a matter of the book's tone. This was not just
another arid treatment of an arcane legal subject, but a thinly disguised polemic
against the detractors of Governor Eyre and his officers, and in favour of a legal
Realpolitik in the empire. The leaders of the Jamaica Committee were among those
critics who thought that Finlason's theses on martial law could not be safely
ignored. Before the end of the year the Committee had commenced a major
literary counter-offensive against the new doctrine of martial law.

The principal figure in this initiative, the radical lawyer and social activist
Frederic Harrison, was aptly prepared for the task. A member of the Jamaica
Committee's executive, Harrison was an academically inclined barrister at
Lincoln's Inn, and was a widely published polemical journalist.[239] For six consecut-
ive weeks commencing on 23 November 1866, Harrison published an open letter
in the *Daily News* on the subject of martial law and the Eyre controversy. In the
Foreword to the collected edition of his letters (published by the Jamaica
Committee) he alleged that they 'were written without concert from any members
of the Jamaica Committee, and without even a knowledge of the course of procedure recommended'.[240] This assurance cannot be accepted at face value.[241] After
all, not only was Harrison a co-founder of the Committee,[242] but he was an active
member of its governing body when he drafted and published the letters.[243] On
the other hand, it is not hard to accept Harrison's assurance that his offerings on
martial law 'were warmly received' by his colleagues.[244] On 20 December 1866,
only eight days after the appearance of the sixth letter, Harrison already had
completed the Preface for the Committee imprint. Early in 1867, the collection
was published under the title *Martial Law: Six Letters to the 'Daily News'*.[245]

Harrison's letters (if more transparently than Finlason's treatise) were also
political tracts covered by a thin veneer of legal scholarship. They were written,
Harrison wrote, to clear the 'public mind' of some 'strange and portentous
doctrines of constitutional law'.[246] In other words, they were written to contradict
the work of W. F. Finlason. This Harrison all but admitted in his first letter to the
Daily News. 'A learned lawyer', he lamented, 'was found to write a book in which
he proved...that the execution of civilians by courts-martial was a striking

---

[239] Vogeler, *Oxford DNB*, online 33732:
[240] Frederic Harrison, *Martial Law: Six Letters to the 'Daily News', Jamaica Papers No. V* (London,
1867), iii.
[241] But Harrison's assertion is supported by the fact that in these months the minutes of the
Jamaica Committee do not indicate that the letters were explicitly commissioned. Some minutes
of November 1866, however, recorded that Harrison was to begin to publish the letters that week. *JC
Minutes*, 19 Nov. 1866.
[242] Harrison's name appears in the Minutes of the first meeting of the Jamaica Committee. *JC
Minutes*, 19 Dec. 1865.
[243] Harrison assumed a position on the Jamaica Committee executive on 9 July 1866. Ibid.
[244] Harrison, *Autobiographic Memoirs*, vol. i (London, 1911), 313.
[245] All quotes from Harrison, *Six Letters*.   [246] Ibid., iv.

feature of the British Constitution.'[247] 'Time was,' he wrote, 'when lawyers and the public watched [basic] liberties with dauntless and far-sighted zeal.'[248] With the leader-writers at the *Saturday Review* and *Pall Mall Gazette*, Harrison perceived that somehow the British people had become complacent about their constitutional rights, that 'some strange change has come over the nation, once so jealous of the power of the Executive, that it again tolerates the servile and despotic language of the Stuarts'. Making matters worse, Parliament, 'controlled by the upper and upper-middle class, has virtually exercised the powers of the Executive'.[249] Power, especially as manifested in the colonies, was slipping its harness. The law of martial law had to be set straight, lest the people once again 'become the accomplices of an arbitrary power'.[250]

Harrison perhaps had had reason to be concerned that the Jamaica Committee was losing the argument. The legal opinion of Stephen and James now was old news. Finlason's treatise, in its girth and ostensible authority, now loomed larger over public debate concerning the Jamaica affair. The Tory government steadfastly refused to prosecute Governor Eyre or any of the regular military officers who had participated in the execution of Gordon and others. The idea of commencing private criminal proceedings against Eyre had met with almost universal derision. It was in this largely inhospitable climate that Harrison had taken up his pen to set the record straight on the law of martial law and its application to the Jamaica affair. The publication and then republication of Harrison's letters in the last days of 1866 was a last-ditch effort to change the drift of public opinion before the Jamaica affair was brought into an English courtroom.

In November 1866, Harrison, at 35 years of age, was one of England's handful of 'radical' barristers.[251] A gentleman of expensive education and independent fortune, Harrison could afford to abstain from the quotidian life of an assize circuit.[252] In the best tradition of the well-bred and well-heeled English recalcitrant, Harrison devoted his time to causes, chiefly the development and validation of the English trade union movement. In 1866 he also was a leading (if somewhat ambivalent)[253] proponent of the extension of the franchise to working men. When he researched and wrote the six letters to the *Daily News*, Harrison, like so many of his confederates on the Jamaica Committee, was concerned mainly about the repercussions of the use of martial law in Jamaica for domestic affairs. His letters were composed as stern warnings: Englishmen could ignore the gross injustices done to Jamaicans only at great peril to their own civil rights.

According to his own statements, Harrison intended his six letters to be a scholarly if not definitive ('I will not pretend that it establishes the law

---

[247] Ibid., 2.　　[248] Ibid., 5.　　[249] Ibid., 3.　　[250] Ibid.

[251] See, e.g., Raymond Challinor, *A Radical Lawyer in Victorian England: W. P. Roberts and the Struggle for Workers' Rights* (London, 1990).

[252] Martha S. Vogeler, *Frederic Harrison: The Vocations of a Positivist* (Oxford, 1984), 2.

[253] Harrison was not a democrat. He supported reform of the franchise, but only as an expedient. His ultimate goal was the complete transformation of British politics and society under the guidance of an intellectual elite. Ibid., 391.

conclusively')²⁵⁴ contribution to public knowledge on martial law. The letters, he recollected, 'were the result of a great deal of legal study'.²⁵⁵ In the Preface to the collected letters, Harrison took pains to answer the criticism of other lawyers that, as a point of professional etiquette, a barrister ought not to comment on a case (such as the criminal prosecution of Governor Eyre) that was soon to come to trial.²⁵⁶ On this point, Harrison argued that it was not clear, at time of writing, that any legal case would be brought against Eyre or military officers.²⁵⁷ The question could thus be argued as an abstraction. Harrison also took pains to emphasize that the views expressed in the letters were his personally, and that they were not to be construed as the views of the lawyers that the Jamaica Committee had, or might in future, retained for the purposes of mounting a prosecution. With these disclaimers in place, Harrison discussed his motives.

Harrison maintained that public discussion of the Jamaica affair had been skewed by the machinations, to adopt a modern phrase, of a vast right-wing conspiracy. 'The most powerful sections of society', he asserted, 'are insisting that a certain line of conduct in a given state of facts is worthy of all honour.'²⁵⁸ It was further asserted that Governor Eyre, the prime mover behind the execution of Gordon and scores of others, was backed by a 'great force of adherents, strong in social and political influence, who are straining every nerve to show that the acts with which he is charged [are matters] of high honour and precious example'. By these (unnamed) men, he continued, a 'learned lawyer was found' to write a book proving that the execution of Gordon had been perfectly legal, and that 'society must come to an end unless Governments might hang obnoxious people'.²⁵⁹ These were notions which Harrison was now moved publicly to refute.

Harrison's letters were not so much an answer to Finlason as an antidote. In contrast to Finlason's work, they were written in an ironical, rhetorical, and deliberately un-academic style. They were the calculated effort of a lawyer (writing from 'Lincoln's Inn') to convince non-lawyers of the truth of some points of law, the untruth of others. Harrison's rhetorical strategy was plain. He wrote as if the argument about martial law was all but lost, as if the majority of his readers already accepted that Governor Eyre and his soldiers had done nothing illegal. When the Jamaica Committee had proposed to 'vindicate great public principles and rights,' he remarked, they were 'openly derided by men of influence and power'.²⁶⁰ But with his letters Harrison sought to rescue the public from a sinister misconception. He wanted to redeem the ancient constitution and the men who sought to uphold it. Harrison summarized his aims in this way: 'The principles with which these letters deal is this – that certain acts alleged to have been

---

²⁵⁴ Ibid., 14.   ²⁵⁵ Harrison, *Autobiographic Memoirs*, 313.
²⁵⁶ After the publication of his first letter in the *Daily News*, Harrison was attacked for having breached this professional protocol by an anonymous writer in the *Morning Post*. The attack obviously stung.   ²⁵⁷ Harrison, *Six Letters*, iii.
²⁵⁸ Ibid., iv.   ²⁵⁹ Ibid., 2.   ²⁶⁰ Ibid., 3.

committed constitute crimes – that certain crimes cannot safely be left uncondemned.'[261]

As Harrison explained in his first letter, these were precisely the principles that had been cast into doubt by the more expansive theories of martial law which had come into currency. In the remaining five letters, Harrison proposed to establish that martial law was 'unknown' to English law and that the Crown had no power to suspend the civil law either at home (or in the colonies), or to try a civilian before a court martial.[262] He would also argue that while officials lawfully could 'repel open force with open force', afterward they had to be called upon to prove that their actions had been based in an unavoidable necessity. Any government official, even the Governor of a colony, could be criminally prosecuted for having used force when it was not imperative to have done so.

In his second letter, Harrison decried the flippancy with which Disraeli and Adderley had endorsed the view that acts committed under martial law could not be illegal.[263] In this way the mistakes of private citizens such as Finlason had taken on new import. When government officials embraced this notion of martial law, the Jamaica controversy was no longer chiefly about 'the punishment of one intemperate ruler'. It became a 'vital question of national liberty and policy', a 'battle-ground of public rights'. However, in a country ruled by laws there was one legitimate means of winning the battle: by 'a formal appeal to the law'. The legality, or not, of the actions of Governor Eyre was a matter rightly to be 'determined by an English judge'.[264] Harrison began to 'draw out the broad features' of the legal case against the Disraelian doctrine of martial law. He began by asserting that the Petition of Right rendered it illegal for a civilian to be tried other than by a civilian court. In support Harrison quoted Coke's statement that any person taking up arms against the Crown ' "may be slain in the rebellion; *but if he be taken, he cannot be put to death by the martial law*" '. The execution of a civilian under colour of martial law was 'murder'. Harrison then quoted from Blackstone, Mansfield, Tindal, Brougham, and Mackintosh in support of the proposition that 'the English constitution and law know nothing, as regards civilians, of any law but the civil law.'[265] Any person, soldier or civilian, who acted against a citizen under the supposed auspices of martial law 'remain for all they do accountable to the arm of civil justice. Civil justice, like the king, never dies.' Once again, Harrison emphasized that his list of authorities was cited that they might amount to a 'strong prima facie case that martial law . . . is repugnant and alien to our system'.[266]

In his third letter Harrison took up the question of the legal status of martial law in the empire. He set out to establish that 'the Crown has no power to suspend civil law in the colonies'.[267] Harrison's basic argument in this regard was

[261] Ibid., 5. [262] Ibid., 6. [263] Ibid., 7. [264] Ibid., 9. [265] Ibid., 13.
[266] Ibid., 3. Significantly, however, Harrison did not directly address the question of emergency powers during a time of armed invasion or insurrection, the key pivot of Finlason's work.
[267] Ibid., 14.

for the transportability of basic legal rights: when an Englishman went to a British colony or dominion, he took his civil rights with him. In the empire, Harrison wrote, 'the Crown does not become, by the chance of place, a despotic power; nor does the subject become, by transplanting his home, a slave'.[268] In fact, for Harrison, the defining characteristic of an *English* place was 'the indefeasibility of civil justice, and subjection to a *limited* Executive'.[269]

At this point Harrison finally began to contest some of the central theses of Finlason's treatise. He began by attempting a definition of martial law, which he understood to describe that state of affairs when public officials announced, in the face of armed insurrection or invasion, that they would have 'recourse to the operations of war'.[270] Harrison readily agreed that government officials had the legal right to meet force with force. His difference with Finlason and his like was over the powers that were conferred by such a proclamation. The advocates of the expansive theory contended that martial law provided a blanket legal immunity to persons who, in good faith, implemented it against rebels or rebel prisoners. According to Harrison, conversely, martial law 'neither suspends, nor abrogates, nor supersedes civil law ... nor withdraws for one instant any citizen, official or not, from complete liability to account for every act in a civil court'. Any person accused of criminal wrongdoing under martial law was free to plead the defence of public necessity.[271] Judges and juries would decide whether the acts of repression had been lawful.

Colonial officials, Harrison argued, decidedly were not exempt from these rules. It did not matter that in places like Jamaica there was legislation on the local statute books, some in place for more than a hundred years, that purported to give colonial officials powers unknown to the British constitution. Harrison made two points in this regard. He quoted long passages of the Jamaican legislation on martial law to demonstrate that it did not intend to create immunities from 'civil and criminal justice'.[272] His second point was that the Jamaica statute would be of no force or effect even if it had *purported* to create such immunities. In this view, Britain was one empire, indivisible, under law.

Harrison's fourth letter turned to the subject of the 'duties and liabilities of a government suppressing an overt rebellion'.[273] On this point Harrison maintained that government officials and military men, whether or not they were acting under a proclamation of martial law, and whether or not they were acting under orders, remained 'individually *liable to trial* for every breach of the law'.[274] In English common law, the exertion of physical force against the body of another person was illegal, *prima facie*. While it was open to an official or soldier accused of a violent crime to plead necessity, like all other legal privileges, the plea had to be 'very strictly proved' that there had been 'no alternative'. In a country and empire which was vigilant of personal integrity and security, it was

---

[268] Harrison, *Six Letters*, 15.   [269] Ibid., 16.   [270] Ibid., 18.   [271] Ibid., 25.
[272] Ibid., 23.   [273] Ibid., 24.   [274] Ibid., 25.

natural that the defence of necessity would have a narrow compass. A wide definition would effectively license men to commit crimes. 'A licence to commit a crime', Harrison opined, 'is so tremendous a condition that nothing can support it but sheer overwhelming palpable necessity.' Moreover, a licence for *government officials* to commit crimes simply could not be countenanced by a constitutional state.

To Harrison's mind, all of these propositions were amply illustrated by the exercise of martial law in Ireland in 1798. In that instance, the Lord Lieutenant of Ireland, on the urging of the Privy Council, instituted martial law by proclamation.[275] However, the Irish Parliament later thought it necessary to pass a bill of indemnity meant to shield the civilian and military officials who implemented martial law from criminal prosecution. That the Irish Parliament took these steps, Harrison argued, proved that they did not believe that martial law could be invoked at the pleasure of government officials and, if it was invoked, that they did not believe it conveyed legal immunity from liability in the civilian courts. These principles were vindicated by the courts in *Wright v. Fitzgerald*, and in the famous case in which the courts wrested Wolfe Tone from the 'illegal fangs of a military tribunal'.[276] Even in the red heat of the Irish rebellion, 'the judges of that day assert[ed] the supremacy of civil justice against military usurpation'.[277]

In his fifth letter Harrison began with a discussion of the Gordon tumults of 1780. In that instance, 'arson, murder and rebellion [were] in full career' and London came very close to being 'reduced to a heap of ashes'.[278] Here, Harrison stated, was an 'insurrection rather than a riot, and [it] was only suppressed by a vigorous use of the military force'. But while the use of the military was widely considered necessary, it was also closely scrutinized by eminent legal and political men. In the House of Lords, Lord Mansfield unequivocally refuted the notion that England was 'living under a military government' or that 'any part of the laws or the constitution are suspended or have been dispensed with'.[279] Nor had Mansfield been contradicted when he stated that any person who broke the law in suppressing the insurrection would be subject to prosecution and punishment in the regular courts. This was not the law only in Britain proper. The same principles had been upheld many times in cases issuing from the larger empire. Harrison cited the cases of Wall and Picton – neither then a hundred years old – in which governors of colonies had been found liable to ordinary citizens for 'crimes done in the provinces'.[280] Here was further proof, Harrison argued, that in former times 'the insignificant character of the accuser mattered as little as the splendid services of the accused'.[281]

Harrison's sixth and final letter addressed the legal implications of the Jamaica controversy. His thesis was straightforward. Some senior government and military

---

[275] For a general description of martial law in Ireland, see Clode, *Military Forces of the Crown*, 168–75.   [276] Harrison, *Six Letters*, 29.
[277] Ibid., 30.   [278] Ibid.   [279] As quoted by Harrison, ibid., 31.   [280] Ibid.
[281] Ibid., 34.

officials had committed crimes for which they must be punished. The case of Gordon's execution was only the most egregious example of wrongdoing. In Jamaica in 1865, civil rights, 'carefully built up in the course of generations', were cast aside like so much straw. If left unredressed, Harrison warned, a dangerous precedent will have been set, one that was bound to 'affect our own civil rights'.[282] This letter, interestingly enough, did not dwell on the moral or legal niceties of the Jamaica affair. The last pages of his epistle instead were a Burkean fulmination against the corrupting effects of the non-Europeanized empire. For Harrison, the 'truly gloomy' aspect of the Jamaica suppression was that such events 'appear to be fatally chronic'.[283] The Jamaica insurrection and suppression, Harrison wrote, was only the most recent event in 'one unbroken weary round of horror'. In the West Indies, in Asia and, at the cost of thousands of lives, during the sepoy rebellion in India, the British were trapped in a regular cycle of rebellion and retribution. Throughout the empire official injustice had bred violent insurrection which, in turn, bred an 'organized reign of terror' by the colonial authorities. In England these events invariably generated 'a murmur of indignation', then defiance by colonial interests, then 'a craven Government, and public apathy'. There was nothing new about the Jamaica affair but the unbending determination of some public-minded men to bring about a decisive legal intervention.

According to Harrison's further analysis, the governance of a sprawling, non-white, empire was having a corrosive effect on the moral fibre of the nation. For decades Englishmen had been embroiled in almost 'constant warfare with half-savage and dark races'.[284] Many English soldiers and civil officials had become both fond of repression, and sure in the belief that it would be accepted, even applauded, at home. 'The terrible Indian rebellion,' Harrison warned, 'has sown evil seeds enough in the military as well as the civil system.' Now, after the martial law in Jamaica, the letters of soldiers reflected an unselfconscious 'delight in slaughter'. The resistance of black men in the empire, combined with the easy accessibility of violence, had made Englishmen cruel, it had in Harrison's striking phrase, 'called out the tiger in our race'. In the empire the violent disposition of Englishmen had been allowed free play. Now, Harrison entreated, 'it must be caged again'.

Finlason's *Treatise* was a work of legal scholarship infused with political aims, rhetoric, and postures. Harrison's *Six Letters* was a work of political rhetoric infused with legal propositions, sources, and language. They were conceived of as a kind of literary antidote to the soporific technicality of the longer and exhaustive work. In the course of time, all of the standard case reports (*Mostyn v. Fabrigas, Grant v. Gould, Wolfe Tone*), eminent authorities (Coke, Hale), and statutes (the Petition of Right) were cited and, sometimes, even generously quoted. But Harrison was writing not so much as a lawyer as a political essayist, and he did not permit mere law to dominate his paragraphs. The tedium of formal legal discourse is supplanted by Harrison's animated paraphrases and hyperbolic invective. In this

---

[282] Harrison, *Six Letters*, 37.   [283] Ibid.   [284] Ibid., 41.

manner of style, the assertion that Jamaican law permitted a man to be tried for his life by a court martial was not wrong, but 'Monstrous and insolent pretence!'[285] This was the order of language, Harrison's letters implied, that might shake the English reading public from its dangerous infatuation with the new doctrine of martial law.

Harrison's stirring rhetoric had a number of interesting features. The first is its relentless anglocentrism. Whether by design or not, Harrison's letters barely mention the plight or suffering of Jamaica's black peasantry. He was primarily interested in the ramifications of the Jamaica affair for Englishmen, not the 'half-savage and dark races'. As those of Carlyle and Carlyle's admirers, Harrison's letters were written on the assumption that the black man was inferior to the white, an unknowable and dangerous 'other'. Where Harrison departed from Carlyle was on the question of what sort of stance to adopt toward the empire's dark-skinned subjects. While Carlyle endorsed rule by the mailed fist, Harrison thought this policy was certain to undermine the most valuable characteristics of English civilization: the juridical equality of all subjects and the rule of law over the 'foul breath of licence'.

In spite of his racial assumptions, Harrison argued strenuously for the principle of the juridical (if not intellectual or social) equality of non-white persons in the empire. It was crucial that 'in the eye of justice, every citizen within it has equal rights'.[286] If the British were to maintain their claim to civilization, then it was imperative that 'British rule shall be the rule of law; that every British citizen, white, brown or black in skin, shall be subject to definite and not indefinite powers'. The bedrock of Britishness was commitment to the principle of 'law, and not prerogative'.[287] But this modern-sounding position was given a pre-modern-sounding justification. Non-white subjects were to be afforded equal rights not because of their equal status as human beings, but because of the dire consequences *for England* of not doing so. 'We cannot make rules for negroes,' Harrison argued, 'without baiting traps for Europeans.' Here was the trap: when negroes were not given the same civil rights and privileges as whites they inevitably rebelled, and with unique 'African ferocity'.[288] In order to cope with these rebellions, colonial officers, always outnumbered by rebels, could do nothing but abandon the one thing that lent credence to their claim to superior civilization: the rule of law. Further to the point, Harrison thought it a dangerous view that the use of unconstrained force could somehow be confined to the non-Europeanized colonies, for the 'contagion of lawlessness spreads fast. What is done in a colony today may be done in Ireland tomorrow, and in England hereafter.'[289]

This last statement went to the heart of Harrison's rhetoric. That unenfranchised majority of British men, as they moved to challenge the powerful at home, should think twice about ignoring tyranny in the empire. Already there were signs

285 Ibid., 21.   286 Ibid., 38.   287 Ibid.   288 Ibid.   289 Ibid.

that some powerful men enjoyed the use of unbridled force. Now was the time to ensure that this taste was not indulged in London, Liverpool, or Glasgow. Now was the time to tell whether the 'vaunted doctrines of English constitution and liberty are either real or sham'.[290]

Harrison's preoccupation with Jamaica as an *English* experience with dire implications for the *English* polity is the first salient theme of his letters. An unshakeable faith in the redemptive qualities of the secular law was the second. If the British polity already had been tainted by the use of terror in the empire, Harrison intimated, the taint could be cleansed. All that was required was for a British judge to affirm, as Coke and Mansfield had done, that the law could neither be suspended nor broken with impunity. All that was required to put things right was for a judge to vindicate the first principle of the constitution: 'throughout our empire, as in this kingdom, government shall be responsible and defined; and there, as here, its basis shall be law, and not prerogative.'[291] For Harrison and his colleagues on the Jamaica Committee, the Jamaica affair was not about the misconduct of 'one intemperate ruler'. It was about correcting the course of a nation that had lost its way. In January 1867, the crossfire of legal polemics having ceased, the Jamaica Committee set about the practical task of putting things right in the courts of law.

In the closing paragraph of his last letter, Harrison returned to the Jamaica controversy. There was ample reason to reject the view (championed by Finlason and others) that some doctrine of martial law immunized Governor Eyre and his senior officers from criminal prosecution for their parts in crimes in the suppression of the Morant Bay rising. But whether Eyre or any other person was 'legally responsible for any criminal act',[292] Harrison ventured, was a matter for judge and jury to determine. The Jamaica controversy, in this way of thinking, boiled down to a struggle over the British nation's basic law. Whether Finlason or Harrison had the correct view of this law, was not for public opinion, or even parliamentarians, to decide. In the not distant future, Harrison trusted, a judge and jury would 'try one of the most solemn and memorable issues' that had ever come before a British court.

V. Conclusion: The Tenets of Terror

It was a natural consequence of the Jamaica affair that it gave rise to an effusion of technical writing on the law of martial law, until then a subject that had been of scant interest. After all, from the moment in November 1865 when news of the suppression reached England, the country's political class had been preoccupied with its legal character and implications. Had it been legal for Governor Eyre to

290 Ibid., 39.   291 Ibid., 4.   292 Ibid., 42.

proclaim martial law over a part of Jamaica? Had Gordon been lawfully arrested, transported, and executed? Had government officials committed crimes during the suppression and, if so, were they open to criminal prosecution and punishment? During the winter of 1866 lawyers began to publish systematic research on these questions. What began as a trickle of newspaper articles and editorial letters became, by the spring of 1866, a torrent of formal memoranda, treatises, and anti-treatises.

But anyone who had hoped that the country's lawyers would supply a clear and uncontentious account of martial law, and its application to the Jamaica case, was sorely disappointed. Like so much of the British constitution, the law of martial law did not have an obvious pedigree or structure. It could not be traced to one or two (or even five) discrete sources of law. For anyone wanting to construct a coherent picture of martial law, there was nothing to do but to excavate and assemble shards from a myriad of case reports, national histories, treatises, official opinions, military dicta, and parliamentary utterances. Martial law was not something that was to be *found* in the sources; it was something that had to be *made* from them. Every account of the subject plainly was the result of numberless choices as between competing authorities (only some of whom were lawyers) and interpretations of those authorities. Inevitably these choices were not random, but were determined by a political predisposition. Arguments about the law of martial law turned on the writer's *a priori* commitments of one of two general kinds: to individual liberty in England or public security in the empire. The legal discourse on martial law was politics by other means.

The account of martial law created and defended by the *Solicitors' Journal*, Stephen, James, and Harrison was starkly different from the account created and defended by the *Law Times*, the *Jurist*, and Finlason. The former took up the subject of martial law, and then made choices about its content, mainly as a result of anxieties about the tenor of domestic politics, specifically, as a result of the 'growing disposition amongst certain classes to applaud "vigour" in the exercise of authority, even when it is accompanied by the setting aside of law'.[293] In these circles it was seen as vital to prove that England's ruling elites, as they moved against agitation for political reform, could not have legal recourse to unbridled military power. They would not permit the Jamaica affair to become a precedent for authoritarianism at home. In their view there was no doctrine of English law that would permit the authorities to suspend the civil law, crush dissent, and claim legal immunity. In this 'liberal' rendering of the subject, martial law was a single instance of the common law defence of necessity, nothing more or less than the plea that some action against person or property that was illegal *prima facie*, was privileged by some demonstrable public necessity. According to this line of

---

[293] Letter to the *Daily News* (16 Jan. 1866), 6.

reasoning, it was obvious that Gordon had been murdered, and that his murderers ought to be brought to book.

If the legal literature of the Jamaica Committee was rooted in liberal anxiety about the sanctity of civil liberties at home, the legal literature of W. F. Finlason was rooted in racial anxiety about white communities in the empire. Finlason argued for a limited imperial exception to the principle of universal legal account-ability. In this account, the reason why the subject of martial law mattered was because in many colonies and dependencies English men and women faced the pervasive and lethal threat of 'servile revolt'. In these places a robust doctrine of martial law was not an academic matter, but utterly essential to the survival of whole populations of white British people. In this regard, Finlason was a political realist. He accepted that in much of the empire the white master class was hated as much as it was outnumbered. Ultimately, British rule over masses of black and uncivilized peoples depended less on consent than on coercion and, even more cru-cially, on the omnipresent threat of coercion. If there was to be even a modicum of security for white administrators and settlers in colonies such as Jamaica, the subjugated peoples had to fear suppression more than they craved resistance. These were the tenets of terror, and they underscored every aspect of Finlason's research and writing on martial law.

The key point being made in Finlason's book was that martial law, once it was lawfully proclaimed, meant that military necessity (as discerned by commanders in the field) trumped any other consideration. It was never to be forgotten that 'the great object under martial law is the safety of the State, and to that the security of the individual must give way'.[294] The law of martial law had its own rules and its own – distinctly military – rationale. While common law was concerned with individual liberty, martial law was concerned with collective security. In determining when to coerce or punish an individual, 'the former mainly regards guilt, the latter chiefly regards danger'. The upshot for the Jamaica affair was plain. If it could be demonstrated that Eyre and his officers genuinely believed that the corporal punishment or execution of a person was necessary to the restoration of peace and order, they were entitled to punish and execute with impunity. From this perspective, for example, if it had been carried out to prevent further insurrection Gordon's execution was a justifiable homicide.

In the thirteen months following the first news of the Morant Bay rebellion and suppression, English lawyers and legal commentators produced thousands of published pages on the law of martial law, and its implications for the Jamaica controversy. But for all their toil the leading authors did not even agree on its nature and import, or whether it condemned or privileged the death of Gordon (and scores of other alleged rebels). In December 1866 a writer to the *Pall Mall Gazette* usefully suggested that the reason why consensus had proved so elusive

---

[294] Letter to the *Daily News* (16 Jan. 1866), 6.

was that its 'nature and extent... appertain to the highest and most difficult chapters of political science'.[295] At the end of the day, the term 'martial law' was a kind of code for a writer's basic attitude toward state power. In drawing the boundaries of martial law, some writers were inclined to err on the side of order, others on the side of liberty. But as the year closed so did the time for scholarly and pseudo-scholarly polemics. It was time to settle matters in the English courts of law.

---

[295] *Pall Mall Gazette* (19 Dec. 1866), 3–4.

5

Marshalling Martial Law: Litigating the Jamaica Controversy

There are some subjects which it is not necessary to discuss until the occasion presents itself – this is one of them.

James Hannen Q.C., Bow Street, 22 Feb. 1867

The Jamaica prosecutions have commenced. We do not wish to say one word to prejudge the case. The question has now passed outside the domain of public discussion.

Daily Telegraph, 8 Feb. 1867

On 22 January 1867 a grand jury consisting of twenty-three gentleman freeholders of Middlesex County was summoned to the opening of the assizes. Its principal function was to assess the evidence supporting indictments for treason, sedition, and, still more exotically, for offences committed 'by governors of colonies abroad'.[1] It was exceedingly rare of course for such a case to be on the docket. But on this day the expectation was different. On 21 January the Jamaica Committee had announced that it was poised to prefer an indictment against Edward Eyre for the murder of George Gordon.[2]

Sir Colin Blackburn, the presiding judge at the Middlesex assizes, was aware of this development. When the grand jurors were assembled and sworn, Blackburn informed them that it 'was possible that an indictment might be preferred against Mr. Eyre; and he had to request that if any of the gentlemen summoned were subscribers either to the fund of the prosecution or defence, they were to withdraw'.[3] The warning was not misplaced. One prospective juror promptly informed the judge that his employer had contributed to one of the two Jamaica-related subscription funds, although he did not know which one. Blackburn told him to stand aside. As for the remaining jurors, they were to make themselves ready to hear the Eyre case upon short notice. In actual fact, however, the Jamaica

---

[1] *Law Times* (26 Jan. 1867), 246.
[2] *The Times* (21 Jan. 1867), 10. The announcement was made as part of an appeal for further subscriptions. Potential donors were informed that the prosecution would commence so soon as key witnesses had arrived from Jamaica.
[3] Ibid.

Committee was not yet in a position to indict Eyre in London. The Middlesex grand jury would eventually be needed, but not for some months to come.

In January 1867 the Jamaica affair had been a matter of controversy in England for more than a year. For the Jamaica Committee, the period of investigation and internal debate was over. Its leaders no longer harboured any doubt that in response to the riot at Morant Bay government and military officials in Jamaica had implemented a reign of terror over the black peasantry of the eastern parishes of the colony. Nor was there any remaining doubt that Gordon had been an innocent man executed in haste, and after a reprehensible sham of a trial. This was not the opinion only of lay Committee members. James and Stephen had publicly averred that Governor Eyre had committed capital crimes during the suppression, crimes that were not excused by the operation of 'martial law'. When Lord Derby's government refused to prosecute these officials, the Jamaica Committee, now under the steadfast leadership of Mill, exercised their right to commence private prosecutions in the English courts of law.

The prosecution of Eyre, the Jamaica Committee repeatedly emphasized, was not about punishing individual wrongdoers, or even securing justice for their victims. The prosecution was promoted as political or 'state' litigation, motivated by a professed reverence for some fundamental principles of law. Eyre was to be put in the dock on a capital charge because this was the only means by which private citizens might vindicate the authentic jurisprudence of political and military power. The prosecution was necessary, not so much because blood had been spilled in a colony, but because so many prominent persons (Disraeli, most prominently) had stated publicly that the blood had been spilled lawfully. These pronouncements, the Committee believed, implied that no British political dissident, even while he stood on home soil, was secure from court martial and summary execution.[4] If left unchallenged the Government's position would subvert the first principle of the constitution: the rule of law over every subject of the realm, including powerful officeholders.

As for Eyre, he and his influential friends did not take it lightly that the Jamaica Committee was preparing to offer him as a sacrifice to their legal gods. It is not a pleasant thing to be indicted for murder, even if one's accusers do not mean for it to be taken personally. While few English observers thought it likely that Eyre would actually be convicted of murder (or any lesser crime), many more were outraged that the former Governor, the saviour of so many white lives in Jamaica, might be so ill-used. Eyre's supporters, and there were plenty of these by the close of 1866, resolved that, if criminal prosecution could not be prevented, it could at the least be vigorously defended. In the final weeks of 1866 the leaders of the Eyre Defence Committee – Murchison and Shrewsbury had emerged as the main actors in this regard – worked closely with hand-picked

---

[4] The 'public cannot feel assured that British subjects who may have given offence to a party in power, will not again be put to death without lawful trial'. Ibid.

lawyers to construct a defence strategy. The centrepiece of their plan was to remove Eyre from London (and from the jurisdiction of its seasoned lawyer–magistrates) to a residence in one of England's remote shires. It was by no accident then, that before the Jamaica Committee was ready to make a legal move against Eyre, he and his family were comfortably ensconced in a country estate in Shropshire.[5]

In January 1867 the Committee was impatient to get the prosecution started. Towards this end, criminal charges were lodged in London against two targets of opportunity: the naval officer Abercrombie Nelson, and the army officer Herbert Brand. While on duty in Jamaica during October 1865, Nelson and Brand had been instrumental in the court martial and execution of Gordon. In January 1867 both men were in London and, although they were aware of the possibility of indictment for the murder of Gordon, were disinclined to flee to the English countryside. In the first week of February 1867, Nelson and Brand were charged as accessories to the murder of Gordon at the Central Police Court at Bow Street. When by the end of March it became obvious to the Committee that Edward Eyre would not soon return to London, they commenced criminal proceedings against the former governor in the county town of Market Drayton, Shropshire. This chapter addresses the history of these prosecutions.

The decision of the Committee to force the Jamaica controversy into the courts of law raises a number of intriguing historical questions about the nature of politically-motivated litigation. How did the Committee conceptualize and then organize these cases? What considerations informed the selection of prosecuting lawyers? How much control could the leaders of the Committee exert over how their cases were handled and argued? How did the lawyers characterize what had happened in Jamaica? On what theory of law did they think the accused culpable for Gordon's murder? What was their courtroom strategy? As for Nelson, Brand, and Eyre, how did they set about the task of defending themselves? On what grounds did their lawyers argue that they were *not* culpable for Gordon's death? How did the urban and rural magistrates cope with the legal and political complexities of the prosecutions? What was their understanding of the law of martial law? How were they evaluated by England's political and legal press?

I. Litigating a Political Case: The 'Coleridge Plot' and After

In July (more than three weeks before Charles Buxton resigned as chair) the Jamaica Committee already had asked Fitzjames Stephen to prepare a formal legal opinion on 'how to obtain justice in this country' for those who had perished during the period of martial law.[6] The opinion was to provide information on the

---

[5] Although Eyre later denied that he had deliberately attempted to evade prosecution by the Jamaica Committee. Eyre to *The Times* (27 Apr. 1868).   [6] *JC Minutes*, 5 July 1866.

legal mechanics of prosecuting a person in England for criminal wrongdoing committed in a colony. Before Stephen could render a report, the Committee instructed John Gorrie to comb through the available evidence and assemble a list of the 'chief criminal acts committed by Governor Eyre and his subordinates'.[7] In August, now committed publicly to the prosecution strategy, the Committee commenced a new fund-raising campaign. Their advertisements stated that 'in light of the contumacious refusal of the Government to do its duty', an additional £10,000 was needed to defray the cost of the legal proceedings.[8] By 28 September the 'Ten Thousand Pound Fund' campaign had attracted nearly £3,000 in subscriptions (a large fraction of the money was secured by John Bright in his constituency at Rochdale).[9] Shaen was asked to make all the final preparations for Eyre's indictment for murder at the next session of the Central Criminal Court in London.[10] Witnesses in Jamaica were sent for. It was time now to retain a trial barrister.

It is important to notice that the Jamaica Committee decided on the prosecution strategy only at substantial cost of control over its destiny. The solicitation and digestion of detailed legal advice became a precondition of all future action. This not only implied some loss of control, but it took time. In November 1866 Goldwin Smith published a letter in the *Manchester Guardian* which chastised pundits who had accused the Committee of being 'dilatory' in bringing charges against Eyre.[11] 'It has been necessary,' Smith explained, 'that before such a course as an indictment for murder was adopted, our counsel should be allowed maturely to deliberate on the case in all its aspects, and examine all the different modes of proceeding.' The Committee had agreed that prudent considerations of law, not 'personal convictions', would be pivotal in the final decisions about if, when, and whom to prosecute. This statement was also meant to reassure supporters that the Committee would quickly rebound from the recent imbroglio involving the famed barrister John Duke Coleridge Q.C.

During its deliberations of the early autumn 1866, the Committee decided to retain a distinguished and experienced trial lawyer (impliedly, one more distinguished and experienced than Fitzjames Stephen) to undertake what was likely to be a highly visible, even sensational prosecution. After some names were bandied about, Shaen approached Coleridge's clerk. The brief proposed that his principal should become the 'Prosecutor' in a criminal case to be styled '*The Prosecutor v. Governor Eyre*'. Coleridge accepted the brief on 19 October 1866.[12]

In choosing Coleridge the Jamaica Committee got the two qualities that it desperately needed in their lead trial counsel: consummate technical skill and unimpeachable professional stature. Coleridge was born in 1820, the son of an eminent barrister and judge (and grand-nephew of the famous poet).[13] After a

---

[7] Ibid., 10 July 1866.   [8] See report in *The Times* (13 Oct. 1866), 6.
[9] *JC Minutes*, 28 Sept. 1866.   [10] Ibid.
[11] As reprinted in the *Daily News* (20 Nov. 1866).   [12] *JC Minutes*, 19 Oct. 1866.
[13] For biographical background on Coleridge, see E. Manson, *Builders of our Law* (London, 1904), 355–67; Pugsley, *Oxford DNB*, online 5886.

brilliant career at Eton and Oxford, Coleridge trained for the bar at the Middle Temple. In 1846 he commenced a practice on the Western Circuit. Coleridge was tall, handsome, and blessed with a 'beautiful voice'. He soon became renowned in the trial courts for his cultivated but forceful eloquence. By 1862 Coleridge was a Queen's Counsel and a bencher. He was also an occasional contributor to liberal political periodicals and, in 1865, was elected as a Liberal M.P. for Exeter. In Parliament, Coleridge advanced a moderate reformist agenda; he led his party's initiative to abolish religious tests at Oxford and Cambridge. In 1868 the *Spectator* pronounced him 'the most mellifluous orator in the House of Commons'.[14] In his pedigree, urbanity, and indisputable reputation, Coleridge was a splendid choice for the Jamaica Committee. He was just the man to give a civilized demeanour to its edgy, not-quite-respectable radicalism. Coleridge was said (by Goldwin Smith) to have another valuable qualification for the brief: he was 'known to be on the side of humanity, a hearty advocate of the cause'.[15] For the pro-Eyre camp, then, Coleridge was a lawyer to be reckoned with, even feared.

We have seen that when he returned to England in August 1866, Eyre was welcomed by supporters moved both by an intense loathing for the 'religious sectarianism and advanced Liberalism' of the Jamaica Committee,[16] and by sympathy and admiration for the former Governor personally. By the late autumn of 1866, the Eyre Defence Committee already had amassed a war-chest of thousands of pounds sterling.

One of the Eyre Defence Committee's first moves was to engage (for Eyre) the services of the solicitor J. Anderson Rose. Rose did not waste time making his presence felt with the Jamaica Committee. On 12 November, Shaen informed his colleagues of some unexpected trouble. The Defence Committee – in what ought to be regarded as one of the most cynical tactical moves in legal history – had attempted to supplant the retainer with Coleridge. As Chesson recorded in his diary: 'Sharp reaction from the Eyre party. On hearing that Mr. Coleridge had been retained by the Jamaica Committee, they sent an emissary to his chambers with a retainer.'[17] When Coleridge's clerk refused it, the emissary did not withdraw. He asserted that Coleridge was obliged to accept the Eyre Committee's brief on grounds that the first retainer had not yet been paid. When informed that the Jamaica Committee had already paid the retainer fee, the emissary changed tack. 'I shall still insist upon retaining [Mr. Coleridge] for Mr. Eyre,' he stated, 'as his retainer for the Jamaica Committee goes for nothing. A committee is an impersonal body and has no power to retain anybody.' Coleridge's clerk was unmoved by this argument, but agreed to raise the issue with his principal upon his return to

---

[14] *Spectator* (11 Apr. 1868), 425.

[15] Letter of Goldwin Smith to the *Manchester Guardian*, as reprinted in the *Daily News* (20 Nov. 1866).

[16] For a highly partisan account of the political and religious orientation of the Jamaica and Eyre Defence Committees, see Finlason, *History of the Jamaica Case*, 368ii–368qq.

[17] *CD*, 26 Oct. 1866.

chambers. Such was the beginning of (what Chesson aptly referred to as) the 'Coleridge Plot'.

When Coleridge learned of the Eyre Committee's brief, he brusquely declined to accept it. But the Eyre camp was not content to leave it there. On the advice of Anderson Rose, the Eyre Committee sent a formal letter of complaint to the Attorney General, Sir John Rolt, alleging that Coleridge was in breach of an important point of bar etiquette. In Rose's view, Coleridge was obliged to accept Eyre's retainer, and for two technical reasons. The first was that the Jamaica Committee's retainer document was a nullity because it purported to retain Coleridge 'in the name of the *Prosecutor* (whomever he may be) *v. Eyre*'.[18] Rose contended that the retainer was bad in form because it was 'not presumed that a private person contemplates a prosecution'.[19] A properly drafted retainer would have styled the action 'in the name of *Regina v. Eyre*', as it was in the retainer that Rose had offered to Coleridge. But there was a second, less picayune, reason why the original retainer was defective: the Jamaica Committee was neither a human nor a corporate person, and (in the words of the *Daily Telegraph*), 'cannot secure by retainer the services of counsel'.[20] Given that Coleridge could not have been retained by the Jamaica Committee, it was a straightforward point of bar etiquette that he was obligated to accept the first valid brief offered him in a case. Just such a brief now was being offered by the solicitors for Eyre. Rose requested that the Attorney General exercise his prerogatives as 'head of the bar'[21] to put things right.

When the leaders of the Jamaica Committee got wind of this ploy, they began immediately to fight back. On 2 November a private letter was sent by Shaen to Coleridge urging him not to renounce his original retainer.[22] Shaen pointed out that voluntary associations 'have been constantly in the habit of tendering retainers, which have been as constantly accepted and acted upon by counsel for many years'. If the objection of the Defence Committee was upheld, Shaen argued, it would 'outlaw' the retainers of barristers with innumerable charitable, literary, and scientific societies. Coleridge replied immediately, assuring Shaen he thought there was 'nothing at all in Mr. Rose's objection'.[23] He then reaffirmed his commitment to the original retainer but with one condition: 'if I am told by the Attorney General that I am bound by professional rule to act for Mr. Eyre, of course I must do so.' Although Coleridge could 'hardly conceive' why the Attorney General would oblige him to accept the defence brief, he would submit to his decision on the question. Professional tradition and discipline, in other words, would trump any personal conviction that he might hold regarding the issue.

The final decision, then, was put into the hands of the Attorney General. Rolt had assumed that office just a few days prior to the Coleridge affair. In his

[18] *Law Times* (17 Nov. 1866), 41.   [19] Ibid (24 Nov. 1866), 62.
[20] *Daily Telegraph* (19 Nov. 1866), 4.   [21] Ibid.
[22] As reprinted in the *Law Times* (24 Nov. 1866), 68.   [23] Ibid.

professional life he had made good in the Court of Chancery. In politics he was a resolute Tory, one unwaveringly opposed to political reform.[24] On his appointment to cabinet, the *Solicitors' Journal* called Rolt 'by far the most distinguished lawyer on the Conservative side of the House of Commons'.[25] A distinguished lawyer though he might have been, Rolt was not the sort of man who would be sorry to damage the ambitions of the Jamaica Committee.

Like so many aspects of the Jamaica affair, the dispute over the Coleridge retainer became the subject of extensive public comment. Not surprisingly, some of the more liberal papers worried that the Attorney General's decision would be tainted by partisan politics. According to the *Daily News*, a newspaper strongly aligned with the Jamaica Committee, the Coleridge case was 'one of a political character and affecting public liberty'.[26] Rolt's finding was certain to affect the ability of voluntary associations to retain the barristers needed to 'defend liberty' in Her Majesty's courts of law. In this view, the courts were a vitally important forum of political conflict. The ability to retain a lawyer of choice, therefore, was an equally important political right. For this reason alone the dispute over the Coleridge retainer gave rise to an important issue of principle. Too bad, the *Daily News* lamented, that such a question was to be decided by a man who, while the head of the London bar, was also a senior member of a government whose leading lights were adamantly opposed to the aims of the Jamaica Committee.

As Attorney General, it was Rolt's absolute prerogative both to make a determination on matters of bar etiquette and, if it suited him, not to offer any reasons for it. Over the protestations of Shaen, some newspapermen, and even Coleridge himself, this was precisely what Rolt opted to do. His decision was that Coleridge was obliged by bar etiquette to accept the retainer offered by Edward Eyre through his solicitor. Rolt did not condescend to justify this determination. When Shaen asked for an explanation, he declined on the basis that such a thing was 'not usual'.[27] If Rolt cared about the imputation that he had been moved by political considerations, he did not show it.

The Jamaica Committee was of course greatly perturbed by the prospect of losing Coleridge. Shaen was instructed to implore Coleridge to treat the Attorney General's decision as merely advisory.[28] But Coleridge, although he did not hide the fact that he thought Rolt's decision incorrect, did not relent. He had told Shaen that he would abide by the finding ('whether I agreed with it or not'), and would keep his word: 'I will not set myself against the authority of the head of the bar in a matter as to which he is the recognised judge.' With a regal disdain for the whole unseemly business, Coleridge expressed his hope that the Committee 'would see, as plainly as I do, that is really of extremely little consequence'.

---

[24] In November of 1866, Rolt had given a speech against the 'threatened despotism of democracy'. As reported in the *Law Times* (24 Nov. 1866), 63.   [25] *Solicitors' Journal* (20 Oct. 1866), 1165.

[26] *Daily News* (20 Nov. 1866), 2.

[27] As quoted in letter of Shaen to Coleridge reprinted in the *Law Times* (24 Nov. 1866), 68.

[28] Ibid.

For an association which had staked everything on the outcome of litigation, losing their first – perhaps ideal – choice of barrister was of rather more consequence. In this regard, the Jamaica Committee garnered some sympathy even from unexpected quarters. The *Daily Telegraph*, a conservative paper which had been scathingly critical of its efforts, had come to accept that there should be a 'test case' of the major legal issues arising out of the Morant Bay uprising. 'In this great duel between what seem conflicting rights – the rights of individual British subjects, and the rights of the Executive during the sharp crisis of an insurrection,' the *Telegraph* stated, 'it is well that the question should be fairly fought out.'[29] Given that the prosecution of Eyre was likely to result in a 'leading case for years, perhaps for centuries', it was essential that both parties were able to retain lawyers of their own choosing. If the nation was to receive the correct legal decision on the vital legal questions thrown up by the execution of Gordon, it was vital that there 'be no advantage or superiority of counsel'. The *Telegraph* thought that Rolt's decision would undermine this important principle. The Jamaica Committee had been deprived of the services of 'a favourite and able advocate', and for reasons that had gone 'utterly unexplained'.[30] In the result, the good of the country had been compromised by an 'arbitrary decision'.

The Committee's response to this setback largely echoed these remarks.[31] Goldwin Smith wrote an open letter accusing the Eyre faction of having set out to 'baffle justice'. Eyre's partisans had attempted – and thanks to a politically friendly Attorney General had succeeded in – the 'abduction, by a technical device, of our counsel, Mr. Coleridge'. For Smith there was a bitter irony in all this. The high-minded 'philosophers' of the Eyre Committee, so ready with their talk of 'higher morality', had resorted to a cheap ruse. It was indeed unfortunate, Smith moaned, that 'a secret and irresponsible conclave of men, full of class feeling, should have the power, in political cases, of locking the gates of justice in the face of public right'. In fact, however, Smith's indignation was naive. While it was true that the Jamaica Committee's horse had been nobbled out of the gate, what had they expected? After all, Mill and his associates were not preparing an afternoon tea for Edward Eyre. Their sworn aim was to put him in the dock for his life. It ought to have been surprising to no one that the Defence Committee and its lawyers were prepared to act fiercely, even unscrupulously, in defence of their man. The only surprising aspect of the Coleridge stratagem was that it had succeeded so brilliantly.

It ought to be noted here that in offering Coleridge a retainer the Eyre Committee never intended that Coleridge would appear for their side in a court of law. As the *Daily News* reported in November, by the time Rolt rendered his decision, the Defence Committee already had retained a number of other eminent barristers,[32] men who were more sympathetic to the plight of the former Governor of Jamaica. In fact, all along the Committee's scheme was

[29] *Daily Telegraph* (19 Nov. 1866), 4.   [30] Ibid.
[31] Letter to the *Manchester Guardian*, reprinted in the *Daily News* (20 Nov. 1866), 2.
[32] *Daily News* (20 Nov. 1866), 2.

calculated only to prevent the Jamaica Committee from being represented by one of England's most distinguished trial lawyers. The Defence Committee was determined that the formidable voice, mind, and bearing of John Coleridge should not become the voice, mind, and bearing of the Jamaica Committee. As events unfolded, this resolve looked ever more prescient.

The Coleridge Plot had wrong-footed the Jamaica Committee, and in his diary Chesson tried to put a brave face on it: 'The Attorney General has decided against the Committee's retainer of Mr. Coleridge. Good! It will only add fuel to the fire.'[33] At a 'heavily attended' executive meeting held on 12 November 1866 (the 'most important meeting we have had yet,' Chesson observed), the Committee voted to press ahead with the criminal prosecution of Eyre, with or without John Coleridge. Solace was taken in the belief that success would turn on the substantive merits of its legal case, not on the personal merits of its lead lawyer. This rather innocent hope soon was reinforced by a new legal memorandum written by Fitzjames Stephen.

In July 1866 Stephen had been asked by the Jamaica Committee to determine which specific Jamaican civilian or military officials had, on the face of the available evidence, committed crimes during the suppression that might be prosecuted in England. In October Stephen reported his findings. In his opinion the Committee might commence viable criminal prosecutions for murder against Eyre, Nelson, and Brand for their respective roles in Gordon's court martial and execution.[34] After the report was discussed, the Committee reaffirmed its resolve to proceed with the prosecutions as soon as possible. But who would undertake the prosecutions in place of Coleridge? There was no immediate commitment to another barrister (perhaps concerned that he too might be 'abducted' by the Eyre alliance). One newspaper confidently announced that Edward James, still on retainer with the Committee, would conduct the prosecution.[35] But while James continued to advise on legal matters,[36] there is no evidence that he was offered the Eyre prosecution brief. (If he was offered the brief, he declined it.) But before the end of November, for reasons that remain unclear, the Committee had retained Stephen to take Coleridge's place as senior prosecuting barrister.[37]

In many respects, Stephen was an obvious second choice. He was an experienced trial lawyer who agreed with the aims of the Jamaica Committee. Over the course of the previous year he had made a systematic study both of the jurisprudence of martial law and the voluminous materials relating to its use in Jamaica. He also understood the relevant criminal law and procedure as well as – probably better than – any man in England. For good reasons, however, Stephen had not been the Committee's first choice. Stephen was an acknowledged master of legal subject matter, not of courtroom advocacy. In fact – and this he himself might have

---

[33] *CD*, 12 Nov. 1866.   [34] *JC Minutes*, 12 Oct. 1866.
[35] *Illustrated London News* (24 Nov. 1866), 495.   [36] *JC Minutes*, 19 Nov. 1866.
[37] On 12 November it was recorded in the Committee's minutes that Stephen had 'submitted his retainer'. The scope of the retainer was not recorded.

admitted without embarrassment – Stephen the trial barrister was decidedly of the second rank. In his decade at the bar, he had worked far more assiduously to make his mark as an intellectual journalist and writer.[38] In an academic debate on the law of martial law, Stephen would perhaps have had no equal in his time. But a murder prosecution is not an academic debate. This was a point which perhaps the leaders of the Jamaica Committee, now with everything riding on success in the courtroom, did not strongly enough appreciate. Stephen became their trial barrister, that is, their most visible public voice and personality, quite by default.

The selection of a prosecuting barrister was not the only problem facing the Jamaica Committee at the close of 1866. Key witnesses still had not arrived from Jamaica. The exact whereabouts of Eyre was uncertain. And of course there was the ever-present problem of money and publicity. Fund-raising efforts were again falling short of expectations, and some of its leading members (Tom Hughes went on another speaking tour)[39] organized new Jamaica meetings and addressed reform rallies to raise money while they 'explained and vindicated' the decision to prosecute Eyre.[40] In the last weeks of November Frederic Harrison published his six letters on martial law in the *Daily News*. This was an impressive body of propaganda, but one that was more than matched by the opposition.

The Coleridge affair was a noteworthy success for the Eyre Committee, but it was only one front in a wider counter-offensive. Since December 1865 the story of George Gordon had been the Jamaica Committee's most potent symbol and rallying point. Of all the widely reported incidents of the suppression, the court martial and execution of Gordon was among the hardest to excuse and easiest to exploit. Being well aware of this the Eyre Committee organized a sustained attack on the image of Gordon as a political martyr. The main platform for the attack was a long pamphlet published in the wake of the Coleridge affair. Along with the Eyre Committee's founding documents,[41] the pamphlet contained a reassessment of Gordon's role in the Jamaica rebellion. 'As a great misapprehension exists in the public mind as to the actual guilt of G. W. Gordon,' the pamphlet began, 'the Committee have thought it advisable to collate from the parliamentary Blue Books sufficient evidence to show his complicity in the insurrection.'[42]

Here the Defence Committee played some very sharp cards. Their pamphlet claimed that Gordon had been 'perfectly aware of what was going to take place' at Morant Bay.[43] But then a bolder assertion: in the weeks prior to the uprising

---

[38] Smith, *Victorian Rationalist*, 8–9.

[39] At these meetings Hughes typically advertised the aims and financial needs of the Jamaica Committee in the context of a speech on electoral reform. For one such speech, see *The Times* (20 Nov. 1867), 7. The *Illustrated London News* (5 Jan. 1867),19, criticized Hughes for having become an 'itinerant M.P.' in the manner of John Bright.   [40] *JC Minutes*, 14 Jan. 1867.

[41] The pamphlet included Carlyle's justification of the Eyre Committee, the minutes of its three previous general meetings, and a long list of eminent subscribers. See *The Eyre Defence and Aid Fund* (London, 1866).

[42] Ibid., 1. The writer was not very specific about the nature of this 'evidence', but insinuated that at least one military officer might have testified to this plot, had he only been called before the Royal Commission.   [43] Ibid.

Gordon had actively conspired with members of the Haitian military to import arms and ammunition into Jamaica. Far from a political innocent, Gordon had been the mastermind of an elaborate plot to arm a rebel army and with it to massacre the white population of Jamaica. The evidence for this allegation consisted solely of the uncorroborated affidavit of a former Confederate naval captain.[44] Neither *The Times* nor any of the other more conservative newspapers lent any credence to the document. By such fabrications, one critic of the Eyre Committee's pamphlet wrote in the *Daily News*, 'the public are deliberately deceived to induce them to subscribe their money'.[45]

One way to bolster the reputation of Edward Eyre was to damage the reputation of George Gordon. Another was to continue to embellish the story of Eyre's life and achievements. In January 1866, Hamilton Hume,[46] the dogged if only modestly able secretary of the Eyre Defence Committee, published the first of a series of published sketches on Eyre's life and character.[47] Unmistakably these were works of a hack journalist, one clumsily determined to exalt his subject. (Even Carlyle thought that the sketches were uncommonly vulgar.)[48] To be fair, however, Hume had no pretence of detached scholarship. His writings were naked efforts to persuade readers that Eyre was the living embodiment of the courageous and humane Englishman. Everything that Hume wrote about Eyre, every anecdote of his exploits, served to 'defend the energetic measures adopted by Mr. Eyre to suppress the negro rebellion'.[49]

According to Hume's account, the Jamaica insurrection of 1865 could not have been averted by Eyre or any other British official. When Eyre arrived in 1863 the island's economy was in ruins, the Assembly riven by faction. The vast negro population of the island had 'almost lapsed into barbarism rather than work',[50] and were cynically manipulated by 'the lowest scum of Baptist missionaries'. And there was yet another reason why Jamaica had been destined for a bloody race revolt: it was a near neighbour of Haiti (Saint-Domingue), that accursed place where 'the black race had conquered the white *by murder*'. This pointed to the essence of Eyre's heroism: 'it was solely owing to [Eyre's] energy,

[44] In the affidavits Captain Henry Edenborough swore that Gordon attempted to buy arms from him in June 1865. The affidavits were taken in connection to two civil actions that had been brought against Edward Eyre by victims of the suppression. *The Times* (20 Sept. 1867), 10; (23 Sept. 1867), 4.

[45] Letter of 'G.O.', *Daily News* (28 Nov. 1866), 2.

[46] In 1865 Hume was the editor of the *British Army and Navy Review*. When news of the Jamaica uprising reached England, Hume penned a series of short pieces defending Eyre's conduct. A biography of Eyre was contracted for. Before the book could be written, however, public opinion had turned so decidedly against Eyre that Hume's publisher ('thinking the volume might be damned') abandoned the idea. Letter of Hume to Carlyle, 13 Nov. 1866, Carlyle Papers, *NLS*, Add. MS. 1768 ff. 168.

[47] The first of these was 'Edward John Eyre, Governor of Jamaica', IV *British Army and Navy Review* (Jan. 1866).

[48] After reading Hume's notes, Carlyle reported that he felt as if he had been 'douched for hours in dirty water'. Letter of Carlyle to Ruskin, 11 Oct. 1866, as cited in Workman, 'Carlyle and the Governor Eyre Controversy', 94–5.   [49] Hume, *Edward John Eyre*, 1.

[50] Ibid., 8.

courage, and determination that an island where there are seven black men to one white, there was not a second edition of all the horrors and atrocities of the Indian mutiny.' In 1858 Canning had been pilloried for not being stern enough with the sepoy rebels. Fewer than ten years later, Hume lamented, the tide of public opinion had turned again. Now, Edward Eyre, this loyal servant of the Crown, was to be arraigned in a criminal court for doing no more than his duty when he 'crushed on the instant, on his own responsibility, a terrible rebellion...a conspiracy unsurpassed in atrocity and cold-blooded vindictiveness'. Such was the character of the Defence Committee's literature at the close of 1866.

In early January 1867, the Defence Committee published a new circular, one with a more decidedly legal message. It was alleged that the Jamaica Committee had recently become 'responsible' for the two civil lawsuits (for unlawful arrest and imprisonment) that had been lodged against Eyre in the English courts[51] in the names of Dr. Robert Bruce and Alexander Phillips, both of Jamaica.[52] The circular then intimated that these lawsuits were the first of what was certain to be a number of desperate and potentially ruinous legal assaults against Eyre personally. This ominous threat underlined the urgency of further subscriptions to the Defence Fund. The accusation that the Jamaica Committee had 'got up' the civil lawsuits was more than superficially credible. Bruce, a Scottish-born physician,[53] and Phillips, a black Jamaican ('gentleman', according to his self-description[54]) were well known to the Jamaica Committee. Both men had been political critics and opponents of Governor Eyre prior to the uprising. Both had been arrested, detained, and otherwise roughly treated under martial law. On the prompting of the Jamaica Committee's lawyers, moreover, both Bruce and Phillips had testified before the Jamaica Royal Commission. Although neither man had yet come to England, by some unknown means Bruce and Phillips had retained Shaen as their solicitor. Shaen's firm prepared and filed the lawsuits against Eyre. For all of these seeming coincidences, the Jamaica Committee flatly denied any 'direct or indirect' involvement with the civil suits or their plaintiffs.[55] On the Committee's direction, Shaen sent a letter to Hume demanding a public retraction. When none was forthcoming, the correspondence was sent to the newspapers. For the time being, the matter of the civil suits then fell from public view.

As January 1867 came to a close, there was talk in the newspapers of a 'hitch' in the Eyre prosecution.[56] In fact there were two. The first was continued delay in the arrival of key witnesses from Jamaica.[57] The second was a more intractable problem of legal geography. After his ostentatious (and profoundly damaging, many believed) arrival at Southampton in August 1866, Eyre had retreated to the

---

[51] The details of the civil lawsuits are discussed below, Epilogue.
[52] *Pall Mall Gazette* (26 Jan. 1867).   [53] Heuman, '*The Killing Time*', 59–60.
[54] See *JRC*, Minutes of Evidence, Q. 17,119.
[55] The dispute is summarized in the *Law Times* (26 Jan. 1867), 240–1. The correspondence between the Committees was published in *The Times* (22 Jan. 1867), 7.
[56] *Law Times* (2 Feb. 1866), 261.   [57] *CD*, 28 Jan. 1867.

relative obscurity and safety of the English countryside. On the advice of lawyers (this was made clear by Eyre's own solicitor),[58] the ex-Governor and his family had removed to a country house (Adderley Hall, a place not connected to the Tory politician) near the town of Market Drayton, Shropshire. There the Defence Committee tried to keep Eyre comfortable and, not easily, quiet.[59]

This was a very prudent – almost certainly not accidental – choice of domicile. While English law permitted 'private' prosecutions, that is, prosecutions initiated by complainants who did not enjoy the formal endorsement of the Crown's agents,[60] there were formidable obstacles to be overcome. In the first place, at least one magistrate would have to be persuaded that there were legal and factual grounds upon which to issue a warrant against the accused person. Secondly, if successful at that preliminary stage, the charges would have to be reviewed by a grand jury before a 'true bill' of indictment could be lodged against the accused. As everyone concerned knew only too well, in the mid-Victorian countryside landowning magistrates – unpaid, untrained, and unrepentant – would determine the fate of the Jamaica Committee's move against Governor Eyre. And, if by some unforeseen event the Committee's warrant was granted by such men, the case against Eyre would then be reviewed by a grand jury made up of Tory squires. For these good reasons the best hope of the Jamaica Committee was for the prosecution of Eyre to take place in a city, preferably London. There the case might be put before a stipendiary magistrate learned in the law, and before a grand jury drawn from a more politically sophisticated and diverse population.

In the liberal press, Eyre, who had been afforded a modicum of respect for personal fortitude, was called a hypocrite and coward for dodging the Jamaica Committee. The *Spectator* observed how the ex-Governor had often affirmed his 'sole responsibility' both for the execution of Gordon and for the larger operation of martial law in Jamaica.[61] Now that he had actually to 'bear the legal responsibility', or so the *Spectator* taunted, 'he seems to wish to evade it, and remains in the heart of a Tory county, where the Great Unpaid would dismiss the application for a committal, and any grand jury would ignore a bill against him'. The weight of this claim increased substantially when, in February 1867, on the advice of Stephen,[62] the Jamaica Committee decided to lay charges in London against the military men Nelson and Brand. Now it was said that the Governor was ducking

---

[58] *Law Times* (16 Feb. 1867), 301.

[59] In October 1866, Eyre learned that the Committee's plan had 'assumed a reality'. In Eyre's first direct correspondence with Carlyle (the men had not yet met), he felt compelled to assure his famous patron that in Jamaica he had been 'actuated by the purest motives' and had done no more than what was 'right, necessary, just and merciful'. While Eyre did not relish the idea of being placed in the 'felons' dock to answer for an imaginary crime', he had 'cheerfully accepted the responsibility' of his former office. In his reply dated 1 November 1866, Carlyle expressed the reassuring view that the Jamaica Committee was unlikely actually to commence legal proceedings, if only for lack of money. See Workman, 'Carlyle and the Governor Eyre Controversy', 95–7.

[60] Douglas Hay and Francis Snyder (eds.), *Policing and Private Prosecutions in Britain, 1750–1850* (Oxford, 1989), 3–4.   [61] *Spectator* (16 Feb. 1867), 174.

[62] *JC Minutes*, 4 Feb. 1867.

the same responsibility that two of his former subordinates 'have incurred more bravely'. These barbs pricked Eyre deeply. In mid-February he informed the Defence Committee of his desire to return to London in order to stand with Nelson and Brand.[63] A meeting was held to discuss options. It was unanimously decided by the leaders of the Defence Committee that Eyre should stay put. On 23 February the *Spectator* confirmed that it had been 'informed privately on the best authority' that Eyre, with the greatest reluctance, had decided that he should accede to the wishes of those who were to pay for his defence. On this intelligence the *Spectator* recanted its earlier claim that Eyre was a coward. At the same time, the paper noted that the incident underlined that the Defence Committee was greatly concerned that, if it was not met with the most astute skill and tactics, the prosecution of Eyre might end badly for the accused.

II. On Bow Street

For more than a year the Jamaica Committee had agitated for the criminal prosecution of Edward Eyre, the man who had become the living embodiment of the argument for (and against) martial law. When the time came to make good on its threat, however, the Committee was forced to settle for the more accessible if less notorious quarry of Nelson and Brand.

During the suppression Nelson had been the senior officer in the field (with the field rank of Brigadier-General) in the areas under martial law. His orders (from Major-General O'Connor) were to suppress the uprising by whatever means possible, and with all possible despatch. This was a challenging assignment, one not made easier by the fact that his headquarters at Morant Bay were easily accessible by sail to the civilian authorities at Spanish Town. Only a few days after Nelson had begun to organize the military response to the rising, the Governor arrived at Morant Bay with George Gordon as his prisoner. Eyre transferred Gordon to Nelson's custody along with a box of documents relating to his alleged complicity in the rebellion. Although Nelson later told the Royal Commission that he had not been given any explicit 'instructions' concerning Gordon's fate,[64] he could have had but little doubt on the point. It was not for nothing that Eyre, the highest-ranking civilian in the colony, had arrested Gordon, had assembled a case against him, and then had personally overseen his delivery to a place under martial law. In short, whatever personal inclination Nelson might have had towards the fate of Gordon, there had been no practical alternative to court martial and an inevitable guilty verdict. Nelson was a soldier. The top executive official in the colony had done everything short of ordering him to try Gordon for the capital crime of treason. That was that.

---

[63] *Spectator* (23 Feb. 1867), 203.

[64] *JRC Minutes*, Q. 31,005. Nelson told the Commission that his only orders were to examine the documents and decide whether there was 'sufficient evidence' on which to try Gordon for treason. Ibid., Q. 31,014.

In almost every respect, however, Nelson was an unsuitable target for a symbolic criminal prosecution. Even more than Eyre, he was likely to attract public sympathy. When he was questioned about Gordon's execution by the Royal Commissioners the previous winter, Nelson's answers were not marked by trepidation. They were broadly candid and free of obvious guile. Nelson had testified that Gordon was subjected to trial by court martial because the documents given him by the Governor indicated that the prisoner was a co-conspirator in an insurrectionary plot.[65] The dearth of experienced officers at his disposal had left Nelson with no choice but to assign three young subalterns (led by Brand, a junior grade naval lieutenant), in charge of the trial. When the court martial tried and convicted Gordon on a Saturday, and sentenced him to death by hanging, Nelson had immediately 'approved and confirmed the finding and sentence'. But he was not a fool. Feeling some unease about executing Gordon on a Sunday, and desirous of confirmation from his superiors, Nelson stayed Gordon's execution.[66] If either O'Connor or Eyre had had any qualms about the court martial, or if for some other reason they had wanted to spare Gordon's life, they were given ample opportunity to intervene. In this way Nelson had hoped to detach himself from ultimate responsibility for an action that (he knew) might later be seen as controversial.[67]

It is understandable, then, that Nelson seemed so confident and at ease when he described his role in the Gordon case to the Royal Commissioners.[68] At the end of the day, he had only followed orders. Nelson must also have been comforted by the fact that the official record of the proceedings was free of any evidence that Nelson had borne Gordon any personal animosity or ill-will.[69] Nor was there anything about Nelson's subsequent (published) letters or comments on Gordon that betrayed race prejudice, malice, or rancour. In his testimony before the Royal Commission Nelson had conveyed the strong impression that during his command at Morant Bay he had conducted himself as a professional soldier who had been given a grim job to do and, with as little fuss as possible, had done it.[70]

---

[65] Ibid., Q. 31,041–31,045. Although there was some doubt as to the chain of command under martial law, whether civilian or military officers held sway, with regard to the treatment of civilian prisoners like Gordon, the military acceded to the authority of the Governor.

[66] *JRC Report*, 37.

[67] Interestingly, in the course of his examination by the Royal Commission, Nelson did not take advantage of opportunities to testify that Gordon's execution was delayed so that his trial and sentence could be reviewed and endorsed by his superiors. Only after repeated questioning did he admit that it might have 'floated through his mind' that it was prudent to wait for an endorsement. *JRC Minutes*, Q. 31,129–31,135.

[68] Neither O'Connor nor Eyre had put his endorsement in writing. These omissions concerned Nelson enough that he asked Eyre for written confirmation that the Governor had in fact endorsed the conviction and execution of Gordon. This the Governor did do. Ibid., Q. 31,104.

[69] It might be revealing that when Eyre wrote of Gordon's execution, even many weeks later, he spoke of the 'justness' of the sentence. In contrast, when Nelson sent a report on the court martial proceedings to General O'Connor, he wrote that it was his 'duty fully to approve and confirm' the sentence. Ibid., Q. 31,097; Q. 31,104.

[70] John Horne Payne, the Jamaica Committee barrister, was present during Nelson's testimony before the Royal Commission. However, nothing in the record suggests that Horne Payne encouraged the Commissioners to engage in an aggressive cross-questioning. Horne Payne asked the

Lieutenant Herbert Brand was an altogether different kettle of fish. A youthful but quite seasoned officer,[71] Brand had been responsible for the trial and punishment of scores of prisoners at Morant Bay during the period of martial law. In the space of a few weeks, courts martial headed by Brand condemned and executed 189 men and women. By the time he was called to give evidence before the Royal Commission in March 1866, a number of witnesses already had testified to Brand's cruelty. On the basis of this testimony Brand was asked whether he had taunted prisoners (Gordon included) about their impending executions,[72] and whether he ordered prisoners flogged before they had been tried and convicted of an offence.[73] He was also asked about his association with the notorious camp commandant, Duberry Ramsay.[74] But the Royal Commission had been even more keenly interested in Brand's role as president of the courts martial that had sent Gordon (and a long list of other men) to the gallows. When pressed to answer probing questions about the manner in which prisoners had been charged, tried, and executed,[75] Brand was by turns evasive, vague, or conveniently forgetful. His testimony about the trial of Gordon was particularly indefinite.[76] Reading his evidence as a whole, it is hard to avoid the conclusion that Brand had relished his role in the suppression. Whatever remorse he felt was prompted by the unanticipated fact that his actions had landed him in hot water.

The less wholesome dimensions of Brand's character were prominently displayed during his widely publicized clash with a leading critic of the Jamaica suppression, Charles Buxton. In August 1866 (ironically, just as Buxton had resigned as chair of the Jamaica Committee), Brand, while still on duty in Jamaica, read a newspaper article written by Buxton some weeks before.[77] The article sternly condemned the courts martial at Morant Bay, and the 'couple of young lieutenants and an ensign' (no names were specified) who had presided over them. Brand was moved to respond. He wrote a letter accusing Buxton of having written 'wicked and malicious lies'. The letter demanded that Buxton retract these 'barefaced lies' or to give 'satisfaction in a way more suited to [Brand's] tastes'. Brand then intimated that his conduct in Jamaica was sure to be vindicated by the Conservative government ('we have a new Admiralty, my friend'), and dared Buxton to publish his letter. Unfortunately for Brand, Buxton called his bluff, sending the letter to all of England's major newspapers. In his published reply,

Commission to put questions to Nelson (which was done), but these were not particularly controversial or searching questions. See for example, ibid., Q. 31,129; Q. 31,142.

[71] Heuman, '*The Killing Time*', 147.   [72] *JRC Minutes*, Q. 32,240–5.

[73] *CD*, 12 Nov. 1866.

[74] When asked about Ramsay's cruelty, Brand, without the slightest hint of irony, remarked that in the circumstances Ramsay 'could not be friends with everybody'! Ibid., Q. 32,607.

[75] It quickly became evident that one after another men had been brought before Brand's court martial charged with 'mutiny, rebellion, and murder', and that Brand had not made any attempt to distinguish as between these charges or the evidence called to substantiate them. Ibid., Q. 33,344.

[76] At one point Brand was admonished by the Committee to give 'direct answers' to the questions put to him. Ibid., Q. 32,543.

[77] For an account of the clash, see *Pall Mall Gazette* (21 Nov. 1866), 10.

Buxton asked whether Brand was the sort of man who 'ought to have been entrusted for a full month with the power of life or death over some hundreds of persons'.[78] Buxton seized the occasion to enjoin the English public to reflect on 'what kind of instruments were employed by the authorities in punishing the alleged rebellion in Jamaica'.[79]

Buxton's letters were read by Brand upon his return to England in October 1866. Nothing if not persevering, Brand sent a another letter to Buxton, calling him a coward, and denouncing his decision to publish the first letter as an 'impertinence for which I shall bring you to book'. Once again, Brand unwisely dared Buxton to publish the letter. This Buxton promptly did. Mortified by Brand's conduct, the Admiralty publicly disavowed his letters, calling them 'shameful'.[80] Steps were taken to discipline Brand for conduct unbecoming a naval officer.[81]

The incident was a nice windfall for the Jamaica Committee and its cause. So much did Brand's 'vulgar little epistles' lend credence to critics of martial law in Jamaica, the *Spectator* commented, that readers could be forgiven for thinking that the Lieutenant 'had been bribed by the Jamaica Committee to expose the recent Courts-Martial'.[82] Brand's outburst tended to reinforce the argument that martial law was a dangerous power to entrust to any man, and that Governor Eyre 'chose exceedingly unfit instruments for working properly so fearful a legal power'. The *Spectator* made another, more interesting, observation. It thought that Brand's letters were indicative of a certain type of man, a type increasingly prevalent among the ranks of young officers. Brand, the paper expounded, was one of those 'underbred, ignorant, *larky* young naval lieutenants ... a young fellow who glories in practical jokes, who is probably cruel in the sort of way in which school boys are cruel ... a fast young man who may hardly know what courtesy and humanity mean'. Increasingly, the *Spectator* remonstrated, it was the Herbert Brands of the country, with their inveterate 'heat of mind, violent prejudices, no experience, complete ignorance of the world except gunrooms, no knowledge of man, contempt for law', who were left to do the unseemly jobs of empire. Such a man as Brand 'was the president of a Court Martial in 189 cases that ended in a capital sentence, that had the duty of considering what evidence was relevant and what was irrelevant'. Such a man as Brand had superintended over the life and death of men while looking on 'the whole affair as a kind of rat-hunt'. If Colonel Nelson was an unpromising candidate for criminal prosecution by the Jamaica Committee, Brand, in all his crass stupidity, presented a more viable target.

The first two Jamaica Committee prosecutions were commenced against Nelson and Brand in the Central Police Court at Bow Street on 6 February 1867. The charges generated multiple hearings over a two-week period. Although the

---

78 *Daily News* (21 Nov. 1866), 5.
79 The complete correspondence was reprinted in the *Daily News* (21 Nov. 1866), 5–6.
80 Letter of Sir John Pakington to Buxton, published in the *Daily News* (26 Nov. 1866), 4.
81 In the result, the Admiralty suspended Brand from the command of a ship. *Daily News* (4 Mar. 1867), 3.   82 *Spectator* (24 Nov. 1866), 1300–1.

hearings have received almost no close scholarly scrutiny, they are important from at least two points of view. First, they marked the beginning of the phase in the history of the Jamaica Committee in which its actions and public demeanour were almost entirely surrendered to lawyers. After February 1867, leading figures of the Committee such as Mill and Bright were very much in the background, passive observers of argument and manoeuvre as orchestrated by lawyers. The move against Nelson and Brand at the Bow Street court is also important because it was there that Fitzjames Stephen established, both for judicial and public consumption, a hybridized political and legal rhetoric with which to advance the Committee's positions.

On the morning of 6 February 1867 the Jamaica Committee, represented as complainants in the persons of Mill and Taylor, and by their lead counsel Stephen (assisted by John Horne Payne),[83] commenced the criminal prosecution of Nelson and Brand. 'At Bow-Street this morning,' the *Pall Mall Gazette* reported, 'an application was made to the Chief Magistrate, Sir Thomas Henry, by Mr. Fitzjames Stephen, for warrants for the apprehension of Colonel Nelson and Lieutenant Brand, on the charge of the wilful murder of Mr. Gordon at Morant Bay, in the county of Surrey, in the Island of Jamaica, in October 1865.'[84] This was the first of five hearings, some brief, some many hours long, the last of which concluding on 23 February.

Stephen commenced his application with an elaborate series of submissions concerning the legal and constitutional validity of the charges being made against Nelson and Brand.[85] The speech, intended as much for the information of the newspaper reporters as for Henry, was given without interruption. In sharp contrast to what was to come later, and before other magistrates, for the entire proceeding Sir Thomas was markedly indulgent of the length, manner, and substance of Stephen's submissions. It is possible to explain why he was. Unlike country magistrates, Henry was a vastly experienced barrister and career ('stipendiary') magistrate who drew a government salary for his work. When he heard the charges against Nelson and Brand, he had been a lawyer for more than thirty-five and a judge for more than twenty-five years.[86] (Henry had presided at the Bow Street court since 1846, and had been the Chief Magistrate since 1864.) On many days his judicial work must have been mundane, repetitive, and often flatly disagreeable. The Nelson and Brand cases would have presented a welcome contrast to daily fare. The case was argued by eminent counsel. It raised points of law and procedure that were widely regarded as being of the utmost legal and political importance. Henry's rulings would be closely scrutinized. He appears to have relished every moment.

---

[83] Horne Payne was chosen to assist Stephen because of his intimate familiarity with the Jamaican evidence and witnesses.   [84] *Pall Mall Gazette* (6 Feb. 1866), 8.

[85] *Report of the Proceedings at Bow Street* (*RPBS*), *Jamaica Papers No. VII* (London, 1867). The report was based on the notes of a shorthand service as edited by William Shaen, the Jamaica Committee's solicitor.   [86] *DNB*, ix, 579–80; Boase, *Oxford DNB*, online 12979.

This brings us to the nebulous subject of mid-Victorian criminal procedure. In 1867, England still had no permanent office of public prosecutor (for this development the country was to wait another twelve years).[87] As stated, another eccentric feature of English justice was that criminal charges could be brought by any private citizen against any other person suspected of criminal wrongdoing.[88] In the context of the Jamaica controversy, this was very significant indeed. It meant that the decision of Lord Derby's government not to initiate criminal prosecutions in England against Eyre or any of his regular military officers was not binding on the Jamaica Committee.[89] 'As the office of public prosecutor is unknown to the English law,' the *Morning Post* observed, 'it is open to any subject who thinks proper to accept the responsibility to call to justice those who in his opinion have violated the law.'[90] The Committee was determined to accept this responsibility, and there was nothing that could be done to stop them. But there was a catch. Lodging a criminal complaint for murder was one thing, and a relatively simple thing, when compared to the procedural obstacles that stood between accusation and trial.

The Jamaica Committee carefully weighed its procedural options, and the implications of those options, before it launched the first prosecution. In the typical murder case, it was possible to proceed against the accused by way of preferred indictment before the grand jury.[91] However, some members of the Committee's executive thought that it would be a mistake to proceed against Eyre (or even Nelson and Brand) in this fashion. According to this view, it was crucial for the Committee to be seen affording the accused every possible opportunity of defending themselves. By encouraging preliminary hearings, the Committee would look scrupulously fair while gaining an opportunity to advertise the importance and soundness of their legal case. In the result, it was a moot point. When he finished his research on procedural options, Stephen informed the Committee that an indictment could not be preferred when the alleged felony had been committed abroad and the accused was not already in custody.[92] There was nothing to do, Stephen advised, but commence the prosecution in a magistrate's court.[93] The decision was taken to prosecute Nelson and Brand at Bow Street on 6 February 1867.

[87] See generally, Manchester, *Modern Legal History*, 226–30; W. R. Cornish and G. De N. Clark, *Law and Society in England, 1750–1950* (London, 1989), 607–9.

[88] As Stephen would later put it, 'it is one of the leading peculiarities of . . . the English law that it can be set in motion by any private person who considers that those in whom he takes an interest have been wronged, or that the interests of the public require that criminal proceedings should be instituted'. Quoted in *The Times* (7 Feb. 1867), 8. See Manchester, *Modern Legal History*, 210.

[89] *Hansard*, xxxiv (31 July 1866), 1789.   [90] *Morning Post* (7 Feb. 1867).

[91] Seymour F. Harris, *Principles of the Criminal Law* (London, 1877), 344–5.

[92] *JC Minutes*, 4 Feb. 1867. Stephen drew this conclusion on the basis of the decision in *Rex v. Shawe*. At Bow Street, Stephen remarked that the case was wrongly decided but binding. *The Times* (7 Feb. 1867), 8.

[93] Finlason did not agree with Stephen's conclusion, or the Jamaica Committee's statement of its motives for proceeding at Bow Street. In his opinion, the Committee chose their course because 'it would afford an opportunity for powerful and impassioned addresses before the magistrates, calculated to prejudice [Eyre] in public opinion, to inflame popular opinion against him, and prevent his chance of a fair trial'. Finlason, *History of the Jamaica Case*, 402.

The procedure triggered a two-stage inquiry. At the first stage, the 'process hearing', the complainants presented their charge in a magistrate's court and then were obliged to show cause why the accused should be compelled to attend the court on an arrest warrant or summons.[94] If the magistrate was satisfied that there was a case for the accused to answer, a bench warrant would be issued for his arrest. When the accused came before the court, it triggered a 'committal hearing' in which the prosecution was required to call enough evidence to establish a *prima facie* case of guilt. Before evidence was called the accused was entitled to challenge the form of the charge or the jurisdiction of the court. Failing this the accused was permitted to cross-question prosecution witnesses on the admissibility or sufficiency of their evidence. If the magistrate was satisfied that the prosecution had made out a sufficient case, and if the accused stood charged with a felony, the indictment was set down for review by the grand jury.[95] A full-blown jury trial of the case would ensue only if the grand jury, upon reviewing the evidence and hearing the charge of a judge, found a 'true bill' of indictment.

The Bow Street hearings in the Nelson and Brand cases were the first formal test of a number of hitherto abstract questions. They were questions that went to the core of the English constitution. Could the Jamaica Committee satisfy a respected judge that as a matter of English law the actions of Nelson and Brand amounted to crimes? Was the crime of murder among them? What was the legal significance, if any, of the fact that Nelson and Brand had acted under a proclamation of martial law? Was there evidence enough to put the allegations to a grand jury? Was it conceivable, in other words, that two officers of Her Majesty's armed forces soon might be standing trial for their lives for acts committed in the line of duty?

The ensuing hearings were minutely transcribed, and then hotly debated, in the English newspaper press. Much was made of the fact that Mill, one of the country's leading thinkers, was one of the two criminal complainants. But it passed without comment that Mill attended all five hearings without being able to utter a single (official) word. No one noticed that Mill and his associates had surrendered the fate of the Jamaica Committee to lawyers and judges. The face and voice of the Committee now was the voice of a man, while doubtlessly sympathetic to their aims, who was not a member of their association. Like any good barrister Stephen maintained an appreciable distance from his clients. He saw the brief as a great responsibility and trust. As the prosecutor of a criminal case, Stephen was duty-bound to proceed against the accused as the nominated barrister of the Crown, not as a shill for a private association. It was for him alone to decide how to craft the relevant legal propositions and, of equal importance (especially in political cases), the courtroom rhetoric in which they were to be presented.

In his opening address to Henry, Stephen assumed a rhetorically muted even clinical posture toward the case. His task was to persuade this experienced criminal

---

[94] David Bentley, *English Criminal Justice in the Nineteenth Century* (London, 1998), 9–10.
[95] Ibid., 131–2.

magistrate that there were law and facts enough to cause the arrest for murder against two serving officers of Her Majesty's armed forces, men regarded in some quarters as heroes. This was a delicate undertaking, and Stephen's address trod gently. He began by citing the statutes that (he contended) established the magistrate's jurisdiction to arrest Nelson and Brand on murder charges.[96] Stephen then made a statement meant for wider consumption: the complainants had hoped also to prefer charges against Edward Eyre.[97] This had not been possible because Mr. Eyre was not physically present within the jurisdiction of the Bow Street court. However, it was Stephen's information that Mr. Eyre had indicated (through his solicitor) that he would soon return to London to face charges.[98]

Stephen then turned to the legal matters at hand. He informed Sir Thomas that his brief in the case at bar was so 'exceptional' that it deserved an exceptional explanation.[99] The prosecutions of Nelson and Brand were predicated on the idea that 'when a great wrong is committed, and a precedent seems to be about to be set up, which if allowed to stand would put in peril the lives and liberties of other persons . . . it is not merely the right but the duty of those who regard such precedent with apprehension to use those means with which by law they are intrusted'. In the case at bar, one of Her Majesty's subjects had been put to death 'deliberately, advisedly, and we say, illegally'. Was this killing (as the Government would have it) merely an 'official mistake', one made good by the dismissal of some civil servants, or was it 'an act of wilful murder'? This question, the complainants submitted, was 'one of the deepest importance, involving the fundamental principles of law'. The prosecution of Nelson and Brand, Stephen submitted, had sprung 'from no party spirit, from no vindictive feeling against the accused, but solely with the desire to obtain from a court of justice – from the highest court in the land – a solemn decision on a question deeply affecting the liberties of us all'.[100] This then was the overarching theme of the case: the criminal prosecution of Nelson and Brand (and, prospectively, Eyre) was motivated by the desire to vindicate constitutional principles, not to punish individuals.

In every respect possible Stephen endeavoured to depersonalize his case. In the first part of his speech, he made only fleeting and dispassionate references to George Gordon and his widow. He did not allege that the accused officers had

---

[96] The Administration of Justice Act, 11 & 12 Vict., c. 42, s. 2, gave an English magistrate jurisdiction to issue arrest warrants for indictable crimes committed in the colonies. The Offences against the Person Act, 24 & 25 Vict., c. 100, s. 9, provided an English magistrate with jurisdiction to arrest a person accused of the crime of murder, even when committed in a colony.

[97] Stephen also told the court that Eyre's solicitor had intimated that 'upon receiving notice, Mr. Eyre would at once come within the jurisdiction [of the Middlesex Police Court]'. *RPBS*, 4.

[98] Stephen made this comment on information given him by Shaen. Shaen fed him the information based on correspondence with Eyre's solicitor, Anderson Rose. Rose latter vehemently denied that he had stated that Eyre would come to London because he 'did not wish to be annoyed in his own neighbourhood at Adderley, Shropshire'. Shaen later alleged that Eyre only changed his mind about facing the charges in London when he learned that he was to be charged with murder. See letters of Rose and Shaen in *The Times* (14 Feb. 1867), 5; (5 Mar. 1867), 5.

[99] This account from *The Times* (7 Feb. 1867), 8.   [100] *RPBS*, 6.

acted in bad faith, or had felt any personal animosity toward Gordon. In reference to Eyre's role in the execution, Stephen actually conceded that he confirmed Gordon's death sentence because he had genuinely believed that it was his duty to do so. Stephen then ventured another and more unexpected comment: '[N]o man,' he emphasized, 'could have shown more gallant determination from first to last to take upon himself every atom of responsibility that belonged to him; whatever else could be said of [Eyre's] conduct, no one could say that he acted otherwise than as a brave man.' These were unusual remarks for a prosecuting barrister to make about a person whom he hoped soon to try for murder. The remarks were noted with absorbing interest both by reporters present in the court, and by the leaders of the Jamaica Committee.

In the remainder of his opening address, Stephen summarized the legal reasons why Nelson and Brand were guilty of murder. His first submission was tersely put: 'by the law of England to put a man deliberately to death is murder, unless you can prove it to be something less'.[101] Clearly the role of Nelson and Brand in the execution of Gordon had been 'deliberate and intentional'. The only contestable issue was whether the accused could proffer some lawful excuse (or 'privilege') for having taken Gordon's life. The bulk of Stephen's submissions related to this issue. He suggested to the court that the only plausible justification that Nelson and Brand could proffer was that their conduct was excused by the operation of 'martial law'. Stephen acknowledged that a possible source of such a privilege was the 'Act of Assembly in Jamaica which empowers the Governor to proclaim martial law'. But there were a number of fatal problems with this theory. First, the Jamaican statute did not specifically define the term 'martial law'. There was nothing to do but to 'look to the common law of England to interpret those words, so that martial law in Jamaica is legal in no other sense than that in which it would have been legal in England'.[102] Second, when they were read carefully the actual provisions of the Act bestowed only two very specific and conditional powers. On the assent of the Council of War, the Governor could conscript men into the colony's militia. Then, once conscripted, the Act provided that the conscripted men were subject to military law and discipline during the period of emergency. Jamaica's martial law statute did nothing to alter the common law of England. It provided no special powers or immunities. For Stephen this was the 'vital point in the case'.

When he reached this juncture of his argument, Stephen asked Henry to fix on a single question: 'Is the law of England supreme, or is there known to the law of England some other power which, in its own discretion, can set aside the law and be supreme over it?'[103] In other words, did the men who put Gordon to death

---

[101] Ibid., 7. In another account of the speech, Stephen was reported to have stated that Gordon was a 'brave though *mistaken* man' (italics added). *The Times* (7 Feb. 1866), 8.

[102] This assertion, in turn, rested on the premiss that when the Spanish population of Jamaica was entirely displaced by English settlers after the conquest of 1688, the island became a 'settled colony' governed by English common law. Ibid., 8.   [103] Ibid.

actually possess 'the prerogative of the Crown to suspend or to override the law'? In Stephen's view it was absolutely clear that they did not. To countenance such a power would be to countenance 'a despotism administered by military officers' who might take life while being 'exempt from any subsequent responsibility to any power, except perhaps to Parliament'. According to Stephen, the term 'martial law', when used to imply some unlimited or despotic power, was a patent self-contradiction. It simultaneously denoted the absence and presence of legal norms. In Stephen's view, it was no less than 'abuse of language to call [martial law] a law at all'.[104] In truth, martial law was 'only a name for a common law power – the power, namely of reducing force by force' in times of state emergency. The proclamation of martial law did not indicate the complete absence of law, but a limited privilege that an action otherwise illegal was 'founded upon necessity'. When the necessity could be proved the illegal actions were excused; but where the necessity could not be proved, 'acts done under martial law became crimes'. This was a proposition grounded in the first principle of the constitution, that the 'law, and nothing else is supreme; that there is no power in this country except the power that exists by law'. Were this not so, if the Crown and not the law were supreme, if martial law was a power 'not governed by law', it would be as if the Petition of Right had never been law, and the Glorious Revolution had never come to pass.

With these statements, Stephen began to set forth his specific legal authorities. He did so in a surprisingly loose fashion. Hale's famous pronouncement, that martial law was a 'thing indulged rather than law – a matter which existed merely so far as the necessity existed',[105] was put to the court. This Stephen followed, oddly enough, by a thumbnail sketch of martial law in the Middle Ages.[106] Stephen then described how the Petition of Right terminated the Crown's prerogative to suspend the common law by executive fiat. While in time of war 'Her Majesty had an undoubted right to use military force at her discretion, to any extent that the exigencies of the case might demand', this prerogative did not imply 'an alternative system of law which was to be substituted for the common law'. The power to use force to restore the peace was 'a power known to law, as much as the power of the policeman to arrest a man under a warrant was known to the law'. If to restore the peace a life is taken, it is incumbent upon the perpetrator to 'show that he has not gone beyond what necessity requires'. If that cannot be shown, Stephen repeated, 'by the law of England, it is called murder. Other codes may call it by a softer name.'

It was now for Stephen to call evidence. He called five witnesses. The first two, Gordon's former physician (Dr. Alexander Fiddes) and a colonial legislator

---

[104] *The Times*, 10.   [105] Ibid., 11.

[106] Stephen tried to demonstrate that the legal limitations on the martial power stretched back '500 years'. By way of example he alleged that the summary execution of the rebel Earl of Lancaster by Edward II was 'distinctly illegal'. Stephen did not offer any specific authority for this assertion, however. Ibid., 12.

(Andrew Lewis) had been brought to England from Jamaica by the Jamaica Committee. These witnesses attested to Gordon's arrest in Kingston (Fiddes), and to his subsequent court martial and execution at Morant Bay (Lewis). Other witnesses certified as true copies the minutes of Gordon's court martial, and a transcript of evidence taken by the Jamaica Royal Commission. Yet another witness stated that Nelson was residing within the jurisdiction of the Middlesex Police Court.

When Stephen finally asked Henry to issue a bench warrant for the arrest of Nelson and Brand, he refused on the technical grounds that there was insufficient proof that Brand was currently residing within the jurisdiction of his court. However, Henry gave the prosecution the chance to repair this defect when court convened the next morning. The following day, 7 February, Stephen produced a witness who put Brand within the court's jurisdiction.[107] Satisfied on the point, Henry issued warrants for the arrest of Nelson and Brand. Stephen then told the court that he wanted to proceed 'with the respect due to gentlemen placed in a most painful situation'.[108] He suggested that the accused be afforded opportunity to surrender to the court before arrests were made. He also wanted to consent to their bail, even if such a gesture was highly unusual in a murder case. Henry complied with both requests. Before the matter was adjourned Henry complimented Stephen on the 'great ability and fairness' with which he had stated the case for the prosecution.

On 8 and 9 February respectively, Nelson and Brand turned themselves in. Nelson's first contact with the criminal process went smoothly enough. He appeared before the magistrate and was quickly released without undue fuss. Brand's surrender did not go so painlessly. When Shaen refused to consent to the release of Brand on his own recognizance, and when Brand could not instantly find sureties of his bail, he was subjected to the indignity of being locked in a gaol cell – that 'horrid, damp, slimy black-hole of Bow-Street'[109] – for nearly two hours.[110] The committal hearing for Nelson and Brand was set for 12 February. There was time now for the prosecutors and the prosecuted to evaluate the proceedings thus far, and for one of the country's opinion leaders, *The Times*, to have its say.

The Times had an interesting, if oddly ambivalent, response to these events. On one hand, it was to be conceded that the prosecution of Nelson and Brand had brought the country 'to the verge of an important State trial'.[111] Many official actions taken in suppressing the Jamaica revolt had been 'deplorable', and when it had the opportunity 'the House of Commons failed to record any protest against the excesses of martial law in Jamaica, and the friends of Mr. Eyre injudiciously held him up as an example for imitation'.[112] *The Times* also agreed that the

[107] *The Times* (8 Feb. 1867), 12.　　　[108] Ibid.
[109] In stark contrast to the neatly kept confines of the courthouse at Market Drayton. See *Morning Star* (27 Mar. 1867), 6.　　　[110] *Law Times* (16 Feb. 1867), 301.
[111] *The Times* (8 Feb. 1867), 8.　　　[112] Ibid. (7 Feb. 1867), 6.

Jamaica litigation raised significant legal questions, ones 'on which lawyers are known to differ, and which can only be settled by solemn judicial decision'.[113] For these reasons the prosecution might be justified. On the other hand, however, *The Times* vigorously objected to Stephen's handling of the Nelson and Brand cases, and particularly for 'importing irrelevant considerations' into the prosecution. In this view, when Stephen attacked a supposed 'Royal prerogative' to suspend law and 'dispose of the lives of subjects with impunity in time of rebellion', he attacked a straw man. No responsible person, *The Times* alleged, had ever made such a claim. The stronger claim was that public officials in Jamaica had acted on the basis of a good faith belief that local legislation gave them the power to stamp out the uprising under martial law. The subsequent prosecution of two serving military officers for murder for doing only what – on the best advice of their superiors – they believed was both legal and necessary, was likely to produce 'evil rather than good'.

As for Stephen, he was so troubled by these comments that he responded to *The Times*' editorial on the very day it was published. (There is no indication that his response was authorized by the Jamaica Committee.) In his letter to the editor, Stephen complained of the oversimplification of his arguments at Bow Street. He then restated his main points in nine numbered propositions, their central thrust being that martial law was a facet of the common law, not a separate body of powers and immunities. Stephen reiterated that the Jamaica Acts did not modify the common law of martial law, nor did they provide a blanket legal privilege to the men acting in their name. The men who put Gordon to death were therefore obliged to prove that the execution was necessary to the restoration of order in the colony.

On receipt of Stephen's letter, *The Times* published another editorial on Jamaica.[114] The editors repeated that the Jamaica Committee had an important point to make, and that the details surrounding the killing of Gordon 'forced every impartial person to confess that a wrong had been done'. Gordon had been guilty of nothing but 'vague incendiary declamation', and his execution was the product of a general panic among the colonial leadership. But what troubled *The Times* was that the Committee, if Stephen's speech at Bow Street was an accurate barometer, was not interested in the 'peculiar circumstances of Gordon's case'. Instead, Stephen had submitted that 'martial law could only apply in time of war, and to members of the military force'. He had endeavoured to show that 'every officer, soldier, or seaman, militiaman or volunteer, who inflicted any punishment after outrage had actually ceased ... was guilty of a breach of the law'. *The Times* thought this an 'abstract turn', one which placed Stephen in the 'radically false' position of prosecuting for murder men he thought guilty of a purely technical wrong. 'Never', the newspaper commented, 'were alleged murderers spoken of in such terms and treated with such courtesy.' It was seen as flatly disingenuous to

---

[113] *The Times* (7 Feb. 1867), 6.   [114] Ibid.

pretend that a murder prosecution could ever be a merely symbolic enterprise. 'A charge of murder is a charge of murder,' *The Times* contended, 'and no courtesy or half assurances that the proceedings are only formal and for the purpose of trying a constitutional principle can lessen the gravity of such an accusation to the defendants.' This was no good way to make an 'abstruse' political point.

It was not long before a number of other newspapers also began to comment unfavourably on Stephen's submissions at Bow Street, especially about his 'very strong expressions of respect for and admiration of Governor Eyre'.[115] How 'very like satire,' wrote the *Law Times*, 'when he is charging the object of his luxations with the highest crime known to the law'. It would have been better if the Jamaica Committee 'were to throw aside all such pretensions of politeness' and 'be content to appear in their true characters'. The *Freeman*, the newspaper of England's Baptist community, also resented the fact that Stephen had referred to the accused with the 'utmost urbanity'.[116] It was as if Stephen saw these men merely as 'mistaken gentlemen, not as culprits; as men who committed some technical mistake, not as men on whom rests innocent blood'.

Stephen's utterances also attracted critics nearer to home. Chesson had been present in the Bow Street court for the process hearings. In his diary he credited Stephen for the 'great clearness and amplitude' of his legal arguments (while noticing that his 'delivery is somewhat marred by indistinct enunciation').[117] But all was not well. In another diary entry Chesson recounted how he (and some unnamed members of the Jamaica Committee) were 'much disgratified at the complimentary tone of Stephen to Eyre', and how they 'thought that the sooner this kid-glove style of prosecuting was given up the better'.[118] Bright had been particularly emphatic as to 'the inexpediency of Mr. Stephen's lavish compliments'. In fact, Bright was so much annoyed with Stephen that he raised the possibility of replacing him with another barrister. And so began a festering conflict between Stephen and his detractors within the Committee.

In the meantime, Nelson and Brand had begun to think seriously about how best to defend themselves at the forthcoming hearing. When Henry issued the warrant for Nelson's arrest, the army officer immediately wrote to the War Office for 'protection'.[119] In response, the Secretary of State for the War Office agreed that Charles Clode, the Ministry's senior solicitor,[120] would coordinate Nelson's defence. The War Office would also pay his legal bills.[121] Clode

---

[115] *Law Times* (9 Feb. 1867), 279.   [116] *Freeman* (15 Feb. 1867).
[117] *CD*, 6 Feb. 1867.   [118] Ibid., 8 Feb. 1867.
[119] For a copy of the request, see *CO* 137/428.
[120] A few years after he acted for Nelson, Clode brought together the research he had done on martial and military law and published an important two-volume treatise, *The Military Forces of the Crown*.
[121] The War Office had already agreed to pay for the defence of civil actions that had been brought against Nelson. This was on the principle, as one civil servant put it, that 'officers exposed to prosecution for conduct whilst on duty under superior authority appear to be entitled to legal assistance in their defence'. Nelson and Brand were subordinate officers who had not exceeded their orders and

retained Harry Poland, an experienced criminal law barrister, to defend Nelson at the committal hearing. Brand appealed to the Admiralty for similar assistance. When he arrived at the committal hearing Brand was represented by an Admiralty solicitor (called Bristow). Henry's decision also had raised the alarm in the Eyre camp. When the committal hearings of Nelson and Brand commenced on 12 February, Anderson Rose, Eyre's solicitor, was in the court ready to read a prepared statement.

This time the main courtroom at Bow Street was full, the clerks having turned away a number of potential spectators.[122] Nelson and Brand took their places in the prisoners' dock. Brand's solicitor, Bristow, requested that the accused be permitted to sit 'on the floor of the court, instead of the dock'. Although Stephen readily acceded to this request, both Nelson and Brand defiantly refused to move. (They remained in the dock for all three sessions of the hearing.) When the matter of seating was settled, Rose stood up to tell the court that Stephen had been sadly mistaken when he asserted previously (on 6 February) that Eyre was soon to return to London in order to face charges laid by the Jamaica Committee. Mr. Eyre, Rose made plain, would do no such thing. On the advice of counsel, he would not be leaving Shropshire for London.[123] Of course, these comments were entirely irrelevant to the case at bar (just as Stephen's comments on Eyre had been). Henry heard Rose out, but then signalled Stephen to get on with the real business at hand.

Stephen stood on his feet, but he was not ready to address points of law. He first wanted to address his previous references to Eyre. 'Some of the remarks which [he] had addressed to the magistrate on a former occasion,' Stephen stated, 'had led to a misconception which [he] desired to remove.'[124] He then (defensively) ventured that it 'was no easy thing in conducting a prosecution of this kind, to hit the exact mean between, on one hand, a tone of improper harshness and, on the other, a tone which may convey to persons little accustomed to criminal proceedings, a false impression of the spirit in which the prosecution was being conducted'. In his references to the accused (and to Eyre) during the previous hearings Stephen had striven to avoid 'the lamentable violence of language which had been used by both sides in reference to this matter'. The reason for this would be plain to any lawyer. *The Queen v. Nelson and Brand* was a criminal prosecution in which Stephen appeared as counsel for the Crown. Stephen's submission was that 'the common law of England was the common law of Jamaica'. He would call 'a distinguished member of the Jamaican bar' to provide expert opinion on the

---

therefore qualified for legal assistance. On the same criteria, Edward Eyre did not qualify. 11 Feb. 1867, *WO* 32/6235, See also 12 Feb. 1867, *CO* 137/428. This policy was confirmed in Parliament by Disraeli, *Hansard*, clxxxviii (14 Feb. 1867), 337.

122 *The Times* (13 Feb. 1866), 12.

123 Rose made the same point in letters written to the editors of England's major newspapers. Rose emphasized that Eyre had been 'determined' to come to London and face the indictment of the Jamaica Committee, and that only by the 'earnest advice of counsel and friends he had been induced to abandon that resolution'. *The Times* (14 Feb. 1867), 5.   124 *RPBS*, 17.

point.[125] This evidence would underpin Stephen's central submission that the actions of Nelson and Brand had been 'wholly illegal in every respect'.[126] While the accused might attempt to privilege these actions on grounds of public necessity, the attempt would fail. That privilege extended only to the suppression of *active* insurrection or resistance, not to the punishment of men who, like George Gordon, had not actually participated in the insurrection. Such persons could only be tried and punished by the regular courts. The contrary notion, that Nelson and Brand had possessed an unlimited discretion to court martial and punish anyone they chose, Stephen argued, was 'utterly irreconcilable with any interpretation whatever of the most fundamental laws of this country from Magna Carta to the present day'.[127]

Stephen then pressed another point: Colonel Nelson not only lacked the legal authority to court martial Gordon, but at the relevant time he had 'actual knowledge – at any rate suspicion – of what the law was'.[128] This would be proved by the contents of an official despatch that Nelson himself had written to General O'Connor on 3 November 1865.[129] While Stephen did not accuse Colonel Nelson (or Lieutenant Brand) of having been motivated by 'personal ill-will' toward Gordon, the court martial and execution had proceeded with reckless indifference toward Gordon's legal rights. Nothing about the circumstances of the case indicated that it had been 'absolutely necessary to put him to death at that time'.[130] In fact, when Nelson ordered that Gordon's execution be delayed for two full days he had tacitly confirmed this. In the final analysis, Stephen contended, it was inescapable that Gordon was hanged for political reasons, for his having been 'an agitator', and that the execution of a man on these grounds was 'wilful murder'.

This concluded Stephen's legal submissions. It now fell upon him (and his assisting barrister, John Horne Payne) to call and examine his witnesses. Over a number of hours the witnesses were called, questioned, cross-questioned, and re-examined. What follows is a summary of their evidence, and the significant admissions made during cross-questioning.

Dr. Fiddes, examined by Payne, testified as to the circumstances of Gordon's arrest. He was not closely cross-questioned.[131] Andrew Lewis, the former Jamaican legislator, described how Gordon had come to be transferred into the custody of Colonel Nelson at Morant Bay. He also described Gordon's execution, and how

---

[125] Stephen called George Phillippo, the Jamaican barrister, who testified that when it was necessary to interpret Jamaica's statutes, the colony's lawyers 'refer to the common law of England and the statute law up to the 1st of George II'. Phillippo also testified that the Spanish law had 'never been the law [in Jamaica] after the conquest'. Ibid., 37.   [126] Ibid., 20.

[127] Ibid.   [128] Ibid., 22.

[129] Stephen also was able to establish that prior to the execution, Nelson had been privy to a letter written to Gordon by his solicitor (Wemyss Anderson). The letter specifically contended that the military lacked jurisdiction to try Gordon before a court martial. Ibid.   [130] Ibid., 27.

[131] But nonetheless admitted to Brand's lawyer that Brand had not been present for the arrest. Ibid., 29.

Nelson (but not Brand) had been present for the execution. On cross-questioning by Poland, Lewis told the court how martial law came to be proclaimed, and the procedures that had been followed. Lewis admitted that he had been one of the thirty privy councillors who had unanimously supported the proclamation of martial law following the Morant Bay rising.[132] In casting his vote, Lewis had been mindful of the extreme vulnerability of the scattered white population of the island. The whites were vastly outnumbered by the blacks and coloureds, and were left to rely on only one white and two black regiments to protect the scattered white population of the island. Further questioning revealed that Lewis's involvement in the suppression of the revolt was more extensive than he had admitted to Stephen's questions. He confessed, for instance, that he had himself presided over courts martial which had rendered death verdicts and had then carried them out. (In fact, Lewis had presided over the court martial and hanging of the charismatic preacher and rebel leader, Paul Bogle.) Lewis also admitted that he was present during much of Gordon's trial and that, upon its conclusion, Gordon did not 'make any application to have the trial postponed'. Finally, Lewis testified that after the rebellion he had voted in favour of presenting Nelson with a valuable ceremonial sword for services rendered during the suppression of the rebellion.[133]

In a few minutes of cross-questioning, Poland had succeeded in establishing that the proclamation of martial law had enjoyed broad support among the white elite of Jamaica, that the population had reason to be frightened of revolt, that many officials had taken part in the fatal courts martial, and that Nelson had been heartily applauded for his role in crushing the uprising. Lewis, a prosecution witness, had been among those who thought that Gordon's court martial and execution had been handled properly and with appropriate alacrity.

One of Stephen's most important witnesses at the committal hearing was Augustus Lake, the former reporter who had taken extensive notes at Gordon's court martial. (Like Fiddes and Lewis, Lake had been brought to England from Jamaica at the expense of the Jamaica Committee.[134]) Lake gave evidence concerning the character of Gordon's trial. He described the witnesses that had been called by the prosecution, and how some of the witnesses were black prisoners who had hoped that their testimony against Gordon would save their own lives. When he was cross-questioned by Poland, Lake testified that in terms of its length, Gordon's trial had been 'very patient'. Lake then stood down. When the lawyers were finished with a few more (inconsequential) witnesses,[135] the committal hearing then adjourned for final legal argument.

---

132 *RPBS*, 31–2.

133 On re-examination, Stephen repaired some of the damage done to his case when Lewis testified that all of the men he had sent to the gallows had been guilty of serious crimes during the actual insurrection. Ibid., 33.

134 The Committee began to arrange for the importing of witnesses from Jamaica at the end of the previous summer. *JC Minutes*, 28 Sept. 1866.

135 Shaen, for instance, was called to authenticate copies of documents that had been tabled by the prosecution, including the proclamation of Charles II which declared that all persons free born

The hearings resumed on 23 February. The War Office, determined to try to prevent the prosecution of Nelson from going before the grand jury, reinforced his defence team with the eminent barrister James Hannen. In 1867 Hannen had been a lawyer for almost twenty years.[136] As a young man he had undertaken extensive legal education at Heidelberg, and it was said that he had a more philosophical attitude toward the law than the average English lawyer. By the time he accepted the Nelson brief Hannen was a busy and successful Queen's Counsel, a man renowned for precision (if not eloquence) in the courtroom. Commercial cases were his speciality. His work in this field helped secure a patronage position as junior counsel for the Treasury, an office which routinely led to a judgeship. As it happened, 1867 was a pivotal year in Hannen's career. When the Nelson hearing was over, he was retained by the Crown in the prosecution of the Manchester Fenians. In 1868 he was appointed a judge of the Queen's Bench. When Hannen's career is looked on as a whole, it would seem that politics had little to do with the fact that he was offered (and accepted) the Nelson brief. The brief fell his way because he was a distinguished barrister who had some connections to government. Hannen appears to have accepted the brief for the simple reason that it was an interesting opportunity to earn his customary fee.

Hannen's appearance for Nelson marked the beginning of a remarkably free-wheeling debate on the law of martial law, and its implications for Nelson and Brand. In his role as prosecutor, Stephen had opened his case (Hannen absent) on 12 February. Only after the last prosecution witness testified, on 23 February, did Hannen reply. After Hannen's speech, Stephen was permitted a long rebuttal, and then both counsel were indulged in a series of short exchanges on particular points of law. It was the first time in the two-year-old history of the Jamaica affair that in a courtroom setting two English barristers had been given the opportunity to exchange legal volleys over the law of martial law.

When Hannen introduced himself to the court he remarked that the cases against Nelson and Brand were 'so closely mixed up' that he would 'speak of them both together'.[137] Interestingly, Bristow, Brand's solicitor, quickly rose to object. Bristow did not think the Nelson and Brand cases were 'altogether identical', and asked to address the court independently of Hannen. This manoeuvre underlined the seriousness with which the charges were viewed. As a young subaltern who for most purposes had been acting under direct orders during the suppression, Brand's legal position in fact was *not* identical to that of the man who had been the senior officer in the field. Without apparent hesitation Henry granted Bristow the right to make separate submissions for his client.

In making his lengthy and detailed submissions to the court, Hannen's object was to demonstrate that the conduct of Nelson toward Gordon had been 'justifiable in

to British subjects in Jamaica were to have the same legal rights and privileges as persons born in England. Ibid., 38–9.

[136] See generally, *DNB*, xxii, 811–12; *The Times* (30 Mar. 1894), 12; *Law Times* (7 Apr. 1894), 527. [137] *RPBS*, 39.

law', and that he should be discharged without further inconvenience. He began by referring to the undisputed fact that in the trial and execution of Gordon, Nelson and Brand had acted from a sense of military duty, not private animosity. Even the prosecuting barrister did not 'for one moment impeach their good faith, or deny they believed that they were acting as they were justified in acting.'[138] Having established this point, Hannen made a bold submission: when Nelson and Brand took action against Gordon and other alleged rebels, they had acted under direct orders from superior officers. If they had balked, or if 'they had refused to do what they did, they would have been liable to be shot'.[139] In such circumstances it was simply unthinkable that the accused might be convicted of murder. Here Hannen also appealed to the Magistrate's sense of practical justice. The certainty that Nelson and Brand would be acquitted on murder charges rendered the prosecution a 'solemn and serious farce, nothing more'. Hannen hoped that Sir Thomas would put an end to the farce, and not by his order subject the accused to the 'pain, trouble and anxiety of being placed on their trial'.

But Hannen was too skilled a barrister to rest his case on this largely emotional appeal. He knew that Henry was an experienced lawyer unlikely to discharge Nelson merely because he was a good officer who had done his duty in a difficult situation. Stephen had treated the case as a formal legal procedure presided over by a legally sophisticated judge. After his opening comments, Hannen did likewise.

Stephen had sought to minimize the scope and effect of the Jamaican statutory law of martial law. Hannen laboured to maximize it. To understand the import of this law one had to understand the history and character of the Jamaican colony. Soon after the island was conquered by Cromwell's forces, the English population of Jamaica was menaced by the 'great dangers' posed by the larger population of blacks.[140] White colonists lived in perpetual fear of slave revolt. By these lights, it was 'perfectly obvious' that when the Jamaican legislature passed a statute on martial law it 'intended to give sanction and authority to martial law in its larger sense'.[141] What the legislators of the colony meant to do was to enable the 'council of the nation' to give the military the powers needed to crush negro rebellions, and without fear of subsequent legal retribution. In the case at bar, the actions of Nelson and Brand were taken only after a 'solemn council of all the great dignitaries of the community' had decided that the colony faced a great emergency.

In this historical and political context, Hannen made more specific submissions about the nature of martial law. He endeavoured to establish that it was not part of ordinary common law but a special body of law that arose during a time of war or open rebellion. Martial law was 'the setting aside of that law which would have been administered in the courts of justice if they were capable of being

---

[138] *RPBS*, 40.　　　[139] Ibid.　　　[140] Ibid., 48.　　　[141] Ibid.

applied to'.[142] The point of martial law was to sanction the use of military force to restore the general peace. Officers charged with this perilous but essential task are 'in fact called upon to fulfil the office of dictator, as it were, and while they act *bona fide* in the interests of the sovereign and the state for the preservation of the peace and for putting down the insurrection; they cannot be called to account by any court of justice whatever'.[143] The fate of those within the jurisdiction of martial law was 'left to the absolute discretion of the military commander'. For these propositions, Hannen told the court, it would be 'easy to multiply authorities'. When called upon to provide these authorities, however, Hannen was not so sure of himself. Rather embarrassingly, in fact, he attempted to cite Blackstone but then could not lay his hands on the relevant quote.[144] When Hannen tried to invoke the Duke of Wellington's famous comments on martial law, Henry chided him for straying from 'legal authorities'.[145] After he made some disjointed references to the Petition of Right, Hannen moved on to discuss the instances when Parliament had proclaimed (or validated) martial law in Ireland. These references were to provide a foundation for the proposition that the statutes governing martial law and indemnity were valid laws.

But Hannen's ensuing legal arguments were weakly researched and organized. Allusions to legal authority were scant and seemingly half-hearted. By the mid-point of his speech, he had all but stopped citing law. The essence of his case was that Nelson's conduct toward Gordon was 'justifiable in law' because he had faithfully carried out his duty during an 'actual insurrection'.[146] He emphasized the importance of the political and military context of Nelson's conduct. Hannen urged the magistrate to imagine himself in the place of Nelson in October 1865, having been asked to subdue scores of black prisoners with few trained soldiers and while surrounded by an 'excited population'.[147] Nelson had been given 'very great discretionary power' but little military might.[148] In these circumstances, Hannen suggested to Henry, 'he has not acted exactly as you, Sir, sitting here quietly in the County of Middlesex, would have acted'. But that did not make him guilty of murder. Even the prosecution had admitted that he had tried only to do his duty, and 'there was no intention to do anything wrong, or any malice express or implied: on the contrary, it is admitted that his *bona fide* intention was to act in conformity with what he believed to be his legal authority'.

But, even accepting these propositions, the execution of Gordon, a non-combatant, had still to be justified. Here Hannen at last made a coherent legal argument.[149]

---

[142] Ibid., 42.   [143] Ibid.   [144] Ibid.

[145] Like the *Pall Mall Gazette* (3 July 1867), 1, Henry no doubt held the view that 'a great soldier is not of necessity a great lawyer'.

[146] This prompted Stephen's objection on grounds that Lewis's evidence did not establish either the gravity of the uprising or the steps needed to quell it. These were the very points that had to be proved at trial in order to make out a defence of necessity. Henry let Hannen's point stand. Ibid., 50.

[147] Ibid., 55.   [148] Ibid., 58.

[149] This argument was strikingly similar to one that had been endorsed by Finlason in his *Treatise on Martial Law*, published the previous year. See above, Ch. 4.

Martial law, Hannen conceded, did not permit civilian or military authorities to conduct courts martial in any manner of their choosing. In the court martial of Gordon, in the trial of any prisoner taken under martial law, Nelson and Brand had been bound to observe the 'common rules of natural justice'.[150] In Hannen's submission, these minimum procedural conditions had been met in Gordon's case. Gordon had been informed of the charges he faced, had been allowed to cross-examine prosecution witnesses, call his own (available) witnesses, and then to offer a legal excuse for his conduct.[151] And even if it were true that Nelson had 'technically exceeded the law', he could not be held liable because he was entitled to an indemnity under colonial legislation. Hannen summarized his position: Colonel Nelson had acted in perfect good faith in the administration of martial law which, Hannen submitted, 'was set by the operation of the municipal law in anticipation of emergencies of this kind'.[152] In so doing he had acted within the extraordinary legal authority given to him by the Governor and the Council of War. Nelson was therefore indemnified for 'anything he did in that capacity _bona fide_'. Hannen asked that Sir Thomas exercise his discretion not to send the case to the grand jury. In his final appeal, he quoted Burke that 'to punish public men acting in extremities', men who had no corrupt motive, was 'repugnant to humanity'.[153] There was no case made out which called upon the magistrate to 'send these gentlemen upon trial for their lives'.

Before Stephen was asked to reply, Brand's solicitor, Bristow, stood up to address the court. As a mere solicitor following in the wake of 'very eminent counsel,' Bristow explained, he did not presume to amend or even supplement Hannen's main arguments. He wanted to communicate to the court only that the defence established for Nelson applied '_a fortiori_, with stronger force to the case of Lieutenant Brand'. Brand, after all, was a young subaltern who had acted on the direct order of a superior officer. Had he not done so, 'he would have been liable, by the law both of Jamaica and of England, as a subordinate officer, to be tried by another court martial and shot'.[154] The same young officer, Bristow continued, 'not being a lawyer', had been ordered to exercise a number of difficult legal tasks and under the most trying circumstances. When he presided over Gordon's court martial, the 'position of Lieutenant Brand is almost identical with that of a juror in this country; he did nothing more than say what he honestly and fairly believed to be true as to the issue delivered in charge to him'. In Bristow's submission, Brand did not act with malice and did not actually kill Gordon. He too had simply followed orders.

Like Hannen before him, in making his last arguments Bristow alluded to Henry's substantial prestige as a judge, and the likely effect of a decision to indict.

---

150 _RPBS_, 55–6.

151 Hannen added that it did not matter that Gordon's arrest and transportation to Morant Bay were of dubious legality. The crimes that Gordon was alleged to have committed were local ones; they related directly to the crimes of the insurrectionists. Ibid.   152 Ibid., 60.

153 Ibid., 61.   154 Ibid., 62.

'If you send [Brand] before a grand jury,' Bristow submitted, 'no doubt it will have a great effect on them, that you, a learned magistrate, a lawyer of great standing and eminence, have thought there was a sufficient case against Lieutenant Brand.'[155] Bristow was concerned that the grand jury would be so much impressed by Henry's endorsement of the case that they would find a true bill 'without exercising their own discretion or judgment'. With this the solicitor reiterated that Brand, after all was said, was 'simply acting in performance of a legitimate and proper duty', and had done nothing criminal in nature.

When Stephen stood to begin his rebuttal, he decided first to 'dispose, in a very few words' the propositions offered by Bristow. That Brand had acted only in the capacity of a juror was quickly dispensed with. English jurors, Stephen acidly reminded the court, do not presume the authority, as did Brand, to sentence men to be 'hanged by the neck until dead'.[156] Stephen's second point applied equally to Nelson: the court martial and execution of Gordon were patently unlawful, and no officer of the English military was obligated to follow an unlawful order. To bolster this point, Stephen elaborated a distinctly liberal conception of military service. When an Englishman chose to join the military, Stephen argued, he did so as a 'free person in a free country'. But the choice having been made, it came with onerous responsibilities, including the risk of disobeying an illegal order and 'being shot in the breach'.[157] This was the necessary footing of military service in any country in which the armed forces were not 'an instrument of tyranny'. Were it otherwise, even the most egregious outrages against 'the life and liberty of every man in this country, or in any part of the dominions' would be excused on the facile grounds that the perpetrators were only following orders.

This brought Stephen back to the main thrust of his rebuttal. For the limited purposes of a committal hearing, the ultimate guilt or innocence of the accused was not at issue. The only important question was whether there were triable issues. Counsel for the prosecution asked only that Henry 'put the matter in train for further investigation'.[158] The finer issues of law and fact arising from the prosecution ought to be resolved at trial.

Stephen then spent some time on the specific assertions and authorities mentioned by Hannen, especially those pertaining to the proposition that Jamaican law had provided the accused with greater legal powers than possessed by persons acting under martial law in England. Stephen's answer was that the term 'martial law' had many possible meanings, but that the Jamaican statute did not specify one.[159] In the absence of a specified meaning, there was no recourse but to 'the common law of England'.[160] Even on a broad reading of the Jamaican law, there had been no military necessity for the transportation, court martial, and execution of Gordon. Mr. Hannen had been in error, moreover, when he suggested that

---

[155] Ibid., 64.   [156] Ibid., 65.   [157] Ibid., 67.   [158] Ibid., 70.
[159] Stephen argued that a proclamation of martial law under the Act had these three effects: to call out the militia; to warn rebels that extreme measures were about to be taken; to stipulate that a complete record be kept in case actions were later called into question. Ibid., 77.   [160] Ibid., 76.

Colonel Nelson had an unfettered discretion to execute one man in order to 'strike terror into others'.[161]

Stephen then addressed a seeming contradiction in his own case. On one hand, he allowed that both Nelson and Brand had acted 'without personal malice against Mr. Gordon in the common sense of the word, and they were under the impression that what they did was a legal act'.[162] On the other hand, he remained adamant that their actions were illegal. But while Stephen did not impute malice to the accused, 'I do impute blame . . . I do impute to them the blame of acting in a tyrannical and oppressive manner, and of taking away human life without due and reasonable cause.'[163] The contradiction was resolved when it was understood that an evil motive was not an element of the crime of murder. What mattered was that the accused intentionally brought about the death of a man. Once it was established that the accused intended to kill the relevant victim, the only remaining legal issue was whether the killing might be privileged by a defence. The relevant defence in the case at bar was public necessity. Stephen did not think that Nelson and Brand could prove necessity, but this was a matter to be weighed by a trial jury, not the police magistrate.

Stephen was equally firm that the prosecution of Nelson and Brand was not a mere symbolic case – a 'feigned issue' – staged either for political reasons or to prepare the ground for proceedings against Edward Eyre. The prosecution was brought because the accused had been party to a political murder. Gordon was hanged, Stephen maintained, not because he had been a violent rebel or criminal but because he was a 'mischievous agitator' who, some months prior to the uprising, was thought to have made some seditious statements. On that principle, the courts martial might have exerted the right to try and hang 'every single member of the Jamaica legislature who had ever taken up a view of politics opposed to the Government'.[164] Stephen thought it a 'monstrous thing that such a right should be proclaimed against any man living under the protection of English law'.[165] The successful prosecution of Nelson and Brand and, in time, Eyre was vital if only because to do nothing would be to validate the principle of justifiable political killing. Nelson and Brand, Stephen stated, 'have done, as I said before, as strong a thing as was ever done in the English dominions, and let them justify it before a jury'.[166]

Had he been more concerned with the law than the rhetorical impact of his speech, Stephen might have ended with that assertion. But he did not. Stephen felt compelled also to erase any doubts which Hannen might have posed regarding jurisdiction and the legal effect of the indemnity statute passed by the Jamaican legislature. Was the alleged homicide of one English subject by another, a

---

[161] *RPBS*, 80.   [162] Ibid., 69.   [163] Ibid.   [164] Ibid., 81.
[165] Ibid.   [166] Ibid., 80.

homicide excused retroactively by local statute, triable in an English court? Stephen contended that there were a number of reasons why it was. First, the relevant procedural statute provided that any murder or manslaughter committed outside the United Kingdom could be tried in England.[167] The effect of this legislation, Stephen submitted, was to make the murder of Gordon 'a crime against the law of England, and that crime…cannot be purged by any other authority than that of the English legislature'. Second, as the Jamaican legislature was not established by Parliament, but was an 'emanation from the Crown', it could only do what the Crown could do. Since 1688, the Crown could not 'give indulgences by Act of Prerogative'.[168] For these reasons, then, the Jamaican indemnity 'has no operation in this country'.[169]

In the remainder of his long (and almost uninterrupted) rebuttal, Stephen emphasized that, whether or not Sir Thomas agreed with all of his submissions on the law of martial law, there were issues here that should properly be presented to a grand jury. What was essential was that the accused be 'put to the proof as to the reasons which induced them to take those extremely strong measures'.[170] In making these last submissions, Stephen was mindful both that the accused officers had been placed in a difficult position, that he [Stephen] agreed that some allowance was due them, and that 'in some quarters [among some leading members of the Jamaica Committee, for instance], that allowance might well be considered excessive'. Here Stephen attempted to stave off further criticism on this point. He emphasized that the accused had acted, if not 'from personal malignity', then from 'that which the law calls malice'.[171] They took a human life when they might have spared it 'with propriety and due regard for the public interest'.

When Stephen finished, Henry complimented the lawyers on their 'very able and elaborate arguments', before quickly coming to the point: both the law and facts of the case remained in dispute. There was nothing to do in this instance than to take the criminal charges against Nelson and Brand and 'to put them in train for further inquiry'.[172] The defendants were to be held on bail to appear before the grand jury of the County of Middlesex on 8 April.

Stephen's advocacy had thus achieved the first objective of his retainer: the Nelson and Brand cases had been captured, as it were, by the English criminal justice system. He had caused a respected criminal judge to conclude that two serving officers of Her Majesty's armed forces *might* have committed murder in the course of their duties, and that the charges ought to be reviewed by a grand jury. This was a major development in the history of the Jamaica affair, one which had been striven for by Stephen's employers for many months. But, as the notices came in, it became increasingly obvious that what Stephen had won in the court-room was more than offset by what had been lost in the arena of political opinion.

---

[167] Criminal Law Consolidation Acts, 24 & 25 Vict. c. 96.   [168] *RPBS*, 83.   [169] Ibid.
[170] Ibid., 86.   [171] Ibid.   [172] Ibid., 86.

It was widely perceived, even among the executive leadership of the Jamaica Committee, that in his bloodless presentation of the criminal case and unwavering civility toward the accused, Stephen had disconnected the Committee from its original inspiration and its base of support.

The dissonance between Stephen's courtroom rhetoric and the Jamaica Committee's *raison d'être* was marked both by friends and enemies of the Committee. The *Saturday Review*, long sympathetic to its aims, observed that the 'courtesy which has thus far distinguished the Jamaican prosecution is creditable rather to the good taste of the promoters than to their consistency'.[173] The 'strict professional propriety' and 'logical precision' of Stephen's presentation, while commendable, had given rise to widespread 'misunderstanding'. While lawyerly decorum might have called for 'an absolutely dispassionate appeal to a criminal tribunal', this was not, the *Review* insisted, what was wanted by the 'uninstructed laymen' who supported the prosecution. The backers of the Jamaica Committee wanted 'revenge', and if they could not have it, they wanted at the very least some forum for the expression of righteous indignation. What they had got was a minutely researched and logically precise argument that the execution of Gordon was 'technically illegal'. Stephen's gentlemanly demeanour toward the accused had been so pronounced, so scrupulously observed in fact, that it won ironic compliments even from Mr. Punch.[174]

It would seem that in the wake of his first appearance before Henry at Bow Street Stephen became aware, probably from newspaper reports, that the compliments directed toward the accused had raised eyebrows. Stephen had addressed the criticism in open court and, to a limited degree, had bowed to it. But it is evident that Stephen's protestations, his attempts to bring a more distinctly accusatory edge to his later speeches at Bow Street, did not appease his critics, especially those on the Jamaica Committee.

In the wake of Stephen's second appearance for the Jamaica Committee as prosecuting counsel, Chesson noted that Stephen had made 'an admirable and closely reasoned speech'. But why, Chesson added, 'does he go out of his way to compliment the accused? This is a cardinal error in judgment and will lead to no end of misconceptions.'[175] This fear was swiftly borne out. Letters of complaint from subscribers already had begun to arrive at the Committee's offices. When the executive of the Committee met on 18 February, the question of Stephen's handling of the prosecution at Bow Street – not yet over – was at the top of the agenda. The letters of complaint were read aloud. Mill and a number of other leading members then 'bore emphatic testimony to the mistake which had been committed'.[176] Shaen, the Committee's solicitor (who had retained Stephen), attempted to reassure his colleagues that in Stephen (and Edward James) 'we have

---

[173] *Saturday Review* (16 Feb. 1867), 192–3.
[174] *Punch* had been a determined adversary of the Jamaica Committee since its inception. See 'If It's Murder, Mention It', *Punch* (16 Feb. 1867), 69.   [175] *CD*, 12 Feb. 1867.
[176] Ibid., 18 Feb. 1867.

got the best men whom we could possibly retain'. According to Chesson, however, Shaen's reassurances 'rather strengthened [than lessened] our apprehension with regard both to Mr. Stephen and Mr. James'.[177] It was resolved that Mill and Taylor would meet with the two barristers and express the concerns of the Committee.

It is not clear whether this meeting took place, or whether it took place before or after the completion of the Bow Street proceedings on 23 February, or, if such a meeting did take place, whether Mill and Taylor tried to prevail on Stephen to alter his courtroom style. We have already noted only that Stephen's second court-room speech did not differ dramatically from what had gone before. The minutes of the Committee meeting of 25 February record that it had received a 'letter of explanation' from Stephen. The minutes do not state whether Stephen defended his courtroom strategy, or simply provided a report of the Bow Street proceedings. In any event, with Nelson and Brand facing indictment before the grand jury, the raw nerves of the Jamaica Committee executive appear to have been soothed. A letter was drafted expressing 'warmest thanks to Stephen for the very able, satisfactory and successful manner in which he has conducted the case for the prosecution'.[178] It was further resolved to publish a lightly edited transcript of the hearings. While Edward James was to be consulted about the 'mode of conducting the prosecution' at the next stage, there was no suggestion that either he or Stephen would be replaced by other lawyers.

At the meeting of 28 February 1867, the Committee executive turned their attention to future litigation. It was decided that Stephen and James should be consulted about the possibility of an additional prosecution of Nelson and Brand for the murder of two other Jamaicans, Clarke and Lawrence.[179] Although this option was considered long enough that it finally got into the newspapers,[180] they ultimately decided not to press ahead with it. The Committee was much more decisive on another point: that 'proceedings should at once be instituted against Mr. Eyre in Shropshire; and that Mr. Shaen was required to lose no time in securing the services of Mr. Stephen for that purpose'. Even with dissension in the ranks, it was time to open the war on the second front.

---

[177] Ibid. It is not clear why Edward James was implicated here. James appears to have played no direct role in the prosecution of Nelson and Brand. It is possible, however, that Stephen had continued to consult with him about the prosecution.   [178] *JC Minutes*, 25 Feb. 1867.

[179] *JC Minutes*, 28 Feb. 1867. Clarke and Lawrence had been arrested near Morant Bay after martial law had been proclaimed, and were condemned and executed by Brand's court martial and under Nelson's (unreviewed) order. Given that Nelson and Brand had already been committed on the charge of being accessories to Gordon's murder, the additional indictments might have been brought against them without further preliminary hearing. The prosecutions would have thrown the personal liability of the accused into sharper relief. *The Times* (18 Mar. 1867), 6.

[180] The two men had been convicted, on flimsy evidence, of complicity in the uprising. Their trials and executions took place some weeks after the rebellion had ceased. More importantly, the executions went ahead without any fiat from Governor Eyre. Nelson confirmed Brand's sentence without consulting his superiors.

III. At Market Drayton

Until early February 1867 the Jamaica Committee had entertained some faint hope that Eyre would come to London to face prosecution. This was not a matter only of wishful thinking. In January Shaen had corresponded with Anderson Rose to work out an arrangement. If Eyre would submit to prosecution in London, the Committee would extend him every courtesy with regard to arrest and bail. After a brief meeting with Rose in mid-January, Shaen formed the impression that Eyre would acquiesce on grounds that he 'did not want to be annoyed by proceedings in his own neighbourhood'. Shaen informed the Committee that if given adequate forewarning, Eyre would 'come forward [in London] to meet the charge, and so avoid being looked after by a policeman'.[181] Stephen had made an announcement to this effect when he opened the case against Nelson and Brand at Bow Street on 6 February.

The announcement appears to have caught the Defence Committee off-guard. Some of its executive members promptly arranged to meet with Rose.[182] They were told that Eyre had expressed his readiness to 'appear at Bow-Street and sink or swim with his subordinates'.[183] After consultation with Rose, the executive unanimously resolved to 'request Mr. Eyre to remain in the county in which he is now residing'. As we have seen, on 12 February Rose had appeared at the Bow Street court to deny that there had been any agreement that his client would cooperate with a London prosecution.[184] If Rose and Shaen once had been *ad idem* on this point, they were no longer. As Rose later reiterated in an open letter to Shaen, 'Mr. Eyre, adhering to the decision of his counsel and friends, declines by any act of his own to countenance or aid the Jamaica Committee in their murder prosecutions.'[185] Rose did offer the Committee the courtesy of Eyre's address in Shropshire. He then wrote to *The Times* to stress that only the 'earnest advice of counsel' had prevented Eyre from volunteering for prosecution in London.[186]

By the end of January 1867, Eyre knew that criminal prosecution – somewhere in England – was inevitable. Accordingly, he wrote to Lord Carnarvon, the Secretary of State for the Colonies, to request that the cost of his defence be paid from the public purse.[187] When similar requests had been made of the War Office and

181 Letter from Shaen to Rose, 22 Feb. 1867, as reported in the *Daily News* (5 Mar. 1867), 3.
182 See the account of these transactions in Hume, *Edward John Eyre*, Appendix C, 277–88.
183 Ibid., 287.
184 Shaen later attempted to explain the misunderstanding on the theory that Rose had thought that any London prosecution would be for a mere misdemeanour under the Colonial Governors Act. Rose repudiated the agreement when he learned that the Jamaica Committee would seek an indictment for murder. Ibid.
185 Letter from Rose to Shaen, reprinted in the *Law Times* (9 Mar. 1867), 368.
186 Rose also accused the Jamaica Committee of trying to include Eyre in one indictment with Nelson and Brand in order to 'prevent them giving evidence the one for the other'. *The Times* (14 Feb. 1867), 5.
187 See Carnarvon diary, 20 Feb. 1867, Carnarvon Papers, *BL*, Add. MS. 69899.

the Admiralty respectively by Nelson and Brand, two commissioned officers in active service, both departments quickly assented to them. Eyre was not so fortunate. Carnarvon was decidedly unsympathetic to Eyre's plight. Already he was on public record that terrible and inexcusable excesses had occurred during the Jamaica suppression. When Eyre's request for financial support reached his desk, Carnarvon rejected it out of hand.[188] Eyre would be compensated if and when he was wholly exonerated of legal wrongdoing. The decision was not reversed by the Cabinet. The Tory government was prepared to *allege* that Eyre was not a criminal, but it was not willing to pay anyone to prove it.

It was well for Eyre, however, that the Government's symbolic endorsement was of more importance to him than its money. By February 1867 his Defence Committee had collected in excess of £4,000 for his legal defence from private donors,[189] enough to fee the very best barristers for many courtroom battles. The main challenge now was in public relations. In a number of prominent newspapers it had been observed that while Nelson and Brand had manfully faced their accusers at Bow Street, Eyre, their civilian chief, was content to hide in the countryside.[190] In order to confront this insinuation, and other issues, on 20 February the leaders of the Defence Committee convened a general meeting of the association at Willis's Rooms, London.

The meeting was organized to permit some of Eyre's more illustrious supporters publicly to support his decision to remain in Shropshire.[191] A succession of speakers made windy speeches about how Eyre had averted an 'incalculable calamity' in Jamaica, and about the indispensability of martial law in the dark-skinned parts of the empire. The physicist Tyndall, now one of Eyre's most visible and vociferous supporters, moved a resolution to endorse the steps taken by the Defence Committee to defend the former Governor.[192] The long-retired army General, Sir William Gomm (a left-over from 'Wellington's wars'), seconded the resolution.[193] Murchison closed the meeting with some comments on Eyre's 'high and spotless character'. He was also careful to comment on Eyre's 'chivalrous desire' to leave Shropshire in order to face his accusers in London, a desire 'only checked by the unanimous resolution of the executive committee'.[194]

---

[188] Ibid. Carnarvon was prepared to resign if overruled by cabinet. In the result, Carnarvon resigned a month later when the Conservatives had committed to the passage of the second Reform Bill.

[189] According to Murchison, the Eyre Defence fund had collected just over £4,000 in 1866. *The Times* (19 Oct. 1866), 10.

[190] 'Mr. Eyre seems to have changed his mind about his assumption of sole responsibility, between the time he thought responsibility a distinction, and the time when it seems at all events a danger.' *Spectator* (16 Feb. 1867), 174.

[191] On 16 February, Eyre was attacked in the *Spectator* for remaining in Shropshire while his subordinates faced prosecution in London. This was seen as a cowardly revocation of his longstanding pledge to assume 'sole responsibility' for the Jamaican suppression under martial law. On 23 February, convinced that Eyre was dissuaded from returning to London only by the unanimous resolution of the Defence Committee, it retracted its accusations. *Spectator* (23 Feb. 1867), 203.

[192] Report of a Meeting of the Eyre Defence Committee, in Hume, *Edward John Eyre*, Appendix C, 278.   [193] Ibid., 285.

[194] Ibid., 287–8.

It is just possible (even the *Spectator* thought as much)[195] that Eyre really *had* felt it his duty to face prosecution in London with Nelson and Brand. But, as a middle-aged family man without means or employment, he had little choice but to accept the advice of his patrons. When the Jamaica Committee announced that it would commence the prosecution in Shropshire on 25 March 1867, Eyre had already ceded control of his defence to his lawyers. They would decide how and by whom he would be defended in court. On 12 March Eyre informed Rose that he wished 'to be entirely guided by yourself and those you consult, as to whether I should voluntarily attend at Market Drayton on the 25th, or not'.[196] After expressing doubts about the efficacy of resistance at the process hearing stage, Eyre repeated himself: 'you will ... doubtless talk the matter over with those best competent to form a just opinion and decide accordingly. I place myself entirely in your hands.'

When he wrote to Rose on 12 March, Eyre, quite understandably, was a frightened man. He had not been able to embrace the view that the impending murder prosecution was a paper tiger. The Nelson and Brand cases were soon to go to a grand jury, and even as he dwelt in the supposed sanctuary of Shropshire, Eyre was not confident of avoiding the same fate. In another letter to Rose, Eyre informed his lawyer that in the course of the previous few months he had become acquainted with many members of the local (lay) magistracy, and he worried that they might easily be gulled by 'the law or sophistry of Mr. Stephen'.[197] Eyre warned Rose that when his case was called in Market Drayton 'there will not I fear be a very full Bench – to [*sic*] many of the Magistrates of this district are debarred from sitting as being contributors to the Defence Fund and amongst these are some of the best.'[198] Of the seven or eight gentlemen magistrates in the county, not more than 'four – if so many – can be got together who have not subscribed'.

If Eyre increasingly was governed by fear, and the lawyers who attended to it, the Jamaica Committee was increasingly governed by fate. Shropshire was among the least auspicious places in England for a group of urban radicals to prosecute a former colonial Governor for the murder of a mulatto political agitator. The presiding magistrates were legal laymen who would be unlikely to place legal principle ahead of personal feeling. On the other hand, the magistrates of Shropshire were likely to be just the sort of conservative Englishmen who would regard Eyre as a beleaguered hero. But time was not on the side of the pursuers. Eyre might easily have waited years, perhaps a lifetime, before returning to the jurisdiction of the Bow Street Police Court. The leaders and benefactors of the Jamaica Committee wanted action. There seemed no alternative but to do battle with the Defence Committee on its chosen ground.

---

[195] *Spectator* (23 Feb. 1867), 203.
[196] Eyre to Rose, 12 Mar. 1867, *BL*, Add. MS. 56373.   [197] Ibid.
[198] In the aftermath of the Market Drayton hearings, the *English Independent* (4 Apr. 1867), 420, credibly supposed that Mr. Eyre 'probably had been the guest of all his judges'.

As promised, a contingent from the Jamaica Committee, minus Mill and Taylor, attended the petty sessions of the peace on the morning of 25 March 1867. In spite of the carping against him after the Bow Street hearings, Stephen once again was retained to act as senior counsel for the prosecution. Horne Payne was there once again to act as Stephen's junior. On the first day Eyre was represented *in absentia* by Rose. Submissions were made to a panel of six magistrates chaired by Sir Baldwin Leighton (about whom more in a moment). The small courtroom was packed with reporters from all the major dailies of the country.[199]

Before Stephen could begin to make submissions, two magistrates,[200] including the senior magistrate for the district, recused themselves from hearing the case because they had subscribed to the Eyre Defence Fund. Their places on the bench would be taken by two alternate magistrates. After this announcement, Stephen stood to inform the court that he had been retained by the complainants Mill and Taylor 'to apply to the bench for a warrant for the apprehension of Mr. John Edward Eyre ... as an accessory before the fact to the wilful murder of George William Gordon'. Stephen then began to describe the facts of the case, and at greater length the reasons why there was jurisdiction to issue a warrant. But he was quickly cut short by Sir Baldwin Leighton. The bench was not interested in hearing submissions on the law at this point. It wanted to know why Mill and Taylor, the actual complainants in the case, were not in court. After an exchange on whether it was necessary for complainants to be present at a process hearing,[201] Shaen offered to serve as complainant. Stephen then called two witnesses (Fiddes and Lake) to establish a case *prima facie*. It was now obvious that process would be issued, and Stephen informed the court that the complainant would be satisfied if the magistrates issued a summons in place of a bench warrant. It was earnestly hoped that Mr. Eyre could be brought to court without any 'unnecessarily harsh' criminal procedure. Rose informed the court that Eyre was 'ready to surrender to the process of the Court at any time they may appoint. He only declines to recognize the Jamaica Committee.' Rose then asked the court for an adjournment until Eyre's counsel, the barrister Hardinge Giffard Q.C., became available two days hence. After consultation among themselves, the magistrates issued a warrant for the arrest of Eyre for murder. The committal hearing would commence in two days.

Once the warrant was issued, the local authorities did everything in their power to shield Eyre from any indignity or discomfort. As a result of prearrangement between the bench and the chief constable of the county,[202] the warrant was executed at Eyre's residence by the chief constable of the county, a local landowner and magistrate called H. Reginald Corbett. (Corbett, it was later reported, was one of the magistrates

---

[199] For a detailed account of the first session before the magistrates at Market Drayton, see *Shropshire News* (28 Mar. 1867).
[200] Tremlow and Donaldson. *The Times* (26 Mar. 1867), 10.   [201] Ibid.
[202] According to the 'special correspondent' of the *Morning Star* (27 Mar. 1867), 6.

who had presided over Eyre's process hearing.[203]) A reporter from the *Morning Star* soon discovered that Corbett's father was Eyre's landlord, and that he and Eyre had met several times. When this information became public, Corbett announced that he would forgo any further participation in the Eyre prosecution.[204]

While the first hearing in the Eyre case had gone almost unnoticed by the people of Market Drayton, the subsequent hearing – held on a market day with Eyre in attendance – was treated as a major event. The slew of journalists despatched from England's principal cities filed reports dripping with condescension toward the locals. The prosecution of the former Governor, one reporter wrote, had 'moved and perturbed the ordinarily sluggish current of life in that quiet rural retreat'.[205] Although it was cold and wet in the hours before the court opened, 'all the inhabitants turned into the Streets, and lined the road from the station to the county courthouse, eager to behold the solicitors, counsel, magistrates, etc., who arrived by early trains.'[206] The irony of all this was manifest: one of the great legal and political controversies of the day was to be contested where nothing of national significance had happened 'since the War of the Roses'.[207] As for the local Tory establishment, it was reported that they were solidly behind Edward Eyre. A number of prominent members of the local elite had subscribed to his defence fund. On the Sunday before the committal hearing, a local vicar had said a special prayer for 'Eyre's safety'.[208] It was also reported that the common people of the county were habitually and deferentially Tory in their politics. They were people, the *Birmingham Post* reported, who were 'never known to differ in feeling or opinion from the landed gentry in the neighbourhood'. It is more than passing strange then that on the morning of the hearing some local officials took pains to ensure that most 'common' people were barred from the courthouse.

An hour before the hearing was to begin, on the morning of 27 March, a sizeable crowd began to converge around the courthouse door, undeterred by the foul weather. Two constables had been assigned to check the name and credentials of every person wanting to enter the courthouse. When the constables entertained doubt as to the suitability of a person, they 'scribbled a line or two on a piece of paper and off indoors the officer went with it', returning with an order (from whom it was not clear) either to admit or reject the prospective entrant.[209] It did not escape the notice of reporters that tradesmen were turned away at the courthouse door, along with three ministers from dissenting chapels.[210] In contrast,

[203] *Morning Star* (27 Mar. 1867), 6.

[204] When the hearing was over, Corbett wrote to Eyre to denounce the 'most disgraceful and malicious attack upon you by the vagabonds styling themselves the Jamaica Committee'. Corbett then explained why he had had to withdraw from the panel of judges. Corbett to Eyre, 31 Mar. 1867, Eyre Papers, *SLSA*, Letter no. 29.   [205] *Daily Telegraph* (26 Mar. 1867), 6.

[206] Ibid.   [207] *Morning Star* (27 Mar. 1867), 6.

[208] *Birmingham Post* reported that the local vicar 'offered up a prayer on Sunday last...for Mr. Eyre's safety'. Quoted in the *Morning Star* (1 Apr. 1867), 5.

[209] *Examiner*, as quoted in the *Morning Star* (1 Apr. 1867), 5.

[210] *Weekly Times* (7 Apr. 1867).

Anglican clergymen, miscellaneous 'gentlemen', and a coterie of 'fashionable ladies' were admitted without delay. 'Not a single person of the humbler classes was admitted to the court,' the *Morning Star* recounted.[211] Someone had arranged for the hearing to unfold in front of an audience only of passionate Eyre sympathizers and supporters.

Eyre arrived at Market Drayton courthouse early in the morning, but quickly withdrew to some rooms for a private consultation with his solicitor and two barristers, Harry Poland and, for the first time, his lead counsel, Hardinge Giffard. At precisely 10.00 a.m. Eyre walked into the small but densely packed courtroom. Lord de Blaquiere, an executive member of the Defence Committee, was close at his side. According to the minutely reported account in the next day's *Morning Star*, Eyre seemed 'exceedingly nervous, and wore a look of deep anxiety'.[212] The reporter from the *Bee-Hive* also recorded that the ex-Governor seemed 'far from robust'.[213] Eyre's entrance was taken by the spectators as a signal for applause. The outburst was quickly and sternly reproached by the magistrates.[214] Eyre bowed repeatedly to the bench of magistrates and sat down at the counsel table (the courtroom did not have a dock) between Giffard and de Blaquiere. Shrewsbury sat down at the same table ready, if necessary, to pledge bail. Stephen, Horne Payne, and Peter Taylor sat opposite at the prosecutor's table.

Not unfairly, one newspaper referred to the five magistrates who entered the courtroom as 'the genuine embodiment of the worst spirit of squirearchy'.[215] Two (Major Broughton and Colonel Hill) were career army officers who had retired to country life. The three other magistrates (Sir Baldwin Leighton, Egerton Harding, and John Tayleur) were members of the county's local landed gentry. All five magistrates owed their appointments to the patronage of the county's Lord Lieutenant. None had formal legal training. The newspapermen from the liberal and radical papers were unkind. Baldwin Leighton was subjected to a particularly harsh drubbing. He was represented as the personification of 'Old Corruption', as a 'self-sufficient, incompetent and arrogant functionary'[216] who stood to benefit from 'less self-esteem and more urbanity'.[217] Leighton's detractors made hay with the fact that, as the former Tory M.P. for South Shropshire, he had championed the Poaching Prevention Act of 1862, a law promulgated to stamp out the poaching of rabbits at night.[218] This episode earned him the nickname 'Rabbitskins' Leighton.[219] With his brother magistrates Leighton frequently suffered by comparison to the London barrister-*cum*-Police Court magistrate, Sir Thomas Henry (a man whom the *Daily News* praised as 'second to none of his colleagues in learning, calmness and impartiality'). Not a single newspaper, not even the conservative dailies, paid similar compliments to the Shropshire judges.

---

[211] *Morning Star* (28 Mar. 1867), 6.   [212] Ibid.   [213] *Bee-Hive* (30 Mar. 1867).
[214] For another account of these events, see *Daily News* (28 Mar. 1867), 6.
[215] *Weekly Times* (7 Apr. 1867).   [216] Ibid.   [217] *Freeman* (5 Apr. 1867).
[218] *Daily News* (1 Apr. 1867), 5.   [219] *Reynolds' Weekly* (7 Apr. 1867).

The committal hearing began with the arraignment of Eyre on a charge that he 'did feloniously aid, abet, counsel and procure certain persons... to wilfully, and of malice aforethought, kill and murder one George William Gordon'. Before Stephen was invited to make submissions, Leighton informed the assembly that Mr. Corbett had withdrawn from the panel of magistrates on grounds that his father was the landlord of the accused person. On Giffard's request, all of the prosecution witnesses were asked to leave the court until called. Leighton then nodded to Stephen. After introducing himself and Horne Payne, Stephen told the court that Peter Taylor M.P. was present as the complainant.[220]

When it is considered that there were obvious and stark differences between pleading a case before Sir Thomas Henry and a panel of rural lay magistrates, Stephen's approach to the Market Drayton hearings was remarkably unsubtle. Stephen must have anticipated that his reception would be sceptical if not openly hostile, that the magistrates would be strongly predisposed to protect Eyre, and that they might not be terribly interested in the technical reasons why he was a murderer. Some advocates might have made some allowances for this. They might, for instance, have shortened or simplified their legal arguments. But Stephen did not. When it was his turn to speak he delivered no less than five hours of technical submissions to judges who probably had not heard so much law quoted in their whole careers on the bench. In only one obvious way did Stephen attempt to massage the biases of the court: at two junctures of his speech, the beginning and middle, Stephen once again reiterated that he thought Edward Eyre a brave and honourable man.

Before he made his first submission on the law, Stephen told the court that Eyre was a man who 'on many accounts was deserving of so much esteem and respect', and that the prosecution for murder of such a man was a 'disagreeable and painful duty'.[221] But if this kind of talk was meant to curry favour with the panel, it did not. From the outset of his speech Stephen met with implacable resistance, most especially from Sir Baldwin Leighton. Neither his formidable erudition nor emotional detachment made the slightest impression on the magistrates, except when it bored or irritated them. After he outlined the material facts pertaining to the death of Gordon, Stephen introduced the central point of his speech: at a committal hearing the prosecution did not have to establish the guilt of the accused, but only that the evidence raised *triable issues*, that 'grave questions, both of fact and law, existed in the case'.[222] If Stephen could convince the bench of this much, then it would be their solemn duty to commit Eyre to the grand jury 'whatever their opinion might be as to the moral or even as to the legal merits of the case'.

Stephen then offered submissions on why Eyre had been an accessory to murder. There could be no doubt that Gordon had been killed intentionally. The issue was the legal status of the court martial which tried and condemned him. Citing

---

[220] There now could be no question of the authenticity of the complaint against Mr. Eyre. For a detailed account of the first day of the committal hearing, see *Morning Star* (28 Mar. 1867), 6.
[221] Ibid.   [222] Ibid.

authorities[223] Stephen took pains to show that the court martial convened by Nelson was not legally constituted, and that 'an irregular military execution was murder'. While Eyre had not been present for the relevant execution, there also could be no doubt that he was 'head and director of all that took place'.[224] As the chief executive officer in the colony he was 'answerable for whatever was done under his direction'. Eyre had personally overseen Gordon's arrest and transfer into military jurisdiction, and had reviewed and endorsed the flawed workings of the court martial. That made him an accessory to the execution. Stephen elaborated: 'Mr. Eyre personally advised everything that was done. Whatever might have been the theory of [command], he was, in fact, at the head of the whole business – he was referred to on every occasion and he gave every order.'[225] Stephen then made a comment which once again would attract trenchant criticism: 'Mr. Eyre himself had avowed his own responsibility, and it was a pleasure to him to pay tribute to a man of undoubted courage and gallantry.' Having so manfully owned up to his actions, and for the motives behind them, Stephen added, 'whatever else anyone might say of Mr. Eyre, it could not be said that he was not a brave – a very brave man'.

There will be more to say about this comment in due course. For now it is enough to observe that Stephen might have thought it apt to compliment Eyre in this way because it accented the impersonal nature of the prosecution, and because, on his reading of the law, it was irrelevant to the question of Eyre's guilt or innocence. Stephen's argument hinged on a subtle, perhaps *too* subtle, argument about the criminal culpability of the former Governor. For Stephen, the central issue was not whether Eyre was a good or bad man, or even whether Eyre had acted on the good faith belief that Gordon's execution was necessary for the restoration of peace and security in the colony. The gravamen of his case was that Eyre had intended to cause Gordon's death by execution, and that in order to avoid conviction for murder he was obliged to prove that 'under all circumstances, the execution was necessary'. This was an issue of fact, one that 'it was impossible for any inferior tribunal to decide conclusively'.[226] Stephen submitted that when, as in the case at bar, the prosecution was able to adduce evidence enough to raise a doubt about the legality of a homicide, it was 'the duty of the bench to commit'.

Until this juncture in Stephen's speech (an hour or so after he had begun) the magistrates had listened in silence. Now Leighton was moved to interject: 'I think you should go on with the facts instead of telling us our duty'. When Stephen assured the magistrate that he had meant no disrespect, Leighton responded that he 'only wished [Stephen] to be short'. Slightly taken aback by this comment,

---

[223] Stephen cited *Russell on Crimes* and Lord Coke to establish that any intentional homicide was murder unless justified at law. He referred to *Governor Wall's Case* (1802) and *Warden v. Bailey* (1811) as case authority for the proposition that an official could be culpable for the wrongful execution of a person either by direct order or illegal court martial. *The Times* (28 Mar. 1867), 10.   [224] Ibid.

[225] *Morning Star* (28 Mar. 1867), 6.   [226] Ibid.

Stephen offered that 'in such a case as this I cannot be short'. Stephen's obvious discomfort raised a titter among the ladies sitting in the front row.[227] Although it was crystal clear now that the magistrates were not prepared to listen to his legal arguments, Stephen soldiered on.

This Stephen did until four o'clock in the afternoon, some five hours after he had stood to address the tribunal. The main points made during the body of his speech were twofold. The first was that martial law 'did not authorize the trial and death of any offenders except soldiers and the Queen's open enemies'.[228] Gordon had been neither. In fact, he had been tried and condemned for conduct that occurred some nine months before martial law was proclaimed in Jamaica. 'Such a proceeding,' Stephen maintained, 'was utterly monstrous, not only according to the elementary principles of law, but according to the ordinary principles of common sense.'[229] Stephen's second theme concerned the issue of Eyre's criminal intent. This element of the charge might be satisfied even if Eyre did not bear 'any private grudge against Mr. Gordon'.[230] He was guilty if it could be proved that Eyre's actions had been reckless, rash, or unreasonable. The intentional killing of a man without lawful justification was, by definition, murder.

This was the most controversial, and seemingly contradictory, aspect of Stephen's argument. On one hand, he contended that Eyre was an otherwise honest and brave man who in difficult circumstances had acted in good faith. On the other, Stephen maintained that in the aftermath of the Morant Bay uprising Eyre came to conflate his personal and political enmity for Gordon with the question of public security. 'Everything', Stephen contended, 'pointed to the conclusion that the evidence given at [Gordon's] trial was not the cause of the execution.'[231] But in pinpointing the actual cause, Stephen was ambiguous. The evidence suggested that Eyre had come to regard Gordon as an immoral and mischievous man long before the outbreak at Morant Bay. After the outbreak Eyre hastily jumped to the conclusion that Gordon was a dangerous traitor. He then personally saw to Gordon's arrest and transportation, and to the collection against him of a criminal case. Eyre had sanctioned Gordon's execution with unseemly haste. In all his dealings with the Gordon case, Eyre had acted like a man 'possessed by the notion that Gordon was an utterly bad man'. And when Eyre was asked by the Colonial Office to justify the execution, he passed over the question of military necessity and vilified Gordon's 'personal and political character'. Gordon was described (Stephen was quoting from Eyre's despatch) as a 'liar, a swindler, dishonest, cruel, vindictive and a hypocrite'. Invoking the ultimate Victorian slur, and as against a dead man, Eyre even had called Gordon 'grossly immoral and an adulterer'. But for all this Stephen did not submit that Eyre had helped kill Gordon knowing he was innocent of treason. In Stephen's view, Eyre's legal sin was that he believed in Gordon's guilt, and the necessity of his

---

[227] *Morning Star* (28 Mar. 1867), 6.   [228] Ibid.   [229] *The Times* (28 Mar. 1867), 10.
[230] Ibid.   [231] *Morning Star* (28 Mar. 1867), 10.

death, when a reasonable man in his position would not have done. In this technical sense, Eyre's conduct was grounded in 'malice aforethought', that key mental prerequisite of a murder conviction.

This part of Stephen's address was delivered with an unmistakable and, for Stephen, uncommon vehemence. Before he finished these submissions, Leighton interrupted him for the second time. 'Mr. Stephen, you are addressing magistrates and not a jury; all this is perfectly irrelevant in our minds.' Incredulous, Stephen asked how submissions pointing to Eyre's 'express malice' could be 'irrelevant' to the proceeding at bar. Leighton retorted that Stephen's submissions were a mere 'abuse' of the accused. When Stephen asked the chairman to specify the words he thought abusive, Leighton referred to prosecuting counsel's emphatic 'tone of voice'. Stephen's response was transparently sarcastic: 'it is rather difficult, sir, to adopt the precise tone of voice which magistrates may consider the most appropriate.' Catching himself, Stephen quickly apologized and asked permission to begin to adduce evidence.[232] When this was granted, Stephen called Fiddes and Lake to testify to the arrest, trial, and execution of Gordon. Another witness certified true copies of government papers on the Jamaica affair. With this the Court adjourned until the next day.

On the second day of the hearing Giffard stood up for the first time, in this instance to dispute a technical point over which parts of official government documents might be read to the court.[233] After some debate of this point, and some (uncontested) submissions by Stephen on the court's jurisdiction, the prosecution rested its case. It was time for Giffard to demonstrate why Eyre should not be bound over to the grand jury on a charge of murder, or any other crime.

In 1867 Hardinge Stanley Giffard was a leader of the South Wales assize circuit.[234] Born in 1823, the son of a Tory newspaper publisher and writer, Giffard was called to the bar in 1850. When on his circuit he accepted a wide range of briefs. When in London, his time was divided between the Chancery bar and the Old Bailey. (On one memorable day in the Old Bailey in 1854, he narrowly escaped assassination at the hands of an insane clergyman wielding a pistol.) In 1865 Giffard 'took silk' as Queen's Counsel. But in spite of this mark of success, Giffard was regarded as a capable but not inordinately talented barrister. He lacked the physical bearing (he was short in stature), power of expression, and the pure animal energy of the very best advocates of his day.[235] But like many

---

[232] Before he sat down, Stephen was informed by Horne Payne that perhaps Leighton had confused Stephen's quotes from Eyre's despatches with Stephen's own words about Eyre. Stephen put this to Leighton as a possible explanation for the unpleasant exchange that followed. Leighton responded that it was 'probably the case, as in a long inquiry like this one it was not difficult to get confused sometimes'. With this the matter was dropped. Ibid.

[233] Stephen wanted to read only some preselected excerpts, while Giffard insisted that the surrounding text also be read. Ibid.

[234] This biographical detail assembled from Rubin, *Oxford DNB*, online 33395; *Law Journal* (17 Dec. 1921), 459; A. Fox-Wilson, *The Earl of Halsbury* (London, 1929), 66–73; R. F. V. Heuston, *The Lives of the Lord Chancellors, 1885–1940* (Oxford, 1964).

[235] *Solicitors' Journal* (17 Dec. 1921), 135; Heuston, *Lord Chancellors*, 15.

modestly gifted persons, Giffard was exceedingly ambitious. He was a fervent and arch Conservative[236] who desired desperately to move up the ladder in law and politics. In 1885, after more than thirty years of toil for the Conservative Party, he was named Lord Chancellor as Lord Halsbury. Until his death in 1921, Giffard was one of Britain's most powerful, and politically reactionary, judges.

In 1867, however, Giffard still was very far from the Lord Chancellor's office. He had yet to make a real mark either at the bar or in politics. In fact, it is not self-evident why (instead of one of a half-dozen more eminent advocates) Giffard was offered the Eyre defence brief. The probable answer is that Giffard offered a combination of three favourable assets. First, he was an experienced and able criminal lawyer, one who shared chambers with Harry Poland.[237] Second, Giffard sympathized strongly with Eyre and his plight.[238] It was his personal belief that Eyre's firm and decisive actions under martial law had saved the white population of Jamaica from massacre. He believed that Gordon deserved to hang.[239] Third, Giffard was available, and wanted the brief. His eagerness in this regard was a product both of ideological affinity and political opportunism. In the spring of 1867 he was positioning himself to contest the next parliamentary election as a Conservative candidate in Wales. The publicity resulting from the case was bound to raise his public profile. The Eyre brief, then, was a snug fit both for client and lawyer. In Giffard, Eyre and his Defence Committee got a man with legal skill and useful conviction. In the Eyre prosecution, Giffard got a chance to do right by a worthy client and himself.

For Stephen, on the other hand, the Eyre prosecution was about principle, not passion. His courtroom manner, in the main, was dry, scholarly, and restrained. This was not, however, entirely a matter of choice. As an advocate Stephen was like an actor with a narrow emotional range. He simply did not have the capacity to become a different kind of lawyer as the occasion demanded. Giffard, by contrast, had more guile. Although his courtroom demeanour was often understated, even stilted,[240] in the Eyre case Giffard was able to adopt a different, even alien, deportment. In its every syllable and gesture the six-hour-long speech he delivered

---

[236] In his youth Giffard wrote for his father's conservative newspaper, the *Standard*. In middle age he cultivated the potentates of the Conservative Party, and in 1868 ran (unsuccessfully) for the Tories. (One of the main themes of his campaign was that a vote for the party of Gladstone was tantamount to a vote for the French Revolution!) Even in the 1860s he still regarded the Reform Act of 1832 as a mistake. Giffard's staunch Toryism persisted to his death in 1921. For description of Giffard's politics, see *Cardiff Times* (25 July 1868); see also, 'Lord Halsbury: An Appreciation', *Solicitor's Journal* (17 Dec. 1921), 134–5.

[237] Harry Poland had acted for Abercrombie Nelson. It is possible that the brief was steered his way through this connection.

[238] In a letter written to Eyre in the immediate aftermath of the Market Drayton hearing, Giffard expressed the 'reverence I feel for the man who saved Jamaica from the horrors of Hayti'. Giffard to Eyre, 2 Apr. 1867, *SLSA*, letter no. 30.

[239] As Giffard's daughter remembered to one of Eyre's sons, 'I often heard [my father] declare that he believed Gordon was guilty, and that he believed Governor Eyre's decision to declare martial law was right.' Evelyn Giffard to Eyre's (unnamed) son, Rhodes House, Oxford.

[240] See Heuston, *Lord Chancellors*, 12.

to the magistrates at Market Drayton was calculated to incite the biases of these rural magistrates. While Stephen's speech mainly was a careful explication of legal propositions, Giffard's speech mainly was a studied avoidance of them. While Stephen had tried to depersonalize the prosecution, Giffard did everything in his power to draw attention to Eyre as a valiant if much-abused man.

It would have been conspicuous to Giffard that Stephen's arguments had done little more than annoy the magistrates. With his speech he hoped to increase that annoyance, while he evaded or obfuscated potentially damaging points of law. These thoughts in mind, Giffard began by reminding the court that Stephen had presumed repeatedly to tell the court what was its 'duty'.[241] On the law and facts of the case, Stephen insisted, its duty was to commit Eyre to the grand jury. In so doing his friend had characterized the court alternately as 'a registry-office for receiving charges that anybody might think fit to make, and a college of doctrinaires discussing nice questions of law for the purpose of amusement'. This was nothing if not a 'disrespectful mode of treating any tribunal'. Giffard took a different view of the court's role. He submitted that magistrates were judges like any other, and as such they were bound not to permit 'private malice from assuming the form of public justice'. If this was another way of telling the court what was its 'duty', the magistrates did not protest.

Having got this bit of flummery out of the way, Giffard turned to Stephen's 'very learned and...very useless investigation of old points of law'.[242] After averring that 'he did not agree with his learned friend as to the law', Giffard informed the court that he would 'say no more about it; and for this reason – he stood there as the guardian of Mr. Eyre's honour, and if by any technical phraseology, by any appeal to points of law, he could induce the Bench to dismiss him without reference to the facts, he would decline...to obtain dismissal on any such ground'. That was not to say that the law was wholly irrelevant. In his first and last reference to legal authority, Giffard spoke of the *Governor Wall Case* and how in that case the prosecuting barrister, a very eminent jurist,[243] had allowed that there should be an acquittal for murder if the accused could prove that he had acted in good faith to suppress mutiny or rebellion. In such a case, the prosecutor admitted, an accused 'was not only not guilty of murder, but an innocent and meritorious man'.

These opening remarks framed Giffard's defence. The remainder of his speech endeavoured to show that Eyre, far from facing the ignominy of a murder charge, deserved the nation's profound gratitude. One of the ways that Giffard sought to achieve this was by bringing the subject of race (a subject not even mentioned by Stephen) back into view. In October 1865, Governor Eyre had to deal with a violent rebellion among a vast population of angry blacks. Before Eyre made his first decision regarding the fate of Gordon, the black rebels already had shed white

---

[241] Giffard's speech as reported in the *Shropshire News* (4 Apr. 1867).   [242] Ibid.
[243] The prosecutor in the *Governor Wall Case* was the Attorney General, Sir Edward Law, later Lord Ellenborough, Lord Chief Justice of the King's Bench.

blood. The complete extermination of the small and scattered white population of the island had been in prospect. In such harrowing circumstances it was not sensible to expect that an executive official would 'conduct himself with the same care and circumspection as people living in the county of Middlesex'. The 'execution of Gordon was not a punishment for past offences, but a most efficient, wholesome, and necessary measure of repression. Gordon was guilty of continuing treason.'[244] Here Giffard came close to accepting Stephen's view that Eyre's guilt or innocence for Gordon's death pivoted on necessity. In Giffard's submission, however, Eyre was not guilty of murder because Gordon's execution *had* been necessary. And this was not a matter only of accepting Eyre's word on the point. Before the Governor endorsed the execution order the senior military officers in the colony, independently of the Governor and in the wake of a full court martial, already had determined both that Gordon had conspired to foment rebellion, and that his living presence in the colony was a grave threat to public safety. All that Eyre had done, in fact, was to decide not to interfere with a military decision made during a state of emergency.

At this juncture, Giffard's words and gestures became increasingly demonstrative. He began to elaborate on Gordon's perfidy, alleging that in making the rebellion his chief aim had been to turn Jamaica into another Haiti, to humiliate and murder every white person in the colony. Only his sense of delicacy, Giffard told the court, prevented him from describing the horrors that Gordon and other 'fiends of lust and wrath' had planned for the colony's white men and women.[245] And what was the Governor's reward for having foiled this plot? Instead of being held up as a national hero he was 'criticized' and 'prosecuted to the death'. 'Good God!,' Giffard bellowed, 'Was this justice?' With this Giffard turned his face away from the magistrates and broke down in a fit of 'tears and sobs'. His speech appeared to move the magistrates deeply.[246] Some moments passed while the barrister fought to regain his composure. Many of the magistrates seemed 'equally moved'.[247]

After he had apologized to the court for this 'exhibition of feeling', Giffard returned to his argument that Gordon's execution was justified by the grounded fear that the black majority had been poised to exterminate all white people in the colony. It was as close as Giffard came to offering a legal argument in defence of his client. The remainder of his address consisted mainly of a fierce attack on the Jamaica Committee and its lawyers. In Giffard's view, the prosecution lawyers had presented a case so one-sided and prejudicial that he could only conclude that they were engaged with the Jamaica Committee in a 'deliberate design to do injustice'.[248] Giffard railed against the fact that the 'prosecution was not instructed by the Government, nor by anybody forming part of the family of the

---

[244] See account of Giffard's speech in the *Shrewsbury Free Press* (6 Apr. 1867), 5.   [245] Ibid.
[246] According to the recollection of Giffard's junior, Harry Poland. Quoted in Heuston, *Lord Chancellors*, 16–17.   [247] *Shrewsbury Free Press* (6 Apr. 1867), 5.
[248] Ibid.

late Mr. Gordon'. The former Governor had been viciously slandered without any opportunity to answer the slanderers 'face to face'. Giffard then denounced the compliments that had been paid to Eyre by counsel for the prosecution. The compliments revealed a fatal contradiction in the prosecution's case. The Jamaica Committee wanted to say about Eyre 'that he was a high-minded and honourable gentleman at the same time that they were accusing him of the basest sort of murder'. Giffard strenuously objected to the notion that there could in the law be 'a divorce between the legal crime of murder and the horrid guilt which was involved in its commission'. He denied that there could be such thing as a 'well-meaning, high-minded, well-intentioned or courageous murderer'.[249] When murder was the charge, law and morality could not, should not, be so neatly separated. Giffard thought that the court now faced a stark choice: either Mr. Eyre was a murderer 'actuated by wicked malice, or he was the most persecuted man the century had seen'.

In summing up the case for dismissal, Giffard contended that the prosecution had not made out even a *prima facie* case that Eyre had done anything more criminal than 'his duty as a man'. While he was confident that a higher court would acquit Eyre of any charge, Giffard 'earnestly trusted and prayed' that the ex-Governor and his family would not be put through the ordeal of further criminal proceedings. The prosecution of Eyre for murder was the 'most malignant conspiracy to prostitute the forms of law that the world had ever heard of', and Giffard asked that the magistrates exercise their judicial discretion to end it. When Giffard finished his speech some six hours after he had started, Stephen did not offer a reply.[250] The hearing was over.

When Giffard was finished, Leighton announced that he and his brother magistrates would retire before making an order. He also pointedly remarked that the judges 'would not be very long'. Only minutes later, time enough to write out a paragraph, the panel returned to the bench. 'Twelve hours of legal argument,' as the *Law Review* wryly observed, 'had provoked only ten minutes of decision.'[251] Recall that what the judges were to decide was only whether there was a contestable issue, either of fact or law, to put to a trial judge and jury. It was the unanimous conclusion of the panel, Leighton announced, that the case before the court 'does not raise a strong or probable presumption of the guilt of the accused'. There was little or no prospect that a jury would find Mr. Eyre guilty of being an accessory to murder. To sustained applause and cheering Eyre was discharged. Eyre stood and shook the hand of his defence counsel. He was then escorted from the courtroom by his benefactors as some men cried out 'Rabbit Skins!!'.[252] A carriage whisked him away to Adderley Hall as the bells pealed from the steeple of the parish church.

---

[249] Ibid.
[250] One paper reported that Stephen relented because he perceived 'the uselessness of further argument'. *Daily News* (1 Apr. 1867), 5.   [251] *London Review* (6 Apr. 1867), 390.
[252] *Morning Star* (1 Apr. 1867), 4.

It is a cliché about trials and other courtroom proceedings that they are like theatre. It was a cliché much indulged in by the pundits who tried to make sense of events at Market Drayton. In fact it was widely appreciated that there was something singularly artificial, something of the 'drawing-room performance',[253] about this particular prosecution in this particular place. After all, the men behind the prosecution openly professed to be manipulating the *form* of criminal prosecution for some other purpose. The Jamaica Committee had wanted to vindicate principles not punish a man. This sense of artifice was intensified by the fact that eminent lawyers had litigated a complex case before a group of unpaid lay judges. An extraordinary amount of attention was paid in the press to the performances of the various players.

The reviews of Giffard's work tended to break down along ideological lines. The *Sun*, an obdurately conservative paper, thought that 'nothing could possibly have been better than the reply of Mr. Giffard, and the skilful manner in which he acquitted himself of his arduous task reflects credit on him.'[254] Giffard's speech 'may fairly be put on record as a full and satisfactory answer to all charges preferred against the ex-Governor, whether past, present, or to come'. In the same vein the *Daily Telegraph* complimented Giffard for his 'able and exhaustive speech', one which had quite properly 'denounced the prosecution as a base pervession of law.[255] W. F. Finlason, Eyre's foremost scholarly defender, believed that as trial counsel Giffard had proved 'fully the equal of Fitzjames Stephen in intellectual rigour, in scholarship, and forensic ability'.[256] The very least that could be said about Giffard's approach to the case was that it had perfectly suited the Shropshire magistrates. He had given them some legal rationale for the decision they were predisposed to make.

As might be expected, the more liberal-minded section of the press was far less enthralled with the counsel for the defence. Giffard's speech, one paper declared, had amounted to more than 'six hours of abuse, bluster and talk'.[257] It was uniformly the opinion of these papers that Giffard's speech had been brazenly dishonest, manipulative, and evasive. It was a dishonest speech, the *Morning Star* lamented, in the sense that it distorted the known record of what actually happened in Jamaica. Giffard, for instance, had alluded to atrocities inflicted by blacks 'which were over and over again shown to be gross and ludicrous exaggerations'.[258] He had also alleged that Gordon had actively plotted to turn Jamaica into another Haiti, allegations which the Jamaica Royal Commission had investigated and rejected.[259] According to the *Saturday Review*, Giffard obviously had moulded his speech 'to suit the prejudices of a non-professional understanding'.[260] He did not hesitate to exploit the fact that the magistrates admired Eyre and were

---

253 *Morning Star* (1 Apr. 1867), 4.   254 *Sun* (30 Mar. 1867).
255 *Daily Telegraph* (29 Mar. 1867).   256 Finlason, *History of the Jamaica Case*, 420.
257 *Shrewsbury Free Press* (6 Apr. 1867), 5.   258 *Morning Star* (1 Apr. 1867), 4.
259 *Saturday Review* (6 Apr. 1867), 423–4.   260 Ibid.

little interested in the legal reasons why this admiration might be misplaced. The bench had wanted to hear the accused praised and his accusers denounced, and Giffard provided exactly what was wanted. He even contrived to give them a glimpse of that rarest of courtroom spectacles, 'a Queen's Counsel in tears'.[261]

The liberal press denounced Giffard's speech for cynicism and guile,[262] but its faults, blatant misstatements of fact excepted, are to be forgiven a trial advocate. Giffard had been retained to stymie the prosecution of Eyre, and this he did. Like any effective lawyer he took the measure of his tribunal and crafted an appropriate rhetoric. Giffard, even the *Saturday Review* observed, was well acquainted 'with the fit occasions for employing sentiment or reason'. The most telling charge made against him – and in adversarial proceedings it was not a *very* telling one – was that he was guilty of rhetorical excess.[263] This was a small thing to say about a lawyer who had achieved a clear-cut win on his brief. The advocacy of Giffard, when it was not actively admired, was only decried in England's most liberal and radical journals, journals which Giffard and the Eyre Committee could afford to ignore. Stephen was not so fortunate. Much to Stephen's dismay, his work at Market Drayton generated a surfeit of bad notices and in papers of all political stripes.

It is interesting that few of Stephen's many critics questioned the plausibility of his arguments on the law of martial law. 'No stronger case for committal was ever laid before a tribunal,' the *Weekly Times* contended.[264] Even the *Law Times*, long an acerbic critic of the Jamaica Committee, conceded that Stephen's submissions on this subject were 'very able and very ingenious', even if their purpose was misguided.[265] Nor was there much criticism of Stephen's general demeanour in the courtroom. On the contrary, the *Daily Telegraph* noted that Stephen had put in his case 'in the cool, positive and determined manner of a counsel who is sure of his facts and safe as to his conclusions'.[266] Where Stephen had gone wrong, his critics universally agreed, was in referring to Eyre as a brave man who had acted in good faith. This concession simply baffled both the friends and enemies of the prosecution.

The Times weighed in on the subject: 'we cannot but think that, when so odious an accusation is brought forward, all compliments and expressions of sympathy on the part of prosecuting counsel are entirely out of place.'[267] Where there is conviction in the assertion of guilt for murder, there can be no room for such 'ghastly courtesy'. The *Morning Herald* thought that any number of John Bright's followers 'caught at haphazard passing through the Temple Bar would have given in five

---

[261] *Daily News* (1 Apr. 1867), 5.

[262] 'The speech for the defence was simply a tissue of abuse for the prosecution . . . a sort of sensational melodrama.' *Shrewsbury Free Press* (6 Apr. 1867).

[263] In this regard, it was fair comment for the *London Review* (6 Apr. 1867), 389–90, that 'Mr. Giffard only wasted a splendid burst of theatrical emotion, which professional economy of dramatic effects should have led him to reserve for the benefit of the common jury.' This was a criticism of Giffard's advocacy not his politics.   [264] *Weekly Times* (7 Apr. 1867).

[265] *Law Times* (6 Apr. 1867), 438.   [266] *Daily Telegraph* (26 Mar. 1867).

[267] *The Times* (30 Mar. 1867), 12.

seconds a better definition of murder than Mr Stephen gave in an address lasting hours'.[268] In offering an explanation for such a poor showing the *Herald* wondered whether Stephen was not 'somewhat ashamed of the work he was doing, but if so, he ought to have retired from it, and not to have professed affection for the gallant stag while leading the bloodhounds'. '[I]t is nothing short of an abuse of the law,' the *London Review* opined, 'to charge a man with murder when you do believe that he is morally not guilty of the crime.'[269] It was as if the Jamaica Committee, or at the very least its senior barrister, could not make up its mind whether Edward Eyre was a murderer or was guilty of a mere 'technical fault'. If there was any hope of mounting a credible prosecution in the future there was nothing for the Committee to do but 'repudiate their representative'.

Such criticisms, coming as they did from journals which had never supported the prosecutions, would have been easier to dismiss if the same ones had not been published by more friendly journals. The labourite *Reynolds' Weekly* had endorsed the prosecution of Eyre, but now, in the wake of Market Drayton, expressed exasperation: 'Mr. Stephen is undoubtedly an able advocate...But the advantage resulting from the admirable statement of the case...was more than lost by his sickening and irrelevant compliments to the accused.'[270] The political motives of the Jamaica Committee, when they were combined with Stephen's benign attitude toward Eyre, 'invested the whole affair with an appearance of unreality...of a solemn judicial farce...got-up to gratify the feelings of a number of sentimental philanthropists'.[271] Similarly, the *Morning Star*, the paper to which Chesson and other members routinely contributed, now felt compelled to distance itself from Stephen's conception of the case.[272] To the *Star*, with his 'ill-timed' compliments Stephen had managed to obscure the defining theory of the prosecution: 'we understood the Jamaica Committee to be of the opinion that Mr. Eyre had in his own handwriting convicted himself of long, bitter and passionate hatred of Mr. Gordon; that Eyre became panic-stricken, and allowed a carnival of useless slaughter.' How were these actions 'consistent with personal bravery, and honour, and public spirit?' Stephen's decision to profess admiration for a man accused of political murder was 'not, we think, exactly the sort of course that Erskine, or Mackintosh or Curran, or Brougham would have taken'.

The criticism stung Stephen sharply enough that on 2 April, days before all the notices were published, for the second time he took the extraordinary step[273] of defending his courtroom work in a long open letter to *The Times*.[274] The letter raises an interesting point of digression. Just as there is no evidence that the Jamaica Committee executive were consulted by Stephen about the content of his arguments, there is no evidence that it was consulted about Stephen's

---

[268] *Morning Herald* (1 Apr. 1867).   [269] *London Review* (6 Apr. 1867), 389–90.
[270] *Reynolds' Weekly* (7 Apr. 1867).   [271] *London Review* (6 Apr. 1867), 389–90.
[272] *Morning Star* (3 Apr. 1867), 4.
[273] Stephen's letter was criticized in the *Law Times* (6 Apr. 1867), 439, as an 'indiscretion' which would not be wisely repeated.   [274] *The Times* (2 Apr. 1867), 12.

apologia.[275] Indeed, it is probable that the letter was motivated in part by the fact that he was not feeling support from the Committee proper, while he was feeling its opposite from the Committee's journalist friends.

Stephen's letter was an attempt to clarify and defend the legal arguments he had made at Market Drayton, arguments, he believed, which had been badly misconstrued by the press.[276] He explained how the compliments he had paid to Eyre 'formed part of an argument from which they ought not to be separated'. He had endeavoured to provide a strictly *legal* explanation of Eyre's guilt for murder, one based on the premiss that the trial and execution of Gordon had been illegal. (If they had been legal, Stephen observed, 'no amount of malice' on Eyre's part would have rendered them illegal.) When it was proved that the trial of Gordon was illegal, Eyre's personal motives were relevant to the privilege of necessity. Stephen admitted that at this stage he had given Eyre 'credit for great courage', but only for having been willing to 'take responsibility and avow the motives of his conduct'. He had not meant to imply that the execution of Gordon or the larger suppression were acts of courage. What Stephen had tried to convey in Market Drayton was that Eyre had bravely assumed responsibility for conduct which he genuinely had thought 'morally and politically expedient', but which was actually immoral and inexpedient. In essence, Eyre had fallen prey to panic and self-deception. In deciding to execute Gordon he had honestly believed what a reasonable man would not. Moreover, Eyre tenaciously held on to this 'rash and erroneous' idea even when his legal advisor (Heslop) had told him that it was illegal, and that only a general indemnity would save him from liability. In fact, Eyre's core motive was to be rid of a political enemy. This, Stephen argued, 'constituted express malice in the highest degree'.[277]

Stephen's theory of his case was that a 'brave but violent and excitable man' such as Eyre was just the sort to 'commit a great political crime'. The great Irish nationalist rebels Fitzgerald and Emmett were 'great criminals', Stephen offered, 'but I could not deny the courage or truthfulness of either'. Sometimes, in times of political excitement especially, great virtue could become great vice. Stephen thought it 'indispensably necessary to the protection of liberty and to the maintenance of the supremacy of the law that such criminals should be brought to justice'. 'I have been surprised', Stephen wrote with obvious anguish, 'at the manner in which my observations on Mr. Eyre have been received.' The 'criticism of his friends', he allowed, might easily have been avoided. It would have been easier to have 'treated Mr. Eyre's case in a simple manner', and to have heaped abuse on the ex-Governor. But this was a path that his notion of professional obligation had prevented him from taking. When Stephen accepted the brief for the prosecution in *The Queen v. Eyre*, he became the lawyer for the Crown, not the Jamaica

---

[275] There are no entries on these issues either in Chesson's diary or the minutes of the Jamaica Committee executive.   [276] Letter to *The Times* (2 Apr. 1867), 12.
[277] Ibid.

Committee. It was his 'duty as counsel for the Crown to state precisely what the evidence appeared to me to prove – no more, no less'. He had accepted the brief in good faith and then 'said exactly what I thought, and not what anyone might think, of his conduct and character ... and I cannot understand how any man of honour can conduct a criminal prosecution on any other principles'.

Although after Market Drayton the Jamaica Committee continued to consult with Stephen on the plausibility of renewed prosecution of Eyre (Stephen opposed the idea),[278] he was finished as the association's lead trial barrister. Although there was no publicized falling-out, the rift which had opened up after Bow Street now had become unbridgeable. Until the Jamaica prosecutions, more-over, Stephen had maintained a very cordial relationship with Mill. As Stephen's wife later recalled, however, in the wake of the hearing at Market Drayton 'by degrees Fitzjames became entirely separated from Mr. Mill'.[279] Mill was among those who believed that Stephen had shown too much courtesy and too little fierceness in pressing the criminal case against Eyre.[280] Mill also backed the idea of another prosecution. The friendship between the two men never fully recovered from this disagreement.

It is possible to see why things had gone so far wrong. The Jamaica Committee had not been able to control the venue of prosecution. They had felt the pressure not to wait until Eyre returned to London. They also had been caught off-guard by Stephen's determination to prosecute the case as he saw fit. Mill and his associates had blithely assumed that Stephen would do their bidding or, that at the least he would not do anything to offend their sensibilities about the case. In this calculation, of course, they were wrong. Stephen had made up his mind that the best way to proceed against Eyre was on the basis that he was not only not comprehensively despised by the prosecution, but that he was actually admired in many respects. Stephen saw it as his task to demonstrate how Eyre had transgressed against the *law*, not against morality. The Committee's criticisms did nothing to move him off this view.

While the courtroom work of Stephen came in for tough criticism in the wake of Market Drayton, sharp attacks also were directed at Sir Baldwin Leighton and the other country magistrates. Even the conservative papers, while they embraced the result, were reluctant to credit the men who decreed it. There was a broad consensus among the urban newspapers that the hearings at Market Drayton had been 'a caricature of justice'.[281] It was as if urban writers had not been aware that in 1867 England still tolerated a rural justice system dominated by (what the conservative *Standard* called) 'unpaid, unprofessional, and, necessarily prejudiced magistrates',[282] and what a Shropshire

---

[278] Stephen was 'strongly adverse' to a criminal prosecution of Eyre under the Colonial Governors Act. *JC Minutes*, 24 Apr. 1867.

[279] Memoirs of Mary Stephen, '1867', Stephen Papers, *CUL*, Add. MS. 8381.   [280] Ibid.

[281] *Morning Star* (1 Apr. 1867), 4.   [282] *Standard* (30 Mar. 1867).

newspaper less politely called 'pig-headed, prejudiced and thoroughly incompetent men'.[283] The *Glasgow Morning Journal* thought it ridiculous that in England a 'few country justices, personal friends apparently of the accused, can dispose of a matter of such gravity in this summary off-hand manner'.[284] The same point was made even more forcefully by the *Morning Star*: 'to leave the game-preserving squires to try poachers is anomalous enough, but to leave it in the power of blind and bigoted partisans to say whether or not foul political murder shall be inquired into is going beyond the tolerance of any civilized community.'[285] So wide now was the gulf between the justice meted out by Sir Thomas Henry and Sir Baldwin Leighton that in England, the *Morning Star* suggested, now 'one law was in force in the metropolis, and another in the provinces'. The squires of Shropshire deserved a vote of thanks, the *Weekly Times* sarcastically noted, for 'calling attention to the rottenness of the entire system, and doing more than they would have dreamt of bringing about a sweeping change'.[286] Even the *Standard* conceded that it was intolerable in an advanced country that weighty legal decisions should be made by amateurs, and that it was time that the system was 'speedily supplanted by some system wiser and more just'.[287]

IV. Marshalling Martial Law at Bow Street and Market Drayton

The criminal prosecutions at Bow Street and Market Drayton were logical consequences of the comparatively mild character of the Jamaica uprising. Historical contingency was at work here. Had Morant Bay been another Indian Mutiny, that is, had scores of Jamaican whites been massacred by greater numbers of marauding blacks, the controversy would have centred on the negligence and indecision of colonial soldiers and officials. But when it became clear in late November 1865 that most white Jamaicans were safe, but that their safety had been assured by a sustained campaign of terror under 'martial law', attention was fixed on the nature and legality of the suppression. Critics began noisily to contend that the terror was unnecessary and politically motivated, and that its perpetrators were criminals. These claims became even more insistent in 1866, as the country grappled with Fenian militancy and the social tension generated by the Reform Bill. It suddenly seemed urgent to ask searching questions about the nation's basic jurisprudence of political power. In times of perceived emergency were government officials entitled to replace civilian law with martial law? Did martial law sanction

---

[283] *Shropshire News* (28 Mar. 1867).   [284] *Glasgow Morning Journal* (1 Apr. 1867).
[285] *Morning Star* (1 Apr. 1867), 4.   [286] *Weekly Times* (7 Apr. 1867).
[287] England's unpaid magistracy had been spasmodically controversial many times prior to the hearings at Market Drayton. Reform of the lay magistracy was not imminent, however. The 'great unpaid' had inertia and patronage on their side, and were not to be easily moved. A much easier thing it was to remove from office a colonial Governor than a rural magistrate. *Standard* (30 Mar. 1867).

summary detention, torture, and execution? Did it immunize officials from the oversight of the courts?

After the parliamentary debates of the summer of 1866, the *raison d'être* of the Jamaica Committee was to cause a high court judge to answer these questions, and to answer them decisively in the negative. The Committee kept the Jamaica affair alive as a public issue, and carried the action forward. They and they alone were so much committed to a decisive judicial resolution of the matter that they were prepared to begin and sustain the criminal prosecution for murder of Nelson, Brand, and Eyre. Without the continued stimulus of this small group of men, the Jamaica affair would have petered out before 1867.

One of the most remarkable collective traits of the Jamaica Committee, true of all of its executive leaders after Buxton resigned as chair, was their intense if innocent belief in the corrective potential of judicial review. They were of one mind that the terror campaign implemented by Governor Eyre and his soldiers, Gordon's execution being but one notorious example, was patently illegal under British law. They were alarmed and infuriated that so many eminent Englishmen either would not admit this fact, or boldly asserted the opposite view. The Committee still earnestly yearned for the day when a judge of the English high court bench would wrench the Jamaica affair from the political muck, and vindicate the true law and constitution. Not once did they express any public doubt that they would succeed in getting a Jamaica case before an eminent judge, and that the judge finally would put things right.

There was more than a little unreality in this yearning. In England it was an easier thing to seek than to attain a judicial ruling on a point of constitutional law. The legal system simply did not provide a convenient mechanism by which a private person or association (or even a department of government) could refer a constitutional case to the judiciary. For lack of any better option, the Committee settled on the rather clumsy device of a private criminal prosecution. This course had several serious drawbacks. First, it personalized issues which the Committee wanted resolved as abstract questions of law. It was inevitable that any person selected for 'test prosecution', fearing conviction, would exercise his appreciable due process rights to prevent a trial. Before a prosecution could get before a high court judge, it had first to pass through a number of preliminary inquiries overseen by magistrates. These hurdles were time-consuming and expensive, and success or failure depended on the quicksilver discretion of lay magistrates and grand jurors. Second, even if the prosecution reached the point of trial in the high courts, it was possible that the constitutional issues would be obscured by more concrete concerns about the guilt or innocence of the accused. The path to a judicial pronouncement on martial law, therefore, was never likely to be smooth. In the case of *The Queen v. Nelson and Brand*, it proved to be bumpy but passable. With regard to the Eyre prosecution at Market Drayton, it proved utterly impassable.

The Jamaica Committee must have reckoned on difficulties, even setbacks. But what they plainly did not anticipate was that going to court would entail a loss of control over the content and public persona of their mission. They did not anticipate that the trial barristers would insist on complete independence in determining how to organize and argue their case. It turned out that the kind of barrister that the Committee needed, one of stature and experience, did not think of himself as the mere mouthpiece of his clients. Certainly Fitzjames Stephen did not. At the cost of friendship with Mill, Stephen was determined to undertake the prosecutions of Nelson, Brand, and Eyre according to his best and autonomous judgement about what to argue, and how to argue it. As Stephen had cause to remind the magistrates at Market Drayton, the first allegiance of a prosecuting barrister was to the Crown, not the complainants. When the prosecution began he was an officer of the court, duty bound to serve the interests of law and justice.

Although the upper echelons of the Jamaica Committee were made up of highly sophisticated men, some of them lawyers, they never came fully to grips either with these ideas, or with Stephen's rather technical theory of Eyre's legal culpability. They also did not fully comprehend the difficulties involved in using the criminal justice system to effect more abstract political and constitutional goals. That is why when things went wrong at Market Drayton, Stephen was a convenient scapegoat.

In most respects, however, Stephen's approach to the Jamaica cases was consonant with the Jamaica Committee's public position that the prosecutions were to be about the vindication of principles not the punishment of individuals. At Bow Street and then Market Drayton, Stephen, perhaps England's leading authority on criminal law, set forth cogent (if highly technical) legal reasons why Nelson, Brand, and Eyre had been accessories to murder, and why the proclamation of martial law did not insulate them from culpability.[288] He also furnished a systematic case for the proposition that civilian and military officials always were answerable to the law for their conduct. Martial law, he maintained, was nothing more than a specific instance of the common law of necessity. At Bow Street Stephen managed to convince a learned magistrate that these theories might be correct, and that it was necessary for a grand jury to decide whether two serving military officers should go to trial for having hanged George Gordon. Given the novelty of the charges and the status of the accused, this was not an inconsiderable success.

Stephen's work at Market Drayton confounded both the press and the Jamaica Committee. On what calculation would it be effective to submit (to a panel of lay magistrates) that Edward Eyre was a brave and honourable man who, while acting in a brave and honourable way, committed murder? 'It is certainly a novelty in criminal prosecutions,' the *London Review* observed, 'to hear a thing described in one breath as murder, and in another as an act which "a brave and public-spirited man might under certain circumstances be tempted to commit".'[289] It defied all

---

[288] The *Law Times* (6 Apr. 1867), 438, a dedicated critic of the Jamaica Committee, conceded that Stephen's advocacy at Market Drayton was 'very able and very ingenious'.
[289] *London Review* (6 Apr. 1867), 389.

reason, *The Times* suggested, that Stephen had not alleged simply that 'political hatred animated the Governor, and that the machinery of martial law was used by him to compass death of a man on whose destruction he had resolved'.[290] Stephen should have alleged that Eyre 'committed the gravest political offence that could be perpetrated by a man in authority, that of having used his official power and the forms of legality to strike down a personal enemy'.

These were forceful points, and leave us wondering about Stephen's approach to the Eyre case. After the criticism felt when he complimented Eyre at Bow Street, why did he *repeat* the compliments in Shropshire? The first thing to be said in answer is that it was not simple contrariness. Stephen thought it was his duty as prosecuting barrister (when before the magistrates at Market Drayton, that it was also prudent) to depersonalize the prosecution. Stephen also genuinely believed that Eyre was an accessory to murder whether or not he had acted in bad faith. Eyre had acted deliberately to take a human life without lawful justification. He was guilty of murder. That was all. And there was another reason to adopt this more technical view of Eyre's criminal guilt: the evidence available to Stephen was not strong enough to establish that Eyre killed Gordon for wicked reasons, and not out of an honest but misguided belief that he was a menace to the public peace. Stephen pleaded in the magistrate courts what he thought he could prove before a trial judge and a jury. In so doing he was always unlikely to satisfy the secret craving of the Jamaica Committee to chasten, if not to humiliate, Edward Eyre in open court. He was congenitally incapable of doing for his retainers what Giffard had done for Eyre and his allies. As it was, Stephen's unyielding sense of professional duty, his intellectual honesty, and his entire inability to bring theatrical panache to his task, all combined to deal him a significant personal and professional failure.

When things went so predictably and embarrassingly wrong for the Jamaica Committee at Market Drayton, someone had to be blamed. That someone was Fitzjames Stephen. But the blame was unfair, mainly wrong-headed, and certainly hypocritical. It was unfair because no barrister in England, neither Coleridge nor anyone else, could have persuaded the Shropshire magistrates to commit Eyre to a grand jury. It was wrong-headed because it was based on a misunderstanding of Stephen's role as prosecuting barrister. Stephen thought it was his duty to put in a case consisting of evidence and law and free of personal invective or rancour. The criticism was hypocritical because it gave the lie to the Committee's own propaganda that they were interested in the vindication of law, not in the ruin of a man.

When it pursued Eyre to Market Drayton, the Jamaica Committee, not Stephen, had given in to impatience and pressure. The decision left Stephen with no alternative than to make the best case he could to deaf ears. In the result, the Committee, not Stephen, was responsible for having squandered its scarce financial resources and its even more scarce credibility and prestige. This was irksome

---

[290] *The Times* (30 Mar. 1867), 9.

enough to its leaders. But it added immeasurably to the pain that in a five-hour address before the court and the assembly of newspaper reporters, Stephen had not drawn even once on the Committee's vast reserves of righteous indignation. That was too much to bear, and it explains why Stephen not only was criticized (by Mill and other erstwhile friends), but for the purposes of further advocacy on behalf of the Committee, effectively dismissed.

In the wake of the Bow Street and Market Drayton prosecutions even some moderate pundits professed to be disgusted with the Jamaica Committee and its legal machinations against Nelson, Brand, and Eyre.[291] This is entirely under-standable, especially given the highly technical theory of their guilt that had been advanced by Stephen at the committal hearings. But it says something more interesting about English political culture in 1867 that a substantial number of writers and journals thought that the prosecutions were vitally important and should be continued. Such 'grave issues for the subjects of Her Majesty in all parts of the world,' the *English Independent* concluded in the wake of Market Drayton, ought to be heard 'before a higher and more competent tribunal'.[292] If the deter-mination of the country magistrates was to go unchallenged, 'it decides a matter of very grave import to every subject of Her Majesty in all her dominions'. The *Glasgow Morning Journal* thought the outcome 'ridiculous'.[293] Their decision had left the 'state of the law, the position of Mr. Eyre, and the whole question, constitutional and executive, in greater confusion than ever'. While the editors of the labourite newspapers had misgivings about how Stephen argued the case for the prosecu-tion,[294] they continued to believe that the prosecution was necessary. The kind of men who loudly supported Eyre and his patrons, the *Weekly Times* pronounced, 'would be delighted to hang John Bright as Eyre hanged Gordon'. The civil liberties of the unenfranchised poor now depended on the decisive intervention of the courts.

As for the Jamaica Committee itself, it did not have time to engage in protracted critical self-assessment. While the prosecution of Eyre had been derailed, the prosecution of the military men was very much on course. Inside of two weeks after the debacle at Market Drayton, the grand jury of Middlesex was ready to receive the judicial charge from a Justice of the Queen's Bench in the case of *The Queen v. Nelson and Brand.*

---

[291] According to the *Saturday Review* (6 Apr. 1867), 423, colonial Governors already had been sufficiently deterred from causing the kind of 'unnecessary bloodshed' that had occurred in Jamaica. Further criminal prosecutions 'would be regarded as measures of persecution, and they would cause a reaction in favour of Mr. Eyre'.   [292] *English Independent* (4 Apr. 1867), 428–9.

[293] *Glasgow Morning Journal* (1 Apr. 1867).

[294] The editors at *Reynolds' Weekly* (7 Apr. 1867) thought that Stephen's compliments for the accused had given the prosecution 'an appearance of unreality'. The *Weekly Times* (7 Apr. 1867) was inclined to blame the Shropshire magistrates for the stumble at Market Drayton.

6

'The Alphabet of Our Liberty': Lord Chief Justice Cockburn in the Old Bailey

Few peculiarities of English society are more noteworthy than the prestige which still attaches itself to the higher Judges.

Spectator, 13 Apr. 1867

Many outrageous things have been done in various epochs of our history in the name of martial law, but arbitrary acts... can never be made lawful, even by their frequent recurrence...

Morning Star, 11 Apr. 1867

I hope the English bar does not compose an individual so lost in spirit and self-respect as to submit to such injustice and such insult. At all events, if there be, I am not that man.

W. F. Finlason to Gladstone, Feb. 1868

For the Jamaica Committee, the prosecution of Edward Eyre at Market Drayton was an embarrassing fiasco. Bad enough that the charge against Eyre had been dismissed; far worse that the Committee's hand-picked prosecutor (for a second time) had handsomely praised an alleged political murderer. But there were innings still to play. On 12 April 1867, inside of two weeks after the Shropshire debacle, the grand jury of Middlesex assembled to assess the bills of indictment against Nelson and Brand. For the dogged leaders and supporters of the Committee, there was still some slender reason to hope that the Court of the Queen's Bench would make an authoritative statement on the legal questions raised by the execution of Gordon.

Because of the vagaries of the English system of criminal justice, however, this outcome was far from certain. In the first place, grand jury proceedings provided only limited scope for a judge to make definitive pronouncements on points of law. At Bow Street, examining magistrate Sir Thomas Henry had already certified that the criminal charge (or 'bill') against Nelson and Brand was legally valid. The single purpose of the grand jury was to investigate the factual basis of the indictment, to determine whether the evidence supporting the charge was sufficient *prima facie.*[1] Grand juries had no jurisdiction to revisit previous findings of law. In the second place, in large cities grand juries were charged mainly by the part-time criminal court judges known as 'Recorders'.[2] It was highly unusual for a Justice of the Queen's Bench to intervene. While Recorders were appointed from the ranks of experienced criminal law barristers, they did not possess the exalted office or prestige of England's fifteen fully constituted common law judges. Further to the point, it was far from clear that a grand jury charge, whoever delivered it, would carry more weight. A jury charge simply did not have the juridical *gravitas* of a trial judgement. The charge was fashioned from the personal knowledge of the presiding judge, unaided by the written or oral pleadings of counsel; it was offered as non-binding advice to the jury on the relevant law and the relevant evidence. The real power over a bill of indictment was fully in the hands of the grand jurors. The role of the judge was to offer learned advice to the jurors and then passively to accept their decision.[3]

But for all this the Jamaica Committee still could reasonably hope for two eventualities. The first was that the Lord Chief Justice of the Queen's Bench, the judge who oversaw the grand jury proceedings, might decide that the problems posed by *The Queen v. Nelson and Brand* were so difficult and urgent that they merited the intervention of a judge of his bench. (As we have seen, Sir Colin Blackburn had been made ready to charge the jury if Eyre had been indicted in Middlesex the previous January.) The Committee could also hope that in making the charge the presiding judge would entreat the jury – successfully – to find 'true bills',[4] thereby committing the accused to be tried before a judge and petit jury. It was also possible that in pressing the bills on the jury the presiding judge would commit the prestige of his office to some compelling pronouncements on the law of martial law. Finally, but with less probability, the Committee could also hope that the grand jury would actually accede to the judge's entreaties and find true bills against Nelson and Brand.

For as long as the Jamaica Committee had threatened to commence criminal prosecutions, however, political pundits had confidently predicted that an English grand jury never would endorse charges against the men who had suppressed the Jamaica uprising, especially charges for murder. There were good reasons for this supposition. At Quarter Sessions of the Peace, grand juries were summoned from the ranks of the county's wealthier freeholding ratepayers.[5] It was thought unlikely

---

[1] J. F. Archbold, *Archbold's Pleading and Evidence* (London, 1862), 66–7; Harris, *Principles of the Criminal Law*, 343; G. Glover Alexander, *The Administration of Justice in Criminal Matters (in England and Wales)* (Cambridge, 1911), 91; Manchester, *Modern Legal History*, 88; Bentley, *English Criminal Justice*, 122.   [2] Harris, *Principles of the Criminal Law*, 343.

[3] In the wake of the judge's charge, the grand jury was entitled to examine prosecution witnesses in a closed session. The witnesses questioned, the grand jury then voted either to indict or not to indict the accused. At least twelve votes were needed to support a finding of 'true bill'. Only the grand jury, after it heard the charge of a judge, and after it examined the prosecution's key witnesses, could actually indict Nelson and Brand.   [4] Alexander, *The Administration of Justice*, 93.

[5] Archbold, *Archbold's Pleading*, 67; Manchester, *Modern Legal History*, 93.

that a majority of any jury pool drawn from this class would permit the Jamaica Committee to use the criminal law to menace the men who had saved Jamaica. In every sense of the word, after all, the prosecution of Nelson and Brand was a *radical* initiative. It was being instigated by men who stood at the radical margin of English politics and causes. The prosecution was being instigated against men of high office and stature, against men who had endeavoured, if imperfectly, to save the lives of white men and women in a dangerous corner of the empire. And this only a handful of years after the traumatic horrors of the Indian Mutiny. When these factors were reckoned, it seemed much more likely that the grand jurors of Middlesex, as of any other English county, would present Nelson and Brand with public honours than bills of indictment.

It is obvious about the leaders of the Jamaica Committee that they were not much moved by received wisdom. Even after the embarrassing setback in Shropshire there was no talk of postponing or withdrawing the proceedings against Nelson and Brand. To an extraordinary degree, moreover, the stubborn persistence of the Committee was about to yield some tangible results. On 10 April 1867, two days before the grand jury convened to hear the Nelson and Brand cases, Sir Alexander Cockburn, the chief judge of the Queen's Bench (the 'supreme court of common law in England', as Blackstone called it)[6], announced that he would go down to the Old Bailey to offer the charge. The result was a monumental pronouncement on the law of martial law in Britain and the empire.

Cockburn's intervention raises a host of unanswered questions. Why was he moved to charge the grand jury in the Nelson and Brand case? How did he characterize the legal issues raised by the prosecution? What was his interpretation of the law of martial law? What were the key suppositions and authorities of his analysis? How did he reconcile the broad constitutional questions posed by the prosecutions with the practical problem of charging the grand jury on a capital case? To what degree, if any, was Cockburn's charge detectably influenced by the political and legal writing on Jamaica to that point? How was the charge comprehended and received by the Committee and the English political class? What does the charge reveal about Cockburn's understanding of law, liberty, and empire? In what sense, if any, was Cockburn's charge a political statement? What bearing did his charge have on the course of the Jamaica affair?

I. Thus Spake Cockburn LCJ

On 10 April 1867, the office of the Lord Chief Justice of the Queen's Bench issued a statement to the press. The Recorder of the County of Middlesex would not be available at the Quarter Sessions to charge the grand jury in *The Queen v. Nelson and Brand*. The Lord Chief Justice himself would take his place at the Old

---

6 As quoted in Manchester, *Modern Legal History*, 128.

Bailey.[7] It was obvious that behind the scenes Cockburn had taken the unusual step of enforcing his prerogative, and the propriety of his having done so was not disputed in the press. The commentators who expressed an opinion on the subject thought it was entirely fitting that a judge of such pre-eminence should address the grand jury in such a significant constitutional case.[8] On this narrow ground at least, the goals of the Jamaica Committee and mainstream political opinion finally coincided.[9]

Which brings us to the subject of the redoubtable Sir Alexander Cockburn. If Cockburn's contemporaries agreed on one thing about him, it was that he lived for the grand occasion. As a barrister, as a politician, as a judge, Cockburn had always sought out and relished moments of concentrated public attention. It surprised nobody in the know that the flamboyant Lord Chief Justice had seized the chance to instal himself at the centre of the Jamaica controversy.

Born in 1802, the son of an ancient family of Scottish noblemen and soldiers, Cockburn was regarded as one of the 'best bred' men at the Bar.[10] He was small in stature but large in personality, vanity, and aspiration. He was a man, a biographer once remarked, 'ambitious of fame'.[11] After his call to the Bar in 1829, Cockburn exploited his keen intellect, melodious speaking voice, and extensive social connections to establish a prominent place both on his circuit (Western) and in politics (Liberal). In the later 1830s Cockburn developed a thriving practice in election and railway petitions. In the 1840s he was lead counsel on a number of noteworthy trials.[12] In 1847 he was elected to Parliament as a reform Liberal. By 1850 he had become an important lieutenant of Palmerston, and in 1851 he was in the cabinet as Attorney General. Offers of judicial appointment soon came his way. But Cockburn demurred. He did not want to give up an immensely lucrative law practice, or his political ambitions, for some nondescript seat on the bench.[13] By 1859, however, having climbed as high as he could go at the bar and in the hierarchy of the Liberal party, Cockburn accepted an appointment as Lord Chief Justice of the Queen's Bench.

When he entered the judiciary Cockburn was a good trial lawyer and political climber. By his own admission, however, he was not a master of common law principles or reasoning. In his work as a judge, Cockburn was famously articulate and fair-minded in putting facts to a jury,[14] but he often struggled to make sense

---

[7] In his opening remarks Cockburn explained that 'the Recorder is not in a position to afford you [the grand jury] the assistance which a grand jury is entitled to expect from judicial authority in a case of difficulty and importance'. He further stated that he 'thought it his duty to attend here today'. Cockburn (ed.), *Charge of the Lord Chief Justice*, 3.   [8] *Daily Telegraph* (11 Apr. 1867), 4.
[9] As the *London Review* (13 Apr. 1867), 420, put the point, 'the charge of the Lord Chief Justice of England to the grand jury . . . goes far to reconcile us to proceedings which not only were a mistake, but which, had they been successful, must have been nugatory.'
[10] 'On Chief Justice Cockburn', *London Society* (11 Jan. 1867), 94. For general biographical detail, see Lobban, *Oxford DNB*, online 5765; *Solicitors' Journal* (27 Nov. 1880); *Law Times* (27 Nov. 1880), 68; *The Times* (22 Nov. 1880).   [11] *DNB*, iii, 636.
[12] Including *McNaughten's Case*, which established that insanity might be a complete defence to a criminal charge.   [13] 'Chief Justice Cockburn', in Manson, *Builders of our Law*, 160–1.
[14] 1 *American Law Review* (1867–8), 757–8.

of complex legal issues.[15] It was said that what the Lord Chief Justice knew of the common law he learned at the side of his brother judge, Blackburn, his conspicuous superior both in legal erudition and acumen.[16] (The exquisite irony of this observation will become only too plain in Chapter 7.) The fact that he was surrounded by better lawyers did not make Cockburn humble. He often exercised the prerogative of the Lord Chief Justice to preside over the most interesting and sensational cases.[17] In the winter of 1867 Cockburn was stricken by a severe respiratory infection. Rumours circulated that his retirement, even death, was imminent.[18] But his illness seems only to have intensified Cockburn's craving of the limelight. The case of *The Queen v. Nelson and Brand* would have appealed to Cockburn's sense of drama at any time in his life. The prospect of it being a last chance to leave his mark on the law – on vital points of constitutional law, no less – made the case irresistible to him.

It was not a routine matter for the Lord Chief Justice of England to come down to the Old Bailey to charge a grand jury. In recognition of the majesty of the occasion, Cockburn was duly greeted at the court by the Lord Mayor, the sheriff, under-sheriff, and aldermen of London. The officials arrived in their finest regalia, Cockburn in his 'magnificent State robes'.[19] Baron Channell, of the Court of Exchequer, accompanied the Lord Chief Justice as did, more discreetly, Cockburn's personal 'medical adviser'.[20] When the proceedings began, the two judges had taken seats at opposite ends of the bench, the London magistrates (and the Liberal politician Lord Granville)[21] sitting between them. 'The incommodious courtroom of the Old Bailey,' the *Morning Star* reported, 'was, shortly before ten o'clock, well filled, not by persons who usually crowd a criminal court, but auditors who obviously felt the full gravity of the case about to be opened.'[22] The decision of the Lord Chief Justice to charge the grand jury, *The Times* observed, imparted to the occasion 'all the manifestations of a State trial'.

Although they had no active role to play in grand jury proceedings, Nelson and Brand were present in the courtroom, as were Shaen and Taylor for the Jamaica Committee. When all were seated, the Court Clerk called the names of twenty-three

---

[15] As the *Solicitors' Journal* (27 Nov. 1880), 69, delicately put it, Lord Chief Justice Cockburn 'never fell into the snare of subtlety'. [16] Lobban, *Oxford DNB*, online 5765.

[17] ' "Lord Chief Justice Cockburn," Lord Bramwell recalled, "liked a page of *The Times* daily devoted to him and his performances, and he picked out of the general list cases which would afford him that gratification. This will account for the number of *cause célèbres* which came before him." ' Quoted in Manson, *Builders of our Law*, 162.

[18] The illness was reported as a severe bronchitis in the *Solicitors' Journal* (9 Feb. 1867), 324. The rumours of Cockburn's imminent retirement were contradicted in the *Law Times* (23 Feb. 1867), 319. [19] *The Times* (11 Apr. 1867), 5.

[20] Shaen spoke with Cockburn's 'medical adviser' during the charge, and was informed that the Lord Chief Justice was 'very unwell'. As reported by Chesson, *CD*, 12 Apr. 1867.

[21] Granville was Liberal leader in the House of Lords, schooled in diplomatic and colonial affairs and, at the time of the grand jury charge in *The Queen v. Nelson and Brand*, was angling for a cabinet post in the next Liberal government. In the result, when Gladstone became Prime Minister in December 1868, Granville was named the Secretary of State for the Colonies.

[22] *Morning Star* (11 Apr. 1867), 5.

prospective grand jurors. Twenty-two men were sworn in. Another man, identifying himself as a civil servant at the War Office, requested through the foreman of the jury that he be excused from serving on the jury on grounds that 'he had formed a strong opinion on the case'.[23] Cockburn directed the man to stand aside (and he left without revealing the gist of his opinion). He informed the remaining twenty-two jurors that it would take a minimum of twelve affirmative votes in order to find a true bill in the case. It was now just past ten in the morning. Without further delay Cockburn commenced to charge the grand jury. His address continued uninterrupted until just before four o'clock in the afternoon.

Cockburn did not read the charge from a prepared script. With only occasional glances at his notes he kept his gaze firmly fixed on the jurors. An admiring reporter from the *Morning Star* wrote that the Lord Chief Justice addressed the jury with 'singular clearness and closeness of sequence', and how his long address was 'listened to throughout with unflagging attention'.[24] Although some commentators later took issue with the content of Cockburn's charge, no one doubted that he had arrived in the Old Bailey fully prepared (if rather unwell physically), and that he spoke with frequent eloquence and impressive learning. Clearly Cockburn seized on the occasion to make (what he hoped would be) an epical statement – an epical *liberal* statement – on the jurisprudence of political and military power. His aim was to make some definitive utterances about the British constitution and the rule of law, and in so doing to rebut the threat posed to them by the proponents of (what he called) the 'wild doctrines' of martial law.

As we will see, the immediate reaction of the political press, particularly the liberal press, to his charge was even more rapturous than even Cockburn might have hoped for. But the resonance of Cockburn's best phrases briefly obscured the fact that his charge in *The Queen v. Nelson and Brand*, when evaluated as a legal argument about the constitution, but especially when evaluated as *oral directions to a jury of laymen*, was deeply flawed. The charge was often unfocused, confusing, and, with respect to some of the most crucial points relating to the culpability of the accused, oddly ambivalent, even self-contradictory. Even more damningly, Cockburn ultimately asked the jury – the triers of fact alone – also to decide the fundamentally important legal issue of the indictments.

Cockburn's address in *Nelson and Brand* was not a boilerplate charge to a jury. He did not intend for it to be once spoken and forgotten. Extensive written notes had been prepared for every section of his address. (Later, these notes were given over to Cockburn's brother to be assembled and edited for a special published edition.) Cockburn drafted the charge to provide the jury with careful direction on the specific points of law and evidence generated by the Nelson and Brand case. But he had far greater ambitions. Cockburn wanted to use the Nelson and Brand case, and the Jamaica suppression as a whole, to canvass all of the legal issues relating to the law of martial law. Cockburn's master plan, in short, was to make an

---

[23] *Daily Telegraph* (12 Apr. 1867), 4–5.   [24] *Morning Star* (11 Apr. 1867), 5.

authoritative contribution to British constitutional jurisprudence. In this task Cockburn invested every particle of his personal and official prestige. His words merit careful exegesis.

It is not an easy matter to recover the structure of Cockburn's long and meandering speech, even for the *reader* of the later, edited, transcription.[25] Conceding that Victorians were far more patient and adept listeners than their counterparts in the twenty-first century, the Lord Chief Justice's charge could not have been easy to follow or comprehend even by the most alert grand juror. The address began with some perfunctory statements about the great 'difficulty and importance' of the Nelson and Brand case,[26] statements offered as justification for the Lord Chief Justice's personal intervention. Sensibly enough, Cockburn then proceeded to boil down the prosecution's case into two general propositions. Although he did not directly refer to submissions of Fitzjames Stephen at Bow Street, the first proposition was of a remarkably similar cast: the prosecution asserted that Gordon's execution was murder because there was 'no jurisdiction in those who tried and sentenced this man to death'.[27] Cockburn's second proposition concerned the motives of the accused. Here Cockburn was perceptibly more blunt than Stephen had been. The prosecution's position was that 'if there was jurisdiction, that jurisdiction was not honestly, but corruptly, exercised, for the purposes of getting rid of an obnoxious individual'. With this Cockburn provided a brief summary of what had happened in Jamaica during October and November 1865.

So far so good. These preliminaries were dispensed with in less than a quarter of an hour.[28] What followed was much heavier sledding, even when considered as a series of differentiated instructions. In the first hour of the charge Cockburn addressed the rather technical question of whether Jamaica's Council of War had the authority to proclaim martial law, and whether the courts martial set up under the proclamation had jurisdiction over British civilians. When that section of the address was completed, Cockburn spent the next ninety minutes on martial law in history. This section preceded a nearly two-hour-long monologue on the relevant legal authorities. In the final ninety minutes of his address, Cockburn charged the jury on the crucial issues of fact as they emerged from the law and evidence. When he was done, he had guided the jury on a five-hour traverse across more than six hundred years of constitutional history, personages, and legal propositions, only rarely stopping to relate this information to the bills against Nelson and Brand. Still, though the charge was convoluted and arcane, it had a perceptible theme.

---

[25] The charge was published in its entirety in a number of the prominent daily newspapers. Quotes are from the official published version of the charge, based on the verbatim notes of a shorthand writer retained by the Jamaica Committee, and as edited by the younger brother of the Chief Justice, Frederick Cockburn. See Cockburn (ed.), *Charge of the Lord Chief Justice.*

[26] Ibid., 3.   [27] Ibid., 4.

[28] The calculations (concerning the time that Cockburn spent on various parts of his speech) are based on the assumption that the speech took just more than five hours and that the transcript of the speech is 160 pages long. On the assumption that Cockburn spoke at an even pace, he covered just more than thirty transcribed pages per hour.

Cockburn was leading the grand jury to the conclusion that George Gordon had been the victim of murder, and that Nelson and Brand were legal accessories to his murder. This had been the unmistakable drift of the charge, that is, until Cockburn – forgiving the pun – suddenly appeared to lose the courage of conviction.

In the first hour of the charge the Lord Chief Justice reviewed the factual background to the court martial and execution of Gordon. Using the findings of the Jamaica Royal Commission as his guide, Cockburn took pains to reconstruct the political and military context of the Nelson and Brand case. He emphasized that Gordon was arrested, tried, and hanged at an historical moment when the colony's dispersed white population faced possible extermination at the hands of a vast black majority. 'This state of things,' the Lord Chief Justice stated, 'as one would naturally have expected, excited in the minds of the white population the greatest consternation and alarm.'[29] By the same token, he also noted many members of the Council of War, and the former Governor Eyre himself, had not thought the threat was so great as to justify the proclamation of martial law over the whole island. And so it was that the civilian courts continued to operate in most of Jamaica, including Kingston. Cockburn reminded the jurors that organized resistance against the authorities was very short-lived. Although the authorities could muster only small numbers of soldiers and militia, 'the moment the soldiers appeared in the field, the whole insurrection collapsed'.

This observation brought Cockburn for the first time to the subject of George Gordon. He described how in October 1865 Gordon 'was generally believed by the authorities and by the white population of Jamaica to have been the instigator of this rebellion, and to be an accomplice with those who were actually engaged in it'.[30] But the mere fact that the authorities believed this of Gordon, Cockburn cautioned, did not make it so. 'The question today,' the judge reminded the jury, 'is whether the right course was taken to bring him to trial if he had been guilty of a crime, or whether his trial and execution were unauthorized, and a violation of law.'[31] Cockburn related how Gordon had been arrested in a place within the jurisdiction of the civilian courts (at Kingston) only to be transported to a military camp (at Morant Bay). These undisputed facts raised the question of 'whether the Governor had authority to proclaim martial law; and, if it should turn out that he had no such authority, then a further question arises'.[32] That question was whether 'the putting him to death under such circumstances amounts or does not amount to wilful murder'. Cockburn told the jury that he would broach these two questions 'in their order'.[33]

Cockburn's reference to this jurisdictional issue justifies a brief digression into the question of the customary division of labour between judge and jury. We have already mentioned that it was an ancient and fixed precept of grand jury proceedings that judges were to advise on the law while juries established the relevant facts. There can be no doubting that cases arise in which it is hard to distinguish

---

[29] Ibid., 5.   [30] Ibid., 4–9.   [31] Ibid.   [32] Ibid.   [33] Ibid.

issues of law from issues of fact. But *The Queen v. Nelson and Brand* was not such a case. The question 'Did Nelson and Brand possess the legal authority to court martial and execute a civilian?' was, by definition, a question of law for the judge alone to decide. Whether Nelson and Brand, two regular military officers, had the legal authority to court martial Gordon, a civilian not taken in arms, did not depend on contentious issues of fact, but on the interpretation of statutes, reported cases, and other formal legal source materials. This job straightforwardly was one for Cockburn to have undertaken by himself. It is not the least perplexing aspect of his charge, therefore, that the Lord Chief Justice ultimately put the jurisdictional issue to the *jury*.[34]

Having completed his introductory remarks, Cockburn broached the subject of the legal character and implications of a proclamation of martial law, 'a question of obviously infinite importance, not only in this case, but in any other similar case which might arise hereafter'.[35] Cockburn's point of departure was the law governing the use of governmental authority. When a governor proclaimed martial law he purported to exert state power over persons and property. To be legitimate, however, the exertion of power had to be traceable to a source in law. In the case of a colonial Governor, his power was derived 'either from the commission which he has received from the Crown, or from some statute, either of imperial or local legislation'. On this reasoning, the legal authority of a governor to proclaim martial law hinged on whether he had all the powers possessed by the Crown, *and if the Crown had the power to proclaim martial law*, or, alternatively, on some discrete statutory power conferred on him by a colonial legislature acting within its jurisdiction.

These propositions are forbidding enough to absorb at one's leisure; they must have posed a daunting challenge to the grand jury. And the jury had far more information still to hear and digest. The legal powers of a colonial governor, Cockburn explained, turned on the distinction in British imperial law between 'conquered' (or 'Crown') and 'settled' colonies.[36] As Cockburn further explained to the jury, in a conquered territory the local populace retain their laws 'subject to the absolute power of the Sovereign of these realms to alter those laws in any way that to the Sovereign in Council may seem proper'.[37] In settled colonies, conversely, 'the inhabitants have all the rights of Englishmen'. While they bear the duty of obedience to the lawful commands of the Sovereign and Parliament, they are also 'entitled to all the rights and liberties as against the prerogative of the Crown which they would enjoy in this country'.[38] Clearly, then, the inhabitants

---

[34] As will be seen, the appropriate question for the jury was not whether Nelson and Brand had the legal authority to court martial and execute Gordon (for the time being this had to be assumed), but whether they acted with a corrupt motive. For some unknown reason, Cockburn had managed to make a muddle of this vital distinction.   [35] Ibid.

[36] The distinction is explained in Kenneth Roberts-Wray, *Commonwealth and Colonial Law* (London, 1966), 540–2.   [37] Cockburn (ed.), *Charge of the Lord Chief Justice*, 10–11.

[38] As Cockburn further explained, the principle that English law governed the colony had in fact been reinforced by acts of Jamaica's infant legislature, and later by the decision of Lord Mansfield in *Campbell v. Hall*. Ibid., 18–19.

of settled colonies were in a stronger legal position *vis-à-vis* the incursions of the colonial state. But was Jamaica a settled or conquered colony? On this point, Jamaican history pointed in both directions. Soon after the colony was conquered by Britain in 1655, the small Spanish population there 'quitted the island'.[39] Cockburn thought that there was decisive fact in this regard. When the Spanish left 'Jamaica was quickly peopled – peopled by Englishmen who settled on lands unoccupied and destitute of other inhabitants'.[40] For this reason the Lord Chief Justice could 'entertain no doubt that Jamaica is entitled to the character of a settled colony'. Therefore, British Jamaica was and had always been a colony of 'freeborn Englishmen'. The upshot of this was made plain: the governor of Jamaica 'can have no further power to declare martial law, as derived from his commission, than that which the Sovereign would have'.[41]

This analysis of imperial law framed what the Lord Chief Justice called 'this great constitutional question'. Has the Sovereign or her agents under commission, 'by virtue of the prerogative of the Crown, in the event of a rebellion, the power of exercising martial law within the realm of England?' Cockburn underlined that the answer to this question could not hinge on the esoterica of a particular body of colonial law. As Cockburn framed the case, the legal implications of the suppression in Jamaica hinged on a reading and application of *English* law. At this juncture Cockburn returned to one of the main themes of his address: that it was of pressing national importance to settle the law governing martial law. Although he assured the jury that the prospect of invoking martial law was unlikely to arise in England, the same could not be said for Ireland. There, 'generations of misrule and of political and religious tyranny and oppression' had enabled 'designing and wicked men to take advantage to produce disturbance and insurrection among the inhabitants'.[42] Cockburn reminded the jury that martial law had been instituted in Ireland only seventy years before. The recent and ongoing activities of the Fenian Brotherhood had made it alarmingly possible that it would be invoked once again. The question was by whom and by what authority.

In giving his answer to these questions the Lord Chief Justice accepted that Parliament, the nation's supreme law-making institution, could pass legislation instituting martial law (or indemnifying its use) either in the home countries or any part of the dominions. Cockburn noted that the Irish Parliament had legislated martial law as recently as 1798.[43] Its prerogatives in this regard simply

---

[39] Ibid., 13.   [40] Ibid., 15.   [41] Ibid., 20.   [42] Ibid., 18–19.

[43] In 1798 the Lord Lieutenant of Ireland proclaimed martial law in order to suppress rebellion. In that instance, the Irish Government did not doubt its authority to exert military authority over civilians. This prerogative later was confirmed by the Irish Parliament. On the other hand, Cockburn noted, the Government did not assume that a proclamation of martial law provided a general legal immunity for those who implemented it. When subsequently the Irish Parliament passed a series of Indemnity Acts, it tacitly recognized that only the assertion of parliamentary sovereignty could prevent soldiers from being convicted for their illegal acts. Further to the point, in 1798 the Irish Court of King's Bench exerted its jurisdiction over the rebel prisoner Wolfe Tone after he had been condemned to die by a military tribunal. All of this, the Lord Chief Justice told the grand jury, '[i]mplies a doubt about the legality of the exercise of the power.' Ibid.

were not at issue. An altogether different and more difficult question was whether the executive branch of a British government had the same prerogative, that is, whether 'the Crown has the power, and whether the representatives of the Crown in our colonies abroad have the power, to call [martial law] into action'. And, if the Crown had such a power, 'then arises the all-important question, what this martial law is'.[44] Before he began to set forth his thinking on these points, Cockburn took the unusual step of condemning the treatise of a living legal writer. 'For, of late,' the Chief Justice explained, 'doctrines have been put forward to my mind of the wildest and most startling character – doctrines which, if true, would establish the position that British subjects, not ordinarily subject to military or martial law, may be brought before tribunals armed with the most arbitrary and despotic power'.[45]

Without mentioning the offending writer by name (but in the published version of Cockburn's charge he was identified as W. F. Finlason)[46] the Lord Chief Justice quoted some passages from Finlason's 1866 work, *A Treatise on Martial Law*. As we have seen, this book contended that the Crown retained a prerogative to proclaim martial law during a civil emergency. Once proclaimed, martial law suspended the operation of common law and common law courts while it licensed the military to exert absolute power until the public peace was restored. In securing this goal, Finlason contended, a military commander might arrest, prosecute, and even execute civilians with impunity. These 'startling' propositions, the Lord Chief Justice informed the jury, had been 'propounded with some pretense of authority', and it was 'high time they should be brought to the test of judicial determination'.[47] Cockburn told the jury that in his view these doctrines miserably failed such a test. He did not mince words. In a single passage Finlason's views were ridiculed as 'unfounded and untenable', 'mischievous', and 'detestable'. His theses about martial law were not only wrong but 'repugnant to the genius of our people, to the spirit of our laws and institutions'.[48] To further underscore his point, Cockburn recited one of the shibboleths of Whig jurisprudence: when charged with a criminal offence, every subject of the realm, whether he is in the home country or a colony, 'though he may be a rebel, though he may be the worst traitor that ever was brought to the block, he is still a subject and entitled to those safeguards which are the essence of justice'. For Cockburn this was a sacred tenet of the British constitution, one 'more especially required in times of excitement and passion, when the minds of men are more apt to be led astray'.[49]

That the Lord Chief Justice of England would so admonish an obscure legal writer, and with such vehemence, was an extraordinary thing, one which points to Cockburn's intense emotional investment in the subject matter of the charge. But this outburst did not in fact presage either the tone or content of the remainder of Cockburn's address to the jury. When he was finished with Finlason, the Lord

---

[44] Cockburn (ed.), *Charge of the Lord Chief Justice*, 21.   [45] Ibid., 22.   [46] Ibid.
[47] Ibid.   [48] Ibid., 22–3.   [49] Ibid., 24.

Chief Justice devoted the next section of his address 'endeavouring to trace the history of martial law back to its fountain-head'.[50] When preparing his charge, Cockburn had wondered 'what light history can throw on the subject of martial law'. It occurred to him that it was vital to know 'when, and where, and how' martial law had been exercised in the past, and whether it conferred legal immunity on the military men who had implemented it with fatal vigour. Like Stephen and Finlason before him, Cockburn was convinced that this was not merely an academic line of inquiry, but essential to an authoritative account of martial law. Cockburn expressed some polite concern that this section of his charge might be 'wearying' to the grand jury, but then plunged ahead for ninety minutes on the results of his historical research.

Cockburn narrowed the scope of his discussion by dispensing quickly with the easiest case. It was self-evident in the legal history of England that the military was entitled to use all necessary force to repel an armed invasion or insurrection. (On this point Cockburn even went so far as to say that rebels captured in arms might be 'put to death afterwards without any trial at all'.)[51] The more urgent question about martial law was the legal position of soldiers *vis-à-vis* civilians arrested or detained outside the field of battle. Cockburn's approach to it, conventionally enough, was historical. Drawing on a series of vignettes from the thirteenth to the eighteenth centuries, the Lord Chief Justice reviewed instances in which persons had been executed without trial. As a dedicated Whig, Cockburn did not have any trouble concluding that these actions were the product of a primitive and lawless era. The actions of Henry VII in suppressing rivals under martial law, for instance, were 'clearly illegal'.[52] When Edward VI used military courts to punish rebels it was by a 'power which the Crown was illegally taking to itself in thus altering the law of the land'.[53] As for the suppression of Catholics by Elizabeth I, that was 'altogether beyond the powers which the constitution of England had intrusted her', an exercise only of mere 'assumed power'.[54]

Then Cockburn turned to the infamous 'usurpations' of the Stuarts, a list of illegal actions that even the Lord Chief Justice thought too numerous fully to recount. These transgressions were not thought intrinsically important, but they stimulated one of the landmarks in English constitutional law, the passage by Parliament in 1628 of the Petition of Right. For Cockburn the Petition of Right was properly understood as 'the supplemental great charter of English liberty'. In the passage of this act, Parliament eliminated the pretension that martial law could be declared or implemented during peacetime. It was not, the Chief Justice stated, a 'statute by which any new limitation was put on the prerogative of the Crown, or by which the subject acquired any new rights or immunities against the prerogative. It is a statute declaring where, according to the law and constitution of this country, the prerogative of the Crown ends, and the rights and liberties of the subject begin'.[55] And, contrary to the opinion of some legal writers, the

---

[50] Ibid., 24–5.   [51] Ibid., 25.   [52] Ibid.   [53] Ibid., 34.   [54] Ibid., 35–41.
[55] Ibid., 65.

Petition had complete 'efficacy' not only in England, but wherever the common law of England applied. If the Petition outlawed the use of martial law against English civilians, it 'beyond question equally does so with reference to the martial law in the island of Jamaica'.[56]

These conclusions had been presaged by Cockburn's foray into the English legal literature on martial law. This sub-section of the charge began with another sweeping generalization: with regard to 'the works of legal writers or judicial decisions, not only is there no authority in support of the power to declare martial law, but what authority there is we shall find directly the other way'.[57] The Lord Chief Justice took pains to show that at some point in their careers, almost all of the country's greatest jurists – Hale, Coke,[58] Mansfield – had decried the idea that officials of the Crown possessed a wide discretion to proclaim martial law and then to enforce it against non-combatants. 'It is hardly conceivable', Cockburn summarized, 'that such authors as these, when writing on the laws of England, and carefully enumerating every species of law obtaining within the kingdom ... have been wholly silent as to the power of applying it to the trial and punishment of civilians.'[59] In driving home this point, Cockburn quoted extensively from the judgement of Lord Chief Justice Loughborough in the 1792 King's Bench decision in *Grant v. Gould*.[60] That case involved the punishment by the regular army of a civilian recruiting agent for the East India Company.[61] In his judgement, Loughborough had distinguished between the law martial (the law applying to soldiers in uniform) and martial law (the replacement of civilian law with military prerogative). He decided that the law martial (or 'military law') might still have application in a place under siege. On the other hand, 'martial law, such as it is described by Hale and such also as it is marked by Mr. Justice Blackstone does not exist in England at all.'[62] For Cockburn, this was a definitive statement of an 'eminent judge [that] there was no such thing within the realm of England as that which is now called "martial law" '.[63]

From the case law on martial law, the Lord Chief Justice moved on to the subject of the standing army. Cockburn considered whether there was any Crown (or executive) prerogative with regard to the disposition and conduct of regular military forces. He quickly concluded that there was not. It was a touchstone of British law, Cockburn told the jury, that the standing army was entirely a creature of Parliament, one renewed and regulated annually by the Mutiny Acts.[64] While in time of war the Crown could exert the right to legislate for 'the government of the

---

[56] Cockburn (ed.), *Charge of the Lord Chief Justice*, 66.   [57] Ibid., 57.

[58] Cockburn seemed unaware, however, that during his career Coke had repeatedly denounced the idea that British subjects enjoyed common law rights and liberties while outside the home countries. See Daniel J. Hulsebosch, 'The Ancient Constitution and the Expanding Empire: Sir Edward Coke's British Jurisprudence', 21 *Law and History Review* (2003), 439–82.

[59] Cockburn (ed.), *Charge of the Lord Chief Justice*, 59.   [60] Ibid., 59–62.

[61] The agent was sentenced by a court martial to receive a thousand lashes for having tried to lure two soldiers away from their service in the army.

[62] Cockburn (ed.), *Charge of the Lord Chief Justice*, 62.   [63] Ibid.   [64] Ibid., 67.

army', it had no similar power to 'legislate in respect of the ordinary subject'.[65] This conclusion was based on what Cockburn called the 'indisputable principle that the Sovereign can only make laws in Parliament with the concurrence of the other estates of the realm'.[66]

But if there was no Crown or executive prerogative to proclaim martial law, and if no statute of the Imperial Parliament had created such a power, what about the Jamaican statute under which Governor Eyre proclaimed martial law? Did this statute give the Governor and the military the legal power to arrest, try, and execute civilians outside the ordinary courts of law? After a close examination of the actual wording of the statute, the Lord Chief Justice told the grand jury that it did not. In Cockburn's view, the statute had a far more limited purchase. It permitted the Governor to convene a Council of War, and to take advice on the existence of some grave public emergency. In the event that the Governor decided that there was such an emergency, the statute entitled him to call out the militia, and to subject the *members of the militia* to military law.[67] According to Cockburn's reading of the statute, it was silent on the application of military law to civilians and, had it not been silent, such a provision would, in any event, have been *ultra vires*. The Lord Chief Justice was firm on this point, even as he acknowledged that in October 1865 the white population of Jamaica had good reason to fear for its security. 'I suppose', Cockburn told the jury, 'there is no island or place in the world in which there has been so much of insurrection and disorder as in the island of Jamaica.' The 'curse' of slavery had left the colony endemically vulnerable to tumult and insurrection. In Cockburn's view, however, these political and military exigencies did not trump the fundamental legal protections of the British subject.

The Lord Chief Justice now had considered, and had ruled out, the notion that there was a Crown prerogative to proclaim and enforce martial law against civilians. Only Parliament could make such a law. He had also spoken against the contention that the Jamaican martial law had been authorized by local statute. The upshot of these findings was that Governor Eyre did not possess the legal authority to proclaim martial law and that Nelson and Brand did not possess the authority to enforce it as against George Gordon. These implications did not stop Cockburn from asking another (seemingly moot) question: 'what is this martial law which is thus to supersede the common law of England?'[68] Before he delved into this inquiry, he restated that in time of war or rebellion it was perfectly legal for the military to execute men 'taken in arms, or taken in pursuit'. Unlawful force could be, *must* be, repelled by lawful force. The real issue was the legal status of

---

[65] Ibid., 69.

[66] But Cockburn was obliged to admit to a seeming contradiction. In a number of its Irish statutes Parliament had referred to the 'acknowledged' or 'undoubted' prerogative of the Crown to proclaim martial law. Cockburn concluded that these references were simply 'unsound', a rare instance when legislators had got it wrong. Ibid., 74.   [67] Ibid., 76–7.

[68] Ibid., 82–3.

civilians or other persons detained while not 'actively engaged' in rebellion. What, if anything, did martial law mean for them?

This issue justified yet another historical digression, and another set of conclusions. For Cockburn the term 'martial law' signified the system of ordinary military law as it applied to crime and discipline among uniformed soldiers and sailors. The main vehicle of military justice was the court martial. In the properly conducted court martial, whether the accused person was a soldier or a civilian, the Lord Chief Justice stated, 'the substance of justice is carefully attended to'.[69] It simply was not the case that martial law might be 'exercised in the arbitrary and despotic form which some persons [Finlason?] contend for, as being something that has no limit'.[70] If in his famous statement on martial law (that it was 'neither more or less than the will of the general who commands the army')[71], Wellington had implied some wider definition, the Lord Chief Justice now repudiated it.[72] It would be a chance not worth taking, Cockburn warned, for a soldier or official to rely on Wellington's statements 'as a protection if called upon to answer for his conduct in a court of justice for any injury inflicted on a fellow-subject in the exercise of martial law'.[73]

To this point in his address, the general drift of Cockburn's charge was that martial law, defined as the Crown's prerogative to exert military authority against civilians, was unconstitutional. Since the passage of the Petition of Right 'martial law' persisted only as the set of codes and procedures governing uniformed soldiers. Those who believed otherwise had, in Cockburn's opinion, been misled by the 'loose language of historians'.[74] (Even some of the country's most distinguished legal writers – Hale and Blackstone, for instance – had used 'inaccurate language' when they discussed this subject.) The English people also had been misled by the fact that the term 'martial law' had been frequently invoked by politicians and writers to justify 'the excesses and abuses which have been committed in the exercise of this power'.[75] In Jamaica, in Ireland before that, martial law had recurrently been used to absolve 'flagrant violations of the law in dealing with persons supposed to be disaffected'. Through sheer force of repetition in the public sphere martial law had become a kind of shorthand for the legitimate use of 'lawless and irresponsible power'.

It is one of the more remarkable aspects of Cockburn's charge that it was offered as a corrective to (what the Lord Chief Justice perceived to be) errors in popular political discourse. In the last third of his address he ruminated at some length on the contention, then so much in currency in England, that in modern imperial statecraft 'the exhibition of martial law in its most summary and terrible form is

---

[69] Cockburn (ed.), *Charge of the Lord Chief Justice*, 100.   [70] Ibid., 98.
[71] As quoted, ibid., 101.
[72] Cockburn was sorry that he 'could not accept the opinion even of so great a man as authority on a question of law'. Ibid. Cockburn also rejected the similar opinions of two Judge-Advocates General, Sir David Dundas and T. E. Headlam, who expressed the view (in 1851 and 1859 respectively) that during martial law military officers were not bound by the ordinary restraints of law. Ibid., 100–3.
[73] Ibid., 101.   [74] Ibid., 104.   [75] Ibid., 105–6.

indispensable'.[76] On this score, Cockburn was adamant. He told the grand jury that he hoped that 'no court of justice will ever entertain so fearful and odious a doctrine'. Here Cockburn drew once again from the Whig catechism. The due constraints of state power by law, Cockburn stated, 'are considerations more important even than shortening the temporary duration of an insurrection'.[77] While public necessity might sanction the killing of armed rebels in the field, it would not sanction the summary trial and execution of persons who had not been taken in arms against the Crown. At the very minimum, prisoners were to be treated according to the procedural protections set forth by the codes of military law. In this regard the Mutiny Act provided that 'wherever martial law is administered by officers in the service, it shall be administered according to the rules of that military procedure which by long experience has been found adapted to the . . . protection of the accused'.[78] There could be no legitimate excuse, then, for the way in which Gordon had been treated by the Governor and military of Jamaica. When he reached this point in his address, the Lord Chief Justice had spoken continuously for almost four hours. He had finally spoken his last words on the general theme of the legal status of martial law. Cockburn now turned to the final section of his charge: the application of the law to the evidence concerning Gordon's arrest, trial, and execution.

Cockburn's charge on the arrest, although largely irrelevant to the charges facing Nelson and Brand, was unmistakably clear. On the assumption that Governor Eyre and his sheriff 'had a really honest belief in the guilt of Gordon, they were legally entitled to apprehend him'.[79] However, once Gordon had been apprehended, the sole lawful recourse of officials was to 'hand him over to the civil tribunals'. Cockburn rejected out of hand the assertion that the authorities had possessed the unfettered right to send Gordon wherever they 'were more likely to get a conviction'.[80] Although on the face of the evidence it was arguable that Gordon committed treason in St. Thomas-in-the-East, it also indicated that he committed treason in Kingston. There had been no justification for sending him *out* of the civilian jurisdiction to a military court except to make it 'more likely to get a conviction'. Cockburn was emphatic on this point: 'I entertain a very strong opinion that the whole proceeding . . . was altogether unlawful and unjustifiable.'[81]

The charge then finally wended its way back to the impugned conduct of the accused men, Nelson and Brand. Cockburn began to set forth the reasons why Gordon's trial by court martial was equally high-handed and illegal. The first problem was that the evidence on which Gordon had been condemned was 'morally and intrinsically worthless'. The second problem was that the tribunal itself (three officers short of the seven required by the Articles of War) was improperly constituted under military law. Third, the officers who presided over the court martial had not viewed the evidence impartially. Their deep-seated bias caused

[76] Ibid., 108.   [77] Ibid.   [78] Ibid., 111.   [79] Ibid., 112.   [80] Ibid., 116.
[81] Ibid., 114.

them to render a decision that 'no jury, however influenced by prejudice or passion' could have made.[82] When the proceeding was looked on as a whole, it was clear Gordon had been charged, tried, and executed by officers who ignored the rules 'not only of ordinary law but military law'.[83] With this analysis the Lord Chief Justice had returned to the key questions. If Governor Eyre had lacked the power to suspend the civil law, if it had been illegal for him to transport Gordon to the military courts, if the court martial lacked jurisdiction, and if Gordon's trial had been conducted improperly, did his subsequent execution 'constitute the crime of wilful murder'?

Cockburn addressed the issue of jurisdiction first. Where a tribunal had the legal authority to put a person on trial for a capital crime, and then to execute him, no criminal responsibility could attach to any member of the tribunal who had acted in good faith.[84] The more problematic question arose when 'judicial functions are exercised by persons who have no judicial authority or power'. In this circumstance, the Lord Chief Justice stated, and when a 'man's life is taken, that is murder: for murder is putting a man to death without a justification'. Echoing one of the slogans of the Jamaica Committee, Cockburn told the jury that 'the law must be vindicated' no matter 'how sorry we may be that gentlemen who have intended to do their duty...should be made amenable to the bar of a criminal court for the crime of murder'.[85]

At this point in the charge, the grand jury could only have thought one thing: in the opinion of the Lord Chief Justice the military tribunal which tried and executed Gordon had lacked jurisdiction, and that Nelson and Brand were culpable as accessories to Gordon's murder. The only factual question for the jury to decide was whether there was evidence to support the assertion that the accused *knew* that they had lacked jurisdiction or, in any event, had acted in bad faith. Based on the charge to that juncture, surely the Lord Chief Justice would urge the grand jury to find a true bill. In fact, however, Cockburn's seeming decisiveness and clarity on the issue suddenly evaporated. Just as he had intimated that the court martial lacked jurisdiction, just as he had depicted the grim implications of this finding for the accused, Cockburn made a comment which undermined their force and credibility. 'I have felt deeply sensible', he suddenly confessed to the jury, 'of the exceeding difficulty of the task. I have been, for the most part, travelling over untrodden ground, with no beaten track to follow, and without the light of judicial decisions or of learned authority to guide me. I have not had the advantage of discussion at the bar...I have not had the benefit of judicial consultation.'[86] The upshot of this was plain. On a crucial issue the Lord Chief Justice could not state categorically that his assessment of the relevant law was correct, that the court martial at Morant Bay *had* lacked jurisdiction, and that the execution of Gordon was murder. Instead Cockburn told the jury that he had done 'the best I could'.

---

[82] Cockburn (ed.), *Charge of the Lord Chief Justice*, 115.   [83] Ibid.
[84] Ibid., 124.   [85] Ibid., 125–6.   [86] Ibid., 127.

Having offered this caveat, Cockburn changed subjects. He began to address the hypothetical case that the court martial law did have jurisdiction. In this instance the issue was whether the jurisdiction was 'corruptly and *mala fide* exercised'. Here it is worth remembering the submissions of Fitzjames Stephen at Bow Street and Market Drayton. At those hearings, Stephen had advanced the theory that when the evidence indicated that one man had intentionally killed another without lawful justification, it did not matter whether the killer had acted in good or bad faith. In order to satisfy the *mens rea* – the guilty mind – element of the crime of murder, it was sufficient to prove that the accused had intended to take a human life. When this was proved, the onus fell back on the accused to justify his conduct by recourse to a legal defence. Significantly, Cockburn took a *different* view of the same vital point, one that was appreciably more generous to Nelson and Brand. He suggested that it was not enough that after the court martial the accused intended to take Gordon's life. It was also essential to prove that Nelson and Brand did not honestly believe that Gordon had conspired to overthrow the government of Jamaica. In other words, the grand jury had to be satisfied on the evidence that they viewed Gordon as a 'mischievous and obnoxious character', and had conspired to 'get rid of him'.[87] In that instance only could Nelson and Brand be found guilty of murder.

In an effort to be scrupulously fair to the accused men, Cockburn stressed that it was a grave and irregular business to charge two regular officers of Her Majesty's forces with so 'nefarious a conspiracy'. The Lord Chief Justice did not take lightly a matter 'which so fearfully affects the character of the parties'. It was crucial that the prosecution provide relevant evidence that, if believed, would sustain a conviction. 'Intention', he then told the jury, 'is at all times of the essence of crime.'[88] Cockburn believed that the prosecution had adduced some circumstantial evidence on this issue which he 'could not withdraw from [the jury's] consideration'.[89] Most damning in this regard was the 'inconclusiveness' and 'moral worthlessness' of the testimony on which Brand had convicted and Nelson condemned Gordon. Even accepting the credibility of the witnesses (a large assumption) who were called before the court martial, their evidence proved nothing more than that Gordon was an 'an agitator and a demagogue'. Cockburn thought it 'absurd' that two soldiers had given to 'such language the colour and complexion of treason'.[90] If inflammatory political rhetoric of this type was evidence of treason, 'no man in troubled times would be safe'. In sum, it was not easy to comprehend how honest men could have sent Gordon to the gallows on the flimsy evidence heard at his court martial. This outcome was strongly suggestive of corrupt motives.

But, once again, at a critical juncture of his charge, the Lord Chief Justice stopped short of making an unqualified recommendation that the jury should find a 'true bill'. In his closing passages Cockburn began to send mixed signals to the jury both on the pivotal issues of law and fact. In one breath he contended that

---

[87] Ibid., 128.   [88] Ibid., 153.   [89] Ibid., 129.   [90] Ibid., 137.

Gordon had been convicted on evidence that was patently and hopelessly flawed; that Gordon's conviction and execution appeared to have been motivated by factors other than his legal guilt on the charges; and that to do nothing about such a repugnant miscarriage of justice was an affront to English law and society.[91] But no sooner had Cockburn spoken these sentences when he told the jury that they were not conclusive of guilt, and that the grand jury should reject the bill if they decided that Nelson and Brand had acted in all good faith that Gordon had committed treason. For Cockburn, the really vital question was whether the execution was 'honestly done or not'. What was in evidence on this issue? Once again Cockburn turned to the conclusions of the Royal Commission, and its finding that after the uprising at Morant Bay Jamaica's colonial leaders had been almost of one mind that Gordon was the 'master spirit' behind the insurrection at Morant Bay. On this premiss, the Lord Chief Justice stated, it was open to the grand jury to find that 'Colonel Nelson and the members of the court-martial, participating in the general belief in Mr. Gordon's guilt, may have suffered their minds to be unduly operated upon thereby to his prejudice, yet without imputation on the honesty of their intention.'[92] If Nelson and Brand had truly believed that Gordon's execution 'would have the effect of at once annihilating the insurrectionary movement, and would . . . be for the future peace of the island', then they were not guilty of his murder. In plainer language, the whole case against Nelson and Brand was to turn on the jury's findings about the honesty of their motivations. They killed Gordon intentionally, but had they done so on the honest belief that it was necessary to the public peace?

But it is equally important here to note what Cockburn did *not* say to the jury on this issue. He did not say (as Stephen had done) that in order to be lawful the decisions made by Nelson and Brand about Gordon had to have been reasonable, or based on credible evidence of guilt. In other words, Cockburn did not invite the jury to evaluate necessity from an objective standpoint. Nelson and Brand were to be discharged by the grand jury even if their honestly held view of necessity had been erroneous, irrational, or untenable. Nelson and Brand must have been much relieved and gratified by the generousness of Cockburn's charge on these crucial points.

What is obvious more generally is that Cockburn was far more comfortable with the abstract analysis and criticism of martial law than with the concrete question of Nelson and Brand's culpability for murder. It was Cockburn's 'very strong opinion' that the transfer of Gordon from Kingston to Morant Bay was 'altogether unlawful and unjustifiable'.[93] It was his equally strong opinion that the court

---

[91] Cockburn suggested to the jury that it was possible that Gordon was hanged not because he had committed treason, but because 'mischief resulted from his acts. . . . even contrary to his intention'. If Gordon was convicted on these grounds, Cockburn stated, then 'I can say only that it was as lamentable a miscarriage of justice as the history of judicial tribunals can disclose'. In the published version of his charge, Cockburn once again directly attacked the contrary position of Finlason. Ibid., 154–5.   [92] Ibid., 152.
[93] Ibid., 114.

martial lacked jurisdiction to try Gordon and that no impartial jury would have convicted on the evidence adduced against him. But as for the implications of all this for the accused, that was another matter. 'It is a very different question indeed,' Cockburn stated some minutes later, 'when you come to deal with the parties who are now charged with murder upon this indictment.'[94] But when Cockburn began to explain *how* the question was different, he was unsure and inexact. On one hand, neither Nelson nor Brand had caused Gordon to be delivered to their prison camp. On the other hand, this did not alter Gordon's right to be convicted only on probative evidence. As Cockburn himself had previously stated, even a court martial operating under military law could not dispense with the rules of natural justice.

Cockburn now had come to the final and pivotal moments of his address. It was time to give a precis of the evidence and crystallize the issues. After some five hours of passive listening on complex and weighty subject matter, the jury must have hoped for a decisive summing up. They did not get it. Once again the Lord Chief Justice lamented that in preparing his charge, he had not had the benefit of 'judicial authority to guide me, nor of forensic argument and disputation to enlighten and instruct me'.[95] Cockburn pointedly restated that he entertained 'some degree of doubt' about the soundness of his conclusions about the relevant law. We can make sensible conjectures about what effect such statements had on the jury, and on the interested parties. Recall the circumstances. An alliance of political radicals was attempting to prosecute two regular officers of Her Majesty's forces on charges of murdering a black agitator in a colony torn by unrest. A grand jury of twenty-two affluent and (probably) habitually conservative men were being asked to decide whether that prosecution should be allowed to proceed. At the crucial point in a highly charged proceeding the Lord Chief Justice had professed to be unsure of his law. If there had been even a remote chance that the jury would find a true bill, Cockburn surely had scuttled it.

By these lights Cockburn's charge was naive, even disingenuous, but never more so than when he summed up on the question of jurisdiction, patently a question of law. One would have expected that having already made some definitive statements about this issue, the Lord Chief Justice would only have reiterated them. But instead the Lord Chief Justice instructed the *jury*, a assemblage of laymen, to undertake a 'review of the authorities to which I have called your attention'.[96] If they 'were of the opinion, upon the whole, that the jurisdiction to exercise martial law is not satisfactorily made out', they were to consider this a reason to 'let this matter *go forward*' (emphasis added).[97] He stated that even if the jury found that Nelson and Brand had had jurisdiction, but that they made a 'most grievous mistake in condemning and sending [Gordon] to death', the jury could still rightly refuse the bill if they found that the proceedings 'were done honestly and faithfully, and what was believed to be in due course of the administration of justice'.[98]

[94] Ibid., 118.   [95] Ibid., 155.   [96] Ibid., 154–5   [97] Ibid.   [98] Ibid., 156.

It is difficult to explain such stark self-contradictions. After having made enormous concessions to the defence, after having hedged on key points of law in a controversial case, the Lord Chief Justice then expressed hope that the grand jury would send the case to trial, 'where all the questions of law incident to the discussion and decision . . . may be fully raised and authoritatively and definitively considered and decided'. Cockburn could not have been so innocent of the political dynamics of the case that, for a fleeting second, he thought the jury would comply. For a judge who in the previous five hours had affirmed and reaffirmed the inviolability of due process and natural justice, these instructions were stunningly favourable to men who had sent another man to the gallows on worthless evidence. Still, Cockburn's final words must have been welcomed by grand jurors. Now they could follow their inclination to strike the bill without controverting the charge of the Lord Chief Justice of England.

Before he concluded his remarks, and having given the grand jury an abundance of reasons to reject the bill, Cockburn suddenly changed tack and made some more earnest and lofty statements about the tragic nature of the Jamaica affair. He observed that these 'sad events have occupied a large portion of the public attention, and few persons have not felt an interest in the discussion of them'.[99] And nor was this an idle debate, for the 'terrible scourgings with instruments of torture' had brought ignominy to the 'very name of Englishmen'. But even here, with the opportunity to make a strong statement against unconstrained violence in the colonies, Cockburn hedged. In fact, he gave voice to some of the very arguments that had been invoked to justify the suppression. He told the jury that the dangers posed in Jamaica to 'white men', even more acutely to 'white women', had been palpable. Had the menace not been speedily suppressed, Cockburn observed, the consequences would have been 'too horrible to think of'. He then amplified the point: 'I think if ever there were circumstances which, if it be lawful to put martial law in force, called for the application of it, it was this case of the insurrection in Jamaica.'[100] Although here the Lord Chief Justice had used the word *if*, his statement could only have further blunted the force of his earlier declarations against martial law. Advertently or not, Cockburn had validated why Nelson and Brand should not be sent to trial.

In the final sentences of the charge the Lord Chief Justice asked the jurors to set aside their personal opinions about the Jamaica affair, to make a decision free of 'passion and prejudice'. As for the law of martial law, once again the jurors were urged 'to ask what is the law so far as we are able to ascertain it, and then whether that law has been truthfully, faithfully, and honestly administered'.[101] The Lord Chief Justice then invited the jurors to begin their work.

---

[99] Cockburn (ed.), *Charge of the Lord Chief Justice*, 156.
[100] Ibid., 158–60.   [101] Ibid., 159.

It was ten minutes to four o'clock. The grand jury recessed until the morning of 11 April. At half past one o'clock in the afternoon, after having interviewed (an unknown number of) the prosecution's witnesses, the foreman of the grand jury returned to the court to declare that a true bill had not been found against Nelson and Brand for the murder of Gordon. The decision was received by Justice Channell. As was customary, no explanation was offered for the finding. However, the foreman indicated to Channell that the jury wished to make a statement: 'the grand jury strongly recommend that martial law should be more clearly defined by legislative enactment'.[102] (Significantly, the jury did not recommend that Parliament make some declaration that 'martial law' was to be explicitly abolished as a means of limiting the jurisdiction of civilian law and law courts.) The grand jury wanted martial law to be clarified, and thereby regularized, as an instrument of state in the empire.

II. 'A Luminous Exposition': First Reactions to Cockburn's Charge

Looked on as a whole, Cockburn's charge was riven with uncertainty and hesitation about virtually every key issue generated by *The Queen v. Nelson and Brand*. Just as he seemed primed to make some definitive pronouncements on the law of martial law, Cockburn suffered a failure of confidence and nerve. At all of the key junctures of his long address the pattern was the same: Cockburn described, analysed, pronounced, and then equivocated.[103] That his performance had been unsteady, the Lord Chief Justice himself later privately admitted. According to his own assessment he had simply not been physically well enough 'to do justice to the subject'.[104]

In the immediate wake of the charge, none of these considerations made much impression on the political and legal press. On the contrary, Cockburn's charge was hailed as a major development, not only in the history of the Jamaica affair, but in the constitutional history of England. Complete transcriptions and editorial commentaries appeared in virtually all of the leading dailies.[105] Many journals published long essays and analyses. The gist of the first wave of published opinion was that Cockburn had rendered a great service to the country. Even those who

---

[102] *Daily Telegraph* (11 Apr. 1867), 3.

[103] For example, after having devoted some third of his charge to the history of martial law, and just before he pronounced a conclusion as to its constitutional status, Cockburn suddenly conceded that 'on this point I speak with considerable diffidence; for I cannot claim to have made history my special study, and my researches in this matter have necessarily been confined to the intervals of constant and severe judicial labours'. Ibid., 47.

[104] Cockburn's comments were noted by Chesson in the wake of a conversation with Frederick Cockburn. *CD*, 12 Apr. 1867.

[105] As the *Saturday Review* noted, *The Times* devoted an entire page to the transcript. *Saturday Review* (13 Apr. 1867), 452.

strenuously disagreed with the prosecution of Nelson and Brand, and with some or all of Cockburn's pronouncements upon it, were willing to acknowledge that the charge was an appreciable and timely contribution to the nation's basic law. The press notices were so many and laudatory that, only days after delivering the charge, Cockburn set his brother to work on a definitive published edition.[106] Eight weeks later, the charge, complete with exact citations and elaborate footnotes, was available on bookstalls.

Cockburn's performance before the grand jury may have been seen as convoluted and wavering, but overwhelmingly his contemporaries, the liberal-minded ones most emphatically, did not see it that way. In these circles, Cockburn's charge was seen as a godsend. The radical, labourite, and Liberal newspapers were nothing short of lavish in their praise. The editors of the *Morning Star*, the newspaper most closely allied with the Jamaica Committee, thought that the charge would 'rank among the most famous judicial deliverances of past times'.[107] Long an admirer of the Lord Chief Justice's 'splendid abilities', the *Star* was awed by the 'exhaustive and luminous completeness of his charge'. After months of partisan and sometimes reckless political wrangling over the Jamaica affair, the legal issues of the case finally had been 'elevated into the serene atmosphere of law and justice'. According to *Reynolds' Weekly*, the charge was no less than a 'magnificent exposition of the law'.[108] The *Bee-Hive* judged it to be 'luminous and exhaustive'.[109] Cockburn's charge in the Nelson and Brand case, the *Pall Mall Gazette* thought, was 'an authoritative and singularly luminous exposition of the law on the subject'.[110]

The more politically moderate papers were only slightly less effusive. The *Examiner* admired Cockburn's charge for its 'energetic precision', and declared it 'one of the most important expositions of law ever delivered'.[111] According to the *English Independent*, Cockburn's address was 'elaborate and masterly'.[112] 'A great and worthy production', the *Morning Advertiser* proclaimed.[113] The *Daily Telegraph* thought that the charge 'will rank as one of the imperishable masterpieces of our judicial records', the importance of which was 'difficult to exaggerate'.[114] Even the ordinarily restrained *Spectator* thought Cockburn's treatment of law to be 'magnificently lucid'.[115]

Liberal journalists thought that there were many good reasons to be grateful for Cockburn's decisive intervention. These reasons clearly were rooted in domestic political anxiety over Ireland and reform of the franchise. By these lights, Cockburn's charge had reaffirmed the rights of Englishmen to engage in

---

[106] As a result of a chance encounter at the Old Bailey between Shaen and the Lord Chief Justice's brother, Frederick, it was agreed that the published version of the charge would be based principally on the notes of the Committee's shorthand writer. *CD*, 12 Apr. 1867.

[107] *Morning Star* (11 Apr. 1867), 4.   [108] *Reynolds' Weekly* (14 Apr. 1867).

[109] *Bee-Hive* (13 Apr. 1867).   [110] *Pall Mall Gazette* (11 Apr. 1867), 3.

[111] *Examiner* (13 Apr. 1867), 226.   [112] *English Independent* (18 Apr. 1867), 494–5.

[113] *Morning Advertiser* (12 Apr. 1867).   [114] *Daily Telegraph* (12 Apr. 1867), 4.

[115] *Spectator* (13 Apr. 1867), 408.

vigorous political dissent without fear of state repression. More specifically, the charge was viewed as a sharp rebuke to those politicians (Disraeli was most frequently mentioned) who had publicly endorsed the notion that officials of state had a broad authority to proclaim and enforce martial law.[116] In delivering his charge, the *Pall Mall Gazette* observed, Cockburn 'did not disguise his alarm' at the notion that 'martial law was the extinction of all law but the will of the military commanders ... Nor did he hesitate to denounce these doctrines as being no less unfounded and untenable than they were mischievous and detestable.'[117] The *Examiner* believed that the Lord Chief Justice had reaffirmed the 'rights of English subjects under English law against encroachments founded upon loose, unconstitutional ideas of martial law'.[118] In the estimation of the *Daily Telegraph*, Cockburn, by virtue of his temperament, training, and acumen, was ideally equipped to deliver the charge: 'it was well that to such a man, and not to a mere black-letter lawyer, the grave questions arising out of the Jamaica insurrection should be primarily referred', the newspaper stated.[119] Cockburn had the intellectual assets needed to comprehend the grave political implications of the Nelson and Brand case. He was a 'man who thoroughly understands political rights, and whose massive intellect would have won him fame in any profession'.

The radical and labour press saw themselves as the front line in the battle for franchise reform. They were thus especially gratified by Cockburn's expressions of hostility toward martial law and its advocates. The Lord Chief Justice, the *Bee-Hive* jubilantly asserted, had 'denounced the wild doctrines that Mr. Disraeli and others have endeavoured to foist upon the laws of England'.[120] Once and for all times, the *Daily News* trumpeted, Cockburn had demolished the proposition, 'repeated by public speakers and writers in every variety of form',[121] that in the event of perceived emergency the Crown possessed an unfettered prerogative to subject civilians to military justice. From this day forward, the paper declared, 'it will be clear to all those who exercise authority that they must conform to the law, and if they put the subjects of the Queen to death without lawful trial they will be themselves liable to be called to account'.[122] In a similar vein, the *Weekly Times* expressed confidence that 'in the future, military and naval officers will know that the highest common law authority holds that they are bound, even in the extremest cases, to secure substantial justice by following legal rules'.[123]

The *Freeman*, the chief organ of the Baptist community in England, gave Cockburn's charge a remarkably similar reading. The 'chief value of the charge,'

---

[116] It will be recalled that in July 1866, Disraeli, the newly appointed Chancellor of the Exchequer and leader of the Conservatives in the House of Commons, had made a brief speech against Buxton's motion to censure Governor Eyre. His remarks had been interpreted in liberal circles as an endorsement of the legality of martial law.   [117] *Pall Mall Gazette* (11 Apr. 1867), 3.
[118] *Examiner* (13 Apr. 1867), 226.   [119] *Daily Telegraph* (11 Apr. 1867), 4.
[120] *Bee-Hive* (13 Apr. 1867).   [121] *Daily News* (12 Apr. 1867), 4.   [122] Ibid.
[123] *Weekly Times* (21 Apr. 1867).

the *Freeman* claimed, 'is that it entirely silences all the utterances common in society of late, as to the powers conferred by martial law . . . the leader of such loose despotic talk being none other than the Honourable Benjamin Disraeli himself'.[124] Two of England's leading legal newspapers also expressed the view that Cockburn had come to the Old Bailey with the express purpose of chastising martial law and those who had spoken in favour of the doctrine. The *Law Magazine* knew of 'no instance in the history of English law, in which a delusion has been more completely scattered to the winds'.[125] Although the grand jury did not find a true bill in the case, the *Solicitors' Journal* stated, 'it is not a trifling gain to have called forth so powerful and emphatic a reassertion of the grand historical principles of English liberty'.[126] If the charge accomplished nothing else, it 'swept away all those theories of the right of the Sovereign to proclaim martial law at his pleasure which of late have been so complacently preached'.

Cockburn's charge earned grudging respect even from *The Times*. After reaffirming his newspaper's opposition to the criminal prosecution of Nelson and Brand, the editor expressed his 'unqualified satisfaction' with Cockburn's 'luminous' (that word again!) exposition of the law.[127] The charge was admired particularly for its scrupulous fairness. It was at once 'unflinching in its vindication of the law, and conspicuous for its assertion of moral right, but equally merciful toward the defendants'. In his speech the Lord Chief Justice had achieved a delicate balance between the vindication of vital constitutional principles and the just treatment of two men accused of murder. Like *The Times*, the *London Review* admitted that Cockburn's charge had done much to 'reconcile us to the proceedings which were not only a mistake, but which . . . kept alive the memory of a tragedy which cannot too soon be forgotten'.[128] In light of the 'lucid examination of the cases' undertaken by the Lord Chief Justice, it was now firmly established that 'neither the Crown by its prerogative, nor its representatives in settled colonies, can proclaim martial law'.

Predictably enough, the more rigidly Tory newspapers were less generous. The *Morning Herald* condemned Cockburn's charge for being as 'favourable to the prosecution as the most rabid negrophilist could have possibly desired'.[129] (At the same time, even the *Herald* admitted that, 'speaking for posterity, and with full consciousness that he had the world for his audience, his Lordship delivered an oration of prodigious length and marvellous attractiveness'.) Only *John Bull*, the organ of ultra-Toryism, had nothing complimentary to say about Cockburn's charge, commenting acidly that it proved only the 'impolicy of raising a merely political Attorney General to the highest judicial seat in the realm'.[130] The Nelson and Brand prosecution was an occasion for the Lord Chief Justice to settle some pressing legal issues, but 'we regret to say that he was not equal to the occasion.'

---

[124] *Freeman* (19 Apr. 1867).   [125] 'Martial Law', 23 *Law Magazine* (1867), 244.
[126] *Solicitors' Journal* (20 Apr. 1867), 567.   [127] *The Times* (11 Apr. 1867), 9.
[128] *London Review* (13 Apr. 1867), 420–1.   [129] *Morning Herald* (12 Apr. 1867).
[130] *John Bull* (13 Apr. 1867), 257.

Cockburn's opinions about the law of martial law were 'unsound', the product of an unhappy mixture of 'rashness' and 'excess of vanity to endeavour to catch a little popular applause'.

This was the flavour of the *early* reactions to Cockburn's charge. The tone and content of published commentary became decidedly more critical as writers began to scrutinize complete transcriptions of the charge. To many readers Cockburn's performance had seemed more convincing at first glance. The Lord Chief Justice, the *Pall Mall Gazette* remarked a week after the charge, had been 'so eloquent in language, so artistic in composition that the first effect produced by it, both on hearers and readers was one of unqualified admiration'.[131] But when the 'first dazzle had passed away, it must be confessed that a sense of disappointment arose in many minds'. The country had hoped to receive definitive answers to a range of issues about the 'functions of citizens, soldiers, judges, jurors, in dealing with a state of insurrection when it occurs'. However, when the answers were closely inspected, it was apparent that 'on none of them did the Chief Justice lay down positive law for the guidance of the grand jury'. Cockburn had begun 'with the air of laying down great and comprehensive propositions, and then showed, without admitting it, that there was no ground whatever on which [they] could rest'. What was wanted was clarity and certainty; what was obtained was obscurity and ambivalence.

The *Saturday Review* was among the journals to conclude that Cockburn's charge had fallen woefully short of just expectations. Although it was true that it contained some decisive-sounding statements against martial law, even on these key points 'the Chief Justice seems to have been harassed by uncertainty and hesitation'.[132] According to the *Review*, Cockburn's charge was demonstrably too long and complex, and infused altogether too much with irrelevant 'political discussion'. What had been required at the Old Bailey was a 'terser and drier exposition of the law...instead of leaving the jury bewildered with conflicting considerations'. The uncertainty of the Lord Chief Justice on the key point of the potential guilt of Nelson and Brand practically guaranteed that the grand jury would dismiss the bill: 'when a Judge, at the end of a prolix address,' the *Review* observed, 'tells a body of Grand Jurymen that...he is in doubt himself, they are not likely to take upon themselves a responsibility which ought to rest with the Bench.' On this point, the *Solicitors' Journal* held a similar view. For the fact that the grand jury refused to find a bill against the accused 'the fault, if any, lies in an excessive straining after fairness which led Sir Alexander Cockburn, after proceeding most lucidly up to a certain point, embarrassed the jury by a show of leaving to their unbiased decision considerations which admitted of no doubt'.[133] In 'dealing with facts,' the *American Law Review* bluntly explained, 'probably no judge living is the equal of the Lord Chief Justice... but questions of pure law seem [to] fall largely outside his province.'[134]

---

[131] *Pall Mall Gazette* (23 Apr. 1867), 1–2. [132] *Saturday Review* (13 Apr. 1867), 452–3.
[133] *Solicitors' Journal* (27 July 1867), 888. [134] 1 *American Law Review* (1867–8), 757–8.

Cockburn's charge was also criticized for having left vital points of law in a state of confusion. But there was another, altogether different reason to look askance at the charge. In 1867, few English political writers, even the most liberal ones, assumed that the empire had seen its last colonial uprising. On the contrary, the active assumption among most observers was that colonial officials, when outnumbered by larger populations of 'alien races',[135] would continue to feel the necessity of extreme measures in order to stave off disaster. In the face of this reality, the Lord Chief Justice was seen to have made statements which, even if they were not definitive, had made it hazardous legally for colonial officials to invoke martial law to put down insurrection. These notions flew in the face of the operative assumptions both of many civilian – but most especially military – officials, assumptions which had been acted upon after the Indian Mutiny with the full approval both of the colonial and central governments, and the great majority of the English political class. *The Times* was quick to identify the seeming incoherence between the prevailing view on martial law, and the view as set down by Cockburn: 'an impression prevails very widely, especially in military circles, that a Colonial governor has an undoubted right to proclaim Martial Law, at least with the advice of his Council. This impression will now have been rudely disturbed by the charge of the Lord Chief Justice.'[136]

In this respect, Cockburn's charge had some extremely unsettling ramifications. When asked to enforce martial law, the officer in the field appeared to be in serious legal jeopardy. For instance, if the Lord Chief Justice had got the law of martial law right, it would be an extremely risky business for military men to exert legal authority over persons in custody. Certainly the military trial and punishment of civilian prisoners was riddled with pitfalls. Paradoxically, in this view, Cockburn's charge had made it a safer course for officers not to take prisoners. 'May it not be questioned,' the *Law Times* queried, 'whether humanity profits by such a limitation?' Was an imperfect court martial not preferable to 'summary vengeance'? The *Pall Mall Gazette*, a liberal paper, thought that: 'it would be better, surely, that [the suppression of rebels] should be done under some general semblance at least of legal authority'. For these commentators, Cockburn's intervention had not settled an important point of law; on the contrary, it had created a legal vacuum, one that was certain to lead to a lethal hesitancy among the men who had been given the arduous task of maintaining order in the empire.

III. Finlason's Counter-Attack

One of the many remarkable aspects of Cockburn's charge in *The Queen v. Nelson and Brand* was that it contained (what the *Law Magazine* called) a 'crushing reference'

---

[135] 'However marked and unfortunate may be the tendency of the planting class to exaggerate the danger of insurrection in such communities, there is little doubt that such danger is not imaginary, and that such insurrections may be extremely formidable.' *Pall Mall Gazette* (13 Apr. 1867), 2.

[136] *The Times* (12 Apr. 1867), 9.

to the work of the legal reporter and treatise writer W. F. Finlason.[137] It was no less remarkable in this regard that Finlason not only took umbrage, but proceeded to mount a sustained and stinging counter-attack against the sitting Lord Chief Justice of England in the newspapers, law journals, and in a seemingly interminable series of monograph books. Of all Cockburn's critics, Finlason by far was the most determined and formidable. Cockburn's charge provided Finlason, already the most prolific scholar on the law of martial law, with the opportunity to develop and advance a more comprehensive argument both about the legal viability of the doctrine, and its indispensability to modern British statecraft.

It is fair to suggest that by the summer of 1867 Finlason had developed a veritable mania for the Jamaica case, one rooted in a mixed soil of professional opportunism, political outlook, and personal insecurity. It is obvious from the thousands of pages he wrote about the legal aspects of the Jamaica controversy that he saw the affair as a main chance to attain a greater measure of renown and respect in his field. Finlason worked tirelessly to become *the* undisputed authority on the English law of martial law.[138] This ambition was bolstered by his seemingly intense personal conviction that a robust doctrine of martial law was essential to peace and security in the empire. It was further bolstered by the fact that his ideas had been publically rebuked by a judge of high office and station, but dubious legal attainment and acumen. Finlason was determined to have his pound of flesh.

We have noted that Cockburn's charge in *The Queen v. Nelson and Brand* was delivered on 11 April 1867. When a short time later it was announced that an official edition of Cockburn's charge would soon be published, Finlason decided not to make a full response until he could read the charge in 'authentic form'.[139] On the very day that Cockburn's charge appeared on the bookstalls, 6 June 1867, Finlason wrote a letter to the *Law Times* complaining both that his work on martial law had been misconstrued by the Lord Chief Justice, and that the Lord Chief Justice had got the law wrong. The letter summarized his most material points.

The Lord Chief Justice had told the grand jury that martial law was synonymous with military law, applicable to soldiers all of the time and civilians during times of state emergency. Finlason rejected this view outright. The statutes governing military law, he contended, clearly stated that they applied to soldiers exclusively. In contrast, Finlason argued that martial law was 'the law of *war*', and as such was entirely distinct from military law. 'The scope of my book', Finlason explained, 'was to establish that the common law allows of martial law when there is a rebellion that amounts to war, and is so formidable as to prevent the common law from having its course.' In Finlason's view it was a 'self-evident proposition' that if the common law cannot operate, 'what must be resorted to [is] but the terrors of war'. In more exact

---

[137] 'Martial Law', 23 *Law Magazine* (1867), 244.

[138] In a long review of Finlason's work the *Law Times* (19 Sept. 1868), 370, an admirer of his commentaries on martial law, wrote that the author's contributions to the subject were so 'exhaustive' and 'lucid' that he deserved the epithet 'The Historian of Martial Law'.

[139] *Law Times* (8 June 1867), 64.

terms, 'martial law for the suppression of rebellion has always been understood to mean the application of irregular military law to civilians'. This was the essence of martial law, like it or not. In the same letter Finlason vigorously objected to having been branded by the Lord Chief Justice as an apologist for the brutal operation of martial law in Jamaica. Finlason wanted readers to understand that his treatise had described 'not what ought to be done, but what *had* been done, and with reference only to bare legality'.[140] Donning the raiment of legal positivism, Finlason 'disclaimed any opinion as to the moral propriety or even policy of the measures taken'. In his book on martial law he had 'dealt only with the law'. It was the common law of England, not of W. F. Finlason, which regarded such measures as lawful.

Having made these (and other) points in his letter of 8 June, Finlason was moved to write another letter to the editor of the *Law Times* on 22 June. In this piece (and in another published in the *Law Journal* on 28 June)[141] he defended himself against the Lord Chief Justice's accusation that his theory about martial law was no more than the 'mere doctrine of despotic power', one utterly bereft of legal authority.[142] Finlason's letter quoted from the leading authorities (Coke, Hale) which defined martial law as the law of war, and then mockingly asked how it was possible that the Lord Chief Justice 'could find no authority for the monstrous doctrines I propounded'. If the judge did not find any, Finlason sniffed, 'he could not have looked for them'.

The letters preceded the appearance in the autumn of 1867 of his second book on martial law, *Commentaries upon Martial Law . . . containing Comments on the Charge of the Lord Chief Justice.*[143] This was a comprehensive (one might say compulsive) effort to redeem the authority of his own work in the face of Cockburn's published speech. In the long and rambling introduction to the *Commentaries*, Finlason endeavoured to justify writing a second book on martial law. He admitted to having been moved both by personal and academic considerations. In the first place, Finlason insisted, a sitting Lord Chief Justice had 'almost challenged him from the judgment seat, to come forward and vindicate his views'.[144] Finlason felt that he owed it 'to the Lord Chief Justice and to himself' to take up the gauntlet. Statements had been made (or implied) about his work and character which demanded reply. It was especially irksome, for instance, that Cockburn had suggested that his first book on martial law was motivated 'not from a sense of justice', but from a sense of revenge, by a vulgar desire to justify the ruthless suppression of black men who had spilt white blood.[145] In reality, Finlason maintained, he had tried mightily to 'confine himself to the question of legality, and declined to enter into that of moral propriety'. At the core of the disagreement, Finlason intimated, was the difference between normative and analytical jurisprudence. In his charge to the grand jury Cockburn had blurred the line between the law of martial law and his moral and political convictions about the law. In a

---

[140] *Law Times* (8 June 1867), 64.   [141] *Law Journal* (28 June 1867), 303–4.
[142] *Law Times* (22 June 1867), 102–3.   [143] Finlason, *Commentaries upon Martial Law.*
[144] Ibid., 28.   [145] Ibid., 18.

phrase, the Lord Chief Justice had confounded the 'is' and the 'ought'. As for Finlason, the 'question he discussed was legal liability and that alone'.[146] He professed not to have taken any position on what, in ideal or abstract terms, the law ought to be. The question at issue was straightforward: taking account of the extant law of England, were Nelson and Brand liable to conviction for murder, or were they not? Unlike the Lord Chief Justice, Finlason had endeavoured to adopt a stance of professional indifference to the answer. His only concern was that the answer accorded with the law of the land.

But in Finlason's view, even these profound philosophical differences between himself and Cockburn did not fully justify the second book on martial law. The main reason for this work was to retrieve the true law of martial law from the error and confusion wrought by Cockburn's charge. Here, in referring to the legal expressions of the Lord Chief Justice of England, Finlason was surprisingly blunt. Those who had invested so much faith in the discernment of the Lord Chief Justice had been 'disappointed'. The charge, although it had been much celebrated in some of the newspapers, was in fact 'utterly indeterminate and indecisive; it laid nothing down clearly and positively on the subject; it appeared even to leave a matter of law to the jury; it avowed a state of entire doubt; and, indeed, assigned this as a reason why bills of murder should be found'. Instead of clearing up a great national controversy over martial law, the Lord Chief Justice left it 'just where it was before'.[147] The country still lacked for 'some clear and decided declaration of the law upon the subject'.[148] It was an unwholesome, even dangerous thing, Finlason further contended, for a great imperial nation to be uncertain about something as fundamental as the legality, or not, of martial law. The kind of trouble that had occurred in Jamaica in October 1865, was only too likely to recur in innumerable other parts of the empire. And then, closer to home, Finlason reminded readers, there was the spectre of political violence, even insurrection, in Ireland. Parliament had suspended the right of *habeas corpus* there. Martial law had been proclaimed in Ireland in the past and it could not be ruled out in the immediate future.[149] That was only one tangible reason why the failings of the charge of the Lord Chief Justice in the Nelson and Brand case were so serious.

Finlason's criticisms were directed at what he took to be the main propositions advanced by Cockburn's charge. Allowing for the fact that Cockburn's specific instructions to the grand jury sometimes contradicted his previous analysis, his charge was seen to have implied or explicitly advanced the following ten theses concerning martial law and its application to the Jamaica affair:

(1) That the Petition of Right extinguished any Crown or executive prerogative to implement martial law with regard to civilians in Britain or a settled colony

(2) That Parliament might enact legislation suspending civilian law and putting martial law in its place

[146] Ibid.   [147] Ibid., 61.   [148] Ibid., 23.   [149] Ibid., 4.

(3)   That in times of open war or insurrection the Crown and its agents are legally justified at common law to execute persons taken in arms against the Crown

(4)   That 'martial law' was properly understood as 'military law,' as the body of statutory law governing serving members of the armed forces

(5)   That military law could not be exerted in an arbitrary or despotic manner

(6)   That in October 1865 the Governor of Jamaica lacked the legal authority to suspend civilian law or try civilians before courts martial

(7)   That the transfer of Gordon from a civilian to a military jurisdiction was illegal

(8)   That the court martial which tried Gordon was improperly constituted and ignored fundamental rules of evidence and justice

(9)   If the court martial lacked jurisdiction to try Gordon, then the accessories to Gordon's execution were guilty of wilful murder

(10)   That the issue of jurisdiction was for the jury to decide.

Finlason took issue with virtually all of these propositions, but centrally with the seeming contradiction between (1) and (3), that is, between the supposed extinction of martial law and its obvious persistence *de facto*. Throughout his jury address, Finlason observed, Cockburn disavowed 'martial law' while he validated most of the powers and immunities associated with the term. As Finlason put it, 'the Lord Chief Justice seems to have been willing to admit everything but the *name* of martial law'.[150] For instance, Cockburn admitted that in time of invasion or insurrection 'there is and must be a power to do all that is necessary for the safety and protection of a country or colony'.[151] (Cockburn had even gone so far as to sanction the execution of rebels who had been captured in the field.)[152] This admission implied another: that in times of public emergency officials of state could proclaim (or otherwise give warning) that the 'course of ordinary law is *de facto* suspended' and that the 'measures of war must be resorted to'. It was clear, then, that thesis (1) not only contradicted (3), but was not applicable in times of invasion or insurrection.

Finlason was also bitingly critical of Cockburn's fourth and fifth theses, that martial law was the law governing the standing army, and that the only extraordinary power bestowed by martial law was the power to impose military law on civilians.[153] In Finlason's view, the proclamation of martial law denoted something far more far-reaching. It was in fact a declaration of *war* made for 'the restoration of peace'.[154] Martial law, then, was not the law applicable to regular soldiers but

---

[150] Finlason, *Commentaries upon Martial Law*, 24.   [151] Ibid., 26.

[152] On this point, Finlason contended that the Lord Chief Justice had erred in the opposite direction. To 'slay prisoners in cold blood,' he declared, 'would be contrary to the usages of war'. Ibid., 24, 38.

[153] In fact, it was Finlason's view that military law 'exists only by statutes, which are expressly limited to soldiers of the Crown'. Ibid., 32–3.   [154] Ibid., 1.

'literally the law of war'.[155] A proclamation of martial law was only justified by 'paramount necessity'.[156] When such necessity arose, it empowered officers not only to apply military justice to civilians (if they saw fit), but to do whatever else 'was necessary for the safety and protection of a country or colony'.[157] Martial law was no more or less than what military men honestly thought was necessary to save the state from invasion or rebellion. It implied 'absolute military command', and as such could not be reduced to a code.[158] That command was limited only by the good faith and military discipline of the men given the task of suppressing the threat to state authority. 'To be anything,' Finlason underlines, '[martial law] must be absolute.'[159]

Finlason evaluated the legally abstract dimensions of Cockburn's charge, but also its contentions regarding their application to the case of Nelson and Brand. Was the Lord Chief Justice correct in his sixth thesis, that Governor Eyre lacked the legal authority to proclaim martial law? Was he correct in his contention that when he was tried by court martial Gordon was entitled to all of the procedural protections guaranteed by the codes of military justice? Was he right, finally, that (if the court martial lacked jurisdiction in Gordon's case) Nelson and Brand were guilty of his wilful murder?

With regard to the first question, Finlason thought that the Lord Chief Justice was plainly wrong when he expressed the view that there was no common law prerogative to proclaim martial law, and that the Jamaica statutes did not confer any special rights in this respect.[160] Like any other chief executive officer in Britain or the empire, Finlason countered, Governor Eyre had possessed both the legal right and responsibility to defend his colony from invasion or insurrection by recourse to military force. Civilian institutions, if they were still operable during the state of siege, had necessarily to give way to the needs of military men in the field.[161] In St.Thomas-in-the-East during mid-October 1865, civilian authority had been violently displaced by rebel action. The Governor's only practical option was to order his military forces to *restore* order. His power to do so did not depend on Jamaica's martial law statute. Even where such laws existed, they were only declaratory of pre-existing common law rights.

Finlason conceded more room for agreement on the subject of Gordon's rights *vis-à-vis* a military court martial. The punishment of a person not taken in arms against the Crown had to be preceded by a trial that respected minimum standards of justice. However, Finlason disagreed with the Lord Chief Justice about what this standard entailed. He reminded readers that martial law could not be equated with military law. Martial law was the law of war as dictated by military necessity. It was not the case, therefore, that every prisoner captured during martial law was automatically entitled to all of the procedural safeguards provided for in the military codes. When military conditions so dictated, a prisoner could be

---

[155] Ibid., 3.   [156] Ibid., 48.   [157] Ibid., 26.   [158] Ibid., 49.

[159] As Finlason elaborated, 'necessity admits of no argument, and overrides all law'. Ibid., 48.

[160] Ibid., 1–3.   [161] Ibid., 6–7.

tried in a summary fashion, even by recourse to 'the rough and summary justice of "drum-head courts martial" '.[162] The one proviso was that the court could only convict and punish a man when the court (however constituted)[163] had made an honest evaluation of some relevant evidence. The court had to conform to the procedural requirements of 'natural justice' not those of the civilian or military courts.

This brought Finlason to Cockburn's charge as it related to the criminal guilt or innocence of Nelson and Brand. Here he broadly agreed with the Lord Chief Justice that this issue should turn, in part, on findings of fact concerning their state of mind at the time of Gordon's conviction and execution. The key issue was not evidence but honesty: did the accused form an honest opinion that enough evidence had been presented in court to prove guilt? Only two findings, either of their bad faith or (in Cockburn's words) of their 'recklessness' could support a true bill for murder.[164] The accused could not be convicted of murdering Gordon merely because they had committed some technical errors of trial procedure. It was right and proper that the grand jury had been asked to decide whether the evidence supported a finding of bad faith. However, Finlason strenuously disagreed with the Lord Chief Justice's charge on two other related points. One was Cockburn's suggestion that Nelson and Brand might have lacked basic jurisdiction to try and execute Gordon. Finlason was certain that their jurisdiction was firmly established by the common law of public necessity. The second point pertained to the fact that Cockburn had put the question of jurisdiction to the jury. Repeating the point made in his June letters, Finlason contended that the question of what martial law was, and whether it gave jurisdiction to Brand's court martial was 'entirely a question of pure law'.[165] It was wholly 'contrary to principle and precedent' to have asked the jury to decide legal issues. There was no way to explain such a fundamental error except to recall that the Lord Chief Justice had made a 'candid avowal that his mind was left in doubt', and that he wanted to indicate to the jury 'that they ought to give the accused the benefit of that doubt, and determine the case, substantially, on the issue of honesty'. The only ground upon which Nelson and Brand could be found culpable for the death of Gordon was that they had acted dishonestly. If this is what the Lord Chief Justice meant, then Finlason had no quarrel with it. The problem was that the statements which preceded this part of the charge indicated a different comprehension of the law.

Finlason confined the direct refutations of Cockburn's charge to the first quarter of his book (some seventy pages of introduction). For the most part, the balance of *Commentaries upon Martial Law* consisted of a (somewhat) more concise restatement of his earlier monograph. But a number of his perspectives on and generalizations about martial law merit our attention.

---

162 Finlason, *Commentaries upon Martial Law*, 65.

163 Finlason thought that the conditions of war would determine how courts would be constituted, and sometimes they would dictate a court consisting of a single judge. Finlason also disagreed with Cockburn about what military law demanded in the trial of capital cases. Ibid., 44–5.

164 Ibid., 40.   165 Ibid., 22.

The first is Finlason's theory of the indispensability of martial law to the viable state. For Finlason martial law was part of the very fibre of politics. The first principle of politics was the state; the first principle of the state was the preservation of law and order. 'There is no prerogative of the Crown so ancient, so important, and so undoubted', Finlason wrote, 'as that of preserving the peace of the realm.'[166] But it was a paradox of these principles in the history of every polity governed by law that in order to save the state from destruction (from external or internal enemies) it was necessary to suspend the law and 'levy war within the realm'.[167] According to this political science, 'the strongest stipulations that justice shall have its regular course only applied when justice *could* have its regular course'.[168] When the state confronted armed invasion or insurrection the civilian law was supplanted reflexively by military necessity. When a country is 'the scene of war,' Finlason argued, 'whether in or out of Queen's dominions and whether the state of war is caused by invasion or rebellion, the common law admits itself suspended or superseded'.[169] In the endemically violent world of men and states, no polity could long survive without the power to set aside the constraints of civil law. In the end, then, martial law is '*legal because it is necessary*' (emphasis added).[170] Martial law was, as Finlason put it, the 'law of social self-defence'.[171]

The second set of generalizations concerned the nature of martial law *as law*. How might any unhindered authority over life, death, and property be worthy of the term *law*? These were thorny questions, and Finlason struggled to make sense of them. One reason that martial law deserved the name law was that it was governed by legal rules regarding when it could be proclaimed and enforced. English history abounded in cases in which monarchs or noblemen imposed martial authority on a populace in time of peace. But these episodes, Finlason insisted, were not instances of martial *law*, 'but in truth were simply assumptions of despotic authority wholly contrary to law'.[172] In 1628, Parliament passed the Petition of Right to stop such usurpations. In 1867 it remained wholly illegal for an executive body to proclaim martial law during *peacetime*. However, when there was tumult, and when executive officials presumed to proclaim martial law, those officials were afterward accountable to the law for their decision. It was a question of fact for a jury whether those who proclaimed and enforced martial law had done so from the honest and reasonable belief that it was necessary.[173]

But there were nagging contradictions to resolve. On one side, 'martial law is in short the suspension of *all* law, but the will of the military commanders trusted with its execution, to be exercised according to their judgement, and the exigencies of the moment' (emphasis added).[174] Under martial law, the commanders were bound by 'no fixed and settled rules or laws; no definite practice, and not bound even by the rules of ordinary military law'.[175] They were entitled to exercise an

---

[166] Ibid., 73.   [167] Ibid., 77.   [168] Ibid., 76.   [169] Ibid., 108–9.
[170] Ibid., 113.   [171] Ibid., 127.   [172] Ibid., 88.   [173] Ibid., 170–1.
[174] Ibid., 141.   [175] Ibid., 142.

'absolute discretion for the doing of anything which possibly could be deemed necessary or expedient... for carrying out the complete subjugation of the rebellion'. But here even Finlason equivocated. Under martial law, he insisted, the commander's will was 'absolute, although... certainly not arbitrary'. For all of his decisions the commander remained 'responsible to the Crown, and subject to the more severe restraints of military subordination and control, according to the law and usages of the army'. In this way, by virtue of the disciplinary customs and structures of the armed forces, absolute military power was actually 'protective of the subject'.[176] Finlason illustrated the point by reference to Jamaica. The 'wild anarchy and unbridled cruelty' that had occurred there in October 1865, he argued, were the result not of too much but too *little* military authority.[177] Things went wrong there when military discipline, especially with regard to the punishment of prisoners, was permitted to break down.

For Finlason martial law deserved the name law because it was limited by the usages of soldiers at war. In elaborating this theory he devoted a long section to the subject of drumhead courts martial. The trial of prisoners in the field, he maintained, was 'necessarily of the very essence of martial law'.[178] The reasons were plain enough. In the event of domestic rebellion, it was inevitable that prisoners would be taken by the forces of the Crown. Finlason argued (again, flatly contradicting the Lord Chief Justice) that not even martial law countenanced the summary execution of these men. On the contrary, 'the law of England' (Finlason did not say *which* law) specified that 'rebels are not less subjects because they are rebels', and 'subjects, even though rebels, cannot be executed without a trial'. Where there was martial law, the ordinary courts being closed, the only recourse was to try prisoners by court martial. The court martial bridged the space between unbridled military power and civilized behaviour. By respecting the conventions of the military court martial, Finlason observed, the commander in the field could avert 'indiscriminate massacre' while 'inspiring a salutary terror by some examples of speedy and summary justice'.

The drumhead court martial of rebel prisoners, Finlason further elaborated, did not need to comply with all of the rules and procedures set down by the military codes.[179] As with all other aspects of martial law, the quality of martial justice was to be dictated by the circumstances encountered by commanders in the field. Commanders were to afford prisoners as much due process as conditions permitted. Prisoners were to be tried only for acts connected with the rebellion.[180] Capital punishment was to be meted out only for crimes of treason or murder, and after some form of trial and conviction on proof.[181] And while the officers of a drumhead court martial would not be obliged to observe all the formal rules of evidence, in all cases 'affecting life or liberty' the substance of those rules was to be respected. No prisoner was to be imprisoned, whipped, or executed except on

---

[176] Finlason, *Commentaries upon Martial Law*, 142.   [177] Ibid., 49.   [178] Ibid., 205.
[179] Ibid., 208.   [180] Ibid., 214.   [181] Ibid., 220–1.

'*legal* evidence, and *enough* of it'.[182] No emergency would justify departure from this most basic principle. Even the most hastily convened battlefield court, Finlason maintained, was 'bound rather by the rules of natural good sense and justice'.[183] His conclusion then was that martial law was absolute, and it was not.

Finlason's martial law was an instrument of controlled terror, one that had an ancient historical and legal pedigree even if it had fallen into disuse in England. Now the Jamaica affair, following in the wake of the great Indian Mutiny, and exacerbated by the Fenian scare, had brought the subject of martial law back into sharp focus. Finlason's second book on the subject was written not only to rebut the facile research and reasoning of the Lord Chief Justice, but also as a way of causing the English political class to get past its liberal-minded squeamishness about an indispensable weapon in the arsenal of imperial statecraft.

IV. The Queen v. Nelson and Brand: *Repercussions for the Jamaica Affair*

On 12 April 1867, the day following the discharge of Nelson and Brand by the Middlesex grand jury, the Jamaica Committee convened a meeting of its executive officers. According to Chesson, the gathering drew a 'very full attendance'.[184] Mill was in the chair. The purpose of the meeting was to review the results to date of the criminal prosecutions instigated by the Committee, both in Jamaica and England. Shaen was asked to explain in greater detail what steps had been taken and what, if anything, was to be done about the fact that the prosecutions of Ramsay in Jamaica, and of Eyre, Nelson, and Brand at home, all had been frustrated by unsympathetic grand juries. Far from securing a conviction, the Committee had failed even to get a case to trial.

The main subject of discussion was whether further prosecutions were necessary, feasible, and, importantly, advisable. The proposition was floated that Cockburn's charge to the Middlesex jury, while it had not led to the full-blown trial of Nelson and Brand, had been a major legal victory, that the Lord Chief Justice had vindicated constitutional government from the scourge of martial law.[185] On this reading of the charge, the Jamaica Committee had achieved its mission. As far as can be reckoned (both from Chesson's journal, and from Committee minutes) no one at the meeting doubted that Cockburn had made some legally significant pronouncements against martial law. In fact, it was agreed without argument that

---

[182] Ibid., 245. By this Finlason meant that the tribunal ought always to seek out and consider the best available evidence; that matters of fact should be proved by witnesses with personal knowledge of their truth; that they should be examined in the presence of the accused. These rules of evidence, while often difficult to apply even by trained lawyers, 'embody principles of sound sense which ought never, in substance, wilfully to be departed from'. Ibid., 238–9.   [183] Ibid., 237–8.

[184] *CD*, 12 Apr. 1867.

[185] Neither Chesson's diary nor the Committee's minutes record whether this view was endorsed by a member of the executive, or whether it was simply debated as a proposition.

the charge should be quickly published and widely distributed, either under the auspices of Cockburn's brother Frederick, or the Committee itself.[186]

But a majority of executive members was not satisfied that their job was done. Mill was particularly emphatic on this point. His contention was that Cockburn's charge, as welcome as it was, should be seen less as an end in itself than as a means to an end. The Committee still had not succeeded in provoking a full-blown jury trial. Mill wanted to invite the Committee's legal advisers to prepare reports on the feasibility of further private criminal prosecutions, especially of Eyre. The motion was debated and carried. As Chesson admiringly recorded: 'there is no shadow of a shade of hesitation in [Mill] when a point of principle or a sound course of action is in question.'[187] On Shaen's suggestion it was further agreed that the Committee's lawyers should evaluate whether Eyre might be prosecuted successfully for the murder of Gordon, but also for criminal transgressions under the Colonial Governors Act[188] (the statute which regulated the conduct of the Crown's officials in the colonies). The executive also agreed that the Committee should issue a circular informing subscribers of these resolutions, and seeking to bring in new revenue.

The passage of Mill's resolution gave rise to another sensitive issue. What new retainer, if any, should be offered to Fitzjames Stephen? A number of Committee executives repeated the view that Stephen's compliments of Eyre, first at Bow Street and then again (over strenuous objections) at Market Drayton, disqualified him from further work on behalf of the Committee. Mill also assumed the lead on this issue. According to Chesson's diary, he argued vociferously that Stephen was to be 'strongly reprobated' for having uttered those words and that, 'with all his regard for him' he (Mill) 'could no longer consent that he should any longer be the mouthpiece of the Committee'. If anyone disputed this assertion, their objection was not recorded. Stephen's tenure as lead trial counsel for the Committee was officially terminated. From that point forward Stephen would be retained solely to provide advice on points of law. Even in the face of the reproof, interestingly enough, Stephen agreed to offer this advice.

At an executive meeting convened on 2 May 1867, the written legal opinion of Edward James on the further prosecutions was read aloud by Shaen. Although James appears not to have commented on the plausibility of a second murder charge, he stated that it would be possible to prosecute and convict Eyre for crimes committed in Jamaica under the Colonial Governors Act.[189] This opinion in hand, the executive revisited the prosecution option. Chesson recorded that 'Mill and every other member of the Committee were unanimous in the determination not to abandon the attempt to procure justice until every means was exhausted.'[190]

---

[186] *CD*, 12 Apr. 1867. When Cockburn's charge was published, the Jamaica Committee paid for copies to be sent to the 'principal officials of various colonies'. *JC Minutes*, 21 Aug. 1867.

[187] *CD*, 12 Apr. 1867.

[188] 42 Geo. III, c. 85. The Act gave jurisdiction to British courts over crimes committed in the colonies by public officials.   [189] *JC Minutes*, 3 May 1867.

[190] *CD*, 3 May 1867.

It was resolved that the Attorney General would be petitioned to initiate criminal proceedings under the Colonial Governors Act. If he refused, the Committee would instruct James to commence a private prosecution. If *this* option also was frustrated the Committee 'would fall back upon civil actions for damages'.

But no sooner had the Committee steeled its resolve than new obstacles cropped up. Some weeks before the commencement of the first prosecution of Eyre, the Committee had arranged for Alexander Fiddes, the Jamaican physician who had been present for Gordon's arrest, to be brought to England from the island as a key witness. Now it was learned that 'contrary to a distinct understanding with him', Fiddes had boarded a ship for home. Any future prosecution of Eyre now would certainly fail for lack for direct evidence. What was to be done? Shaen ventured a possible answer. He informed the Committee that he knew of two Jamaicans, Alexander Phillips and Dr. Robert Bruce, both victims of abuses during the martial law, who were soon to arrive in England in order to pursue civil lawsuits against Eyre. Shaen thought that they could be persuaded to testify in support of new criminal charges. The Committee asked Shaen to look into this urgently.

When the executive met again on 21 May, the problem of witnesses still had not been resolved.[191] To make matters worse, on 24 May Shaen informed the Committee that Fitzjames Stephen had written the Committee to indicate that he 'was strongly adverse to the institution, at present, of any proceedings against Mr. Eyre under the *Colonial Governors Act*'.[192] (The grounds of Stephen's opposition were not recorded in the minutes.) Having lost a vital witness, and confronted now with conflicting legal advice, the Committee's executive decided to postpone the instigation of any criminal proceedings against Eyre. In subsequent weeks Shaen continued to search for potential witnesses. Finally, on or about the first day of July 1867, he reported to the Jamaica Committee executive that Phillips was in England and had agreed to act as a prosecution witness in any proceedings against Eyre. Phillips (and two other potential witnesses) was promptly invited to address the next meeting of the executive on 4 July.

But before this meeting could take place Cockburn's charge in *The Queen v. Nelson and Brand* became the subject of discussion in the House of Commons. It is not every day, then or now, that British parliamentarians debate the merits and demerits of a jury charge. On 2 July 1867, however, an Irish Liberal M.P. named O'Reilly stood in the House in order at once to praise the charge as 'masterly' and to recite its inadequacies as constitutional law. O'Reilly was moved by two concerns. The first was that the Fenian rising would cause government officials to proclaim martial law in all or part of Ireland. The second was that Cockburn's charge had lulled the British political class into complacency about martial law. While the Lord Chief Justice (O'Reilly believed) had denounced the doctrine of martial law, a mere jury charge did not carry the force of law. For the Irish people, then, martial

[191] *JC Minutes*, 21 May 1867.   [192] Ibid., 24 May 1867.

law still was a subject of 'vital and thrilling interest'.[193] There were good grounds to fear 'such a barbarous law being revived in that country'. That was why O'Reilly now moved a resolution in the House that 'no commission for proceeding by Martial Law may issue forth to any person . . . without consent of Parliament'. It was a matter of vital importance that any lingering doubt about the legality of martial law should be erased by a definitive resolution of Parliament.[194]

O'Reilly's motion touched off an intense exchange. W. E. Forster, the Liberal philanthropist and long-time anti-slavery activist, while thinking the motion 'not necessary', agreed with the general thrust of O'Reilly's comments. In Forster's view, there still was too much danger that martial law would be revived, if not in Ireland, in one of the colonies. Although Cockburn had demonstrated that martial law (defined as the 'arbitrary will of the Executive') was a 'fallacy of recent growth',[195] the present Government had not done enough to ensure that the Jamaican atrocities would not be repeated. As far as he knew, a number of colonies had not revoked laws which sanctioned the use of martial law. In Forster's view, the Government was simply unwilling to rule out the future use of martial law in the colonies.

The Government's response was offered by Tory Cabinet minister (and barrister) Gathorne Gathorne-Hardy, who called attention to the many passages of Cockburn's charge in which the Lord Chief Justice had qualified his denunciation of martial law. For instance, the Lord Chief Justice plainly acknowledged the 'necessity which might arise of setting aside the law of the land and securing with great vigour the military law'.[196] The Lord Chief Justice also had conceded that 'though an insurrection were suppressed it might be necessary to continue the enforcement of martial law in order to strike terror in the minds of the people for their better order in the future'. In this account of the charge, Cockburn had fully accepted that Governor Eyre was justified in 'resorting to military law in putting down the rebellion'. Gathorne-Hardy then made a further point. The House of Commons would be ill-advised to support Mr. O'Reilly's resolution because, after months of public debate and legal intervention, the law of martial law remained uncertain. Even the Lord Chief Justice in his charge, 'he [Gathorne-Hardy] would not say vacillated, but apparently had gone from one side to another'.[197] The Lord Chief Justice also had admitted that in preparing his charge he had laboured under many pressures and disadvantages. The judge had not had the benefit of arguments from learned counsel. In these circumstances it was understandable that the charge was not definitive on the law of martial law, and that it should not be the subject of a Parliamentary resolution. But there was yet another, more practical, reason not to support O'Reilly's motion: it was crucial that the House not 'place an impediment in the way of those who were acting in distant spheres, and to whom . . . was committed the authority of the Crown and the rights of the

[193] *Hansard*, clxxxviii (2 May 1867), 899.   [194] Ibid., 902.   [195] Ibid., 906–7.
[196] Ibid., 908.   [197] Ibid., 910.

country'.[198] In the empire, in other words, martial law continued to be an essential instrument of statecraft.

Thus, for a second time in a year, a Tory cabinet minister had publicly sanctioned a doctrine of martial law in the House of Commons. For the first time, moreover, the same official cited the words of the Lord Chief Justice of the Queen's Bench as a *supporting* authority. This alarming development spurred Mill to his feet. Mill began by remarking on Gathorne-Hardy's 'obvious desire to explain away and get rid of the effect of the Charge of the Lord Chief Justice'.[199] While admitting that the charge was 'not law', Mill urged the House to embrace it as an 'exceedingly strong corroboration' of the principle that 'there is not, properly speaking, as regards non-military persons, such a thing as martial law'.[200] If necessary, new steps would be taken to expunge the notion that 'any proceeding, such as a declaration of martial law, can or ought to exempt those who act upon it from amenability to the laws of their country'. It was a principle of the highest importance that no one, not even the highest officers of the land, could 'escape or get out of the region and jurisdiction of the law'.

This statement did not attract any rejoinder either from Gathorne-Hardy or any other member on the Tory benches. The remainder of the discussion was devoted mainly to reasons why it would be a bad idea for the House to support O'Reilly's motion. T. E. Headlam, a lawyer and former Judge-Advocate General, thought that if the House was to alter the law of martial law (which he thought unwise) it should be by bill, not by resolution.[201] Edward Cardwell voiced his support for the view that martial law was no more or less than an instance of the common law defence of necessity. No British official acted under 'martial law' 'except under a great responsibility and the liability to render a future account to the ordinary tribunals of the country'.[202] Then, after some quibbling interventions by two other members, O'Reilly stood to tell the House that he would comply with the request (of Cardwell) not to press his motion to a vote. O'Reilly claimed, somewhat hopefully, that the motion had achieved its purpose. He believed that 'no Government in this country, in the face of the opinions which had been expressed, and in the face of a clear statement of the law which they had had, would venture to assume the power of proclaiming any law which was not the law of the land'.[203]

Some weeks later, Cockburn's charge was discussed in the House of Lords. The Earl Russell initiated the discussion when he complained to the Colonial Secretary, Lord Buckingham, that a Mr. Purcell, a temporary stipendiary magistrate in Jamaica, had made intemperate and public criticisms of the Lord Chief Justice

---

[198] Ibid., 912.   [199] Ibid., 899.   [200] Ibid., 913.

[201] Ibid., 914. In 1859, Headlam had prepared a report on martial law for the Government. The report took the position that the Crown possessed the power to proclaim martial law, and thereby to empower the military to override the ordinary civil rights of civilians, in times of great emergency. The legality of acts taken under martial law would later be dealt with by Parliament in an indemnity statute. See *PP* (1860) xxiii, Appendix 11, 60.   [202] Ibid., 916.

[203] Ibid., 918.

and his charge.[204] (Purcell claimed that Cockburn's opinions on law were 'worthless' in that he 'never was a lawyer', but that his appointment to the bench had been the result only of the political patronage from Lord Palmerston.) Russell wanted to know what steps would be taken to discipline the offending magistrate. Before the question could be answered (Purcell's appointment would be terminated), Lord Melville interjected of Cockburn's speech that 'a more unjust, unfair, and partial Charge never was delivered by any Judge from the bench'.[205] This remark caused the Lord Chancellor (Lord Chelmsford), a 'personal friend' of Cockburn's, to come to the defence of the Lord Chief Justice. Lord Chelmsford replied that it was 'impossible to do ample justice to the research and ability which the charge displays. As to the law on the subject, persons might differ from the learned Lord Chief Justice; but there can be no doubt that the Charge was the result of the conscientious conviction of the Lord Chief Justice, expressed after due deliberation.'[206] If the Lord Chief Justice had displayed as much 'partisan feeling' as was alleged by Melville, the Lord Chancellor derisively suggested that he be made the subject of an impeachment. The final word on the subject was had by Lord Shrewsbury, a leading member of the Eyre Defence Committee. While he himself was in no position to pronounce on the authority of the charge, he knew that 'many persons say there were grave errors of judgment in it, and that many matters which were asserted by the learned judge could be contradicted'.[207] Shrewsbury hoped that the proponents of Cockburn's charge 'had also read the answers to it'.

By now, July 1867, it must have been obvious to the Jamaica Committee that Cockburn's charge had not settled the law of martial law. On 19 July the Committee met to receive Alexander Phillips, and to resume its discussion of further legal actions. Their principal guest, Phillips, was a black man (a maroon) of some education, a self-described colonial 'gentleman'.[208] Before the uprising of October 1865, Phillips had associated with critics of the Governor and his policies. In the days following the uprising he was arrested in the sweep of persons in the colony, white and black, viewed by the authorities as sympathizers – or co-conspirators – of the Morant Bay rebels. Like Gordon, Phillips was arrested in a place still under civilian law, only to be transported (in shackles) by military steamer to a makeshift prison in the part of the island under martial law. There he was given over to the not-so-tender oversight of Duberry Ramsay. According to Phillips' testimony before the Royal Commission, on Ramsay's order he was locked in a tiny cell for several days, and brought out only to witness the execution of suspected rebels. Then, without trial (or even charge) Ramsay ordered that Phillips be given a hundred lashes with a cat-o'-nine-tails. He was whipped, and then released to the care of friends. It was Phillips whom, after he attended the Jamaica Committee meeting of 4 July, Chesson patronizingly described as one of the 'coloured witnesses' whose expressions of gratitude were 'quaint in their language but genuine in their spirit'.[209]

---

[204] *Hansard*, clxxxviii (19 July 1867), 1718.   [205] Ibid.   [206] Ibid., 1721.
[207] Ibid., 1722.   [208] *JRC Minutes*, 345.   [209] *CD*, 4 July 1867.

The fortuitous appearance on the scene of Phillips (and his fellow Jamaican, Robert Bruce) caused the Jamaica Committee to make some firm decisions. The Committee would pursue a further criminal prosecution of Eyre. At the same time, some members of the Committee would, in their private capacity, raise money for the support of Phillips and Bruce while they were in England.[210]

In a letter of 10 July 1867, Shaen asked Attorney General Rolt to consider laying charges against Eyre for seventeen counts of criminal misconduct (the charges were specified and supported in a separate appendix) arising from the period of martial law, and after.[211] The charges were to be lodged in the Court of Queen's Bench under the authority of the Colonial Governors Act. Shaen cited the Jamaica Committee's 'want of success' in previous prosecutions as a 'strong additional reason for the institution of proceedings by the Attorney General, in order to prevent an absolute failure of justice'. To fortify their entreaty, the Committee enclosed a complete copy of Cockburn's charge in *Nelson and Brand*. Three days later, however, Rolt returned all of the papers to Shaen, stating that he had already once considered a prosecution of Eyre and had not thought it necessary to proceed against him. In the latest letter and enclosures of the Jamaica Committee, Rolt tersely stated, he did not 'find anything to induce me to alter the conclusion at which I had previously arrived'.[212] The Committee responded by sending the entire correspondence to the newspapers.

The Government's position on martial law was clarified somewhat when in late June 1867 (making good on an undertaking to Parliament given in May by the Lord Chancellor) it tabled a copy of a despatch which had been sent to every colonial Governor by the Colonial Office the previous January.[213] The document had been prepared under the auspices and signature of the Secretary of State for the Colonies, Lord Carnarvon. The despatch informed Governors that any colonial statute which invested executive authority with the 'permanent power of suspending the ordinary law of the colony . . . is, I need hardly say, entirely at variance with the spirit of English law'.[214] Such statutes were to be repealed forthwith. But the despatch made another important statement: 'Her Majesty's Government must not be supposed to convey an absolute prohibition of all recourse to martial law under the stress of great emergencies.' Martial law might still be proclaimed 'on the pressure of the moment'. However, any official who proclaimed martial law would

---

[210] *JC Minutes*, 1 Aug. 1867. The Committee pressed ahead even as its public prestige was further damaged when one of its executive members, Edward Beesly, made an inflammatory public speech at Exeter Hall on 2 July 1867, one which queried why the Sheffield outrages had generated so much public anger when the Jamaica atrocities had not. Beesly further asserted that the murder of some recalcitrant working men by trade unionists was no more or less criminal than the murders committed by Eyre. These statements were strongly condemned in the press. See *Pall Mall Gazette* (3 July 1867), 11; *London Review* (16 July 1867), 15; *Spectator* (13 July 1867), 774–5.

[211] As reprinted in the *Daily News* (29 July 1867), 3.   [212] Ibid.

[213] The despatch had been written to the Governor of Antigua, but expressed the position of the Government on the use of martial law throughout the empire. See Despatch from the Earl of Carnarvon, 26 Jan. 1867, *CO* 323/287. See also below, Epilogue. The despatch was reprinted in a number of newspapers, and in the *Law Times* (29 June 1867), 132.   [214] Ibid.

be 'held strictly accountable for acts which indicate not merely a mistaken judgment, but a recklessness of human life and suffering'.

Although in some quarters Carnarvon's despatch was compared favourably to Cockburn's charge,[215] the two documents reflected the same deeply divided consciousness about law and coercion in the empire. The despatch was also the product of men who wanted it both ways: an empire governed by laws when possible and by terror when necessary. Henry Taylor – a senior bureaucrat in the Colonial Office – was unembarrassed by these contradictions. In a letter to his superior, Frederic Rogers, dated 13 June 1867, Taylor endorsed what he read as an emerging public consensus that martial law was an extreme measure but 'that it cannot always be dispensed with'.[216] Taylor had been asked to consider whether Cockburn's charge obliged the Colonial Office now to revise the policy on martial law set forth in Carnarvon's general despatch. His conclusion was that it did not. The charge, he warned Rogers, was 'somewhat deficient, largely redundant, and more or less unsteady'. Even the later edition of the charge, having been 'revised and amplified into a sort of treatise', provided no good reason for the Colonial Office to change course. The central recommendation of the Lord Chief Justice that martial law 'be defined and regulated by legislative enactment', Taylor thought a particularly bad idea. Not only would such law be terribly difficult to draft but would almost certainly render it impossible for Governors to respond adequately to dire emergencies of state.

In Taylor's view, in making his charge the Lord Chief Justice 'seems hardly to present any other side of the question than that which the evils and outrages suffered and perpetrated in the execution of martial law should have suggested to his mind'.[217] Cockburn clearly believed that 'the maintenance of principles essential to the due administration of justice [are] more important to mankind than the saving of a particular community at a particular time from insurrection or massacre'. It was Taylor's thinking, thinking which prevailed in the Colonial Office, that a more pragmatic approach toward martial law was essential for colonies 'where the ruling race are but a handful among the multitude of the subject race'. As Taylor later recorded in his memoirs, what he had contended for is 'that the stumbling block of law should not be intruded upon the minds of men at the moment when they are suddenly charged with the rescue of a community from imminent destruction'.[218]

It was not necessary to be privy to the internal correspondence of the Colonial Office in order to discern the drift of Colonial Office policy on martial law.[219] The remarks first of Disraeli and then Gathorne-Hardy in the House of Commons,

---

[215] The *Law Times* (13 July 1867), 156, applauded Carnarvon for having set a 'practical course' in the wake of an 'unpractical discussion'.

[216] As quoted in the *The Autobiography of Henry Taylor, 1800–1875*, vol. ii (London, 1885), 260–3.   [217] Ibid.

[218] Ibid.

[219] This correspondence, incidentally, also included the recent opinion of the law officers of the Crown that the Jamaica Indemnity Act would 'supply a defence' to any new criminal or civil litigation commenced against Governor Eyre. See Law Officers to Colonial Office, 2 Feb. 1867, *CO* 885/11.

followed later by the terse rebuff of the Jamaica Committee by the Attorney General, made it abundantly clear to the Committee that the Government was not prepared to offer a blanket condemnation of martial law either in principle or practice. For this reason they decided to press on with new prosecutions, knowing perfectly well that the policy was unlikely to be warmly received by the general public or the press. The Committee, the *Saturday Review* remarked of its determination to begin new legal actions, had become nothing less than a 'Limited Liability Company organized for the purpose of persecution'.[220] In the wake of the charge of the Lord Chief Justice in *Nelson and Brand*, the only possible explanation for the Committee's persistence was the 'gratification of political hatred'. The editors at the *Review* called for 'men of sense and knowledge of the world' to demonstrate their disdain of the Jamaica Committee and its policies.

It is tempting to read the history backwards and assume that it was inevitable that the grand jury would not indict Nelson and Brand. In the days leading up to the jury charge, however, the War Office did not take such a sanguine view. We have noted that when the Chief Magistrate at Bow Street issued process in *Nelson and Brand* in early February 1867, the War Office was alarmed enough both to underwrite the legal defence of the officers, and to seek expert legal advice. Upon the request of Lord Longford, the chief solicitor to the department, Charles Clode, was asked to prepare a memorandum on the legal position of the accused officers. On 11 March a copy of the document was sent to the barrister James Hannen.[221] Hannen was asked to comment on the best course of action 'in the event of a true bill being found by the Grand Jury'. Neither the request nor Hannen's prompt reply betrayed any sign that the result of the grand jury inquiry was seen as a foregone conclusion. In fact, Hannen advised that the War Office, among other things,[222] prepare itself to 'give evidence generally in support of the defence', and to acquire certified copies of the Jamaica indemnity statute, as well as affidavits from the accused that their actions were 'bona fide in order to suppress the rebellion'.[223]

None of this deflected the Jamaica Committee from its course. In the remainder of the summer, and then into the autumn of 1867, the executive planned and then prepared to prosecute Eyre for a second time. Additional monies were raised for this purpose, and for the 'relief and assistance' of Phillips and Bruce while they remained in England.[224] As for Eyre, his movements were now kept under constant surveillance. The policy of the Committee was to seek his arrest when he visited a city, preferably London. When he was charged again, it would be in a city and before city magistrates. But time and again, Chesson recorded, Eyre 'slipped through our fingers'.[225] In the autumn, Eyre was tracked from Southampton to Dover to Paris and Brussels. When it became clear that Eyre would remain abroad

---

[220] *Saturday Review* (3 Aug. 1867), 146.
[221] Clode to Longford, 15 Mar. 1867, *WO* 32/6235.
[222] If there was to be a trial, Hannen thought that the War Office should counsel Nelson and Brand to exercise their right to be tried in the Court of Queen's Bench. Ibid.   [223] Ibid.
[224] *JC Minutes*, 1 Aug. 1867.   [225] *CD*, 8 Aug. 1867.

for some weeks, it was resolved that prosecution would be attempted sometime early in 1868. The Committee would wait as long as was necessary. They began the task of retaining new trial counsel, just as they watched attentively as the Jamaica civil suits proceeded through the courts.

V. 'The Alphabet of Our Liberty': Making Sense of the Cockburn Charge

It was remarkable, even extraordinary business when in April 1867, Alexander Cockburn went down to the Old Bailey to charge the grand jury in *The Queen v. Nelson and Brand*. Why had he taken it upon himself to do this? In his oral address, and even more elaborately in the published edition of the charge, Cockburn provided a surprisingly candid answer. In the first place, the Nelson and Brand prosecutions had given rise to legal issues of unusual urgency and complexity. Did government officials, in the colonies or at home, possess a general prerogative to proclaim martial law? If so, what legal powers were conferred by such a proclamation? Could the civilian and military officials who implemented martial law be held accountable for their conduct in the common law courts? Cockburn thought these questions of 'infinite importance, not only in this case, but in any other similar case which may arise hereafter'.[226]

But, as Cockburn himself acknowledged, his motivations were more complex. He did not go down to the Old Bailey, his full entourage and appointments of office conspicuously on display, only to comment on some abstract questions of law. Cockburn took it upon himself to charge the grand jury in *Nelson and Brand* in order to alter the course of public debate on martial law. Since November 1865 many of the country's leading figures had contested the implications of the Jamaica suppression. The focal point of the controversy was the accountability, or not, of political and military officials who had used martial law to crush resistance to state authority. By April 1867, Cockburn clearly believed, the argument was being carried by the wrong side. By then a number of distinguished politicians and legal writers had endorsed conceptions of martial law 'of the wildest and most startling character'.[227] Although a Royal Commission had established beyond question that terrible atrocities had been committed in Jamaica, yet, Cockburn lamented, 'among the educated classes... persons can be found to uphold and applaud such proceedings'. In the result, an aura of legitimacy had been lent to 'the most arbitrary and despotic power'. The English body politic had been infected by wrong and retrograde ideas, and Cockburn thought it time to put things right. The Nelson and Brand case presented an occasion for the Lord Chief

---

[226] Cockburn (ed.), *Charge of the Lord Chief Justice*, 9.   [227] Ibid., 22–3.

Justice of the Queen's Bench to exert, in his own words, the whole 'weight and authority' of his office 'against the exercise of martial law in the form in which it has lately been in force'.[228] Cockburn went down to the Old Bailey to remind the English people of their great (Whig) political and legal inheritance, to school them, as the *Daily News* put it, in 'the alphabet of our liberty'.

About all of this, Cockburn was remarkably free-spoken. The dragon of unfettered military power had got loose in the land, and he had slain it. But there were still other, unstated, reasons why the Lord Chief Justice had been beguiled by the role of judicial St. George. Cockburn was an able man, but in equal measure he was also an egotistical, vainglorious, and, in the months preceding the charge, chronically ill man. (This might help explain why, in his long address on martial law, Cockburn conveniently forgot that in 1851 he had stood in Parliament to defend the proclamation and use of martial law in Ceylon.)[229] When he went down to the Old Bailey in April 1867 Cockburn was uncomfortably aware of his own mortality. Cockburn latched on to the Nelson and Brand prosecution as a means of consolidating his place among the great British judges.

Cockburn charged the jury in *Nelson and Brand* in order to alter the rightward drift of political discourse in England and, in the immediate aftermath of his charge, it looked as though he had succeeded brilliantly. The charge, although ostensibly a mere advisory opinion on points of law, was a sensation. Cockburn's intervention had struck a chord, at least among liberal journalists, in a country tensed by democratic agitation and Fenian violence. A score of leading newspaper editors exalted in Cockburn's stirring affirmations of constitutional government and fundamental liberties.[230] Cockburn also garnered praise – even by some conservative writers – for having admonished the draconian theory of martial law. Few writers could remember the last time that a high court judge had pronounced so clearly and powerfully on matters of such fundamental importance.

It is striking about the commentary on Cockburn's charge, however, that it became markedly less favourable as time advanced. On a sober and deliberate reading of *all* that the Lord Chief Justice had said about the law of martial law, of

---

[228] In a postscript to the published edition. Ibid., 160.

[229] When the Ceylon issue was debated in the House of Commons in 1851, Cockburn was Lord Russell's Attorney General. In the course of the debate he spoke in defence of Torrington and his use of martial law. Is it possible that in 1867 Cockburn had forgotten his role in the Ceylon affair? Or was he simply too embarrassed to speak of the episode, now nearly 20 years old?

[230] Cockburn's admirers made very generous assumptions about the charge's clarity, coherence, and likely impact. The rapturous early reception of Cockburn's charge can perhaps be put down to three things. First, nothing was so much savoured by the Victorian political class as a high-mindedly Whiggish speech about the timeless glories of the English constitution. The Lord Chief Justice's charge provided a number of tasty passages of this kind. Second, when they penned their first responses to the charge, few commentators appear to have read the entire charge carefully. The Lord Chief Justice's obvious ambivalence, his hedging and self-contradiction on key points, were obscured by the tendency of journalists to focus only on its most grandiloquent passages. Finally, the fact that the charge had not led to the bill against Nelson and Brand, a result welcomed by most of the press, made it easier for some writers either to ignore or forgive the charge's many flaws.

all he had said about its application to the Nelson and Brand case, and of all his instructions to the grand jury, all that glistered was not gold. On close inspection, the charge was marred by hesitancy, vagueness, and flat self-contradiction. According to a number of discerning newspaper and legal critics, Cockburn's charge did not provide a coherent alternative account of the law of martial law. When looked at as a whole, the charge seemed at the same time to denounce and embrace martial law.

If Cockburn's charge had any theoretical mooring, it was to the notion that in England and her colonies all human conduct occurred inside the compass of the law. As for the law itself, it consisted not only of case judgements and legislative enactments, but of natural rights. Thus, every official of state was legally accountable for every action. By the same token, every subject of the realm was entitled both to his rights under common law and 'the eternal and immutable principles of justice, principles which can never be violated without lasting detriment to the true interests of a civilized community'.[231] The contrary idea, that during a perceived emergency agents of the Crown were empowered to act in a 'purely arbitrary, despotic, and capricious' manner, Cockburn brushed aside as 'repugnant to the genius of our people'.[232] This form of martial law had no basis 'in those repertories of the law of England which have been compiled by the sages and fathers of the law'.[233] For these reasons, then, it was 'utterly illegal' to try a civilian (like George Gordon) by court martial 'after a rebellion had been suppressed'.[234] As Cockburn gravely assured the grand jury, 'there are considerations more important even than the shortening of the temporary duration of an insurrection.'[235]

These were clear and confident words. But Cockburn's charge ultimately recanted them. He was willing only to reject martial law on the level of *theory*. When the time came for him to give clear instructions to the jury on these points, Cockburn balked. Suddenly he lost faith in the authority of his own high-minded pronouncements. When the grand jury craned their necks to hear his final words on the law of martial law, the Lord Chief Justice of England did not, *would not*, say definitively that Nelson and Brand had lacked the legal authority to take Gordon's life. In fact, Cockburn now was so unsure of himself that he put the question – this the central *legal* question raised by the prosecution – to the jurors.

One explanation for Cockburn's hesitations and self-contradictions can be ruled out. The problem was not a *momentary* loss of concentration or nerve. We can know this because some weeks after the charge, when Cockburn drafted the postscript to the published version of his address, he repeated the same doubts and ambivalence. Time for sober reflection had not made him more certain. In these paragraphs, his last word on the subject, Cockburn reiterated that martial law was a menace to the British idea of civilization. 'Thrice in little more than half-a-century,' he reminded readers, '. . . in Ireland, in Demerara, in Jamaica, has martial law been

---

231 Cockburn (ed.), *Charge of the Lord Chief Justice*, 108.   232 Ibid., 23.
233 Ibid., 99.   234 Ibid., 29.   235 Ibid., 108.

carried into execution under circumstances of the most painful character.'[236] These episodes were offered as grim object lessons in 'what human nature was capable of when stimulated by the fierce passions engendered by recent conflict or [when]... vengeance is let loose in the shape of martial law, to be exercised by a dominant class on an inferior and despised race'. In the sentences that followed, however, Cockburn admitted that there might be moments (the first moments of the Morant Bay uprising were cited as an example) when it 'might be well to have the means of immediate and summary punishment... hanging, as it were, over the heads of the population, to strike terror into their minds in the event of any further disposition to disorder manifesting itself'. While he continued to maintain that martial law had been abused in Jamaica, and that henceforth it ought to be 'placed under strict and well-defined restraints', Cockburn could not bring himself to condemn martial law – this ultimate instrument of state terror – categorically. As a practical matter, the Lord Chief Justice acknowledged, no imperial power could do without a doctrine of martial law. In the end, Cockburn left it to others, to political theorists, to reconcile martial law with the rule of law.

The most comprehensive and searching criticisms of Cockburn's charge were written by W. F. Finlason. In his *Treatise on Martial Law*, Finlason established himself as the leading English authority on the law governing public emergency. He was not prepared to give up this hard-won standing without a fight, even if it meant taking on the presiding Lord Chief Justice of England. Finlason's attack had two facets. The first was to expose the stark contradictions within Cockburn's charge, to demonstrate that the Lord Chief Justice had declaimed martial law in name but not in substance. The second was to criticize Cockburn from the point of view of legal positivism. In this vein Finlason claimed that Cockburn's charge was tainted by normative thinking; it confused what the law was with what it ought to be. Conversely, Finlason asked readers to accept that his own analysis of the law of martial law did not make this mistake, that it was purely dispassionate and empirical. Finlason's martial law was presented as the law as hard fact.

Finlason's most telling criticism of Cockburn's charge actually grew out of a shared premiss. Both agreed that martial law, whatever its specific content, could only be invoked when the state was threatened by armed invasion or insurrection. According to Cockburn's theory, however, the invocation of martial law had very limited implications. It entitled the armed forces to apply military law and measures against persons in arms against the Crown. It did not entitle the military to exercise limitless power without fear of legal repercussions. Finlason dissented from this narrow reading of the doctrine. In his opinion, martial law was the law of war, if always of *defensive* war; it was invoked so that the state might survive armed invasion or insurrection. It was invoked so that military commanders, experts in coercion, might exert whatever force they judged necessary to re-establish peace

---

[236] Ibid. Once again, Cockburn did not mention the period of martial law in Ceylon during 1848, or his speech on the subject in the House of Commons.

and good order. Martial law was the name given the regime that existed so long as civilian jurisdiction was mortally threatened. This regime was not reducible to specific rules or codes. Martial law was law only in the restricted sense that military commanders responded to threats in a systematic manner. Its content was dictated solely by the exigencies of the moment as perceived by commanders in the field. Martial law might countenance any action that was honestly thought necessary for the restoration of order, including the use of terror. If it was to have any possible efficacy as an emergency measure, martial law had to have the capacity to demoralize and frighten an opposing force. 'To be anything,' Finlason plausibly asserted, 'it must be *absolute*.'[237]

Finlason's criticisms were compelling, if only because they focused on what Cockburn accepted or implied, but would not plainly say. Cockburn accepted that the empire was often a dangerous and hostile place for white officials and colonists. He also accepted that it sometimes was necessary for the military to use brutal and exemplary force to re-establish public safety and order. Even more tellingly, Cockburn implied that if martial law was to serve its purpose then men like Nelson and Brand could not later be held accountable for killings perpetrated in perfect good faith. As Finlason pointedly remarked in his second book, Cockburn had been willing 'to admit everything but the *name* of martial law'.[238]

It is not the place of an historical study to say that Finlason's account of martial law was correct, or at least more correct than Cockburn's. That is the job of a law book on martial law. What can be said, however, is that Finlason presented an internally coherent view of the sources. But it is also appropriate to observe that Finlason's writings on martial law were just as much skewed by political convictions as those of the Lord Chief Justice. In Finlason's account of the law of martial law, the foundational 'hard fact' is the perception that nations, particularly imperial nations, cannot get along without a robust doctrine of martial law. Finlason thought that the British Empire was a good, even inevitable institution, but that it could not be run on civilian laws and procedures alone. Since the Indian Mutiny it was patently obvious that small and scattered communities of white Britons could not dominate multitudes of non-white, non-Britons without raw coercion or, better, the *threat* of raw coercion (the very essence of martial law). In the final analysis, the main difference between Finlason and Cockburn on martial law was that the former was more forthright about the implications of empire for constitutional government. More honestly than Cockburn, Finlason was willing to accept that what happened in Jamaica, however regrettable, underlined the indispensability of terror as an instrument of imperial government. For Finlason the law and politics of martial law were mutually and wholly complementary.

---

[237] Finlason, *Commentaries upon Martial Law*, 33.   [238] Ibid., 24.

By the early summer of 1867 the euphoria that some members of the Jamaica Committee had felt about Cockburn's charge had given way to a far more sober assessment of the situation. Once again the question of martial law had been problematized in the press and in Parliament. Not only were Nelson, Brand, and Eyre still free and unpunished, but the most draconian ideas of martial law still had not been condemned by a high court judge while acting in his formal capacity as an oracle of the law. The central mission of the Jamaica Committee had not yet been realized. For all of Alexander Cockburn's posturing and pretence, the waking dragon of authoritarian politics manifestly had not been slain.

7

'The Most Law-Loving People in the World': The Denouement of the Jamaica Litigation

Ex-Governor Eyre, like some troublesome ghost, refuses to be laid to rest . . . he has been the cause of a strange dissension amongst some of the most distinguished men in the country . . . And now he has succeeded in setting the judges by the ears.

Morning Advertiser, 9 June 1868

We presume that such an incident as that which took place in the Court of Queen's Bench yesterday is unexampled in history.

Morning Star, 9 June 1868

The fact is that great lawyers are almost as much divided as the unlearned public on the conduct of Mr. Eyre, and it would not be right, even if it were possible, to disguise this fact.

The Times, 11 June 1868

[N]o one knows what negroes are and what treatment they require until he has lived among them, and the benevolent but unscientific theory that all men and all races of men are equal misleads an immense number of people who ought to know better.

The Globe, 4 June 1868

For weeks on end in 1865 and 1866, even as late as April 1867, the Jamaica controversy had dominated public literature and debate. By the close of 1868, however, Jamaica had been overtaken by (what *The Times* called) 'a succession of stirring events at home and abroad'.[1] In the domestic sphere Jamaica was displaced by the wrangle over parliamentary reform, and by Fenian violence in Ireland and then England herself. The Jamaica affair also had to compete for attention with a sensational military expedition to Abyssinia.[2] The progress of

---

[1] *The Times* (2 May 1868), 10.

[2] After the Reform Bill passed in August 1867, the Derby Government funded and despatched a substantial military force to rescue British consular officials and missionaries being held captive in Abyssinia. See generally, Ian Hernon, *Massacre and Retribution: Forgotten Wars of the Nineteenth Century* (Stroud, 1998), 99–129.

this operation was followed with unflagging interest and, for the most part, patriotic pride.[3] In short, this was very far from a hospitable climate in which to mount new criminal prosecutions of Edward Eyre.

At the close of 1867 the leaders of the Jamaica Committee did not bother even to claim that their cause was widely supported. Indeed, in virtually every quarter of English political life, the idea of persisting in the criminal prosecution of Eyre was viewed either with disdain or outright contempt. Most of the (few) journalists who had supported the Committee's original criminal prosecutions now urged them to quit the field.[4] Thus, when the Jamaica Committee announced in January 1868 that it would commence a new private prosecution of Eyre for the murder of Gordon, they were vigorously denounced in almost every quarter. When the renewed prosecution failed, and when the Committee had the temerity to persist against Eyre on still different criminal charges, most English journalists thought that the leaders of the Committee had taken leave of their senses. The mission of the Committee, so the catch-phrase went, had degenerated from prosecution to persecution.

But leaders of the Jamaica Committee were nothing if not zealous. Two days after the grand jury decision in *Nelson and Brand*, on 12 April 1867, the executive already had resolved to prosecute Eyre a second time.[5] But there were impediments. As in the past, the Committee did not make a move until they had received copious legal advice. When this advice was in hand, the Committee needed to find more money before retaining trial lawyers. Before these tasks could be completed, however, a number of vital witnesses left England for Jamaica. Then, in late May 1867, the Committee's detectives reported that Eyre and his family had left Shropshire. Eyre's whereabouts remained unknown until August, when he was finally spotted on a street in Southampton. But before the Committee could commence criminal proceedings against him there, Eyre and his family had sailed for Europe. Eyre remained abroad for many months. The leaders of the Committee were dismayed but not deterred. Eyre was kept under close watch in France and then Belgium.[6] Charges were to be laid against him as soon as he returned to England. There was nothing to do but wait.

That the Committee had come to be so profoundly out of step with their country's preoccupations and sympathies, and yet soldiered on with their programme, is among the most revealing things about it. While the Committee doubtless would have welcomed broad public support, it was never viewed as essential. Going to court to settle issues of law and constitution is not by its nature a 'popular' or democratic cause, either in its aims or methods. The Committee existed as a

---

[3] *Annual Register* (1867), 156–7; Spencer Walpole, *The History of Twenty-Five Years, 1855–1880*, vol. ii (London, 1904), 282–3.

[4] For the opinion that the Jamaica Committee had long outstayed its usefulness, see, for instance, the *Pall Mall Gazette* (31 July 1868), 2.　　　　　[5] *JC Minutes*, 24 May; 8, 19 Aug. 1867.

[6] Eyre was followed from Dover to Paris and then to Brussels. The Committee's detective reported on Eyre's lifestyle and reception, and on matters as trivial as the 'bright new suits of livery' being worn by Eyre's servants. *JC Minutes*, 7 Oct. 1867.

means of enforcing what were seen as the basic legal commitments of the English nation. Its single and unwavering goal was to provide an occasion for a high court judge – an unelected official – to vindicate what was viewed as the country's 'true' constitution. More specifically, the Committee wanted to provide an opportunity (in the form of a criminal case) for a high court judge to pronounce that the summary arrest, court martial, and execution of civilians was illegal even when done under the banner of martial law. Such a ruling, it was understood, would reinforce the hallowed principle that British civilian and military officials everywhere and always were accountable to the common law. The Committee held fast to these goals and assumptions even when they were frustrated, first by rural magistrates, then by urban grand jurors. In fact, the rejection of the first two prosecutions only steeled the Committee to commence a third. If they did not relish the disdain and vilification that this decision attracted, neither were they deeply troubled by it. The Jamaica Committee were slaves to principle not popularity.

It is striking about Mill and the other leaders of the Committee that in the face of severe setbacks they remained tenaciously optimistic that the English legal system would ultimately yield the main prize. Even the damaging equivocations of Lord Chief Justice Cockburn were not enough to discourage this belief. The Committee were supremely confident that if one of their prosecutions actually got to trial, if their lawyers were given full opportunity to present evidence and argue law, then as night follows day the presiding judge would provide them with the decision they wanted. Moreover, not for one second did the leaders of the Committee doubt that such a decision would establish permanent limits on the use of state power, limits which politicians, administrators, and military men would be bound to respect. As for Eyre, he never faltered in his belief that the true *raison d'être* of the Committee was to torment the men who had saved Jamaica. What is interesting about Eyre, then, is that he *shared* with the Jamaica Committee the belief, in his case the fear, that judges like Cockburn might sacrifice him to the gods of Whig constitutionalism.

In this final chapter of the study we will trace the genesis of the final attempts by the Jamaica Committee to use the vehicle of criminal prosecution to vindicate their jurisprudence of power in the English courts. In February and March 1868 the Committee brought new charges against Eyre, first for murder and then under the Colonial Governors Act. After some legal setbacks the Committee's lawyers persuaded a police court magistrate to send a bill of indictment against Eyre before the Middlesex grand jury. In May 1868, the grand jury was charged by Sir Colin Blackburn, the senior subordinate judge of the Queen's Bench. After a long and detailed address, Blackburn recommended that the grand jury dismiss the indictment. When Blackburn's charge was accepted by the grand jury, the incident touched off the most public and acrimonious dispute between high court justices in the Victorian period, perhaps in all English legal history. The charge also terminated the efforts of the Committee to secure its goals through the criminal courts.

These events raise a number of historical questions. Why and how did the Jamaica Committee reformulate its legal strategy? Whom did they retain to prosecute Edward Eyre, and what explains their choice? How did the Eyre Defence Committee orchestrate the defence of the former Governor? How was it that Blackburn was assigned to charge the grand jury in *The Queen v. Edward Eyre*? How did Blackburn comprehend the legal issues raised by the case? How did he comprehend the law of martial law? We will discover that Blackburn's vision of the Eyre prosecution differed markedly from that of the Lord Chief Justice. How and why did it differ, and why did Cockburn lash out so bitterly and publicly against Blackburn's view of the law? How was this intra-judicial conflict compassed by political and legal journalists? What were their ramifications for the public image and prestige of the English high courts? Where did these developments leave the law of martial law? What does the episode reveal about the legal and political commitments of the judiciary? How did the Jamaica Committee react to these developments? Were its leaders correct when they claimed to have achieved its central aims?

I. The Second Criminal Prosecution of Edward Eyre

In the early summer of 1867, the former Governor Eyre thought himself the most harassed and persecuted man in England. His efforts to avert a potentially catastrophic rebellion in Jamaica, though many of his countrymen thought them nothing short of heroic, had cost him his career and pension. Although Eyre had staved off one criminal prosecution for murder, he was certain that a second prosecution loomed, perhaps for crimes under the Colonial Governors Act. Eyre also was the principal defendant in two civil actions arising from the suppression.[7] Although most journalists believed that there was little chance that a criminal case against Eyre would ever get to trial, Eyre himself was not so sanguine. He certainly did not assume that the professional judges would take his part. In the wake of the *Nelson and Brand* case, Eyre complained bitterly to Murchison about the 'violent partisanship of the Lord Chief Justice'.[8] In a letter to his barrister, Hardinge Giffard, written in April 1867, Eyre worried that in the next prosecution the Committee would proceed by direct (or 'preferred') indictment, 'and thereby force a trial without a chance of the interposition of the good sense of justice of an English Jury'.[9] He confessed that he was loath to be 'left to the tender mercies of Chief Justice Cockburn', who, Eyre snidely added, 'would act as immorally in this

---

[7] Eyre claimed that these lawsuits had been 'got up' by the Jamaica Committee, a charge which the Committee denied. Privately Eyre feared that years might pass before these cases were resolved. Eyre to Murchison, 14 Aug. 1867, Murchison Papers, *BL* Add. MS. 46,126, f. 112. See also below, Epilogue.

[8] In August 1867 Eyre wrote to Murchison to complain that the 'civil actions begun months ago make no progress and may so remain, or only advance a step or two for years'. Ibid.

[9] Eyre to Hardinge Giffard, 17 Apr. 1867, Giffard Papers, *BL* Add. MS. 56,373.

further capacity as he is said to do in his private life'.[10] Eyre wanted to know what might be done to avert a second prosecution.

The answer was that nothing could be done. But before a new prosecution was commenced the Eyre Defence Committee did take some action. In late April, a deputation led by Murchison attempted to intercede with the Derby Government to restore Eyre's pension, advocating his cause to the new Colonial Secretary, Lord Buckingham. They did not succeed. Buckingham refused to consider Eyre's case until all of the criminal and civil litigation against him had been resolved. Buckingham also refused to predict that Eyre's pension would be restored even if everything eventually came right for the former Governor. When the Government's intransigence on this point became a matter of public record, Eyre was convinced that it had only lent 'encouragement to the Jamaica Committee to "persevere" '. Frustrated by the 'suspense, anxiety and annoyance' of the civil litigation, worried about another criminal prosecution, and (according to self-pitying letters to Murchison) in order to save money ('I have not the means to live in England as I have been accustomed to live'),[11] he resolved to remove his family to a less expensive residence in continental Europe. He left England in August 1867.

Eyre was absent the country until January 1868. Although the Jamaica Committee had kept track of his movements in Europe, in the end they did not have to rely on spies for his whereabouts. Eyre returned England bent on having all of the legal cases against him 'terminated one way or another'.[12] Accordingly, when he arrived in London his solicitor was instructed to visit the offices of William Shaen, and to inform the Committee of his intention to submit to prosecution. At an executive meeting of 18 February, Shaen informed his colleagues that Mr. Eyre was 'evidently tired of the delay, and wants the matter [of his prosecution] settled'. Shaen had received Eyre's undertaking that he would remain at a specific London address long enough to establish the jurisdiction of the Bow Street Police Court. This information provoked yet another debate, as one member put it, 'on the propriety of going on with the matter'.[13] Two members of the Committee[14] moved a resolution to abandon the second criminal prosecution of Eyre. (It is not clear whether the objection was against prosecution for murder or prosecution 'full stop'.) Once again, Mill made the most forceful and decisive interjection. He told the Committee that 'rather than to give up the prosecution he would go on with it at his own expense'. This intervention, Chesson recorded in his diary, 'virtually settled the affair and the resolution was negatived by a decided majority'. The prosecutions were to proceed, even in the absence of unanimous support from the executive.

The Committee's decision prompted Lindsey Aspland, an executive member and barrister, to communicate his resignation to Mill. It was Aspland's view that the

---

[10] Eyre to Hardinge Giffard, 17 Apr. 1867, Giffard Papers, *BL* Add. MS. 56,373.

[11] Eyre to Murchison, 14 Aug. 1867, Murchison Papers, *BL* Add. MS. 46,126, f. 112.

[12] As quoted in *CD*, 18 Feb. 1868. Eyre later took umbrage at the suggestion that he had fled prosecution. Eyre to *The Times* (27 Apr. 1868), 10.   [13] Ibid.

[14] They were Edward Stanley and George Hopwood, two men not previously mentioned in the minutes of the Jamaica Committee.

Committee had exhausted every prudent option in trying to bring Eyre to justice. It was time to abandon him to the 'contempt' of public opinion. In Mill's reply to Aspland's letter, he was emphatic that there was a compelling reason for the Committee to stay the course with the law: 'ours is, morally, a protest against a series of atrocious crimes, & politically an assertion of the authority of the criminal law over public delinquents. This protest & vindication must be made now or never.'[15] Because the aims of the Committee had nothing to do with popular or party politics, but rather a point of fundamental principle, it did not matter that they were distasteful or widely disliked. Nor did it deter Mill that the decision to renew the prosecution of Eyre had provoked some men to threaten his life.[16] What mattered was the moral goal, the ultimate victory of law over licence. It was the duty of the Committee to exploit every 'unexhausted chance' to secure the victory of law, lest it become complicit with its defeat.

Having committed itself to another prosecution, the Committee needed still to resolve the important and delicate business of selecting trial lawyers. As matters stood in January 1868, it was highly unlikely that Fitzjames Stephen would be offered the brief. As we have seen, only a few months previously Mill (and some of the other leading Committee members) had been unsparingly critical of Stephen for having made complimentary remarks about Eyre at Market Drayton.[17] Stephen was also on record as being 'strongly adverse' to another prosecution of Eyre. It is difficult to fathom, then, why Chesson recorded in his diary that 'Stephen was actually to have been retained [for the second Eyre prosecution], but even he seems to have become conscious of the absurdity of his position and to have written such a letter as compelled Mr. Shaen to retain new counsel.'[18] Astonishingly, for all of the acrimony between the Committee and Stephen, the majority of executive members had been prepared to fall back on the devil they knew. Only when Stephen formally withdrew his name did they endeavour to find a new man.

Their first alternate choice, the eminent barrister Sir John Quain Q.C., declined the brief because of previous commitments.[19] But by chance Shaen quickly succeeded in getting another qualified man. While crossing the street in legal London before the executive meeting of 18 February, Shaen recognized Sir Robert Collier Q.C., the former Solicitor General (in Lord Russell's last government). Knowing his reputation as an able lawyer and Liberal parliamentarian, Shaen offered him the brief on the spot. Collier had been delighted to accept, adding that he was gratified to 'represent the Committee's views which are his own'.[20]

In some respects, however, Collier was an awkward choice. In his favour he was widely regarded as a fine and experienced lawyer who, at the age of 51, had gained eminence both on the Western Circuit and, after 1859, as Judge-Advocate and

---

[15] Mill to Aspland, 23 Feb. 1868, in Mineka and Lindley (eds.), *Later Letters*, no. 1192.
[16] As Mill informed Goldwin Smith in May 1868, 'I receive abusive letters at the rate of three or four a week, & the other day I received one threatening me with assassination.' Ibid., no. 1247.
[17] *JC Minutes*, 18 Feb. 1868.   [18] *CD*, 18 Feb. 1868.   [19] Ibid.   [20] Ibid.

Counsel for the Admiralty.[21] Indeed, even Finlason, no admirer of the Jamaica Committee, regarded Collier as nothing less than 'a great Crown lawyer',[22] one who possessed an unusually thorough knowledge of military law. Collier was also a well-connected Liberal politician who had held a seat in Parliament since 1852. In 1863 he had been promoted by Lord Russell to the office of Solicitor General. During the Derby Government, Collier remained as part of Gladstone's inner circle. (In fact, when the Liberals returned to power later in 1868, Collier became the Attorney General.) Which brings us to the reasons why Collier might not have been the most felicitous choice as senior counsel in the prosecution of Eyre. During the first eight months of the Jamaica affair, he had been one of the Crown's two senior law officers. In this period not only had he *not* urged the criminal prosecution of Eyre (he was not the Attorney General and the incident was under investigation by the Royal Commission), but he had co-signed memoranda of law, now part of the public record, which set forth positions on martial law (and related matters) contrary to those that were to be advanced in the forthcoming case. In these memoranda Collier had endorsed (from the perspective of the Jamaica Committee) a number of potentially embarrassing legal propositions.[23] When Collier was retained in February 1868, these memoranda already had been discussed in public journals and by Finlason.[24] He nonetheless was offered, and eagerly accepted, the prosecution brief.

II. 'I Am in England!': A Return to Bow Street

On 27 February 1868, Collier (assisted by the reliable second, Horne Payne), together with the usual complainants, Mill and Taylor, appeared at Bow Street to obtain a warrant for the arrest of Edward Eyre, not for charges under the Colonial Governors Act, but for being an accessory to the murder of Gordon.[25] Once again, the presiding magistrate was Sir Thomas Henry. The Committee had decided to pursue Eyre on the same theory of liability in murder that had failed (before the

[21] Pugsley, *Oxford DNB*, online 5921; *The Times* (28 Oct. 1886), 6; *Solicitors' Journal* (30 Oct. 1868), 14.   [22] Finlason, letter to the *Law Times* (8 June 1868), 64–5.
[23] One was that the 'Legislature of Jamaica was fully competent' to pass legislation enabling the Governor of the colony (with the assent of his Council of War) to proclaim martial law. Another memorandum informed Cardwell that where a proclamation of martial law was justified by state emergency, 'no limit can be placed *a priori*, to the powers exercisable'. Still another subscribed to a limited doctrine of martial law as the Crown's 'unquestionable right to meet war with war, in case of an armed insurrection against its authority...and in so much as the exercise of summary military authority...is unavoidably necessary, *flagrante bello*'. See, for example, Law Officers to Cardwell, 24 Jan. 1866, *CO* 885/1.
[24] See, for instance, Finlason's reference to Collier in the *Law Times* (8 June 1867), 64.
[25] It is worth noting that the Committee might have proceeded against Eyre by way of preferred indictment directly to the grand jury, bypassing the police court. But thinking that this procedure would be seen as unfair to the accused, the Committee declined to do so. *Solicitors' Journal* (25 Apr. 1868), 514; *CD*, 3 Mar. 1868.

grand jury) in *Nelson and Brand*. This was an interesting and risky legal tack. On the positive side of the ledger, the Committee could rely on the professional knowledge and demeanour of the magistrate. They knew that if they were to present Sir Thomas with a sound legal case and relevant evidence, he would not permit extraneous considerations to interfere with his duty. In a nearly identical case, moreover, Henry had committed Nelson and Brand to the grand jury. But, on the other side of the ledger, the (lay) magistrates of Market Drayton already had refused to issue process against Eyre. More significantly, a grand jury, charged by no less an authority than the Lord Chief Justice of England, had thrown out the bill against Nelson and Brand. Did Henry have the authority either to ignore or overrule these decisions? The Jamaica Committee had staked what was left of its credibility on the theory that he did.

It is not clear why the Committee decided to start a new prosecution for murder. Neither the minutes of executive meetings nor Chesson's diary provide clear answers. What is clear, however, is that Mill believed that Eyre was, in his words, a 'great public criminal' whose conduct in Jamaica merited the most serious charge that could be brought.[26] But at the same time Mill could only have been aware that there were high legal hurdles to clear before any Eyre prosecution could be brought to trial. At this point he could be certain only that there would have to be a process hearing in the Police Court, and that their barrister would make submissions on the relevant law and evidence. But because he could not be certain that the case would go farther, Mill believed that it was of 'great importance that [Collier's] speech should be correctly and fully reported'.[27] In fact, Mill invested so much importance in this speech that he arranged for a shorthand writer to record it verbatim for publication in the *Daily News*.[28]

Collier tried to anticipate objections from the bench.[29] He began by explaining why Eyre had not been prosecuted with Nelson and Brand in 1867 (he was not then residing within the jurisdiction of the Middlesex court)[30]. He then moved on to the stickier issue of the negative result in the prosecution of Eyre on the same charge at Market Drayton. On this point, Collier submitted that one magistrate was not bound by the previous decision of another. In the case at bar, Sir Thomas was entitled to exercise 'his own discretion'.[31] Moreover, Collier asked the judge to recall that the decision at Market Drayton 'was given prior to the delivery of the charge of the Lord Chief Justice to the grand jury in reference to the case of Nelson and Brand'. Had this 'luminous statement of martial law' been available to the Shropshire magistrates, he suggested, 'they would have come to a different conclusion'. Collier then turned to the motivations of the complainants, Mill and Taylor (the Jamaica Committee was not mentioned). In England, it often behooved private citizens to ensure that serious crimes did not go unpunished. Collier assured the court that in

---

[26] Mill to Walker, 26 Feb. 1868, *Later Letters*, no. 1194.   [27] Ibid.   [28] Ibid.
[29] Just as in the prosecution of Nelson and Brand, the jurisdiction of the English courts was established by Sir John Jervis' Act, 11 & 12 Vict., c. 4, and by 24 & 25 Vict., c. 100, s. 9.
[30] All quotes from the *Pall Mall Gazette* (27 Feb. 1868), 8–9.   [31] Ibid.

the case at bar the complainants 'were certainly not influenced by any personal motives, but by a very painful sense of duty, believing that a great crime had been committed – that a British subject had been put to death without warrant, and under circumstances that constituted what the law called murder'. This was a case, Collier added, which affected the 'tenure under which every man in the colonies, and indeed in the British dominion, holds his life and property'.

When he was finished this prologue, Collier provided Henry with a concise summary of the alleged facts of the case, and the legal grounds on which the facts gave rise to an inference that Edward Eyre had been an accessory to murder. While the newspapers did not report the specifics, Collier's arguments were said by one reporter to be 'to a great extent, identical with those urged by Fitzjames Stephen in the case of Nelson and Brand'.[32] These arguments were buttressed with citations from Cockburn's charge.

Henry listened to Collier's submissions without interruption. He then made a terse ruling on the application. He would not grant it. His reasons were straightforward. Although it was no obstacle to the application that it had been rejected by other magistrates, the 'judicial investigation' that had occurred in the case of *The Queen v. Nelson and Brand* was another matter.[33] In that case, the 'highest authority has laid down the law on that subject, and has charged a jury, putting before them all of the arguments you [Collier] have used'.[34] The grand jury of Middlesex had heard an exhaustive and authoritative charge on the relevant law as it applied to two parties who had participated directly in Gordon's trial and execution, and then had not found a true bill. In effect, the grand jury 'decided, not only that the charge of murder was not established, but that there was not even a *prima facie* case to go before a jury'. In his twenty-eight years as a magistrate, Sir Thomas could not recall even a single case in which 'a bill against the principals on a charge of murder had been ignored, a magistrate has afterwards granted a warrant against an accessory'. When Collier repeated his submission that the grand jury's decision was not 'conclusive', Sir Thomas referred to what he thought was the decisive point. The Lord Chief Justice had told the grand jury that if they thought that Nelson and Brand 'ought not to be harassed by criminal proceedings, you will say so by ignoring the indictment'. So the grand jury did say, and Sir Thomas thought it fruitless to cause them to say it again.

This latest legal foray into the courts met with a cold reception, most especially in the conservative papers. The *London Review* thought it 'ill-advised'.[35] The reaction of the Middlesex jury to the Nelson and Brand case underlined the 'utter hopelessness' of further prosecutions. The most likely outcome of any new action against Eyre, the *Review* warned, would be to make him into 'a kind of martyr, and of earning him the commiseration of the whole community'. The *Sun* condemned the Jamaica Committee for 'misguided zeal and ill-directed energies'.[36] As for the

[32] *Pall Mall Gazette* (27 Feb. 1868), 8–9.   [33] As quoted in *The Times* (28 Feb. 1868), 6.
[34] *Solicitors' Journal* (29 Feb. 1868), 363.   [35] *London Review* (29 Feb. 1868), 200.
[36] *Sun* (28 Feb. 1868).

Law Times, it relished the fact that this most recent 'persecution' of Eyre had been ignominiously defeated: 'these repeated endeavours to ruin a public servant by putting him to never-ending costs deserves, as it will receive, the severest reprobation.'[37] As for *The Times*, while it found much to regret in the conduct of the former Governor, it hoped that it had 'heard the last of Governor Eyre and the Jamaica Committee'.[38] Eyre's offences had been political rather than legal; for those he had been adequately punished by loss of position and disgrace. 'Those who would make him a murderer', *The Times* grimly concluded, 'provoke those who would make him a hero.' The *Globe* was not nearly so restrained.[39] In an editorial called 'Mill versus Eyre', the magazine decried the humiliating spectacle of an eminent philosopher ('one of the very few making any pretensions to that character in this practical nineteenth century') 'quite willing to parade himself as the remorseless persecutor of a public servant', and by a distinguished lawyer 'gravely asking an inferior court of justice to reverse the judgment of an English jury, and to violate the law of the realm *as expounded by himself in his previous capacity as legal adviser to the Crown*' (emphasis added).[40] While Mill lacked the dignity and judgement that befitted an important thinker, Collier had revealed himself 'an inconsistent advocate pleading in direct opposition to one of his own professional opinions'. Together the two men had orchestrated what could be explained only as a 'stunt' for the 'ultra-Liberal party'. Nothing could be 'more treasonable to the commonwealth', the *Globe* railed, 'than the machinations of the Jamaica Committee, with its philosophic head and legal cat's paw'.

Since 1865 England's other legal weekly, the *Solicitors' Journal*, had been cautiously supportive of the goal of the Jamaica Committee to 'vindicate' the constitution. But now, two years and three prosecutions later, it thought that the 'process of "vindication" has gone far enough'.[41] Similarly, the *Daily News*, a paper that had long championed the Committee's aims and methods, now doubted the efficacy and wisdom of further prosecutions.[42] The Jamaica Committee, the paper contended, 'have done their duty to society ... They have proved that the old association of law and liberty is as dear to Englishmen of this generation as it was to those of ages gone by'. The likely result of another charge was to cause 'delay in the civil proceedings which are being taken against Mr. Eyre by private individuals whom his acts have brought to ruin'. It was to these actions that the Committee and its supporters were now to look for justice.

The executive of the Jamaica Committee met again on 3 March.[43] Shaen briefed members on the failure of the Bow Street proceedings. He then read a report from Collier recommending that a case be mounted against Eyre under the

---

[37] *Law Times* (7 Mar. 1868), 343.   [38] *The Times* (28 Feb. 1868), 6.

[39] *Globe* (28 Feb. 1868).

[40] The article alluded to the fact that in one of his memoranda, Collier (with Palmer) had concluded that the proclamation of martial law under the Jamaica statute gave 'as complete an indemnity as the Indemnity Act itself'. Ibid.   [41] *Solicitors' Journal* (7 Mar. 1868), 373.

[42] *Daily News* (28 Feb. 1868).   [43] *JC Minutes*, 4 Mar. 1868.

Colonial Governors Act. Collier opined that the Government's indifference to such charges was not to be viewed as an obstacle. Under the Colonial Governors Act, he explained, executive officers of the Crown could be prosecuted privately in England for any crime (except if it was a felony[44]) committed in the empire. There was agreement among those in attendance that another prosecution should be mounted. But on what charge? For his own part Shaen recommended that the Committee proceed by a preferred indictment for murder. This idea was supported by Harrison. The issue was debated at some length. Once again, the decisive intervention was made by Mill, who spoke in favour of Collier's plan. According to Chesson's diary, Mill's endorsement 'carried the point'.[45] Collier was to be instructed to commence all necessary preparations for a new prosecution. The caveats and criticisms, even of the friendly press, had fallen on deaf ears.

The Colonial Governors Act was passed by Parliament during the reign of William III in 1700,[46] after Britain's first century of experience in the administration of a far-flung empire. The Act reflected the anxiousness of Whig legislators to extend the rule of domestic law over executive officers of the Crown who exercised public authority 'beyond the seas'. In the preamble to the Act, it was observed that 'divers governors, lieutenant governors or commanders in chief of plantations and colonies...have taken advantage, and have not been deterred from oppressing His Majesty's subjects within their respective governments and commands'. The authors of a broad range of 'crimes and offences' while abroad were henceforth to be answerable exclusively in the Court of King's Bench.[47] For the next 100 years the Colonial Governors Act sat in the statute books unimplemented. Then, in 1802[48] the statute was amended in the wake of the celebrated murder trial of Governor Wall.[49] In the preamble to the amended statute, Parliament reaffirmed that 'persons holding or exercising publick [sic] employments out of Great Britain often escape punishment for offences committed by them for want of courts having sufficient jurisdiction'. The former statute was revised so as to apply to the holders of minor public offices, and to give the authorities discretion to try an official either in the locality of the offence or in England.[50] In 1804, General Thomas Picton, accused of torturing a woman when he was the military governor of the island of Trinidad, was the first public servant to be prosecuted for offences under the revised statute.[51]

[44] The non-applicability of the statute to felonies was decided in *Rex v. Shawe*, (1816) 5 M. & S. 403; 105 E.R. 1098.   [45] *CD*, 3 Mar. 1868.

[46] 11 & 12 Wm. III, c. 12.

[47] Prior to the passage of the Colonial Governors Act, the only crimes committed abroad for which the British courts exerted jurisdiction were murder and treason. This jurisdiction was established by 33 Henry VIII, c. 23.   [48] 42 & 43 Geo. III, c. 85.

[49] Wall was prosecuted in England for the flogging to death of a soldier on the West African island of Goree. See David Dean, 'Joseph Wall of Goree Island', 57 *African Affairs* (1958), 295–301.

[50] See generally, Roberts-Wray, *Commonwealth and Colonial Law*, 312–13. The revised statute also provided prosecutors with new allowances in terms of procedure and evidence. The statute clearly was designed to facilitate prosecutions.

[51] See Donald Thomas, 'The Trial of Thomas Picton (1806)', in Donald Thomas (ed.), *State Trials: The Public Conscience*, vol. ii (London, 1972), 158–63.

Although Picton was convicted, his trial did not portend a wave of new charges. In 1816, in the only other prosecution under the Act, it was held that the option of trying an executive official in England did not apply to a felony.[52] This decision affected the criminal prosecution of the former Governor Eyre in 1868.

Under the provisions of the Colonial Governors Act, complainants were entitled to proceed by preferred indictment to the grand jury.[53] When they so proceeded, however, the accused was deprived of the safeguard of a 'preliminary inquiry before the grand jury'. Given the problems that the Jamaica Committee had experienced with grand juries (both in Jamaica and England), the more direct form of prosecution offered obvious benefits. In the result, the Committee, the *Solicitors' Journal* noted, 'thought it more proper to apply in the first instance to a justice for a summons'.[54] This was both a principled and strategic choice. As Collier later stated, the preferred indictment is 'not a fair proceeding toward the person charged, and is a disadvantage to the prosecutor, inasmuch as there are ... no depositions for the judge wherewith to charge the jury'.

The new proceedings were commenced by Collier at Bow Street on 20 April 1868. The prosecution alleged that Eyre had committed twenty-one distinct misdemeanours under the Colonial Governors Act. The list of charges related to the 'illegal and oppressive' proclamation of martial law, and to a list of unlawful arrests, trials, and punishments. After Collier specified the charges, presented evidence (including evidence that Eyre dwelled within the court's jurisdiction), and summed up the prosecution's case for a summons, Vaughan granted the application. The summons directed Eyre to appear in the Bow Street court on 22 April. But when the case was called two days later (Eyre now in attendance), Vaughan suddenly announced that he lacked jurisdiction to commit the case directly to the Queen's Bench. His reasons were highly technical.[55] Collier's arguments to the contrary were rejected. Vaughan granted a stay of proceedings subject to the complainants' motion to compel (by a writ of *mandamus*) Vaughan to commit the case to trial in the Queen's Bench.

The Jamaica Committee was willing to spend the extra time and money to remove this new obstruction. The first hearing on the *mandamus* writ was held before a panel of the Justices of the Queen's Bench on 30 April. After a brief exchange with the Lord Chief Justice, it was decided that the panel (sitting *in banco*)[56] was not entitled to grant the order without a formal hearing in which the position of the magistrate might be fully explicated and defended by counsel. The motion was finally heard on 8 May and, interestingly enough, *Fitzjames Stephen*

---

[52] See generally, Roberts-Wray, *Commonwealth and Colonial Law*, 313.

[53] *Solicitors' Journal* (25 Apr. 1868), 514.

[54] *Pall Mall Gazette* (30 Apr. 1868), 9; *The Times* (2 May 1868), 9.

[55] Vaughan explained that the relevant provision of the applicable statute (11 & 12 Vict., c. 42, s. 25), permitted him only to bind over the witnesses to appear at a court of 'oyer and terminer', and that the Queen's Bench was not such a court. *Solicitors' Journal* (25 Apr. 1868), 514.

[56] *In banco* hearings were held at Westminster Hall in order to settle disputed points of law prior to trial.

appeared to make submissions with Collier. (Clearly Stephen was not so much estranged from the Committee that he would turn down an opportunity to address a subtle point of criminal procedure.) As events turned out, however, the Queen's Bench granted the writ without asking to hear from the Committee lawyers. Speaking for the court, Blackburn ruled that since the magistrate held that there was evidence sufficient to merit a trial, he had jurisdiction to send the Eyre case before the grand jury.

With this detour out of the way, the renewed prosecution of Eyre was commenced before Vaughan on 15 May. It is abundantly clear from the transcript that this case was treated with great seriousness on both sides. Collier did not take for granted that he would get the committal. He endeavoured to put in a very strong and comprehensive case, one designed to cast Eyre in the worst possible light. (Not the slightest trace here of the compliments that had been paid to Eyre by Stephen.) On behalf of the defence, Hardinge Giffard vehemently resisted every aspect of the prosecution's case. Neither side entertained pat assumptions about the outcome.

When the hearing commenced Mill and Taylor were present in the courtroom as complainants. Collier and Horne Payne introduced themselves as counsel for the prosecution. Eyre was in court, represented once again by Giffard and Poland. His jurisdiction no longer at issue, Vaughan's task was to determine whether the prosecution had made out a case *prima facie*, one meriting the committal of Eyre to the grand jury.

Collier opened his case by stating that the complainants might have prosecuted the accused for murder instead of misdemeanour, but that 'for his own part he [Collier] felt it to be a great relief not to find it his duty to urge the more serious charge'.[57] The facts of the case were not in dispute. The prosecution's case was 'entirely a question of law', specifically, the liability of a colonial Governor for the proclamation and enforcement of martial law. Collier offered that British colonies were 'generally well governed' and that for this reason there 'had been no authority as to the construction to be put upon' the Colonial Governors Act. But based on the language of that statute, Collier submitted, it was self-evident that colonial officials might be prosecuted in the Queen's Bench for any 'oppression' of Her Majesty's subjects. And if the issuance of a proclamation of martial law was 'not oppressive,' Collier 'did not know what would be considered oppressive'.

Collier then contended that the proclamation issued by Eyre was 'such a one as no governor could have the power to issue. It amounted, in fact, to a declaration of war against all the inhabitants of Jamaica, whether white or black'. In essence, the Governor had tried to give power to his soldiers to kill men without trial. This was a power that 'the Crown of England had no authority to issue at home'. If it could not be issued by the Crown in Britain, it could not be 'delegated to an inferior power' in the colonies. Collier conceded only this much to the defence: that the common law of necessity permitted a soldier to kill persons openly engaged in

---

[57] *Pall Mall Gazette* (15 May 1868), 8.

armed rebellion. However, if 'he overcame and bound his enemy he could not kill him then, but must give him up to the ordinary tribunals'. In support of these propositions Collier cited the decision of Lord Mansfield in the Gordon riots case.[58] Collier also quoted extensively from the charge of Cockburn in *The Queen v. Nelson and Brand.* While he paid no compliments to Eyre, Collier did not think it necessary to his case to impute 'corrupt motives' to the accused. Eyre's state of mind had 'nothing to do with his case'.[59] The issue was whether certain of the former Governor's actions in Jamaica were illegal. If they were, 'the responsibility must rest with the author of those acts, who should have made himself acquainted with the proper limit to his authority'.[60] The entire purpose of the prosecution, Collier explained, was to cause the limits of a Governor's authority to proclaim martial law to be 'fully and fairly argued' before a high court. If Vaughan asked questions of these submissions, they were not recorded by reporters. When Collier finished his preliminary submissions, he began to call evidence for the prosecution.

In order to establish the charges *prima facie*, Collier read into evidence some of Eyre's despatches from the parliamentary Blue Books, as well as his testimony before the Jamaica Royal Commission. When this was done, he called witnesses. Some (Shaen and a clerk from the Colonial Office) were called to prove the authenticity of relevant documents. Others (Augustus Lake, the Jamaican newspaper reporter and, as *The Times* noted, 'man of colour'[61]) testified as eyewitnesses to various 'oppressions' which Eyre had either ordered or countenanced during the martial law. Lake told the court how Dr. Bruce, an elderly friend of the witness, was arrested outside the area of martial law only to be transported and imprisoned at Morant Bay. Lake also testified to the travails of Alexander Phillips. Before he finished giving evidence, the hearing was adjourned for three days.

When the hearing resumed on 19 May 1868 Collier finished with Lake, and the witness was cross-examined by Giffard. Giffard made some headway. Lake was led to admit that, fourteen months earlier, his passage to England had been paid for by the Jamaica Committee, and since that time he had been gainfully employed as a clerk by 'Messrs. Shaen and Roscoe, the attorneys for this prosecution'.[62] That was not all. Giffard asked Lake if he knew that Bruce and Phillips had commenced civil actions against Eyre. Giffard must have been gratified by Lake's bumbling response: he (Lake) declined 'to say whether actions have been brought by Dr. Bruce and Phillips because I don't think I should divulge the secrets of my employer – I mean I decline to answer any questions with reference to actions brought by my employers.'[63] The Jamaica Committee had always denied that it

[58] Ibid.   [59] *The Times* (16 May 1868), 12.

[60] Collier cited a case (*Rex v. Sainsbury*) in which a justice of the peace was found guilty for the illegal issuance of licenses. In that case it was held that the 'absence of corrupt motive was no answer to an indictment or an illegal act'. Ibid.   [61] Ibid.

[62] The evidence was reproduced in detail in W. F. Finlason, *Report of the Case of The Queen v. Edward Eyre on his Prosecution in the Court of Queen's Bench containing the Charge of Mr. Justice Blackburn* (London, 1868), 3.   [63] Ibid., 4.

had been moved by any personal animus. Now it had come out that at least one key witness against the accused was on the payroll of the accuser's solicitors, the same solicitors who were also overseeing civil litigation against the former Governor.

Collier's next witnesses were sailors who had been on board the naval ship *Wolverine* when Gordon was transferred from Kingston to Morant Bay. While on shore, the sailors had also witnessed acts of violence against unarmed black civilians. Under cross-questioning, one sailor described the capture, on 24 October 1865, of a ship which had run aground while carrying gunpowder, arms, and a Haitian General.[64] Here Giffard was able to adduce some support for the defence theory that Eyre had acted out of a well-grounded fear that the colony was facing an armed conspiracy of black Jamaicans backed by Haitian allies. That this theory had no basis in fact, and that Eyre knew it, did not deter Giffard.[65]

But surely the 'star' witness for the prosecution was Alexander Phillips, the black Jamaican and self-described 'gentleman' freeholder. Collier called Phillips so that he could testify to his personal suffering at the hands of Eyre and his subordinates. This was the first time that an actual victim of martial law had given such testimony in an English court. Phillips provided a harrowing account of having been arrested without charge at his place of residence (outside the jurisdiction of martial law) on the order of the Governor. Along with some other prisoners he had been handcuffed and roughly transported to Spanish Town. There, Phillips, Bruce, and another prisoner were brought before the Governor. After a brief interrogation, Eyre ordered them transported by ship to the charge of Ramsay at Morant Bay. During the next ten days of harsh captivity Phillips was forced to witness the execution of forty-nine men condemned by courts martial. Despite protestations of infirmity and ill-health, despite not having been charged or tried for a crime, Phillips was brought out into the prison yard and tied to a post. Under the supervision of a naval officer four sailors proceeded to give Phillips a hundred lashes with a 'navy cat'. After the flogging Phillips was left on the side of a nearby road. After some time lapsed Phillips was found by his brother and taken home. Some months later, the authorities charged Phillips with having conspired to foment rebellion. He was acquitted.

On cross-questioning by Giffard, Phillips was obliged to disclose a number of facts that were unflattering of his impartiality. He admitted that his passage from Jamaica had been paid for by William Shaen. Throughout his (eleven-month) stay in England Phillips had been supported from a fund raised by Louis Chamerovzow and administered through Shaen's law offices. He admitted that he was the plaintiff in an active civil suit against Eyre. He also admitted that some prominent

[64] Finlason, *Report of The Queen v. Edward Eyre*, 6.
[65] The Court did not hear that when the Haitian General established that the arms were to overthrow the government in Haiti, Eyre ordered him deported. By the end of October, some weeks before the period of martial law was ended, Eyre knew that there was no reliable evidence supporting the theory that Haitians had supported Jamaican rebels. See Heuman, *'The Killing Time'*, 158.

members of the Jamaica Committee had set up and endowed a fund 'to enable me to bring this action'. Prior to issuing the writ Phillips had used the names of Mill and Taylor 'in getting subscriptions' for the fund (although he confessed that he had lacked 'any direct authority' for this).[66] Collier was concerned enough by Giffard's cross-questioning that he re-examined his witness. Phillips then told the Court that he had not 'volunteered' to give evidence in the prosecution of Eyre, but had responded to a subpoena. He stated that he had 'nothing to do with any criminal proceedings'. His only purpose for being in England was to succeed in his civil action against Eyre. With this, Phillips was invited to stand down. Collier called another witness to enter and prove documents and closed the case for the prosecution.

Giffard, before he opened the defence, asked for Shaen to be recalled for cross-examination. At this point Giffard became very bellicose. Shaen was shown a newspaper clipping of a letter written by Charles Buxton to Mill after the committal hearings had begun. (In that letter Buxton indicated his support for the prosecution of Eyre under the Colonial Governors Act and enclosed a cheque in the sum of £300 to help defray costs.)[67] When asked how this letter had got into the newspapers, Shaen admitted that it had been given to him by Mill for immediate publication. With this Giffard turned to Vaughan, and submitted that Shaen's actions constituted a 'gross contempt of court'. The letter had been published in an effort to influence the magistrate's decision in a case *sub judice*. When Vaughan rejected this submission out of hand, Giffard tried to cause Shaen to admit that Mill and Taylor had contributed personally to a fund set up to finance the civil actions of Bruce and Phillips against Eyre. Shaen denied this, but was obliged to admit that Mill and Taylor knew about and had 'recommended' the actions both to Shaen and prospective donors as 'deserving support'.[68] Still not finished with Shaen, Giffard questioned him about the civil litigation that had been started against Eyre from his law office. Shaen described how he had filed two writs against Eyre on behalf of Bruce, but that they since had been abandoned. He explained how he expected that his fees would be paid out of a 'fund' that had been set up for this purpose. Giffard asked for the names of the persons who had contributed to the fund. He wanted to know if either or both of the complainants against Eyre, Mill and Taylor, were subscribers or sponsors. Shaen testified that the complainants had not backed Bruce's action, but offered that they *had* supported Phillips' lawsuit. For what it was worth, and it had very little to do with whether the accused had committed misdemeanours under the Colonial Governors Act, Giffard had shown that the complainants were orchestrating a multi-faceted legal campaign against Eyre.

[66] Finlason, *Report of The Queen v. Edward Eyre*, 11.

[67] As Buxton's letter explained, he was prepared once again actively to support the Jamaica Committee because the idea of prosecuting Eyre for murder finally had been abandoned, and because a judge had still to establish the 'legal limits' on the power of a colonial governor to 'inflict vengeance'. *The Times* (16 May 1868), 12. Buxton later explained his motives in a letter to his constituents published in the *Pall Mall Gazette* (25 May 1868), 6. See also Buxton's letter to *The Times* (7 Dec. 1868), 4.

[68] This in the *Morning Star* (20 May 1868), 5.

This testimony brought the second full day of evidence to a close. In all the prosecution had called six witnesses to testify that Eyre had either ordered or endorsed acts of extreme cruelty. This was many more witnesses than had been needed to justify a committal to the grand jury.[69] The Times plausibly suggested that the prosecution's evidence had been deliberately excessive and 'sensational' in order to 'create a prejudice' against the accused.[70] Giffard was seen to have had his work cut out for him in sparing Eyre from a committal.

Even though the committal hearing did not place Eyre in immediate jeopardy, the Eyre Defence Committee did not take it lightly. In a show of solidarity with the accused, Eyre was joined in the courtroom by Murchison (who sat at the counsel table) and Lord de Blaquiere (who sat on the magistrate's bench). More remarkably, de Blaquiere was flanked on the bench by none other than Sir Baldwin Leighton, the Shropshire squire–magistrate who had refused to commit Eyre to trial at Market Drayton. Then there was Giffard. It was obvious from the forceful manner of his cross-questioning that Giffard meant to offer a ferocious defence. Although it was unlikely that Giffard would succeed at this first stage of the litigation (the prosecution only having to prove its case *prima facie* before a stipendiary magistrate), he hoped to weaken the prosecution's case in the eyes both of prospective grand jurors and public opinion. So it was, then, that on the third day of the hearing, Giffard made his submissions.

Giffard's position was based on three different contentions.[71] The first was that the prosecution's case had been mounted in bad faith and was inherently unreliable. The charges had been brought by the complainants in order to pursue a personal vendetta against the accused. The complainants and their witnesses, some of whom were pursuing civil suits against the accused, had conspired to convict the former Governor on any conceivable criminal offence. In order to achieve this goal they had engaged in character assassination. While pretending to repudiate 'any imputation of corrupt motives to Mr. Eyre', claiming all the while that their only object was 'to obtain a judicial decision on an abstruse point of law',[72] the complainants in fact 'continued to circulate atrocious calumnies against him'. Giffard cited an example of the complainants' bad faith. Shaen himself had admitted that after the present proceedings had begun, Mill had instructed him to provide a private communication (Buxton's letter) to the newspapers. The letter accused Eyre of a litany of crimes and oppressions, none of which the prosecution had proved in court. Giffard thought that this was a tawdry and illegal attempt to 'influence the case'; that it was tantamount to the late prosecutors of the Fenians having circulated denunciations of the accused before their trial.[73]

[69] According to *The Times* (22 May 1868), 9.   [70] Ibid.
[71] By coming to Bow Street Leighton could only have meant to offer symbolic support for the accused. This must have been a highly unusual course of conduct for a man who was himself a magistrate. However, Leighton's presence in the courtroom, while remarked upon, was not criticized. *Morning Star* (21 May 1868), 5.   [72] *The Times* (22 May 1868), 9.
[73] Collier was permitted to respond to Giffard's opening address. To the first assertion, Collier responded that 'there had been a good deal of abuse in the papers, more abuse indeed of the prosecutors than of Mr. Eyre'. Ibid.

Giffard's second line of defence was that the prosecution had failed to prove a case *prima facie* that Eyre was guilty of any of the charges. Not only did the evidence fail to place Eyre at the scene of any of the alleged crimes, but it could not even substantiate that he had *known* of them. At the relevant times Eyre had known 'only that [some persons] had been convicted by courts martial, at one of which the Attorney General presided'.[74] There was no evidence that Eyre had ordered or even been aware of the specific acts mentioned in the indictment. For this reason, Giffard submitted, there was no case to be answered before the grand jury.[75] Giffard then argued a final line of defence: that the doctrine of *res judicata* applied to the case. By this Giffard meant that the accused had – *de facto* – twice before been acquitted of the same charges, once at Market Drayton, and then again by Sir Thomas Henry at the Bow Street court. In these different instances the charges differed in name only, and it would amount to abuse of process for the accused to be tried for them a third time.

Magistrate Vaughan quickly dispensed with the notion that any of these objections were cogent enough for him to end the hearing. He assured Giffard that even if it were true that the Jamaica Committee had tried to influence the outcome of the hearing by publishing Buxton's letter, it was of no effect. With respect to the question of Eyre's conduct and state of mind, Vaughan thought that these were issues for a jury. And with regard to the plea of *res judicata*, the magistrate took no time to conclude that the previous cases had proceeded on 'a different charge and under a different statute'. The plea, therefore, did not apply.

When it became apparent to Giffard that he was making no headway with his first submissions, he became petulant. He told Vaughan that 'he was not anxious to go on speaking for the mere sake of hearing his own voice. If the magistrate had made up his mind, he should not pursue the argument any further.'[76] Vaughan was unmoved, and replied that 'unless Mr. Giffard could address to him arguments of such cogency as to make him entirely reverse the view he had formed so far, it was his duty to send the case before the jury'. Giffard expressed his 'great discouragement' that the magistrate appeared to have 'already formed an opinion adverse to his case', but then went on with his remaining submissions.[77]

Eyre stood accused of issuing an illegal proclamation and of committing various acts of oppression against British subjects. With regard to the first accusation, Giffard repeated that it was incurably vague, and that it did not seem to entail what was the hallmark of a valid criminal charge: that the accused had *mens rea*, a guilty mind. In this vein, Giffard urged Vaughan to consider that Eyre proclaimed martial law only after having convened a Council of War. At that Council, 'all the persons in authority, all of the most intelligent people of the place   including the Chief Justice and the law officers of the Crown – came to the conclusion that

---

[74] Ibid.

[75] Collier was allowed to reply on the point, and stated that the evidence indicated that the Governor had been physically present at the place where the offences had taken place. It was for the trial jury to decide whether he ordered or knew about illegal floggings and executions.   [76] Ibid.

[77] Ibid.

the proclamation was necessary'. Whatever Eyre had done, he had done with the active encouragement of 'those persons who were his legal and constitutional advisers', men whom 'he was bound to consult'. It was nothing if not unfair that Eyre alone stood accused of what was a collective decision and responsibility. Giffard did not cite any law in support of this point. Instead, he recommended his attack on the motives of Eyre's accusers. Giffard submitted that the reason why the Jamaica Committee had not preferred an indictment directly before the grand jury (which was their right) was that they knew that 'no grand jury would find a true bill, but that a magistrate hearing the case would enable them to gratify their malignant spite'.[78] When Vaughan wondered aloud about the relevance and propriety of these remarks, Giffard reasserted his right both to question the motives of Eyre's accusers, and to suggest that the prosecution had been brought for the purpose only of causing 'vexation and annoyance'. To any honest observer, on the other hand, it was obvious that the former Governor had proclaimed and then maintained martial law because, and only because, 'the disturbed state of the island required strong measures'. None of the witnesses heard by the magistrate, Giffard contended, had been in a good position to discredit the Governor's judgement on this crucial point.

Giffard then returned to the evidence regarding the alleged oppression of individuals. It was quite proper, first, that those arrested in civilian jurisdictions had been transported to Morant Bay. In every case their offences were said to have been committed in that parish. On the same principle, Giffard offered, alleged Fenians arrested in London were often sent to Ireland for trial.[79] 'In regard to all the persons who had been arrested,' Giffard contended, 'there was at the same time reasonable cause for believing them concerned in . . . a conspiracy to overthrow the Government, to murder all the whites, and to make Jamaica a second Hayti.' At the relevant moments, then, persons such as Phillips had been real suspects in real crimes. If errors had been made by the Governor they were errors made in good faith, not ones that might later generate criminal liability. (Just as the magistrate himself would not be liable 'even if the person erroneously committed had been ill-treated in prison'.) There was no evidence that directly implicated the former Governor in any of the 'excesses or irregularities' that had been committed in Jamaica. If Mr. Eyre's attention had been called to these cruelties, Eyre would have stopped them. 'But could it be supposed', Giffard asked, 'that he [Eyre] was a sort of universal eye, seeing every detail of every occurrence?' Eyre simply had not known about any illegal or cruel conduct in time to stop it.

But some other things, Giffard submitted, the Governor had known all too well. He had known about the vagaries of the black race, of the 'Negro character'.[80] He had known that although 'capable of much ferocity in organized outrages, [negroes] were incapable of acting without leadership'. At the critical juncture, Eyre 'knew that the general populace would be easily reduced to peace

---

[78] *The Times* (22 May 1868), 9.   [79] Ibid.   [80] Ibid.

and order when they saw their leaders executed'. In adopting this strategy, Eyre, in his 'admirable promptitude, justice and wisdom, had saved a valuable colony, and preserved the lives of the respectable inhabitants of the island, whether white or coloured'. Giffard then attempted to buttress these submissions with quotations from the findings of the Royal Commission. That posed a problem. Vaughan already had ruled that this document was not admissible as evidence, and could not be the source of quotations. Giffard objected to this ruling. When his objection was overruled, Giffard once again became peevish. He stated that 'if that was the magistrate's opinion he should not address him any further'. With this Giffard sat down and made no more submissions.

Vaughan, who only weeks before had declined jurisdiction over the case, then rendered a brief judgement on the committal. Despite Giffard's 'most able address', and in spite of some personal misgivings about the prosecution, the magistrate had concluded that it was his 'duty to commit Mr. Eyre to take his trial at the next court of oyer and terminer, at the Court of Queen's Bench'.[81] There was evidence enough before the Court that amounted to a *prima facie* case on all the charges. Specifically, there was evidence that some persons had been subjected to 'cruel and oppressive acts . . . committed long after the restoration of peace'.[82] Vaughan mentioned the case of Phillips 'especially as one of great hardship, and if Mr. Eyre did not expressly sanction the treatment of Phillips, he was in the city [of Kingston] at the time, and had been in correspondence with his subordinate officers upon the subject of his detention'. With respect to the questions of law generated by the prosecution, the magistrate 'considered himself bound imperatively by the well-considered and luminous charge of the Lord Chief Justice in the case of *The Queen v. Nelson and Brand*'.[83] It was not the place of a mere magistrate to 'lay down anything as an addition or gloss upon the law as stated in that charge'. Eyre was bound over to appear on a bond of £1,000. As a matter of course, his case would come before the grand jury prior to any full-blown trial on the merits. Eyre was cautioned and then invited to make a statement in answer to the charge.

Eyre stood up, and exhibiting 'considerable agitation', spoke for himself.[84] He stated that the disgrace of the day fell not upon him, but those of his accusers who had subjected him to more than two years of 'wearing and most rancorous prosecution'. Here stood a man who had served Britain faithfully for a quarter of a century, in the last months of service 'saving indubitably a great British colony from ruin', but now finding himself 'committed to a felon's dock'. Eyre then stated that he was comforted by the certain knowledge that his persecutors 'formed but a very small section of the community'. This statement, even the *Morning Star* reported,

---

[81] Ibid.   [82] *Pall Mall Gazette* (21 May 1868), 6–7.
[83] *Morning Star* (21 May 1868), 5.
[84] The *Daily News* (21 May 1868), admittedly no friend to Edward Eyre, thought that the former Governor's speech was emblematic of a man who had 'lost his self-control' out of simple amazement 'that the indiscriminate shootings and hangings and burnings which he authorized were to become the subject of judicial inquiry'.

prompted a loud burst of applause in the court. Eyre expressed confidence in his final vindication and sat down, once again to 'renewed and tumultuous applause'. Above the din a person was heard to shout, ' "You are not alone, I am England!" '[85]

While Eyre's words were widely admired in the newspapers for their earnestness and dignity,[86] the committal hearing could only have injured the former Governor's public reputation and standing. For the first time in more than a year – for the first time ever in the capital city – the Jamaica Committee had produced sworn evidence that Eyre had either ordered or countenanced the summary execution and physical abuse of prisoners. It was equally clear that the abuses were rooted in racially motivated anger and revenge, not military necessity. 'The damaging part of the case against Mr. Eyre,' *The Times* observed, '. . . was that which showed him to have been present in person where barbarous punishments were being inflicted without any reason being given, and persons were hanged after being recommended to mercy.'[87] To be sure, *The Times* report continued, the 'evidence for the prosecution was sensational, but the same may be said with equal truth, of the arguments of the defence'. Despite his best efforts, Eyre's lawyer manifestly had been unable to slow the main thrust either of the prosecution's evidence or its law. Now it was inevitable, with Ireland simmering probably imperative, that the 'whole story of the Jamaica Rebellion will come once again under judicial cognizance'.

It was to be expected that England's most reliably radical newspapers would write approvingly of the Jamaica Committee's success at Bow Street.[88] It is more interesting that so many more moderate (even conservative voices like *The Times*) now reversed themselves, and offered at least grudging support for the idea that finally there would be a decisive legal test of the constitutional issues arising from the Jamaica suppression. The *Daily Telegraph* (a Liberal paper in 1868) was particularly firm on this point: 'after many unsuccessful efforts, some of which failed on technical grounds . . . the Jamaica Committee have at length gained a point which enables us to anticipate a solemn judicial decision on the matters debated with such acrimony for the last two years.'[89] According to the *Telegraph* there was no well-founded basis for thinking that the Jamaica Committee (Mill was named individually) were moved by any motive other than to obtain 'an authoritative exposition of the law'.[90] Some vital questions still were unanswered: 'whether the original proclamation of martial law in Jamaica was legal, and whether, if legal, it could [be] considered in force after amnesty had been declared – these are matters

---

[85] *Imperial Review*, as quoted in the *Pall Mall Gazette* (23 May 1868), 4.
[86] See review of newspaper reports in the *Pall Mall Gazette* (21 May 1868), 2. At least one man was so moved by Eyre's plight that he sent Eyre's defence fund a draft for £300. As John Humphrey wrote in a letter to Eyre, 'Every man who feels, with me, that your energetic measures alone saved our colony and should be held up to every Colonial Governor as an example and not a reproach will I feel certain come forward with material help.' Humphrey to Eyre, 22 May 1868, Eyre Papers, *SLSA*, f. 37. Lord Overton wrote a similar letter enclosing a generous cheque on 26 May 1868. Ibid., f. 38.
[87] *The Times* (22 May 1868), 9.   [88] As quoted in the *Pall Mall Gazette* (21 May 1868), 2.
[89] *Daily Telegraph* (21 May 1868).   [90] Ibid.

on which every English subject, of whatever creed or colour, has a personal interest.' More to the point, these were matters that could be settled only by 'distinct judicial utterance'.[91]

Of course, not all political commentators had changed their minds, either about the evidence or the motives of the Jamaica Committee. The *Saturday Review*, for instance, scoffed at the pretension that the aims of the Committee were 'merely intellectual', and that this new prosecution of Eyre was motivated by the 'same noble thirst for judicial knowledge' as was the first.[92] The tenuous credibility of this view was utterly shattered when it was revealed that 'a host of sable witnesses have been hired from Jamaica at large cost, and that salaries and subsidies paid out of the funds of the Jamaica Committee have curiously sharpened African memories'. And what was the English public to look forward to upon the conclusion of the current prosecution? To the spectacle of 'every "victim" of every Court-martial, everybody who has been flogged or frightened, no matter by whom... bringing civil actions in the English Courts against Mr. Eyre'. This was unvarnished legal harassment 'in the prostituted name of public conscience'.

The *Standard* and the *Globe* newspapers were more vitriolic. The *Standard* asserted that 'no reasonable man, not being of the venomous clique of philanthropists, can expect or desire to see this cold-blooded and iniquitous proceeding succeed'.[93] For the *Globe* the Jamaica Committee was a cabal of 'dastardly conspirators' led by the 'materialist philosopher', Mill, a man so blinkered by hatred that he 'attached more value to the life [of] a dusky rebel like Gordon than to the lives of a few thousand British soldiers. The real philosopher knows that [the] negro race is lower than our own.' Mill and his minions had deigned to torment a man who in Jamaica had succeeded in averting 'outrage and massacre as horrible as anything in the Indian Mutiny'. Who would be their next victim, the journal queried, 'Sir Robert Napier for the murder of Theodorus of Abyssinia?'

III. Back before the Grand Jury: Blackburn on Martial Law

The twenty-one-count indictment in *The Queen v. Eyre* was sent to the Middlesex grand jury on 21 April 1868. The hearing was scheduled for the next session of Oyer and Terminer in the Court of Queen's Bench. Those proceedings opened on the early morning of 2 June. Present to deliver the charge was Sir Colin Blackburn.

Like Alexander Cockburn, Blackburn was Scottish born but English educated (at Eton and Cambridge). Called to the bar in 1838, he was renowned, even as a young barrister, as an accomplished scholar of common law.[94] Not so high born or

---

[91] Ibid.   [92] *Saturday Review* (23 May 1868), 680–1.
[93] As quoted in *Pall Mall Gazette* (22 May 1868), 3.
[94] Specializing in commercial law. In 1860 Blackburn published a treatise on contracts of sale. *Law Times* (18 Jan. 1896), 274–5; Manson, *Builders of our Law*, 258–9; Jones, *Oxford DNB*, online 2510.

socially connected as Cockburn, Blackburn progressed in his career as a pleader more slowly. Twenty years after his call, Blackburn occupied a prosperous but uncelebrated position on the Northern Circuit. He had not 'taken silk', nor had he cultivated the patronage of the bar's political cliques. In the late 1850s Blackburn was more highly regarded as a treatise writer than a trial barrister.[95] Nonetheless, in 1859, and to the general astonishment of the English bar, Blackburn was appointed to a vacancy on the Queen's Bench. To many observers, it simply beggared belief that this man, a veritable stranger to the upper echelons of law and politics, might be elevated to the high court bench. The Lord Chancellor's (Lord Campbell) official explanation for his choice, that Blackburn had been promoted because he was 'the fittest man in Westminster Hall', was widely dismissed as absurd.[96] But critics of the appointment soon bowed to two facts: the appointment could not be undone, and Blackburn quickly proved himself a tireless, learned, and astute judge. While his 'burly figure, strong face, and round bullet head' did not make for a prepossessing judicial bearing,[97] Blackburn was a formidable presence in the courtroom. He was greatly respected by counsel. Before he had been on the bench for a decade the *Law Journal* described Blackburn as 'one of the greatest judicial lights of the nineteenth century'.[98]

Cockburn had a host of compelling reasons to select Blackburn to charge the grand jury in *The Queen v. Eyre*. There are two preliminary points to be made in this regard. The first is that Cockburn might have exercised his prerogative to charge the jury himself, but did not. Although it is not clear why he did not, the safest conjecture is that he feared that another intervention by the Lord Chief Justice in a Jamaica case would be viewed as untoward. His own Jamaica charge had generated praise, but also no little controversy. As its Chief Justice Cockburn had to be mindful of the reputation of the Queen's Bench for probity and impartiality. The second point is that Cockburn was immensely proud of his work in *The Queen v. Nelson and Brand* (proud enough to have assisted in its publication). He saw the charge as an important part of his judicial legacy, something jealously to be protected. Cockburn would not have appointed any judge whom he thought would undermine his achievement in *Nelson and Brand*. But on the assumption that Blackburn would adopt, and by adopting reinforce, Cockburn's earlier pronouncements on the law of martial law, he was an artful choice for the charge in *The Queen v. Eyre*.

Blackburn had many formal qualifications for the assignment. As the senior subordinate or 'puisne' judge of the Queen's Bench, it often fell upon him to deliver grand jury charges for the entire court.[99] Blackburn had presided over other overtly

[95] Blackburn had edited a highly regarded set of law reports. Jones, ibid.

[96] He was selected by Lord Campbell over a number of senior Whig silk gownsmen even though he was not himself Queen's Counsel, and had no obvious connections to either major political grouping. Manson, *Builders of Law*, 259–60.   [97] Jones, *Oxford DNB*, online 2510.

[98] III *Law Journal* (1868), 384–5.

[99] And the senior judge was paid slightly more to reflect this additional responsibility. *London Review* (13 June 1868), 584.

political cases (only eight months earlier he, with Mr. Justice Mellor, presided over the Special Commission tribunal instituted to try the Manchester Fenians). The English press had generally been laudatory of Blackburn's work on these trials.[100] From the point of view of the Lord Chief Justice, however, there was a much more compelling reason to select his senior puisne judge. Unlike Cockburn, Blackburn was renowned for his prodigious legal knowledge and technical skill. In these respects, Cockburn could not hold a candle to his brother judge. (In fact, in the 1860s a jibe circulated to the effect that Cockburn 'had acquired his great legal knowledge by sitting on the bench with Mr. Justice Blackburn'.[101]) When Blackburn endorsed the general outlines of Cockburn's charge in *Nelson and Brand* – and this must have been Cockburn's active assumption – the endorsement would carry real weight. In the event, however, if these were Cockburn's calculations, they proved embarrass-ingly, even humiliatingly, wrong. To his shock and consternation, Blackburn's charge, far from paying fealty and homage to Cockburn's vision of the law of martial law, did much to undermine its prestige and authority. To make matters worse, and to the palpable fury of the Lord Chief Justice, Blackburn told the grand jury that his charge had been endorsed by the entire Court of the Queen's Bench.

The Middlesex grand jury was assembled for the charge in *The Queen v. Eyre* on 2 June 1868. More than eighteen months after the first Jamaica prosecution, two and half years after the trouble at Morant Bay, the *Eyre* case drew a large assem-blage of newspaper reporters, casual onlookers, and interested barristers.[102] The partisans of the Jamaica and Eyre Defence Committees also were well represented. When Blackburn began the charge at half-past nine, every seat in the courtroom was filled and the doors locked to newcomers. A substantial overflow gazed down at the proceedings from the open windows of an upper corridor. As on past occa-sions, spectators would require considerable patience. Blackburn's address took some four hours to complete.[103]

Blackburn approached the charge with anxiety to be thorough and precise. Unusually, he committed his key points to writing.[104] In the first minutes of his charge Blackburn told the grand jury that if Eyre had committed any crimes at all, they were crimes committed 'under colour of his office'.[105] All of the twenty-one counts of the indictment related to official functions. Even at this early point in his address, Blackburn sent signals that he was not entirely unsympathetic with the plight of the accused. His opening remarks went on to emphasize the serious predicament that Eyre had faced prior to making the decisions that now had been impugned. There could be no doubting, Blackburn underlined, but that Eyre had

---

[100] *The Times* (14 Nov. 1867), 8, not an impartial source of course, observed that 'no bias on the side of severity can be traced in the judicial conduct of the inquiry'. For a contrary view, see Paul Rose, *The Manchester Martyrs: The Story of a Fenian Tragedy* (London, 1970), 62.

[101] Manson, *Builders of our Law*, 2nd edn (London, 1904), 161.

[102] *Morning Star* (3 June 1868), 5.

[103] While the charge was printed in the newspapers from the shorthand notes of a number of reporters, I rely here on the edition published (verbatim) by Finlason. See Finlason, *Report of The Queen v. Edward Eyre*.   [104] Ibid., 59.

[105] Ibid., 54.

faced an armed rebellion in Jamaica, and that it had been his legal *duty* to suppress it. The main question for the grand jury was whether Eyre was guilty of any *neglect* of that duty, and whether the 'neglect is such and to such an extent as to amount to criminal negligence'. Both the legal duty and responsibility, Blackburn stated, would vary according to the 'power he has, either by the general law or the particular statutes referring to his particular case'. Further to the point, Blackburn thought the powers of the Governor of a colony were 'more extensive' than the Lord Lieutenant of a county or the Mayor of an English borough.

In the first passages of the charge, then, Blackburn had established two important premises. First, that whether Eyre should be indicted on any or all of the charges would hinge on the extent of Eyre's legal authority under *Jamaican* law. Second, that the case concerned the accused's potential criminal *negligence*; it was about whether the former Governor, when he proclaimed and implemented martial law, had acted reasonably.

In elaborating the question of Eyre's possible criminal negligence, Blackburn relied on a single case, one that had been given scant attention by Cockburn, the 1832 trial decision in *The King v. Pinney*.[106] In that case Charles Pinney, the former Mayor of Bristol, had stood accused of the gross dereliction of his duty as chief magistrate of the city during a period of civil unrest. The indictment specified that for two days and nights in October 1831 Pinney repeatedly failed to implement measures to suppress a series of furious riots (sparked by clashes over the first Reform Bill). The principal issue raised by the prosecution was 'whether the defendant had done all that ... could be reasonably expected from a man of honesty and of ordinary prudence, firmness and activity under the circumstances in which he was placed'.[107] From Lord Littledale's decision in the case Blackburn distilled the legal criterion for the assessment of Eyre's criminal culpability. The key question for the jury was as follows: what might 'reasonably be expected from a man of honesty and ordinary prudence, firmness, and activity under the circumstances'?[108]

Blackburn elaborated on the legal standard of culpability. A culpable wrong was not a 'mere error of judgment'. It was malicious, reckless, or high-handed. With regard to a public official, the culpable wrong was usually associated with a gross abuse of authority or some other 'great failure of duty'. In deciding such an issue, Blackburn added, 'much allowance should be made for the difficulty of his position, but not too much.'[109] In the end, it was for the jury to decide whether misconduct had occurred and whether it was pardonable in the circumstances.

In the charge delivered by Cockburn, the question of the Crown's authority to proclaim martial law was prominent. Blackburn did not raise this issue until he had already decided that the case raised an issue of criminal negligence. It was so 'very important' that this point of law was 'accurately laid down' that Blackburn

---

[106] B. & Ad. 947.   [107] Finlason, *Report of The Queen v. Edward Eyre*, 57.
[108] Ibid.   [109] Ibid., 59.

told the jury that he was going to read directly from his notes.[110] It was alleged by the prosecution, Blackburn began, that Eyre's actions in proclaiming and conducting martial law were 'utterly beyond his competence'. Were this true, the impugned acts of Governor Eyre would have been 'totally illegal' and there would be nothing to do but find a true bill against him. This was a critical juncture of the charge. Recall that in his charge Cockburn described many legal reasons to doubt whether Nelson and Brand had jurisdiction to court martial Gordon (even though he ultimately left the point to the jury). In arriving at this conclusion the Lord Chief Justice had explicitly rejected the idea that the Jamaica statutes provided this jurisdiction. For his part, not only did Blackburn almost entirely ignore Cockburn's analysis of these points, he arrived at a radically different view of the 'law that was in force in Jamaica at the time'.[111]

Just as Cockburn had done, Blackburn examined the constitutional history and status of Jamaica. He agreed with Cockburn that soon after its conquest from Spain, Jamaica had become a settled colony complete with the laws of England. He observed that during the reign of Charles II the Crown exercised its prerogative to establish a Legislative Assembly in Jamaica. In so doing, Blackburn maintained, the Crown contemplated that the law of England would thereafter be *altered* by local statutes, subject to the ultimate control of Parliament.[112] On this point Blackburn did 'not entertain any doubt'. And here Blackburn made a decisive break from Cockburn's charge. The Lord Chief Justice had laid it down that under the Jamaican statutes the Governor was not to 'do anything contrary to the laws of England and the island'.[113] If Jamaica's Governors had become habituated to believe that they had the 'full power to declare and exercise martial law in the amplest sense of the term', this was a regrettable mistake.[114] In fact, the Jamaica statutes had given the Governor the legal power only to organize a militia and to subject the population to the justice laid down under the military codes. But Blackburn held an entirely different view of the issue. By his reckoning the Jamaica assembly held 'the supreme legislative power within the limits of the colony subject to the control of Parliament'.[115] As Governor of Jamaica, Eyre had a perfect right to assume that the laws passed by the legislature, including laws regarding martial law, were *intra vires* until and if they were invalidated by the higher authorities in London. Blackburn doubted very much 'that we ever could punish a person, in Jamaica or any other colony, where there is a Legislative Assembly, for acting *bona fide* and honestly under a Legislative Act'. He emphasized that *The Queen v. Eyre* raised 'a question of *criminal law*, and I think I should be wrong if I left you in any doubt about it' (emphasis added). In such cases the due process rights of the accused were paramount. Any statute bearing on

---

[110] Ibid.   [111] Ibid., 61.   [112] Ibid., 67.

[113] Cockburn (ed.), *Charge of the Lord Chief Justice*, 78.

[114] For Cockburn, military law was a type of ordinary law with regular rules and procedures. About military law there was 'nothing arbitrary, nothing capricious, nothing unsettled'. Ibid., 98.

[115] Finlason, *Report of The Queen v. Edward Eyre*, 68.

criminal liability was to be construed in favour of the accused. Governors of
colonies were not obliged also to be subtle lawyers, and to say ' "I will not obey [a
law] because it is unconstitutional." ' The law of England could not be so
perverse, Blackburn told the jury, that a Governor could be 'bound to disobey the
law at any risk, and it would, I think, be impossible, if he obeyed it, for anyone to
support the proposition that he could be criminally punished for that'.

At this point in his charge, however, this was a hypothetical conclusion.
The actual legal content and status of martial law, both as Crown prerogative
and as a product of a Jamaica statute – Cockburn's charge in *Nelson and Brand*
notwithstanding – had yet to be determined. At English law, he informed the jury,
'the general rule was that a subject was not to be tried or punished, except by
due course of law'.[116] In the context of foreign invasion or insurrection, however,
it was clearly impractical to try offenders by regular courts and juries; in such
extraordinary circumstances it was necessary to 'exercise summary proceedings by
martial law' in order to restore the peace. But, because Britain came to enjoy a
long period of domestic security and comparative tranquillity, 'it never has come
to be decided what this precise power is'.[117] This was because English judging was
a 'practical science' and judges decided only 'so much as was necessary for the
particular case'. Still, Blackburn ventured some generalizations about the law of
martial law. Since the passage of the Petition of Right, he concluded, there was no
general Crown prerogative to replace civilian with martial law 'in time of peace'.
However, the extent of the Crown's prerogative in time of insurrection or invasion
has 'not been quite settled'.[118] Whatever its true extent, Blackburn added, martial
law was 'by no means that unbounded, wild and tyrannical prerogative which
some persons have lately been saying it is'.

Blackburn now returned to the specific question of the potential criminal liability of Edward Eyre. The Crown prerogative to proclaim martial law, he stated,
'if it exists at all, is strictly limited to necessity'.[119] However, on the preliminary
evidence in the case at bar it appeared that the former Governor had continued to
implement martial law for some weeks 'after all armed resistance had ceased, [and]
when it would have been quite practicable to try anyone by the ordinary tribunals'.
For this reason Blackburn thought that 'there can be no reasonable doubt that he
did exceed much that would be authorized on the most extended view of the prerogative'. To this Blackburn added the even more frank assertion that 'if it stood
solely and entirely on the question of what was the power which Mr Eyre had in
exercising the common law prerogative of the Crown, I think I should be obliged
to say to you that, though there might be good reasons for an Act of Indemnity or
a Pardon, you must find this bill'. 'But then,' Blackburn hastened to add, 'the law
by no means remains in that state in Jamaica; it has been completely altered by
Jamaica Statutes, as I construe them, and very greatly extended power is given to

---

[116] Finlason, *Report of The Queen v. Edward Eyre*, 69.   [117] Ibid., 71.
[118] Ibid., 74.   [119] Ibid.

the Governor of Jamaica more than ever was possessed by the Crown in this country.'[120] Blackburn did not tell the jury (he was under no technical obligation to do so, as Cockburn's charge was not a binding precedent) that this reading of the colonial law flatly contradicted that of the Lord Chief Justice of England.

Instead of hedging on this point, Blackburn defended his theory of martial law in Jamaica. It was a natural by-product of history, he informed the jury, that the laws of England and Jamaica should have diverged on this point. From its inception, after all, Jamaican legislators knew 'perfectly well that they were a slave colony, and that insurrections were very likely to occur, and they were a freshly conquered colony surrounded by Spanish colonists, and likely to be invaded from abroad'. Slavery, of course, became the only persistent source of anxiety for the white minority. '[I]n slave states,' Blackburn observed, 'there is very likely to have been very fearful legislation.'[121] Jamaica was no exception. There the colony's legislators quite sensibly had promulgated a set of laws which suited their peculiar security needs. They had been given the power to make their own laws of martial law, and had used them. For this reason, the key to the prosecution in *The Queen v. Eyre* was one of statutory interpretation. Blackburn's view was that the early Jamaican acts bearing on martial law mainly concerned raising and regulating the militia. In the course of time, however, the Jamaican legislators had amended their martial law statutes to give the governor 'very extensive power' to cope with public emergency. What the Jamaica legislature had meant to do, what Blackburn thought that they *did* do, was to give their Governor, on the advice of the Council of War, the power to proclaim martial law and thereby to 'supersede the common law altogether, and to punish all manner of offences that were then done . . . by summary process'.[122] In short, the legislature created a mechanism by which their Commander-in-Chief might be vested with 'very arbitrary and great power' – powers unknown in the mother country – in order to meet exigencies also unknown in the mother country.

This analysis framed Blackburn's charge on the central point of Eyre's legal powers and duties under the martial law statutes of Jamaica. In his view, Blackburn bluntly told the jury, these statutes permitted a Governor to convene a Council of War and, having taken their advice, to suspend the common law in all or some part of the colony. Blackburn stressed that this was not only a power, but in the circumstances of real emergency, it was a positive duty. Here the Justice referred again to the common law decision in *The King v. Pinney*. There it was laid down by Lord Littledale that the Mayor of Bristol had been legally obligated to take reasonable steps to quell a riot. His failure to do what a reasonable man in his place would have done was criminally negligent. So it was in the case at bar. Had Eyre *not* used his power under the martial law statutes, 'when a reasonable man would have felt that he ought to have used it', he would have been 'punishable for it'.[123] By the same token, Blackburn told the jury, if Eyre did his duty in a manner

---

[120] Ibid, 75.   [121] Ibid., 79.   [122] Ibid., 77.   [123] Ibid., 81.

consistent with reason he was not culpable. For this reason, when the time came to make their decision the grand jurors would be obliged to put themselves 'in his [Eyre's] place, knowing what he did know, and see whether there was a criminal neglect to bring that reasonable firmness, self-control, and moderation to bear on the question'.

Blackburn then made a claim which later proved explosively controversial. He told the jury that prior to his appearance before the grand jury he had previewed the main legal propositions of his charge with the Lord Chief Justice and the three puisne judges of the Queen's Bench.[124] The jury was to feel great confidence in his 'view of what I think the law should be' for the simple reason that he had had 'frequent opportunity of consulting' with his brother judges of the Queen's Bench, including the Lord Chief Justice. The day prior to giving his charge, Blackburn added, he had stated to the other judges 'the effect of what I am now stating to you, and they all approved of it, and authorized me to say . . . they agree in my view of the law, and thought it right.' He did not want the jury to think that the crucial direction he had given on the law of martial law in Jamaica was 'only my own view'. He assured the jury that his view of the subject was also 'the view that has been entertained by the best authorities we can get upon the subject'. On this key point Blackburn was crystal clear: 'I think that you should follow the view that I am telling you'.[125]

In the final third of his charge Blackburn turned to the factual issues that were to be answered by the grand jury. Was it reasonable of Eyre to have convened the Council of War and to have proclaimed martial law?[126] Once proclaimed, had he possessed reasonable grounds to continue martial law for a month? Finally, was it a 'justifiable thing' for Eyre to have ordered the removal of some men from the jurisdiction of civilian law into the hands of the military? Then as now, an English judge is permitted to impart his personal opinion on the evidence as it relates to the questions of fact, so long as the jurors are reminded that final decisions are theirs alone to make. Blackburn exercised this prerogative, sometimes boldly.

On the subject of whether Eyre should have proclaimed martial law, Blackburn candidly told the grand jury that Eyre 'would have been culpable if he had not'. Then he dealt with the charges relating to the fact that Eyre had ordered Gordon, Phillips, and other civilians to be removed from civilian jurisdiction to the military courts at Morant Bay. On this score, Blackburn stated that 'all crime was local' and was rightly prosecuted where it was committed. In the case at bar, he stated, there were factual ambiguities. The alleged sedition and treason of men like Gordon did not occur only in one place. Furthermore, Gordon had close personal and political associations with rebel leaders in St. Thomas-in-the-East, the parish under martial law. On this basis Blackburn thought (once again in contradiction to Cockburn's charge in *Nelson and Brand*) that it had been lawful, under Jamaican legislation, to remove Gordon and the others to the courts martial. After

---

[124] Finlason, *Report of The Queen v. Edward Eyre*, 88.   [125] Ibid.   [126] Ibid., 82–3.

all, he reminded jurors, one of the main purposes of Jamaica's martial law statute law was to cure the 'impracticality' of full-blown common law trials in times of public emergency.[127] Thus, Eyre had the legal authority to do what he did; the question for the grand jury was whether in the circumstances it had been reasonable, and therefore justifiable, to take these steps. In making this decision, Blackburn stressed, the jurors were to put themselves in Eyre's position 'to see with his eyes, and hear with his ears'.

Blackburn then addressed the specific charges relating to the military execution of Gordon and other alleged rebels. He thought that these charges also had to be evaluated in their proper political context. Gordon, for instance, had not been just any prisoner; he was a committed and zealous opponent of Eyre and the British colonial regime in Jamaica. While Blackburn did not think that the evidence was good that Gordon was 'a party to any organized conspiracy to cause an insurrection throughout the island', it did indicate that he was 'a violent, pestilent agitator, and that he used very improper and seditious language which caused the insurrection'.[128] This pointed to a critical issue. It was trite law that a British subject could not be tried before a military tribunal for being a political agitator. Still less would this procedure be justified because the agitator might (inconveniently for the authorities) be acquitted by a civilian tribunal. If Gordon was subjected to a court martial for either of these reasons, Blackburn stated, 'that would be a grave act of lawless tyranny and oppression, and a bill should be found at once'. On the other hand, the judge continued, if based on the information available to him at the time, Eyre reasonably concluded that 'there was a dangerous insurrection and conspiracy spreading ... and that it was really proper for suppressing it that Mr Gordon, whom he believed to be the head, should be summarily tried', then Gordon's arrest and execution might be 'fully justified'.[129] In short, if Eyre had acted in honest and reasonable good faith, 'he would be excused for acting under the powers which the Colonial Legislature had given him'. Blackburn emphasized again that the grand jurors were to put themselves in Eyre's shoes, to take notice of how matters stood in Jamaica in October 1865. They were told to remember that it was the 'general belief in the colony' (Blackburn did not say among *whites* only) that strong measures were needed if general insurrection was to be averted. The grand jury was told to make 'great allowances for the position in which he was, and for his responsibility for the colony'.

As he summarized the evidence Blackburn reminded the jury that decisions on matters of fact were theirs alone to make. At the same time, Blackburn summarized in ways which were plainly favourable to the accused. (In at least one instance he even went so far as to pay Eyre a direct compliment.)[130] Then there was the potentially damaging question of Eyre's criminal responsibility for

---

[127] Ibid., 84.   [128] Ibid., 85.   [129] Ibid., 86.

[130] For instance, Blackburn praised the former Governor for having testified before the Jamaica Royal Commission, even at risk of self-incrimination. Ibid., 89.

atrocities committed by subordinates. Blackburn did not entertain the 'slightest doubt' that 'letting persons run riot in the exercise of martial law, without having taken the proper care to see it rightly regulated, a vast number of things were done that ought not to have been done'. The 'frightful story' concerning the arrest, detention, and flogging of Alexander Phillips was offered as an example. Phillips, it was obvious, had been the victim of a 'most atrocious tyranny'. But when it came time to summarize the evidence, Blackburn was strangely selective. He did not mention, for instance, that Eyre had ordered Phillips arrested without charge, and then transported to military camps at which, the Governor knew, prisoners were being subjected to harsh punishments as a matter of routine. Nor did Blackburn mention that many of the most brutal and arbitrary punishments were meted out days and even weeks after the uprising had been crushed. More specifically, instead of citing the reasons why Eyre might be *culpable* for the outrages visited on Phillips, Blackburn said only that he 'could not find throughout the whole evidence that Mr Eyre in any way was made aware of this, or sanctioned it'. After earnestly acknowledging that martial law could quickly degenerate into a violent tyranny if it was not closely supervised,[131] and that Eyre had failed to closely supervise his forces in the field, and that 'terrible things were done' in the Queen's name, Blackburn still 'could not say that the neglect to take proper precaution to see that martial law was fairly exercised could be charged upon Eyre'.[132] He then summed up his position: 'I think the defence of Mr. Eyre is complete that these things were to be regulated by the military'. A Governor was not culpable for transgressions caused by the poor discipline of soldiers. On this point, Blackburn had every confidence in the jury: 'I do not think you will say the civil officer, the Governor, is responsible for the faults of the military'.[133] Eyre could not have asked for a more sympathetic charge on this issue.

In his final words to the jury Blackburn urged each man 'to draw your own inference as to what really were the circumstances and position of Jamaica – how things came to Mr. Eyre's mind in Jamaica in the very difficult position in which he was'. When they came to hear the evidence and to make a final decision upon it, Blackburn declared, they were not to consider that Eyre might have recourse to a legislated indemnity. That would be an issue for the judge to decide should the jury find a true bill. Blackburn completed his charge in the early afternoon. The grand jury retired for just less than four hours before returning to the court. Blackburn was sent for and returned (with, for no apparent reason but for a symbolic show of solidarity, Mr. Justice Lush) a few minutes past four o'clock. The verdict 'No bill' was read aloud, and the jury discharged. The *Manchester Guardian* described the scene: 'Few people were present when the grand jury gave

---

[131] Finlason, *Report of The Queen v. Edward Eyre*, 93.

[132] Ibid., 94. This was precisely the charge that the prosecution had made in the third count of its indictment. For reasons that are not entirely clear, Blackburn stated to the jury that 'this particular charge had not been brought forward'.   [133] Ibid., 95–6.

their decision, and there was no manifestation of feeling.'[134] It was later reported that the vote had been twenty-one to two against the finding of a bill on any of the twenty-one counts.[135] One juror (perhaps one of the two who had voted in favour of indictment) was quoted as stating that 'Mr. Justice Blackburn's charge did produce its intended effect on the minds of a large majority of the grand jury, and served as the ostensible ground for their not finding a true bill on several of the counts.'[136]

Blackburn's assessment of the law of martial law, especially his assessment of the effect of colonial statutes on this law, differed markedly from Cockburn's. This point merits some brief elaboration. The Lord Chief Justice had found that Nelson and Brand lacked the legal authority, either as a result of Crown prerogative or colonial legislation, to supersede the common law. He also believed that while he entertained some doubt about his analysis, that it would be 'safer' for the grand jury to find a true bill. We have also seen, however, that when he summed up his charge in *The Queen v. Nelson and Brand*, Cockburn left it to the *jury* to decide (what looks to be the legal question) whether the accused had the legal power to try and execute Gordon and the (more clearly factual) question of whether the court martial proceedings had been carried out by the accused 'honestly and faithfully'.[137] Strikingly, however, whatever were his personal convictions about the case, Cockburn signally had *not* used his position as a bully-pulpit. If he erred in this aspect of his charge, he erred on the side of the jury's discretion.

In Cockburn's charge there was ironic tension between the judge's ideas about martial law and his unwillingness to urge them strongly on the jury. In this respect, Blackburn's charge was far more coherent. First, he quite properly treated the issues relating to martial law as being within the exclusive province of the presiding judge. Second, he decided unequivocally that Eyre had possessed the legal power to suspend the ordinary operation of civilian law. And when it came time to comment on the key issue of fact – whether Eyre had proclaimed and implemented martial law with sufficient honesty and prudence – Blackburn adopted a consistent approach. Just as he reasoned that Jamaica's martial law statute had to be understood within the context of the island's political history, he also reasoned that Eyre's conduct had to be understood within the context of the security crisis created by the Morant Bay rebellion.

The case of *Nelson and Brand* involved the charge of accessory to murder. The *Eyre* case involved various charges under the Colonial Governors Act. For this reason alone the charges of Cockburn and Blackburn were bound to be dissimilar in some ways. However, in both cases criminal culpability turned on the legal nature and effect of a proclamation of martial law. In both cases the prosecution contended that such a proclamation did not bestow any extraordinary powers or immunities on the accused. In both cases, too, the defence argued that the

[134] *Manchester Guardian* (3 June 1868), 5.   [135] *Spectator* (6 June 1868), 665.
[136] From the *Daily News*, as quoted in the *Pall Mall Gazette* (11 June 1868), 6.
[137] Cockburn (ed.), *Charge of the Lord Chief Justice*, 156.

impugned conduct was privileged by the operation of martial law. With regard to these *overlapping* issues, one would expect the two charges to be more alike than different. After all, the charges emanated from the same Court and within the period of only one year. In the result, however, Blackburn's charge was markedly different from its predecessor both in terms of structure and content. Given that they later became a matter of public contention, these differences also deserve further amplification.

In the opening section of his address, Cockburn told the jury that he would focus mainly on one point: whether the proclamation of martial law signed by Governor Eyre gave Nelson and Brand the legal authority to detain, court martial, and hang George Gordon. If they had no such authority, so the jury was informed, they could be indicted for murder. Accordingly, the Lord Chief Justice devoted the majority of a five-hour address (some three-quarters of the published transcript) to the legal status of martial law within the constitution. In half a dozen places in his speech he reminded the jury that the case before them was of 'great', 'grave', and even 'infinite' importance, and for the very specific reason that the legal definition and status of martial law raised questions about the core principles of the English constitution. In other words, Cockburn more or less embraced the view of the Jamaica Committee that the prosecution in *The Queen v. Nelson and Brand* was about issues of far greater moment than the criminal culpability of two men.

The introductory section of Blackburn's address, by contrast, made no direct comment on the larger constitutional ramifications of the Eyre prosecution. Instead he moved quickly to a terse (if not uncontroversial) statement of the factual background of the case. In almost every respect Blackburn treated *The Queen v. Eyre* as a more or less routine criminal case. The only thing which marked it from more mundane cases was the fact that the accused was the senior executive official of a colonial government at the time of the alleged offences, and that the offences related to official conduct. More specifically, Blackburn reminded the jury that the charges against Eyre arose from putting down an armed insurrection. Among these steps he caused 'what is called martial law, in the sense of summary process, superseding the common law, to be put in force'.[138] This had led to the infliction of a number of summary executions and other 'severe punishments'. The task for the grand jury, Blackburn stated, was not unusual: it was to decide what the former Governor had done, 'and whether, in doing these things, he did anything for which he is criminally responsible'. While Blackburn acknowledged that it was of 'very great importance' (at another point of 'grave and great importance')[139] that the law governing the Eyre prosecution 'should be accurately known', he did not say why this was so. The grand jurors were left to draw their own conclusions. This was characteristic of the entire address. In the introduction, body, and conclusion of the charge Blackburn's rhetorical posture was understated and unemotional.

---

[138] Finlason, *Report of The Queen v. Edward Eyre*, 53.   [139] Ibid., 55.

In this respect, the contrast with Cockburn's charge was stark. The Lord Chief Justice had taken every opportunity to emphasize that the *Nelson and Brand* prosecution was a matter of uncommon significance. Before he addressed the issues he reminded the jury that his very *presence* in the courtroom was meant to underline its gravity.[140] The accused officers had adopted a summary military procedure to take human life, and had contended that their conduct was privileged by the operation of martial law. Cockburn was explicit that this claim was a milestone in British constitutional law, a potentially pivotal test of the nation's commitment to the constitutional norm of the rule of law. In his oratory (the case was portrayed as a contest between 'arbitrary, despotic, and capricious' power on one hand, the 'genius' of British 'laws and institutions' on the other) Cockburn had tried to lift the *Nelson and Brand* prosecution onto the highest possible plane of political significance. Blackburn, conversely, endeavoured to downplay the political dimensions of the Eyre case.

In terms of specific legal issues, Cockburn had reduced *Nelson and Brand* to three main questions: was there a Crown prerogative to replace civilian with military law? Did the accused officers possess the legal authority to court martial and hang Gordon? If so, was their authority exercised in good faith? During his charge Cockburn informed the jury that if the accused lacked jurisdiction to try and execute Gordon, they were liable to the charge of murder. The same was true if they had jurisdiction but did not use it honestly. One of the crucial findings of Cockburn's charge was that Jamaica was a 'settled colony' to which all of the laws of England applied. From this point forward the focus was on the law of martial law in *English* legal history. Cockburn devoted fully three-quarters of his long address to demonstrate that as a matter of English law 'martial law' – defined as the unlimited power of military men over civilians in an emergency – was neither a prerogative of the Crown nor the product of a Jamaican statute. This section of his charge ended with strong pronouncements about the illegality of martial law in peacetime, about the definition and limitation of martial law as a defence of necessity, and of the 'eternal and immutable principles of justice'.[141] Very little time was spent on the nature and effect of Jamaican law. Cockburn defined the case as principally one of constitutional law, and relied on a wide range of legal and historical sources. In *The Queen v. Eyre*, however, Blackburn clung to the idea that this was mainly a criminal case. Accordingly, the compass of his research was limited to the local statutes (and a small number of English law reports) that set forth the legal powers and responsibilities of a Jamaican governor. Strikingly, at no point in his charge did Blackburn quote from or even refer to Cockburn's address in *Nelson and Brand*. It is obvious that he meant to set a distinct legal course.

In the final analysis, Cockburn's charge was an effort to adopt the format of the jury charge in order to distil a set of constitutional propositions. The Lord Chief

[140] 'I have thought it my duty to attend here to-day [sic] that I might render you such a service as the circumstances of the case require.' Cockburn (ed.), *Charge of the Lord Chief Justice*, 3.

[141] Ibid., 108.

Justice had tried everything in his power to make an enduring statement about issues of enduring importance. To the accused men, the presence and decision-making authority of the grand jury was almost an afterthought. Blackburn's charge took an altogether different approach. It sought to pull the issues down from the rarified air of constitutional principle, and discuss them on the more mundane ground of criminal law. Where Cockburn had focused on the implications of the prosecution for the country, Blackburn focused on the implications of the prosecution for a man accused of more than a score of serious criminal charges. But in insisting on this focus, in neglecting to validate Cockburn's central propositions about martial law, Blackburn's charge had done much to corrode the prestige and authority of its predecessor. By these measures it is hard to comprehend why Blackburn was so obviously surprised to be the subject of a fearful backlash.

IV. Cockburn v. Blackburn

Blackburn's charge was widely transcribed and then furiously discussed in England's newspapers and political sheets. Where there had been some predisposition in favour of Eyre and against the Jamaica Committee, the charge was praised for its clarity and good sense. The charge 'is most luminous and complete', the *Sun* proclaimed.[142] It is the exertion of the 'calmest and shrewdest of our judges', declared the *Illustrated London News*.[143] While some writers thought that the chief virtue of the charge was its scrupulous impartiality ('there was no bias beyond the strict line of justice'),[144] others complimented its commonsensical approach to the politics of the Eyre case. On this reading of the charge, Blackburn's many specific comments on law and evidence all had been informed by an unsentimental view of race and security in the empire. It was also noted with satisfaction that the charge had been given by the 'most learned of the Queen's Judges, and the opinion of all of his brethren'.[145]

To his lasting credit, or so the argument went, Blackburn had impressed the jury with the importance of the political context of Eyre's decisions. He had urged them 'to see with his eyes, and to hear with his ears'. And what had been seen and heard? Blackburn had reminded the jury that when he proclaimed martial law, Eyre was confronted by a situation in which the blood of a tiny white minority already had been spilt by black men, and on an island colony in which blacks outnumbered whites by forty to one. According to the *Globe* newspaper, Blackburn's portrayal of the predicament of Eyre was so fair-minded and thorough that it left the jury with no doubt but that 'the right way to crush the rebellion was to strike

---

[142] *Sun* (3 June 1868).   [143] *Illustrated London News* (13 June 1868), 575.
[144] *Age We Live In* (6 June 1868).
[145] *Saturday Review* (6 June 1868), 747. Blackburn's charge, the *London Review* (6 June 1868), 556, stated, has the 'advantage of expressing the views of the Lord Chief Justice and the other Judges of the Court of Queen's Bench'.

terror in the hearts of the insurgents'.[146] 'Mr. Eyre knew well the character of the negro,' wrote the *Age We Live In*, 'and on the outbreak of the revolt he foresaw what must be the end if he did not, with a strong and unflinching hand, punish the ringleaders.'[147] Blackburn was credited both for having known these things and, in an appropriately judicial manner, for having incorporated them in his charge.

The most fervent admirers of Blackburn's charge thought that it was a subtle affirmation of the view that in the non-white empire Governors would sometimes need to have recourse to brutal repressive force. The most fervent detractors of the charge held much the same view, if with fear and loathing. In a long leader the editor of the Baptist paper, the *Freeman*, deeply regretted that the charge (and the jury's findings) reflected an unmistakable hardening of public opinion – most especially among better-educated Englishmen – on matters of race and empire: 'The melancholy fact is but too evident that what is called "society" in England, is deeply impregnated with contempt and hatred toward inferior races. Anything is lawful against negroes or Hindoos.'[148] These racialist notions, the *Freeman* claimed, were rapidly corroding some of the fundamental principles of the English constitution, including the idea of the juridical equality of all subjects.[149] Any close reader of Blackburn's charge, it was asserted, 'must think that these unworthy sentiments have even tainted the administration of justice'.[150] Blackburn had stood before the grand jury and denounced Gordon as a 'pestilent firebrand' while he blamed the 'regime of killing, shooting and burning without restraint' on the 'bad discipline of the military'. In all of his crucial statements to the jury Blackburn had conveyed the idea that 'hanging a man not deserving death may be excused by honest intentions'.

Blackburn's charge was brusquely denounced in the newspapers of the radical and labourite left. For the *Morning Star* the charge was 'entirely in the teeth of that of the Lord Chief Justice'.[151] When closely inspected the charge revealed an 'extraordinary series of blunders' which could only be explained by the judge's tendency to view the subject of race and security in Jamaica 'too much from the point of view of the Jamaica planters'. The *Bee-Hive* described the charge as the 'grossly indecent' production of 'one of the most dangerous men on the judgment seat'.[152] In a long article published under the title 'Mr. Justice Blackburn's Unconstitutional Law', the *Weekly Times* complained that 'very much of Justice Blackburn's charge would justify our describing it as an appeal made by the prejudices of a judge to the prejudices of a Grand Jury'.[153] Blackburn was seen as having decided every

---

[146] *Globe* (4 June 1868).   [147] *Age We Live In* (6 June 1868).
[148] *Freeman* (5 June 1868), 451–2.
[149] 'Men may be our fellow subjects, but we feel towards them as lords, if they are of a different race or religion. It is not for them to pester us with complaints of *unequal* treatment; they are not our equals.' Ibid.   [150] For a similar view, see the *Daily News* (3 June 1868).
[151] *Morning Star*, as quoted in the *Pall Mall Gazette* (3 June 1868), 2.
[152] *Bee-Hive* (6 June 1868).   [153] *Weekly Times* (7 June 1868), 1.

point of dispute 'absolutely in Mr. Eyre's favour',[154] and in so doing having breathed new life into the doctrine of 'arbitrary power when it is exercised to put down the "common people" '. The *Weekly Times* agreed that Blackburn had committed a 'terrible blunder' when he directed the grand jury's attention to whether Eyre had been 'right or wrong' in what he did. The jury had thus been distracted from the real job of assessing whether there was evidence enough for the case to go forward. In effect, Blackburn had encouraged the grand jury to usurp the role of a trial jury. The editor professed not to 'remember any instance in modern times in which a Judge has committed so many serious errors or expounded law in a manner so fatally and alarmingly opposite to all sound maxims of jurisprudence and Constitutional principles'. *Reynolds' Weekly* concurred in this assessment, and suggested that Blackburn, before he rendered the charge, had made common cause with the 'higher classes' in a blatant 'conspiracy against justice'.[155]

A few of the leading newspapers and political reviews undertook very minute comparisons of the Blackburn and Cockburn charges. The *London Review* thought that Blackburn's charge differed 'rather in appearance and tone than in substance from that of Lord Chief Justice Cockburn'.[156] Similarly, the *Pall Mall Gazette* asserted that the 'differences between the two judges is, we think, rather apparent than real, and depends more on the style in which the two judges expressed themselves'.[157] The *Saturday Review* contended that Blackburn had provided as satisfactory a charge as could be hoped for in the context of so much 'heat and passion'.[158] *The Times* thought that Blackburn had been absolutely correct to have invited the jurors to look at the case from the point of view of Governor Eyre and what he knew at the crucial moments, and then to measure the legal quality of his conduct by the standard of 'ordinary political intelligence'.[159] This was the right test, and the jury applied it fairly. It was time to abandon the whole affair to history. Among the more mainstream periodicals only the *Spectator*, while it proudly admitted being out of step with public opinion on the Jamaica affair, was adamant that Blackburn's charge should not be allowed to stand as the 'final judgment of English law upon what has happened'.[160] The first thing noticed by the *Spectator* was that Blackburn's address to the grand jury could be read as a 'clever reply to the Chief Justice'. In fact the key elements of the charge so flatly contradicted Cockburn's that it was as if it had come from 'opposite counsel'. The divergence between the two charges was especially evident regarding the effect on martial law of a colonial statute.[161] Cockburn had stated that local

---

[154] More particularly, Blackburn had told the jury that Eyre had faced a widespread insurrection, not a local riot. This was contrary to the finding of the Jamaica Royal Commission. Ibid.

[155] *Reynolds' Weekly* (7 June 1868).   [156] *London Review* (6 June 1868), 556–7.

[157] The writer noted that the 'whole tone of [Blackburn's] charge is no doubt greatly more favourable to what might be called the prerogative view of the question', but insisted that Blackburn qualified his words enough to diminish this impression. *Pall Mall Gazette* (3 June 1868), 1–2.

[158] *Saturday Review* (6 June 1868), 747–8.   [159] *The Times* (4 June 1868), 8.

[160] *Spectator* (6 June 1868), 665–6.

[161] Here Blackburn was criticized for failing to take into account that the Jamaican statute expressly provided that 'nothing therein contained should authorize any act contrary to the law of England'. Ibid.

laws could not alter the English law of martial law. Blackburn's charge flatly contradicted the Lord Chief Justice on this issue, one of vital importance in the empire.

The *Spectator* saw other and equally consequential contradictions between the charges. Not only had Eyre benefited from a generous interpretation of his legal powers, but also from a deeply skewed discussion of how and why they had been used. Blackburn, it was noted, had taken great pains to describe the clamour for martial law while mentioning nothing of Eyre's duty to 'stand decidedly *above* the violence and party passions'. By the same token, the judge repeatedly stressed that Eyre had been responsible for the security of the colony's white population while he did not even once mention that he had been equally responsible for *everyone* in the colony, including black subjects. And then there was the question of Eyre's liability for crimes committed by soldiers. The jury was told that the former Governor bore no legal responsibility even though many of the worst transgressions occurred to his knowledge, and as long as three weeks after the rebellion had been crushed. In the opinion of the *Spectator*, Blackburn had offered every conceivable reason to absolve Eyre but none of the 'counter-considerations'. Looked on as a whole, then, Blackburn's charge 'read exactly like a speech for the defence'.[162] Further to the point, the charge appears to have had a great effect on the jury.[163] How to account for the apparent bias? For the *Spectator* the only plausible explanation was that Blackburn had embraced, if only unconsciously, the 'implicit assumption that British subjects...cannot for a moment expect the same treatment as British subjects of Anglo-Saxon or even Celtic descent'.[164] Given the deeply slanted character of the charge, it was inescapable that this racialism was 'the true axiom at the bottom of Mr Justice Blackburn's mind, and at bottom of the mind of the great majority of both of the grand juries which have ignored the bill against Nelson, Brand and Eyre'.

The *Spectator's* scathing criticism of Blackburn's charge was something of an anomaly, but it presaged another stunning development in the Jamaica controversy. On Monday 8 June 1868 Cockburn, together with Blackburn and Lush, were present at Westminster Hall to commence a new session of the Queen's Bench. A rumour had circulated among the barristers that the Lord Chief Justice intended to comment on Blackburn's charge in *The Queen v. Eyre*.[165] Thus, when Cockburn and his brother judges took their seats, the court was crowded with curious lawyers and reporters. A hush fell over the room. In a solemn voice the Lord Chief Justice began to read a prepared statement concerning the Eyre prosecution. As the law reporter for *The Times* (none other than Finlason) later put it, 'the Bar and the public this morning were somewhat startled by a recurrence to the case of *The Queen v. Eyre*.'[166]

---

[162] Ibid., 665.
[163] At least one juror reported that Blackburn's charge had been decisive. *Pall Mall Gazette* (11 June 1868), 6.   [164] *Spectator* (6) June 1868), 666.
[165] *Law Times* (13 June 1868), 124.   [166] *The Times* (9 June 1868), 11.

The Lord Chief Justice quickly explained how he had 'thought it necessary to say a few words on a subject which appears to me too important to pass over in silence'.[167] That subject was the 'charge recently delivered by Mr. Blackburn to the grand jury of the county of Middlesex, in the case of "The Queen v. Eyre" '. Cockburn recounted how it had 'gone forth to the world' that his brother Blackburn's charge had 'received the assent and approbation of the other members of this court'. The Lord Chief Justice regretted to report that 'there has been a very serious misapprehension on the point', one vitally important to 'clear up at the earliest moment'. With this dramatic introduction out of the way, Cockburn proceeded to describe just 'how far the legal doctrines enunciated on the occasion in question have the sanction and authority of the court'.

Cockburn acknowledged that he and a number of other Justices of the Queen's Bench *had* consulted with Blackburn before he delivered the charge in the Eyre case. As a result of this consultation, the Justices agreed on the proposition of law that ought to form the basis of the charge, that 'the governor of a colony had by virtue of authority delegated to him by the Crown or conferred on him by local legislation, the power to proclaim martial law'. However, the main proposition agreed upon was that in this specific case 'all that could be required of [the Governor], so far as affecting his responsibility in a court of criminal law, was that of judging of the necessity ... either of putting this exceptional law in force or prolonging its duration'. The 'sole justification' of martial law was necessity, and the pertinent question for the jury was whether the Governor had acted 'with an honest intention' and with that 'careful, conscientious, and considerate judgment which may be reasonably expected from one vested with authority'. If the evidence suggested that the Governor met this standard, 'he would not be liable for errors of judgment, and still less for irregularities committed by subordinates ... if committed without his sanction or knowledge'.

If this was the core of their agreement, the judges had also been allied on two other subordinate points. The first concerned the proper criteria of guilt. While a Governor would not be criminally liable for proclaiming martial law when he had been so advised by those persons 'competent to advise him, ... mere honesty of intention would be no excuse for the reckless, precipitate, and inconsiderate exercise of so formidable a power, still less for any abuse of it in regard to the lives and persons of her Majesty's subjects'. And just as an abuse of power could not be excused, the judges also agreed that 'neither could the continuance of martial law be excused, even as regards criminal responsibility, when the necessity which can alone justify the law, ceased by the entire suppression of all insurrection'. These propositions taken together, so the Lord Chief Justice summarized, were 'the substance of what we all concurred in thinking was the proper direction to be given to the jury ... This was all that appeared to us to be necessary to lay down in point of law.' Cockburn was adamant that 'not only was the legal doctrine to which I have

---

[167] All quotes from the account of Cockburn's statement published in *The Times*, ibid.

referred all that the rest of the court assented to; but I feel justified in saying that it was all they expected to be embraced in the charge'.

According to the Lord Chief Justice, it had been the mutual understanding of the Court that Blackburn would confine his charge to these propositions only. As it transpired, however, he had not. The reason *why* Blackburn's charge had departed from the agreed script, whether 'through misconception on the part of the learned judge, or from the language of the charge not being sufficiently precise', Cockburn did not profess to know. What was more certain was that 'an erroneous impression has been created that the court has sanctioned all the legal propositions asserted in the charge'. Given that the case involved 'great constitutional principles', Cockburn wanted to eliminate all uncertainty on this point. (The Lord Chief Justice thought this so important, in fact, that he was willing to subject Blackburn to no small measure of public humiliation in order to put the record right.) Cockburn was not finished. He wanted now to 'declare the extent to which alone the assent of the court must be considered as having gone'. Cockburn thought it his 'duty' to 'point out the error which has arisen'. Cockburn was emphatic on this point: 'but, so far as I am individually concerned, I must go further, and declare that there are in the charge of the learned judge [Blackburn] as it appeared in print... propositions of law in which not only am I not prepared to concur, but from which I altogether dissent.' Cockburn then took the opportunity carefully to enumerate the nature and basis of his objections.

First, Cockburn dissented from the view expressed by Blackburn that 'martial law, in the modern acception of the term, was ever exercised in this country... against civilians not taken in arms'. Second, while it was conceded that the legislature of Jamaica was competent to confer on the Governor the power to proclaim martial law, Cockburn contended that the Jamaican statutes made 'no reference to martial law except for the purpose of compelling the inhabitants of the island to military service and subjecting them while engaged in it to military law'. In Cockburn's view, in the absence of 'argument at the bar and of judicial decision', there was simply 'too much doubt on the subject [of the legal status of statutory provisions for martial law] to warrant a judge... to direct a grand jury authoritatively'. Given that it had been agreed by all the Justices that Eyre could not be held criminally liable if he followed the advice of his law officers, Blackburn had had no need to pronounce on the meaning of martial law under the Jamaican statutes. Cockburn still was not finished: 'but, above all,' he stated, 'I dissent from the direction of [Blackburn]... that the removal of Mr. Gordon from Kingston into the proclaimed district for the purpose of subjecting him to martial law was legally justifiable.' Cockburn 'emphatically repudiate[d] the notion of sharing that opinion'.

Cockburn knew that what he was doing would be seen as controversial, even extraordinary. He quickly moved to justify himself. He reiterated that he had felt duty bound to correct the record because Blackburn had claimed the concurrence of the entire Court of Queen's Bench. This implicated a principle of general import-ance, because 'the collective authority of the court is pledged in every charge delivered to the grand jury of Middlesex'. When a judge of the Queen's Bench gave a charge, he 'speaks not of his own authority, or on his sole responsibility alone – he is the organ and mouthpiece of the court'. For this reason, when a Justice felt compelled to dissent from a proposed charge, it was his duty to go down to the grand jury and 'deliver his own charge'. The Lord Chief Justice informed listeners that, had he known beforehand that Blackburn was to make pronouncements of law with which he disagreed, had he known more particularly that Blackburn was to address 'the question of the legality of martial law or the effect of the Jamaica statutes', he would 'have felt it his duty to attend his place in court . . . and to declare his view of the law'. It was because he had been deprived of the opportunity to offer a parallel charge that Cockburn felt compelled to correct the record *ex post facto*.

By way of illustration, Cockburn referred to Blackburn's discussion of the 'very serious case of Mr. Gordon'. Cockburn thought that 'he was right in saying that almost on the eve of the delivery of the charge the opinion of Mr. Justice Blackburn himself was that the apprehension and removal of Mr. Gordon were in point of fact unjustifiable'. This was the impression also of the other members of the court. For this reason, Blackburn's recorded statements to the jury on this point 'surprised' all concerned. Had it been otherwise, had the Lord Chief Justice known that 'in my own court my opinion, declared to the grand jury in the case of "The Queen v. Nelson and Brand", would have been thus authoritatively over-ruled, I assuredly should have deemed it my duty to declare my own opinion to the grand jury, and to apprise them that the statement of the law thus made to them had not the sanction of any other member of the court'. At this point Cockburn stated (rather emptily) that these observations were made 'not without much pain and imperious sense of public duty'. The 'bar have now known me too long to mis-construe my motives, or to believe that I am actuated by any vain desire to uphold my own opinion against any other judge'. The Lord Chief Justice gave his assur-ance that he was 'influenced only by the desire of protecting myself against being held responsible for opinions from which I dissent, and from preventing doctrines going forth with the authority of this, the highest court of criminal jurisdiction in the realm . . . to which doctrine its assent has not been given'. Cockburn feared that 'the question as to the exercise of martial law may again present itself'. When that day came, it would be open to lawyers to quote from the charge of 'so distinguished a judge as Mr Justice Blackburn, so long as they also stated that Justice Blackburn's charge had not enjoyed the sanction of the entire Court of Queen's Bench'.

Cockburn's remarks were not addressed only to lawyers. He desired for his words to 'operate as a salutary warning' to public officials that an action 'such as the seizure of Mr. Gordon was, in the opinion of the majority of this court, alto-gether unjustifiable and illegal'. That official who felt moved to proclaim martial law would be held 'responsible to the law if he acts otherwise than under a sense of imperious and impending necessity, or without due regard to what reason and humanity alike require'. Cockburn's statement was now concluded.

Blackburn, remember, had been sitting silently at the side of his Lord Chief Justice throughout this extraordinary, and for Blackburn we can rightly presume, extraordinarily painful exercise. He (with what Finlason described as 'great calmness of tone')[168] then made a brief statement of his own. He would neither defend nor deny the accuracy of his charge on the key points of law. Blackburn wanted to make it clear only that he had considered himself 'bound to direct the jury according to my own view of the case, but also bound to take every means in my power to secure that my view of the law be the correct one'. With this in mind Blackburn carefully inspected the charge in *The Queen v. Nelson and Brand*. He came to the conclusion, one which he did not now retract, that his exposition of the law of martial law did not differ materially from that of the Lord Chief Justice. Still, Blackburn had thought it prudent to consult with his brother judges before he charged the jury. The 'most important proposition' of the charge, that relating to the potential criminal responsibility of a Governor who had suppressed a rebellion, he had read aloud from prepared notes. Then, when he had finished reading his notes, Blackburn recalled, the Lord Chief Justice had himself invited him to tell the grand jury that his charge was approved of by the entire Court of Queen's Bench.

Cockburn listened intently to Blackburn's statement. It did not square with his own recollection. Just as Blackburn was completing the last portion of his statement (so Finlason reported) 'the Lord Chief Justice shook his head to intimate dissent'.[169] Cockburn then declared that Blackburn *continued* to misapprehend what had happened. The Lord Chief Justice reiterated that Blackburn's statements of law in the conference room were confined to 'the responsibility of the governor'. He suggested that Mr. Justice Lush would be able to corroborate this version of what had been said. With a nod of the head, Lush signalled his concurrence. This marked the end of the exchange, and the Court finally moved on to other business.

Cockburn's comments astonished English legal and political journalists. In the estimation of the *Law Times*, the remarks of Lord Chief Justice Cockburn were of a kind 'unprecedented in . . . the history of any other of the Superior Courts of law'.[170] Why had things gone so far awry? Was the Lord Chief Justice correct when he intimated that Blackburn had changed his mind on key issues after his consultation with his brother judges? Blackburn's answers to these questions had been somewhat (if understandably) inexact. Having been publicly admonished by his Lord Chief Justice, Blackburn had little practical recourse other than to take blame on himself. And so he did, if in a circumscribed way. Blackburn accepted responsibility for the misunderstanding concerning judicial support for his view of the law. He conceded that he 'ought to have taken more care to ascertain that there was no misunderstanding' as to the contents of his charge. Blackburn was certain that had he done so, and had his brother judges had indicated their dissent, he would have 'felt bound to deliver the same direction to

---

[168] Ibid.   [169] Ibid.   [170] *Law Times* (13 June 1868), 124.

the jury'. As matters stood, Blackburn wanted to make it abundantly clear that he believed his charge was correct in law, but that it 'had not more weight than was to be attached to my own individual opinion, conscientiously, deliberately and laboriously formed, but still mine alone'. On the law of martial law Blackburn was bloodied but unbowed.

The remarkable public clash between Cockburn and Blackburn still was not over. The following day Cockburn learned that it was the talk among some senior barristers that he himself had been responsible for, as he put it, 'bringing about the unfortunate misapprehension which has occurred in the case of *The Queen v. Eyre*'.[171] A rumour was in currency that before he gave his charge Blackburn had circulated a 'paper which embodied the substance of the law he intended to lay down'. The upshot of the rumour was that the Lord Chief Justice's account of the misunderstanding was wrong and self-serving. Cockburn felt compelled to respond publicly to this rumour, and he did so by initiating and then publishing correspondence with Mr. Justice Lush. In his letter to Lush, Cockburn asked whether his brother judge might confirm Cockburn's recollection of the judicial conference, particularly, how he [Cockburn] had been the last to enter the room when Blackburn briefed his fellow judges. Cockburn wanted Lush to corroborate that he had arrived in the room late, and had *not* seen the written summary that was given over to Lush. Cockburn also asked Lush to confirm that Blackburn's notes had 'contained more than the statement of the propositions to which we all [heard and] assented'. Lush, in his brief written reply (also given to the newspapers), affirmed that the notes 'contained only the general propositions mentioned by you in court yesterday', and that they had made no mention either of martial law or the Gordon case. In Lush's view, the Lord Chief Justice's perceptions of the incident were correct. In essence, Lush agreed that Blackburn's charge contained propositions which had not been approved by the other judges, and for which Blackburn alone was responsible.

Observers found it hard to absorb what had happened here. No one could recall another instance when a high court judge had made such 'a direct appeal to the newspapers'.[172] No one could remember another example of such a public and unseemly dispute between two judges of high office and exalted stature. No one could remember another instance in which one high court judge had asked a brother judge to corroborate a story which had been recalled differently by yet another judge. No one could remember when the private conversation and consultation as between judges had been publicized. In making his statement, in publishing his correspondence with Lush, the Lord Chief Justice of England had stepped outside of the prevailing concept of conventional judicial decorum. In so doing, moreover, the Lord Chief Justice had gone so far, in open court and then in an open letter, as to accuse a subordinate judge 'of something like bad faith'.[173]

---

[171] As printed in the *Pall Mall Gazette* (10 June 1868), 6.
[172] *John Bull* (13 June 1868), 405.   [173] *Morning Advertiser* (9 June 1868).

For all these reasons the intervention of the Lord Chief Justice amazed, even stunned, England's political and legal pundits. *The Times* thought that Cockburn's actions were 'not only unusual, but, we believe, unprecedented'.[174] According to the *Morning Star*, 'such an incident as that which took place yesterday is unexampled in history'.[175] The *Saturday Review* called it an 'unprecedented incident', the *Illustrated London News* an 'unprecedented occurrence'. 'We venture to say,' the *Morning Advertiser* declared, 'that a more extraordinary event...is not within the recollection of the oldest member of the bar. We repeat that we cannot recall one instance in which the Chief of one of our superior courts has found it necessary to express his dissent from the opinions of a judge of his own court in language so emphatic.'[176] '[A] *fracas* between the two learned Judges of the first court of the realm,' *John Bull* remarked, 'is, we should hope, almost unprecedented in our forensic history.'[177] At the opposite end of the political spectrum, *Reynolds' Weekly* was in accord that the 'spectacle of English judges flatly contradicting each other on the bench of justice on a vital principle...is strange, and, we dare say, scandalous'.[178] The editors of the *Law Times*, perhaps in a better position to offer an informed opinion, thought that the actions of the Lord Chief Justice were of a kind that 'has never been witnessed before, and, we trust, will never recur'.[179]

The press was of one mind that Cockburn's intercession had been shockingly irregular. It was being spoken of, so reported the *Imperial Review*, 'as the greatest scandal that has arisen in the courts since the Trial of the Seven Bishops'.[180] The preponderance of opinion among the more liberal papers, however, was that it also had been essential, even if it came at some cost to the tranquillity and prestige of the English judiciary. By these lights, the Eyre case was one of the 'utmost constitutional moment'.[181] If left unchallenged, Blackburn's charge would reverse all of the (perceived) gains that had been made in the reaffirmation of England's canonical jurisprudence of political and military authority. Hence the *Morning Star* praised the Lord Chief Justice for the 'courage and firmness' of his conduct. In this view, Cockburn had been right to intercede, even 'seeming to humiliate a learned brother', in order to vindicate the 'most cherished principles of freedom'.[182] According to the *Daily News*, 'the Lord Chief Justice only did his duty yesterday, and for so doing he deserves the hearty thanks of every lover of constitutional freedom'.[183] 'Mr. Alexander Cockburn,' the *Weekly Times* proclaimed, 'has just vindicated the true majesty of the law, in opposition to the interpretation of another Judge, containing the most atrocious doctrines and the most alarming

---

[174] *The Times* (9 June 1868), 9.   [175] *Morning Star* (9 June 1868), 4.
[176] *Morning Advertiser*, (9 June 1868).   [177] *John Bull* (13 June 1868), 405.
[178] *Reynolds' Weekly* (14 June 1868).   [179] *Law Times* (13 June 1868), 120.
[180] *Imperial Review* (13 June 1868), 548. In 1688 seven bishops were prosecuted for having petitioned against the dispensing of indulgences by James II. In that case four judges each delivered different charges to the grand jury. *Pall Mall Gazette* (9 June 1868), 1.
[181] *Saturday Review* (13 June 1868), 768. For similar remarks on the significance of the point, see *London Review* (13 June 1868), 583.   [182] *Morning Star* (9 June 1868), 4.
[183] As quoted in the *Pall Mall Gazette* (9 June 1868), 2.

errors.'[184] The Lord Chief Justice had prevented constitutional rights from becoming a 'vague tradition of the past'. The *Spectator* devoted a long and detailed article to a proof that on key points Blackburn's charge was 'diametrically opposite' those of his Lord Chief Justice.[185] According to this reading of the incident, Blackburn had been moved by unmistakable 'political prejudices' (his slander of Gordon was cited as evidence) to use the charge to exonerate Edward Eyre while he revived the doctrine of martial law, and all this in the teeth of a 'legal opinion so elaborately laid down by his superior judge'. For this reason the 'remarkable censure' delivered by the Lord Chief Justice was 'not more grave or more startling than the occasion really required'.

From the liberal and radical papers these were predictable reactions. But many other less strident voices also supported Cockburn's bold intercession. *The Times* thought that the clash between the two senior judges was to be regretted, but, by the same token, 'the Bar and the public had the right to know whether the Lord Chief Justice had changed his considered opinion, and it was inevitable that his dissent from the reversal of it should be declared sooner than later.'[186] And 'however much it was to be regretted,' the *Law Magazine* remarked, 'that any necessity should have arisen for the Chief Justice to repudiate the views stated by Mr. Justice Blackburn ... the former did no more than his duty in publicly expressing his disapproval of the charge'.[187] Had he deferred to professional niceties, 'the only inference that could be adopted was that the Chief Justice had materially modified his opinions on a question of great importance'. The issues at bar were of such magnitude that Cockburn's truculent dissent was 'not only perfectly justified, but imperatively called for'. In a similar vein, the *Morning Post* conceded that 'Mr. Blackburn transgressed equally against the canons of good taste and the usages which govern the procedure of the court of which he is a member.'[188] It was obvious that Blackburn had 'seized the opportunity' to pronounce on 'a point of great constitutional importance', and in a manner which 'in effect overruled the expressed opinions of the chief of that court'. The *Saturday Review* agreed that 'Mr. Justice Blackburn's great and remarkable mastery of the English law', and the weight which that mastery lent his decisions, 'made it the more necessary that the Queen's Bench should disavow any of his expressions which appeared to commit them to too much.'[189] Even among those inclined toward a 'natural sympathy with Mr Eyre's position,' the *Review* warned, it was important for the English to watch with the 'utmost jealousy the unconstitutional pretensions of martial law'.

When the dust began to settle on *The Queen v. Eyre*, the political and legal journals were broadly of one mind, as one put it, that the case had raised 'the gravest constitutional principles'.[190] There was also a rough consensus that these principles, far from being clarified, had fostered unprecedented and, in a law-loving country,

---

[184] *Weekly Times* (14 June 1868), 1.   [185] *Spectator* (13 June 1868), 697–8.
[186] *The Times* (11 June 1868), 8.   [187] 25 *Law Magazine* (1868), 257.
[188] As quoted in the *Pall Mall Gazette* (9 June 1868), 2.
[189] *Saturday Review* (13 June 1868), 768.   [190] *London Review* (13 June 1868), 584.

disconcerting levels of public conflict among the highest judges of the country. The final point of agreement was that it was time for the Jamaica Committee to wind up its affairs. But this last was more easily wished for than achieved.

V. Vindicating Martial Law: Finlason as the Carlyle of Legal Letters

The Jamaica Committee undoubtedly were surprised and dismayed by Blackburn's charge in *The Queen v. Eyre*. They were not so innocent, however, as to be surprised by the finding of the grand jury. As Goldwin Smith confided to an American friend prior to the charge, 'the state of opinion among the upper class from which grand juries are taken . . . is such as scarcely to give us any hope of success'.[191] The Committee now had been rebuffed by two English and one Jamaican grand juries, and separately by a panel of rural magistrates. But still they were not willing to give up. On 7 June, the day after the grand jury refused the bill in the second Eyre prosecution, Shaen was asked to provide a summary report on the feasibility of proceeding against Eyre by way of preferred indictment (thus bypassing the grand jury). On 12 June he gave his reply, advising the Committee that it would be 'inexpedient to take further proceedings against Mr. Eyre'.[192] (It is not clear whether Shaen had consulted with Stephen, or with some other barrister before rendering this advice.) Shaen's recommendation was accepted, apparently without opposition, even from Mill. Thirty months after its inception, the Jamaica Committee no longer was in the business of private criminal prosecutions. In fact, the Committee braced itself for a legal counter-attack from the Eyre camp in the form of an indictment for criminal conspiracy.[193]

Before the meeting of 12 June adjourned, Smith was invited to compose a public statement to the subscribers of the Jamaica Committee that would justify the previous prosecutions of Eyre, and the decision not to initiate further criminal cases. On 1 July, Smith presented a draft to the Committee's executive. After some minor amendments were made, the text was sent to the newspapers (under the signature of executive officers Mill, Taylor, and Chesson). The statement was published in many of England's newspapers on 16 and 17 July 1868.

The July statement began with an iteration of the most unsavoury facts about the Jamaica suppression, and their significance from 'a constitutional point of view'.[194] It explained that the Jamaica Committee had initiated prosecutions, not only because of the intrinsic importance of these issues, but because so many English parliamentarians, journalists, and legal writers had actually 'applauded the arbitrary

---

[191] Smith to Forbes, 30 May 1868, Smith Papers, *CUL*.   [192] *JC Minutes*, 12 June 1868.

[193] The plausibility of such an indictment was discussed in the *Law Times* (30 May 1868), 79. It is not known whether the Eyre Committee seriously weighed this option.

[194] 'The Statement of the Jamaica Committee', 15 July 1868, in John Robson *et al.* (eds.), *Collected Works of John Stuart Mill*, vol. xxi (Toronto, 1984), 429–35 at 431.

violence of Mr. Eyre' and 'took occasion to uphold martial law as exemplified in the acts of the governor and his subordinates'. Before the Jamaica affair, so the statement claimed, it had been generally (if somewhat complacently) assumed in England that such acts unquestionably were illegal, and would inevitably result in criminal prosecution and punishment. When they did not, when successive home governments refused even to declare categorically that Eyre and his soldiers had committed crimes, or indeed to 'take any steps for submitting the conduct of the principal agents to a judicial investigation', the void had to be filled by 'private citizens'. In the result, the Jamaica Committee had been formed to accomplish three related goals: 'to obtain a judicial inquiry into the conduct of Mr. Eyre and his subordinates; to settle the law in the interest of justice, liberty and humanity; and to arouse public morality against oppression generally, and particularly against the oppression of subject and dependent races'.

The roots of the Jamaica Committee were in Exeter Hall, as was duly acknowledged by the reference to the 'dependent races'. But this second July statement made it patently clear that the main preoccupation of the Committee was the integrity of the English constitution. The association had been formed and initiatives had been undertaken in order to vindicate certain constitutional principles, especially the principle that English law was always to prevail over English men. This precept had given rise to the chief aim of the Committee: to cause a judge of the English high courts to pronounce that Governor Eyre and his officers had contravened the basic law of nation and empire. For this reason, because its *raison d'être* was legal in character, the July statement underlined that the Committee had 'acted throughout under the legal guidance of counsel at once eminent and dispassionate'.[195] Expert legal advice had been the cornerstone of each of the Committee's key decisions, including the decision to prosecute on those acts of repression which had been inflicted 'after the insurrection had, in the opinion of the Governor himself, been put down, and when, in the judgment of his chief military subordinate, the military necessity was at an end'.[196]

The statement concluded with a self-assessment of how far the Jamaica Committee had accomplished its three main aims. With regard to the goal of arousing public opinion against the oppression of 'dependent races', the Committee thought that its efforts had been 'well repaid'. According to its reading of the record, the Committee had elicited a 'great amount of sound public opinion'. Moreover, it was 'not unreasonable to think' that its efforts in this regard had helped prevent similar abominations during the 'recent disturbances in Ireland'.[197] But with regard to the goal of gaining a fully realized trial of the legal issues created by the Jamaica martial law, there was a frank admission of failure. These efforts all had been 'baffled by the forms of law'. It was for the educated public to decide whether the Committee failed for the 'want of ground for an

---

[195] *Collected Works of John Stuart Mill* (Toronto, 1984), 429–35 at 431.   [196] Ibid., 433.
[197] Ibid., 434.

inquiry, or to the determination of those who interposed that no inquiry should take place'.

Regarding the related goal of settling the constitutional law in the interests of liberty and justice, the statement was more self-congratulatory. The charge of Lord Chief Justice Cockburn in *The Queen v. Nelson and Brand* was hailed as 'a lasting barrier against the encroachment of martial law and its upholders on the rights and liberties of British subjects'. The fact that Blackburn's subsequent charge 'differed' from that of the Lord Chief Justice was explained away on the basis that 'the opinion of the Lord Chief Justice is known to be shared by every other member of the Court'. Furthermore, Blackburn's charge 'did not maintain, as some lawyers had maintained, that the power of proclaiming martial law formed part of the prerogative of the Crown in England'. Insofar as Blackburn had given the doctrine of martial law a wider reading, that reading was 'limited to Jamaica, and founded on the Acts of the Colonial Legislature'. This legislation, and legislation of its kind in other colonies, the Committee reminded readers, had been repealed by consequence of Lord Carnarvon's circular on martial law. These facts were offered as justification for a bold statement: 'British jurisprudence, therefore, has been finally purged of martial law'.

It was one thing for the Jamaica Committee to herald the death of martial law, quite another for it to be so. In fact, in 1868 both as a legal doctrine and a state practice martial law was very far from dead;[198] the evidence to the contrary was tendentious and misleading. It simply was not true, for example, that Carnarvon's circular had banned the implementation of martial law in the empire.[199] Its only obvious effect was to direct that colonial statute books be cleansed of any 'permanent power' to suspend the ordinary law.[200] So that there would be no mistake about it, however, the circular also informed colonial officials that it 'must not be supposed to convey an absolute prohibition of all recourse to martial law under stress of great emergencies'. Carnarvon had meant to regulate the use of martial law, not to ban it outright.

This was one reason to doubt the authority of the Jamaica Committee's claims. Another was Blackburn's grand jury charge in *The Queen v. Eyre*. The Committee had tried to explain the charge away, but this was not easily done. As matters stood in July 1868, Blackburn's charge was the last *official* pronouncement on martial law from the English high court bench. The charge might be criticized – by the Lord Chief Justice himself – but it could not be undone or overruled. While Blackburn had cast doubt on there being a Crown prerogative to proclaim martial law, and on the assertion that martial law bestowed an 'unbounded' authority, he had not stated that martial law was illegal. On the contrary, Sir Colin had declared to the grand jury that sometimes, in the empire especially, it would become

---

[198] The continued use of martial law after 1868 is discussed below, Epilogue.

[199] It required only that colonial Governors move to repeal legislation which sanctioned the proclamation and use of martial law. For an overview of Lord Carnarvon's circular, see *The Economist* (6 July 1867), 752.   [200] See Carnarvon's Circular, 27 Jan. 1867, *CO* 323/287.

necessary for colonial officials to proclaim and implement martial law *as a reign of terror*. Where blacks or indigenous peoples outnumbered whites, there would be no other way to cope with the threat of race war. Blackburn also had underlined that when martial law was implemented honestly and reasonably (in the circumstances of a real emergency) it was unlikely that there could be criminal culpability. If martial law had not endured as a Crown prerogative, at the very least it endured as an instance of the common law defence of public necessity.

But there was yet another reason to doubt that martial law was dead. One of the ironic effects of the Jamaica Committee's July declaration was that it incited Finlason to publish new proofs that all of the Committee's central claims about martial law were either misleading or wrong. If Blackburn was in no position to defend his ideas on martial law from attacks, Finlason did not labour under this handicap. In the second half of 1868 he took it upon himself to vindicate his thesis that martial law was the law of war, unfettered by civilian notions of constraint and right conduct. In its July statement, the Jamaica Committee attempted to resurrect the authority of Cockburn's charge. In his last work on the Jamaica affair, Finlason attempted to entomb the charge for eternity.

In his capacity as chief legal reporter for *The Times*, on 9 June Finlason published an account of the wrangle between Justices Cockburn and Blackburn.[201] The piece contained some unusually piquant assertions about Cockburn and his charge. One was that Cockburn, in his recent statements to the press, had overstated the degree to which his address in *Nelson and Brand* enjoyed the support of his brother judges of the Queen's Bench. Cockburn had insinuated that only Blackburn dissented from his views on martial law. Finlason tried to undermine this claim, if with very inexact evidence. '[I]t was believed in the profession,' his article stated, 'that Mr. Justice Hannen concurs generally with Mr. Justice Blackburn'.[202] Finlason further alleged that with regard to the 'other learned judges it was well known in the profession that some of the most eminent and learned among them concur with Mr. Justice Blackburn'. Finlason concluded these remarks with the rather more serious allegation that Cockburn, when he made his charge, had wrongly claimed the 'concurrence of Mr. Baron Channell'. Finlason noted how this claim was 'omitted from the published charge, and was well known to have been mistaken'. Here Finlason had come perilously close to impugning the integrity (or at the very least, the mental competence) of the presiding Lord Chief Justice of England. In his zeal to fortify Blackburn and diminish Cockburn, Finlason had resorted to vulgar gossip and innuendo. For this he was admonished both in the *Pall Mall Gazette* and the *Solicitors' Journal*.[203]

---

[201] *The Times* (9 June 1868), 9. See also *Pall Mall Gazette* (9 June 1868), 997.

[202] Finlason reported that when Hannen was a law officer of the Crown in 1866, he had advised Cardwell that 'martial law for all acts done under its authority carried an indemnity'. *The Times* (9 June 1868), 9.

[203] *Pall Mall Gazette* (9 June 1868), 4. In the opinion of the *Solicitors' Journal* (13 June 1868), 669, an experienced legal journalist should have known better than to 'speculate as to the individual opinions of the other judges'. But there was another important reason to admonish the *Times* reporter:

More pointedly, the day after Finlason's report was printed, *The Times* ran a retraction.[204]

But by no means did this embarrassing incident signal the end of Finlason's engagement with these issues. On the contrary, during a sixty-day period from the beginning of July to November 1868 Finlason published no fewer than *four* book-length collections of documents and commentaries on martial law and the Jamaica case, every one a refutation of the notion that martial law was illegal or moribund.[205] This was an astonishing level of output for a legal writer – for any writer – and it is a fact about Finlason, his publishers,[206] and the historical moment which will deserve further comment when these works have been properly excavated.

Not the least reason that Finlason was such a prolific writer on martial law was that he was not too ashamed to publish old material under a new title. This stated, an impressive fraction of the material he published in 1868 was the product of fresh research and new thinking. At least two important inferences can be made about the historical significance of this unusual body of work. The first concerns Finlason's motivations and mindset. It is obvious that the author felt impelled, by professional ambition and political animus, to have the last word on the national debate on martial law. Every one of the hundreds of pages he published on the subject, especially after 1866, was invested with a sense of deep personal conviction and urgency. Finlason wrote as if he was one of a tiny handful of English lawyers who comprehended the *true* law of martial law, and how the true law had been corrupted by politics. Finlason also wrote as if the law of martial law was a matter of critical importance, from the premiss that, at the very least, the security of English men and women in the empire would be imperilled by doctrinal error. The second inference arises from the sheer volume of this work. While it is hard to know whether these books had a readership (given the arcane nature of the material, presumably it was a small one), it is plain that the books had a *market*. A sufficient number of people bought Finlason's first book on the legal aspects of the Jamaica affair to justify a second, and then respectively, a third, fourth, and fifth. How else to explain why Finlason's publishers[207] were

Finlason was 'well known in the profession as the author of a work on martial law which advocates views opposed to those of the Lord Chief Justice'. Given this personal interest in the story, Finlason's surmises about the opinions of other judges had been, at the very least, in 'bad taste'.

[204] The editor explained that the author of the story had had recourse to the shorthand notes of Cockburn's charge and 'desires to say … that those words were not used'. *The Times* (10 June 1868), 11.

[205] Finlason's *Report of The Queen v. Edward Eyre* and *The Repression of Riot or Rebellion* ran to 150 and 225 pages respectively, and were published in July 1868. *Justice to a Colonial Governor* was a 170-page script, and was published by the same two houses in August 1868. Finlason's *History of the Jamaica Case* ran to nearly 700 pages, and was published in 1869.

[206] Finlason's first book (*Commentaries on Martial Law*, 1866) had a single publisher, Stevens & Sons, which specialized in legal books and was located in Lincoln's Inn. Two of his later books (*The Queen v. Eyre*, and *The Repression of Riot and Rebellion*) were published both by Stevens & Sons and a house which did not specialize in law books, Chapman & Hall. Finlason's other books were brought out by one or the other press.

[207] Ibid.

prepared to release four (highly repetitious) volumes on the same subject in the space of six months?

There is an unmistakable evolution in the tone and content of Finlason's work on martial law. His first book on the subject, *A Treatise on Martial Law* (1866) was mainly an empirical survey of legal sources. Its stated purpose was to identify and explicate the disparate and largely unknown legal history of martial law. We have seen that the first treatise was not altogether neutral on the politics of martial law, that it advanced arguments about its utility as an instrument of imperial administration. In the main, however, this was a work of presentational scholarship, one executed with a minimum of stridency. Finlason's publications of 1868 were markedly different. Their author no longer was writing in a doctrinal vacuum. Now he took up his pen to discredit extant but *wrong* ideas about the law and policy pertaining to the Jamaica affair. Each one of Finlason's last four books on the subject was a fusion of legal sources and political stances. Each was rooted in the unshakeable conviction that martial law was a legitimate part of the English constitution *and* that it was vital that it should remain so. Increasingly, Finlason's legal writing was harnessed to the racial and political perspectives of England's extreme conservatives. In fact, Finlason ultimately began to posture himself as the Tom Carlyle of legal letters.

Finlason pursued his polemic fully within the conventions of legal writing and publishing. His first book of 1868, published in July, was devoted entirely to the exoneration of Blackburn's charge in *The Queen v. Edward John Eyre*.[208] The body of the work consisted of an annotated transcription of the charge,[209] as amended by Blackburn's personal corrections.[210] This section of the book was preceded by a long introductory essay. In this section Finlason candidly admitted that his book had been provoked by the 'unfortunate attempt made by the Lord Chief Justice to disparage the authority of the charge of his learned brother and to uphold his own'. The entire thrust of the introduction was to set forth the multiple reasons why Blackburn, not Cockburn, had got the law of martial law right.

In Finlason's view, it had not been clearly understood, either by the Lord Chief Justice or the press, that the *Eyre* case was 'wholly different' from *Nelson and Brand*. In *Nelson and Brand* the accused stood charged with murder and the subject of martial law figured only incidentally. In the *Eyre* prosecution the accused was charged with a list of misdemeanours arising from the proclamation,

---

[208] *Report of The Queen v. Edward Eyre*, xl.

[209] The book also included a copy of the indictment, and a transcription of evidence from the Bow Street hearing. Ibid.

[210] Before he published, Finlason sent Blackburn a transcript of his charge assembled from a shorthand writer's notes. At some point Blackburn 'revised' and returned it. It is obvious, then, not only that Blackburn had not changed his mind about the propriety and accuracy of his charge, but that he was not afraid to validate his views on martial law even in the face of the public criticism of his Lord Chief Justice. Ibid., xl.

implementation, and continuance of martial law. For this reason alone the Eyre prosecution 'directly and necessarily involved the whole subject of martial law'.[211] By Finlason's reckoning, Blackburn's charge on these issues was a model of judicial probity and precision. As far as possible, for instance, he chose to 'ground himself upon the enactment of the Colonial Act allowing martial law to be declared'.[212] By the same token, Blackburn saw that the very existence of the statute implied a 'precedent power to declare martial law'. In Finlason's view, moreover, Blackburn, unlike Cockburn, used the term 'martial law' in its correct sense, that it denoted 'the temporary establishment of military power in suspension of, and substitution for, the ordinary law of the land, as in time of war'.[213] There was no doubting, then, that Governor Eyre had possessed the legal authority to declare war on the Jamaican rebels. The only issue regarding his possible criminal liability was whether in proclaiming and implementing martial law the Governor had acted on best advice and in honest good faith. As Blackburn had correctly recognized, this was an issue of fact for the grand jurors alone to decide. His remarks quite properly had been confined to the legal implications of a particular finding of fact. Were it found that the ex-Governor had recklessly ignored advice that martial law was not to be proclaimed, or once proclaimed to be quickly ended, then the jury might find a true bill for offences under the Colonial Governors Act. However, if the jury decided that Eyre acted on the best available advice, then there would be no basis for a finding that he was 'gravely culpable' and therefore 'criminally liable'.[214]

It was Finlason's contention that in dealing with the issues raised by the Eyre prosecution, Blackburn had 'rigidly confined himself to his own province or function'.[215] He gave 'clear, plain, positive directions on such questions of law as *were* relevant'. In contrast to the charge of the Lord Chief Justice, everything Blackburn stated on the subject had 'judicial authority'. For this reason, 'if there is any inconsistency between [Blackburn's] charge and that of the Lord Chief Justice,' Finlason bluntly concluded, 'the *latter* must be discarded.'

These were reasons why Blackburn's charge was worthy of praise. But Finlason was even more forceful on the reasons why Cockburn's charge was not. The list was long and, for the most part, familiar to readers. To begin, Finlason thought that Cockburn had charged the grand jury on the wrong points of law. In this view, the main issue in *Nelson and Brand* was 'the *law of murder*, especially as to the doctrine set up of a sort of constructive murder by reason of the assumed illegality'.[216] As such, the Lord Chief Justice's charge ought mainly to have concerned the law of 'felonious malice'. Instead Cockburn expressed his opinion on the 'collateral' issue of martial law. In doing so, the Lord Chief Justice proceeded to make a number of additional mistakes. First, he incorrectly equated martial law with military law (instead of the law of war). Then, distrusting his own analysis,

---

[211] Ibid.   [212] Ibid., xx.   [213] Ibid., xxi.

[214] As Finlason put it, 'he could not be deemed to have acted without ordinary sense and judgment.' Ibid., xxvi.   [215] Ibid., xviii.

[216] Ibid., x.

Cockburn informed the jury that 'he was *not* able to give a distinct direction as to the legality or illegality of martial law'.[217] In the result, the Lord Chief Justice 'neither laid down as a matter of law, what martial law was, nor whether or not it was allowed in time of rebellion, in the sense in which it was understood and exercised by the accused'.[218] To compound the problem, and for a reason known only to the Lord Chief Justice, he invited the grand jury to resolve the key legal issue.

Finlason still was not finished with this final demolition of Cockburn's charge. The Lord Chief Justice had committed another serious error when he construed the political and military context of the Nelson and Brand case.[219] Cockburn had been utterly incapable of coming to grips with the concrete political, racial, and military realities of a colony like Jamaica. During his review of the evidence concerning the Morant Bay disturbances, Cockburn 'told the jury, in effect, that there was no rebellion, but a mere outbreak of insurrection put down in a day ... and that there could be no need for martial law'.[220] For Finlason, this not only was a highly contestable claim, it was a claim that ought to have been left to the grand jury to decide. Instead Cockburn had made a factual assumption that was not within his province to make, while he left purely judicial matters to the jury. When looking on Cockburn's charge as a whole, Finlason summarized, it indicated nothing more decisive than 'mere argument, one half upon the law, the other half upon the facts'.[221] More damningly, 'upon none of the great questions of law ... did the Lord Chief Justice venture to lay down any proposition of law.'[222]

All, or almost all of this, Finlason had written or intimated before. Where his final books on martial law departed from the script was with respect to Cockburn's underlying motivations. Finlason had come to think, and more than that to *publish*, the contention that Cockburn's errors were not innocent mistakes but were the product of deep-seated ideological bias. In this view, the errors of the Lord Chief Justice had been so many and so flagrant, his outburst against Blackburn so vehement and perverse, that there was no other plausible explanation. In the material published in the last months of 1868, especially in a book, *The Repression of Riot and Rebellion*, Finlason made his personal mission, his vendetta, to subject the mind and motives of the sitting Lord Chief Justice of the Queen's Bench to relentless and vitriolic attack.

Finlason's attack against the Lord Chief Justice had a number of facets, but all of them were subordinated to a central thesis: that there was no *innocent* reason for him to have concluded that the law of martial law was shrouded in obscurity and doubt. Cockburn's anguished references to a 'deficiency of authority' were simply unsustainable. In fact, Finlason maintained, the English law of martial law 'had been settled for centuries and declared by the greatest legal authorities, attested by judicial decisions, [and] affirmed by Parliament'.[223] Martial law was the unfettered law of war. Before

217 *Report of The Queen v. Edward Eyre*, xi.
218 See also *The Repression of Riot and Rebellion*, 201–2.   219 Ibid., ii–iii.
220 Ibid., xiii.   221 Ibid., xvii.   222 Ibid., xv.   223 Ibid., 202–3.

Cockburn muddied the water, this point had been definitively settled. If this law was to be unsettled, Finlason argued, 'it is not enough . . . for a judge to come down and declare that he is in doubt; that he cannot find the authorities, or that, so far as he does find them, he does not like them; that he thinks our historians inaccurate, and our legal constitutional writers in error; that Parliament and statesmen were mistaken, the lawyers were wrong, the legislature itself misled; all of this is not enough to create even a doubt as to law.' Given that the legal authorities were clear, it could have been rendered as unclear only by 'a fault in the will, as well as from a defect of the intellect'.[224]

Finlason did not suppose that Cockburn's mistakes were a consequence of deficient intellect. Rather, the Lord Chief Justice quite literally had been *unwilling* to countenance that martial law is the law of war. 'A mind, from any causes', Finlason audaciously wrote, 'strongly *adverse* to some branch of law, will naturally be extremely averse to acknowledge it.'[225] It was plainly an *idée fixe* of Cockburn's mental world that martial law was 'odious and oppressive'. Before he researched his charge in *Nelson and Brand* the Lord Chief Justice already had made up his mind that martial law was military law, and that what had been done in Jamaica under its banner was entirely illegal. This predisposition, Finlason believed, was 'wholly fatal to anything like calm judicial enquiry'. It was Finlason's belief that Cockburn, when he began actually to sift through the authorities, had encountered an unexpected fact: overwhelmingly they supported the proposition that martial law gave officials the legal authority to do whatever they honestly thought necessary to overcome armed resistance to the Crown. In the *Nelson and Brand* case, the accused officers *had* possessed the legal authority to execute Gordon. However, Cockburn had found this fact so inconvenient and repulsive that he simply refused to give it voice. Instead of professing the law the Lord Chief Justice had professed doubt, and then quite improperly had asked a jury of laymen to resolve the matter.

Thus far Finlason had provided an explanation of *what* Cockburn had done in *Nelson and Brand* and in the wake of the charge in *The Queen v. Eyre*. In a long book on the Eyre controversy published later in 1868,[226] Finlason offered a more fully realized theory of *why* he had done it. By the polite and deferential standards of the Victorian bar, Finlason's previous criticisms of Cockburn had been exceptionally bold. Now they grew bolder.

After he had indulged himself in another long description of the apparent weaknesses and contradictions of the Lord Chief Justice's reasoning in the *Nelson and Brand* case, Finlason observed that the judge had 'all through betrayed a singular disregard of historical testimony or legal authority'.[227] As a matter of political instinct, he asserted, Cockburn was an unfaltering Whig who, like many

---

[224] Ibid., 203.   [225] Ibid.
[226] *Justice to a Colonial Governor, or Some Considerations on the Case of Mr. Eyre: Containing the Substance of All the Documents, Discussions and Proceedings relating Thereto* (London, 1868).
[227] Ibid., 187.

English judges, had 'an intense aversion to anything like military rule or law'.[228] This liberal cast of mind was not only deeply rooted, but it was stubbornly anglocentric. Judges like Cockburn could not think about martial law in Jamaica without treating 'the subject in the same way as if it regarded this country'.[229] The Lord Chief Justice, in other words, was incapable of accepting that martial law might be practically obsolete in England but indispensably important in the empire. His political assumptions had blinded him to the extreme perils faced by white minorities in the tropical colonies, and to the need for some institutionalized recourse to terror: 'the Lord Chief Justice cannot tolerate the trial of rebels by court-martial even during rebellion because he cannot realize to himself the necessity for such deterrent measures, the reason being that he is always thinking of *this country*'.

Finlason ventured some further speculations about the wellsprings of Cockburn's aversion to martial law. It was possible, he suggested, that the Lord Chief Justice had 'become imbued with the animosities and prejudices entertained by the abolitionist party against the English inhabitants of our former slave colonies'.[230] Finlason trusted (with bitter irony) that this was not the case, for it was notorious that that party was 'composed of well-meaning but narrow-minded men' who had always relied on 'the weapons of calumny and misrepresentation' in advancing their causes. Such men steadfastly ignored, sometimes even celebrated, the 'wholesale massacre' carried out by mobs of negro insurrectionists while they denounced white settlers and officials. And so it was, Finlason maintained, in the context of the recent Jamaica affair. The anti-slavery party had stigmatized 'their fellow countrymen in the West Indies as monsters' just as they discounted the 'horrors of negro insurrection'.[231] If the 'Lord Chief Justice had in any degree become imbued with these ideas,' Finlason reflected, 'it would be perfectly impossible for him . . . to do justice on such a question'. Later in the same paragraph, Finlason went still farther, suggesting that Cockburn's charge, 'from the outset to the end, betrayed the effects of the influences [of the abolitionist view] thus exercised, to an extent entirely incompatible with his taking a fair view of a negro rebellion'.

Finlason was not finished. In subsequent passages he contended that Cockburn was not only biased but hypocritical. He reminded readers that in 1852, when Cockburn was Attorney General in Lord Russell's government, he had provided Parliament with an 'energetic vindication' of the brutal regime of martial law instituted in Ceylon by Lord Torrington. In that instance, Cockburn had frankly admitted 'the legality of martial law' and 'the lawfulness, under martial law, of summary punishment of rebels . . . as a means of deterring others'.[232] In Finlason's judgement, the discrepancy between Cockburn's opinion in 1852 and 1867 was not explicable on grounds that circumstances had dictated a harsher response in Ceylon. In fact, the Jamaica suppression had been 'marked by infinitely less

---

[228] Ibid., cxxiii.   [229] Ibid., cxxxvi.   [230] Ibid., cxxxviii.   [231] Ibid., cxxxix.
[232] Ibid., cxxv.

severity, as compared to the degree of danger than in the case of Ceylon'.[233] In Ceylon, Torrington had overseen 'wholesale military executions' without benefit even of courts martial. These had been exceptionally rare in Jamaica.[234] Finlason was prepared to concede that in 1852 Cockburn had been 'speaking in his official capacity as the law adviser of the Crown'.[235] But the Lord Chief Justice, Finlason observed with venomous irony, 'would be the last man on earth to take refuge in the excuse of office'. The Lord Chief Justice would never bear any imputation that he had spoken then as a 'mere paid partizan, whose views of the law, even in cases where human lives had been sacrificed, are to be regarded as . . . the mere result of party exigencies of the moment'. Were the question ever put to him, Finlason plausibly suggested, Cockburn would have little choice but to 'avow that his views on the Ceylon case were the views he honestly at the time entertained'.

In the final analysis, Finlason was inclined to believe that whatever ideas Cockburn might have entertained about martial law in 1852, he had come viscerally to detest the doctrine by 1867, so much so that he was willing to compromise his impartiality in order to expunge it. It was obvious to Finlason that in dealing with the Jamaica prosecutions the Lord Chief Justice had been motivated by 'some unconquerable prejudices against the exercise of martial law in this case of Jamaica, quite precluding him from doing justice to those engaged in it'.[236] The main consideration behind this bias, Finlason speculated, derived from its 'supposed bearing on the legal right to exercise it in this country, or in Ireland'. At every turn Cockburn had demonstrated his sympathy for the legal political preoccupations of the 'philosophical Liberals' associated with the Jamaica Committee.

In *Justice to a Colonial Governor*, Finlason's prose displayed a palpable and emotive contempt for anti-slavers, philosophical liberals, and their fellow-travellers on the high court bench. More explicitly than in his previous books on Jamaica and martial law Finlason had assumed the tone, vocabulary, and stances of Thomas Carlyle. We have seen that in his notorious essays on the 'Nigger Question' (1853) and 'Shooting Niagara' (1867),[237] Carlyle fulminated against racial equality, abolitionism, liberalism, and political democratization.[238] In a choice passage in the later essay, 'Shooting Niagara', Carlyle digressed from his polemic against the second Reform Bill to castigate the Jamaica Committee and Cockburn; the first for launching its feeble-minded sally against martial law, the second for giving it undeserved respectability. For Carlyle the Jamaica Committee were a 'knot of rabid Nigger-Philanthropists, barking furiously in the gutter', men so blinded by misguided idealism that they forgot that martial law was not an aberration, but

---

[233] Ibid., cxxvii.

[234] The Jamaica Royal Commission estimated that about eighty Jamaicans had been 'shot down hastily'. The number was thought to have been twice as high in Ceylon. Ibid., cxxviii.   [235] Ibid.

[236] Ibid., cxxix.

[237] 'Occasional Discourse on The Nigger Question' and 'Shooting Niagara: And After?', in Thomas Carlyle, *Critical and Miscellaneous Essays*, vols. iii, v (London, 1899).

[238] See generally, Hall, 'Rethinking Imperial Histories: The Reform Act of 1867' and 'Competing Masculinities'.

the very bedrock of any 'Human Society'.[239] The coercive power of the state, pitiless and unfettered, permitted civilization to arise and be sustained. To Carlyle's mind, there was no clearer sign of the degraded condition of political life in England than that a Governor, for 'putting down the frightfulest Mob-insurrection, Black or White, shall do it with a rope round *his* neck'. Finlason greatly admired 'Shooting Niagara', and in *Justice to a Colonial Governor* he quoted from it liberally. 'It is given to genius', Finlason wrote, 'to see in a moment, as by intuition, or by inspiration, truths which ordinary minds discover by laborious inquiry.'[240] Although he was not a lawyer, Carlyle (that 'illustrious writer', 'an historic genius')[241] had penetrated to a 'matter of legal and historical verity'. Carlyle had intuited what was plain in the legal authorities: that in England it was and always had been the law that when faced with armed insurrection officials of state might (now quoting from the charge of Blackburn) exercise 'the power of martial law to punish the insurgents by summary proceedings, and thus to check the spread of rebellion and to "trample it out" '.[242]

For Finlason, Carlyle also had been the country's most perceptive and sober observer of the implications of race for imperial security and law. He altogether agreed with 'the illustrious writer' that the egregious mistakes of the Jamaica Committee and Lord Chief Justice Cockburn were attributable to their insistence upon an 'entire identity, for all purposes, of the men of negro and of British blood, and treated a negro rebellion precisely as if it were one of British-born subjects'.[243] He also agreed that the Jamaica Committee's legal initiatives had been predicated on the patent absurdity that black Jamaicans, these ex-slaves and progeny of slaves, were entitled to equal regard under the law. The Lord Chief Justice himself had forgotten that by the 'very terms of the [Jamaica] charter it was restricted to English-*born* subjects and their descendants; and that nothing was further from the notions of our ancestors than restraining them from the recourse to martial law against subjects of an alien race'. In reality, the majority of men in a place like Jamaica, 'although they may be entitled to the rights of free-born Englishmen in the colony, are not, as a matter of fact, of British *blood*, and are always more or less animated by feelings of dislike for our rule'. As Finlason summarized the point, there was a 'monstrous fallacy in supposing that those considerations of personal liberty which might preclude or restrain the resort to martial law in this country could possibly have any application when it is resorted to by those of our own blood for their protection against subjects of an alien race'. Martial law, if it was obsolete in the home countries, remained indispensable in the empire of black men.

In *Justice to a Colonial Governor*, Finlason laboured to integrate Carlylean ideas about race and power with the legal materials associated with martial law. His

---

[239] 'Shooting Niagara', *Critical Essays*, 12.
[240] Finlason, *Justice to a Colonial Governor*, clviii.
[241] The 'historic genius' reference was made in Finlason's last book on the Eyre controversy, *History of the Jamaica Case*, 370.   [242] Finlason, *Justice to a Colonial Governor*, clviii.
[243] Ibid., cxxxi.

thesis was that the racial disparities and tensions endemic to tropical colonies had given renewed life and relevancy to the superannuated treatises and dicta which set forth the English law governing the suppression of rebellion by force. Taking the Jamaica affair as his example, Finlason postulated that anything that had been done to suppress the insurrection, no matter how brutal or irregular, was legally privileged if it had been done honestly. On the best information available to Jamaica's civilian and military officials in October 1865, the Morant Bay violence signalled the start of a 'murderous insurrection, a dangerous insurrection, an insurrection of a race for the purpose of extermination'.[244] Eyre, as Carlyle had put it, had been asked to put out a fire in a ship's powder room at mid-ocean.[245] In such dire circumstances, Finlason contended, 'it was necessary not only to put down the outbreak of the rebellion, but to inspire terror by the speedy punishment of a great many of those who had engaged in the rebellion'.[246] In these circumstances terror was a necessary and entirely lawful counterweight to the threat. When the Governor decided to meet this threat with overwhelming and terrible force he assumed that later he would be shielded by the laws of his colony and his homeland. In Finlason's estimation, Eyre 'was *right* in that view'.

VI. 'The Most Law-Loving People in the World': The Denouement of the Jamaica Prosecutions

'We are the most law-loving people in the world,' Mr. Punch acidly jibed in March 1868, 'but we are not prigs and pedants.'[247] In this brief excoriation of the Eyre prosecution, the editors at *Punch* had, if inadvertently, exposed a fissure in England's domestic political culture. On the one hand the English *were* a law-loving people, at least in the sense that their political elites were steeped in the idea that even the most exalted and powerful were liable to legal constraints and penalties. On the other hand, in an era of rapidly expanding empire, it was only prudent to consider the practical limits of the rule of law over men. In such a world it made good sense to think about the rule of law as contingent upon racial geography. It was one thing to constrain officials in Weston-super-Mare, Devon, quite another in St. Thomas-in-the-East, Jamaica. In the sprawling and turbulent empire of non-white men, inevitably there would be moments when civilian officials and military men would need to be unharnessed from the ordinary law. In such places and at such times there could be no effective substitute for ruthless and unrepentant coercion.

In the English broadsheets of 1868 the final episodes of the Jamaica litigation competed for space with one of the great foreign military adventures of the mid-Victorian period: the Magdala campaign. In 1867 an Abyssinian prince

---

[244] Ibid., lxxi.   [245] As quoted by Finlason, ibid., clvii.   [246] Ibid., xxvii.
[247] *Punch* (7 Mar. 1868), 99.

called Tewodros (in the English papers, 'Theodorus') decided that it would be useful to take as hostages the handful of British diplomats and European missionaries in his midst.[248] The hostages and their retainers were spirited to a mountain redoubt called Magdala. Ransom demands were made and wended their way back to London. The Derby Government soon felt pressure to organize a military intervention. In June 1867 a force of 13,000 troops was despatched to Abyssinia under the command of General Robert Napier. The following March they were poised to besiege Magdala. Before the attack could be commenced, Theodorus released all of the European hostages unharmed. But Napier did not withdraw. Magdala was bombarded, sieged, and sacked, Theodorus dying by his own hand. Napier and his force returned to England to a hero's welcome.

In July 1868 *Blackwood's Magazine* sarcastically suggested that the men who prosecuted Edward Eyre, they being so much preoccupied with the 'honour of England', ought now to bring the 'machine of the law' to bear against Sir Robert Napier.[249] That Napier is 'mainly responsible for the death of Theodore,' the editor wrote, 'I believe no lawyer of any eminence will dispute'. Here was an instance of 'Like case, like rule. Eyre convicted, it will not be difficult ... to bring Sir Robert to condign punishment.' The *Law Times* published a similar remark: 'why do not the Jamaica Committee try the question [of martial law] again by indicting Sir Robert Napier for bombarding Magdala after the surrender of the prisoners?'[250] In both cases English officials had taken human lives with no legal justification outside the exigencies of war. If Eyre had no legal authority to take lives in Jamaica, Napier had none in Abyssinia.[251] This line of reasoning, *Blackwood's* suggested, was plainly absurd.

These were taunts; but they were not nonsensical ones. They were based on the well-grounded perception that the Abyssinian expedition, in spite of its enormous cost to the public treasury,[252] had been overwhelmingly popular in England. The taunts were issued on the confident assumption that most readers would think it preposterous that Napier should be prosecuted for the death of Theodorus and his followers. The typical Englishmen, it was confidently understood, actually savoured the fact that Napier had razed Magdala, slaying Theodorus in the process. After all, Napier had been sent on a morally justifiable mission: to rescue British nationals from a wrongful captivity and punish the culprits. This was the orthodox view of the Magdala expeditions, and not only among the conservative sheets. The *Morning Star* newspaper, for instance, although it was the journalistic arm of political radicalism, published long,

---

[248] Hernon, *Massacre and Retribution*, 99–129; D. G. Chandler, 'The Expedition to Abyssinia, 1867–8', in Brian Bond (ed.), *Victorian Military Campaigns* (London, 1967), 107–60.

[249] *Blackwood's Magazine* (July 1868), 100–3.

[250] *Law Times* (13 June 1868), 120. See also *Law Times* (20 June 1868), 139.

[251] On this point a writer to the *Solicitors' Journal* (20 June 1868) ventured that the two cases were different because there was 'no shadow of question as to the legality of Napier's proceeding'. The writer did not explain the legal basis for this assertion.

[252] The bill came to £8,600,000. Hernon, *Massacre and Retribution*, 126.

detailed, and praising reports on the siege. In May 1868 the *Star*, without the slightest sense of irony, published reports from Abyssinia on the same page as the Eyre prosecution.[253] None of this raised an eyebrow among the Jamaica Committee. Mill himself thought that the country had been right to send the military to Magdala, and that 'the manner in which the war has been carried on by Sir R. Napier does honour to him & our country'.[254] Here an important line was being drawn. Mill was not squeamish about the use of governmental force. He was not a pacifist. Mill's concern was with the use and abuse of military force within British territories, especially with regard to British subjects. With the majority of his countrymen, on the other hand, Mill accepted that Britain was a great and global power, and that from time to time would be obliged to engage in small wars and punitive expeditions.[255]

For all the bluster of their final public statement of July 1868, the stalwarts of the Jamaica Committee must have been displeased by the state of legal affairs in England at the close of 1868. The thing that they had so doggedly striven for – a decisive vindication of the rule of law over political and military licence – had not been achieved. Where certainty, coherence, and clarity had been wanted in the law of martial law, most observers saw only uncertainty, contradiction, and confusion. 'In our wide Colonial empire,' the *Irish Law Times* observed, 'any day may witness some catastrophe similar to that of Morant Bay.'[256] Closer to home, there was reason to 'dread a Fenian outbreak'. But just as it had become imperative to settle the law concerning 'the power of the supreme magistrate of the locality to repress disturbances', the whole field had sunk into a 'state of haze'. For the *Irish Law Times*, it only aggravated an already unwholesome situation that 'two such distinguished authorities as [Cockburn and Blackburn] differ on an important constitutional question'. The last Jamaica prosecution, so timely and potentially decisive, had generated more smoke than fire.

The legal programme of the Jamaica Committee was founded on the assumption that the high court judges would seize the moment decisively to resolve the constitutional questions engendered by the Jamaica affair, especially the question of the legal status of martial law. Prior to the second prosecution of the former Governor Eyre, this had been the assumption also of most journalists. Blackburn's charge, and the spectacle produced when Cockburn publically assailed both the content of the charge and the conduct of its author, dramatically disproved this premiss. Suddenly the prestige of the law and the judicial law-makers had been cast into doubt. The *Imperial Review* expressed its profound regret that 'on a

---

[253] These reports were reprinted from the *Pall Mall Gazette*. See, e.g., *Morning Star* (20, 21 May 1868), 5.

[254] Mill believed that Britain was fully entitled to 'recover its envoy even if by war'. Mill, however, did profess some concern that Napier continued hostilities after the citadel had fallen and the hostages had been freed. Mill to Pratten, 9 June 1868, *Later Letters*, 1412.

[255] In the ten years preceding the Jamaica controversy, Britain had participated in no fewer than ten wars and punitive expeditions. For a comprehensive list, see Brian Bond (ed.), *Victorian Military Campaigns* (London, 1967), Appendix 1, 309–11. [256] *Irish Law Times* (13 June 1868).

question of such magnitude' as the law of martial law two eminent judges could express opinions that were 'diametrically opposite'.[257] A matter of fundamental public importance had been left in an 'embarrassing state of uncertainty'.

For its part, *The Times* also lamented that the law of martial law had become such a muddle. The editors regretted that Blackburn had not submitted a more detailed written script to his brother justices before he gave the charge in *The Queen v. Eyre*.[258] By doing so he might have averted a damaging public disagreement between 'the highest judicial authorities on a case of the highest interest'. It had been hoped by many observers, the Jamaica Committee only most prominently, that the judges would extricate martial law from the mire of political expedience and partisanship. Unfortunately, at the end of June 1868 it was glaringly apparent that, as *The Times* put it, the 'great lawyers are almost as much divided as the unlearned public on the conduct of Mr. Eyre, and it would not be right, even if it were possible, to disguise this fact'. This was a conclusion that the labour sheet *Reynolds' Weekly* also endorsed, if with greater regret. *Reynolds'* thought that the English nation had been put through two and a half years of agonizing conflict concerning the law of martial law – over the ultimate limits of political and military action – only for the issue to be left 'wholly unsettled'.[259] But, worse than that, the country had been subjected to the 'spectacle of English judges flatly contradicting each other on the bench of justice on a vital principle'.[260] The end result, *The Times* declared, was 'a scandal in the administration of our law for a parallel to which we must vainly seek in recent years, perhaps not in a generation'.

But why had things gone so badly wrong? One theory was that when they engaged with the issues raised by the law of martial law, the judges concerned had been too much influenced by political prejudices and preconceptions. With surprising bluntness the *Law Journal* observed that it was 'idle to disguise the fact that where historical and political theories, mixed up with the whole course of English history, are necessarily brought into play, the minds of judges work under the same advantages and disadvantages as do the minds of other intelligent men'.[261] In this view, one most fervently advanced in the writings of Finlason, the Lord Chief Justice was by far the worst sinner. According to Finlason, Cockburn had tried to superimpose his liberal predilections onto the categorically *illiberal* grid of martial law. The result was an internally incoherent account of martial law as mere military law. Cockburn's thesis did not issue from the detached analysis of legal authorities, but from the *a priori* premiss that martial law was incompatible with the English constitution. Other writers made similar assertions about Sir Colin Blackburn. As the *Spectator* put it,[262] he had been guided by an 'extraordinary prepossession by political prejudices'. When he made his charge in *The Queen v. Eyre*, the *Spectator* contended, Blackburn had rendered martial law as the law of

[257] *Imperial Review* (13 June 1868), 548–9.   [258] *The Times* (11 June 1868), 8.
[259] *The Times* (9 June 1868), 9.   [260] *Reynolds' Weekly* (14 June 1868).
[261] *Law Journal*, as quoted in *Pall Mall Gazette* (13 June 1868), 4.
[262] *Spectator* (13 June 1868), 698.

war because this view of the subject was consonant with another extra-legal consideration: that it was essential to the security of white minorities in the empire that imperial officials had ready access to uninhibited military power.

No reasonably informed student of English political history would be surprised to learn that Mill and Disraeli disagreed about the nature and content of martial law, or about the significance of the Jamaica affair. Nor is it extraordinary that the Jamaica and Eyre Defence Committees were able to find lawyers to advocate opposite positions on the criminal culpability of Eyre for the death of Gordon. What is far more interesting is that leading *English judges* also divided on the law of martial law, and on more or less the same grounds as the politicians. The *Manchester Guardian* offered a sophisticated hypothesis about this phenomenon.[263] With regard to the great issues thrown up by the Jamaica affair, the newspaper asserted, 'law is only part of the question'. For these questions the 'letter of statutes and dicta' could not alone be conclusive. What was genuinely pivotal to the outcome of the Jamaica cases was the 'moral medium through which [judges] regard facts'. In this respect, the *Guardian* soberly maintained, judges 'differ as widely as other men'. The public conflict between Cockburn and Blackburn was really a clash of 'political prepossessions'. On its face, this was a remarkably uncluttered and demystified view of what had happened. The courtroom, it was commonly thought, was a 'sphere that ought to be free from all disturbance'. The Jamaica affair had done much to dispel this myth.

---

[263] *Manchester Guardian* (10 June 1868), 4.

Epilogue

Phillips v. Eyre and the Problem of Martial Law

When Mill assumed the leadership of the Jamaica Committee his single-minded goal was to induce an English high court judge to find that martial law was unconstitutional, and that actions taken under its authority were answerable to the common law. This was to be achieved primarily by way of the private criminal prosecution of Edward Eyre. When this endeavour was derailed for a third time in the spring of 1868, Mill and his allies decided, if with great reluctance, to abandon the criminal prosecution strategy. But this did not mean that they had abandoned their goal. In fact, rather than wind up the affairs of the association, the Committee contemplated new but different legal initiatives. Their most feasible option was further to facilitate civil litigation in the English courts, litigation against Eyre and or other military officers and officials who had figured prominently in the implementation of martial law in Jamaica during October 1865. Success in such a lawsuit, it was thought, would be underscored by the principle that the declaration of 'martial law' in a British territory did not engender any special legal immunities or privileges.

In January 1867, two British subjects resident in Jamaica, Alexander Phillips and Dr. Robert Bruce, filed writs in England's Court of Exchequer against Eyre, and jointly against Abercrombie Nelson and Herbert Brand.[1] The lawsuits pleaded for £10,000 in money damages as compensation for a list of trespasses including assault, battery, and false imprisonment. The leaders of the Jamaica Committee were fully aware of these developments. Although Phillips and Bruce were in Jamaica when the writs were filed, both plaintiffs had somehow arranged to retain Shaen & Roscoe, the Committee's solicitors. William Shaen, of course, was an executive member and chief solicitor of the Committee during the entire course of the Phillips and Bruce litigation. It is understandable, then, that the *Law Times* queried whether these were 'volunteer litigants', or whether their lawsuits had in fact been 'instigated' by the Committee.[2] When the writs were served, Hamilton Hume, Secretary of the Eyre Defence Committee, publicly accused the

---

[1] *Law Times* (5 Jan. 1867), 181. In one source there is a suggestion that the plaintiffs had issued a writ in the Court of Exchequer in December 1865, but abandoned the earlier action. *Daily News* (13 Sept. 1866), 7.　　　　　　　　　　　　　　[2] *Law Times* (5 Jan. 1867), 181.

Committee of having 'got up' the suits as another facet of a larger campaign of legal persecution.[3]

After the Phillips and Bruce writs garnered publicity, the Jamaica Committee continued to deny that they had played any direct role in the litigation. The veracity of this claim turned on a very nice usage of the word 'direct'.[4] The seed capital for the litigation, it is true, did not come directly from the coffers of the Committee.[5] Nor was it directly financed by the Committee after the writs were served. In a letter to *The Times* published in November 1868, Shaen stated categorically that the Jamaica Committee 'never, in any way, promoted or assisted the only pending action against Mr. Eyre which is brought by Mr. Phillips on his own responsibility'.[6] But here Shaen was being less than candid.

In reality, the patronage of leading members of the Committee, if not the Committee proper, was the very lifeblood of these lawsuits. Since 1866, Louis Chamerovzow (chairman of Exeter Hall, and founding member of the Jamaica Committee) had used his position at Exeter Hall to channel financial, logistical, and legal support to both plaintiffs.[7] In 1868, so that Phillips and Bruce might serve as witnesses in the second prosecution of Eyre, Exeter Hall had paid their passage to England. Then, as was admitted by Phillips during a proceeding against Eyre in May 1868, the living expenses of both men had been defrayed from a fund collected and sustained by active members of the Jamaica Committee, and administered by Shaen & Roscoe. And, as Eyre's solicitors carefully documented in the press,[8] the Phillips and Bruce litigation fund had been promoted by recourse to a printed circular prepared and distributed by the same law firm. That document declared that Mill, Taylor, and Bright endorsed Phillips' litigation in order to 'raise ... by civil procedure the important constitutional questions involved by the attempts of the Jamaica Committee to obtain an authoritative decision upon them'.[9] This campaign garnered donations of more than £620. When the time arose, the plaintiffs had money enough not only to remain in England while their cases made their way to trial, but to retain barristers of the highest skill and reputation.

While the cost of the civil litigation against Eyre was underwritten by third parties, it is probable that the impetus for the actions originated in the sense of outrage and injustice felt by Phillips and Bruce themselves. Both men had the

---

[3] This accusation is reported in the *Law Times* (26 Jan. 1867), 240.

[4] In his diary, Chesson recorded that the Jamaica Committee 'had nothing whatever to do with [it]'. *CD*, 14 Jan. 1867.

[5] According to Chesson's private diary. *CD*, 3 May 1867. According to later records, at a meeting of the Committee held in the spring of 1869, Mill proposed that money be donated from the coffers of the association to help support an appeal of a verdict against Phillips. *JC Minutes*, 5 Apr. 1872.

[6] Letter to *The Times* (4 Nov. 1868), 8.

[7] Finlason, *Report of The Queen v. Edward Eyre*, 9–11.

[8] The accusations were raised soon after the writs were filed. See *Spectator* (26 Jan. 1867), 87. The Jamaica Committee's activities on behalf of the plaintiffs were described in detail by Anderson Rose (employing ample quotes from a circular prepared by Shaen) in a letter to *The Times* (9 Nov. 1868), 7.

[9] There was some uncertainty as to whether Shaen had specifically got permissions to use these names.

social and psychological resources to contemplate and start the process. In October 1865, Phillips, we have seen, was a landowning 'gentleman' in St. Thomas-in-the-East.[10] Bruce was a medical doctor and coroner in the same parish.[11] Before the trouble at Morant Bay, both men had been involved in the agitation for political reform and had cultivated dependable contacts among Baptist missionaries. When the violence broke out, both men had quickly been identified by the authorities – on scant evidence – as co-conspirators in the uprising.[12] On the order of Governor Eyre, both also had been placed under arrest, roughly handled, and transferred to the makeshift military prison at Morant Bay. There they were confined, in miserable conditions, for almost a month in the camp run by Duberry Ramsay. Perhaps because he was a black man, Phillips was pitilessly flogged. When martial law ended, however, both were tried in the civilian courts for conspiracy to commit treason and were acquitted. It would appear then that their ordeal wounded them not only in body, but also in their sense of dignity as British subjects.

One of the putative legal rights of a British subject was to be free of unjustified trespass to the person; another was to sue for damages should this right be infringed, even if on the order of an executive official of state. Had it not been for the obstacle presented by the indemnity statute passed by the colonial assembly in November 1865, and then assented to by the British government in June 1866, Phillips and Bruce might have pressed their causes in the local courts.[13] But the statute left them with no sensible alternative but to pursue the civil actions in the English courts, and on the theory that a colonial legislature lacked the legal authority to limit the civil rights of a British subject in the English courts.[14]

Some time in the first weeks of 1867, before Phillips and Bruce had arrived in England, Shaen & Roscoe served their writs in the Court of Exchequer against both Eyre and Abercrombie Nelson. The defendants wasted no time in making written appeals to their respective ministries (the Colonial Office and War Office) for support in defending the actions.[15] As we have seen, because he was a subordinate officer at the time of the alleged wrongdoing, Nelson's application was granted.[16]

---

[10] When asked by the Royal Commission if he had a business, Phillips replied that he was 'in the position of a gentleman', that he was 'living off his own means'. *JRC Minutes*, Q. 17,119.

[11] *JRC Minutes*, Q. 12,218–43.

[12] In a despatch to Cardwell written after the uprising, Governor Eyre referred to Phillips as 'another of the principal agitators'. Eyre to Cardwell, Jan. 1866, *JRC Eyre Papers, PP* (1866), 15.

[13] At least one civil action brought against a colonial official in Jamaica was dismissed on this ground in 1867. Ibid.

[14] This view was not held by the plaintiffs only. When it learned of these lawsuits, *The Times* was of the view that the 1775 decision, *Mostyn v. Fabrigas*, had decided that an action in trespass arising in a colony or dominion might be litigated in England. *The Times* (11 Feb. 1867), 9.

[15] With regard to the requests of Nelson, see Forster to Duke of Cambridge, 19 Dec.1866; Clode to Lord Longford, 15 Mar. 1867, *WO* 32/6235.

[16] As Disraeli stated to the House of Commons in February 1867, 'when an officer in Her Majesty's service, obeying the commands of his superior officer, performs acts which are afterwards legally impugned, it will, of course, be the duty of the Government to defend him'. *Hansard*, ccxii (14 Feb. 1867), 337.

Eyre, we have also briefly noted, was not so fortunate. On 21 January 1867, Eyre informed the Colonial Office that he was about to be the target of criminal prosecutions and civil lawsuits.[17] He pointed to the 'enormous expenditure which must be incurred in any attempt adequately to meet charges brought forward under such circumstances'. He wanted the official documents needed for a full defence in court,[18] and to be fully indemnified for the financial cost of his defence. These requests caused a considerable stir at the upper echelons of the Colonial Office. There was uncertainty about the scope and effect of the Indemnity Act, and whether it would protect Eyre. There was equal uncertainty about the government's obligation to pay Eyre's legal costs. Certainly there was no eagerness to do so. Frederic Rogers, after he made enquiries about the policies extant in other ministries, ultimately recommended that Eyre ought to be reimbursed only 'if it is shown that he acted lawfully and in good faith'.[19] Rogers thought that the government 'can look better by leaving Eyre's defence to him and his friends and by waiting to see what he has done'. He did not want a civil jury to think that an award of damages would be paid from the 'public purse'. But before Lord Carnarvon was asked to make a final decision on these matters, Rogers sought further legal advice on Eyre's prospects. In the result, Eyre was informed that the 'Jamaica Indemnity Act, though not confirmed by an Imperial Act, will supply a defence in criminal or civil proceedings brought against you'.[20] As for his legal costs, Carnarvon was steadfast that Eyre would be reimbursed only after he successfully defended the claims.

Left to his private resources, Eyre did well enough. By November 1868 some £13,000 had been raised by the Eyre Defence Committee to defray expenses associated with the criminal prosecutions.[21] However, it is not clear that the Eyre Committee paid for all (perhaps not *any*) of the costs associated with defending the civil actions. In fact, there is evidence that before the Phillips suit was resolved in the spring of 1870, Eyre was out of pocket by many thousands of pounds.[22] But, whoever was paying the bills, Eyre's lawyers mounted an aggressive defence to the civil suits. On 26 January 1867, less than two weeks after the Phillips writs were served, his lawyers brought a motion to stay proceedings against Eyre.[23] Bramwell dismissed the motion.

[17] Eyre to Frederic Rogers, 21 Jan. 1867, *CO* 137/429.

[18] In particular, Eyre requested all of the documents which contained the legal advice he had received from the law officers of the Crown prior to and during the proclamation of martial law. Eyre also wanted a copy of the Act of Indemnity. Ibid.

[19] See Henry Taylor's personal notation on the file. Ibid.

[20] Carnarvon to Eyre, 7 Feb. 1867, *CO* 137/429.

[21] According to Charles Buxton. 'Letter to the Electors of East Surrey', *The Times* (7 Nov. 1868), 4. This figure was repeated in the House of Commons. See Bowring, *Hansard*, ccxii (8 July 1872), 807. Another £3,000 had been raised for Eyre in the shape of a 'Testimonial Fund'. Ibid.

[22] Eyre to Murchison, 3 Mar. 1869, Murchison Papers, *BL* Add. MS. 46126.

[23] They argued that as the plaintiffs resided outside the jurisdiction of the court, they were obliged to post security for costs or face dismissal. *Law Times* (26 Jan. 1867), 243.

Bruce arrived in England, physically unwell, in April 1867.[24] Phillips arrived in May.[25] After a consultation with Shaen, both men decided to abandon their actions in the Court of Exchequer, only to start two new lawsuits, now against Eyre only, in the Court of Queen's Bench.[26] The editor of the *London Review* believed he knew the reason behind this seemingly strange move. He noted that lawsuits as notorious and significant as those brought against Eyre 'are generally tried by the Chief Justice or Chief Baron in the court in which they are brought; and consequently, the present action, if proceeded with, will come to Sir Alexander Cockburn'.[27] Before the civil actions were commenced, Cockburn had rendered his grand jury charge in *The Queen v. Nelson and Brand*. For this reason, the *Review* wondered whether the plaintiffs 'hoped for some advantage' in having their cases heard in the court of the Lord Chief Justice.

Phillips registered his new pleadings on 7 November 1867. By early January 1868, Eyre had entered a defence, its essence being that he 'was not guilty to the action, and also that he was protected by the Act of Indemnity passed by the Jamaica legislature'.[28] Phillips' solicitors then quickly responded by seeking (by way of preliminary motion) a counter-pleading called a 'demurrer'.[29] By this procedural device, they wanted to admit the material facts alleged in Eyre's pleadings while objecting to the legal validity of his assertion of legal privilege or defence. In short, Phillips wanted to knock out Eyre's contention that the indemnity statute provided a complete defence to the action. Phillips' lawyers reckoned that if their client prevailed on this point, he was sure to prevail in the litigation as a whole. But, in order not to gamble everything at once, they sought to amend his pleadings with the averment that 'part of the trespasses complained of were committed outside the jurisdiction of the Jamaica Legislature'.

The motion was argued before a Mr. Brewster, the 'master' (an officer of the court) who presided over motions in the Queen's Bench chambers. Over the objections of Eyre's solicitor on the application (a Mr. Petheram), Brewster granted Phillips' application.[30] The upshot of this decision was that before *Phillips v. Eyre* could be tried on its merits, there would be a preliminary hearing on the 'declaration' (or formal legal restatement)[31] of Phillips' demurrer.

---

[24] *Daily News* (13 Sept. 1867), 7.   [25] *CD*, 3 May 1867.

[26] It is possible that there were both procedural and substantive advantages to be realized by starting afresh in the Queen's Bench. Procedurally, the plaintiffs would no longer face harassing questions about why they had done so little to advance their lawsuits.

[27] *London Review* (1 June 1867), 619.

[28] For an account of the application, see *Pall Mall Gazette* (10 Feb. 1868), 6.

[29] For an explanation of the demurrer, see J. H. Baker, *An Introduction to English Legal History*, 4th edn (London, 2002), 79.

[30] The substance of his objection was not recorded. *Pall Mall Gazette* (10 Feb. 1868), 6.

[31] In this sense, the procedure by which a party would provide a systematic restatement of the law and facts supporting the cause of action. *Black's Law Dictionary*, 5th edn (St. Paul, Minn., 1979), 367.

Although Dr. Bruce, perhaps for reasons of failing health, did not pursue his action to this next stage,[32] Phillips stayed the course.[33] In April 1868 some of Phillips' witnesses were examined out of court (including, as an expert in Jamaica law, the colonial barrister George Phillippo).[34] Then, in mid-June, the second criminal prosecution of Eyre was dismissed after Blackburn's charge to the Middlesex grand jury. Phillips' civil action now was the only active litigation against the former Governor. As *Phillips v. Eyre* slowly made its way through the courts in the autumn of 1868, Charles Buxton, who had recently fallen out with the Jamaica Committee over the further prosecution of Eyre, attempted to bring a halt also to Phillips' civil proceedings.[35] Convinced that further litigation against Eyre was pointless, Buxton offered to pay Phillips money 'out of his own pocket' if he would agree to abandon his lawsuit. Although it was far from certain that he would ultimately prevail in his case, Phillips refused. The tempting inference here is that for this plaintiff the lawsuit had exceptional or symbolic importance. More than money, this obviously proud black gentleman craved public vindication of his rights and privileges as a British subject.

When *Phillips v. Eyre* came before the Court of Queen's Bench on 17 November 1868, it was not, as has been stated, as an ordinary trial matter. No witnesses were called; no facts were decided. The case came forward as proceedings *in banco*[36], as an adversarial hearing on the demurrer. Although *in banco* proceedings conventionally were heard by a panel of four judges, in this instance only three judges presided on the case: Lord Chief Justice Cockburn with Mr. Justice Lush and Mr. Justice Hayes. (A fourth judge, Mr. Justice Hannen, had recused himself because he once had acted as defence counsel for Colonel Nelson in *The Queen v. Nelson and Brand*.)[37] The *Law Times* recognized that *Phillips v. Eyre* was an 'important case', one meriting an extensive report.[38] *The Times* also provided readers with nearly three full columns of broadsheet on the oral submissions.[39] Between these two accounts, and that of the law report,[40] a good if incomplete picture can be pieced together of what was said by the lawyers and judges.

[32] In an application made in the same proceedings, Bruce's lawyers asked for an additional three months to file his formal pleadings. These documents were never filed. Ibid.

[33] There were further if ultimately inconsequential preliminary proceedings in *Phillips v. Eyre*. For a summary, see *Pall Mall Gazette* (20 Apr. 1868), 7.

[34] Phillippo testified as an expert on Jamaican statutory law. *Pall Mall Gazette* (20 Apr. 1868), 7.

[35] *Pall Mall Gazette* (4 Nov. 1868), 5. Buxton opposed the civil actions on the same grounds that he had opposed the criminal prosecutions, i.e. that they would generate sympathy for Eyre while not producing a clear judicial statement on the law of martial law. Buxton's good faith in this intervention was questioned publicly by Eyre's solicitor, Anderson Rose. See Letter to *The Times* (9 Nov. 1868), 7.

[36] In contrast to trial proceedings 'at *nisi prius*' involving issues of fact, the *in banco* procedure was invoked so that a panel of four judges (sitting 'in bench') might decide an issue of law. *Black's Law Dictionary*, 684.   [37] *The Times* (18 Nov. 1868), 11.

[38] *Law Times* (21 Nov. 1868), 47.   [39] *The Times* (18 Nov. 1868), 11.

[40] *Phillips v. Eyre* (1869), L.R. 4 225 (Q.B.).

Phillips's revised pleadings set forth seven separate but related allegations of tortious wrong.[41] The first six pertained to various counts of wrongful detention and physical ill-treatment during the period of martial law, the seventh to detention and ill-treatment after martial law had ceased. Specifically, Phillips alleged that on 24 October 1865, Phillips had been arrested at his home and then conveyed in irons to the Governor's residence thirty miles away at Spanish Town. After a brief interrogation, he was forcibly conveyed to a temporary military prison at Uppark Camp, before being put on a ship bound for the military prison at Morant Bay. Phillips asserted that, on 4 November 1865, he was 'cruelly beaten, flogged, wounded, and tortured' before being released. It was further alleged that these wrongs had caused the plaintiff significant pain, sickness, and disability. When granted the demurrer a year earlier, Phillips's lawyers amended their pleadings to make the potentially important assertion that 'the defendant committed such trespasses as are complained of and not included in the Act on other occasions, for longer periods of time, and in other places than are attempted to be justified or excused, and in excess of the alleged right or excuse'. Phillips further contended that some of the wrongful acts of the defendant were committed when Phillips was imprisoned 'on the high seas' and therefore 'beyond the territorial limits' of the Jamaica legislature.[42] In other words, the plaintiff had prepared a 'fall-back position' in the event that the Queen's Bench found that the Act of Indemnity privileged any wrongdoing that had occurred during martial law.

Both sides chose lawyers with great care. The eminent barrister Sir John Quain Q.C.[43] (who, a few months earlier, had declined the prosecution brief in *The Queen v. Eyre*) was retained to argue the case for Phillips. Once again, Horne Payne was briefed as the assisting barrister. The defence retained Sir George Mellish Q.C., a lawyer renowned for his work in hearings *in banco*.[44] Mellish was assisted by Harry Poland, another veteran of the criminal prosecutions of Eyre.

Before delving into the legal arguments and decisions rendered in the case it is worth stating a point that was conspicuous to contemporary observers, but has been largely lost on subsequent scholars:[45] *Phillips v. Eyre* was anything but a mundane civil action waged between private parties. This was a rare example of what might be called 'national litigation'. It was plain to every educated English person in November 1868 that *Phillips v. Eyre* was yet another battle in the legal proxy-war being waged between the proponents of a liberal conception of the constitution and the

[41] The pleadings had been transposed into a 'replication, demurrer, and a new assignment'. *The Times* (18 Nov. 1868), 11.   [42] *Phillips v. Eyre* (1869), L.R. 4 225 (Q.B.), 228.

[43] Thirty years at the bar, Quain was one of the leading lawyers of his day. He was appointed to the Court of Queen's Bench in 1871. Polden, *Oxford DNB*, online 22938.

[44] Mellish also had been thirty years at the bar, and was appointed to the bench in 1870. Hamilton, *Oxford DNB*, online 18530; *DNB*, xiii, 220–1.

[45] Since 1870 *Phillips v. Eyre* has often been cited in the legal textbooks as a 'leading case' in the law governing 'conflict of laws'. However, in describing the precedent, the treatise writers have not been concerned with its historical antecedents or context. See J. A. Foote, *Private International Jurisprudence* (London, 1878), 393–402; A. V. Dicey, *Conflict of Laws* (London, 1896), 659–66; G. C. Cheshire, *Private International Law*, 3rd edn (Oxford, 1947), 368–84.

proponents of (what they viewed as) a pragmatic conception of security in the empire. This was the civil equivalent of a state trial.

The central matter at issue in the hearing in *Phillips v. Eyre* was the legal validity of Eyre's blanket plea of 'not guilty' on grounds that his actions, even if wrongful at law, were privileged by the indemnity legislation passed by the Jamaica Assembly in 1866, and then assented to by the government later that year. Quain opened the case for the plaintiff. His first submission was that 'immediately on commission of the wrongful acts . . . there vested [in the plaintiff] a right of action, so that he could at once have come over to England and issued the writ in the court of Queen's Bench'. His second submission was that 'no *ex post facto* act of the Jamaica Legislature could deprive a British subject of a right of action once vested in him'.[46] In support of these two submissions, Quain cited the principle set down in the 1775 case *Mostyn v. Fabrigas*.[47] In that case, Lord Mansfield decided that every otherwise good cause of action must be amenable to the jurisdiction of some court in some part of the empire. When the defendant denied that a court had jurisdiction, it was incumbent upon him to 'shew a more proper and sufficient jurisdiction'. In the case at bar, Quain contended, the Jamaica indemnity law inconvenienced the plaintiff solely to the extent that he could not pursue his action against Eyre in that colony. His right to maintain the suit in England, however, could not be extinguished without overruling the principle laid down by Lord Mansfield. Quain also pressed on the panel that there was 'no difference between a prosecution under the act generally known as the *Colonial Governors Act* and a civil action'. No one had suggested in *The Queen v. Eyre* that the Jamaica indemnity statute foreclosed a criminal prosecution.

All of the sources indicate that Quain's submissions attracted immediate and stiff resistance from the panel, especially, if unexpectedly, from Cockburn. Interrupting Quain in mid-argument, Cockburn asked whether, in the wake of an insurrection in England, would it not 'surely be valid' for Parliament to pass an indemnity law even after indictments had been found.[48] The Lord Chief Justice also strongly suggested that there were salient differences between criminal and civil proceedings, and that there might be a stronger case that the indemnity should extinguish a civil action. At this point, Cockburn abruptly broke off his exchange with Quain and called upon Mellish to take up these questions for the defence.

Mellish's argument focussed on the principle of parliamentary sovereignty. 'By the law of England,' he maintained, 'the legislature of a colony is supreme within its boundary.'[49] In passing the indemnity statute, an Act that had not been repealed by the central government, the legislature of that colony made law 'as

---

[46] In support of this view Quain cited Justice Blackburn in *The Queen v. Eyre. The Times* (18 Nov. 1867), 11.   [47] Ibid.

[48] Quain submitted that whatever Parliament might do, the jurisdiction of a colonial legislature was more limited. *The Times* (18 Nov. 1867), 11.   [49] *Phillips v. Eyre* (1869), L.R. 4 225 (Q.B.).

binding as the laws of the Imperial Parliament'.[50] While Mellish conceded that a colonial legislature could not deprive a British subject of a 'remedy', he contended that it could 'discharge a right of action which has accrued within the limits of their territory'. Mellish submitted that the indemnity law had been passed with the express purpose of erasing any right of action that accrued to the plaintiff during the period of civil unrest in Jamaica. Between the colonies and home country, such statutes had been promulgated more than a dozen times before. Legislative indemnity was thus 'well known to the law'.[51] Further to the point, Mellish argued that 'it was a fallacy to speak of the [Act of Indemnity] as a local act. The local Act was valid by reason of Imperial law ... The prerogative of the Crown had created colonial legislatures in the colonies.' It was to be remembered that after the Jamaica Royal Commission made its final report, the Government assented to the indemnity law. Just as Parliament could pass or approve any laws, including retroactive laws, so too could a colonial legislature pass any law *intra vires*. No one disputed that it was competent for a colonial legislature to make laws on civil and criminal liability.

Like Quain, Mellish was frequently interrupted by Cockburn. However, the questions put to Mellish were conspicuously of a friendly kind. Cockburn even offered his own examples of indemnity statutes, including others previously passed by the Jamaica Assembly.[52] By the time Quain was asked to make his reply, his position was precarious. When he tried to mount an argument that the Jamaica indemnity law was *ultra vires* because it tended to contradict the provisions of the Colonial Governors Act, Cockburn pointed out that the law would still be valid with regard to civil cases. He suggested that Quain's submissions, if accepted, would tend to undermine the authority and effectiveness of colonial legislatures. The Lord Chief Justice then began to propound on why this would be a very unwelcome consequence, that neither colonial officials nor subjects would have any clear idea of their real legal rights and obligations.[53] At this juncture, Quain might have advanced his alternative pleading that some of the wrongs done to the plaintiff occurred after the period of martial law and potential indemnity. (Had he been of a mind to do it, moreover, Cockburn might himself have *initiated* some discussion of this pleading. Neither did.) By way of conclusion, Quain made the rather fatuous submission that as a signatory of the indemnity law, Governor Eyre was not entitled to its protection. But making little headway with this, as *The Times* reported, Quain 'fell back on his main argument that a right of action had vested, and could not be divested by a Colonial Act'.[54]

That was his final submission. Cockburn complimented both counsel on their 'admirable arguments', and informed them that judgement would be reserved. The written judgement in *Phillips v. Eyre* was delivered in open court by Cockburn more than two months later, on 29 January 1869.

---

[50] Ibid., 231–2.   [51] Ibid., 232.   [52] *The Times* (18 Nov. 1867), 11.   [53] Ibid.
[54] Ibid., 11.

It is trite legal theory that when judges decide cases, they make choices. They choose between alternative characterizations of law and facts, and the envisioned consequences of choices about law and facts. The personality, sometimes the political disposition, of the individual judge is a factor in the outcome of cases. Certainly this was the active assumption of the lawyers and benefactors of Alexander Phillips. When Phillips abandoned his writs in the Court of Exchequer, and began new actions in the Court of Queen's Bench, it was because he had been advised that when choices were to be made about the law and facts of his lawsuit against Eyre, it was more likely that advantageous choices would be made by Lord Chief Justice Cockburn. After all, in his charge in *The Queen v. Nelson and Brand*, Cockburn had chosen against the expansive doctrines of martial law, and against the authoritarian tendency which informed them. In that instance, in other words, he had proved willing to subordinate doctrine to justice.

But the striking aspect of Cockburn's judgement in *Phillips v. Eyre* is that it conveys the sense that there were *no* choices to be made at all. Cockburn wrote as if he were powerless to find for the plaintiff, no matter how just his cause. At the same time, the Lord Chief Justice was not insensible to the fact that *Phillips* raised issues of 'great importance'. Cockburn understood perfectly well that the Jamaica indemnity statute was *ex post facto* law, and that it was designed to pardon the unpardonable. 'There can be no doubt', he wrote, 'that every so-called Indemnity Act involves a manifest violation of justice ... It is equally true ... that such legislation may be used to cover acts of the most tyrannical, arbitrary, and merciless character, – acts not capable of being justified or palliated even by the plea of necessity, but prompted by local passions, prejudices or fears ... by reckless indifference to human suffering and an utter disregard of the dictates of common humanity.' Thus, while Cockburn's judgement in *Phillips v. Eyre* was not indifferent to the plight of the plaintiff (and others like him), in this regard it was perceptibly fatalistic. The decision was written as if he were no more than the purveyor of bad news.

With regard to the first question of the validity of the indemnity statute, for instance, Cockburn thought that it could not be disputed that 'the Jamaica legislature, having full legislative authority within the limits of the colony, had full power to pass the statute in question so far as to take away the right of action before the local tribunals of the island'.[55] Indemnity laws, he noted, had been passed both by the English and colonial legislatures many times in history. The only contestable issue was whether the Jamaica Assembly might 'take away the right of action in this country'. Cockburn grimly concluded that it could. But when he explained *why* it could, Cockburn did not allude (as he had done in *Nelson and Brand*) to the moral and political implications of the indemnity for British subjects. Instead he asked readers to suppose that the Act was 'the law of another country'.[56] The problem with finding that the Jamaica legislature could

---

[55] *Phillips v. Eyre* (1869), L.R. 4 225 (Q.B.), 238.   [56] Ibid., 239.

not extinguish a right of action was that it would have 'startling consequences' for the 'comity of nations'. Cockburn was troubled that 'an arrest and imprisonment might be perfectly justified by the law of a foreign country under circumstances in which it would be actionable here'.[57] In contrast, Cockburn seemed wholly untroubled by the fact that Phillips, a British subject who was unlawfully imprisoned and tortured by public officials, was to be deprived of a remedy.

In the end, whatever other thoughts Cockburn harboured about Phillips's claims, they were subordinated to the principle of parliamentary sovereignty. A colonial legislature had exercised its plenary power to pass a statute concerning rights and obligations arising within the jurisdiction of the colony. More specifically, the Jamaica legislature had 'taken away' a right of action *ab initio*.[58] That right was a nullity, and a nullity is not divisible. While the indemnity law might have been abusive or tyrannical, it was no less a law for that. Cockburn reminded that 'against any abuse of local legislative authority in such case a protection is provided by the necessity of the assent of the Sovereign, acting on the advice of ministers, themselves responsible to parliament'.[59] He then made a statement that must have deeply rankled his erstwhile admirers among the Jamaica Committee: 'we may rest assured that no such enactment would receive the royal assent unless it were confined to acts honestly done in the suppression of existing rebellion, and under the pressure of most urgent necessity.' In fact, for three years it had been hotly debated whether the acts of suppression had been done as a matter of good faith and necessity, and whether the Government had been well advised to assent to the Indemnity Act. It is hard to fathom why Cockburn, of all judges, thought it necessary to make such an inane assertion.

As we have noted, as an *in banco* proceeding *Phillips v. Eyre* was contested solely on issues of law. As for the facts, Cockburn simply acknowledged that the defendant's pleadings contained the 'necessary averments that the grievances complained of were committed during the continuance of the rebellion, and were used for its suppression, and were reasonably and in good faith considered by the defendant to be necessary for the purpose'.[60] But this acknowledgement raises another puzzle. The conceded facts of the case, so unflattering of the defendant, might have spurred Cockburn to find some plausible way to preserve the action. To be sure, the legal issues posed by the *Phillips* litigation were different – more narrow – than those raised in *Nelson and Brand*. But the moral and political issues overlapped. If he was very much moved by these issues, the Lord Chief Justice might have had ample scope to keep Phillips's lawsuit alive. More particularly, had

---

[57] As *The Times* remarked, the same principle would rightly obtain for the more advanced colonies of the empire: 'a colony like New South Wales or the Canadian Confederation would ill bear to find its Legislature treated with less courtesy than those of foreign States.' Quoted in *Pall Mall Gazette* (30 Jan. 1869), 2.   [58] *Phillips v. Eyre* (1869), L.R. 4 225 (Q.B.), 242.

[59] Ibid., 243.

[60] Cockburn added here that it would be 'incumbent on the defendant to make good these averments in order to support his plea'. It is not clear when or where the defendant would have to make these pleas good. Ibid.

he been of a mind to do it, Cockburn might have seized on the plaintiff's separate pleading that some of the impugned acts of the defendant had taken place on the 'high seas', and outside the physical jurisdiction of the Jamaica legislature. He might also have considered the pleading that some of the counts of harm took place after martial law had ceased. But Cockburn did not choose to do these things, or any other thing, to save the cause for the plaintiff.

Why he did not must remain a matter of unconfident conjecture. The suggestion here is that Cockburn was fatigued by the controversy generated by his previous contacts with the Jamaica affair. He was stung by the criticism (by Finlason and others) of his charge in *Nelson and Brand*, and then stung again and even more painfully by the criticism that followed his public statements about the charge of Sir Colin Blackburn. In his decision in *Phillips v. Eyre*, Cockburn strove to restore general confidence in his abilities as a good technical judge, and as a judge who would not permit mere political considerations to taint his findings of law.

The Queen's Bench decision in *Phillips v. Eyre* touched off an intriguing discussion in the news journals on the nature of government and citizenship within the British Empire. In this regard, the *Law Times* thought that the court had arrived at the only decision possible. Readers were reminded that a contrary finding would have been a 'practical denial to our colonies of that complete power of self government which in theory we have conferred on them'.[61] The extinction of Phillips's right of action was the unavoidable price of devolved governmental power in the empire. The *Saturday Review* agreed that despite the obvious hardship to the plaintiff, the decision was 'not only intelligible, but inevitable'.[62] *The Times* reasoned that the case had exposed an unavoidable contradiction between the supremacy of the imperial Parliament and efficient colonial government.[63] While the word of the Parliament in London had to be final, 'for an Empire to remain an Empire the Colonial Legislature cannot be permitted to legislate in a way which might result in the State at the same time and in the same place holding different relations to its subjects'. This latter principle was particularly sacrosanct in the field of criminal law. In civil cases, however, the Court was right to put colonial legislatures on exactly the same footing as foreign states.

Not everyone, however, was so sanguine about the decision. One of its implications, cautioned the *Law Times*, was that 'British subjects may be abandoned to the caprice and malignity of colonial legislatures'.[64] One colonial lawyer expressed concern that if the decision in *Phillips v. Eyre* was undisturbed, that a person 'on becoming a colonist [would] deliver up entirely, and without remedy or power of recall, his rights and privileges as a British subject to the control of the colonial legislature'.[65] The prospect now was for the concept of British imperial citizenship to become even more contingent and fragmented. Which leads to a point that was

---

[61] *Law Times* (20 Feb. 1869), 304.   [62] *Saturday Review* (6 Feb. 1869), 180–1.
[63] *The Times* (30 Jan. 1869).   [64] *Law Times* (20 Feb. 1869), 304.
[65] Ibid. (19 June 1869), 143.

not discussed in the newspapers and professional journals. What about the legal position of the millions of imperial subjects, mainly (like Alexander Phillips) persons of colour, who could exert little or no influence over the law and policies of their colonial government? Was it acceptable that the common law rights and liberties of these people might be routinely unheeded, overridden, or eliminated? The single safeguard against this eventuality, and it proved no safeguard at all to Phillips, was the refusal by the Government in London to assent to such draconian legislation.[66]

The result in *Phillips v. Eyre* did not garner widespread attention in the newspapers. The conservative *Evening Standard* was one of the few to comment. In the opinion of the *Standard*, Phillips's courtroom defeat signally was the defeat, it was hoped the *final* defeat, of the Jamaica Committee. The editor observed with pleasure that 'on every occasion upon which they have appealed to the law to endorse their mischievous, captious, and unpatriotic machinations they have been signally defeated, and they may now close their accounts.'[67] Once again, however, this proved a forlorn hope. In February 1869 it was announced that Phillips would take his case to a court of error, the Court of Exchequer Chamber.[68]

On 23 April 1869 the executive members of the Jamaica Committee met to discuss these developments. After £200 was voted from the Committee's coffers to compensate Chesson for having expended so much time and money on Committee business, discussion turned to the *Phillips* case.[69] Mill moved that the Committee vote some of its remaining funds 'toward promoting an appeal from the Court of Queen's Bench to the highest judicial authority, with a view if possible to reverse a decision according to which a colonial legislature has power to legalise *ex post facto* any acts, however illegal, of the colonial executive'. The motion was debated indecisively. The executive revisited the subject on 13 May. After hearing from Mill and Shaen on the matter (there is no record of what they said), the Committee 'deemed it inexpedient to take any steps in support of the civil actions against Mr. Eyre'. The Committee did not meet again until after Phillips's appeal was heard.

As for Edward Eyre, for all his legal troubles he had never completely given up on the reinstatement of his position (or pension) with the colonial service. But until Cockburn's decision in *Phillips v. Eyre*, all efforts to nudge the Government in this direction (Murchison had worked hard to persuade the Government that Eyre was at least owed financial compensation and a pension)[70] had failed. Liberal and Conservative governments had been firm that there would be no payments until all litigation had been concluded, and in Eyre's favour. In February 1869,

---

66   *The Times* (30 Jan. 1869).   67   As quoted in the *Pall Mall Gazette* (30 Jan. 1869), 2.
68   *Law Times* (13 Feb. 1869), 281.
69   *JC Minutes*, 23 Apr. 1869. The matter of Phillips's appeal also had been raised at a meeting of the BFASS held on 5 February 1869. The BFASS appointed an ad hoc committee to inquire into Phillips's expenses and consider a donation. On 5 March the matter was considered again and then dropped. *BFASS Minutes*, 5 Feb.; 5 Mar. 1869.
70   Murchison's overture was supported by a petition signed by 10,000 persons. Dutton, *Hero as Murderer*, 391.

Eyre expressed confidence that the Queen's Bench decision in 'the action by the negro Phillips has practically brought to a close all further legal proceedings against me'.[71] He was optimistic that Lord Granville, the new (Liberal) Secretary of State for the Colonies, would honour the promises made by previous Governments. Granville promptly informed Eyre that he should not look forward to 'the prospect of early re-employment as a Governor'. A few days after this exchange, Eyre learned that Phillips was to launch an appeal against the decision of the Queen's Bench.

The appeal was argued before the judges of the Exchequer Chamber on 2 and 3 February 1870.[72] Quain and Horne Payne again appeared as counsel for the plaintiff–appellant. Once again, George Mellish acted for Eyre, this time assisted by Poland and Eyre's lead counsel in the criminal prosecutions, Hardinge Giffard.

Quain began his submissions for the appellant by attacking the proposition that the Jamaican legislature had the jurisdiction to deprive a British subject of a civil remedy in England. When the history of the Jamaica Assembly was looked at closely, it was found to be a creation of a Crown Charter, not an Act of Parliament. As a matter of constitutional law, Quain contended, this meant that the Jamaica legislature was a subordinate body with limited powers. More exactly, the Crown 'could not confer upon the legislature the authority to pass an indemnity law; it could not do so in express terms, and certainly not by implication'.[73] While it was true that in the past other imperial legislatures had passed indemnity acts, these bodies all were creatures of Parliament; they were therefore 'omnipotent' with regard to the rights and obligations of local persons.[74] Quain also set forth a number of alternative arguments. He argued that the Indemnity Act was void because it attempted to 'relieve the governor from liability to legal proceedings of every kind', from criminal as well as civil law. It was 'therefore repugnant to the law of England'. Quain further contended that Cockburn had erred when he stated that it was essential to uphold the indemnity statute in order to preserve the principle of legal comity as between foreign states. This doctrine, Quain submitted, 'does not extend to *ex post facto* legislation rendering acts legal which were previously illegal'.

In his reply for the respondent, Mellish was content mainly to reassert arguments made during the first hearing. His main contention was that colonial legislatures, whatever their origins, 'possess supreme legislative power; but that power is subordinate to parliament'.[75] It was not correct, therefore, to state that the Act of Indemnity left persons in the position of the appellant without a remedy. In fact, Mellish submitted, 'they have two remedies. The Crown may disallow the Act, or the imperial parliament may declare it void as to England.' In the case at bar, both the Crown and Parliament assented to the Act, and in so doing permitted the Act to have its intended effects. One of the effects of this law was

---

[71] Eyre to Murchison, 5 Feb. 1869, Murchison Papers, *BL* Add. MS. 46126.
[72] *Phillips v. Eyre* (1870), L.R. 6 (Q.B.) 1 (Ex. Ch.).   [73] Ibid., 6.   [74] Ibid., 8.
[75] Ibid., 9.

that no right of action had ever accrued to Phillips for what had been done to him during martial law. If he had no right of action in Jamaica for a matter occurring in that colony, it followed that he could have no right of action in England for the same matter. Mellish also reasserted that 'the comity of nations requires that a person indemnified by a law in one country for acts done in that country, shall be protected in every other country against legal proceedings in respect to those acts.'[76] It was not germane to the operation of this principle that the law was retroactive in effect.

The decision on the appeal in *Phillips v. Eyre* was rendered on 23 June 1870 by Mr. Justice James Shaw Willes. On the woolsack since 1855, in 1870 Willes was generally regarded as one of the most learned and astute judges of his day.[77] His extensive reasons in the *Phillips* case have been cited extensively by common lawyers litigating issues in the conflict of laws. But although Willes was renowned as a great technician of common law, as a judge unlikely to permit non-legal considerations to influence his legal reasoning, at least one of his main findings in *Phillips v. Eyre* did not turn on formal legal sources or precedents, but on a view of public security in the empire. In these passages of his judgement, Willes did what Cockburn had avoided doing: he revisited the larger political context of the *Phillips v. Eyre* litigation, including the rationale for martial law and statutory indemnity.

The first issue of the litigation was the 'validity and effect' of the Jamaica Indemnity Act.[78] In resolving these issues, however, Willes did not have recourse first to case precedents. He thought it more pertinent to launch into a long discussion of a political abstraction: the 'condition of a governor of a colony, and other subjects of Her Majesty there, in case of open rebellion'.[79] In this section of his judgement Willes constructed the kinds of security problems that might be encountered by the archetypal colonial Governor faced with an archetypal uprising among a subjugated majority. As Willes explained, 'to act under such circumstances within the precise limits of the law of ordinary peace is a difficult and may be an impossible task, and to hesitate or temporize may entail disastrous consequences.'[80] Willes thought it was incumbent upon colonial Governors to take speedy and vigorous action on the best available information, even to circumvent the common law, in order to nip rebellion in the bud. But Willes also understood that such a policy was certain to generate accusations that the Governor had been 'violent and oppressive'. It was equally certain that the accusations would give rise to '[legal] actions at the suit of individuals dissatisfied with his conduct'. Willes was worried that the sheer weight of such lawsuits (the 'bare litigation to which [the Governor] and those who acted under his authority may be exposed')[81] might prove 'harassing and ruinous' to that executive official. It was

---

76 *Phillips v. Eyre* (1870), L.R. 6 (Q.B.) 1 (Ex. Ch.), 12.
77 *DNB*, xxi, 287; Simpson, *Oxford DNB*, online 29442.
78 *Phillips v. Eyre* (1870), L.R. 6 (Q.B.) 1 (Ex. Ch.), 15.   79 Ibid., 14–15.
80 Ibid., 16.   81 Ibid., 17.

on this basis, on the basis of this overtly *political* calculation, that Willes felt entitled to conclude that, in 'these and like circumstances it seems to be plainly within the competence of the legislature, which could have authorized by antecedent legislation the acts done as necessary or proper for preserving the public peace . . . to adopt and ratify like acts when done'. Willes's view of this matter was only encouraged by the fact that in other places 'similar laws have been passed after great troubles'.[82] Eyre himself could not have improved on Willes's defence of the indemnity statute.

The appellants had objected to this line of reasoning on grounds that the Jamaica Assembly was a creature of the Crown, and that the Crown did not have the authority to endow an assembly with jurisdiction over the rights of Englishmen in the mother country. Willes decided that this objection was misplaced, and that there was 'even greater reason for holding sacred the prerogative of the Crown to constitute a local legislature in the case of a settled colony [like Jamaica]'.[83] These reasons, however, all were rooted in notions of effective and right government, not legal precedent. The Crown needed to have this power in order that 'in colonies distant from the mother-country' the colonists might have the 'due government of the country in dealing with matters best understood upon the spot, and with emergencies which do not admit of delay, and also for giving the subjects there resident the benefit of voice by their representatives in the councils by which they are taxed and governed'.[84] Lest his passage sound too much as if it had been written by an American revolutionary, Willes began to cite the (disparate) cases in which English courts, explicitly and implicitly, had recognized the right of a colonial assembly to limit the rights of colonists in the English courts. In the end, however, Willes himself was not wholly convinced that the case law established the point irrefutably. He ultimately fell back on the statement that the Crown '*should* have the power of creating a local government' (emphasis added). This was in accordance with the available law and treatises and, vitally, 'with just principles of government'. Once again, this finding squared with Willes's opinion of prudent and effective security arrangements in the empire.

In the first half of his written judgement, Willes had drawn on a mixture of case law and political theory to establish that the Jamaica legislature had the jurisdiction to pass a valid indemnity law. In the remainder he moved on to consider the alternative issues raised by the appellant. If the Indemnity Act was good law, what was its effect for Phillips's lawsuit? Was the Act void for being repugnant to other imperial law such as the Colonial Governors Act? To this question Willes offered a perplexing and convoluted answer that relied in part on the assertion that in criminal cases, circumstances and motives had to be accounted for 'which would be excluded in deciding the dry question of civil liability'.[85] The upshot of this was unclear, as was Willes's further suggestion that criminal cases 'would be subject to

[82] Ibid., 15.   [83] Ibid., 18.   [84] Ibid., 19.   [85] Ibid., 21.

the control and restraint of the Crown'. It is unclear, for instance, in what sense the Jamaica Committee (or any other private prosecutor) was subject to such control. While offering these curious explanations, Willes did not confront the real argument of the appellant: that if the colonial legislature could not extinguish the right to prosecute Eyre in England, it could not extinguish the right to bring a civil suit against him.

Willes was far more convincing in dispensing with the appellant's second argument, that Eyre could not have the advantage of any legislation he himself had signed into law.[86] But the question of whether the retroactivity of the Indemnity Act was contrary to natural justice (that it was 'naturally or necessarily unjust') was more thought-provoking. 'Retrospective laws', Willes conceded, 'are, no doubt, *prima facie* of questionable policy.'[87] But that was not to say that it was always illegal for a legislature to make such laws, or even retroactively to 'take away a vested right of action'. It was a trite point of law that some rights, when not exercised, might be ratified by 'subsequent confirmation of competent authority'.[88] Willes further observed of English history that 'numerous rights of action have been swept away' by Parliament and subordinate legislatures. Doubt might be expressed about whether a British legislative body retrospectively could make a lawful act a crime. However, Willes thought there was no doubt that such a body could make an unlawful act lawful. In fact, Willes stated, now returning to matters of political abstraction, 'there may be occasions . . . involving the safety of the state, or even the conduct of individual subjects', when the want of prospective law 'may involve practical public inconvenience and wrong'.[89] Whether any given circumstance called for retrospective legislation was a 'matter of policy and discretion for debate and decision in the parliament which would have the jurisdiction to deal with the subject-matter by preliminary legislation'.

The first four-fifths of Willes's judgement in *Phillips v. Eyre* should be of interest to historians of the legal history of the British empire, but it has been of scant interest to British and Commonwealth lawyers. Although the case has been frequently cited,[90] it has been cited almost exclusively with regard to Willes's concluding statements regarding an issue in the conflict of laws, whether the Jamaica Indemnity Act could have 'the extra-territorial effect of taking away the right of action in an English court'.[91] In this regard Willes undertook some analysis of the 'true character of a civil or legal obligation'. A legal obligation, he stated, 'is the principal to which a right of action is only an accessory'. Legal obligations, and the rights of action to which they might give rise, were 'equally the creature of the law of the place and subordinate thereto'. By this logic, Willes explained, if the supreme law-making authority, even if

---

[86] This objection rested on the assertion that the Indemnity Act permitted Eyre to act as his own judge and jury in deciding who was entitled to immunity. But, given that the litigation at bar did not raise the issue of whether Eyre had acted in good faith, the point was irrelevant. Ibid., 22.

[87] Ibid., 23.   [88] Ibid., 24.   [89] Ibid., 27.

[90] See Foote, *Private International Jurisprudence*, 393–402; Dicey, *Conflict of Laws*, 659–66; Cheshire, *Private International Law*, 368–84.   [91] *Phillips v. Eyre* (1870), L.R. 6 (Q.B.) 1, 28.

by retroactive legislation, moves to erase a legal obligation it cannot later or somewhere be the source of a right of action. In the next paragraph, Willes set forth a rule of law that was to govern when a lawsuit could be brought in England for a tort committed abroad: Willes decided that 'two conditions must be fulfilled. First, the wrong must be of such a character that it would have been actionable if committed in England...Secondly, the act must not have been justifiable by the law of the place where it was done.'[92] Although Willes did not trouble himself to apply the test to the facts at bar, the implication here was plain. Phillips could pass the first, but not the second part of Willes's test. The wrongs visited on the appellant would have been actionable in England, had they not been negated by the Jamaica Indemnity Act. That particular expression of legislative sovereignty erased the original wrongs *ab initio*. From the moment that the Crown gave its assent to the Indemnity Act, Phillips had had no right of action. Any other result, Willes summed up, would diminish the law-making power of other sovereign states and, in so doing, would be 'an unprecedented and mischievous violation of the comity of nations'.[93]

The *Law Times* had long been a critic of the Jamaica litigation, and its editors hailed Willes's decision as a major victory for political and legal realism about martial law. They warmly embraced the principle that a 'justification or discharge in the colony is valid everywhere'.[94] But the editor at the *Law Times* wanted to make far bolder claims for the decision. In his view, the Exchequer Chamber had used the *Phillips* case to resolve 'questions of vast constitutional interest'. On this reading of the decision, the justices of the Queen's Bench had entertained the notion that statutory indemnities were null as contrary to natural law, and that 'men who had acted as magistrates or governors in times of great public peril, might be liable to be harassed by actions or prosecutions for any errors or excesses'. The judgement of the Exchequer Chamber, conversely, quite deliberately had purged the law of all vestiges of this view. The general result of their decision was that 'indemnity in such cases was so obviously of the essence of justice, that to a great extent it was afforded by common law'. It now was doubtful that in 'any case of honest error or excess, an Indemnity Act was necessary at all'. However, when such legislation was enacted, there could no longer be any doubt as to its validity throughout the empire. In the concluding passages of his leader, the editor of the *Law Times* gave the decision an even wider reading. In his view, the 'whole tendency' of the Exchequer Chamber's decision in *Phillips v. Eyre* was to validate the idea of martial law as the unfettered law of war.[95]

The leader-writer at *The Times* was not prepared to go quite so far. He did hope, however, that this decision would mark the end of the Jamaica litigation.[96] With the

---

    [92] Ibid., 29.   [93] Ibid., 30.   [94] *Law Times* (2 July 1870), 160.
    [95] The editor noted that the plaintiff had been seized outside the jurisdiction of martial law and then subjected to detention and severe flogging, without benefit of trial. From the fact that the Exchequer Chamber did not flinch from the indemnification of such acts, the Court concluded that 'there was no necessary oppressiveness in the infliction of flogging on a civilian'. Ibid.
    [96] *The Times* (24 June 1870), 9.

Law Times, The Times thought that *Phillips v. Eyre* raised 'most important points of constitutional law'. This litigation was not merely about the grievances of a single plaintiff, but related to matters of general political importance. In this respect the editors at *The Times* were struck by how much the decision of Willes resembled that of Sir Colin Blackburn in *The Queen v. Eyre*. In both cases, they observed, 'the duty of the defendant to put down the rebellion was recognized, and the general principle that acts performed *bona fide* for such a purpose may be protected was admitted'. The great novelty of the *Phillips* case, however, was the issue of whether a colonial legislature could 'take away the right of a plaintiff in this country'. The appeals court ruled that it did, and *The Times* welcomed this decision as 'just and expedient'. It was agreed that the Court had been correct to focus on the import of their decision for international law and commerce, not the 'special circumstances of the Jamaica case'. While it was tempting to brush aside the laws made by the legislature of a poor and weak colony, to have done so would mean that the laws made in Canada for Canadians would not be binding in an English court. A judgement in favour of the plaintiff in *Phillips v. Eyre* would have 'put an end to the self-government of all the young and vigorous communities of the English race'. The suppression of the Morant Bay rebellion occurred in Jamaica, and the rights and penalties flowing from it were better resolved there than in the mother country. *The Times* contended that this decision placed imperial law on a 'sound basis and intelligible principle'. That was seen as a propitious consequence of the Jamaica affair, and the newspaper hoped 'now to have taken leave of the Jamaica controversy for ever'.

The Times did not devote a single sentence to the plight of Alexander Phillips, or to the fact that he would not be compensated or vindicated for the sadistic cruelty suffered at the hands of Eyre and his soldiers. From the point of view of Phillips, then, but also from the view of those who had hoped that the Phillips litigation might advance the legal cause against the oppressive use of state power, *Phillips v. Eyre* was a comprehensive disappointment. Indeed, in this sense the lawsuit was counter-productive. Now it had been established by a court of high authority that colonial legislatures had sovereign jurisdiction to pass laws which might legitimate even the worst excesses of martial law, and shield its worst offenders. It was also beyond dispute that a colonial legislature could prevent the victims from seeking recourse to justice in the mother country. British citizenship, in other words, now was officially divisible. The nature and extent of the most basic civil and constitutional rights were to be a function of local legislation, not imperial citizenship. To the bitter disappointment of Phillips and his allies, English judges had sealed them off from the English courts. For future victims of summary justice under martial law, for the few who might have attempted to use the English courts to obtain justice, their only hope was that the Government in London would see fit to withhold royal assent from indemnity legislation.

Eyre had returned to England from Jamaica in August 1866. For the next three and a half years he was almost constantly embroiled in litigation. While Eyre eventually avoided liability in every case, the experience left him a broken man. In 1869 he wrote a series of despairing letters to Murchison. Eyre complained that he had expended £4,000 on Jamaica-related litigation.[97] Having gained nothing from quiet negotiation, he hoped that Murchison could arrange for the matter of his legal expenses to be raised in the House of Commons. While Murchison did not think the timing right for this move, he did confer on the matter with the other executives of the Eyre Committee. In June 1869 the Committee met for the final time and voted to give Eyre £7,000 from its remaining funds.[98] But in February 1870, in the wake of the final arguments in the *Phillips* appeal, Eyre complained that he had now spent £8,000 on the litigation and that his financial straits now were so desperate that he had begun 'looking for a job managing a nobleman's large property'.[99] Eyre wanted to be given the £5,000 that (so he calculated) the Defence Committee still held in reserve, even though even this sum would be 'quite inadequate to enable me to live'. There are no extant records showing that this money was given to Eyre, although it had no other likely destination.

Some months after the *Phillips* case concluded, Eyre once again pressed the Government to pay legal bills in the sum of £4,133 (for expenses relating only to the criminal prosecutions).[100] He reminded officials that the previous (Conservative) government had promised to make good on the cost of any successful legal defence. Eyre's appeal involved a delicate political decision, one now in the hands of Gladstone and the leaders of the Liberal Party. With two former members of the Jamaica Committee in his cabinet (Bright and Collier), and many other members and sympathizers in his caucus, Gladstone did not rush to make a decision. There were more pressing and less divisive matters to address. And then, in the winter of 1872, there was the eerily familiar matter of the Kooka uprising.

In early January 1872, approximately one hundred armed men from a Sikh sect called the Kookas attacked two predominately Muslim villages in the British Punjab.[101] The purpose of the attacks was to suppress Muslim ritual practices (specifically, to stop the butchering of cows) and to secure arms. After killing some ten Muslim villagers, the Kookas withdrew. Fearing the onset of religious war, the senior British official in the district, a man called Forsyth, authorized his deputy, Cowan, to take whatever steps were necessary to subdue the Sikh insurgency. Soon thereafter a British force made up mainly of native police and fighters defeated the Kookas in the field. Some sixty or seventy Kooka men (and two women) surrendered to Cowan. Cowan then took the position that it was necessary to set an example.[102] On his own initiative he carried out the summary execution of forty-nine Sikh men. In keeping with precedents set during the

---

[97] Eyre did not specify whether these expenses were related to the criminal or civil litigation. Eyre to Murchison, 3 Mar. 1869, Murchison Papers, *BL* Add. MS. 46126.

[98] Tyndall to Murchison, 16 June 1869, ibid.   [99] Eyre to Murchison, 11 Feb. 1870, ibid.

[100] The history of the claim was reviewed by Sir John Bowring. See *Hansard*, ccxii (8 July 1872), 799–810.

[101] For general accounts, see *The Times* (13 Feb. 1872), 9, (19 Feb. 1872), 9; letter to *The Times* (7 June 1872), 12.   [102] Letter to *The Times* (7 June 1872), 12.

suppression of the Mutiny fifteen years earlier, moreover, forty-nine prisoners were blown to pieces at the mouths of cannon. When Forsyth learned of these punishments, he ordered that no prisoner was to be executed until he had been tried and convicted by a military court. Ignoring this order, Cowan proceeded to take the lives of six more prisoners. Later, Forsyth himself executed sixteen Kooka men after they were condemned by drumhead courts martial.

In February 1872, the conduct of Forsyth and Cowan was under investigation by the British authorities in India. On 29 February 1872, questions were raised in the House of Commons about the execution of the Kooka prisoners.[103] Mountstuart Grant Duff, the Liberal Under-Secretary for India, confirmed that the punishments had taken place, most of them in the grisly manner described in the press.[104] The Government undertook to review the matter. In the meantime, in the spring of 1872 the British authorities in India sacked Cowan and reassigned Forsyth to another district.

The Kooka incident demonstrated that the Jamaica controversy had done little to resolve the legal and moral questions associated with unrest in the empire. The English political class still had not developed a coherent legal framework or policy for the suppression of resistance. The episode was noticed and questioned in England, but it did not trigger a major controversy or push for criminal prosecution. One reason it did not is that the incident took place under a Liberal regime; the most vociferous critics of martial law did not want to embarrass Gladstone's government. Another reason is that the proponents of liberal constitutionalism in the empire were something of a spent force. And whatever righteous anger was felt in these circles, it was curbed when the British government in India had moved so swiftly to discipline the offending officials.

In the conservative reaches of English political life, however, Cowan's actions were either endorsed in principle or approved of in fact. One writer to *The Times* cogently defended the underlying principle of his actions.[105] In this view, the Kooka prisoners had been 'obviously guilty of a very great crime' and, had they not been firmly subdued, would have 'spread anarchy and rebellion far and wide'. While the wholesale execution of so many men was excessive, had Cowan 'selected the ringleaders, or half-a-dozen of the most determined fanatics, and blown them away from the guns[106] in order to strike terror into the whole sect, and to impress the natives with awe, a great deal might be said for this view of the case'. Still other writers, however, were not prepared to concede even this guarded criticism. The Indian correspondent to *The Times*, for instance, emphasized that Cowan's 'precipitate action... nipped in its bud what might have been a dangerous outbreak'.[107] By this way of reckoning, Cowan was an 'old and energetic servant'

---

[103] Haviland-Burke, *Hansard*, ccix (29 Feb. 1872), 1157.

[104] Although the Under-Secretary corrected the record in one respect: only forty-nine men had been killed by cannon fire. Ibid.　　　[105] Letter of 'A Civilian' to *The Times* (7 June 1872), 12.

[106] A punishment the writer soberly judged 'more immediate and less painful than hanging'.

[107] *The Times* (3 Apr. 1872), 4.

of the empire.[108] To have cashiered such a fellow 'because he did not act to the letter of the law seems monstrous'.

There is another noteworthy fact about the Kooka episode. Only five years after Lord Carnarvon laid down new rules on the use of martial law in the empire, the British government in India promulgated yet another set of rules for the 'guidance of civil and military men who may be similarly situated hereafter'.[109] Clearly the Jamaica affair had done little to remove the uncertainties associated either with the use or excuse of martial law. In fact, Finlason seized on the Kooka incident to pen yet another clarification of the basic principles.[110] He reasserted that the 'essence of martial law was military authority'. He also suggested that dispute had arisen over the suppression of the Kooka insurgents because civilian officials had tried to exercise powers better 'intrusted to military men'. When there was a public emergency, it was well known, 'civilians may be carried away by the cruelty of panic or the excesses of inexperience'. Repression was better left to the professionals. For these reasons, Finlason thought that the authorities in India had been right to dismiss Cowan. When civilians or soldiers exercised the powers of martial law, Finlason concluded, they 'were undoubtedly liable for their own errors of judgment'. The irony of this remark, made by Edward Eyre's greatest champion, seems to have been entirely lost on its author.

Although the Kooka episode did not become the subject of general discussion in Parliament, in July 1872 the subject of Eyre's legal expenses finally did. Gladstone's position on the issue was clear: the previous Government had entered a 'substantial engagement' to pay Eyre's legal bills, and the present Government was 'bound in honour and policy to fulfil the engagement'.[111] But while this was the Prime Minister's position, he would not (or, politically, could not) avoid a debate on the subject. On 8 July 1872 the appropriate supply motion was introduced by the Government in the House of Commons.[112] The ensuing debate was led by many of the same politicians (making many of the same arguments) who had clashed in July 1866.[113] All of the main particulars of the uprising and suppression were revisited. In accord with tradition, both sides sought to bolster their positions by references to law and legality. Conservatives supported the resolution on the principle that Eyre's honesty and good faith had been proved in the courts of law. The radicals opposed it on the principle that the Lord Chief Justice of England had explicitly condemned Eyre's conduct, and that the payment would amount to a tacit endorsement of criminal wrongdoing.

For the Tories, Charles Adderley, if less fervently than in July 1866, opened the defence by referring to Eyre as a 'doubly-ruined man' who, as a result only of an

---

[108] Letter to *The Times* (20 May 1872), 13.
[109] This is reported in the letter of 'A Civilian' to *The Times* (7 June 1872), 12.
[110] Letter to *The Times* (25 May 1872), 6.   [111] *Hansard*, ccxii (8 July 1872), 845.
[112] Their speeches will be considered below, in the concluding essay of the present study.
[113] For a contemporary account of the debate, see *The Times* (10 July 1872), 9. See generally, Dutton, *Hero as Murderer*, 390–1; Semmel, *Governor Eyre Controversy*, 174–5.

honest error of judgement, had lost both office and promotion.[114] Adderley stressed that Eyre had been 'tried by every sort of tribunal, [and] had been acquitted by them all'.[115] Other Conservative M.P.s were not prepared to concede that Eyre had made serious errors of judgement in Jamaica. '[H]ad it not been for the promptitude with which Eyre acted,' Mr. Wheelhouse opined, 'it was most likely that within five days a White man would not have been left in Jamaica.'[116] Wheelhouse also recalled that 'Grand juries of [Eyre's] countrymen had declared that there was even no *prima facie* case against him.' These arguments were addressed by veterans of the Jamaica Committee. As Tom Hughes informed the House, despite all efforts to the contrary Eyre 'had never been tried in this country on the merits of the case'.[117] In a longer and more impassioned speech, Peter Taylor was emphatic that 'all the talk we have had about repeated verdicts of acquittal . . . is a mistake'.[118] In fact, every one of the criminal prosecutions of the former governor 'failed through a series of what I may call secondary or even tertiary causes, or technicalities'. Taylor (in contrast to what had been asserted in 1868) candidly admitted that in this respect the Jamaica Committee had 'failed'. It had failed in its attempt to win a decisive legal victory for a liberal jurisprudence of power. Taylor very much regretted this failure, and the fact that incidents of 'shameless barbarity' (he alluded to the 'killing of the Kooka prisoners in India')[119] continued to mar the reputation of England as a country governed by laws.

The issue continued to be debated until Gladstone's speech (offering his reluctant support for the motion) signalled closure. On the ensuing division, the Government's motion carried, but only over the negative votes of 130 members, most of them Liberals. This was not Eyre's final political victory. Two years later, Disraeli's Tory Government voted to grant Eyre the full pension of a retired Governor. His finances secure, Eyre moved to Devon, where he lived in obscurity until he died, in 1901, at the age of 86.

The legal expenses debate of July 1872 marked the final death spasm of the Jamaica controversy. It also marked the beginning of a long period, nearly three decades long, in which the English political class shunted the law and politics of martial law to the margins of public attention and discussion. This is not to suggest that the many substantial questions associated with martial law had been settled. (The Kooka incident and legal expenses debate surely belied that notion.) Nor does it mean that martial law had been rejected as a viable instrument of imperial policy and administration. In fact, in the late-Victorian era martial law was very much alive both as idea and as practice. Near to home, for instance, more than once it seemed conceivable that in Ireland the British government would replace an inchoate authoritarianism with a full-blooded regime of martial law.[120]

---

[114] *Hansard*, ccxii (8 July 1872), 811. As for the money which had been raised privately for Eyre's defence, that had been sucked up by 'that leech – the legal profession'.   [115] Ibid., 810.

[116] Ibid., 824.   [117] Ibid., 825.   [118] Ibid., 829.   [119] Ibid., 830.

[120] For a discussion of British repression in Ireland, and the spectre of martial law, see Goldwin Smith, letter to *The Times* (15 Apr. 1885), 10.

But the more pressing exigencies were a product of imperial expansion and insecurity. In the last quarter of the nineteenth century, the British Empire grew larger and more dangerous. In the empire and on its frontiers, martial law not only did not become obsolete, it persisted as a conventional practice of the British military as it waged a myriad of 'small wars'.[121] In this context, martial law was understood broadly as the 'laws and usages of war',[122] as a capacious label for the techniques employed by British field commanders to deal with armed insurgents and contiguous civilian populations.[123] (These techniques were informed by provisions of the *British Manual of Military Law*,[124] although the book offered few specific guidelines.)[125] There can be but little doubt, furthermore, that in the suppression of rebels and their communities the British military often had recourse to terror.[126] In fact, there is evidence that the use of terror in these cases was official doctrine at the War Office.[127] The important difference between the

[121] In this period a myriad of small wars were fought for a variety of reasons, including the conquest of territory (e.g. Burma, 1885), the expansion and protection of frontiers (Afghanistan, 1878–80), the rescue of British nationals (e.g. Abyssinia, 1868), to relieve besieged forces (Sudan, 1884), and the suppression of colonial insurrection (South Africa, 1880). For this taxonomy, see C. E. Callwell, *Small Wars: Their Principles and Practice*, 3rd edn (London, 1899), 25–7. For an overview of these wars, see generally, Bond (ed.), *Victorian Military Campaigns*, 3–27.

[122] See generally, Simpson, *End of Empire*, 58–9; 62–3.

[123] For examples, see references to the use of martial law by the British military in Afghanistan, *The Times* (14 Feb. 1880), 9; and in Burma, *The Times* (13 Sept. 1886), 4. For a discussion of martial law in Afghanistan in 1879, see Keith Terrance Surridge, *Managing the South African War, 1899–1902: Politicians v. Generals* (Woodbridge, 1998), 10–11. For comments on the relations between civilian and military authority in the late Victorian empire, see generally, Surridge, *Managing the South African War*, 5–14.

[124] War Office, *Manual of Military Law* (London, 1899), c. 5, 49. In this period, British officers received formal training in the law governing military and martial law. See generally, G. R. Rubin, 'The Legal Education of British Army Officers, 1860–1923', 15 *Journal of Legal History* (1994), 223–51, at 227–9, 233–4.

[125] The absence of precise guidelines frequently led to confusion and conflict between British civilian and military officials in South Africa. See generally, Keith Terrance Surridge, 'British Civil–Military Relations and the South African War, 1899–1902', unpublished manuscript (1994), 207–12.

[126] For a brief discussion of Lord Roberts' tactics in Afghanistan and Burma, see Surridge, *Managing the South African War*, 10–12.

[127] Colonel Callwell's book, *Small Wars*, is highly instructive in this regard. First published in 1896 (it went through three editions, the last in 1906), the book was a semi-official training manual written by an active Major in the British army, an artillery officer who had seen extensive action in India, Afghanistan, and South Africa. The book was published under the official imprimatur of the War Office, and 'remained a standard textbook on the subject up to the Second World War' (see Moreman, *Oxford DNB*, online 32251). With regard to the suppression of insurrection, Callwell thought that the object of such campaigns was 'not only to prove to the opposition force unmistakably which is the stronger, but also to inflict punishment on those who have taken up arms' (41). For the punishment to be felt by the insurgents, Callwell believed, sometimes 'their villages must be demolished and their crops and granaries destroyed' (ibid.). Callwell cautioned that there was 'a limit to the amount of licence in destruction which is expedient', but he did not say what it was. Throughout his book, Callwell emphasized that warfare in the uncivilized parts of the empire was radically different from 'regular warfare between two nations' (72). Frequently it called for strenuous engagement with far greater numbers of 'barbarous' and 'irregular warriors' in remote and 'savage' places. In such circumstances it was necessary for the military to 'overawe' and demoralize the enemy to seize and keep the initiative by 'vigour and promptitude' (73). (Here Callwell quoted Napoleon

use of martial law in Jamaica in 1865 and, citing but two examples, its use in South Africa in 1880 or Burma in 1885, was that the former case became the subject of intense and prolonged controversy among the English political class. From 1870 until 1899, the implementation of martial law in the empire barely raised a ripple. While the profound moral and jurisprudential issues linked to martial law were not resolved, they were coped with, as one historian has noted, 'by never calling the military to account after an insurrection ended'.[128]

The single noteworthy theoretical contribution to the jurisprudence of martial law in the late-Victorian era was made by Albert Venn Dicey. The scion of Clapham Sect activists, Dicey was raised on the same broth of evangelical religion and philosophical radicalism that had also fired the mind of his distinguished cousin, Fitzjames Stephen.[129] Like Stephen, in the early 1860s Dicey tried his hand at journalism, advocating for anti-slavery and the Northern cause during the American Civil War.[130] When the Jamaica controversy began in November 1865, Dicey was an enterprising young lawyer seeking, with modest success, to make his way at the bar. Although it is not clear whether Dicey joined the Jamaica Committee,[131] he moved in the same circles as its leaders, and was an admirer of Mill. (On one occasion at least in this period, Dicey undertook some legal work connected to the Jamaica affair on behalf of Charles Buxton.)[132] In the 1870s, Dicey practised law and wrote journalism and legal treatises. In 1880 he accepted the Vinerian Chair at Oxford and, in 1885, published his first important work, *An Introduction to the Study of the Law of the Constitution*.[133] In this book Dicey advanced the thesis that the 'rule of law' as upheld in the high courts was (with the supremacy of Parliament) one of the two fundamental tenets of the British constitution.[134] In elaborating this thesis Dicey was obliged to confront the problem of martial law.

Dicey approached the history and content of the constitution in the venerable if not wholly coherent tradition (Lord Chief Justice Cockburn was another adherent)

---

with approval: 'in Asia he is the master who seizes the people piteously by the throat and imposes on their imagination'(ibid.).) While at no point in his book did Callwell explicitly endorse the use of terror tactics against insurgents or civilians, he strongly implied that such practices could be justified by the exigencies of these conflicts. The later editions of Callwell's book, moreover, were published in the wake of the controversies over the commission of atrocities by the British military during the Boer War. Callwell did not use this as an occasion to retract or amend his views.

[128] Simpson, *End of Empire*, 62.   [129] Cosgrove, *Oxford DNB*, online 32811.

[130] See generally, Richard A. Cosgrove, *The Rule of Law: Albert Venn Dicey, Victorian Jurist* (Chapel Hill, NC, 1980), 23–30; Trowbridge H. Ford, *Albert Venn Dicey: The Man and His Times* (Chichester, 1985), 79–100.

[131] Dicey's name did not appear on the list of eminent members which invariably was published with the Committee's advertisements and pamphlet literature.

[132] Dicey attested to the accuracy of certain statements that Buxton had made about the Eyre Defence Committee during the election of 1868. See letter to *The Times* (7 Dec. 1868).

[133] Albert Venn Dicey, *Introduction to the Study of the Law of the Constitution*, 4th edn (London, 1893).

[134] Cosgrove, *Victorian Jurist*, 67. See also, H. W. Arndt, 'The Origins of Dicey's Concept of the "Rule Of Law" ', 31 *Australian Law Journal* (1957), 117–23.

of English Whiggery.[135] His book set out to prove that England's basic law was rooted in the nation's historical commitment to individual legal rights and immunities.[136] It is not surprising, then, that Dicey's first proposition about martial law was that it was 'unknown to the law of England'.[137] Unlike some nations of continental Europe (Dicey cited France as an example), the British constitution did not make any formal provision for military rule during emergency. Dicey took this as 'unmistakable proof of the permanent supremacy of law under our constitution'.[138] But Dicey's second thesis about martial law tended to contradict the first. He contended that martial law, when defined as the Crown's prerogative to 'repel force by force in case of invasion, insurrection, riot or generally of any violent resistance to the law', was 'most assuredly recognised in the most ample manner by the law of England'.[139] In these circumstances, in fact, the proclamation of martial law not only was a prerogative right but a positive legal duty which could not be shirked without risk of penalty.[140] But true to his precept that a fundamental tenet of the English constitution was the rule of law, Dicey insisted that the soldier or official who exercised martial powers had 'no exemption from liability to the law for his conduct in restoring order'. More exactly, any person called upon by duty to enforce martial law was 'liable to be called to account before a jury for the use of excessive, that is, of unnecessary force'.[141] In Dicey's view, therefore, martial law decidedly was not a regime of absolute or unfettered power. As a legal proposition, it amounted to no more or less than the common law defence of necessity.

Although he did not credit these influences in *The Law of the Constitution*, Dicey's account of martial law did not differ markedly from those expressed during the Jamaica controversy by Stephen and Cockburn. Dicey's analysis exhibited the same conviction that martial law existed within British law, but as something subordinate to its basic strictures. With his predecessors, moreover, Dicey did not attempt to resolve, or even squarely to confront, a number of the thorny issues engendered by martial law. Could Parliament pass laws that implemented and indemnified martial law while still respecting the precept of the rule of law?[142] If martial law was a prerogative of the Crown, could it be invoked and implemented while the civilian courts continued to operate? Were authorities acting under martial law justified in using *terror* as a means of pacifying a recalcitrant civilian population? Did its powers extend to prisoners and civilian detainees? If martial law extended to detainees, were they entitled to a military trial prior to punishment?

[135] In this respect Dicey's theory of the rule of law stood in a tradition elaborated by Locke, Blackstone, and the less celebrated Victorian constitutional lawyer, W. E. Hearn. See generally, ibid.
[136] Cosgrove, *Victorian Jurist*, 69.
[137] At least when martial law was defined as the 'suspension of ordinary law and the temporary government of a country or parts of it by military tribunals'. Dicey, *Law of the Constitution*, 268–70.
[138] For strenuous criticism of Dicey's reasoning on this point, see Simpson, *End of Empire*, 60.
[139] Dicey, *Law of the Constitution*, 269.   [140] Ibid., 270.   [141] Ibid.
[142] For discussion, see Cosgrove, *Victorian Jurist*, 82–5.

The timing of Dicey's book on the constitution had been influenced, perhaps inspired, by the contemporaneous debate over Irish Home Rule.[143] He had felt it was an apt moment for a legal scholar to distil and vindicate the British constitution as a repository of liberty. Interestingly, however, Dicey had not felt it an apt moment to distil and clarify the constitution as an instrument of repression.

As matters stood at the turn of the century, martial law persisted in two distinct senses. It persisted as military practice, as a tool in the hands of the men who, quite literally, represented the leading edge of British imperialism.[144] Martial law also persisted as a legal problem, as a disparate body of judicial and academic statements about putative legal rights and liabilities. For more than twenty-five years after the Jamaica affair, the English political class did not much care about the growing disengagement between martial law as theory and as praxis. This insouciance was jolted during the Boer War of 1899–1901.

The obdurate resistance of the Boers placed enormous strain on relations between the British civilian and military institutions.[145] The grimly violent business of subduing the Boer population exposed the perils of unclarity about the jurisprudence of military power. The British conducted the Boer War almost entirely under martial law.[146] And when things went badly wrong on the battlefield in 1899, the repression of the Boers was escalated both in degree and kind. By 1900 the 'pacification' of the Boers had come to involve the wholesale destruction of farms and food supplies, the concentration of civilians in detainment camps, and the summary court martial and execution of Boer guerrilla fighters. These policies touched off a series of clashes between British civilian and military officials.[147] Attempts by the former to rein in the more extreme and arbitrary practices of the latter were not entirely successful.[148] There was lack of agreement even on the rather fundamental point of whether captured Boer guerrillas were to be treated as traitors or prisoners of war.[149] In the result, these issues gave rise to a significant legal case in the law of martial law[150] and to a spasm of renewed, if inconclusive, scholarly attention to the subject.[151]

---

[143] For discussion of these influences, see Ford, *Dicey: Man and His Times*, 124–46.

[144] For this bifurcation, see Simpson, *End of Empire*, 60–3.

[145] See generally, Surridge, *Managing the South African War*, 1–5.

[146] Martial law was declared (by Governors Milner and Hely-Hutchinson) over most of British-controlled South Africa in October 1899, and remained in place until June 1900. See Surridge, *British Civil–Military Relations*, 213–80.   [147] Ibid., 222.

[148] Ibid., 222–30.   [149] Ibid., 233.

[150] In *ex parte Marais* [1902] A.C. 109, the applicant, a Boer civilian, applied to the ordinary courts in the Cape Colony for immediate release from military detention pursuant to a regulation posited under martial law. The applicant contended that it was unlawful under British law for the military to arrest and detain a civilian when the ordinary courts were still open. The continued operation of these courts tended to falsify the plea of military necessity. The Judicial Committee of the Privy Council refused the application on grounds that the respondent had established a *prima facie* case (in the form of an affidavit) for continued detention on grounds of military necessity. The Privy Council refused to impugn professional military judgement on this point.

[151] In April 1902, stimulated by the *Marais* case, the *Law Quarterly Review* 18 (1902), 117–58, published four separate articles on martial law. In 'Martial Law Historically Considered', W. S. Holdsworth

If the use of martial law in South Africa generated internecine conflict within the imperial state, it did not give rise to great disquiet in the home countries. Even at the cusp of the twentieth century, the (now much larger and more diversified) English political class remained broadly disengaged from the problem of martial law.[152] And so it remained until the military's doctrine of martial law was implemented to shameful effect by Brigadier Dyer and his troops against unarmed civilians at Amritsar, India in 1919.[153] But this incident, while it generated discord in England, did not lead to a major reformulation of colonial policy on the use of military force. Although in the 1920s government officials became disinclined to entrust the military with unsupervised authority over civilian populations in the empire, brutally coercive practices continued.[154] In fact, as late as 1952 the British authorities in Kenya suppressed the Mau Mau rebellion with a campaign of repressive terror far more prolonged and fearsome than anything instituted by Edward Eyre.[155] When the British empire expired in the 1960s, the Jamaica suppression and the intense controversy it spawned, for those who knew of these events, could only have seemed distant and quaint.

(because the subject had been largely forgotten since the Jamaica controversy?) reviewed the historical sources on martial law, and defended the view that martial law was an instance of the common law defence of necessity. In 'Martial Law', H. Erle Richards similarly contended that the proclamation did not create legal powers or immunities to cope with insurrection apart from those extant at common law. However, Richards understood the *Marais* decision to support the proposition that there could not be liability for actions under martial law, however violent, done honestly (140). 'To suspend the law [during an emergency]', Richards wrote, 'is in general to annul it altogether' (141). In 'The Case of Marais', Cyril Dodd reviewed the speeches of the Privy Council and set forth grounds to doubt the reasoning of the majority that the military detention of a civilian could be justified when 'the Courts are open' (146). Dodd contended that the authorities supported the contrary view that the operation of civilian courts was a decisive indication that peace existed in a district (147). Finally, in 'What Is Martial Law?', Sir Frederick Pollock called into question both the broad reading of powers and immunities under martial law ('its exercise requires to be justified on every occasion by the necessity of the case' (153)) and the legal reasoning of the *Marais* decision. Pollock thought that as a matter of imperial law the case stood for the narrow principle that 'the absence of visible disorder and the continued sitting of the courts are not conclusive evidence of a state of peace' (157). Pollock also reminded readers (as Dodd had done) that a decision of the Judicial Committee of the Privy Council was not in any event binding in the English courts (144, 158). The case, in other words, had not finally decided any important point of the law of martial law.

[152] This might in fact have reflected the growing indifference of late Victorians to imperial issues. See John Darwin, 'Bored by the Raj', a review of Bernard Porter, *The Absent-Minded Imperialists: What the British Really Thought about Empire* (Oxford, 2004), in *The Times Literary Supplement* (18 Feb. 2005), 6–7. For the most comprehensive and perceptive account of the use of martial law in the British empire during the twentieth century, see Simpson, *End of Empire*, 64–90.

[153] For discussion of martial law and Amritsar, see generally, Simpson, ibid., 64–6; Nassar Hussain, *The Jurisprudence of Emergency: Colonialism and the Rule of Law* (Ann Arbor, Mich., 2003), 99–102, 124–31.   [154] Simpson, *End of Empire*, 69–71.

[155] During the eight-year period of emergency in Kenya, the British authorities hanged more than 1,000 suspected rebels, subjected no fewer than 150,000 to periods of detention, and killed an estimated 12,000 in combat. Many thousands more Kenyans died in British detention camps. See Bernard Porter, 'How Did They Get Away with It?', a review of books by David Anderson and Caroline Elkins, 27 *London Review of Books* (3 Mar. 2005); Justin Willis, 'In the Noose', a review of the Anderson and Elkins books, *The Times Literary Supplement* (18 Mar. 2005), 32; Neal Ascherson, 'The Breaking of Mau Mau', a review of the Anderson and Elkins books, *New York Review of Books* (7 Apr. 2005), 26.

Conclusion

A Jurisprudence of Power: Victorian Empire and the Rule of Law

> The bloody transactions in Jamaica form a national question...This is a matter of law and right, of mercy and humanity; and our moral weight in the world will depend, to an incalculable extent, on the mode in which we deal with this imperial calamity.
>
> *Fortnightly Review*, 1 Jan. 1866

'The rebellion of the negroes comes very [near] the national soul', *The Times* remarked – tellingly yet misleadingly – in mid-November 1865.[1] For if news of the Jamaica rebellion had come near the national soul, news of the suppression had pierced to its core. As the *Fortnightly Review* observed at the close of November, 'the outrages of the negro have sunk into the background, and the foreground is now filled by the spectacle of the punishments inflicted indiscriminately on the coloured race in two parishes'.[2] The episode presented a disturbing paradox. In order to 'save' Jamaica, colonial officials – *British* colonial officials – had engaged in the 'flagrant violation of the commonest principles of justice and of law'. The image of George Gordon hanging dead from a courthouse railing, the *Review* commented, 'has made an impression on the public far deeper than the Maroons in their warpaint'.

The Jamaica suppression was a source of great disquiet among the English governing class, far more so than the rebellion which had preceded it. The diverse body of journalists, social activists, and politicians who pressed the issue shared the perception that their countrymen had betrayed the minimum demands of civilized conduct. Their criticisms stemmed from a *moral* theory of government, one grounded in deep misgivings about the human craving for mastery. The 'general inclination of all mankind,' as Thomas Hobbes hauntingly put it, is 'a perpetual and restless desire of power after power, that ceaseth only in death'.[3] By these

---

[1] *The Times* (18 Nov. 1865), 8.

[2] *Fortnightly Review* (27 Nov. 1865), 240. This and the other Jamaica editorials written in this period were authored by the radical thinker and writer G. H. Lewes. See Edwin M. Everett, *The Party of Humanity: The* Fortnightly Review *and its Contributors, 1865–1874* (Chapel Hill, NC, 1939), 49–50.

[3] As quoted in Colaiaco, *Crisis of Victorian Thought*, 29.

lights empire was a dangerous blessing. On one hand it could be the means of sharing the bounty of superior civilization. On the other it could be the occasion of wantonness and tyranny. For those who spoke out against Governor Eyre, the Jamaica suppression was a painful example of the second case. In this view the prolonged period of state-sanctioned violence under martial law was a grievous breach of trust. On the pretext of crushing a dangerous rebellion, British officials had indulged in a racially charged reign of terror. The primitive instincts of men had been freed from the strictures of law. Absolute power, borrowing Lord Acton's dictum, had corrupted absolutely.

For the moralizing fragment of the governing class, the Jamaica suppression was a matter of intense shame. But it was also a moment of exceptional opportunity. What had been done in Jamaica was so patently wrong, so patently *illegal*, that it presented a ripe opportunity for the nation to confront and resolve some of the most pressing questions of the era, questions which had been discreetly set aside after the suppression of the Indian Mutiny. Late in 1865, the leaders of the Jamaica Committee put these questions back on the national agenda. The division over Jamaica, in Huxley's striking phrase, became a 'touchstone of ultimate political convictions'. How was a civilized nation, one emphatically committed to the principle of the rule of law over men, to govern a burgeoning empire of dark-skinned and often violently recalcitrant subjects? How to govern such an empire, moreover, without betraying revered tenets of British statecraft? If the nation were made to come to grips with these questions, and to answer them well, it might reinforce the world's most majestic and stringent jurisprudence of political and military power.

For all their acerbity and partisanship, English commentators on the Jamaica affair were united in their unabashed chauvinism. They thought their country the most civilized in the world. They also were of one mind about the hallmark of its superiority. It was not her established church, but her established law that made England great. In an era of increasingly fragmented religious belief, of increasingly widespread unbelief, the primacy of secular law was the essential sinew of society. Law, not religion, secured personal security and property from the innate selfishness and savagery of all men. Law, not religion was the deeper reservoir of public conscience. No one knew law better, lived it better, than did the English. Or so it was more easily assumed before the bloody Jamaica suppression.

The moral perils of empire were quintessentially English preoccupations, and they had surfaced many times before. In the late 1780s, Edmund Burke advanced the case that Britain's imperial ambitions in India had led inexorably to brazen tyranny in that territory and insidious corruption at home.[4] The nation which encouraged or countenanced such abuses, Burke warned, would earn the 'wrath of Heaven'. In 1824 Sir Henry Brougham and Sir James Mackintosh stood in

---

[4] Frederick Whelan, *Edmund Burke and India: Political Morality and Empire* (Pittsburgh, Penn., 1998), 7–9.

Parliament to denounce the ruthless application of 'martial law' in the slave colony in Demerara, and to warn against the normalization of martial law as an instrument of imperial government.[5] In the 1830s Thomas Macaulay strove to find an intellectually respectable middle ground between Britain's discordant passions for global empire and natural justice.[6] In 1850 and 1851 a series of eminent statesmen, Gladstone among them, made earnest speeches against the abuse of martial law in Ionia and Ceylon.[7] The outcry against the brutal suppression of the Indian Mutiny was comparatively muted. But even in that supercharged atmosphere of race hatred and revenge, some dissent was registered and some steps were taken (by 'Clemency' Canning, famously) to curb the worst abuses of the martial law.

The tendency of the Victorian English to brood (at least spasmodically) over the clash between 'liberty and despotism' in the empire has been noticed by a number of historians.[8] In the 1880s J. R. Seeley reflected on the stark divergence in British policy toward its Europeanized and non-Europeanized colonies: 'how can the same nation pursue two lines of policy so radically different without bewilderment, be despotic in Asia and democratic in Australia...?'[9] Seeley's ruminations were symptomatic of what the historian Peter Marsh has described as the Victorian 'penchant for moral rhetoric. The strong tendency of Victorians to analyse their society, to attack each other, and to defend their various interests in moral terms.'[10] In no context was this tendency more pronounced than with regard to the administration of empire. The Jamaica suppression was only the most intensely and protractedly controversial of the more than seventy instances during Queen Victoria's reign that the British military was called upon to crush rebellions or riots in its dominions.[11] The disconcerting violence of these episodes, as Kathryn Tidrick has remarked, called into question 'the English ideal of themselves as a ruling race'.[12]

The principal theme of the present study is that in the late-1860s the political customs and ideals of the English governing class were deeply infused with legalistic ways of seeing, expressing, and acting. The inveterate legal-mindedness of the mid-Victorian English elite has been noticed, but not often documented or

---

[5] *Hansard*, xi (11 June 1824), 968, 1046.

[6] William Roger Lewis, 'Introduction', in Robin Winks (ed.), *The Oxford History of the British Empire*, vol. v, *Historiography* (Oxford, 2001), 5.

[7] See speech of Joseph Hume, *Hansard*, xii (23 July 1850), 175; speech of Gladstone, *Hansard*, cxvii (27 May 1851), 209.

[8] For this quote and a discussion of the historical writing of J. R. Seeley, see Lewis, 'Introduction', 10.

[9] J. R. Seeley, *The Expansion of England* (Chicago, Ill., 1971), 141.

[10] Peter Marsh, 'Conscience and the Conduct of Government in Nineteenth Century Britain: An Introduction', in Peter Marsh (ed.), *The Conscience of the Victorian State* (Syracuse, NY, 1979), 1–17, at 3.

[11] John Cell, 'The Imperial Conscience', in Peter Marsh (ed.), *The Conscience of the Victorian State* (Syracuse, NY, 1979), at 174.

[12] Kathryn Tidrick, *Empire and the English Character* (London, 1990), 1. It must be counted as a serious defect of Tidrick's book, however, that it fails to consider that law and legality were important elements of the self-idealization of the British governing class. The index of this work does not contain entries for either 'law' or 'martial law'.

discussed.[13] The most compelling exceptions have focused on the importance of constitutionalism in English political language and conflict. 'If there was unanimity about anything in the world of nineteenth century politics,' historian James Vernon has suggestively written, 'it was that the English constitution was, or, at the very least, had been, the best in the world…the most sacred symbol of Englishness.'[14] In this account, the constitution was the central, if *ceaselessly contested* 'master narrative' of Victorian political discourse.[15] Of course, this line of historical thought owes a very great debt to the path-breaking work of Edward Thompson. In the final section of his book *Whigs and Hunters*, Thompson wrote cogently of how law was both an intrinsic element of the modern English world-view, and how it operated as a detectable constraint on the exercise of political power.[16] According to Thompson (and this proposition is adopted and expatiated on in the book at hand), the English governing class was defined by its persistent allegiance to the *ideal* that the mark of a truly civilized community was the accountability of office and authority to a tangible and effective political jurisprudence.[17]

In the mid-1860s, the English moral imagination, at least among those of a broadly 'liberal' cast of mind, fundamentally was a legal imagination. Its first principle was that the conduct of powerful men and institutions had everywhere and at all costs to be constrained through the comprehensive application of secular law. But while the main actors of the Jamaica affair were preoccupied with law and legal process, historians have not been.[18] In this literature, legal perceptions, principles, personalities, and procedures are consigned to the margins of focus. The actual Jamaica litigation is variously discounted as irrelevantly technical,[19] pointlessly vindictive,[20] or abjectly unsuccessful.[21] On these grounds, scholars have permitted themselves to be largely indifferent to such matters as the selection of lawyers, the style and content of legal argument, the technical literature on martial law, and the structure and contours of judicial pronouncements. The

---

[13] For some of the most noteworthy general discussions of the legalistic character of modern English history, see John Brewer and John Styles (eds.), *An Ungovernable People: The English and Their Law in the Seventeenth and Eighteenth Centuries* (Camden, NJ, 1980), 11; David Sugarman and G. R. Rubin, 'Introduction: Towards a New History of Law and Material Society in England, 1750–1914', in G. R. Rubin and David Sugarman (eds.), *Law, Economy and Society, 1750–1914: Essays in the History of English Law* (Abingdon, 1984), 1–123.

[14] James Vernon, *Politics and the People: A Study in English Political Culture, c.1815–1867* (Cambridge, 1993), 298. See also, James Vernon (ed.), *Re-Reading the Constitution: New Narratives in the Political History of England's Long Nineteenth Century* (Cambridge, 1996). For a study of the centrality of the 'constitutionalist idiom' in radical politics, see James A. Epstein, *Radical Expression: Political Language, Ritual, and Symbol in England, 1790–1850* (New York, 1994).

[15] Vernon, *Re-Reading the Constitution*, 2; idem., *Politics and the People*, 295–6.

[16] E. P. Thompson, *Whigs and Hunters: The Origins of the Black Act* (London, 1975).

[17] For sympathetic critical assessment of Thompson's ideas on law and power, see Daniel H. Cole, ' "An Unqualified Human Good": E. P. Thompson and the Rule of Law', 28 *Journal of Law and Society* (2001), 177–203.

[18] For more exact critical explication and evaluation of this work, see below, Appendix.

[19] Ford, 'The Governor Eyre Case in England', 233.

[20] Dutton, *Hero as Murderer*, 365–92.   [21] Hall, 'Rethinking Imperial Histories', 13.

historiography of the Jamaica controversy, for all its undoubted strengths, has not counted law, lawyers, and judges as among the important elements of English political consciousness and conflict. It has neglected the role of the English legal system as a forum for the negotiation of the basic terms of political power. Still less has the extant literature considered two related hypotheses: (1) that the history of English law in the Victorian era merits investigation in its own right; (2) that the course of this history might have been affected in some important ways by the Jamaica affair. The notable exceptions to this generalization[22] prove its merit.[23]

This study has taken a different view. Its chapters have endeavoured to show how legal ways of seeing and doing were central features of English political discourse and conflict. I have argued that the men who transformed the Jamaica suppression from a news story into a prolonged controversy were informed and enlivened by the view that the suppression threatened something fundamental in the moral framework of their political world. An influential fraction of the English governing class was moved by the idea that the bulwark of a *moral* politics (i.e. the only politics which could be embraced conscientiously) was an unbreakable commitment to the principle of the rule of law over men. Many of the same fraction not only believed – they feared – that some powerful members of their community wanted to *renege* on this commitment. This fear was not alleviated by the fact that the authoritarian impulse had been expressed mainly against black men in the empire. In this light, therefore, the Jamaica prosecutions were not esoteric indulgences. They represented the concerted effort of an alliance of English private citizens to enforce the secular commandments of civil society, to enforce political modernity against backsliding conservatives.

These general thematic and historiographical points having been set forth, our focus properly returns to the main interpretive questions of this study. Why, to begin, did some members of the English governing class move to transform the Jamaica suppression from a colonial news story into a domestic controversy? Why did they respond with so much apparent emotion, conviction, and determination? Why did they turn to lawyers and legal procedures? Why this paroxysm of bad conscience in 1865?

---

[22] Historian Charles Townshend has written intelligently of the use of martial law in British and imperial civil emergencies generally, and during the Jamaica affair specifically. This work, however, is content to provide a narrative overview of the clash over the use of martial law in Jamaica, one which focusses on the implications of the dispute for the administration of the empire after 1870. See Charles Townshend, 'Martial Law: Legal and Administrative Problems of Civil Emergency in Britain and the Empire, 1800–1940', 25 *Historical Journal* (1982), 167–95. For a related discussion of the legal dimensions of the English 'image of order', see Charles Townshend, *Making the Peace: Public Order and Security in Modern Britain* (London, 1993), 1–23.

[23] By far the most significant work on the historical and theoretical significance of martial law is Nassar Hussain's recent monograph, *The Jurisprudence of Emergency*. See below, Appendix. For other modern historical works on the history of English martial law, see generally, Minattur, *Martial Law*; Richard A. Cosgrove, 'The Boer War and the Modernization of British Martial Law', 22 *Military Affairs* (1980), 124–7. See Kostal, 'A Jurisprudence of Power'.

One reason is that so many political activists and journalists were outraged that British officials had instituted a reign of terror in Jamaica and, in more than a few instances, had boasted about it upon their return to England. But these facts, as disgraceful as some thought them to be, were not combustible enough to have ignited the Jamaica controversy. In fact, the most explosive feature of the episode, the main reason why it was so vehemently contested and litigated, was that Edward Eyre, his senior officers, and their apologists in England, fervently maintained that the suppression had taken place in strict accordance with law. Specifically, Eyre and his allies claimed that even the most ruthless measures – the whippings, burnings, and hangings – were perfectly legal under the English law of martial law. According to Mill, Bright, and Smith, to all of the leaders of the Jamaica Committee, it was this contention, this *legal* contention, which had to be impugned and, by the best available means, judicially refuted.

By the summer of 1866, only six months after it was formed, the Jamaica Committee was operating essentially as a bureau of legal warfare. Its strategic aim was to fund and coordinate a sustained legal campaign to defeat the resuscitation and normalization of martial law as an instrument of British statecraft. Its primary tactical weapon was the private criminal prosecution. Mill and his adjutants sought to use the criminal prosecution as a means of providing an English high court – the seat of the country's secular priesthood – with an occasion to pronounce definitively against martial law, and in favour of the undivided accountability of political and military power to civilian law. The Committee was committed to these goals for two reasons. First, the invocation of martial law in the empire operated as licence for otherwise civilized men to revert to barbarism. In Frederic Harrison's memorable phrase, it 'called out all the tiger in our race. That wild beast must be caged again.'[24] Second, the use of martial law in the empire was viewed as a grave threat to civil liberties and the rule of law in the home countries. 'The contagion of lawlessness spread fast,' Harrison warned in a publication of the Jamaica Committee: 'What is done in a colony to-day may be done in Ireland to-morrow, and in England hereafter.'[25]

One of the trademarks of English liberalism in the nineteenth century was the fear that men invariably were corrupted and debased by political power. As Lord Brougham put it (paraphrasing Hobbes), power was a perpetual threat because it was wielded by 'frail men, the sport of sordid propensities'. This theme cropped up repeatedly in the Jamaica literature. And as the *Glasgow Sentinel* lamented in November 1865, it was alarmingly apparent about the suppression that 'British soldiers had imbibed a good share of the savage spirit so much condemned in the negro'.[26] The white men of Jamaica were so menaced by the prospect of a general rebellion among blacks, *The Economist* observed a few days later, that 'the natural decree seemed to be to let those whites loose. They were let loose.'[27] The editor

[24] Harrison, *Six Letters*, 41.   [25] Ibid., 39.
[26] *Glasgow Sentinel* (25 Nov. 1865).   [27] *The Economist* (2 Dec. 1865), 1455–6.

reflected on what he called the 'latent force' in white men, that 'terrible reserve of unscrupulous energy which lies as [if] it were bottled and sealed among our kins-men'. Deep in the breast of all Englishmen, the editor concluded, there was an 'instinct for dominance which is their vice as well as their greatest political power'. The *Fortnightly Review* described how, in a moment of numb panic, Governor Eyre had encouraged his soldiers to forsake their humanity, and to 'hunt down a race, and perpetrate indiscriminate slaughter'.[28] They had been overtaken, another newspaper suggested, with the 'savage passion of race hatred'.[29] The regu-lar and militia officers of Jamaica, as one commentator remarked in 1866, had presided over nothing less than a 'hell-like saturnalia' of torture and killing.[30]

In an article published in the wake of the final report of the Jamaica Royal Commission in June 1866, even the staunchly conservative *Quarterly Review* was obliged to acknowledge that British officials were capable of dreadful atrocities, particularly in the non-white empire. In those places where Englishmen feel threatened by a mass of 'dusky complexions', the *Review* observed, 'acts are perpet-rated which reveal the unextinguished savageness of the human heart, beneath the superficial gloss of a partial civilization'.[31] In an article called 'The Anglo-Saxon Let Loose', the *Spectator* made a strikingly similar observation. The Jamaica suppression was cited as only the most recent example of the 'terrible ferocity which the Anglo-Saxon . . . when once released from conventional bonds, almost invariably displays'.[32] The Anglo-Saxon, it continued, this 'good-humoured, just, and law-bound individual', was fully capable of the 'most hideous cruelty'. When liberated from 'external discipline', he could evince 'a mad crave to destroy, an anger which nothing except slaughter can appease, a lust of bloodthirstiness such as towards the end of a battle it has often perplexed English generals to control'. This primitive facet of the British character (the 'element of the tiger', the *Spectator* called it, 'the tiger in our race', as Harrison had put it) had always to be held in check by external constraints.

Critics of the suppression were appalled by the sheer animal savagery that white British men had exhibited in Jamaica. Sympathy was felt, if in varying degrees of intensity, for the victims of martial law. In some quarters, too, there was genuine resolve to come to the aid of those who had suffered. But 'justice for the negro', as Mill himself admitted, was a secondary justification of the Jamaica controversy. In their texts and testimonies, most of the critics made it abundantly clear that they were interested mainly in the ramifications of the suppression for public life in the home countries. Liberal-minded journalists, politicians, thinkers, and activists were profoundly worried that the Jamaican bloodshed was symptomatic of (what one commentator called) 'the military spirit which was

---

[28] *Fortnightly Review* (27 Nov. 1865), 242–3.   [29] *Pall Mall Gazette* (19 Dec. 1866), 3–4.
[30] Charles Roundell, as quoted by John Gorrie, *Illustrations of Martial Law in Jamaica, Jamaica Papers No. VI*, 3–4.   [31] 120 *Quarterly Review* 120 (July–Oct. 1866), 236.
[32] *Spectator* (24 Mar. 1866), 321–2.

engendered by the Indian Mutiny'.[33] The main purpose of the Jamaica agitation, the *Daily News* contended in the summer of 1866, was to resist the 'importation of West Indian maxims into England'.[34]

The Jamaica agitators feared that authoritarianism was on the march. Their instinct was to respond with the affirmation of law. Even the ardently religious men of Exeter Hall decried the Jamaica atrocities mainly because of their despotic lawlessness. 'The Englishman loved his country,' Jacob Bright told an audience in November 1865, 'but he loved it because it was the country of law, and because he was never subject to the caprices of a despotic will.'[35] It was abhorrent enough that Governor Eyre had orchestrated a reign of terror, far worse that he claimed, and in some quarters was supported in the claim, that everything he had done was legal under the law of martial law. As the Quaker industrialist and Radical politician W. E. Forster protested, 'those in favour of martial law were declaring a *legal* massacre.'[36] As for Conservative leaders and newspapers, the *Morning Star* commented, they 'have given unqualified approval to manifestly illegal and ruthless acts'.[37] This trend could not be left unchallenged. England was a country that might tolerate disagreement about the accountability of men to religion, but not about their accountability to the constitution. As the authority of religious dogma waned there was a redoubled commitment to (what Fitzjames Stephen later called) the 'English gospel of law'.[38] In this view, the one absolutely essential property of the civilized community was accountability to secular law. The Jamaica agitators, its pious men such as John Bright no less than its secular men such as John Stuart Mill, were united in the belief that legality, not faith, was the fundamental creed of modern English society.[39] Comprehensive legal accountability was the nation's 'civil religion'.[40]

The focal point of the Jamaica affair in England was the military trial and execution of Gordon. The Gordon case became a *cause célèbre*, in part because he was a fair-skinned Christian man who had many influential English friends. But the particulars of Gordon the man were not nearly so important as the particulars of Gordon the political symbol. The most important fact about Gordon in England was that he had been Jamaica's leading opposition politician. Nothing could be more profoundly antithetical to the liberal catechism than the military execution of a politician. In a country of law and liberty, political murder was the most grievous crime of them all. The editor of the Irish news journal the

[33] Charles Roundell, *England and her Subject Races, with Special Reference to Jamaica* (London, 1866), 18.   [34] *Daily News* (31 July 1866).

[35] *The Times* (28 Nov. 1865), 7.   [36] *Daily News* (11 Jan. 1867), 3.

[37] *Morning Star* (9 Dec. 1865).

[38] Stephen, as quoted in W. W. Hunter, *Life of the Earl of Mayo*, vol. ii (London, 1875), 169.

[39] For a more cautious assessment of secularization in the mid-Victorian era, if one that does not evaluate the role of secular law and the courts, see Jose Harris, *Private Lives, Public Spirit: A Social History of Britain, 1870–1914* (Oxford, 1993), 150–79.

[40] R. Bellah, as quoted in David Sugarman, ' "A Hatred of Disorder": Legal Science, Liberalism, and Imperialism', in Peter Fitzpatrick (ed.), *Dangerous Supplements: Resistance and Renewal in Jurisprudence* (London, 1991), 34–67, at 59.

Dublin Review was particularly alive to this point. In his opinion, the most damning charge against Governor Eyre was 'for hanging the leader of the opposition to himself'.[41] This was not merely a crime but a 'great political crime', one which called into question England's proud international reputation as the fount of all constitutional government. 'In causing Mr. Gordon to be hanged,' Walter Bagehot opined, 'Eyre's greatest offence is that he put an affront on the majesty of law, and, for a time, cancelled the ripest fruits of our civilization.'[42]

The Jamaica affair had yet another source of momentum. The Jamaica martial law had done untold damage to England's international prestige. As the *Quarterly Review* lamented in January 1866, 'the [Jamaica] tale is known throughout the world, and there is a dark stain on the honour of our country which neither we, nor our neighbours on the Continent or in America, are likely to forget'. The *Glasgow Sentinel* thought that a more 'unconstitutional proceeding never took place in a so-called constitutional country'.[43] The Jamaica atrocities had lowered Britain to the same level as 'Austrians and Russians'. 'It has truly been stated,' the radical sheet *Reynolds' Weekly* contended, 'that the character of England for justice and humanity throughout the world is now at stake'.[44] The more staid *Athenaeum* was of the same view: 'such a crime as the Jamaica massacre ... has not been committed in the name of England for a hundred years ... and unless the offence is promptly disowned, denounced and punished, our honourable name in the world will have received a stain which twenty generations will not suffice to clear away'.[45] In these accounts, Governor Eyre and his soldiers, in their zeal to quiet a restive colony, had betrayed their country's most sacred ideals. That could not be left uncorrected.

It was far from accidental, then, that the Jamaica suppression became the subject of fierce debate. The controversy arose from the tectonic stresses generated by the collision between global imperial ambition and bedrock moral and legal sensibilities. The Jamaica affair was a prolonged and intense argument about how to relieve these stresses, about how and whether it might be possible to govern a vast, racially diverse, and endemically dangerous empire by civilian legal norms. In the wake of Morant Bay a significant number of voices were raised in support of the view that it was not possible, that it was time for a candid reassessment of the exactions of imperial rule. In July 1866, a writer to the *Pall Mall Gazette* (he signed his letter 'Anglo-Colonus') summarized the dilemma: 'We British govern many millions of what we call inferior races – Indians, Chinese, negroes, savages. Almost everywhere we are in number an absurdly small minority. Everywhere ... they nourish an antipathy against the ruling race, and are ready at times to combine ... for its overthrow.'[46] The editor of the *North British Review* was moved to place the insurrection in a broader historical context.[47] 'Servile insurrections and proconsular

---

[41] *Dublin Review* (Oct. 1866), 398.
[42] *The Collected Works of Walter Bagehot*, ed. Norman St. John-Stevas (London, 1986), 41.
[43] *Glasgow Sentinel* (2 Dec. 1865).   [44] *Reynolds' Weekly* (10 Dec. 1865).
[45] *Athenaeum* (16 Dec. 1865).   [46] 'Anglo-Colonus', *Pall Mall Gazette* (30 July 1866).
[47] *North British Review* (June 1866), 388, 392–3.

delinquencies', he wrote, 'not unfrequently reminded the Roman that he was a citizen of a vast Empire.' It was time now for the British to take stock: 'for more than a century,' the *Review* reflected, 'we have affected to rule one-fifth of the habitable globe, through the agency of a mere handful of Anglo-Saxons'. The dangerous and perplexing problems associated with this task now threatened the tranquillity of the mother country. As abandonment of the empire was 'out of the question', the 'only remaining alternative is to face the difficulties involved in its retention'.

In the wake of the Indian Mutiny, and eight years later the Jamaica uprising, some leading members of the English governing class began to advocate openly and vigorously for a policy of imperial security based on racial *Realpolitik*.[48] According to this doctrine, the fact had to be faced that in much of the empire it was folly to speak of government by consent.[49] Plainly, the dark-skinned peoples of the empire hated, and always would hate, their white masters, and spoiled for the moment of their extermination. In the aftermath of the massacre at Cawnpore, more lately at Morant Bay, it was time to make some sober changes to the manner and style of imperial administration. The only sure way of avoiding an endless succession of Cawnpores was to rule through force or, better, the omnipresent threat of force.

Thomas Carlyle is rightly recalled as the leading mid-Victorian theorist of this brand of racial authoritarianism.[50] One of the reasons why the Jamaica affair began to gain momentum after December 1865 is that Carlylean ideas about imperial government were becoming (to some liberals) alarmingly ubiquitous. 'Anglo-Colonus', the correspondent to the *Pall Mall Gazette*, was especially blunt about what needed to be done, and why: 'we are few and they are many, therefore we must repress disloyalty by terror . . . the amount of terror . . . depends . . . simply on the numerical proportion between us and them, and the consequent necessity of acting with vigour.'[51] The editor of the *Morning Herald* had arrived at a similarly unvarnished view of the issue. '[R]evolutions', he remarked (on the publication of the final report of the Jamaica Commission), 'are not made with rosewater, and rebellions are not put down with kid gloves. When a handful of whites find themselves suddenly menaced by a multitude of blacks . . . it is almost a moral necessity that things should be done of which calm and cool judgment will disapprove.'[52] The black multitudes of the colonies, even the *Law Times* grimly concluded, 'are restrained from violence only by fear'.[53]

---

[48] For elaboration of this point, see Eric Stokes, *The English Utilitarians and India* (Oxford, 1959), 282, 288.

[49] See Peter Burroughs, 'Imperial Institutions and the Government of Empire', in Andrew Porter (ed.), *Oxford History of the British Empire*, vol. iii (Oxford, 1999), 171–2; Cell, 'The Imperial Conscience', 202.

[50] See generally, Hall, 'The Economy of Intellectual Prestige', 178–80; Holt, *The Problem of Freedom*, 280–2.   [51] 'Anglo-Colonus', *Pall Mall Gazette* (30 July 1866).

[52] *Morning Herald* (20 June 1866), 4.   [53] *Law Times* (1 Sept. 1866), 762.

In December 1865, the medical journal *The Lancet* waded into the question of imperial security with an article bluntly titled 'The War of Race'.[54] The piece commenced with an endorsement of the racial theory of the Scottish anatomist Dr. Robert Knox. 'Human character, individual and national,' Knox had proved, 'is traceable solely to the nature of the race to which the nation or individual belongs.' Knox had advanced another key idea. The white and black were static, unequal in mental and moral attributes, and permanently and lethally antagonistic. On this view, the Jamaica revolt, like the Indian Mutiny before it, was 'foretold on scientific principles', the inevitable outcome of the violent resentment felt by the 'dark races' toward their white masters. While the editor of *The Lancet* conceded that it was 'impolitic to say so', there was only one reliable means by which white communities could ensure their safety in the 'deltas of the Indus, or the Ganges, Australia, the Antilles, or the Cape'. The black men there had either to be 'constantly kept down with a rod of iron, or be slowly exterminated'. There was no practical alternative. 'If [the British] are to hold places within the tropics,' the editor asserted, 'it can only be as military masters lording it over a sort of serf population, and under the continual fear of whose terrible vengeance we must always live.' Whatever the 'philanthropist' and 'dreamy essayist' might say about it, in a world riven by racial enmity there could be no such place as a 'liberal' empire. The British were urged to 'polish up [their] revolvers and mountain artillery; there was nothing else to be done'.

Such views were extreme but widely held. As *The Times* remarked in the immediate aftermath of the Jamaica rebellion, 'a rising of this sort must be crushed at once ... Immediate justice is the best mercy in the long run, for to the lower class of minds death loses nearly all its terrors if it is seen at a considerable interval.'[55] The more liberal-leaning editor of the *Pall Mall Gazette* held a strikingly similar viewpoint. The Jamaica rising, he contended,

is another proof and another warning of two conclusions ... that two races originally and essentially different in type and character, and in utterly different stages of civilization, cannot live together on terms of absolute legal and social equality ... Real peace and harmony under such circumstances are out of the question ... The second conclusion is that perfect political and civil freedom – freedom, that is, from surveillance, freedom to bear arms and form organizations, freedom, as Englishmen understand the word – can scarcely be safely granted to races at present (to say no more) as ignorant, and therefore as easily misled, deluded, and maddened, as the negroes of the West Indies or the Sepoys of the East.[56]

Even more strident versions of the same opinion were offered by a succession of speakers at the Anthropological Society of London in February 1866. The retired naval commander Bedford Pim expressed his frustration that England's leading Ministers did not seem to comprehend 'how hazardous it is to vacillate with savages'.[57]

---

[54] *The Lancet* (2 Dec. 1865), 626–7.   [55] As quoted in the *Pall Mall Gazette* (18 Nov. 1865).
[56] *Pall Mall Gazette* (17 Nov. 1865).
[57] Unidentified speaker, quoted in Bedford Pim, *The Negro and Jamaica* (London, 1866), 49–50.

That had been done in India before 1857, with catastrophic results. The country simply had not learnt 'the true art of governing alien races'. A speaker called Winwood Reade made the point even more starkly: 'What he had always said about native wars was this: Avoid them as long as you can: but if you must fight with natives, kill them down. Kill them down not only for self-protection, but from a philanthropic principle. It seems paradoxical to say so, but there may be mercy in a massacre.'[58]

In the late-1860s England was a country which could foster a theory of extreme racial authoritarianism. But it was not a country which could foster the theory without qualms. For every publication which endorsed racialized despotism in the empire, there was another which either rejected the policy outright or, more often, posed searching questions about its moral and legal implications. Could the English nation govern subjugated peoples without betraying its most cherished principles? Could it cope with insurrection while respecting the rule of law? There were those who thought that these questions were important, and that they might be answered affirmatively. The key here was a reinvigorated doctrine of martial law.

The *Pall Mall Gazette* once observed (amidst the Jamaica litigation) that if 'a small number of whites is established in the middle of numerous alien races, . . . it is better that this should be done under some legal semblance at least of legal authority, than in a state of mere legal chaos'.[59] If it was nothing else, the doctrine of martial law imposed some minimal constraints on power. Martial law might be a debased sort of law, it might be antithetical to English norms, but at least it was a form of *law*. As the *Evening Standard* explained in January 1866,

There is something in the very nature of martial law which is repugnant to the English temper, and it is well that it should be so. Yet that in extreme cases it is necessary no one can deny, and especially in places where the power of government is so weak and so ineffectually supported by armed force . . . Such seems to have been most emphatically the case in Jamaica . . .[60]

The editor of the *Law Times* held a similar view. While martial law was a fearful business, it was essential to public security in the colonies.[61] It signalled to the subject population that 'any attempt . . . to avail themselves of the power of numbers will be instantly suppressed'. In the empire, 'the submission of that multitude is secured only by their consciousness of the multitude that the force of Government will be used promptly, resolutely and thoroughly'. For whites living among hostile populations in the colonies, this was not a point of abstract political theory. As one white Jamaican clerical wrote in 1865:

We argue that laws should be adapted to the state of the people for whom they are made. We want protection, however it may come, from a system which gives power to a class of men, who, after thirty years of kindness and education have turned round like savages on

---

[58] Winwood Reade, quoted ibid., 63.   [59] *Pall Mall Gazette* (23 Apr. 1867), 1–2.
[60] *Evening Standard* (26 Jan. 1866).   [61] *Law Times* (6 Jan. 1866), 125.

the white man. We want, if needed, martial law. In short, we want to live under any form of government so be that we shall not have our throats cut.[62]

We have seen that among some sections of the English intelligentsia, this kind of racially charged tough-talking about martial law was highly fashionable. Among other sections, however, it was detested and feared. As the *Spectator* generalized in September 1866,

The truth seems to be that the literary aristocracy of England are contracting one of the worst vices of aristocracies of all kinds, the entire loss of reverence for inferiors... Mr. Carlyle and Mr. Ruskin have made up their minds that the lower races should be managed and governed by the higher, and they decline to recognise any evil which results from the application of their principle.[63]

Walter Bagehot gave the same point a different gloss:

Mr. Carlyle's defence of Mr. Eyre means, if it means anything, that we are to reverse our system of government by law... and set up instead the will of one man... We say this would be a step backward towards barbarism – nay, it would *be* barbarism, for it would carry us back to the strife of the strong with the strong. . . .[64]

Bagehot was among those who would not stand by while the integrity of English political jurisprudence was undermined in the name of imperial security.

While one plane of English political tectonics in the 1860s was a rock-solid commitment to global imperialism, another and contrary plane was the country's habitual veneration of legality. We have seen that by early December 1865, a small but potent alliance of politicians, journalists, social activists, evangelicals, and secular intellectuals had become united in the view that the Jamaica suppression could not be allowed to pass unchallenged. It was bad enough that British officials in Jamaica had orchestrated a 'red anarchy' of racially motivated violence,[65] but still worse that so many prominent Englishmen had gone on record that even the most calculated bloodshed had been perfectly legal under the law of martial law. More than the violence itself, this thesis about its *legality* shocked English liberals into action. As the *Daily News* commented,

It is one of the compensations of the evils of this terrible Jamaica tragedy that it is finding out some of the least expected weak points of our character at home. Last summer nobody would have believed that there were people here... who deliberately approve of hanging accused persons without trial, and justify the slaughter of a whole population in revenge for a local outbreak....The most extraordinary feature of their conduct is that they offer their justification of the utter subversion of the law in the name of Conservatism.[66]

The editor of the *Solicitors' Journal* made a similar point: 'there is now, we believe, a party in England which holds the Crown to be above the law; but if there be, we are politically opposed to that party.'[67]

---

[62] The Revd. J. Radcliffe to *The Times* (18 Nov. 1865), 6.   [63] *Spectator* (15 Sept. 1866).
[64] 'Mr. Carlyle on Mr. Eyre', *Economist* (15 Sept. 1866), 1080.
[65] Roundell, *England and her Subject Races*, 18.   [66] *Daily News* (30 Jan. 1866).
[67] *Solicitors' Journal* (16 Dec. 1865).

The *raison d'être* of the Jamaica Committee was to defend a liberal jurisprudence of power. It was organized and sustained to fight what its members saw as creeping ideological *regression* among the conservative wing of the English governing class; regression starkly manifested in their endorsement of a robust and expansive doctrine of martial law. Some liberals feared that the use of martial law to suppress dissent in Jamaica presaged the use of martial law to suppress dissent at home. They feared that the normalization of martial law as an instrument of imperial administration represented a severe threat to constitutional government at home. In a speech made on behalf of the Jamaica Committee in August 1866, Goldwin Smith emphasized the 'practical bearing of the [Jamaica suppression] ...on the securities for public liberty in our own country. It is almost exclusively from this point of view that I have myself taken up the question.'[68] Mill later recalled the point in this way: 'There was far more at stake than only justice to the negroes, imperative as was that consideration. The question was whether the British dependencies, and eventually perhaps, Great Britain itself, were to be under the government of law or of military licence.'[69] The primary aim of the Jamaica Committee, as Mill once privately explained, was not to defend negroes, over even the principle of liberty, but to vindicate the 'first necessity of human society, law'.[70] In this view, there was no safe way for the English to be lawless tyrants abroad and constitutional liberals at home.

Even at the inception of their association in December 1865, the leaders of the Jamaica Committee were preoccupied with the legitimation of martial law, and its ominous ramifications for (what one historian has called) England's 'fragile democratic culture' in the mid-Victorian era.[71] Two recent political developments in the home countries, the Fenian agitation and the agitation for constitutional reform, only exacerbated the Committee's sense of alarm and urgency. Irish nationalism and electoral reform were extremely raw points of domestic political life, and the Jamaica affair only aggravated the injury. As the *Morning Advertiser* remarked,

Men have been *illegally executed* in Jamaica,...and some London papers are actually defending or extenuating these sham trials and judicial murders, and eagerly advocating Governor Eyre's cause. This is the worst feature of the whole case; for if such doings as these can find 'Liberal' defenders, we may soon have them repeated in Ireland – aye, even in England also.[72]

The *Glasgow Sentinel* held the same opinion: 'if such be accepted as a precedent, we may...in case of a Fenian rising in Ireland...have sympathizers in Glasgow seized upon police warrants and the prisoners packed off by the first steamer to Cork or Dublin to be tried by drum-head law.'[73]

---

[68] *Bee-Hive* (25 Aug. 1866).   [69] John Stuart Mill, *Autobiography* (London, 1873), 283.
[70] Mill to Urquart, 4 Oct. 1866, in Mineka and Lindley (eds.), *Later Letters*, 1205.
[71] Lorimer, 'Race, Science and Culture', 23.   [72] *Morning Advertiser* (14 Dec. 1865).
[73] *Glasgow Sentinel* (2 Dec. 1865).

By the summer of 1866, critics of the Jamaica suppression had achieved some appreciable successes. The Russell Government had undertaken a remarkably thorough and impartial investigation of what had happened in Jamaica. The final report of the inquiry firmly condemned the colonial authorities for having tolerated excessive punishments under martial law. An experienced and respected public official had been unceremoniously dismissed from the colonial service. The new regime in Jamaica, moreover, was ordered to prosecute Jamaicans, white and black, who had committed atrocities before and during the suppression. And when Lord Derby formed a Conservative government in June 1866, all these findings and decisions were upheld. In the judgement of the Jamaica Committee, however, these measures were wholly subverted when, in the course of the parliamentary debate on the Jamaica suppression of late July 1866, Disraeli announced that neither Eyre nor any senior military officer would be prosecuted criminally for their parts in the military trial and execution of Gordon (or any other person). The Government's policies on Jamaica, Disraeli had stressed, were 'based on the assumption that everything which was done [there] was legal'.[74] No senior official would be prosecuted because none had committed crimes. They had not committed crimes, Charles Adderley reminded the House of Commons, because their actions 'took place under the proclamation of martial law'.[75]

That was not to say that the Tory Cabinet was of one undivided mind about Jamaica. We have seen that Lord Carnarvon, Cardwell's successor at the Colonial Office, was greatly perturbed both by what had happened under martial law in Jamaica, and by his Government's unwillingness more forcefully to condemn it. Like Cardwell, like Mill, like Cockburn, Carnarvon was a moralizing imperialist. He firmly believed that empire was creditable only when it was justified by the upstanding conduct of its masters. Like any other expression of political power, the legitimate empire could not be tyrannous or arbitrary. The hallmark of English civilization, the endowment which warranted its imperial dominions, was its jurisprudence of power. That was why Carnarvon was appalled that British officials, under cover of some bastardized 'martial' law, had implemented a bloody reign of terror in Jamaica. He was equally appalled when some members of the Government had tried to defend actions which Carnarvon thought 'indefensible'.[76] But like most of his contemporaries, conservatives and liberals, Carnarvon thought that it was possible to put things right. He thought it possible that England's sprawling, non-Europeanized empire of the late 1860s might yet be reconciled with the rule of law. His circular on the new regulatory framework for martial law, sent to all British colonial Governors in January 1867, was an attempt to resolve the contradiction between the dual commitment to empire and law.

Did this measure succeed? A writer to the *Pall Mall Gazette* was right to harbour doubt.[77] It was one thing to establish rules governing the use of martial law, quite

---

[74] *Hansard*, clxxxiv (31 July 1866), 1838.   [75] Ibid., 1788.
[76] Ibid. (2 Aug. 1866), 1894.   [77] Letter of M. H. to *Pall Mall Gazette* (19 Dec. 1866), 3–4.

another to comprehend the *sense* of the doctrine: 'the great questions respecting the nature and extent of martial law', he contended, 'itself are of a very different nature.' These questions 'appertain to the highest and most difficult chapters of political science'. From this perspective, then, the question 'what is the law of martial law?' was really an oblique way of asking, 'what are the right limits on the use of political and military power?' 'Once identified, was it possible for these limits to be respected where the British community was a vulnerable minority?' These questions the nation had yet to answer.

The British military, for their part, could not wait for the nation, or even the Colonial Office, to resolve the key issues concerning martial law. It is probably right to suggest that the intensity and staying-power of the Jamaica controversy took senior British military officials by surprise. Few among them predicted in October 1865 that the court martial and execution of some black rebels would have led to so much 'obloquy',[78] to say nothing of criminal prosecution for murder. Just as the Colonial Office had done in 1866, senior officials at the War Office and Admiralty began to consult their lawyers. The first order of business was to arrange for the legal defence of Nelson and Brand. Of greater moment, however, was the long-term posture of the military toward martial law. If another unseemly imbroglio was to be avoided, it was essential for the army and navy to devise a set of protocols pertaining to martial law. Rules were needed to govern the interaction as between military and civilian officials, and as between military officers in the field and detainees. With this in mind military lawyers were asked to prepare a series of legal memoranda. At the War Office, a departmental lawyer called Charles Clode advised the Ministry both on the defence of Nelson and on the general legal issues that might arise out of the implementation of martial law.[79] Another important study on the subject was prepared in November 1866 by Sir William Power, the army's Commissary General-in-Chief.

Power's memorandum is particularly revealing about the contradictory character of British imperialism. It focused on how the army and navy might avoid trouble when called upon to aid colonial authorities in the suppression of insurrection. In Power's judgement, the law was not the key point. While martial law bestowed great theoretical powers on military men, as a practical matter, these powers could be exercised only at great peril. This was because in British colonies, even during a period of martial law, the army operated within an essentially *civilian* framework. In these places the expectations and conventions of civilian conduct never were entirely displaced. For that reason, the only prudent course for military officers was to 'permit the Civilian Government to carry on its ordinary functions concurrently with Martial Law'. With regard to civilian prisoners and detainees, moreover, the prudent course was for the military to give them over for trial by the

---

[78] This memorandum also can be found at *CO* 885/3.

[79] This memorandum was found among Cardwell's state papers. Clode to Lord Longford, March 1867, *CO* 137/428. The bulk of this work was done by Charles Clode. Clode eventually was able to assemble his researches into two volumes of published work: see Clode, *Military Forces of the Crown*.

'ordinary Civil Courts of the land'. In 1866, the Lord Commissioners of the Admiralty developed a similar protocol for naval officers who (like Herbert Brand) were ordered to assist in the implementation of martial law.[80] The protocol was based on the premiss that under martial law the 'arbitrary will of such an officer in such cases supersedes the Ordinary Law'. However, the thrust of the remaining articles of the protocol was that the will of the officer was *not* to be used arbitrarily. In fact, naval officers were instructed to seek written orders from the senior commander in the field in all matters of conduct, but 'especially in regard to the treatment of prisoners'. Further, the naval officer was not to destroy lives or property 'except under the exigencies of military operations or of self-defence'. Power's memorandum concluded with one more word of advice: when asked to participate in any military court martial or tribunal, naval officers were to 'take care, if so employed... to apply for the assistance, if possible, of a legal adviser'.

In one form or another, perceptions of law and illegality always had been the conceptual linchpin of the Jamaica affair, especially for those who had taken the offensive. Readers will recall that the first step of the newly formed Jamaica Committee (a step decided on before the first official meeting of the association) was to retain first-class lawyers to provide a formal opinion on the legal culpability for the military execution of Gordon. The second step was to publish the opinion. In this way the Jamaica Committee tried to place its stamp on a hotly contested subject of public discourse. When the government refused to take legal action against the principal figures of the suppression, the third step was to go to court. The purpose of this litigation, as was explained in one of the Committee's many pamphlets, was not to punish individual men, but 'to vindicate, by appeal to judicial authority, the great legal and constitutional principles which have been violated in the late proceedings, and deserted by Government'.[81] The Jamaica Committee wanted to cause a high court judge to state that there were no exceptions, not even in the most dangerous reaches of the empire, to England's secular constitution.

The Committee's decision was derided in England's mainstream press, liberal and conservative.[82] But here historians have been insufficiently precise about the focus of criticism. To be sure, most commentators rejected the notion that a murder prosecution could be a legitimate vehicle for a constitutional test case. By the same token, however, many of the same commentators were sure that the legal powers associated with the term 'martial law' had been abused in Jamaica, and that these abuses had not been sufficiently acknowledged or admonished. As things stood at the end of 1866, the Jamaica suppression offended a defining principle of English political culture, i.e. that political and military conduct was comprehensively accountable to the law.

---

[80] W. G. Romaine, Secretary of the Admiralty, to Vice-Admiral Sir J. Hope, 25 May 1866, *CO* 885/3. [81] *Statement of the Jamaica Committee, Jamaica Papers No. III* (London, 1866), 4.
[82] The conservative *Morning Herald* (30 July 1866), thought the intended prosecution 'vindictive and cowardly'. The *Manchester Guardian* (11 July 1866), 2, thought that the prosecution was 'vain, foolish and uncalled for', and that it had no 'reasonable prospect of success'.

Even those who denounced the Jamaica prosecutions were prepared to concede that issues of vital importance remained unresolved. In the estimation of the *Solicitors' Journal*, for example, the Jamaica episode posed one of the 'gravest constitutional questions which could arise in the present day.... Was it competent for the representative of the Queen ... to abrogate the common law of England?'[83] The actions of the Jamaican authorities in proclaiming and enforcing martial law, the *Journal* further contended, had called into question 'the all-important dogmas which are the boast of our national jurisprudence, that no rank or station is above the law, and that the life of the meanest British subject is not to be taken from him except in pursuance of the lawful judgment of his peers, and in accordance with the Common Law of the land'. The *Daily Telegraph* reminded readers that 'the case of Mr. Eyre today may, at any future time, be the case of some other colonial governor. In her dependencies all over the world England stands confronting hostile races.'[84] The editor of the *Irish Law Times* had related concerns: 'in our wide colonial empire ... it is a monstrous thing to consider that the power of the Governor of the colony to declare martial law is in a state of haze.'[85] The *Saturday Review* concluded at the close of 1866 that 'the whole subject of martial law is a mere chaos. No one can say what effect the proclamation has on the ordinary legal position of British subjects ... The true position of a colonial governor, again, is a matter which is of the highest importance to determine legally.'[86] On the eve of the prosecution of Nelson and Brand, even *The Times*, a tireless critic of the litigation, conceded that the country had been 'brought to the verge of an important state trial. Important indeed are the principles involved in this prosecution.'[87]

By 1867 there was also broad agreement that the issues posed by the Jamaica controversy would never be acceptably resolved by politicians. In the past eighteen months Jamaica had become (what the *Fortnightly Review* called) a 'national question',[88] one that could not be answered by recourse to political wrangling or 'party tactics'. The only viable option was for the conflict to be resolved in the courts of law. Before Jamaica was laid to rest, the *Fortnightly* exhorted, the English 'should make a point of getting a clear and decided opinion touching martial law, and its limits'. The *Pall Mall Gazette* made a similar point: 'you may discuss such questions in fifty ways, but the only way of settling them at all is to try them in a *court of law*, and this is the strong point of the proceedings of the Jamaica Committee' (emphasis added).[89]

The English high court judges of the mid-Victorian era enjoyed an enormous and perhaps unrivalled institutional prestige, even in the eyes of groups – radical liberals and democrats for instance – who had reason to mistrust them. After all, the judiciary was an unreconstructed bastion of unaccountable power in an era of increasing democracy. Judicial appointments were owed to patronage, sometimes

---

[83] *Solicitors' Journal* (16 Dec. 1865), 140. [84] *Daily Telegraph* (14 Dec. 1865).
[85] *Irish Law Times* (13 June 1868), 313. [86] *Saturday Review* (17 Nov. 1866), 595–6.
[87] *The Times* (8 Feb. 1867), 8. [88] *Fortnightly Review* (1 Jan. 1866).
[89] *Pall Mall Gazette* (8 Feb. 1867).

rank political patronage. Judges presided over an arcane, forbidding, and still largely unreformed system of principles and procedures, a system which buttressed the social and political status quo. But for all this, the impartiality and sagacity of the elite judiciary were almost universally acknowledged. 'Few peculiarities of English society', the *Spectator* declared in 1867, 'are more noteworthy than the prestige which still attaches itself to the higher Judges. A Judge is almost the only kind of man left in this country whose utterance can change opinion at once.'[90] In a nation rife with political partisanship and discord, judges alone could claim 'absolute impartiality in the application of exhaustive knowledge'. In the wake of the indecisive parliamentary debates on Jamaica in the summer of 1866, *Lloyd's Weekly*, the radical Sunday paper, pledged to agitate on the question 'until the law speaks from the dispassionate lips of English judges'.[91] The more moderate *Daily Telegraph* offered a similar opinion:

The Jamaica prosecutions have commenced. We do not wish to say one word to prejudge the case... The question has now passed outside the domain of public discussion, and we may fully rely on the acumen of our bar, the intelligence of an English jury, and the judicial learning of our bench for the thorough investigation of a very grave problem.[92]

In the result, when the Jamaica affair was moved into the courts during the winter of 1867 it did *not* pass outside the domain of public discussion. The form and focus of that discussion, however, changed irrevocably. After the first criminal complaints were laid down, the Jamaica affair was transformed into a series of legal pleadings, oral arguments, judicial pronouncements, and the seemingly unending slew of published legal commentaries. In essence, the country turned to lawyers and judges to accomplish what had not been accomplished by politicians: to reconcile the nation's conflicting passions for legality and imperial dominion.

For the parties involved, litigation means a loss of control, a surrender of office. When the Jamaica prosecutions were commenced in February 1867, the fate of the contestants and their goals was handed over to lawyers. (As we have seen, the personal reputation, skill, and bearing of lawyers was thought so vitally important to the outcome that the Eyre Defence Committee went to extraordinary lengths to prevent the Jamaica Committee from securing the services of John Coleridge.) In the first stages of litigation, the Jamaica Committee entrusted its fate to Fitzjames Stephen. It is right to use the word 'entrusted' here. Stephen was no one's legal marionette. To the immense discomfort and irritation of his clients, Stephen placed his own mark on the key issues of the case. He criticized 'wild doctrines' of martial law and upheld the traditional jurisprudence of power, but he did so while praising the courage of Edward Eyre. On the other side of the bar, the barristers James Hannen and Hardinge Giffard were retained to deliver their clients from criminal jeopardy. In doing so Hannen and Giffard defended the

---

[90] *Spectator* (13 Apr. 1867).   [91] *Lloyd's Weekly* (12 Aug. 1866).
[92] *Daily Telegraph* (7 Feb. 1867).

broadest possible reading of martial law, and carried the brief of its indispensability to public security in the non-white empire.

Although he was the paid partisan of the Jamaica Committee, Stephen reflected the conflicting (Karl Marx saw them as the canting)[93] currents of the Jamaica affair. Stephen was a lawyer, a moralist, and a passionate imperialist. His brief was an extremely onerous one. While the leaders of the Jamaica Committee were free to fulminate against the 'crimes' of Governor Eyre, to make portentous references to 'uncaged tigers', 'ultimate political convictions', and 'great constitutional principles', it fell to Stephen to take this high-minded talk into hand, and fashion it into compelling legal propositions. In effect, Stephen had been hired to *prove* that a proclamation of martial law did not curtail the common law. It fell to him to prove that it did not immunize officials from legal culpability. His task was made still more difficult by the fact that he was being asked to prove these points while prosecuting murder cases. The quest for a definitive judgement on martial law had somehow to be balanced with the legal rights and real personal jeopardy of the accused men.

Stephen was painfully aware of this tension. He was also aware of the political and moral ambiguity of the Jamaica cases. This was consistent with his sturdy realism about imperial administration. Stephen recognized that empire was a dangerous enterprise; the dangers faced by tiny white communities of settlers and administrators were constant and palpable. There were times, in other words, when their survival would depend on the quick and decisive use of force. As an intellectually honest man, as a barrister of great professional integrity, Stephen came to court ready to concede this much to the defence. Thus, when he opened the prosecution of Eyre in February 1867, he admitted that in the last days of crisis the former Governor had acted decisively in the context of a genuine and dangerous crisis. Stephen candidly expressed his 'regret at having to appear to make such a charge against a man who upon many accounts was deserving of so much esteem and respect'.[94] We have seen that this statement (and a subsequent comment of the same kind) infuriated the Jamaica Committee, and eventually precipitated a personal break between Stephen and Mill.[95] But Stephen repeated and then refused to disown these remarks, remarks which faithfully reflected a morally complex view of the issues. With Carnarvon (and Mill, too) Stephen shared a romantic theory of empire as properly the benevolent despotism of advanced societies over their less advanced cousins.[96] Imperial dominion was justifiable – in fact, it was (as John Calhoun had said of slavery) a positive good – so long as the imperial state governed

---

[93] Marx thought that the hand-wringing of English liberals over the Jamaica suppression was conclusive evidence of their 'utter turpitude'. Marx to Engels, 20 Nov. 1865, *Karl Marx and Frederick Engels: Collected Works*, vol. xlii (New York, 1987), 198–9.   [94] *Morning Star* (28 Mar. 1867), 6.

[95] Stephen's wife later recalled that Mill 'never forgave' Stephen for the manner in which he handled the Eyre prosecution. Memoirs of Mary Stephen, *CUL*, Add. MS. 8381.

[96] Smith, *Victorian Rationalist*, 123–38. See generally, Lynn Zastoupil, *John Stuart Mill and India* (Stanford, Calif., 1994), 201–4.

in the long-term interest of subjugated peoples.[97] The legitimacy of imperial government was a product of paternalism, not consent.[98] At the same time, Stephen also subscribed to the notion that the hallmark of any civilized government, domestic or imperial, was the existence of a vigorous state governed by law.[99] The main job of the state was to constrain the natural selfishness and aggression of men (still more so 'primitive' men), but to do so by resorting to transparent legal principle and procedures.

Stephen tried to incorporate all of these ideas into his formal legal submissions. The 'great public wrong' of the Jamaica suppression, he stated to Sir Thomas Henry in February 1866, was not that a Governor had used force, but that the use of force had become unharnessed from law.[100] If this precedent 'were allowed to pass unquestioned,' Stephen submitted, '[it would] seriously imperil the life and liberty of every man in the British Empire, whether in this country or elsewhere'. At Bow Street in February 1867 Stephen argued that Eyre had 'wilfully' put Gordon to death, and that such an action was a serious crime unless it was legally justified. Moreover, a proclamation of martial law, on whatever basis it was made, did not shield officials from the legal consequences of their actions. Any transgression against person or property that required justification at common law, required justification at martial law. With respect to the charge against Eyre, the relevant privilege was public necessity. In order to be acquitted of Gordon's murder, Eyre was obliged to prove that a reasonable official in his position would have thought it vital to public security that Gordon should be summarily tried and executed. For Stephen, these technical points of law had a much broader thrust. He wanted a court to affirm that English law applied – comprehensively and unremittingly – even to political decision-making during an emergency.

In his reply to Stephen's submissions, Hannen, Eyre's lead barrister, argued strenuously for a much more capacious doctrine of martial law. If Stephen's submissions were right, if the term 'martial law' denoted nothing more than the common law of necessity, Hannen submitted, executive officials would never trouble themselves to proclaim it.[101] Logic required there to be some definite legal advantage in making the proclamation. In fact, there was. Martial law was proclaimed, in England and in the empire, in order to warn persons living within a defined jurisdiction that ordinary common law principles and procedures had been suspended in favour of a far more 'terrible instrument'. It was a warning that Her Majesty's military officers had been duly authorized to do whatever they judged necessary to restore public order. In essence, it was a declaration of war on armed invaders or

---

[97] Mill's views on imperialism and race are canvassed in David Theo Goldberg, 'Liberalism's Limits: Carlyle and Mill on "The Negro Question" ', in Julie K. Ward and Tommy L. Lott (eds.), *Philosophers on Race: Critical Essays* (Oxford, 2002), 199–203; see also, Zastoupil, *Mill and India*.

[98] Stokes, *English Utilitarians*, 283–4.

[99] Ibid., 274–81. Mill and Stephen parted company on the sources and boundaries of individual liberty. Colaiaco, *Crisis of Victorian Thought*, 29–35.   [100] *RPBS*, 4.

[101] Ibid., 47.

rebels. And just as martial law bestowed the powers of war, it also granted the immunities of war. If in implementing martial law an officer in the field exercised judgement reasonably and in good faith, he had nothing to fear when civilian law was reinstated. Martial law enabled military men to make war without fear of legal consequences. Any more restricted view of the subject, Hannen submitted, would render it 'a mockery, a delusion' and just as surely 'a snare' to any officer foolish enough to use his authority.[102] And this being the law governing martial law in England, surely it was the law in those places, like Jamaica, where English rule is 'subject to great dangers'.

Hannen and Stephen clarified the lines of legal argument about martial law, but, as partisan advocates in a criminal case, they were constrained in what they could and could not say about the subject. The legal writer William Finlason was not so encumbered. In a minutely researched stream of works published between 1866 and 1869, Finlason not only re-excavated the English law of martial law, he wholly remade it. Finlason's writings on martial law represent the most sustained and cogent attempt by a Victorian writer to forge a credible theoretical synthesis of expansive imperialism and the rule of law.

Finlason's account of martial law was predicated on what he took to be two indisputable political facts. The first was that Britain's imperial commitments and aspirations were sacrosanct. Retrenchment was unthinkable. This first fact implied a second. In many colonies the British population would be perpetually small, isolated, and vulnerable to attack by the 'millions of a hostile race jealous of their rule, and often thirsting for their blood'.[103] 'A negro rebellion,' Finlason pointedly reminded readers, 'is necessarily, sooner or later, a war of *extermination.*'[104] Although his legal authorities were far from conclusive on this point, Finlason believed that the great jurists had fashioned not one but *two* bodies of martial law jurisprudence. There was the law of martial law pertaining to England and the home countries (and the 'advanced' dominions), and the nearly distinct law of martial law pertaining to the non-white colonies. By the mid-nineteenth century, martial law in England was 'rather of historical than practical interest'.[105] In the empire of dark-skinned peoples, however, martial law remained of the greatest possible relevance. For Finlason, this explained why common law rights and privileges always prevailed in England, and why, in the non-white empire, the common law 'only applies to British-*born* subjects and their descendants, and not

---

[102] Ibid., 51.
[103] Finlason, *Justice to a Colonial Governor*, cxxxi. The same point had been made by the editor of *The Times* (17 Nov. 1865), 8, two years earlier: '[with negroes] martial law is the law of necessity, for there is small choice under such circumstances... The truth is, a rising of this sort must be crushed at once, and if a few hundred soldiers and volunteers are to do the work of a large army they must make themselves ubiquitous, and they must every where finish their work thoroughly... Immediate justice is the best mercy in the long run, for to the lower class of minds death loses nearly all its terrors if it is seen at a considerable interval.'   [104] Finlason, *Justice to a Colonial Governor*, vi.
[105] Finlason, *Justice to a Colonial Governor*, cxxx Although in case of public emergency (in Ireland, for instance) it was possible that Parliament might enact martial law.

to alien races'.[106] Martial law did not undermine the common law rights of subjugated peoples because they did not have any.

Finlason's martial law was the unalloyed law of war. He contemplated that at some times and places British officers and soldiers would be permitted, even required, to commit acts of the most extreme brutality. More, Finlason unblinkingly accepted that British officials sometimes would be called upon to orchestrate campaigns of proactive and calculated terror. In the right circumstances, that is, when colonial white men and women were menaced by teeming populations of black men and women, all of this was justifiable at law. At the same time, however, Finlason was an Englishman and, more exactly, an English lawyer. It was a mark of his Englishness that he believed that the use of unbridled power – even in the most alien and harrowing of circumstances – required legal justification. In this unshakeable allegiance to law, Englishmen separated themselves from mere Russians or Austrians. In fact, the English were so much devoted to law that even their doctrine of force was understood as a kind of law, *martial* law. Martial law was the repressive instrument of civilized men because it comprehended limits. Under martial law, soldiers might kill, torture, and maim rebellious men, but they could not do so wantonly, maliciously, or dishonestly. Under martial law, scores of rebels might be hanged on the order of drumhead courts martial, but only when the purpose for doing so was rationally connected to the restoration of public order. Under martial law, as Finlason solemnly insisted, the military were obliged to observe 'those rules of common justice and humanity, which are universally obligatory, which are independent of all positive laws'.[107] When they failed to live up to this minimum standard, soldiers were accountable for their actions in the courts of law.

Finlason, like so many of his countrymen, wanted it both ways. He wanted England to continue with its imperial mandate within a flexible but substantive legal framework. He wanted an empire based on laws, but laws flexible enough to sanction and excuse the expedient use of terror. In this regard, Finlason's differences with Stephen and the Jamaica Committee were more in the manner of degree than kind. Finlason wanted a vast, secure, and strong empire but one with a relaxed legal accountability of authority. Stephen, too, wanted a vast, secure, and strong empire, but one with the *same* legal accountability of authority which prevailed in the home countries. By initiating the Jamaica prosecutions, and persisting with them for more than two years, the Jamaica Committee had hoped to establish definitively that Stephen's vision was correct. In spite of numerous obstacles and setbacks, the Committee never wavered in its confidence that a high court judge would settle these questions in favour of a comprehensive vision of the rule of law. In the result, however, this *faith* – the word is used advisedly – proved misplaced.

The grand jury charge provided by Cockburn in *The Queen v. Nelson and Brand* is an archetypal study in liberal confusion and self-contradiction about law

---

[106] *Justice to a Colonial Governor*, cxxx.   [107] Finlason, *Treatise on Martial Law*, 84.

and empire. Cockburn was emphatic that martial law was certainly 'not the wild, extravagant exercise of arbitrary and despotic jurisdiction which has lately been represented'.[108] Martial law did not – could not – give men licence to negate the 'eternal and immutable principles of justice, principles which can never be violated'.[109] On the most expansive reading of the sources, martial law was 'military law applied to civilians' during some great emergency of state.[110] With respect to the military trial and execution of Gordon, Cockburn seemed to take the position that they were illegal. The military court had lacked jurisdiction. The trial had not respected even the most rudimentary principles of procedure and evidence. The Lord Chief Justice suggested that Gordon had been executed because the authorities thought him a 'mischievous and obnoxious character'.[111] That being the case, Gordon's executioners were guilty of murder. Had the Lord Chief Justice stopped there, the Jamaica Committee rightly would have claimed victory. But the Lord Chief Justice, we have seen, did not stop there. He proceeded to tell the jury that he actually entertained 'some degree of doubt' that he had got the law right on the pivotal issue of jurisdiction. In fact, so great was his doubt that he invited the *jury* to decide the issue! Although in his closing statements Cockburn urged the jury to find true bills against the accused, his vacillation on the key points of law all but assured that they would not.

In the immediate aftermath of the Cockburn charge, liberal journalists almost uniformly agreed that the Lord Chief Justice had performed magnificently, and that his remarks on martial law would be counted among the great statements on the constitution. Cockburn basked in the praise. Nor was he chastened when readers of the whole charge noticed that it was actually riven by doubt and self-contradiction. In a postscript to the published edition of his address, Cockburn did not recant or recast even one of his instructions to the jury. As for the key question of 'the legality of what was done under martial law', Cockburn 'purposely abstained from expressing any opinion' for fear of prejudicing any 'further judicial proceedings'. Instead, Cockburn took the opportunity to address another theme: the terrible savagery of men, even white men, when released from law to strike against an 'inferior and despised race'.[112] The Lord Chief Justice 'shuddered to think what human nature was capable of...when vengeance is let loose in the shape of martial law'. But, tellingly, Cockburn qualified these remarks. In fact, he was 'quite ready to admit' that when confronted by armed insurrection in the empire the authorities were warranted in replacing civilian with military law. He also admitted that in these circumstances 'it might be well to have the means of summary and immediate punishment at hand, hanging, as it were, over the heads of the population, to strike terror into their minds'. Here the Lord Chief Justice took pains to underline the pragmatism of his views on law and imperial security. He accepted the fact of empire and the need to use force in order to preserve it.

---

[108] Cockburn (ed.), *Charge of the Lord Chief Justice*, 121.   [109] Ibid., 108.
[110] Ibid., 121.   [111] Ibid., 128.   [112] Ibid., 161.

Cockburn's single recommendation was for the 'necessity of legislation if martial law is ever again to be put in force'.[113] For the liberals who had already lavished praise on Cockburn for his magnificent contribution to the rule of law, these annotations were very inconvenient. But if the liberals chose to ignore or forget them, at least one of Cockburn's brother judges did not.[114]

When, on 2 June 1868, Sir Colin Blackburn began to charge the grand jury in *The Queen v. Eyre*, he was aware that, whatever else his Lord Chief Justice had said about martial law, certainly he had *not* condemned the doctrine outright. There still was very considerable doubt about the law of martial law, and the 'rule or test of criminal responsibility for such acts'.[115] Like so many other members of the governing class, Blackburn thought that it was 'of very great importance indeed that the law [upon this subject] should be distinctly understood'. An imperial nation could not afford for its officials in the colonies to be uncertain of their legal position when they moved to crush rebellion. Blackburn was so much convinced of the need for clarity on this point that he risked the wrath of his Lord Chief Justice in order to achieve it.

As we have seen, Blackburn's explanation of the law of martial law plainly controverted the charge of the Lord Chief Justice. Specifically, he found that the colonial statute used by Edward Eyre to invoke and implement martial law was valid, and gave the Governor 'very arbitrary and great power' to put down insurrection.[116] Blackburn thought that this statute quite properly reflected the security concerns of a former slave society, concerns that persisted as the white population of the island was dwarfed by the progeny of the former slaves. More than a generation after emancipation, the tiny white community of Jamaica still was menaced by the prospect of race war. That was why the Governor (with his Council of War) had been given unusually wide powers to proclaim and enforce martial law.[117] The main question for the jury was whether Governor Eyre had used those powers reasonably and in good faith.[118] As they deliberated on this question, the grand jurors were urged to 'see with [the Governor's] eyes, to hear with his ears'. Concretely, that meant that the jury was to take into account that when he decided how to respond to the insurrection at Morant Bay, Eyre was responsible for the lives of every white person in the colony. The jury was to take into account the possibility that the wrong decisions might have led to loss of these lives in a war of racial extermination. Blackburn's charge, in other words, had been unmistakably generous to the accused. To underline the authority of his

---

[113] Cockburn (ed.), *Charge of the Lord Chief Justice*, 163.

[114] When Mill later claimed for the Jamaica Committee, that 'we had elicited from the highest criminal judge in the nation an authoritative declaration that the law was what we maintained it to be', his famous memory appeared to have failed him. Mill, *Autobiography*, 283.

[115] Finlason, *Report of The Queen v. Edward Eyre*, 54.   [116] Ibid., 77–8.

[117] According to the *Spectator* (6 June 1868), 5, Blackburn had concluded that 'negroes cannot expect for a moment the same treatment as British subjects of Anglo-Saxon or even Celtic descent...That is the true axiom at the bottom of Mr. Blackburn's mind... [I]t is not a pleasant interpretation.'   [118] Finlason, *Report of The Queen v. Edward Eyre*, 85.

words, moreover, Blackburn informed the jury that the charge had been endorsed by the entire Court of Queen's Bench.

Blackburn's charge, and the unprecedented attempt by the Lord Chief Justice to disclaim it, led to an extraordinary explosion of critical commentary. The conservative *Standard* deplored the fact that after two years of legal wrangling over questions of the greatest constitutional importance, the 'legal history of the Eyre case is hardly yet completed'.[119] The unseemly clash between the two eminent judges, the *Pall Mall Gazette* concluded, had cast the subject of martial law 'back into the confusion in which it was involved before the proceedings against Mr. Eyre were instituted'.[120] *Reynolds' Weekly*, the radical sheet, was scandalized by the 'spectacle of English judges flatly contradicting each other on the bench of justice, and on a vital principle'.[121] The *Law Times* was appalled by the public rift between Cockburn and Blackburn, and by the 'divided opinion of the great Judges as to [a colonial official's] power to employ the military, or to put down revolt'.[122] All over the globe British civilian and military proconsuls did not know the limits of their powers, or the liabilities that might flow from their use. 'The hands of all our colonial rulers', the editor of the *Law Times* ventured, 'are paralysed by the existing uncertainty of the law.' The law of martial law, the *Imperial Review* drily commented, 'could hardly be left in a more unsatisfactory state.'[123]

By the summer of 1868 it was glaringly apparent to informed observers that the English jurisprudence of power was in a state of alarming unclarity. It was equally obvious that the high court judiciary, that most venerated of English law-making institutions, could not furnish a coherent resolution to the problem. The *Manchester Guardian* was astute about the reasons for this. 'Whatever precision may be attained in stating the law applicable to the case,' it offered, 'every one must perceive that law is only part of the question.'[124] The other part was politics, or, more accurately, the moral basis of politics. The martial law in Jamaica had engendered the kind of fundamental disagreement that no mere legal authority 'can rule into concurrence'. 'Even the judges delivering their opinions from the Bench', the *Guardian* observed, 'are not exempt from this danger of irreconcilable variance.' They might come to some agreement about the applicable legal principles, and yet still 'differ as widely as other men in the moral medium through which they regard the facts'. Martial law, the *Saturday Review* once observed, was 'pre-eminently a historical study'.[125] The editor at the *Pall Mall Gazette* made a similar, if better realized, observation: [126] 'it is idle to disguise the fact that where historical and political theories, mixed up with the whole course of English history, are necessarily brought into play, the minds of judges work under the same advantages and disadvantages as do the minds of all other intelligent men'. If the legal system had failed to deliver a decisive answer to the contradictions thrown up

[119] *Standard* (9 June 1868).   [120] *Pall Mall Gazette* (9 June 1868), 1.
[121] *Reynolds' Weekly* (14 June 1868).   [122] *Law Times* (13 June 1868), 120.
[123] *Imperial Review* (13 June 1868), 549.   [124] *Manchester Guardian* (10 June 1868), 4.
[125] *Saturday Review* (14 July 1866), 40–2.   [126] *Pall Mall Gazette* (13 June 1868), 4.

by law and imperialism, it was because they could not be answered decisively, not, at least, by citing legal authorities. The constitutional law of England was not so much a fixed body of precedents as a deep reservoir of public conscience, one roiled by powerful cross-currents.

If it seems obvious that all constitutions, even those that have been arranged systematically, are dynamic and contestable, this point was not obvious to the main protagonists of the Jamaica affair. Even Mill, the enormously erudite leader of the Jamaica Committee, advanced a strangely naive view of constitutional law and interpretation. Throughout the duration of the Jamaica controversy Mill spoke of 'great legal and constitutional principles' as if they were rules of arithmetic. Throughout the duration of the Jamaica litigation Mill spoke of English judges as if they were legal automata preprogrammed to expunge martial law from the constitution. When they did not do so, when Cockburn balked, and when Blackburn explicitly endorsed the use of martial law in the empire, Mill had nothing to say about it. In the final analysis, it is plain that Mill simply did not have a subtle theory either of the English constitution or its interpretation. The decision to send the Jamaica affair into the courts was the result more of hopefulness than discernment. When finally left with no better options, the Jamaica Committee decided to promote a skewed reading of Cockburn while disregarding Blackburn. But, in retrospect, the judges, especially Blackburn, had been more honest than Mill. Like Mill, a former functionary of the East India Company,[127] they accepted the justice of England's imperial mission in the world. But, unlike Mill, the judges were willing to confront the fact that – for an *imperial* nation – the issues raised by the Jamaica suppression were morally and politically equivocal.[128] What in fact *were* the ultimate political convictions of England's liberal elite? Could there be such thing as a liberal empire? In the late 1860s, even as the Jamaica controversy raged, few liberals were willing even to pose such questions. Ironically, even as Edward Eyre was being prosecuted for murder in the English courts, those who supported this action tacitly accepted two theses constantly advanced by their opponents. They accepted that England would retain an extensive foreign empire, and that the empire could not everywhere and all the time be governed by recourse only to civilian legal norms. If the country was to avoid an endless succession of Cawnpores and Morant Bays, colonial officials sometimes would need to implement extremely violent measures. The question, then, was not whether violence would be used against recalcitrant peoples, but whether its use was to be regulated by civilian legal authorities. In this way, and for English liberals and conservatives alike, the abrasive logic of empire stripped away the placid surface of English constitutional law, exposing a fluid mantle of stark moral and political choices.

[127] Ironically, Mill was employed at the East India Company when it faced and suppressed the Mutiny of 1857. For Mill and empire, see generally, Kinzer *et al.*, *Moralist In and Out of Parliament*, 185–227; Goldberg, 'Liberalism's Limits', 199–203; Hussain, *The Jurisprudence of Emergency*, 119–20.   [128] For Mill as public moralist, see Collini, *Public Moralists*, 121–89.

When it is thought about, that in the mid-nineteenth century the English political class was engaged in a violent and racist imperialism is among the *least* remarkable facts about it. Far more noteworthy, far more exceptional historically, is that so many of its members could, at least for an historical moment, become so strongly agitated by these policies. Surely the most striking and revealing aspect of the Jamaica controversy is that it should have occurred at all. Recall what had happened. The Governor of a remote island colony had taken decisive steps to quell a potentially catastrophic rebellion among overwhelming numbers of blacks, a race renowned for its savagery. The Governor took these steps only a handful of years after the Indian Mutiny, and after white blood had been spilt by black men and women at Morant Bay. While the ensuing suppression was stringent, it was far less so than the suppression of the mutineers eight years earlier. As for the Governor, all his major decisions had been approved by lawyers and privy councillors. The uprising was quickly and successfully suppressed, and under a modicum of legal regularity. Nonetheless, when this information reached England, an appreciable number of eminent white men loudly insisted that what had happened in Jamaica was immoral and illegal. The Government did not wholly disagree. Within a few weeks, Eyre was suspended, and a contingent of lawyers sent to the colony to investigate. Six months later, Eyre had been cashiered without pension and was menaced by criminal prosecutions for murder. A London magistrate thought there were facts and law enough to send Jamaica cases to the grand jury. The Lord Chief Justice of England, while he professed uncertainty about the applicable legal principles, recommended that the case go to trial. While the prosecutions were denounced in some quarters, they were carefully monitored and evaluated in every quarter. For all these reasons, the Jamaica affair was one of the most extraordinary moral and legal spectacles of the era. While some writers were fond of suggesting that the Jamaica suppression had lowered the English to the debased level of mere Russians and Austrians, the evidence suggests that in the nineteenth and twentieth centuries continental European Colonialism was far more repressive and far less answerable to forms of law.[129]

The second remarkable feature of the Jamaica controversy is the pervasive degree to which it was defined and pursued as a problem of law. The rallying point of the Jamaica controversialists was that Governor Eyre and his soldiers had transgressed against the fundamental law of the nation, and that, if the precedent was not checked, it would undermine the domestic constitution. There was broad agreement among the English elite that the law of martial law, at least as it related to imperial administration, ought to be settled by the courts. There was even broader agreement that some manner of law, even if it was the law governing war, ought always to prevail over human desire. It is noteworthy that even Edward Eyre, as he pondered his response to bloodshed at Morant Bay, did not think that

---

[129] For an excellent overview of the habitually ruthless response of European colonial states to native insurrection, see L. H. Gann and Peter Duignan (eds.), *African Proconsuls: European Governors in Africa* (Stanford, Calif., 1978).

he could suppress the Jamaica rising in any way he liked. In 1866, Mr. Justice Alan Ker of the Jamaica Supreme Court was strongly of the opinion that Duberry Ramsay and other Jamaican militia officers had committed serious criminal offences during the period of martial law. In their turn, Carnarvon and Blackburn also imagined that the officers charged with authority under martial law were legally accountable for their actions. Even Finlason, the zealous champion of imperial security, thought that the exertion of force under martial law was constrained by the requirements of natural justice. In this period it was still hoped that an accommodation could be forged between the love of law and the love of imperial domination. It seems not to have occurred to these distinguished lawyers and politicians that empire – this 'fatal heritage'[130] – might be the Trojan horse of English political jurisprudence.

Edward Eyre died at the age of 86 in Devonshire in December 1901. When he was nine years old Brougham had stood in Parliament to denounce the implementation of martial law in Demerara. In the last days of his long life the newspapers bristled with reports on the war against the Boer guerrillas and their communities. Once again the vocabulary of repression – martial law, courts martial, summary execution – was in widespread use. Once again the English political class, if only listlessly, was grappling with the dark implications of empire. Eyre's death was an occasion for reflection. Of the Jamaica controversy, the writer for *The Times* was moved to observe, 'its passions have long since died away, its issues have never been finally decided.'[131] But there can be comfort in this. For of course the struggle over the moral and legal predicates of political action, over the jurisprudence of power, never can be 'finally decided'.

---

130 *The Times* (21 May 1858), paraphrasing John Bright.
131 As quoted in Ford, 'The Governor Eyre Case in England', 233.

APPENDIX

The Jamaica Controversy as Historiography

Why did the suppression of an uprising in Jamaica in 1865, then one of Britain's second-tier colonies, engender a prolonged and acrimonious public controversy in the mother country? Who initiated and sustained the Jamaica affair, and what were their defining ideas and aims? By what means was the Jamaica affair contested, and what was its final outcome? In what ways was the Jamaica controversy linked to the political, intellectual, and cultural history of mid-Victorian England? What is the historical significance, if any, of the episode? These questions, taken together, have spawned a large body of scholarly writing, one that has doubled or tripled in size since 1990. This bibliographical essay provides a critical assessment of the historiography of the Jamaica controversy. It attempts to identify trends in the historical questions, methods, evidence, and interpretations that have been implemented by the scholars of the episode.

We have already noted that the Morant Bay uprising of 1865 has given rise to two largely distinct bodies of historical writing. The first examines Morant Bay mainly as an episode in Jamaican and Caribbean history. This work is interested mainly in the predicament of the black population of Jamaica, and in the specific causes and outcomes of the uprising. These historians also want to situate their data within the larger historiography of slavery and post-slavery in the Americas. In this regard the most important contributions to the literature have been made by Gad Heuman and Thomas Holt.[1] Their books are the most comprehensive guides to the causes, contours, and significance of the Morant Bay uprising.[2] But the second branch of this historiography, the branch of greater relevance to this study, has focused on the Jamaica rising, and especially the violent suppression of that rising, as an episode in the history of mid-Victorian politics in England. For more than forty years the standard work in this regard has been Bernard Semmel's self-described 'narrative essay', *The Governor Eyre Controversy*.[3] Published in England in 1962, Semmel's (un-footnoted) study did not purport to be a 'definitive treatment'.[4] Instead Semmel provides readers with an interpretive overview of the controversy, one predicated on the 'interdependence of British imperial and domestic politics'.[5] He describes the

---

[1] The work of Heuman and Holt largely superseded the pioneering work of Eric Williams, *British Historians and the West Indies* (London, 1966). Williams, in turn, had displaced *The Myth of Governor Eyre*, (London, 1933), a polemic against British imperialism published by Lord Sydney Olivier, and William L. Mathieson, *The Sugar Colonies and Governor Eyre, 1849–1866* (London, 1936).

[2] As will be discussed below, in Thomas C. Holt, *The Problem of Freedom: Race, Labor, and Politics in Jamaica and Britain, 1832–1938* (Baltimore, Md, 1992), 263–309. Holt also furnished a long chapter on the Jamaica controversy in England. See also, Catherine Hall, *Civilizing Subjects: Colony and Metropole in the English Imagination, 1830–1867* (Chicago, Ill., 2002).

[3] Bernard Semmel, *The Governor Eyre Controversy* (London, 1962), 7. Also published under the title *Jamaican Blood and Victorian Conscience* (New York, 1962).

[4] Ibid. The book was fewer than 200 pages long and provided a short bibliography, but no citations to documents.

[5] And in this regard superseded the best preceding account, Arvel B. Erickson, 'Empire or Anarchy: The Jamaica Rebellion of 1865', 44 *Journal of Negro History* (1959), 99–122.

Jamaica affair as a prolonged public debate of one of the great and vexed questions of nineteenth-century English politics: whether 'the maintenance of a colonial empire is compatible with liberal democracy'.[6] This theme is of enduring importance, and it stands at the core of the present study.

Semmel's main methodological premiss is that the Jamaica controversy could be faithfully reconstructed from the writings and newspaper accounts of the famous political and literary men who took up sides on the issue. His book treats the controversy as a clash between two political tendencies, one exemplified by the arch-liberal John Stuart Mill, the other by the arch-conservative Thomas Carlyle. An historian of Victorian high culture, Semmel is interested in how the English intelligentsia seized on the Jamaica affair as a means of contesting fundamental questions about social equality, political democracy, and empire. By the same token, Semmel's narrative is not insensible of the fact that law figured prominently in the Jamaica controversy ('The question most directly at issue', Semmel wrote, 'was martial law')[7]. But in a pattern frequently repeated by subsequent scholars of the Eyre controversy, Semmel poses questions about the significance of law, lawyers, and litigation for domestic and imperial politics in mid-Victorian England, but then does not excavate the relevant sources. His book identifies 'martial law' as a central subject matter of the conflict without undertaking systematic study of its historical nature, its technical legal literature, or its linkage to politics and political ideology.

In the 1960s the most notable addition to the historiography of the Jamaica affair was Geoffrey Dutton's deeply felt and researched biography of Eyre, *The Hero as Murderer*. In the Foreword Dutton recalled a time when Australians remembered Edward Eyre as 'one of their greatest explorers'.[8] By the mid 1960s, however, Eyre's reputation had suffered something of a drubbing at the hands of writers such as Olivier and Semmel. Dutton's biography is offered as a corrective. It endeavours to place Eyre's (admittedly dubious) conduct as Governor of Jamaica, especially his handling of the Morant Bay emergency, in the more flattering context of an eventful and largely admirable life. In *The Hero as Murderer*, Dutton draws on an extensive array of primary sources to portray Eyre as a fundamentally decent man who happened also to be tragically ill-equipped to navigate the political riptides of post-emancipation Jamaica. Impulsive and imperious, Dutton's Eyre lacked the cool and measured judgement needed to deal effectively with an armed uprising. In proclaiming martial law, Dutton concludes, Eyre created a 'monster which got away from him'.[9] But if Dutton was sometimes a stern judge of his hero, he was even more scathing (to the point of unreason) in his criticism of the 'savage philanthropists' who hounded Eyre upon his return to England.[10] In his view, Mill and his Jamaica Committee were moved by a romantic and misplaced sympathy for Jamaica's black population on one hand, an unreasoning antipathy toward the domestic and imperial ruling class on the other. The litigation mounted by the Committee against Eyre, Dutton contends, was gratuitous and vindictive. It had no significance beyond the level of personal annoyance to the former Governor Eyre.

The tendency to marginalize the role of law and litigation in the Jamaica affair is equally pronounced in one of the thickest limbs of its historiography, the body of work which has

---

[6] Semmel, *The Governor Eyre Controversy*, 7.   [7] Ibid., 128.

[8] Geoffrey Dutton, *The Hero as Murderer: The Life of Edward John Eyre, Australian Explorer and Governor of Jamaica, 1815–1901* (London, 1967), 9.   [9] Ibid., 283.

[10] Ibid., 309.

focussed on the words and deeds of the many illustrious political and literary men who led public debate on the issue. In one of the first published academic pieces on the controversy, George Ford's 1948 article 'The Governor Eyre Case in England',[11] the author quoted extensively from the pertinent writings of Mill, Carlyle, Ruskin, and Bright, and even from bit players such as Darwin and Dickens. In Ford's view, the Jamaica controversy could be summarized as a protracted intellectual joust between the leading lights of English liberalism and conservatism. While Ford acknowledged that in its 'final stages' the Jamaica controversy was immersed in law and legal procedures, he observed that the legal aspects of the 'Eyre case involve a maze of legal technicalities which need not concern us here'.[12] This disinclination to explore the legal dimensions of the Jamaica affair continues to resonate in the later scholarship.

In 1974 Gillian Workman published a sophisticated and insightful short article on the importance of the Jamaica affair in the late career and writings of Carlyle.[13] Workman exploits Carlyle's previously unexamined letters to demonstrate that the 'sage of Chelsea' took up the issue of Governor Eyre and the alleged oppression of Jamaican blacks 'to make a point about the condition of England'.[14] In fact, in Workman's perceptive view, most of the key actors in the controversy were less interested in the position of black subjects of the empire than with the 'political and legal implications of the case' for Englishmen.[15] For Carlyle, Jamaica was a cynical diversion staged by English liberals and hypocritical do-gooders. He mocked radicals like John Bright who could moan so sorrowfully about the plight of black Jamaican peasants while they overlooked the exploitation of white English workers. On the basis of this evidence Workman advances the controversial argument that in his Jamaica interventions Carlyle was not moved 'by any racist views', but only by his paternalistic concern for the woeful state of the English underclass.[16] What Carlyle had wanted to do was use the Jamaica affair to fix public attention on (what he saw as) the real moral crisis facing the country. In the rehabilitation of Eyre he hoped that the country would be inspired to embrace an authentically conservative form of government.

Carlyle's legacy has been far less sympathetically treated in recent work on his part in the Jamaica affair.[17] In a 1989 article on how middle-class intellectuals used Jamaica to contest the unreformed political status quo,[18] Catherine Hall argues that Carlyle used his prestige as a public sage to champion Eyre and in so doing, the cause of racism, public order, and social hierarchy. For Carlyle a soundly constructed polity would reflect the natural intellectual and moral inequality as between whites and especially as between whites and blacks. Hall's Carlyle was a dogmatic racist, but also a relentless critic of 'effeminate' white men (like Mill and the philanthropists) who denied and desecrated their responsibilities as members of a privileged caste.[19] In Hall's account of Mill and the Jamaica affair, Mill

---

[11] George H. Ford, 'The Governor Eyre Case in England', 27 *University of Toronto Quarterly* (1947–8), 219–33.   [12] Ibid., 233.

[13] Gillian Workman, 'Thomas Carlyle and the Governor Eyre Controversy: An Account with Some New Material', 18 *Victorian Studies* (1974), 77–102.   [14] Ibid., 82.

[15] Ibid., 81.   [16] Ibid., 85.

[17] See particularly, Holt, *The Problem of Freedom*, 284–6; Catherine Hall, 'Competing Masculinities: Thomas Carlyle, John Stuart Mill and the Case of Governor Eyre,' in Catherine Hall (ed.), *White, Male and Middle-Class: Explorations in Feminism and History* (Cambridge, 1992), 255–93, at 268–76.

[18] Catherine Hall, 'The Economy of Intellectual Prestige: Thomas Carlyle, John Stuart Mill, and the Case of Governor Eyre', 22 *Labour/Le Travail* (1989), 167–96.

[19] Hall, 'The Economy of Intellectual Prestige', 180–1. For largely complimentary accounts of Carlyle and the Jamaica affair, see Fred Kaplan, *Thomas Carlyle: A Biography* (Ithaca, NY, 1983), 487–95; Chris R.

attempted to use the episode to 'construct a particular version of England' which insisted 'on the idea of formal equality between the races, equality before the law'.[20] Both Mill and Carlyle shared a 'profound belief in centrality of individual action'. In Mill's ideal state, however, the citizenry was to be encouraged to achieve a masculine independence from arbitrary authority of all kinds. The suppression in Jamaica, and the willingness of the British state to validate it, Hall offers as an object lesson in the use of such authority. With his colleagues on the Jamaica Committee Mill wanted to use the courts to chastise the usurpers, and to encourage more egalitarian social norms.

Like many of her predecessors, Hall was fully cognizant that the Jamaica Committee tried to achieve their programme by hiring lawyers and going to court. When Carlyle and the Eyre Defence Committee resisted these designs, the Jamaica litigation became a 'site of struggle over the dignity, prestige, hierarchic and legal status of whole categories of people'.[21] But what was the nature of this 'site of struggle'? How did the site – its lawyers, traditions, and procedures – influence its shape and outcome? Such questions were left unposed and unanswered.

In his otherwise compelling and elegantly written account of Mill as the foremost of mid-Victorian England's 'public moralists', Stefan Collini also was content to provide readers with a gloss on Mill's perspectives on law and legality, and on the legal dimensions of the Jamaica affair.[22] For Collini the Jamaica affair was 'one of those great moral earthquakes of Victorian public life', and Mill was at its epicentre. In the years prior to the Jamaica episode, Collini's Mill already had assumed the role of England's 'moral coach, keeping the national conscience in trim'.[23] As a dedicated critic especially of the English governing classes, Mill was instantly attracted to the story of the Morant Bay rising. For not only had Jamaican officials overseen a lawless massacre, but their masters at home refused to state unreservedly that such a thing had indeed occurred. It seemed to Mill that (in the wake of the American Civil War) the English ruling cliques were exhibiting renewed interest in authoritarian forms of government. Mill was determined that this trend should be vehemently confronted and reversed. Although Mill was appalled by the savagery of the suppression, he was moved to intervene in the case because of its sinister implications for the constitution. From the outset Mill was convinced that in its profligate use of martial powers the suppression in Jamaica was 'illegal',[24] and his main goal was to prove it in a court of law. In Collini's view, however, in this mission Mill and his colleagues abjectly failed both in rhetorical and legal terms.[25] Few of Mill's countrymen were persuaded by his Jamaica arguments. As for the legal initiatives, 'no court had proved willing to put [Eyre] to trial'.[26] The Jamaica affair underlined that even the most astute and determined public moralist could not reverse a strong contrary tide of opinion.

While Collini's depiction of Mill as a 'moral coach' deeply preoccupied with the Jamaica issue is convincing enough, his account does not squarely confront the question of why

---

Vanden Bossche, *Carlyle and the Search for Authority* (Columbus, Ohio, 1991), 168–71; Simon Heffer, *Moral Desperado: A Life of Thomas Carlyle* (London, 1995), 353–5.

[20] Hall, 'The Economy of Intellectual Prestige',186.   [21] Ibid., 196.

[22] Stefan Collini, *Public Moralists: Political Thought and Intellectual Life in Britain, 1850–1930* (Oxford, 1991), 144–62.   [23] Ibid., 133.

[24] Ibid., 145.   [25] Ibid., 164.

[26] Ibid., 146. As readers of this study will know, however, the Lord Chief Justice of England had been willing to send Eyre to trial. It was the Middlesex grand jury which had been unwilling.

Mill invested so much faith in the intervention of English lawyers and judges. Collini's essay also does not consider the theoretical tensions within Mill's views on law, and the more bedevilling problem of his commitments at once to liberal constitutionalism and the empire. In 1992, the year following the publication of Collini's essay, Bruce Kinzer and Ann and John Robson (Kinzer–Robson) published a more microscopic study of Mill and the Jamaica affair, one that is broadly consonant with its predecessor.[27] The Kinzer–Robson book addresses Mill's brief but eventful career (1865–8) as a parliamentarian. In this regard it is a model of minute research and measured judgement. Here Mill's parliamentary career is consequential in terms both of the issues he chose to take on, and for what he did and said about them. Mill had stood for office in order to champion advanced causes, and his stance on Jamaica was among his most controversial as an elected politician: 'nothing Mill did in or out of Parliament during the second half of the 1860s aroused such strong feeling as his conduct as a member of the Jamaica Committee.'[28] Upon his return from France in November 1865, Mill made speeches emphasizing the illegal and unconstitutional character of the suppression. Within the Jamaica Committee he was unbending that state officials had committed serious crimes in Jamaica, crimes that needed to be redressed by recourse to criminal prosecution in the English courts.

Unlike that of Collini, the Kinzer–Robson study contains a detailed survey of the litigation pursued by the Jamaica Committee. But in this regard the book has some distinct limitations of sources and perspective. The parliamentary clash over Jamaica is viewed as the decisive moment in the controversy; the move into (what is revealingly referred to as) 'the narrow confines of the courts' as anticlimactic and largely irrelevant. But in what sense the Jamaica controversy was 'narrowed' by litigation is not clear. There is no assessment here of what was lost or gained by the interventions of lawyers and judges. (In fact, it is possible to hypothesize that the litigation actually widened the controversy in the sense that the discussion of the political dimensions of notions such as martial law were elaborated in specific legal pleadings, oral arguments, and judicial dicta.) And like Collini, Kinzer–Robson conclude that the 'legal remedies invoked by the Jamaica Committee had all proved unavailing'.[29] While the authors observe that the Committee claimed that its legal initiatives had been at least partly successful (especially in having provoked the grand jury charge of Lord Chief Justice Cockburn), Kinzer–Robson dismiss these claims as smugly self-serving.[30] Perhaps they were. But if it is to be convincing, surely such a conclusion must be based on some criteria of how constitutional law is made. Is it correct to say that the decision of a grand jury is more important legally (or politically) than the charge of the Lord Chief Justice of England? On what theory of the English constitution is it certain that Cockburn's charge was not a major contribution to the law of martial law? Moreover, what theory of law entitles an author to state categorically that Blackburn's charge, or the findings of the Middlesex grand jury, obviated Cockburn's charge? In the end, the Kinzer–Robson essay, so perceptive on so many issues, fails to offer any compelling reasons to accept its contentions about the legal aspects of the Jamaica affair.

When the works of Collini and Kinzer–Robson are examined as a whole, both their strengths and weaknesses are readily apparent. Mill is skilfully reconstructed as a major

---

[27] Bruce L. Kinzer, Ann P. Robson, and John M. Robson, *A Moralist In and Out of Parliament: John Stuart Mill at Westminster, 1865–1868* (Toronto, 1992), 184–217.

[28] Ibid., 185. In contrast, Mill's role in the Jamaica affair is given short shrift in a recent large-scale biography. See Nicholas Capaldi, *John Stuart Mill: A Biography* (Cambridge, 2004), 326.   [29] Ibid., 210–11.

[30] Ibid., 212.

intellectual, didactic, and rhetorical force in England in the mid-1860s. His criticisms of martial law and its apologists are comprehensively assembled. But at the point when Mill and his allies turned over the Jamaica project to lawyers, the trail runs cold. Some important questions are left unasked, some leads unpursued. Further to the point, a glaring contradiction about Mill and the Jamaica Committee is undetected. The Mill scholars are of one mind that he was a relentless critic of the insularity and arrogance of the English governing classes. By training and temperament he was unwearyingly hostile toward men who had effective power but ineffective accountability. But why then did Mill place so much faith in the ability and willingness of judges, these among the most privileged and insular of English officials, to bring men like Eyre to book? Why did Mill place so much faith in the integrity and sagacity of English courts? Why, even in the face of setbacks, did he insist so long and so strenuously that the Jamaica affair be channelled into courtrooms?

Jamaica affair historiography, especially the work that has peered through the lens of key political and intellectual figures, has also been interested in the fact that both the controversy and the controversialists overlapped with the ferment over the second Reform Bill. In his influential 1965 monograph, *Before the Socialists*,[31] Royden Harrison devotes a long chapter to this connective tissue. Virtually all of the most prominent executive members of the Jamaica Committee – Bright, Mill, Beales, Beesly – also were leaders of the Reform League. For the bourgeois radicals at the helm of the League, the extension of the franchise and the attempt to achieve justice for the illegal excesses in Jamaica were two sides of the same coin. Both cases, at bottom, were about the accountability (or not) of political power. For Harrison, however, the Jamaica affair was very much a sideshow of the more consequential struggle over the political destiny of the British working class. For this reason he commits only a few sentences of his essay to the actual aims, ideas, or methods of the Jamaica Committee. In an article published thirty years later, Catherine Hall attempts to show why Jamaica deserved more attention from historians of the Reform Bill.[32] In the industrializing cities and towns of England, Hall suggestively argues, 1867 was a year of 'conjuncture' between domestic and imperial politics. The debates over political reform and Jamaica both were 'concerned with defining the different ways of belonging to nation and empire, who were subjects and who were citizens, and what the hierarchies were within those categories'.[33] That year, 1867, the year of the Hyde Park riot, was also a year in which the theme of legal limits – of legitimate dissent and of legitimate repression – was at the forefront of public discussion. In Hall's view, the Jamaica affair was pressed in the courts as a means of galvanizing the support of urban working men for the democratization of political power. And although, in Hall's dismissive estimation, Cockburn's charge on martial law 'had absolutely no effect',[34] the legal agenda of the Jamaica Committee was a success as liberal propaganda. The ultimate irony was that the Jamaica affair had arisen from the suffering of black men in the empire, but had been reshaped as a rallying cry for white men at home.

The legal historiography of the British Empire has been confined mainly to constitutional and administrative developments. Insofar as the Jamaica uprising of 1865 led to pivotal changes in the government of this and other British colonies, it has attracted historians. The first detailed references to the subject appeared in a work published in the 1930s.[35]

[31] Royden Harrison, *Before the Socialists: Studies in Labour and Politics, 1861–1881* (London, 1965), 78–136.

[32] Catherine Hall, 'Rethinking Imperial Histories: The Reform Act of 1867', 208 *New Left Review* (1994), 3–29.   [33] Ibid., 10.

[34] Ibid., 13.   [35] Mathieson, *Sugar Colonies*.

The modern historiography of this subject began with two articles published by Arvel Erickson in 1959. In these pieces Erickson argued that the Colonial Office, when it was under the 'humane and legally-minded' auspices of Edward Cardwell, made an honest and determined effort to get to the bottom of what had happened in Jamaica. When the investigatory stage was complete, moreover, Cardwell was prepared to hold Jamaican officials, Eyre included, fully accountable to the 'traditions of British justice'.[36] In these informative (if tentative) essays, Cardwell was portrayed as an earnest Peelite whose only ambition was to put the work of the Colonial Office on a more efficient and rational footing. One of the main tenets of Cardwell's thinking was that British imperial officials – even during moments of public emergency – were legally and morally obligated to respect the minimum requirements of justice. If it was inevitable that England should build and maintain a vast empire, it was essential that it be an empire built and maintained around a legal cornerstone.

In 1976, the question of the Jamaica affair and imperial administration was explored in greater depth in a carefully rendered essay by Bruce Knox.[37] Knox's exhaustive examination of the despatches and ministerial correspondence generated by the Jamaica affair broadly corroborates the hypotheses of Arvel Erickson. Cardwell's response to the rebellion and suppression was described as a model of caution and especially scrupulousness. And just as Cardwell was willing to bring Eyre (and some other officials) to book for the excesses of the suppression, so too was his successor as Secretary of State for the Colonies, Lord Carnarvon. Both Cardwell and Carnarvon were genuinely outraged, even ashamed, by what had been done in Jamaica; both men were also unwavering in their determination (even when their subordinates waffled) to discipline those who were guilty of misconduct.[38] Throughout the controversy, even when things heated up politically, their only preoccupation was 'with the proper exercise of imperial power'.[39] Neither Cardwell nor Carnarvon embraced the notion that the use of 'martial law' immunized colonial officials from political (and, in cases of malicious conduct, from legal) accountability for their actions.

In W. P. Morrell's 1969 monograph, *British Colonial Policy in the Mid-Victorian Age*, the significance of Jamaica for imperial administration was looked at through a wider lens. Morrell's book concerns the struggle of the mid-Victorian Colonial Office to devise effective colonial constitutions.[40] In this regard the Jamaica crisis was portrayed as an object lesson in the futility of one model: local government by an assembly dominated by an entrenched oligarchy.[41] In colonies where power was so much concentrated, the mandarins at the Colonial Office began to advocate for direct rule from London. On the tensions generated by such choices, Ronald Hyam's 1976 work, *Britain's Imperial Century, 1815–1914*, is more instructive. In Hyam's account, the tumult caused in England by the Jamaica affair exposed a festering contradiction within imperial administration. Just as the British government was moving to devolve powers to some colonies, to liberalize and

---

[36] Arvel B. Erickson, 'Edward T. Cardwell: Peelite', 49 *Transactions of the American Philosophical Society, Part 2* (1959) 5–6, 42–53; Erickson, 'Empire or Anarchy', 107.

[37] Bruce A. Knox, 'The British Government and the Governor Eyre Controversy, 1865–1875', 19 *Historical Journal* (Dec. 1976), 877–900.

[38] For a similar conclusion, see also Susan H. Farnsworth, *The Evolution of British Imperial Policy during the Mid-Nineteenth Century: A Study of the Peelite Contribution, 1846–1874* (New York, 1992), 237–50.

[39] Knox, 'British Government', 899.

[40] W. P. Morrell, *British Colonial Policy in the Mid-Victorian Age* (Oxford, 1969), 399–432.

[41] Ibid., 432.

democratize their constitutions, it 'decided in favour of semi-despotic government over millions of coloured peoples'.[42] In the work of Hyam, a key variable was race and racial theory. In colonies where the majority of men were of European origin, there was increasing liberalism. But where whites were greatly outnumbered by black and indigenous populations, there was increasing paternalism from the centre. This bifurcated policy was justified by the searing memory of the Indian Mutiny, and by the concomitant rise of new and more systematic theories about racial inequality. Here Hyam suggestively touches upon a subject – the role of race and racial identity in the Jamaica affair – that has attracted an extensive and rich historiography.

The pivotal role of racism in mid-Victorian imperial and domestic politics generally, the Jamaica affair specifically, has received intensive historical scrutiny in the past thirty years. In the 1970s Christine Bolt,[43] Douglas Lorimer,[44] and later, Catherine Hall,[45] published important studies of the racial dimensions of the Eyre controversy. While this body of scholarship features different points of emphasis,[46] it broadly agrees on a key point: the Jamaica conflict was at once a by-product of and a reaction against 'a new vigorous racist ideology', one which had put the 'humanitarian traditions of the anti-slavery movements' on the defensive.[47]

This body of scholarship yielded a number of important generalizations about both the historical context and content of the Jamaica affair. In the 1860s Britain continued to expand its dominion over the world's non-caucasian populations. In the far-flung outposts of the new empire, however, British hegemony often depended on the application of brute force. Racism, now burnished by science,[48] was frequently invoked to resolve the painful contradiction between England's liberal ideals at home and coercive practices abroad. By the time of the Jamaica suppression (only seven years after the trauma of the Indian Mutiny), growing numbers of influential Englishmen had embraced two racialist tenets of imperial government. The first was that non-white persons were members of an inferior, inherently violent human sub-species.[49] The second was that in the teeming non-white empire, England's comparatively tiny and scattered white subjects were vulnerable to annihilation. For this reason, the theory of imperial administration was skewed by the spectre of race war, by mortal fear of 'another Haiti' or 'another Cawnpore'. Despite (or perhaps because of) the efforts of the liberal–philanthropic alliance to make the Jamaica suppression into a *cause célèbre*, it actually tilted the balance of influential opinion in favour of the 'war of races' doctrine.[50] Jamaica came to symbolize the need for more openly authoritarian forms of government in the non-white empire.[51]

---

[42] Ronald Hyam, *Britain's Imperial Century, 1815–1914: A Study of Empire and Expansion*, 2nd edn (London, 1993), 78.   [43] Christine Bolt, *Victorian Attitudes to Race* (London, 1971).

[44] Douglas A. Lorimer, *Colour, Class, and the Victorians: English Attitudes to the Negro in the Nineteenth Century* (Leicester, 1978).

[45] Hall, 'The Economy of Intellectual Prestige', 167–96; '"From Greenland's Icy Mountains...to Africa's Golden Sand": Ethnicity, Race and Nation in Mid-Nineteenth-Century England"', 5 *Gender and History* (1993), 212–30; 'Imperial Man: Edward Eyre in Australasia and the West Indies 1833–65', in Bill Schwarz (ed.), *The Expansion of England: Race, Ethnicity and Cultural History* (London, 1996), 130–70. Mill's views on imperialism and race are canvassed in David Theo Goldberg, 'Liberalism's Limits: Carlyle and Mill on "The Negro Question"', in Julie K. Ward and Tommy L. Lott (eds.), *Philosophers on Race: Critical Essays* (Oxford, 2002), 199–203.

[46] For insight into this nuance, see Douglas A. Lorimer, 'Race, Science and Culture: Historical Continuities and Discontinuities, 1850–1914', in Shearer West (ed.), *The Victorians and Race* (Aldershot, 1996), 13.   [47] Ibid., 16.

[48] Ibid.   [49] Bolt, *Victorian Attitudes*, 202.   [50] Ibid., 105

[51] Lorimer, *Colour, Class, and the Victorians*, 197.

Since 1995 new writing on race and English society in the Victorian era has been plentiful.[52] The authors of this material have drawn heavily on literary and cultural theory, on the idea of the historical contingency and political potency of labels such as 'race'. In this essay commentary will be restricted to those works which have commented directly on the problem of the Jamaica affair. The most important and prolific historian in this regard is Catherine Hall. We have seen already that Hall has considered the Jamaica controversy from a number of angles, including its significance for mid-Victorian and intellectual and political history.[53] But her more recent work has focussed on the controversy as a window onto the dynamic social psychology of the era. Hall has wanted to know the degree to which the Jamaica conflict – viewed here as a war of words between intellectuals exemplified by Carlyle and Mill – contributed to and/or reflected the 'discursive construction' of distinct social identities such as 'English', 'white', and 'black'.[54] For Hall, the Jamaica affair was not a struggle over political or constitutional ideas as much as a struggle over the meaning of authentic manhood or 'masculinity'.[55] In the eyes of Carlyle, Edward Eyre embodied the heroic white man who had struggled mightily to impose order on the insensible mass of degraded black sub-humans. In the eyes of Mill, Eyre embodied the omnipresent threat posed by powerful statesmen to the rights of freeborn Englishmen. In this way the Jamaica affair was exploited as an opportunity to advance and contest theories about who was, and who was not, a fully constituted subject of the realm.[56]

These themes Hall brought powerfully together in *Civilizing Subjects: Colony and Metropole in the English Imagination*,[57] an ambitious and comprehensive study of mid-nineteenth-century Birmingham's vigorous evangelical community, and of their missionary ambitions and activities in Jamaica. The book addressed the 'mutual constitution of colonizer and colonized', and how this dialectic contributed to the making of empire. Hall returned again to the subject of the Jamaica affair of 1865–8, seen here as a pivotal event for the Birmingham Baptists because it indicated the stark failure of their attempt to rally fellow citizens to the cause of oppressed black men and women of the empire. In Birmingham news of the suppression caused a brief flutter of public interest in the plight of black subjects. It was not long, however, before the Jamaica issue was supplanted by the debate over the second Reform Bill.[58] Domestic political preoccupations trumped imperial politics. By 1867, Hall concluded, 'being a "friend of the negro" was no longer a mobilizing identity'.[59] It had been superseded by the preoccupation of white Englishmen with their own political identity and privileges.

The historians of race and the Jamaica affair have contributed substantially to general understanding of the episode and what it reveals about English history in the late 1860s. That human beings organize the world into linguistic categories such as 'black', 'male', and 'citizen'; that such categories are historically contingent; that they are contested and sometimes reinvented; that they have enormous political importance; all of this now is widely

---

[52] See, for example, Simon Gikandi, *Maps of Englishness: Writing and Identity in the Culture of Colonialism* (New York, 1996); Shearer West (ed.), *The Victorians and Race* (Aldershot, 1996); Bill Schwarz (ed.), *The Expansion of England: Race, Ethnicity and Cultural History*; Kathryn Tidrick, *Empire and the English Character* (London, 1990); Catherine Hall (ed.), *Cultures of Empire: Colonizers in Britain and the Empire in the Nineteenth and Twentieth Centuries* (New York, 2000); Marcus Wood, *Slavery, Empathy and Pornography* (Oxford, 2002).

[53] Hall, 'The Economy of Intellectual Prestige',166–98; 'Rethinking Imperial Histories'.

[54] Hall, 'Competing Masculinities'; 'Imperial Man'. [55] Hall, 'Competing Masculinities', 279.

[56] Hall puts forward a similar argument in a slightly different context in ' "From Greenland's Icy Mountains" ', 212–30. [57] Ibid., 13.

[58] Ibid., 423. [59] Ibid., 424.

regarded as a commonplace. With regard to the Jamaica affair proper, the historians of race have established a number of hypotheses beyond sensible doubt. In the 1860s theories of racial inequality – theories enhanced by their supposed scientific respectability – were being invoked to justify the use of state coercion against non-white peoples in the empire. There is compelling evidence that among the educated elites in England these theories were increasingly accepted, and that their acceptance was corrosive of the notion that every person living in the empire (every adult male person, at minimum) shared an equal and indivisible legal status as a subject of the British sovereign. Neither is there much room for doubt that in the 1860s there was increasing anxiety about the prospect of bloody uprisings among vast non-white populations in the empire, and that this anxiety contributed greatly to renewed interest in the law of martial law. Neither is there room for doubt, finally, that one of the reasons why Edward Eyre enjoyed so much support in England is that he had used martial law to torture and kill recalcitrant black men and women. The Jamaica suppression was a *cause célèbre*; but never was it, or not for long was it, a popular cause. Here race was the key factor.

But, when the formidable oeuvre of Catherine Hall and the other historians of Victorian race and culture is looked at as a whole, does it yield illuminating answers to the wider cluster of questions raised by the Jamaica affair? Does it penetrate to the heart of the controversy? In the opinion of this writer, the candid answer is that it does not. The principal limitation of this historiography is that race, even when it is thought of as a 'contingent' or 'discursive' cultural artifact, is simply too narrow an aperture for seeing something as unruly and complex as the Jamaica affair. This limitation, however, is only one facet of a larger one. Ironically enough, the historians of race and culture almost invariably have treated the affair as ahistorical, as an episode free of contradiction and change. The Jamaica Committee, for example, is depicted as having been devoid of internal tension, as if it had been created by one man, Mill, and as if that man had imposed a single and coherent agenda on his associates. It assumes that the main goal of the Committee was to obtain justice for the oppressed black men of Jamaica, and the wider empire. The histories of the racial dimensions of the Jamaica affair, in their sometimes overweening determination to show that English society in the nineteenth century was monolithic in its anti-black racism, ignores or minimizes some important facts. It must be significant, for instance, that Cardwell, Carnarvon, and other English state officials were not unwilling to prosecute (and in other ways punish) white men for the abuse of black men and women. Colonial judges such as Alan Ker operated their courts on the assumption that black Jamaicans were British subjects, and that their unjustifiable homicide was murder.

The race historians of the Jamaica controversy have not lent much credence to law as a historical variable. English lawyers, legal writers, and judges, when they are present in these studies, are rarely portrayed as having said, written, or done anything of genuine importance. When legal developments, texts, and decisions are mentioned at all in these works, they are passed over quickly, or dismissed with a facile comment.[60] Here, one perceives that two kinds of academic prejudice are at work: a prejudice against law as an important element of history, and a prejudice against the (presumed) hypocrisy and deception of liberal legal systems.

---

[60] In her essay 'Imperial Man', 163–4, for instance, Hall touches on the subject of martial law (she even quotes from Finlason) but then moves quickly to conclude that 'successive prosecutions were thrown out by the juries...who determined that an Englishman's rights and liberties were more important than those of Jamaicans.' The reasons why this is an unreliable generalization are too many to list here.

Historians of modern English law have never been numerous, and among this tiny order few have concentrated on the historical integration of legal and political culture.[61] Before the study at hand, the Jamaica affair had never had an historian who wanted to dig systematically into its legal character and archive. In 1982, however, the historian Charles Townshend published a highly innovative article on the use of martial law in British domestic and imperial history from 1800 to the Second World War.[62] Here Townshend argued that the British state, having seldom worried about foreign invasion or civil insurrection, never developed 'formal arrangements for the exercise of power during civil emergencies'. But while British politicians did not need a well-realized system of emergency law, increasingly British imperial administrators did.[63] In the empire armed resistance to British authority was comparatively commonplace and potentially lethal. Martial law, Townshend notes, had been proclaimed more than ten times in British colonies between 1800 and 1864. But only after martial law was implemented in Jamaica in 1865, Townshend (mistakenly[64]) asserted, did the incident occasion a 'legal and moral crisis... an intellectual civil war'.[65] At the centre of the conflict was the content and constitutional status of martial law. Townshend's article provided a brief survey of the energetic but ultimately indecisive legal debate inspired by the Jamaican martial law.[66] This section supported Townshend's general thesis that the British government's response to civil emergency continued to be ad hoc and haphazard long into the twentieth century.[67] The essay ended with a resonant remark (reminiscent of one made in 1962 by Semmel[68]): 'the essential dilemma remains: how far can the liberal–democratic polity justifiably employ force against domestic opponents, without altering its own nature?'[69]

The role of the law, and especially of one important imperial lawyer, John Gorrie, in the Jamaica affair was canvassed in depth in a 1997 monograph by Bridget Brereton.[70] As we have seen, Gorrie was a Scottish-born barrister who at the close of 1865 was selected by the Jamaica Committee to travel to Kingston in order to be their legal eyes and ears during the investigation by the Jamaica Royal Commission. As Brereton's book skilfully documents, Gorrie was a radical liberal and anti-slavery activist, one strongly committed to the notion of the legal equality of all British subjects before the law. When Gorrie agreed

---

[61] David Sugarman and G. R. Rubin, 'Introduction: Towards a New History of Law and Material Society in England, 1750–1914', in G. R. Rubin and David Sugarman (eds.), *Law, Economy and Society, 1750–1914: Essays in the History of English Law* (Abingdon, 1984), 1–123; David Sugarman, 'In the Spirit of Weber: Law, Modernity and the "Peculiarities of the English"', *Institute for Legal Studies, 2 Working Studies Series* (1987), 2–9, at 3.

[62] Charles Townshend, 'Martial Law: Legal and Administrative Problems of Civil Emergency in Britain and the Empire, 1800–1940', 25 *Historical Journal* (1982), 167–95.

[63] For further development of these themes, see idem., *Making the Peace: Public Order and Public Security in Modern Britain* (Oxford, 1993). This book, while it makes only fleeting references to the Jamaica affair, offers a number of arguments which have been addressed in the concluding essay of the study at hand.

[64] Without wanting to put too fine a point on the term 'intellectual civil war', the martial law in Ceylon in 1848 generated a prolonged and very intense public dispute. See my 'A Jurisprudence of Power: Martial Law and the Ceylon Controversy of 1848–51', 28 *Journal of Imperial and Commonwealth History* (2000), 1–34.   [65] Townshend, 'Martial Law', 169.

[66] Ibid., 172–3.

[67] See also, Townshend, *Political Violence in Ireland: Government and Resistance since 1848* (Oxford, 1983), 94–6.   [68] Semmel, *Governor Eyre Controversy*, 7.

[69] Ibid., 195.

[70] Bridget Brereton, *Law, Justice and Empire: The Colonial Career of John Gorrie, 1829–1892* (Kingston, Jamaica, 1997).

to travel to Jamaica for the Jamaica Committee, he did so largely for idealistic reasons. Gorrie was genuinely outraged by the suffering of the black peasantry under martial law, and wanted to ensure that justice was done by them.

Brereton's is one of the few studies to acknowledge that legal ideas and procedures were not tangential to the Jamaica affair, but its unifying feature, and that lawyers (although Gorrie is not the leading example here) were not just passive instruments but active agents. Although it does not theorize the point, Brereton's book strongly implies that when the Jamaica Committee went to law they trusted their fate to professional men over whom they would have only limited control. However, her chapter on the Jamaica affair, while informative, also betrays some serious inadequacies.[71] The focal point of the book, after all, is John Gorrie. But when Gorrie returned from Jamaica to England, he did not assume a place either as a leading member of the Jamaica Committee or as one of the Committee's leading courtroom lawyers. Thus, with her main character in the wings, Brereton covered all of the permutations of the litigation against Nelson, Brand, and Eyre in eight terse pages.[72] The treatise literature on martial law, the arguments of counsel, jury charges, and the response of the political press were ignored or only superficially discussed. As for Brereton's concluding statement, it focussed on the significance of the Jamaica affair, not so much for English law or political culture, but for the career of John Gorrie.[73]

Easily the most penetrating study of law and the Jamaica affair appeared recently in Nassar Hussain's incisive if sometimes confounding monograph, *The Jurisprudence of Emergency: Colonialism and the Rule of Law*.[74] A hybrid of historical studies and legal theory, Hussain's book examines the 'extension of English law and constitutionality to the colonies'.[75] It is important to note about this study that its historical elements are subordinated to theoretical aims. As Hussain explains, his book uses historical evidence (relating to episodes in nineteenth- and twentieth-century British imperial history) in order to develop 'notions in legal theory of the meaning of the rule of law, the function of the legal exception, and the range and features of emergency powers'. The theoretical premiss of the study is the supposed tension in all advanced polities between state power and legality, between what the 'state perceives as a necessary power for survival... and what the law makes available'. Hussain wants to use history – British imperial history – to investigate how law can be used to develop 'notions in legal theory of the meaning of the rule of law, the function of the legal exception, and the range and features of emergency powers'.

As mentioned, Hussain's study is not history for its own sake. It wants to dismantle historical episodes and then to bring the pieces together as a model, in this case, of the political and ideological functioning of law, and specifically of the notion of the rule of law. Its principal mission, then, is to construct theoretical generalizations about the 'possibilities and predicaments of modern law'.[76] Hussain himself locates his work within the burgeoning literature of post-colonialism, 'in a larger movement of intellectual inquiry that attends to the complex of power/knowledge in discourses about the colony'. By studying the 'problematic of the rule of law and emergency' from an historical perspective, the author seeks to make a contribution to the theory of the rule of law. It proceeds by defining three keywords – 'rule of law', 'emergency', and 'colonialism' – and then retracing their usage and

---

[71] Ibid., 32–65.

[72] Ibid., 56–62.   [73] Ibid., 62–4.

[74] Nassar Hussain, *The Jurisprudence of Emergency: Colonialism and the Rule of Law* (Ann Arbor, Mich., 2003), 110–16.   [75] Ibid., 2–3.

[76] Ibid., 6.

significance in his case studies. Of course, Hussain's treatment of the Jamaica affair is of greatest pertinence here.

As he attempts to achieve these theoretical goals, Hussain engages in some very fertile thinking about law and the later British Empire. In much the same way as the study at hand, Hussain hypothesizes that the British justified the physical, social, and economic domination of foreign peoples and places by recourse to 'a much-vaunted tradition of ancient liberty and lawfulness'. For British governing classes of the era, 'legality became the pre-eminent signifier of state legitimacy and of "civilization"'. Still, at the core of the British Empire there was a ceaseless dialectic of resistance and coercion. In the result, the British imperial state of the era veered between the 'contrary impulses' of formal legality and brute force.[77] The suppression of the Morant Bay uprising, and the controversy which followed, is offered as a prime example.

In a chapter called 'Martial Law and Massacre',[78] Hussain examines the ways in which British imperial regimes understood and used the notion of 'martial law'. His methodology is to compare the repression of colonial (the Jamaica suppression and the Amritsar massacre) and domestic (Gordon and Bristol riots) disturbances in order to 'extrapolate the deeper relation between law and violence that martial law demonstrates'.[79] With regard to Jamaica, Hussain examines how the suppression exposed glaring contradictions in the British state's commitments both to legality and domination in the empire. In dissecting these contradictions he delves more insightfully than any previously published historian into the judicial and extra-judicial literature generated by the subsequent controversy.[80] Here he begins the task (in the space of a few pages)[81] of connecting legal literature with currents in mid-Victorian racial and imperial theory. But once this task is usefully begun, the analysis loses momentum and clarity. In these pages martial law is not viewed as a contested legal doctrine, or even an amalgam of contested law and politics. Hussain prefers to see martial law as a 'deeply cognitive problem'.[82] The difficulties presented by such a phrase, alas, are not alleviated by what follows this introduction.[83] Hussain's once-promising line of analysis degenerates into a mire of obtuse phrases and abstruse terms. By the end of his discussion of the Jamaica affair the historical sources have all but disappeared under this theoretical detritus.

As this manuscript went to press, the signs were not promising that historians of the Victorian empire now are convinced of the centrality of law, lawyers, and legal institutions to their subject matter, or of the larger significance of the Jamaica controversy. The new edition of *The Oxford History of the British Empire*, published in five volumes between 1998 and 2001, almost entirely overlooks legal ideas, events, and variables. With regard to the volume on the nineteenth century, not even one of thirty essays tackles law and empire as a central theme.[84]

---

[77] Ibid. [78] Ibid., 99–126. [79] Ibid., 101. [80] Ibid., 111–13.
[81] Ibid., 112–13. [82] Ibid., 113.

[83] By way of example, Hussain summarizes the martial law writing of W. F. Finlason in the following manner: 'We can now recognise the anxiety over the slippage between the same act of violence as it can appear within the authority of the law and opposed to it, so that excessive cruelty can easily be mistaken for a warranted severity. Necessity is the legal category of a correct cognition.' Ibid.

[84] The essays make only cursory references to the subject. There are four isolated references to 'martial law'. Gad Heuman's essay on 'The British West Indies' (admittedly a very large subject) does not mention the repercussions in England of the Jamaica suppression of 1865. See Andrew Porter (ed.), *The Oxford History of the British Empire*, vol. iii, *The Nineteenth Century* (Oxford, 1999), 486–7. Strangely, Niall Ferguson's *Empire: The Rise and Demise of the British World Order and the Lessons for Global Power* (New York, 2003), although it makes a strong case for the positive residue of British empire, also only superficially considers the subject of English lawyers and law.

Bibliography

Primary sources
Government publications
Legal treatises and commentaries
Other printed sources
Newspapers and periodical journals
Manuscript collections

Secondary sources
Books and theses
Journal articles and chapters in books

PRIMARY SOURCES

Government publications

Reports of the British House of Commons
Second Report from the Select Committee on Ceylon (1850) xii
Papers Laid before the Royal Commission of Inquiry by Governor Eyre (1866) xxx
Report of the Jamaica Royal Commission (1866) xxx, xxxi
Papers Relating to the Disturbances in Jamaica (1866) li

Parliamentary Papers
Hansard's Parliamentary Debates, 3rd series

Manuals
War Office, *Manual of Military Law* (London, 1899).

Legal treatises and commentaries

Agabeg, Aviet, *Principles of Criminal Law*, 4th edn (London, 1886).
Amos, Sheldon, *Fifty Years of the English Constitution, 1830–1880* (London, 1880).
Anson, Sir William R., *The Law and Custom of the Constitution, Part I, Parliament* (Oxford, 1897).
Archbold, J. F., *Archbold's Pleading and Evidence* (London, 1862).
Bagehot, W., *The English Constitution* (London, 1867).
Bernard, Montague, 'The Growth of Laws and Usages of War', in *Oxford Essays*, vol. ii (London, 1856), 88–136.
Black's Law Dictionary, 5th edn. (St Paul, Minn., 1979).
Blackstone, William, *Commentaries on the Laws of England* (4 vols., Oxford, 1765–9).
—— *Blackstone's Commentaries on the Laws of England*, ed. Herbert Broom and E. A. Hadley, vol. i (London, 1869).
Broom, Herbert, *Constitutional Law: Viewed in Relation to Common Law, and Exemplified by Cases* (London, 1866).

Brougham, Henry Lord, *The British Constitution: Its History, Structure and Working*, 3rd edn (London, 1860).

Cheshire, G. C., *Private International Law*, 3rd edn (Oxford, 1947).

Clode, Charles M., *The Military Forces of the Crown: Their Administration and Government* (2 vols., London, 1869).

Cockburn, Frederick (ed.), *Charge of the Lord Chief Justice of England to the Grand Jury at the Central Criminal Court, in the Case of The Queen against Nelson and Brand* (London, 1867).

Coke, Sir Edward, *Coke's First Institutes*, ed. J. H. Thomas (Philadelphia, Penn., 1836).

Dicey, Albert Venn, *Introduction to the Study of the Law of the Constitution*, 4th edn (London, 1893).

—— *Conflict of Laws* (London, 1896).

Eyre Aid and Defence Fund (London, 1867).

Finlason, W. F., *A Treatise on Martial Law as Allowed by the Law of England in Time of Rebellion: With Illustrations Drawn from the Official Documents in the Jamaica Case, and Comments Constitutional and Legal* (London, 1866).

—— *Commentaries upon Martial Law: With Special Reference to its Regulation and Restraint, With Comments upon the Charge of the Lord Chief Justice* (London, 1867).

—— *Report of the Case of The Queen v. Edward Eyre on his Prosecution in the Court of Queen's Bench containing the Charge of Mr. Justice Blackburn* (London, 1868).

—— *A Review of the Authorities as to the Repression of Riot or Rebellion, with Special References to Criminal or Civil Liability* (London, 1868).

—— *Justice to a Colonial Governor, or Some Considerations on the Case of Mr. Eyre: Containing the Substance of all the Documents, Discussions and Proceedings Relating Thereto* (London, 1868).

—— *The History of the Jamaica Case* (London, 1869).

Foote, J. A., *Private International Jurisprudence* (London, 1878).

Forsyth, William, *Cases and Opinions on Constitutional Law* (London, 1869).

Hale, Matthew, *The History of the Common Law of England*, 6th edn (London, 1820).

Hallam, Henry, *Constitutional History of England from the Accession of Henry VII to the Death of George II*, 7th edn (London, 1854).

Harris, Seymour F., *Principles of the Criminal Law* (London, 1877).

Hawkins, William, *A Treatise on the Pleas of the Crown* (London, 1716).

Hough, W., *Precedents in Military Law: Including the Practice of Courts Martial, the Mode of Conducting Trials, the Duties of Officers at Military Courts of Inquest, Courts of Inquiry, Courts of Requests, etc.* (London, 1855).

Lieber, Francis, *Lieber's Code and the Law of War*, ed. Richard Shelly Hartigan (Chicago, Ill., 1983).

McArthur, J., *Principles and Practice of Naval and Military Courts Martial* (2 vols., London, 1813).

May, Thomas Erskine, *The Constitutional History of England* (2 vols., London, 1861–3).

Phillips, O. Hood, and Jackson, Paul, *O. Hood Phillips' Constitutional and Administrative Law*, 6th edn (London, 1978).

Phillips, S. March, *A Treatise on the Law of Evidence* (2 vols., New York, 1823).

Roscoe, Henry, *Lives of Eminent British Lawyers* (2 vols., London, 1841).

Russell, William O., *Russell on Crimes and Misdemeanours* (2 vols., London, 1843).

Simmons, Thomas F., *Remarks on the Constitution and Practice of Courts Martial*, 2nd edn (London, 1835).

Stephen, Sir James Fitzjames, *A General View of the Criminal Law of England* (3 vols., London, reprinted, 1863; New York, 1964).
—— *Liberty, Equality, Fraternity*, ed. R. J. White (Cambridge, 1967).
Tovey, Hamilton, *Martial Law and the Customs of War* (London, 1886).
Tytler, A. F., *An Essay on Military Law* (London, 1800).

Other printed sources

Annual Register: A Review of Public Events at Home and Abroad, n.s. (London, 1865–70).
Bagehot, Walter, *The Collected Works of Walter Bagehot*, ed. Norman St. John-Stevas (London, 1986).
—— *The Works and Life of Walter Bagehot*, ed. Mrs. Russell Barrington (10 vols., London, 1915).
Ball, Charles, *The History of the Indian Mutiny* (New York, c.1860).
Bright, John, *Speeches by the Rt. Honourable John Bright, M.P.*, ed. Thorold Rogers (London, 1869).
—— *The Public Letters of the Right Hon. John Bright, M.P.* (London, 1885).
—— *The Diaries of John Bright*, ed. R. A. J. Walling (New York, 1931).
Carlyle, Jane Welsh, *Letters and Memorials of J. W. Carlyle* (New York, 1883).
Carlyle, Thomas, *Collected Works* (London, 1867).
—— *Thomas Carlyle: Critical and Miscellaneous Essays in Five Volumes*, vol. v (London, 1899).
—— and Ruskin, John, *The Correspondence of Thomas Carlyle and John Ruskin*, ed. George Allan Cate (Stanford, Calif., 1982).
Fletcher, D., *Personal Recollections of the Honourable George W. Gordon* (London, 1867).
Foulkes, William, *A Generation of Judges, by Their Reporter*, 2nd edn (London, 1888).
Gorrie, J., *Illustrations of Martial Law in Jamaica* (London, 1867).
Harrison, Frederic, *Martial Law: Six Letters to the 'Daily News'* (London, 1867).
—— 'The Religion of Inhumanity', *Fortnightly Review* (June 1873).
—— *Autobiographic Memoirs* (London, 1911).
Harvey, Thomas and Brewis, William, *Jamaica in 1866* (London, 1867).
Hunter, W. W., *Life of the Earl of Mayo* (2 vols., London, 1875).
Hume, A. Hamilton, *The Life of Edward John Eyre* (London, 1867).
Huxley, Thomas Henry, *Life and Letters of Thomas Henry Huxley*, ed. Leonard Huxley (London, 1900).
—— *Autobiography and Selected Letters*, ed. Ana Snell (Boston, Mass., 1909).
Kingsley, Frances E., *Charles Kingsley: His Letters and Memories of His Life* (2 vols., London, 1877).
Lee, Sir Sidney, and Stephen, Sir Leslie (eds.), *Dictionary of National Biography: Founded in 1882 by George Smith, from the Earliest Times to 1900* (22 vols., London, 1921–2).
McCarthy, Justin, *A History of Our Own Times* (3 vols., New York, 1895).
—— *Reminiscences* (New York and London, 1899).
—— *Portrait of the Sixties* (London, 1903).
Manson, E., *Builders of our Law*, 2nd edn (London, 1904).
Marx, Karl, and Engels, Frederick, *Karl Marx, Frederick Engels: Collected Works*, vol. xlii (New York, 1987).
Mill, John Stuart, *Autobiography* (London, 1873).
—— *Collected Works of John Stuart Mill*, ed. John M. Robson *et al.*, vol.xxi (5 vols., Toronto, 1984).

—— *The Later Letters of John Stuart Mill, 1849–1873*, ed. Dwight N. Lindley and Francis E. Mineka (Toronto, 1972).

—— *John Stuart Mill: Autobiography and Literary Essays*, ed. John M. Robson and Jack Stillinger (Toronto, 1981).

—— *Essays on Equality, Law, and Education*, ed. Stefan Collini and John M. Robson (Toronto, 1984).

—— *Public and Parliamentary Speeches: November 1850–November 1873*, ed. John M. Robson and B. L. Kinzer (Toronto, 1988).

—— *Writings on India*, ed. Martin Moir, Zawahir Moir, and John M. Robson (Toronto, 1990).

—— *Additional Letters of John Stuart Mill*, ed. Marion Filipiuk, Michael Laine, and John M. Robson (Toronto, 1991).

Pim, Bedford, *The Negro and Jamaica* (London, 1866).

Price, George, *Jamaica and the Colonial Office: Who Caused the Crisis?* (London, 1866).

Roscoe, Henry, *Lives of Eminent British Lawyers* (2 vols., London, 1841).

Roundell, Charles, *England and her Subject Races, with Special Reference to Jamaica* (London, 1866).

Smith, Goldwin, *Reminiscences by Goldwin Smith*, ed. Arnold Hamilton (New York, 1910).

—— *Goldwin Smith Papers*, ed. Patricia H. Gaffney (Ithaca, NY, 1971).

Spencer, Herbert, *An Autobiography* (2 vols., New York, 1904).

Taylor, Sir Henry, *The Autobiography of Henry Taylor, 1800–1875*, vol. ii (London, 1885).

Underhill, Edward Bean, *The Tragedy of Morant Bay: A Narrative of the Disturbances in the Island of Jamaica in 1865* (London, 1895).

Walpole, Spencer, *The History of Twenty-Five Years, 1855–1880* (4 vols., London, 1904).

Williams, B. T., *The Case of G. W. Gordon, with Preliminary Observations on the Jamaican Riot of Oct. 11, 1865* (1866).

Young, George A., *Notes on the Recent Events in the Island of Jamaica, and on the Right of the Crown to Proclaim Martial Law* (London, 1866).

Newspapers and periodical journals

Age We Live In

Albion

Army and Navy Gazette

Athenaeum

Bee-Hive

Birmingham Post

Blackwood's Magazine

British Army and Navy Review

Cardiff Times

Colonial Standard (Jamaica)

Cornhill Magazine

Daily Gleaner (Jamaica)

Daily News

Daily Telegraph

Dublin Review

Edinburgh Review

English Independent

Evening Standard

Examiner

Falmouth Post (Jamaica)

Fortnightly Review

Fraser's Magazine

Freeman

Glasgow Morning Journal

Glasgow Sentinel

Globe

Illustrated London News

John Bull

Jurist

Law Magazine

Law Times
London Review
London Society
Lloyd's Weekly
Manchester Guardian
Morning Advertiser
Morning Chronicle
Morning Herald
Morning Post
Morning Star
Newcastle Weekly Chronicle
New York Daily News
New York Times
North British Review
Pall Mall Gazette

Punch
Quarterly Review
Reynolds' Weekly
Saturday Review
Shrewsbury Free Press
Shropshire News
Solicitors' Journal
Spectator
Standard
Sun
The Economist
The Lancet
The Times
Weekly Times
Westminster Review

Manuscript collections

British and Foreign Anti-Slavery Society (Rhodes House, Oxford)
Brougham Papers (University College Library, London)
Bright Papers (British Library)
Carlyle Papers (National Library of Scotland)
Carnarvon Papers (British Library)
Chesson Diary (Rylands Library, Manchester)
Gladstone Papers (British Library)
Eyre Papers, State Library of South Australia
Eyre Defence Committee Papers (Rhodes House, Oxford)
Harrison Papers (London School of Economics)
Jamaica Committee Papers (Rhodes House, Oxford)
Murchison Papers (British Library)
Smith Papers (Cornell Library)
Stephen Papers (Cambridge University Library)

SECONDARY SOURCES

Books and theses

Adams, George Burton, *Constitutional History of England* (New York, 1956).
Alexander, G. Glover, *The Administration of Justice in Criminal Matters (in England and Wales)* (Cambridge, 1911).

Allan, T. R. S., *Law, Liberty, and Justice: The Foundations of British Constitutionalism* (Oxford, 1993).

Anderson, D. M., and Killingray, D. (eds.), *Policing the Empire: Government, Authority and Control* c.*1830–1940* (Manchester, 1991).

Armitage, David, *The Ideological Origins of the British Empire* (Cambridge, 2000).

August, Eugene, *John Stuart Mill: A Mind at Large* (New York, 1975).

Babington, A., *Military Intervention in Britain: From the Gordon Riots to the Gibraltar Incident* (London, 1990).

Baker, John H., *The Law's Two Bodies: Some Evidential Problems in English Legal History* (Oxford, 2001).

—— *An Introduction to English Legal History*, 4th edn (London, 2002).

Barrows, Floyd D., and Mock, David B. (eds.), *A Dictionary of Obituaries of Modern British Radicals* (New York, 1989).

Baylen, Joseph O., and Gossman, Norbert L. (eds.), *Biographical Dictionary of Modern British Radicals*, vol. ii (New York, 1977).

Belliotti, Raymond A., *Justifying Law: The Debate over Foundations, Goals, and Methods* (Philadelphia, Penn., 1992).

Bentley, David, *English Criminal Justice in the Nineteenth Century* (London, 1998).

Benton, Lauren, *Law and Colonial Cultures: Legal Regimes in World History, 1400–1900* (Cambridge, 2002).

Biagini, Eugene F., *Liberty, Retrenchment and Reform: Popular Liberalism in the Age of Gladstone, 1860–1880* (Cambridge, 1992).

Bibby, H. Cyril, *The Essence of Thomas Huxley* (New York, 1967).

Biddulph, General Sir Robert, *Lord Cardwell at the War Office: A History of His Administration, 1868–1874* (London, 1904).

Birkhimer, W. E., *Military Government and Martial Law* (Kansas City, Mo., 1914).

Black, Clinton V., *The Story of Jamaica: From Prehistory to the Present* (London, 1965).

Blackett, R. J. M., *Divided Hearts: Britain and the American Civil War* (Baton Rouge, La., 2001).

Blakeley, Brian L., *The Colonial Office, 1868–1892* (Durham, NC, 1972).

Bolt, Christine, *Victorian Attitudes to Race* (London, 1971).

Bond, Brian (ed.), *Victorian Military Campaigns* (London, 1967).

Bond, J. E., *The Rules of Riot: Internal Conflict and the Law of War* (Princeton, NJ, 1974).

Bradley, A. W., and Wade, E. C. S., *Constitutional Law: An Outline of the Law and Practice of the Constitution including Central and Local Government, the Citizen and the State and Administrative Law*, 7th edn (London, 1968).

Brereton, Bridget, *Law, Justice and Empire: The Colonial Career of John Gorrie, 1829–1892* (Kingston, Jamaica, 1997).

Brewer, John and Styles, John (eds.), *An Ungovernable People: The English and their Law in the Seventeenth and Eighteenth Centuries* (Camden, NJ, 1980).

Burnard, Trevor, *Mastery, Tyranny and Desire: Thomas Thistlewood and his Slaves in Anglo-American World* (Chapel Hill, NC, 2004).

Burns, W. L., *The British West Indies* (Westport, Conn., 1975).

Callwell, Col. C. E., *Small Wars: Their Principles and Practice*, 3rd edn (London, 1899; reprinted 1976).

Campbell, Mavis Christine, *The Dynamics of Change in a Slave Society: A Sociopolitical History of the Free Coloreds of Jamaica, 1800–1865* (Rutherford, NJ, 1976).

Capaldi, Nicholas, *John Stuart Mill: A Biography* (Cambridge, 2004).

Cassidy, Cheryl Marguerit, 'Islands and Empires: A Rhetorical Analysis of the Governor Eyre Controversy, 1865–1867', Ph.D. thesis University of Michigan (Ann Arbor, Mich., 1988).

Cell, John W., *British Colonial Administration in the Mid-Nineteenth Century: The Policy-Making Process* (New Haven, Conn., 1970).

Challinor, Raymond, *A Radical Lawyer in Victorian England: W. P. Roberts and the Struggle for Workers' Rights* (London, 1990).

Chaudhuri, S. B., *Civil Disturbances during the British Rule in India, 1765–1857* (Calcutta, 1955).

Chowdhury, S. R., *Rule of Law in a State of Emergency: The Paris Minimum Standards of Human Rights Norms in a State of Emergency* (New York, 1989).

Cocks, Raymond, *Foundations of the Modern Bar* (London, 1983).

Colaiaco, James A., *James Fitzjames Stephen and the Crisis of Victorian Thought* (London, 1983).

Collini, Stefan, *Public Moralists: Political Thought and Intellectual Life in Britain, 1850–1930* (Oxford, 1991).

Cooke, James L., *New French Imperialism, 1880–1910: The Third Republic and Colonial Expansion* (Hamden, Conn., 1973).

Cornish, W. R., and Clark, G. de N., *Law and Society in England, 1750–1950* (London, 1989).

Cosgrove, Richard A., *The Rule of Law: Albert Venn Dicey, Victorian Jurist* (Chapel Hill, NC, 1980).

—— *Scholars of the Law: English Jurisprudence from Blackstone to Hart* (New York, 1996).

Craton, Michael, *Testing the Chains: Resistance to Slavery in the British West Indies* (Ithaca, NY, 1982).

—— *Empire, Enslavement and Freedom in the Caribbean* (Kingston, Jamaica, 1997).

Curtin, Philip D., *Two Jamaicas: The Role of Ideas in a Tropical Colony, 1830–1865* (Cambridge, 1967).

Da Costa, Emilia V., *Crowns of Glory, Tears of Blood: The Demerara Slave Rebellion of 1823* (New York, 1994).

David, Saul, *The Indian Mutiny 1857* (London, 2002).

Desmond, Adrian J., *Huxley: From Devil's Disciple to Evolution's High Priest* (Reading, Mass., 1997).

Duman, Daniel, *The English and Colonial Bars in the Nineteenth Century* (London, 1983).

—— *The Judicial Bench in England, 1727–1875: The Reshaping of a Professional Elite* (London, 1984).

Dutton, Geoffrey, *The Hero as Murderer: The Life of Edward John Eyre, Australian Explorer and Governor of Jamaica, 1815–1901* (London, 1967).

Egerton, H. E., *A Short History of British Colonial Policy, 1606–1909*, 9th edn (London, 1932).

Eisenach, Eldon J., *Mill and the Moral Character of Liberalism* (University Park, Penn., 1998).

Elias, T. O., *British Colonial Law: A Comparative Study of the Interaction Between English and Local Laws in British Dependencies* (London, 1962).

Eldridge, C. C., *Victorian Imperialism* (London, 1978).

——— (ed.), *British Imperialism in the Nineteenth Century* (London, 1984).

Epstein, James A., *Radical Expression: Political Language, Ritual, and Symbol in England, 1790–1850* (New York, 1994).

Everett, Edwin Mallard, *The Party of Humanity: The* Fortnightly Review *and its Contributors, 1865–1874* (Chapel Hill, NC, 1939).

Fairman, Charles, *The Law of Martial Rule*, 2nd edn (Chicago, Ill., 1943).

Farnsworth, Susan H., *The Evolution of British Imperial Policy During the Mid-Nineteenth Century: A Study of the Peelite Contribution, 1846–1874* (New York, 1992).

Ferguson, Niall, *Empire: The Rise and Demise of the British World Order and the Lessons for Global Power* (New York, 2003).

Feuchtwanger, E. J., *Gladstone* (London, 1975).

Fitzpatrick, Peter (ed.), *Dangerous Supplements, Resistance and Renewal in Jurisprudence* (London, 1991).

Ford, Trowbridge H., *Albert Venn Dicey: The Man and His Times* (Chichester, 1985).

Fox-Wilson, A., *The Earl of Halsbury* (London, 1929).

Francis, Mark, and Morrow, John, *A History of English Political Thought in the Nineteenth Century* (New York, 1994).

Gann, L. H., and Duignan, Peter (eds.), *African Proconsuls: European Governors in Africa* (Stanford, Calif., 1978).

Gash, Norman, *Politics in the Age of Peel: A Study in the Technique of Parliamentary Representation, 1830–1850*, 2nd edn (Boston, Mass., 1977).

Gikandi, Simon, *Maps of Englishness: Writing and Identity in the Culture of Colonialism* (New York, 1996).

Gopal, S., *British Policy in India, 1858–1905* (Cambridge, 1965).

Gough, J. W., *Fundamental Law in English Constitutional History* (Oxford, 1971).

Greaves, H. R. G., *The British Constitution* (London, 1958).

Green, William A., *British Slave Emancipation: The Sugar Colonies and the Great Experiment, 1830–1865* (Oxford, 1976).

Greene, Jack P., *Negotiated Authorities: Essays in Colonial Political and Constitutional History* (London, 1994).

Greenleaf, W. H., *The British Political Tradition* (4 vols., New York, 1983).

Greenwood, Murray, and Wright, Barry (eds.), *Canadian State Trials* (2 vols., Toronto, 1996, 2002).

Hall, Catherine (ed.), *Cultures of Empire: Colonizers in Britain and the Empire in the Nineteenth and Twentieth Centuries* (New York, 2000).

——— *Civilizing Subjects: Colony and Metropole in the English Imagination, 1830–1867* (Chicago, Ill., 2002).

Hall, Henry L., *The Colonial Office: A History* (London, 1937).

Hardman, Malcolm, *Six Victorian Thinkers* (Manchester, 1991).

Harris, Jose, *Private Lives, Public Spirit: A Social History of Britain, 1870–1914* (Oxford, 1993).

Harrison, Royden, *Before the Socialists: Studies in Labour and Politics, 1861–1881* (London, 1965).

Hay, Douglas, and Snyder, Francis (eds.), *Policing and Private Prosecutions in Britain, 1750–1850* (Oxford, 1989).

Heffer, Simon, *Moral Desperado: A Life of Thomas Carlyle* (London, 1995).

Hernon, Ian, *Massacre and Retribution: Forgotten Wars of the Nineteenth Century* (Stroud, 1998).

Heuman, Gad J., *Between Black and White: Race, Politics, and the Free Coloreds in Jamaica, 1792–1865* (Westport, Conn., 1981).

——'*The Killing Time': The Morant Bay Rebellion in Jamaica* (Knoxville, Tenn., 1994).

Heuston, R. F. V., *The Lives of the Lord Chancellors, 1885–1940* (Oxford, 1964).

Hibbert, Christopher, *The Great Mutiny: India 1857* (London, 1978).

Hill, Roland, *Lord Acton* (New Haven, Conn., 2000).

Hinton, Tim, *John Ruskin: The Later Years* (New Haven, Conn., 2000).

Hobson, J. A., *Imperialism: A Study*, 3rd edn (London, 1988).

Hochschild, Adam, *King Leopold's Ghost: A Story of Greed, Terror and Heroism in Central Africa* (Boston, Mass., 1998).

Holdsworth, Sir William, *A History of English Law* (17 vols., London, 1922–72).

Holt, Thomas C., *The Problem of Freedom: Race, Labor, and Politics in Jamaica and Britain, 1832–1938* (Baltimore, Md., 1992).

Hoppen, K. Theodore, *The Mid-Victorian Generation, 1846–1886* (Oxford, 1998).

Hunt, John Dixon, *The Wider Sea: A Life of John Ruskin* (Toronto, 1982).

Hussain, Nassar, *The Jurisprudence of Emergency: Colonialism and the Rule of Law* (Ann Arbor, Mich., 2003).

Hyam, Ronald, *Britain's Imperial Century, 1815–1914: A Study of Empire and Expansion*, 2nd edn (London, 1993).

Jacobs, H. P., *Sixty Years of Change, 1806–1866: Progress and Reaction in Kingston and the Countryside* (Kingston, Jamaica, 1973).

James, Lawrence, *The Rise and Fall of the British Empire* (London, 1994).

Joyce, Patrick, *Democratic Subjects: the Self and the Social in Nineteenth-Century England* (Cambridge, 1994).

—— *Visions of the People: Industrial England and the Question of Class, 1848–1914* (Cambridge, 1991).

Judd, Denis, *Empire: The British Imperial Experience, from 1765 to the Present* (New York, 1996).

Kaplan, Fred, *Thomas Carlyle: A Biography* (Ithaca, NY, 1983).

Keir, D. L., and Lawson, F. H., *Cases in Constitutional Law* (Oxford, 1954).

Keith, Arthur Berriedale, *An Introduction to British Constitutional Law* (Oxford, 1931).

Kinzer, Bruce L., Robson, Ann P., and Robson, John M., *A Moralist In and Out of Parliament: John Stuart Mill at Westminster, 1865–1868* (Toronto, 1992).

Kirchheimer, Otto, and Neuman, Franz, *Social Democracy and the Rule of Law* (London, 1987).

Klingberg, Frank J., *The Anti-Slavery Movement in England: A Study in English Humanitarianism* (New Haven, Conn., 1926).

Lawson, F. H., *The Rational Strength of English Law* (London, 1952).

Lawson, Philip, *The East India Company: A History* (London, 1993).

LeMay, G. H. L., *The Victorian Constitution: Conventions, Usages, and Contingencies* (London, 1979).

Lewis, J. R., *The Victorian Bar* (London, 1982).

Lieberman, David, *The Province of Legislation Determined: Legal Theory in Eighteenth-Century Britain* (Cambridge, 1989).

Lorimer, Douglas A., *Colour, Class, and the Victorians: English Attitudes to the Negro in the Mid-Nineteenth Century* (Leicester, 1978).

Louis, Wm. Roger (ed.), *The Oxford History of the British Empire* (5 vols., Oxford, 1998–2001).

Lowry, James M., *Martial Law within the Realm of England* (London, 1914).

Maclagan, Michael, *'Clemency' Canning: Charles John, 1st Earl of Canning* (London, 1962).

Maitland, F. W., *The Constitutional History of England* (Cambridge, 1961).

Majumdar, R. C., *The Sepoy Mutiny and the Revolt of 1857* (Calcutta, 1957).

Manchester, A. H., *A Modern Legal History of England and Wales, 1750–1950* (London, 1980).

Marriot, Sir John A. R., *The Mechanism of the Modern State* (2 vols., Oxford, 1927).

—— *This Realm of England* (Toronto, 1938).

Marsh, Peter (ed.), *The Conscience of the Victorian State* (Syracuse, NY, 1979).

Marshall, P. J., *Cambridge Illustrated History of the British Empire* (Cambridge, 1996).

Masterman, J. Howard, *A History of the British Constitution* (London, 1920).

Mathieson, William Law, *The Sugar Colonies and Governor Eyre, 1849–1866* (London, 1936).

Meek, C. K., *Colonial Law: A Bibliography* (Oxford, 1948).

Mills, L. A., *Ceylon under British Rule, 1795–1932* (London, 1933).

Minattur, Joseph, *Martial Law in India, Pakistan and Ceylon* (The Hague, 1962).

Morrell, W. P., *British Colonial Policy in the Mid-Victorian Age* (Oxford, 1969).

Neff, Emery, *Carlyle and Mill: An Introduction to Victorian Thought* (New York, 1926).

Olivier, Lord Sydney Haldane, *The Myth of Governor Eyre* (London, 1933).

O'Sullivan, R., *Military Law and The Supremacy of the Civil Courts* (London, 1921).

Packe, Michael St. John, *The Life of John Stuart Mill* (New York, 1954).

Pagden, Anthony, *Lords of All the World: Ideologies of Empire in Spain, Britain and France, c.1500–1800* (New Haven, Conn., 1995).

Phillips, Kevin, *The Cousins' Wars: Religion, Politics and the Triumph of Anglo-America* (New York, 1999).

Porter, Andrew (ed.), *The Oxford History of the British Empire*, vol. iii, *The Nineteenth Century* (Oxford, 1999).

Pulling, A. (ed.), *Manual of Emergency Legislation* (London, 1914).

Radzinowicz, L., *Sir James Fitzjames Stephen, 1829–1894 and His Contribution to the Development of Criminal Law* (London, 1957).

Ramanathan, P., *Riots and Martial Law in Ceylon, 1915* (London, 1916).

Rankin, R. S., *When Civil Law Fails* (Durham, NC, 1939).

Roberts-Wray, Kenneth, *Commonwealth and Colonial Law* (London, 1966).

Robson, John M., *The Improvement of Mankind: The Social and Political Thought of John Stuart Mill* (Toronto, 1968).

Rose, Paul, *The Manchester Martyrs: The Story of a Fenian Tragedy* (London, 1970).

Ryan, Alan, *J. S. Mill* (London, 1974).

Schwarz, Bill (ed.), *The Expansion of England: Race, Ethnicity and Cultural History* (London, 1996).

Searle, G. R., *Entrepreneurial Politics in Mid-Victorian Britain* (Oxford, 1993).

Seeley, J. R., *The Expansion of England* (Chicago, Ill., 1971).

Semmel, Bernard, *The Governor Eyre Controversy* (London, 1962).

—— *Jamaican Blood and Victorian Conscience* (New York, 1962).

Shaen, M. J. (ed.), *William Shaen: A Brief Sketch* (London, 1912).

Sharpe, R. J., *The Law of Habeas Corpus* (Oxford, 1989).

Sheller, Mimi, *Democracy after Slavery: Black Publics and Peasant Radicalism in Haiti and Jamaica* (Gainesville, Fla., 2000).

Simpson, A. W. Brian, *In the Highest Degree Odious: Detention without Trial in Wartime Britain* (Oxford, 1992).

—— *Human Rights and the End of the Empire: Britain and the Genesis of the European Convention* (Oxford, 2001).

Skorupski, John, *John Stuart Mill* (London, 1989).

Smith, Herbert A., *The Legislative Competence of the Dominions* (London, 1927).

Smith, K. J. M., *James Fitzjames Stephen: Portrait of a Victorian Rationalist* (Cambridge, 1988).

Spiers, Edward M., *The Late Victorian Army, 1868–1902* (Manchester, 1992).

Stafford, William, *John Stuart Mill* (New York, 1998).

Stembridge, Stanley R., *Parliament, the Press and the Colonies, 1846–1880* (New York, 1982).

Stephen, Leslie, *The English Utilitarians*, vol. iii (London, 1900).

—— *The Life of Sir James Fitzjames Stephen* (London, 1895).

Stokes, Eric, *The Peasant Armed: The Indian Revolt of 1857*, ed. C. A. Bayly (Oxford, 1986).

—— *The English Utilitarians and India* (Oxford, 1959).

Suret-Canale, Jean, *French Colonialism in Tropical Africa, 1900–1945* (New York, 1971).

Surridge, Keith Terrance, *Managing the South African War, 1899–1902: Politicians v. Generals* (Woodbridge, 1998).

—— 'British Civil–Military Relations and the South African War, 1899–1902', unpublished manuscript (1994).

Swinfen, D. B., *Imperial Control of Colonial Legislation, 1813–1865: A Study of British Policy towards Colonial Legislative Powers* (Oxford, 1970).

Taylor, Hannis, *The Origin and Growth of the English Constitution: An Historical Treatise*, Part 2 (Littleton, Col., 1992).

Taylor, Miles, *The Decline of British Radicalism, 1847–1860* (Oxford, 1995).

Temperley, Howard, *British Antislavery, 1833–1870* (Columbia, SC, 1972).

Thomas, Donald (ed.), *State Trials: The Public Conscience*, vol. ii (London, 1972).

Thompson, E. P., *Whigs and Hunters: The Origins of the Black Act* (London, 1975).

—— *The Poverty of Theory and other Essays* (London, 1978).

Thornton, A. P., *The Imperial Idea and its Enemies: A Study in British Power* (London, 1985).

Tidrick, Kathryn, *Empire and the English Character* (London, 1990).

Townshend, Charles, *Political Violence in Ireland: Government and Resistance since 1848* (Oxford, 1983).

—— *Making the Peace: Public Order and Public Security in Modern Britain* (Oxford, 1993).

Turley, David, *The Culture of English Antislavery, 1780–1860* (London, 1991).

VanArsdel, Rosemary T., and Vann, J. Don (eds.), *Victorian Periodicals and Victorian Society* (Toronto, 1994).

Vanden Bossche, Chris R., *Carlyle and the Search for Authority* (Columbus, OH, 1991).

Vernon, James, *Politics and the People: A Study in English Political Culture, c.1815–1867* (Cambridge, 1993).

—— (ed.), *Re-Reading the Constitution: New Narratives in the Political History of England's Long Nineteenth Century* (Cambridge, 1996).

Vogeler, Martha S., *Frederic Harrison: The Vocations of a Positivist* (Oxford, 1984).

Walker, Geoffrey De Q., *The Rule of Law: Foundation of Constitutional Democracy* (Carlton, Victoria, 1988).

Wallace, Elisabeth, *Goldwin Smith: Victorian Liberal* (Toronto, 1957).

Watson, Bruce, *The Great India Mutiny: Colin Campbell and the Campaign at Lucknow* (New York, 1991).

Whelan, Frederick, *Edmund Burke and India: Political Morality and Empire* (Pittsburgh, Penn., 1998).

Wiener, Frederick Bernays, *A Practical Manual of Martial Law* (Harrisburg, Penn., 1940).

—— *Civilians under Military Justice: The British Practice Since 1869, Especially in North America* (Chicago, Ill., 1967).

Wilkinson, Rupert, *The Prefects: British Leadership and the Public School Tradition* (London, 1964).

Williams, Eric, *British Historians and the West Indies* (London, 1966).

Wilson, David Alec and MacArthur, David Wilson, *Carlyle in Old Age, 1865–1881* (New York, 1934).

Winks, Robin (ed.), *The Oxford History of the British Empire,* vol. v, *Historiography* (Oxford, 2001).

Wolters, J. F., *Martial Law and its Administration* (Houston, Tex., 1930).

Wood, Marcus, *Slavery, Empathy and Pornography* (Oxford, 2002).

Worth, George J., *Thomas Hughes* (Boston, Mass., 1984).

Wright, T. R., *The Religion of Humanity: The Impact of Comtean Positivism on Victorian Britain* (Cambridge, 1986).

Zastoupil, Lynn, *John Stuart Mill and India* (Stanford, Calif., 1994).

Zoller, Peter, 'Revolt in Jamaica: A Study of Carlyle, Ruskin, Mill and Huxley', Ph.D. thesis Claremont Graduate Center (Claremont, Calif., 1970).

Journal articles and chapters in books

Arndt, H. W., 'The Origins of Dicey's Concept of the "Rule of Law"', 31 *Australian Law Journal* (1957), 117–23.

Arnold, Frazer, 'The Rationale of Martial Law', XV *American Bar Association Journal* (1929), 117–23.

Ascherson, Neal, 'The Breaking of Mau Mau' (a review of books by David Anderson and Caroline Elkins), *New York Review of Books* (7 Apr. 2005), 26.

Barringer, Tim, 'Images of Otherness and the Visual Production of Difference: Race and Labour in Illustrated Texts, 1850–1865', in Shearer West (ed.), *The Victorians and Race* (Aldershot, 1996), 34–52.

Bayly, C. A., 'Two Colonial Revolts: The Java War, 1825–30, and the India Mutiny of 1857–59', in C. A. Bayly and D. H. A. Kolff (eds.), *Two Colonial Empires* (Dordrecht, 1986).

Beehler, Rodger, 'Waiting for the Rule of Law', 38 *University of Toronto Law Journal* (1988), 298–316.

Belcham, John, 'Republicanism, Popular Constitutionalism and the Radical Platform in Early Nineteenth-Century England', 6 *Social History* (1981), 1–32.

Belliotti, Raymond A., 'The Rule of Law and the Critical Legal Studies Movement', 24 *University of Western Ontario Law Review* (1986), 67–78.

Birch, Dinah, 'Review: *John Ruskin: The Later Years*', London Review of Books (10 Aug. 2000), 30.

Bowman, Harold M., 'Martial Law in England', 15 *Michigan Law Review* (1916), 93–126.

Boynton, Lindsay, 'Martial Law and the Petition of Right', 79 *English Historical Review* (1964), 255–84.

Brewer, John, 'The Wilkites and the Law, 1763–74: A Study of Radical Notions of Governance', in J. Brewer and J. Styles (eds.), *An Ungovernable People: The English and Their Law in the Seventeenth and Eighteenth Centuries* (Camden, NJ, 1980), 128–71.

Burroughs, Peter, 'Imperial Defence and the Victorian Army', 15 *Journal of Imperial and Commonwealth History* (1986), 55–72.

—— 'Imperial Institutions and the Government of Empire', in Andrew Porter (ed.), *The Oxford History of the British Empire,* vol. iii, *The Nineteenth Century* (Oxford, 1999).

—— 'The Law, the Citizen, and the State in Nineteenth-Century Australia', 22 *Journal of Imperial and Commonwealth History* (1994), 542–54.

—— 'The Mauritius Rebellion of 1832 and the Abolition of British Colonial Slavery', 4 *Journal of Imperial and Commonwealth History* (1974–5), 243–65.

Burton, Antoinette, 'Who Needs the Nation? Interrogating "British" History', in Catherine Hall (ed.), *Cultures of Empire: Colonizers in Britain and the Empire in the Nineteenth and Twentieth Centuries* (New York, 2000), 137–53.

Capua, J. V., 'The Early History of Martial Law in England from the Fourteenth Century to the Petition of Right', 36 *Cambridge Law Journal* (1977), 152–73.

Catherall, G. A., 'George William Gordon: Saint or Sinner?', 27 *Baptist Quarterly* (1977), 163–72.

Cell, John, 'The Imperial Conscience', in Marsh, Peter (ed.), *The Conscience of the Victorian State* (Syracuse, NY, 1979).

Chandler, D. G., 'The Expedition to Abyssinia, 1867–8', in Brian Bond (ed.), *Victorian Military Campaigns* (London, 1967), 107–60.

Chomsky, Carol, 'The United States–Dakota War Trials: A Study in Military Injustice', 43 *Stanford Law Review* (1990), 13–95.

Cohen, William B., 'The French Governors', in L. H. Gann and Peter Duignan (eds.), *African Proconsuls: European Governors in Africa* (Stanford, Calif., 1978), 19–50.

Cole, Daniel H., ' "An Unqualified Human Good": E. P. Thompson and the Rule of Law', 28 *Journal of Law and Society* (2001), 177–203.

Conklin, Alice L., 'Colonialism and Human Rights: A Contradiction in Terms? The Case of France and West Africa, 1895–1914', 103 *American Historical Review* (1998), 419–42.

Cormack, William S., 'Victor Hugues and the Reign of Terror on Guadeloupe, 1794–1798', in A. J. B. Johnston (ed.), *Essays in French Colonial History: Proceedings of the 21st Annual Meeting of the French Colonial Society* (East Lansing, Mich., 1997), 31–41.

Corwin, E. S., 'Martial Law Yesterday and Today', 47 *Political Science Quarterly* (1932), 95–104.

Cosgrove, Richard A., 'The Boer War and the Modernization of British Martial Law', 22 *Military Affairs* (1980), 124–7.

Cowling, Maurice, 'Disraeli, Derby and Fusion, October 1865 to July 1866', 8 *Historical Journal* (1965), 31–71.

Darwin, J., 'Imperialism and the Victorians: The Dynamics of Territorial Expansion', 112 *English Historical Review* (1997) 614–42.

—— 'Bored by the Raj' (a review of Bernard Porter, *The Absent-Minded Imperialists: What the British Really Thought about Empire* (Oxford, 2004)), *The Times Literary Supplement* (18 Feb. 2005), 6–7.

Dean, David, 'Joseph Wall of Goree Island', 57 *African Affairs* (1958), 295–301.

Dennison, George M., 'Martial Law: The Development of a Theory of Emergency Powers, 1776–1861', 18 *American Journal of Legal History* (1974), 52–79.

Dickinson, H. T., 'The Eighteenth-Century Debate on the Glorious Revolution', 61 *History* (1978), 28–45.

Dodd, Cyril, 'The Case of Marais', 18 *Law Quarterly Review* (1902), 143–51.

Drescher, Seymour, 'The Ending of the Slave Trade and the Evolution of European Scientific Racism', 14 *Social Science History* (1990), 415–50.

Duman, Daniel, 'Pathway to Professionalism: The English Bar in the Eighteenth and Nineteenth Centuries', 13 *Journal of Social History* (1980), 615–28.

Emsley, Clive, 'Repression, "Terror" and the Rule of Law in England During the Decade of the French Revolution', 100 *English Historical Review* (1985), 801–25.

Endicott, Timothy A. O., 'The Impossibility of the Rule of Law', 19 *Oxford Journal of Legal Studies* (1999), 1–18.

Engdahl, David E., 'Soldiers, Riots, and Revolution: The Law and History of Military Troops in Civil Disorders', 57 *Iowa Law Review* (1971), 1–73.

Erickson, Arvel B., 'Edward T. Cardwell: Peelite', 49 *Transactions of the American Philosophical Society*, Part 2 (1959), 5–67.

—— 'Empire or Anarchy: The Jamaica Rebellion of 1865', 44 *Journal of Negro History* (1959), 99–122.

Fairman, Charles, 'Martial Rule and the Suppression of Insurrection', 23 *Illinois Law Review* (1929), 766–88.

Fine, Robert, 'The Rule of Law and Muggletonian Marxism: The Perplexities of Edward Thompson', 21 *Journal of Law and Society* (1994), 193–213.

Fisher, William W. III, 'The Jurisprudence of Justice Marshall', *Harvard Blackletter Law Journal* (1989), 131–40.

Ford, George H., 'The Governor Eyre Case in England', 27 *University of Toronto Quarterly* (1947–8), 219–33.

Francis, Mark, and Morrow, John, 'After the Ancient Constitution: Political Theory and English Constitutional Writing, 1765–1832', 9 *History of Political Thought* (1988), 283–302.

Fulweiler, Howard W., 'The Strange Case of Governor Eyre: Race and the "Victorian Frame of Mind"', 29 *Clio* (2000), 119–42.

Gann, L. H., 'German Governors: An Overview', in L. H. Gann and Peter Duignan (eds.), *African Proconsuls: European Governors in Africa* (Stanford, Calif., 1978), 467–72.

Gardinier, David E., 'French Colonial Rule in Africa: A Bibliographical Essay', in Gifford Prosser and Wm. Roger Louis (eds.), *France and Britain in Africa: Imperial Rivalry and Colonial Rule* (New Haven, Conn., 1971), 787–949.

Gilbert, Arthur N., 'Law and Honour Among Eighteenth-Century British Army Officers', 19 *Historical Journal* (1975), 75–87.

—— 'Military and Civilian Justice in Eighteenth-Century England: An Assessment', 17 *Journal of British Studies* (1978), 41–65.

Gocking, C. V., 'Early Constitutional History of Jamaica (with Special Reference to the Period 1836–1866)', 6 *Caribbean Quarterly* (1960), 114–33.

Goldberg, David Theo, 'Liberalism's Limits: Carlyle and Mill on "The Negro Question"', in Julie K. Ward and Tommy J. Lott (eds.), *Philosophers on Race: Critical Essays* (Oxford, 2002), 199–203.

Goldman, Lawrence, 'The Social Science Association, 1857–1866: A Context for Mid-Victorian Liberalism', 101 *English Historical Review* (1986), 95–134.

Hall, Catherine, 'The Economy of Intellectual Prestige: Thomas Carlyle, John Stuart Mill, and the Case of Governor Eyre', 22 *Labour/Le Travail* (1989), 167–96.

—— 'Competing Masculinities: Thomas Carlyle, John Stuart Mill and the Case of Governor Eyre', in Catherine Hall (ed.), *White, Male and Middle-Class: Explorations in Feminism and History* (London, 1992), 255–93.

—— ' "From Greenland's Icy Mountains . . . to Africa's Golden Sand": Ethnicity, Race and Nation in Mid-Nineteenth-Century England', 5 *Gender and History* (1993), 212–30.

—— 'Rethinking Imperial Histories: The Reform Act of 1867', 208 *New Left Review* (1994), 3–29.

—— 'Imperial Man: Edward Eyre in Australasia and the West Indies 1833–65', in Bill Schwarz (ed.), *The Expansion of England: Race, Ethnicity and Cultural History* (London, 1996), 130–70.

—— 'Thinking the Postcolonial, Thinking the Empire', in Catherine Hall (ed.), *Cultures of Empire: Colonizers in Britain and the Empire in the Nineteenth and Twentieth Centuries* (New York, 2000), 1–33.

Hamburger, Philip A., 'Revolution and Judicial Review: Chief Justice Holt's Opinion in *City of London v. Wood* ', 94 *Columbia Law Review* (1994), 2091–153.

Harcourt-Smith, Simon, 'The Rising at Morant Bay, 1865', 24 *History Today* (1974), 625–32.

Harrison, Royden, 'Professor Beesly and the Working-Class Movement', in Asa Briggs and John Saville (eds.), *Essays in Labour History* (London, 1967), 205–41.

Henley, Kenneth, 'The Impersonal Rule of Law', 5 *Canadian Journal of Law and Jurisprudence* (1992), 299–308.

Heuman, Gad, 'The British West Indies', in Andrew Porter (ed.), *The Oxford History of The British Empire*, vol. iii, *The Nineteenth Century* (Oxford, 1999), 470–94.

Holdsworth, W. S., 'Martial Law Historically Considered', 18 *Law Quarterly Review* (1902), 117–32.

Hulsebosch, Daniel J., 'The Ancient Constitution and the Expanding Empire: Sir Edward Coke's British Jurisprudence', 21 *Law and History Review* (2003), 439–82.

Jeffery, Keith, 'Military Aid to the Civil Power in the United Kingdom: An Historical Perspective', in P. J. Rowe and C. J. Whelan (eds.), *Military Intervention in Democratic Societies* (London, 1985), 51–67.

Johnson, Howard, 'Oil, Imperial Policy and the Trinidad Disturbances, 1937', 4 *Journal of Imperial and Commonwealth History* (1974–5), 29–54.

Jowell, Jeffrey, 'The Rule of Law Today', in Jeffery Jowell and Dawn Oliver (eds.), *The Changing Constitution*, 3rd edn (Oxford, 1994), 57–78.

Knox, Bruce A., 'The British Government and the Governor Eyre Controversy, 1865–1875', 19 *Historical Journal* (Dec. 1976), 877–900.

—— 'Colonial Influence on Imperial Policy, 1858–1866: Victoria and the Colonial Naval Defence Act, 1865', 11 *Historical Studies: Australia and New Zealand* (1963), 61–79.

—— 'The Earl of Carnarvon, Empire, and Imperialism, 1855–90', in Peter Burroughs and A. J. Stockwell (eds.), 25 *Journal of Imperial and Commonwealth History, Special Edition, Managing the Business of Empire* (1998), 48–65.

—— 'Reconsidering Mid-Victorian Imperialism', 1 *Journal of Imperial and Commonwealth History* (1973), 155–72.

—— 'The Rise of Colonial Federation as an Object of British Policy, 1850–1870', 11 *Journal of British Studies* (1971), 92–112.

Knox, Graham, 'British Colonial Policy and the Problems of Establishing a Free Society in Jamaica, 1838–1865', 2 *Caribbean Studies* (1963), 3–13.

Kostal, R. W., 'A Jurisprudence of Power: Martial Law and the Ceylon Controversy of 1848–51', 28 *Journal of Imperial and Commonwealth History* (2000), 1–34.

Lewis, William Roger, 'Introduction', in Robin Winks (ed.), *The Oxford History of the British Empire*, vol. v, *Historiography* (Oxford, 2001), 5.

Lorimer, Douglas A., 'Race, Science and Culture: Historical Continuities and Discontinuities, 1850–1914', in Shearer West (ed.), *The Victorians and Race* (Aldershot, 1996), 12–33.

Malchow, H. L., 'The Half-Breed as Gothic Unnatural', in Shearer West (ed.), *The Victorians and Race* (Aldershot, 1996), 101–11.

Martin, G., ' "Anti-Imperialism" in the Mid-Nineteenth Century and the Nature of the British Empire, 1820–70', in R. Hyam and G. Martin (eds.), *Reappraisals in British Imperial History* (Toronto, 1975), 88–120.

McCamie, Charles, 'Martial Law', 32 *Columbia Law Review* (1932), 1073–4.

Morris, Jan, 'Eyre: a Portrait', 35 *Encounter* (1970), 3–13.

Mukherjee, R., ' "Satan Let Loose upon Earth": The Kanpur Massacres in India in the Revolt of 1857', 128 *Past and Present* (1990), 92–116.

Murray, R. N., 'The Road Back: Jamaica after 1866', 6 *Caribbean Quarterly* (1960), 134–41.

Nasson, W. R., ' "Doing Down their Masters": Africans, Boers, and Treason in the Cape Colony during the South African War of 1899–1902', 12 *Journal of Imperial and Commonwealth History* (1983–4), 29–53.

Nippel, W. E., ' "Reading the Riot Act": The Discourse of Law Enforcement in 18th Century England', 1 *History and Anthropology* (1985), 401–26.

O'Higgins, Patrick, '*Wright v. Fitzgerald* Revisited', 25 *Modern Law Review* (1962), 413–22.

Pollock, Sir Frederick, 'What is Martial Law?', 18 *Law Quarterly Review* (1902), 152–8.

Porter, Bernard, 'How Did They Get away with it?' (a review of books by David Anderson and Caroline Elkins), *London Review of Books* (3 Mar. 2005).

Quinault, Roland, '1848 and Parliamentary Reform', 31 *Historical Journal* (1988), 831–51.

Radin, Margaret Jane, 'Reconsidering the Rule of Law', 69 *Boston University Law Review* (1989), 781–819.

Radzinowicz, Leon, 'New Departures in Maintaining Public Order in the Face of Chartist Disturbances', *Cambridge Law Journal* (1960), 51–80.

Reckord, Mary, 'The Jamaica Slave Rebellion of 1831', 40 *Past and Present* (1968), 108–25.

Reynolds, Noel B., 'Grounding the Rule of Law', 2 *Ratio Juris* (1989), 1–16.

Richards, H. Erle, 'Martial Law', 18 *Law Quarterly Review* (1902), 133–42.

Robotham, Don, ' "The Notorious Riot": The Socio-Economic and Political Bases of Paul Bogle's Revolt', 3 *Anales del Caribe* (1983), 51–111.

Rosen, F., 'Eric Stokes, British Utilitarianism, and India', in Martin I. Moir, Douglas M. Peers, and Lynn Zastoupil (eds.), *J. S. Mill's Encounter with India* (Toronto, 1999), 18–33.

Rubin, G. R., 'The Legal Education of British Army Officers, 1860–1923', 15 *Journal of Legal History* (1994), 223–51.

—— 'Parliament, Prerogative and Military Law: Who Had Legal Authority over the Army in the Later Nineteenth Century?', 18 *Legal History* (1997), 45–84.

Scheuerle, William H., 'Henry Kingsley and the Governor Eyre Controversy', 37 *Victorian Newsletter* (Spring 1970), 24–7.

Schlueter, Captain David A., 'The Court-Martial: An Historical Survey', 87 *Military Law Review* (1980), 129–66.

Schwarz, Bill, 'The Expansion and Contraction of England', in Bill Schwarz (ed.), *The Expansion of England: Race, Ethnicity and Cultural History* (London, 1996), 1–8.

Sedley, Stephen, 'The Common Law and the Constitution', 8 *London Review of Books* (May 1997), 8–11.

Semmel, Bernard, 'The Philosophic Radicals and Colonialism', 21 *Journal of Economic History* (Dec. 1961), 513–25.

Shklar, Judith N., 'Political Theory and the Rule of Law', in Allan C. Hutchinson and Patrick Monahan (eds.), *The Rule of Law: Ideal or Ideology* (Toronto, 1987), 1–16.

Sires, Ronald V., 'Governmental Crisis in Jamaica, 1860–1866', 2 *Jamaican Historical Review* (1953), 1–26.

Simpson, A. W. B., 'The Rise and Fall of the Legal Treatise', in A. W. B. Simpson, *Legal Theory and Legal History: Essays on the Common Law* (London, 1987), 273–320.

Steele, E. D., 'J. S. Mill and the Irish Question: Reform, and the Integrity of the Empire, 1865–1870', 13 *Historical Journal* (1970), 419–50.

Stepan, Nancy Leys, 'Race, Gender, Science and Citizenship', in Catherine Hall (ed.), *Cultures of Empire: Colonizers in Britain and the Empire in the Nineteenth and Twentieth Centuries* (New York, 2000), 61–86.

Stockwell, A. J., 'Power, Authority and Freedom', in P. J. Marshall (ed.), *The Cambridge Illustrated History of the British Empire* (Cambridge, 1996), 147–71.

Stokes, Eric, 'Bureaucracy and Ideology: Britain and India in the Nineteenth Century', *Transactions of the Royal Historical Society* (1979), 131–56.

—— 'Macaulay: The Indian Years, 1834–38', 1 *Review of English Literature* (1960), 40–50.

Sugarman, David, 'In the Spirit of Weber: Law, Modernity and "The Peculiarities of the English" ', *Institute for Legal Studies, Working Papers* 2:9 (1987).

—— 'Legal Theory, the Common Law Mind and the Making of the Textbook Tradition', in William L. Twining (ed.), *Legal Theory and Common Law* (Oxford, 1986), 26–61.

—— ' "A Hatred of Disorder": Legal Science, Liberalism and Imperialism', in Peter Fitzpatrick (ed.), *Dangerous Supplements: Resistance and Renewal in Jurisprudence* (London, 1991), 34–67.

—— and G. R. Rubin, 'Introduction: Towards a New History of Law and Material Society in England, 1750–1914', in G. R. Rubin and David Sugarman (eds.), *Law, Economy and Society, 1750–1914: Essays in the History of English Law* (Abingdon, 1984), 1–123.

Taiwo, Olufemi, 'The Rule of Law: The New Leviathan?', 12 *Canadian Journal of Law and Jurisprudence* (1999), 151–68.

Taylor, Miles, 'Imperium et Libertas? Rethinking the Radical Critique of Imperialism during the Nineteenth Century', 19 *Journal of Imperial and Commonwealth History* (1991), 1–23.

—— 'The 1848 Revolutions and the British Empire', 166 *Past and Present* (2000), 146–80.

Townshend, Charles, 'Martial Law: Legal and Administrative Problems of Civil Emergency in Britain and the Empire, 1800–1940', 25 *Historical Journal* (1982), 167–95.

Walvin, James, 'Abolishing the Slave Trade: Anti-Slavery and Popular Radicalism, 1776–1807', in Clive Emsley and James Walvin (eds.), *Artisans, Peasants and Proletarians 1760–1860* (London, 1985), 32–56.

Weinrib, Ernest J., 'The Intelligibility of the Rule of Law', in Allan C. Hutchinson and Patrick Monahan (eds.), *The Rule of Law: Ideal or Ideology* (Toronto, 1987), 59–84.

Wheeler, Douglas, L., 'Portuguese Colonial Governors in Africa, 1870–1974', in L. H. Gann and Peter Duigan (eds.), *African Proconsuls: European Governors in Africa* (Stanford, Calif., 1978), 415–26.

Williams, Gerald R., 'The King's Peace: Riot Law in its Historical Perspective', *Utah Law Review* (1971), 240–58.

Willis, Justin, 'In the Noose' (a review of books by David Anderson and Caroline Elkins), *The Times Literary Supplement* (18 Mar. 2005), 32.

Wilson, Kathleen, 'Inventing Revolution: 1688 and the Eighteenth-Century Popular Politics', 28 *Journal of British Studies* (1989), 349–86.

Winter, James, 'The Cave of Adullam and Parliamentary Reform', 81 *English Historical Review* (1966), 38–55.

Workman, Gillian, 'Thomas Carlyle and the Governor Eyre Controversy: An Account with Some New Material', 18 *Victorian Studies* (1974), 77–102.

Index